Springer Proceedings in Business and Economics

Springer Proceedings in Business and Economics brings the most current research presented at conferences and workshops to a global readership. The series features volumes (in electronic and print formats) of selected contributions from conferences in all areas of economics, business, management, and finance. In addition to an overall evaluation by the publisher of the topical interest, scientific quality, and timeliness of each volume, each contribution is refereed to standards comparable to those of leading journals, resulting in authoritative contributions to the respective fields. Springer's production and distribution infrastructure ensures rapid publication and wide circulation of the latest developments in the most compelling and promising areas of research today.

The editorial development of volumes may be managed using Springer Nature's innovative EquinOCS, a proven online conference proceedings submission, management and review system. This system is designed to ensure an efficient timeline for your publication, making Springer Proceedings in Business and Economics the premier series to publish your workshop or conference volume.

This book series is indexed in SCOPUS.

Nicholas Tsounis • Aspasia Vlachvei
Editors

Applied Economic Research and Trends

2023 International Conference on Applied Economics (ICOAE), Brno, Czech Republic, June 29-July 1, 2023

Volume 2

Editors
Nicholas Tsounis
Department of Economics
University of Western Macedonia
Kastoria, Greece

Aspasia Vlachvei
Department of Economics
University of Western Macedonia
Kastoria, Greece

ISSN 2198-7246   ISSN 2198-7254 (electronic)
Springer Proceedings in Business and Economics
ISBN 978-3-031-49104-7   ISBN 978-3-031-49105-4 (eBook)
https://doi.org/10.1007/978-3-031-49105-4

© The Editor(s) (if applicable) and The Author(s), under exclusive license to Springer Nature Switzerland AG 2024

This work is subject to copyright. All rights are solely and exclusively licensed by the Publisher, whether the whole or part of the material is concerned, specifically the rights of translation, reprinting, reuse of illustrations, recitation, broadcasting, reproduction on microfilms or in any other physical way, and transmission or information storage and retrieval, electronic adaptation, computer software, or by similar or dissimilar methodology now known or hereafter developed.

The use of general descriptive names, registered names, trademarks, service marks, etc. in this publication does not imply, even in the absence of a specific statement, that such names are exempt from the relevant protective laws and regulations and therefore free for general use.

The publisher, the authors, and the editors are safe to assume that the advice and information in this book are believed to be true and accurate at the date of publication. Neither the publisher nor the authors or the editors give a warranty, expressed or implied, with respect to the material contained herein or for any errors or omissions that may have been made. The publisher remains neutral with regard to jurisdictional claims in published maps and institutional affiliations.

This Springer imprint is published by the registered company Springer Nature Switzerland AG
The registered company address is: Gewerbestrasse 11, 6330 Cham, Switzerland

If disposing of this product, please recycle the paper.

Preface

The 2023 conference was co-organised by the Faculty of Business and Economics of the Mendel University in Brno and the Department of Economics of the University of Western Macedonia, Greece, after the kind invitation by Profs. Martina Rašticová and Veronika Solilová who were also co-chairs of the conference.

The aim of the conference was to bring together economists from different fields of Applied Economic Research in order to share methods and ideas.

The topics covered include:

- Applied Macroeconomics
- Applied International Economics
- Applied Microeconomics including Industrial Organisations
- Applied work on International Trade Theory including European Integration
- Applied Financial Economics
- Applied Agricultural Economics
- Applied Labour and Demographic Economics
- Applied Health Economics
- Applied Education Economic

All papers presented in ICOAE 2023 and published in the conference proceedings were peer reviewed by at least two anonymous referees. In total, 105 works were submitted from 22 countries while 73 papers were accepted for publication in the conference proceedings.

The acceptance rate for ICOAE 2023 was 69.5%.

The full-text articles will be published on-line by Springer in the series Springer Proceedings in Business and Economics, and they will be included in the SCOPUS database for indexing.

The organisers of ICOAE 2023 would like to thank:

- The Scientific Committee of the conference for their help and their important support for carrying out the tremendous workload organising and synchronising the peer reviewing process of the submitted papers in a very specific short period of time.

- The anonymous reviewers for accepting to referee the submitted conference papers and submitting their reviews on time for the finalisation of the conference programme.
- Prof. Svatopluk Kapounek, Dean of the Faculty and Professors Martina Rašticová and Veronika Solilová, for accepting to host the conference at the Faculty of Business and Economics of the Mendel University in Brno and providing the required resources.
- Dr. Hana Vránová and Barbora Šiklová, members of the local organising committee, for the time and effort they put for the successful organisation of the conference.
- Mr. Gerassimos Bertsatos for running the reception desk of the conference and Mr. Lazaros Markopoulos and Mr. Stelios Angelis from the Department of Economics and Informatics, of the University of Western Macedonia, respectively, for technical support.

Kastoria, Greece

Nicholas Tsounis
Aspasia Vlachvei

Contents

Volume 1

1. **The Nexus Between Geopolitical Risks and Confidence Measures in G7 Countries** 1
   Milan Christian de Wet

2. **International Trade Flows and Geo-Political Episodes—Network Perspective** 17
   Ahaan Shah, Keyaan Shah, and Homa Hosseinmardi

3. **A South African Perspective on the Corporate Cash Holding Conundrum** 37
   Ilse Botha and Carol Thompson

4. **Simulating the Impacts of Productive Development Policies in Algeria: Computable General Equilibrium Model Analysis** 51
   Mohammed Touitou

5. **Forecasting the Main Energy Crop Prices in the Agricultural Sector of Thailand Using a Machine Learning Model** 63
   Jittima Singvejsakul and Chukiat Chaiboonsri

6. **Extreme Events and Stock Market Efficiency: The Modified Shannon Entropy Approach** 77
   Joanna Olbrys

7. **Examining Public Expenditure on Education and the Relationship Between Expenditure and Corruption in Greece Through a Nonparametric Statistical Analysis Method** .. 91
   Kyriaki Efthalitsidou, Nikolaos Sariannidis, Marina Vezou, and Konstantinos Spinthiropoulos

8. **Does Clove Export Cause Economic Growth in Nigeria?** 113
   Okezie A. Ihugba, Alexander A. Orji, Erasmus E. Duru, and N. C. Ebomuche

9	The Share of Dependent Work Income in Greece: Main Domestic and External Determinants 143
	George Petrakos, Konstantinos Rontos, Chara Vavoura, and Ioannis Vavouras

10	Export-Led and Import-Led Growth Hypotheses: Empirical Evidence from Greece 159
	Melina Dritsaki and Chaido Dritsaki

11	An Empirical Analysis of the Trade Impediments in Greece's Global Trade Relationships: A CGE Approach 187
	Gerasimos Bertsatos and Nicholas Tsounis

12	Employee Benefits Required by Women of Generation Y in the Food and Agricultural Sectors 205
	Jiří Duda

13	How Is Economic News Tone Driven: An Analysis of the Longitudinal Data (1998–2017) of Korean Economic News 219
	Wansoo Lee

14	The Role of Trust and Contracts in the Expansion of Technology-Intensive SMEs 235
	Ewa Baranowska-Prokop and Jacek Prokop

15	Improving Employee Retention: Evidence from "Best Practices" in the Craft Sector to Tackle the Labor Shortage of Skilled Workers 245
	Romina Klara Haller

16	Blockchain Research Trends in Information Systems: A Systematic Review 265
	Van Nguyen Nhu Tam and Cao Tien Thanh

17	Analysis of Customer Perception of E-banking Services in India ... 283
	Amit Kumar Gupta, Manoj Kumar Srivastava, Imlak Shaikh, and Ashutosh Dash

18	Defense Spending and Economic Growth: An Empirical Investigation in the Case of Greece 299
	Antonis Tsitouras, Nicholas Tsounis, and Harry Papapanagos

19	Quality of IFRS Reporting: Developed, Transitional, and Developing Economies 321
	Patrik Svoboda and Hana Bohušová

20	Influencer Marketing and Its Impact on Consumer Behavior: Case Study from Slovakia 337
	Roman Chinoracky, Tatiana Corejova, and Natalia Stalmasekova

21	**The Reflection of COVID-19 Pandemic in the State Budget of the Slovak Republic: Selected Problems** .... Janka Grofčíková and Katarína Izáková	351
22	**Role of Information Technology in the Efficiency of HR Processes in Educational Institutions: A Case Study of Greece** ..... Olympia Papaevangelou, Stavros Kalogiannidis, Dimitrios Syndoukas, Zacharias Karantonis, and Despoina Savvidou	367
23	**US Museums: Digitization, Social Media Engagement, and Revenue Diversification in the Pandemic** .... Angela Besana, Martha Friel, Enrico Giorgio Domenico Crisafulli, and Cristina Rossi	393
24	**Understanding Customer Perception and Brand Equity in the Hospitality Sector: Integrating Sentiment Analysis and Topic Modeling** .... T. D. Dang and M. T. Nguyen	413
25	**Business Ethics and Green Taxonomy in an Era that Energy Consumption and Prices Are Defined by a War: An Empirical Study in Western Macedonian Enterprises** .... A. Metsiou, G. Broni, E. Papachristou, M. Kiki, and P. Evangelou	427
26	**Economics and Marketing of Skills.** *Pass the Point of No Return* **in Arts and Tourism** .... Angela Besana, Annamaria Esposito, Chiara Fisichella, and Maria Cristina Vannini	445
27	**Risk-Taking Behavior and Effects of Framing in Group and Individual Decisions: Evidence from Chamas and Student Subjects in Kenya**... Mercy Inyangala Kano, Gülnur Muradoğlu, and John Olukuru	465
28	**Empirical Study on the Role of Cultivation in the Acceptance of ICT Technologies in the Agricultural Sector of Kozani** .... Deligiannis Dimitrios, Saprikis Vaggelis, Avlogiaris Giorgos, and Antoniadis Ioannis	487
29	**How Has the COVID-19 Pandemic Affected the Utilization of the Company's Working Capital?** .... Janka Grofčíková	499
30	**Trainer's Characterization of Entrepreneurs to Reduce Unemployment Gap, Lambayeque** .... Vidal Taboada Silvia Lourdes, Guillermo Segundo Miñan Olivos, Jairo Jaime Turriate Chávez, Luis Alberto Vásquez Caballero, Mercedes Alejandrina Collazos Alarcón, and Mónica del Pilar Pintado Damián	521

31	LNG Carriers' Discharge Waiting Time and Energy Inflation...... Stavros Karamperidis, Nektatios A. Michail, and Konstantinos Melas	531
32	Big Data Analytics in Management Reporting: A Systematic Literature Review .... Simon Luca Kropf	537
33	Using Enterprise Social Media Networks to Foster Team-Level Collaboration in a Project Organization .... Thomas Ruf	559
34	Bankruptcy Prediction Using Machine Learning: The Case of Slovakia .... Hussam Musa, Frederik Rech, Zdenka Musova, Chen Yan, and Ľubomír Pintér	575
35	Value Creation in Automotive Industry in Slovakia .... Ľuboš Elexa	593
36	Does German Hospital Financing Lead to Distorted Incentives in the Billing of Intensive Care Ventilation Therapy? ... Peter Kremeier	613

Volume 2

37	Life Cycle Cost Analysis: Applying Monte Carlo Simulation on Energy Costs in Case Studies for Investments in Natural Gas Infrastructure.. Stefan Wieke	625
38	Examination of the Beliefs About the Role of Psychological Approaches in Economic Growth and National Development....... Stavros Kalogiannidis, Christina Patitsa, Dimitrios Syndoukas, and Fotios Chatzitheodoridis	641
39	Heterogenous Consumption Responses and Wealth Inequality over the Business Cycle .... Rachel Forshaw	667
40	Consumer Behavior When Buying Clothes in Slovakia in the Context of Environmentally Responsible Trends .... Simona Bartošová, Zdenka Musová, and Zlatica Fulajtárová	701
41	Impact of Gender Diversity Boards on Financial Health SMEs .... Mário Papík and Lenka Papíková	729
42	Sustainable Banking Practice: The Role of Environmental, Social, and Governance Factors... Imlak Shaikh, Ashutosh Dash, Amit Kumar Gupta, and Manoj Kumar Srivastava	741

43	Corporate Social Responsibility as a Swap for Reducing Firm Risk: Evidence from Stock Market Reaction to FDI Announcements .... Mei Liu and Qing-Ping Ma	757
44	The Impact of Housing Market Policy on House Prices in China... Mei Liu and Qing-Ping Ma	793
45	Changes in the Use of Employee Training Methods in Slovakia in the Context of the COVID-19 Pandemic: A Quantitative and Qualitative Perspective .... Jozef Ďurian, Lukas Smerek, and Ivana Simockova	815
46	Centralized Governance in Decentralized Autonomous Organizations .... Ivan Sedliačik and Kamil Ščerba	831
47	Do Consumers Seek Terroir Elements When Choosing a Wine? Insight from Four Generational Cohorts .... Spyridon Mamalis, Irene (Eirini) Kamenidou, Aikaterini Karampatea, Elisavet Bouloumpasi, and Adriana Skendi	839
48	Recreational Uses of the Protected Natural Ecosystem of Grammos in the Region of Western Macedonia .... Katerina Melfou, Georgia Koutouzidou, Dimitrios Kalfas, Stergios Loudovaris, and Ioannis A. Giantsis	853
49	National and Regional Disparities: How Recovering?............... Anna Maria Bagnasco, Viviana Clavenna, and Federica Fortunato	867
50	The Impact of Insurance Needs Satisfaction on Consumers' Purchase and Repurchase Intention.................................... Dimitrios Karnachoritis and Irene Samanta	889
51	Factors Determining Business Eco-Innovation Activities: A Case of Slovak SMEs... Miroslava Vinczeová, Ladislav Klement, and Vladimíra Klementová	907
52	The Impact of COVID-19 and Lockdowns on Media: The Greek Case .... Athanasios Papathanasopoulos	923
53	The Impact of Macroeconomic Indicators on Exchange Rates of the Visegrad Group .... Kitty Klacsánová, Mária Bohdalová, and Nico Haberer	939
54	Working Capital Management Policy and Its Financing Across Selected Enterprises According to Size in the Czech Republic .... Markéta Skupieňová	955

55	**Effects of Monetary Policy and the External Sector on Peru's Economic Cycles** Vony Sucaticona-Aguilar and Polan Ferro-Gonzales	969
56	**Importance of Business Digitization: The Case of the Region of Western Macedonia, Greece** Ioannis Metsios, Vaggelis Saprikis, and Ioannis Antoniadis	987
57	**Using the Predictive Model IN05 to Assess the Business Environment in Czechia** Tomáš Pražák	1009
58	**The WWW Factor: Understanding Generation Z's Website Preferences** Tereza Ikášová	1021
59	**Factors Affecting the Effectiveness of Email Marketing** Lola Maria Sempelidou, Giorgos Avlogiaris, and Ioannis Antoniadis	1035
60	**E-commerce to Increase Sales in a Peruvian Importer of Hardware Items** Guillermo S. Miñan Olivos, María Y. Del Busto Valdez, Johan H. Espinoza Tumpay, Williams E. Castillo Martínez, and Jairo Jaime Turriate Chávez	1051
61	**Big Data in Economics Research** Aristidis Bitzenis and Nikos Koutsoupias	1063
62	**Testing Horizontal Support and Resistance Zones on Cryptocurrencies** Prodromos Tsinaslanidis	1073
63	**Pre-bankruptcy Consolidation Process and Business Reorganization: A Case Study** Araviadi Ioanna and Katarachia Androniki	1085
64	**Tourist Clusters and the Tourist Experience as a Tool for Smart, Sustainable, and Integrated Development of Rural Areas: The Case of Troodos in Cyprus** Electra Pitoska and Panayiotis Papadopoullos	1095
65	**Entrepreneurship of Winemaking Enterprises in Mountain Less-Favored Areas: An Empirical Study** Electra Pitoska, Evagelia Theodorli, and Agapi Altini	1113
66	**Consumer Attitudes Toward Artificial Intelligence in Fashion** Katerina Vatantzi, Aspasia Vlachvei, and Ioannis Antoniadis	1127

67	What Determines Supply and Demand for Occupational Pension Provision in Germany? Results of a Current Expert Surveys..	1143
	Robert Piotr Dombek	
68	Population Aging: How Much Time Do We Still Have?..............	1175
	Jure Miljevič and Cveto Gregorc	
69	The Impact of Capital Adequacy on Banking Risk-Evidence from Emerging Market	1209
	Osama Samih Shaban	
70	Digital Entrepreneurship Activities Among Gender Groups in Greek Agrifood Firms...	1223
	Afroditi Kitta, Ourania Notta, and Aspasia Vlachvei	
71	The Dynamics of Tourist Flows in Greece	1241
	G. Bertsatos, Z. Kalogiratou, Th. Monovasilis, and N. Tsounis	

Index... 1249

Chapter 37
Life Cycle Cost Analysis: Applying Monte Carlo Simulation on Energy Costs in Case Studies for Investments in Natural Gas Infrastructure

Stefan Wieke

Abstract Decision makers in companies of the natural gas infrastructure establish their decisions on case studies. The case studies are usually prepared according to life cycle cost analysis in combination with the net present value method.

Seven case studies, which were prepared by experts from consulting companies, are examined with regard to the robustness of the results obtained. The case studies investigate different options of compressor units for installation in gas facilities in Germany with the aim of finding the best option.

The focus is on the evaluation of energy costs as the main cost driver and their future development. The authors of the case studies have to make assumptions for the future development of energy costs. These assumptions are associated with large uncertainties and are not backed up by risk analyses.

Based on the seven case studies from 2001 to 2015 and the knowledge of the actual historical energy costs, it is possible to assess with which uncertainties case studies are associated and how robust the results are. Monte Carlo simulation is used to predict future energy prices.

In addition to risk assessment with Monte Carlo simulation, other measures to identify the best option for an investment are proposed.

Keywords Life Cycle Cost Analysis · Monte Carlo simulation · Case studies · Energy costs · Risk assessment · Net present value

S. Wieke (✉)
Mendel University, Brno, Czechia
e-mail: xwieke@mendelu.cz

37.1 Introduction

It is of tremendous importance for commercial companies to make the right decisions for business development. In this context, decisions on investments in the company's technical facilities and equipment, which have a primary impact on its success and market assertion, are of crucial importance. In many cases, this investment is a strategic decision. Technical equipment, such as production facilities and machinery, represents a significant financial investment over a long-term period.

The decision makers need a reliable basis to decide on the option that meets the requirements best for the investment project.

The evaluation of investment projects is mostly based on discounted cash flow methods. The NPV (net present value) method is the most commonly applied method. In some business areas such as the energy sector the life cycle cost analysis (LCCA) in combination with NPV is the preferred method.

A definition of LCCA is as follows:

To evaluate the economics of a paving project, an analysis should be made of potential design options, each capable of providing the required performance. If all other things are equal, the option that is the least expensive over time should be selected (Lee, 2002).

The costs are composed of CAPEX (capital costs) and OPEX (operational costs), whereas CAPEX represents the initial investment and OPEX consists of operation costs and maintenance costs. Also, other cost factors could be considered if these are the main cost drivers in this context. The cost drivers in operation are the energy costs and maintenance costs.

Life cycle calculation (LCC) analysis represents the state of the art for the evaluation of projects in the energy sector. These projects have a long-term horizon into the future in terms of preparation (engineering), execution (construction), and operation lifetime. It is not uncommon for the lifetime to be 30 years or more. It is obvious that the input data and their future development are associated with high uncertainties. The uncertainties in the input data have to be addressed to avoid wrong decisions about an investment project.

In LCC analysis for the energy sector, the uncertainties in input data and the prediction of the future development of input data have inherent risks and are mainly related to the difficulty in predicting future energy prices.

The use of inaccurate input data can lead to inaccurate results in the LCC analysis. Not only can the NPVs of the option be calculated incorrectly, but also the order of the options examined can change. As a result, an option may be selected that is not the most advantageous.

These uncertainties can be addressed, among others, with risk assessment by using Monte Carlo simulation (MCS).

This paper assesses eight case studies on investments in compressor stations for natural gas infrastructure in Germany.

The calculations of the NPV in the models in the case studies examined are recalculated by using real historical energy costs and in a second step by using real historical energy costs and Monte Carlo simulation for prediction of their future development. This work analyses if the results of the calculated NPVs are improved by applying Monte Carlo simulation.

None of the authors of these case studies has applied risk assessments such as Monte Carlo simulation.

A detailed examination of executed case studies in Germany's energy sector is very rare in the literature because these studies are usually not published and not accessible for scientific research.

The research objective of the work is to determine what the risks for NPV calculations in the course of selecting an option for an investment project are and to what extent risk assessment based on Monte Carlo simulation can secure the results of LCCA modeling.

37.2 Material and Methodology

37.2.1 Case Studies

Seven case studies and one publication have been analyzed.

The studies cover investment in compressor stations, which is long term and is associated with considerable monetary resources. In the decision-making process, the gas pipeline operators in Germany rely on case studies for decision-making.

The studies are aimed at determining the optimum investment option. They proceed in the order of LCCA in conjunction with NPV calculations.

Most case studies follow life cycle calculation (LCC) as outlined in EN ISO 15663 part 1 – part 3, 2000. LCC analysis aims to find the best option for an investment project.

This paper assesses the approach in case studies to identify the best option for an investment in compressors in Germany's natural gas infrastructure. The assessed case studies were executed by experts from consulting firms and were reviewed by experts from gas suppliers. These seven studies served as the basis for decision-making on investments in the natural gas infrastructure. These studies represent expert opinions, whereas the experts are with both, the consulting firms and the operators of pipelines for natural gas Fernleitungsnetzbetreiber (FNB).

One publication about the same subject is included in the analysis (Cierniak, 2001).

The evaluated seven studies were executed in the period from 2005 to 2015. Additionally, the publication issued in 2001 is also subject to evaluation. In total, eight (8) studies were assessed.

The asset life cycle used in the case studies ranges from 10 years to 30 years.

37.2.2 Models

Shafiee et al. (2019) explain that the LCC method calculates all direct costs associated with the project or a policy without taking indirect costs (or benefits) into account. The evaluation process involves the summation of discounted cash flows that accrue cost elements over the life cycle of the project/asset/policy with an appropriate discount rate.

The costs are composed of CAPEX and OPEX, whereas CAPEX represents the initial investment and OPEX consists of operation costs and maintenance costs. Also, other cost factors could be considered but these are of minor interest in this context. The cost drivers in operation are the energy costs and maintenance costs. This work focuses on energy costs.

LCC analysis is widely used in the hydrocarbon industry. Kawauchi et al. (2014) conducted a detailed literature survey, Internet-web browsing, and interviews with experts and focused on the basic process of LCC analysis. They break down the basic process of LCC analysis and provide the literature on the broken-down topics. Kawauchi et al. (2014) give an overview of the codes and standards establishing the details and procedure of LCC analysis. Case studies had not been the subject of the paper.

The rules established in the codes and standards are also applied in the German gas sector.

A systematic survey on the current state-of-the-art and future perspectives of the application of various DMS (decision-making support) methods in the upstream oil and gas industry was conducted by Shafiee et al. (2019). Figure 37.1 shows that LCC is by far the most relevant method for decision-making in the last four decades:

The systematic literature review conducted by Shafiee et al. (2019) focuses on the upstream sector of the oil and gas business, whereas the infrastructure for the transmission and distribution of natural gas relates to the downstream sector.

Life cycle cost analysis is established in codes and standards such as ISO 15663 "Petroleum and natural gas industries – Life Cycle Costing" part 1–3 as an international standard (EN ISO 15663 part 1 – part 3, 2000). This code is recognized and provides a guideline for LCCA.

The case studies examined in this paper provide a model for the calculation of NPV. These models are sound and the results can be reproduced.

Risk analyses are the exception in LCC modeling in publications and are not used in the case studies examined.

37.2.3 Input Data of the Case Studies

The input data and especially their assumed development in the future are reviewed. These input data are not only macroeconomic data such as inflation rate, price

37 Life Cycle Cost Analysis: Applying Monte Carlo Simulation on Energy...

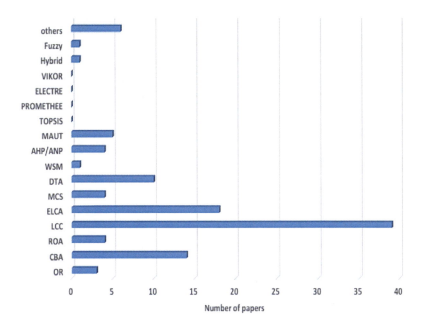

Fig. 37.1 Distribution of decision-making methods applied to the upstream sector during the past four decades. (Shafiee et al., 2019)

indices, and energy prices but also economic data such as maintenance costs and discount factor.

This paper assesses the energy costs, namely, costs for electricity and costs for natural gas. Both energies are used to propel the prime movers of the compressors, either gas turbines, or electric motors.

The authors made assumptions for the energy prices and treated these values with an inflation rate (or escalation factor in percent) in order to establish the future development of energy costs. In consequence, the authors assume a linear increase in the energy prices for the future.

37.2.4 Real Historical Energy Costs

The development of energy prices can be easily obtained. The market price developments for electrical energy and natural gas are publicly available and shown in Figs. 37.2 and 37.3.

The energy prices include all fees and taxes but do not include value added tax (VAT). CO_2-certificate costs are not included and must be analyzed independently.

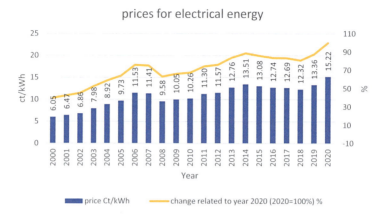

Fig. 37.2 Development of prices for electrical energy for industrial consumers in Germany. (Destatis 2008 until 2020 (Schwenke & Bantle, 2021), 2000 until 2007)

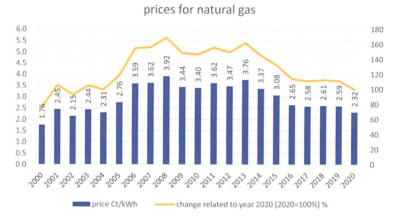

Fig. 37.3 Development of prices for natural gas for industrial consumers in Germany. (BMWi, 2000 until 2020)

The energy prices implemented in the case studies can be correlated with real historical energy prices, and it reveals if the prices utilized are in line with the real historical costs over the lifetime.

The development of energy costs over the years is of considerable importance. The authors in the studies use an escalation factor for the annual rise to incorporate the development of energy costs across the life span. The factor is the inflation rate, which is set as a fixed rate. The values are set between 1.5% and 3% and are based on the expectation of the authors.

It is clear that an incorrect assumption could distort the result of a case study.

A combination of incorrect figures for the applied energy price and an inappropriate escalation factor could distort the result even more.

The examined feasibility studies were prepared from 2001 to 2015 and have the advantage that the predictions in the studies can be compared to the real historical data with today's knowledge. An assessment of how the assumptions affect the results of the calculation of the NPV is easily possible.

In fact, in the studies, the DCE (discounted cumulated expenditure) and not the NPV has been calculated. DCE represents the NPV based on CAPEX and OPEX. Revenues are not considered, as they are the same for all candidate options for the defined operating cases.

DCE can be considered as the total cost of ownership (TCO) comprising CAPEX and OPEX.

For this reason, the option with the lowest NPV is the most advantageous. In fact, not the NPV is calculated but the discounted cumulated expenditure (DCE).

37.2.5 Risk Assessment with Monte Carlo Simulation

Monte Carlo simulation (MCS) is part of probabilistic methods for managing uncertainties and risks.

What is the basic idea of Monte Carlo simulation? Gleißner and Wolfrum (2019) provide an explanation:

Random events can be used if they occur frequently enough to answer the most diverse questions. Since the core of such a simulation is the generation of random numbers the name Monte Carlo simulation was set.

The general sequence for carrying out a Monte Carlo simulation can be described in a few stages as follows:

- Generate the random number needed for the Monte Carlo simulation.
- Convert the random numbers into the required probability distribution function (pdf).
- Perform one step of a Monte Carlo simulation according to the drawn random numbers and the underlying probability distribution.
- Repeat the aforementioned steps in a sufficient number of simulations (i.e., 1000 times) in order to generate stable distributions and relevant statistical data.
- Final evaluation: Formation of the probability distributions of the calculated variables (i.e., NPV), median, percentiles, range, standard deviation, etc.
- From the data, histograms, cumulative distributions, confidence levels, and subsequently box plots can be generated in the context of descriptive statistics for the evaluation of probability (risk).

Monte Carlo simulation is a particularly suitable methodology to quantify the uncertainty of an LCC because the key inputs of the model can be randomly and independently varied about their normal value by a probability distribution function (PDF) to generate a new set of LCC results (Ally & Pryor, 2016).

Today, MCS can be run with 10,000 iterations in a reasonable time, and the number of iterations is not an issue in terms of generating stable results.

Monte Carlo simulation is applied to each option in each case study for the assessment. This means that all models for calculating the DCE undergo a re-run with probability distributions for costs for natural gas and electricity.

Consequently, the following results are available for further evaluation of the DCE calculations of the examined options in the feasibility study:

- DCE calculation with input data from the studies (not part of this work).
- DCE calculations with real historical input data.
- DCE calculations with input data generated from the probability distributions of the Monte Carlo simulation.

The probability distribution functions (PDF) for the following input values have to be defined:

- Cost of electricity.
- Cost of natural gas (fuel gas).
- Costs for CO_2 certificates, if included in the respective case study.

The Beta Pert function is selected as the probability distribution function (PDF) in the MCS-software.

For the Beta Pert function, a minimum value, a maximum value, and a most likely value must be specified as input data for the above costs.

Different approaches to determine these values are possible.

In order to set the min/max/most likely values, the level of knowledge of the authors of the study about the historical data of the energy costs must be considered. For example, the author of a study from 2008 has only firm data up to 2007 (in the best case till 2008) but not later. How shall he establish future costs and how shall he predict future costs?

For example, the assumed cost value from the studies could be taken as the minimum value. The maximum value then results from the escalation with the inflation rate used in the individual study. The arithmetic average could be used as the most likely value. This could be a simple and possible approach. This approach is not chosen because it does not reflect the knowledge of the development of historical data (i.e., if the study is prepared in 2008, historical data until 2008 are known).

A more realistic approach is to consider the possible knowledge of a study author about the historical data of energy costs. Here, a graph of the annual costs for the period from the year 2000 to the year of study preparation is created in a chart in MS Excel (compare charts in Fig. 37.4 through Fig. 37.6). For this graph, a trend line and the corresponding linear function or quadratic function in the form $y = a \times x + b$ or $y = a \times x^2 + bx + c$ are generated in MS Excel. With the help of these functions, the values for the costs are extrapolated into the future. This approach provides the min/max and most likely figures.

The following graphs are samples of the corresponding case studies.

The red line represents the historical costs from the author's view (up to the year of the preparation of the study). The blue line represents the historical data until 2020. The dotted line is the trend line for calculating the min/max/most likely values.

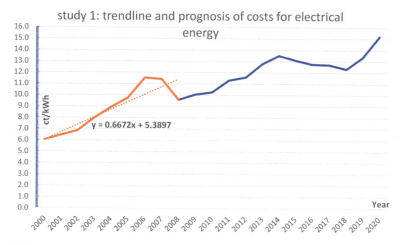

Fig. 37.4 Study 1, trendline and prognosis of costs for electrical energy

As input data for the probability distribution function, the costs from the year the study was carried out, and the extrapolated costs up to the end of the period under consideration (usually the year 2020) are used as the minimum and maximum values. The arithmetic average of both is taken as the most likely value. For the quadratic function, the value for the year 2020 is taken as most likely.

Each simulation is carried out with 10,000 iterations.

The calculated DCEs are presented graphically in the same way as the calculations of DCE with the study values and the calculations with real historical values.

37.3 Results

The following diagrams show the results from using Monte Carlo simulation as explained before.

The DCEs were recalculated for the cost models developed from the studies using Monte Carlo simulation. Three diagrams of three case studies are subject to further analysis. This publication shows typical graphs for three studies and not all graphs for all case studies. The chosen graphs represent typical cases.

The graphs for case studies 1, 2, and 4 show the following:

- DCE calculations with real historical input data.
- DCE calculations with input data generated from the probability distributions of the Monte Carlo simulation.

Each graph shows the calculated DCE for several discount rates. Option 1, option 2, ... are different from each other and represent specific compressor-driver configurations in the case studies.

37.4 Discussion

The discrepancies for DCE, which are calculated with real historical values and with Monte Carlos simulation based on real historical values, are evaluated.

The DCE calculation with real historical data is done with the real historical data over the life span up to the year 2020.

The DCE calculation with Monte Carlo simulation based on real historical data is an assumed approach for an author of the case studies. The author has knowledge of real historical data only up to the date on which he created the case study. To forecast future energy costs, he can set trendlines and apply Monte Carlo simulations.

In contrast, the calculation of DCE using real historical data is based on the complete knowledge of energy costs. Calculating the DCE using Monte Carlo simulation includes only the knowledge of the real historical data up to the time the case study was created.

Ideally, the results of these two calculations are the same. Both methods use the same model, one with full knowledge of the real historical data and the other with MCS.

The trendlines in Figs. 37.4, 37.5 and 37.6 show when the Monte Carlo simulation is expected to produce reliable and less reliable results.

Graph 4 shows the real historical data for electric energy from the year 2000 to 2020. A trend line based on knowledge of energy costs up to the year 2008 produces useful values for energy costs.

The extrapolation of the trendline until the year 2020 also produces reliable results because the trend for electric energy costs continued with slightly higher values from 2008 until 2020. Matching results of DCE calculations can be expected

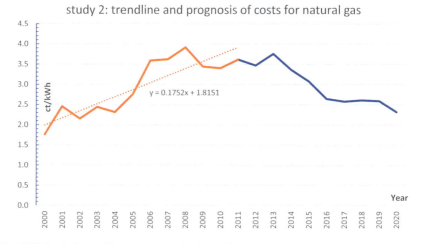

Fig. 37.5 Study 2, trendline and prognosis of costs for natural gas

37 Life Cycle Cost Analysis: Applying Monte Carlo Simulation on Energy...

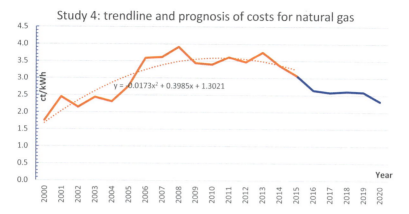

Fig. 37.6 Study 4, trendline and prognosis of costs for natural gas

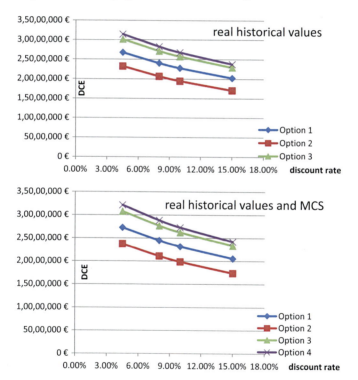

Fig. 37.7 Study 1, DCE calculation with different data basis

with higher values for DCE calculated with MCS. In Fig. 37.7, the expectation shows almost the same DCEs for both approaches.

For the cost of natural gas, the situation is different. The cost of natural gas is not continuously increasing, but decreasing from the year 2013. In 2020, the costs for

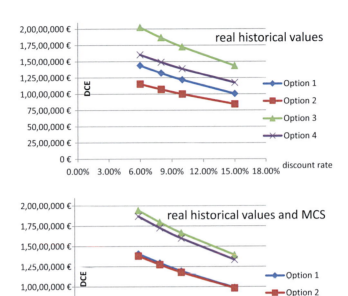

Fig. 37.8 Study 2, DCE calculation with different data basis

natural gas reached about the same value as in 2003. This is shown in Figs. 37.5 and 37.6.

A forecast in 2008 of the future development of the price would suggest a trend line of increasing natural gas prices (Fig. 37.5).

A forecast in 2015 would show a good match between the forecast and actual values for the year 2020. However, this curve would forecast lower costs for further extrapolation into the future, such as the year 2023. Today's knowledge (2023) shows very volatile prices.

In Fig. 37.8, Options 2 and 4 of case study 2 are driven by natural gas. As expected, DCEs calculated with Monte Carlo simulation have higher values. Options 1 and 3 are electricity driven. The MCS-calculated ranking of options is not so clear as for calculation with real historical data. The comparison clearly shows that the extrapolation (in fact the forecast) of future energy cost has uncertainties, even though MCS is used.

The ranking between options with the full knowledge of energy costs (real historical data) is more explicit.

In Fig. 37.9, in case study 4 option 1 is natural gas powered and option 2 is electric powered. The trendline in Fig. 37.6 for natural gas results in higher predicted

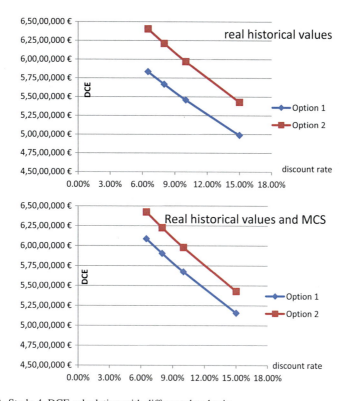

Fig. 37.9 Study 4, DCE calculation with different data basis

values. Therefore, the calculated DCE for the Monte Carlo simulation is higher. For option 2, as expected the calculated DCEs show a good match. The ranking between the options does not change.

Not only does the prediction of energy costs have a significant influence, but also the number of operating hours per year and the number of years in operation (with a direct effect on the number of operating hours). In case study 4, only 3 years in operation contribute to DCE. The influence is of lower influence.

Case studies 1 and 2 are from 2008 and 2011 with higher operating hours and the time period to predict future prices is much longer. Also, these aspects must be taken into consideration when analyzing the results.

37.5 Conclusion

In the LCCA, a model is created in which the NPV (or, as in this case, the DCE) is calculated. This procedure is standardized and described, for example, in ISO 15663. Part of this procedure is to define a life span for the investment project, which is 15–20 years or more in the future. For the life span, input data into the model must be defined and their future development must be forecast over the period of time. There is no standardized procedure for this.

Because of the great uncertainty in predicting the future development of input data, it is recommended in the technical literature and also in ISO 15663 to carry out risk analysis. Monte Carlo simulation is a recognized and proven risk analysis tool.

For risk assessment, it is recommended to identify the main cost drivers and apply risk assessment to these data. In the case study examined, these are the energy costs for natural gas and electric power. It is shown that considering real historical data, a forecast of future prices is associated with uncertainties and that predicted data may significantly differ from real historical data. The uncertainties may lead to results that differ from those calculated under full knowledge of energy costs. This raises the question of the robustness of the results of an LCCA.

Monte Carlo simulation can be used for predicting future energy prices. However, MCS allows more than just forecasting future data. The results of a Monte Carlo simulation can be evaluated and assessed with respect to their reliability by statistical methods.

Risk assessment based on Monte Carlo simulation provides decision makers with a more reliable basis for an investment project.

Since uncertainty remains about the future development of the input data, the decision maker must be given further options for evaluation to back up the results.

For this purpose, the technical literature and also ISO 15663 propose sensitivity analyses. Sensitivity analysis for the discount factor is already included in this publication (see Figs. 37.7, 37.8 and 37.9).

The basis for decision makers must be improved and should be as broad as possible. The improvement requires an extension of the case studies with several elements.

However, the analysis shows that the use of Monte Carlo simulation does not always improve the results of the model calculations. The Monte Carlo simulation can only be as good as the input data. Even if the Monte Carlo simulation does not clearly lead to improvements, the statistical evaluation of the results allows a risk assessment of the investment decision.

It turns out that the extension of the LCCA model is not limited to Monte Carlo simulation. Further elements should secure the results and make them more reliable for decision makers. These elements could be as follows:

- Sensitivity analyses for deterministic input variables, such as energy costs, operating hours, and discount rate.
- Equal DCE for the ratio of energy costs (natural gas vs. electricity).
- Definition of criteria outside the cost model (social, environmental).
- Weighted scoring of criteria outside the cost model.

Further research to improve LCCA as the basis for decision-making shall examine the mentioned measures and the impact on finding the most appropriate investment option.

References

Ally, J., & Pryor, T. (2016). Life cycle costing of diesel, natural gas, hybrid and hydrogen fuel cell bus systems: An Australian case study. *Energy Policy, 94*, 285–294.
Cierniak, S. (2001). Life cycle costs von Kolben- und Turbokompressoren. *Erdöl Erdgas Kohle, 117*, 511–517.
EN ISO 15663 part 1 – part 3. (2000). *EN ISO 15663-1 petroleum and natural gas industries – Life cycle costing – Part 1 – Part 3.*
Gleißner, W. & Wolfrum, M. (2019). *Grundlagen des Risikomanagements* (pp. 3–13). https://doi.org/10.1007/978-3-658-24274-9_2
Kawauchi, Y., Cooperation, T. E. & Rausand, M. (2014) *Life cycle cost (LCC) analysis in oil and chemical process industries life cycle cost (LCC) analysis in oil and chemical process industries*. ResearchGate.
Lee, D. B. (2002). Fundamentals of life-cycle cost analysis. *Transportation Research Record, 1812*(1), 203–210. https://doi.org/10.3141/1812-25
Schwenke, T. & Bantle, C. (2021). *BDEW-Strompreisanalyse, Juni 2021.*
Shafiee, M., Animah, I., Alkali, B., & Baglee, D. (2019). Decision support methods and applications in the upstream oil and gas sector. *Journal of Petroleum Science and Engineering, 173*, 1173–1186. https://doi.org/10.1016/j.petrol.2018.10.050

Chapter 38
Examination of the Beliefs About the Role of Psychological Approaches in Economic Growth and National Development

Stavros Kalogiannidis ⓘ **, Christina Patitsa, Dimitrios Syndoukas, and Fotios Chatzitheodoridis**

Abstract Experts in development now recognize that development is more than simply an economic issue. Before it is an issue of economy, politics, culture, or society, development is first and foremost a psychological issue. The rate of change in the attitudes, minds, and behaviors of these civilizations' citizens determines how quickly societies evolve in a variety of ways. This study assessed the efficacy of psychology in national development. Data were collected from different 379 participants in Greece using an emailed questionnaire. It was established that the different aspects of psychology particularly cognitive, social, and clinical psychology, have an influence on national development. Clinical psychologists' activities and efforts, for instance, might be perceived as helping patients learn to better adapt to and deal with various life circumstances, even while the social environment may be the source of their poor mental health. The results showed that to see the birth of a contemporary human person, and, subsequently, a modern society, development must occur in both cognitive and behavioral dimensions. In light of this, national expansion, which includes economic, political, cultural, and

S. Kalogiannidis (✉)
Department of Business Administration, University of Western Macedonia, Kozani, Greece
e-mail: aff00056@uowm.gr

C. Patitsa
Department of Tourism Management, University of West Attica,
e-mail: cpatitsa@uniwa.gr

D. Syndoukas
Department of Business Administration, University of Western Macedonia, Greece
e-mail: dsyndoukas@uowm.gr

F. Chatzitheodoridis
Department of Regional and Cross Border Development, University of Western Macedonia, Kozani, Greece
e-mail: fxtheodoridis@uowm.gr

© The Author(s), under exclusive license to Springer Nature Switzerland AG 2024
N. Tsounis, A. Vlachvei (eds.), *Applied Economic Research and Trends*, Springer Proceedings in Business and Economics,
https://doi.org/10.1007/978-3-031-49105-4_38

social as well as security and military development, is ideal and reasonable when a society's inhabitants are cognitively and behaviorally evolved. In other words, the process of development starts with the growth of the mind, the mind's psychology, and the mind's conduct. The first stage of growth is the maturation of the intellect, which moves from simple to complex. Each person's cognition, which consists of a collection of beliefs, ideas, and higher mental processes such as thoughts, perceptions, thinking, problem-solving, and decision-making, must be qualitatively improved if there is any chance of national growth. Cognitive growth results in behavioral development, which then shapes conduct in the direction of the best and most advantageous acts. The belief in progress among the populace of a society and the rotation of that populace's conduct in the direction of growth are hence indicators of the development of a nation and society. An analysis of psychological factors and their impact on the growth and underdevelopment of societies has been attempted in this article.

Keywords Psychology · Attitude change · Individual behaviorism · National development

38.1 Background to the Study

Psychology has traditionally taken a second seat to other social disciplines in Greece when it comes to nation-building and societal development. Psychology is highly positivistic and individualistic, which has kept it from becoming more applicable to society and the country (Abdolmalaki, 2022). Psychology has evolved into a "culturally decontextualized" study of behavior as a result of psychologists' emphasis on research. According to the prevalent behaviorist paradigm, there is no distinction between humans and animals at the level of behavior. Because of its individualistic orientation, it was unable to provide the comprehensive viewpoint needed to recognize the most significant societal challenges and problems (Tatarko et al., 2020). Psychology is now seen as having importance for individuals and society since it will influence how people live in the future. All aspects of education, including curriculum design, instructional strategies, discipline, good study habits, and personality development, increasingly depend on an understanding of psychology (Patitsa et al., 2021).

In psychology, the "individual" is the subject of investigation and analysis. Results may be generalized by investigating and researching the traits of people within a community (Gomes & Fradkin, 2015). To achieve national development, it is thus just as necessary to empower and develop each individual member of society as it is to research and understand the individual (Carr & Maclachlan, 1998). Basically, the route to national growth involves individual development, and it is inevitable that the society's citizens must develop as individuals (Abdolmalaki, 2022). The perception of one's power to impact the world generally, one's physical or mental abilities, one's interpersonal connections, one's physical activity, one's confrontation with nature or suppression, and one's ability to regulate one's own emotions are just a few places where this perception may arise (Cefai et al., 2018).

According to Spolaore (2012), literary development refers to a process of steady expansion in order to become more sophisticated, strong, and even bigger. Different definitions of development have been put forward by development specialists like Emile Durkheim, Karl Marx, Max Weber, and Mikhail Todaro, among others. The majority of them think that progress began with meeting fundamental human needs and eventually expanded to include all facets of life, including those related to culture, society, welfare, education, the arts, economics, politics, and defense (Sánchez et al., 2022). Growth is a quantitative phenomenon, but development is an objective economic class phenomenon that is complex and multidimensional and cannot be easily measured by quantitative indicators like per capita income, increased investment and savings, and the transfer of cutting-edge technology from contemporary industrialized nations to countries (Prado-Abril et al., 2019; Siegler, 1976; Vassilopoulos & Malikiosi-Loizos, 2016). Because substantial qualitative changes in the social, political, and cultural structures are necessary in addition to improving the economic situation, developing technology, and expanding national wealth. The three most crucial things to keep in mind when defining development are that it should be seen as a value category first, a multifaceted and complex process second, and that it should be related to the idea of improvement third (Purdy, 2013; Sánchez et al., 2022; Tatarko et al., 2020).

The vast majority of development specialists, including UN employees and authorities, emphasize culture as one of the most crucial elements in attaining development. Since culture is often one of the most significant variables in the accomplishment of progress, cultural development is both one of the essential prerequisites for and one of the primary goals of development in every civilization. Human development is another essential concept in development-related themes. The UN report on human development defined human development as a process in which human capacities grow. In this regard, the three most significant indicators of human development—longevity, level of knowledge, and a decent standard of living—have been identified. It has been asserted that by providing these three elements in a society, it is possible to say that society has attained human development. The attempt to replace the production-oriented development viewpoint with a more humanistic one led to the creation of the Human Development Index (Griffin & McConnell, 2001, p. 229). As presented in Fig. 38.1, Greece's Human Development Index (HDI) score grew from 0.759 in 1990 to 0.887 by 2021, indicating that the nation has attained extremely high levels of development, according to data from 1990 to 2021. The HDI is a metric that combines GDP per capita, life expectancy, and educational attainment. Compared to nations with lower ratings, those with scores above 0.700 are seen to have high levels of development.

Development specialists are now working to make the concept of human development a reality. This comprises a variety of elements, such as psychological aspects of existence. In the framework of development, the concept of social development has also been taken into account (Purdy, 2013). By enhancing the social system, social structure, institutions, services, and resource utilization strategies, the United

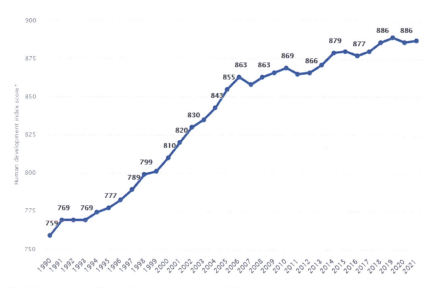

Fig. 38.1 Greece's Human Development Index (HDI) score. (Source: Statista, 2023)

Nations calls for social development to raise living standards in a broader sense (Cefai et al., 2018). Aspects of social development include achieving social equity and justice, social integration, a meritocracy system, social involvement, attending to the requirements of different transitions, embracing social plurality while preserving national cohesiveness, and enhancing human talents (Hanitio & Perkins, 2017). Another definition uses the measures of social development, life expectancy, infant mortality, and accessibility to public education. The World Bank claims that people, their well-being, prosperity, and the growth of civil society by them are at the heart of development, particularly social development (Patitsa et al., 2022). In essence, social development is one of a society's growth mechanisms. Social development may be seen as the manifestation of a fundamental shift in society's beliefs, moral standards, attitudes, actions, and social structures (Cefai et al., 2018). The history of emerging nations after 1945 demonstrates that without a thorough transformation of the political, social, and cultural structure, economic advancement is all but impossible. The application of ideas in their particular meanings has grown along with the division of labor, variety of enterprises, specialization of sciences, and propensity to improve conceptions. Because of this, there are currently at least four different types of development in the four spheres of social life: economic, political, cultural, and social. These developments are distinct from one another even though they are all involved in the process of national development in every society (Abdolmalaki, 2022; Odedoyin, 2019). "National development" refers to the process of change in all nations and communities (Guiso et al., 2020; Vassilopoulos & Malikiosi-Loizos, 2016). There is still another aspect of growth at play here, and that aspect is "psychological development," which has so far been disregarded or disregarded. It is a crucial and deciding factor in the growth process at the same time (Cefai et al., 2018; Prado-Abril et al., 2019).

One psychological sign of underdevelopment is a lack of "motivation" (Guiso et al., 2020). In general, people in Third World nations have constrained intellectual scopes and weak acquired motives. They do not hold the conviction that society can and should be changed, or that change is both desirable and essential. In other words, they lack the drive to become involved in development issues. The underlying problem of underdevelopment in the cultural or psychological components of Third World cultures' inhabitants, who are reportedly superstitious, fate-conscious, conservative, and docile, is taken into consideration by the psychological theory of development (Guiso et al., 2020; Vassilopoulos & Malikiosi-Loizos, 2016). Based on his study of religious values in the East and their inhibitory impact on economic development, Ralph Pierce concludes that the value system that recommends religious order and withdrawal from the outside world in order to achieve salvation is based on the development of modern social organization and technology (Pickren & Rutherford, 2010; Van Vlaenderen, 2001). This study focused on examining the role played by psychology in regard to national development.

38.1.1 Objectives

1. To understand the beliefs about the effect of cognitive psychology on national development.
2. To examine the beliefs about the influence of the different aspects of clinical psychology on national development.
3. To determine the beliefs effect of social psychology on national development.

38.1.2 Research Questions

1. What are the beliefs that cognitive psychology may play a role in national development?
2. How do the different aspects of clinical psychology influence national development?
3. What are the beliefs that social psychology may play a role in national development?

38.1.3 Hypotheses

Hypothesis one (H1): The different aspects of cognitive psychology positively affect national development.

Hypothesis two (H2): The different aspects of clinical psychology have a significant influence on national development

Hypothesis three (H3): Social psychology positively affects national development.

38.1.4 Significance of the Study

The findings on the role of psychology in national development provide important knowledge in the area of national growth but most importantly on how development in most countries is influenced by the different aspects of clinical, cognitive, and social psychology. People need to understand psychology because it enables them to create environments that promote emotional stability, maximum stability, and the eradication of crime (Selzam, 2008, p. 168). In light of this, psychology plays a significant role in a number of areas of human and societal life. It has evolved into a practical instrument for changing attitudes, mannerisms, deeds, and other things.

38.2 Literature Review

38.2.1 Emergence of Global Psychology

We are departing the realm of a globalized civilization as a result of current global events. Globalization could not be stopped. In time, it would follow its own path and turn back toward traditionalism (Guiso et al., 2020). As a result, a universal psychology must be developed. International organizations, conferences, and accessibility to modern media like the internet, Facebook, and other social media have made it possible for a global psychology to emerge where every person would have a "say," including small, developing nations next to the largest first and second world economies (Moghaddam et al., 2013; Siegler, 1976; Vassilopoulos & Malikiosi-Loizos, 2016). Ruchi (2022) noted that it is important to allow for the expression of all indigenous knowledge from all cultures in their own distinctive ways if we are to make psychology universal and available to all people and nations on the planet.

The upshot of the world's drastic change is the emergence of a global psychological paradigm. Environmental, social, cultural, and political issues are seriously threatening its survival (Hanitio & Perkins, 2017). The task at hand is to figure out how to integrate with it, as opposed to existing independently of one another (Oladipo, 2010). There seems to be an irreconcilable confrontation between secular, scientific, religious, technical, and spiritual cultural traditions as a result of the current pressures of globalization (Abdolmalaki, 2022; Moghaddam et al., 2013). These fundamental disparities are being utilized to illustrate a rising sense of ambiguity and bewilderment about how to live successfully within the evolving global framework of human life (Cefai et al., 2018). The scope and complexity of global events and forces indicate a major obstacle for psychology as a science and profession due to the enormous demands placed on individual and collective psychological theories around the world as well as the threats they pose to our sense of identity, control, and wellbeing (Gomes & Fradkin, 2015; Spolaore, 2012).

38.2.2 Elements of Psychology

38.2.2.1 Social Psychology

The scientific study of how individuals affect one another's ideas, emotions, and actions is known as social psychology. Advertising attempts to sway you by using straightforward visuals or catchy jingles, but it may also be subtle. Even those who are not physically there may have an impact on us; for example, recalling our parents' or friends' pleased grins and desires for the future might alter how we behave in morally troubling circumstances (Prado-Abril et al., 2019). In addition, our culture, national standards, societal expectations, and local community norms can have an impact on us without us even being aware of it (Abdolmalaki, 2022; Tatarko et al., 2020).

Social influence, social behavior, and social thinking. Social thinking, social influence, and social conduct are the three core themes of social psychology. The overlap between each of these research areas is shown in Fig. 38.2. The rings overlap because these three forces interact with one another as they have an impact on us on a daily basis. This book's first portion discusses social thought, covering issues like how we identify the self and how we see other individuals. The second part of the essay discusses social impact and includes inquiries into bias, conformity, and persuasion. Third, chapters on social conduct touch on benevolence, hostility, and love ties. This book examines each component separately before bringing them together in a number of mini-chapters on different applied psychology subjects (Abdolmalaki, 2022; Guiso et al., 2020; Hanitio & Perkins, 2017).

Social psychology is a popular choice for both college electives and professional careers. However, compared to many other fields of study, it is still a very new science—it has only been around for around 100 years, give or take a few decades (Vassilopoulos & Malikiosi-Loizos, 2016). The Society for Social and

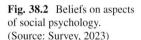

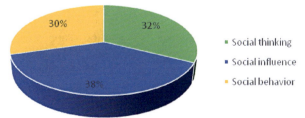

Fig. 38.2 Beliefs on aspects of social psychology. (Source: Survey, 2023)

Personality Psychology and the Society of Experimental Social Psychology are two distinct professional organizations that are exclusively for social psychologists. The American Psychological Association also has a separate branch dedicated to social and personality psychology (Hanitio & Perkins, 2017). Since we can now connect and exchange information online, cross-cultural partnerships among social psychologists are becoming more common. Being involved in social psychology right now is thrilling on both a personal and professional level (Moghaddam et al., 2013; Pritchett, 2022).

38.2.2.2 Clinical Psychology

Clinical psychology is a branch of psychology that is used to diagnose and treat psychological disorders such as aberrant behavior, mental disease, and psychiatric issues. Clinical psychology combines the study of psychology with the treatment of difficult psychological issues in people. Like everything else, clinical psychology has a history that surrounds its continual evolution. Clinical psychology also includes a substantial amount of research and data (Prado-Abril et al., 2019; Rosa Maria et al., 2015). However, there are differences between working in clinical psychology and other mental health fields, such as social work or school psychology. Although clinical psychology is a very complex, interconnected system, it may nevertheless be easily disassembled in order to be understood (Cefai et al., 2018).

The evolution of clinical psychology throughout its history provides a useful starting point for deconstructing the idea of what clinical psychology really is. Clinical psychology has a lengthy history that dates back to the Greek philosophers, Sigmund Freud's theories, and even current forms of psychology that take all of their knowledge not just from philosophy but also from science and other fields. In the development of clinical psychology, there have been numerous significant turning points. Greek philosophers were among the first to recognize connections between the mind and body that aided in understanding how illnesses were affected by this interaction. The concepts of the "spirit or soul is in charge of the body and that issues residing in the soul might end up in physical illness" were understood by Aristotle, Hippocrates, and Plato. The next major turning point for clinical psychology was the Middle Ages, when mental and physical impairments were seen as more than just moral failings and the treatment of illnesses and insanity was seen as a spiritual problem. The third stepping stone appeared later, during the Renaissance. By this time, scientific investigation had shown that beliefs in the supernatural and religious perspectives were unscientific. It was discovered that biomedical reductionism was able to prove that disease was studied more correctly by scientific investigation and observation as opposed to spiritual metaphysical ideas (Siegler, 1976). Sigmund Freud and his associates made a breakthrough in clinical psychology in the nineteenth century when they begin to understand the relationship between the body and the mind. According to Sigmund Freud's theories, which are based on the Greek philosophy of the relationship between a person's body and mind, there are unconscious instructions that have a significant impact on a person's wellbeing and health (Moghaddam et al., 2013).

Clinical psychology is a field that is continually changing, and it may be characterized by its connection to contemporary medicine and its use of what is often referred to as the scientific method. New understandings of the relationship between a person's brain and behavior and mind are constantly being created with the aid of neuroscience and contemporary medicine (Vassilopoulos & Malikiosi-Loizos, 2016). The tremendous human battle to comprehend anomalous behavior in the context of the mind and body has been at the heart of this development. This specific branch of psychology advances science and contributes to a deeper comprehension of the human mind or even the very spiritual character of people (Moghaddam et al., 2013). The practice and research of the aforementioned branch of psychology are always changing in order to better the treatment that patients get (Purdy, 2013; Spolaore, 2012).

Research is situated in the base camp of clinical psychology. As the field of psychology continues to develop, learn, and evolve, research is employed to assist in offering answers to various problems. This ongoing process gives the impression that nature is always changing (Prado-Abril et al., 2019). Clinical psychology researchers use the scientific method and statistics to gather the data required to expand the field's conceptual framework. It has been established that "research is fundamental to both the science and practice of clinical psychology" (Hanitio & Perkins, 2017; Oladipo, 2010). Without research and statistics, clinical psychology would not advance, and things that were improving people's quality of life might not continue to do so the next day because no statistics were provided to clinical psychologists on how to adjust methods to ensure they are operating as intended and no research was conducted to improve the methods already in use (Odedoyin, 2019).

Compared to other branches of psychology, clinical psychology is unique. The training and specialization within the subject, as well as the possibility of needing a different form of graduate degree, are some of the distinctions between clinical psychology and other sciences. For instance, a school psychologist must have a master's degree and work in an elementary or secondary school context. A school psychologist's major objective is to assist and collaborate with kids and their families (Van Vlaenderen, 2001). The majority of social workers place a strong emphasis on maintaining and monitoring individual case studies (Ruchi, 2022). The biological elements of sickness and their potential effect on a person's behavior are given greater attention in social work training than the research component. When compared to one another, counseling psychology and clinical psychology are quite similar and have no discernible differences (Wagemans, 2004). However, psychiatrists are doctors who have received specialized training in various forms of mental medicine. The molecular underpinnings of both behavior and behavioral issues will be thoroughly studied by the psychiatrist (Ibrahim & Ibrahim, 2018). Other occupations such as counseling specialties, psychiatric nursing, and occupational therapy provide therapeutic services that are comparable to those provided by school psychologists, social workers, and psychiatrists. Clinical psychologists, on the other hand, vary from other mental health-related specialists in several aspects (Prado-Abril et al., 2019).

Although clinical psychology is regarded as a separate subject, it is made up of a variety of different elements. Because of the fresh information being gathered in fields like biology, technology, and even physics as well as chemistry and physics, clinical psychology is always evolving (Rosa Maria et al., 2015). The history of psychology has contributed to the development of clinical psychology by incorporating a variety of factors (Kornegay, 2014; Minibas-poussard, 2018; United & Commission, 2012). Clinical psychology differs from other psychological disciplines, but they all share the same fundamental goal of trying to meet all of humanity's psychological needs while also helping to provide enduring and realistic ability to not only thrive but also to cater for the human spirit (Rosa Maria et al., 2015).

38.2.2.3 Cognitive Psychology

The study of cognitive development focuses on how a child grows in terms of information processing, conceptual resources, perceptual skills, language learning, and other characteristics of the fully developed adult brain and cognitive psychology. It is well acknowledged that children and adults view their waking experiences in different ways in terms of quality (Siegler, 1976). Cognitive development is the formation of the ability to actively observe, grasp, and articulate one's knowledge in adult terms (Reyes, 2001; Nick & Angus, 2005). The process through which a person learns to perceive, analyze, and understand their environment is known as cognitive development (Dupuy & Neset, 2018). Both inherited and environmental factors have an impact on it. Four stages are involved in the creation of cognitive information. They are intelligence, reasoning, language, and memory (Hertzman & Melton, 2010; Nordhaus, 2004). Anything that holds a baby's attention, such as playing with toys, watching television, or listening to their parents speak, aids in the development of their cognitive skills when they reach these phases, which start around 18 months of age (Joossens et al., 2022; Moghaddam et al., 2013).

In the last 50 years, cognitive psychology (CP) has made tremendous strides, providing a sizable amount of information mostly focused on certain components of the intricate cognitive architecture of the mind (Spolaore, 2012). The creation of universal notions, paradigms, and models that can be applied to all fields of psychology has not been hindered by the emphasis on particular processes, which is in large part necessary restricted and detailed (Tatarko et al., 2020). Strong cognitive processes that seem to be crucial determinants of high-level intelligence and underpin many cognitive tasks have been identified by cognitive psychology (Abdolmalaki, 2022). Referring to these systems may be useful in defining the core elements of human intellect. In this context, a few traditional cognitive studies have been able to demonstrate the connection between cognitive ability and accuracy in a few fundamental calculations. In a ground-breaking research, Siegler

(1976) demonstrated that IQ was predicted by the speed and accuracy of simple comparisons and short-term memory tasks.

Bruno (2019) noted that it is vital to comprehend the connections between working memory and the other major cognitive processes. Considerations should be made for executive functions, processing speed, and attentional resources in particular (Sánchez et al., 2022). The most fascinating instance involves processing speed. For instance, Bruno (2019) found that in the investigation of the link between working memory and processing speed, the first variable sometimes seemed to explain the second, but the reverse relationship may also exist (Gomes & Fradkin, 2015; LEG Training Workshops, 2013). Since they have been detected more often, situations involving executive functions and attention seem to be more in line with this theory (Ibrahim & Ibrahim, 2018). It is unclear, however, if working memory may be considered to encompass additional active manipulation activities that do not necessarily entail a stronger attentional request in comparison to low-level short-term memory processes, or whether attention can be equated with the active component of working memory (Hanitio & Perkins, 2017). Also unclear are the connections between working memory and other executive functions as well as why vocabulary, which is frequently linked to a person's cultural background, may not be as sensitive to sociocultural influences as working memory, which is ingrained in the neurological makeup of the individual (Minibas-poussard, 2018).

38.2.3 Psychology in National Development

The process of globalization and its effects have been extensively explored in various social science subjects, but psychology has shied away from the problems (Miller, 2023). The nation is grappling with pressing challenges including terrorism, caste strife, and regionalism, yet few Greek psychiatrists have given these problems any consideration (Purdy, 2013). Even though human behavior and a lust-filled mindset are tied to climate change and global warming, Greek psychologists have given little attention to these issues (Doyle, 2014).

In the areas of crime, delinquency, rehabilitation of criminals, police work, population management, public health, etc., psychologists have made substantial contributions; yet, they were unable to make a macro-level influence or address the larger social concerns that affect society as a whole (Moghaddam et al., 2013). They have disregarded the focal points of complex societal problems in many civilizations. In Greece, research on poverty, inequality, and social transformation continues to be a low priority, and its effects are only marginal (Abdolmalaki, 2022). Psychologists feel "left out" of the national conversation when they compare themselves to other social sciences, notably economists and sociologists.

Psychologists now feel strongly compelled to do research that is pertinent to the process of societal evolution as a result of feeling "left out" (Prado-Abril et al., 2019). Greek psychologists have been consumers of knowledge rather than knowledge brokers. With the possible exception of more recent years, information has only ever flowed in one way. Greek psyche has thereby evolved into something that is boring and replicative in addition to being just imitative and obedient (Hanitio & Perkins, 2017; Vassilopoulos & Malikiosi-Loizos, 2016). One could hardly expect Greek scholars to concentrate on issues that are important to the nation given this mentality (Hanitio & Perkins, 2017). Given social and national concerns, the significance of psychological research in Greece has not yet been established. Similar to the scientific policy, some social scientists have made an effort to develop a social science policy for the nation (Abdolmalaki, 2022).

People in Greece mostly utilize their cultural and religious beliefs to justify their behavior. In Greece, people are aware that taking part in politics involves doing something that is neither fully nor completely pure. It seems that social morality and justice norms only show up at cultural events, despite the academics' claims to the contrary. Democracy's core principles may never be a good fit for Greece. Modern conceptions of development originally focused on economic expansion but have now expanded to include social, economic, and environmental factors that contribute to human progress (Kalantonis et al., 2021). As a result, it increasingly drew sociologists, anthropologists, political scientists, and other social sciences into its fold; nevertheless, psychologists stayed far (Chatzitheodoridis & Kontogeorgos 2020; Kalfas et al., 2023; Hanitio & Perkins, 2017; Prado-Abril et al., 2019).

Among the social sciences, social psychology may be one of sociology's closest allies, but not in Greece. Social psychology is still quite undeveloped in terms of ideas that are suitable to study in developing countries (Hanitio & Perkins, 2017; Qatar Government, 2014). Until psychology alters its technique and goals and pays more attention to medium-range generalization relating to certain kinds of socio-cultural systems in third world countries, its impact is likely to remain, at best, limited and marginal (Moghaddam et al., 2013). This analysis identified clinical research on cross-disciplinary problems in developmental, clinical, physiological, and comparative psychology. Some of the topics they addressed included the psychology of labor, political events, the psychology of the natural world, the psychology of inequality and poverty, the psychology of population growth and reproductive health, the dynamics of social change, and a critical analysis of how these works were applied (Nicolene, 2023). However, the majority of the work falling under certain topics was done by individuals who were not psychologists (Chatzitheodoridis et al., 2023; Cefai et al., 2018; Hanitio & Perkins, 2017).

Studies on social tension and intergroup connections, rural development dynamics, educational social psychology, etc., were all well worth reading (Oladipo, 2010). There isn't enough ongoing research being done on important subjects, either theoretical or applied. In that they seldom improve upon the work of their colleagues in the area, psychologists exhibit the worst type of individualism. Since science is the outcome of the continuous and cumulative efforts of the whole scientific community, it evolves piece by piece (Pezirkianidis & Stalikas, 2020; Kalogiannidis et al., 2022a, b, c, d). Without this mentality, research becomes ad hoc in character and is subject to unending duplications and replications. As Gomes and Fradkin (2015) note, research has concentrated on issues where there has already been a lot of work done. It is only reasonable that useful ideas pertinent to the Greek context have not developed in light of such lone and dispersed efforts (Nezlek, 2020; Noh Bin Amit & Rafidah Aga Mohd Jaladin, 2007; Tatarko et al., 2020). The inadequacy of the Greek psychologists to place their empirical data and analyses into suitable theoretical frameworks is likely caused by this isolated mentality (Kalogiannidis et al., 2022a, b, c, d; Moghaddam et al., 2013).

Psychologists only look at little parts of human issues, disregarding their intricacy and the core of the issue. Psychology is microcosmic, giving disproportionate attention to a specific, broad component of a significant societal issue (Moghaddam et al., 2013). The issues that are of the greatest importance to emerging nations nearly often include institutional and structural elements for which psychology is insufficiently prepared (Sinha, 1986). Generally speaking, psychology must acknowledge its limits. What psychology can and cannot achieve is still up for discussion, and, psychology currently only has a limited role to play at the national level of planning (Minibas-poussard, 2018).

38.3 Methodology

38.3.1 Research Design

The study used a quantitative research methodology and a cross-sectional survey research design. The cross-sectional research strategy depends on a detailed investigation of a group or event in order to unearth the roots of numerous underlying principles related to the research topic or study subject.

38.3.2 Target Population

The research was directed at various psychology professionals across. The best suitable sample for the research to understand the efficacy of psychology in national development was chosen from this community.

38.3.3 Sample Size Determination

The researcher utilized Krejcie and Morgan (1970) to determine the required sample size for this study. Based on the target population of Greece, a corresponding sample size of 379 participants as per the Krejcie and Morgan (1970) model was used for this study.

Table 38.1 Variables, guiding question, and measurement

Variable	Guiding question	Measurement statement	Measurement scale
Dependent variable			
National development	What are the different aspects of national development	1. Handling of growth in urban areas 2. Eradication of poverty 3. Improved literacy levels 4. Increased agricultural production	Nominal scale
Independent variables			
Beliefs about the contribution of cognitive psychology in national development	RQ1: What are the beliefs that cognitive psychology may play a role in national development?	1. Ability to critically evaluate 2. Ability to learn 3. Intellectual thinking 4. Ability to memorize events 5. Perceptions towards growth and development	Nominal scale
Beliefs about the contribution of clinical psychology in national development	RQ2: How do the different aspects of clinical psychology influence national development?	1. Psychological wellbeing 2. Individual behavioral traits 3. Ability to manage stress 4. Ability to manage emotions	Nominal scale
Beliefs about the contribution of social psychology in national development	RQ3: What are the beliefs that social psychology may play a role in national development?	1. Social influence 2. Social thinking 3. Social behavior	Nominal scale

38.3.4 Data Collection

An online survey questionnaire was used to collect data from the selected different experienced psychologists in Greece. Only after receiving participants' informed permission and verifying that they were willing to take part in the research was data gathered. In order to identify the relationship between the study variables and provide answers to the research questions, the data collected will be helpful. Different investigative questions regarding the belief that psychology and especially different psychological fields may have an influence in national development were included in the questionnaire (Table 38.1).

38.3.5 Data Analysis

The quantitative data was coded, and SPSS was used to analyze it. The findings were tabulated, and frequencies and percentages were used to interpret them. The overall predictive power of the independent factors on the study's dependent variable was calculated using regression analysis. In order to determine various predicted values in this situation, a multiple regression model is required.

$$Y = \beta_O + \beta_1 X_1 + \beta_2 X_2 + \beta_3 X_3 + \varepsilon \tag{38.1}$$

Where

Y = national development
$\beta 0$ = constant (coefficient of intercept);
X_1 = Beliefs about the contribution of cognitive psychology in national development
X_2 = Beliefs about the contribution of clinical psychology in national development
X_3 = Beliefs about the contribution of social psychology in national development
ε = Represents the error term in the multiple regression model
The hypotheses of the study were tested at the 5% (0.05) level of significance throughout the study.

38.3.6 Ethical Considerations

The researcher ensured that informed permission was acquired in order to validate participants' willingness to participate in the study. Confidentiality and privacy were also preserved while dealing with respondents' data. Finally, respondents were allowed to answer questions depending on their understanding of the various opinion questions. This aided in gaining wide responses to specific queries.

38.4 Results

This section presents the different results obtained after analysis using SPSS.

38.4.1 Univariate Analysis

The majority of the participants (78.3%) were male, and the females were only 28.7%. Most study participants (46.7%) had a bachelor's degree, 22.4% had

Table 38.2 Showing demographic data of study respondents

Characteristic	Frequency	Percentage (%)
Gender		
Male	297	78.3
Female	82	28.7
Education level		
Certificate	32	8.4
Diploma	71	18.7
Bachelors	177	46.7
Masters	85	22.4
PhD	14	3.7
Experience in psychology and sociology		
Below 5 years	61	16.1
5–10 years	121	31.9
Above 10 years	197	60.0
Total	**379**	**100**

Source: Survey (2023)

Table 38.3 Beliefs about cognitive psychology aspects on national development

Beliefs about cognitive psychology aspects on national development	Frequency	Percentage (%)
Ability to critically evaluate	51	13.5
Ability to learn	47	12.4
Intellectual thinking	112	29.6
Ability to memorize events	71	18.7
Perceptions towards growth and development	98	25.8
Total	**379**	**100**

Source: Survey (2023)

a master's degree, and only 3.2% had PhDs. Most participants (60%) had an experience of above 10 years in the area of psychology followed by 31.9% had an experience of 5–10 years and only 8.1% had an experience of less than 5 years in the psychology sector (Table 38.2).

38.4.2 Descriptive Statistics

The study sought to establish the effect of cognitive psychology on national development, and focus was first put on the aspects of cognitive psychology, and the results are presented in Table 38.3.

The results in Table 38.3 show that cognitive psychology largely relates to intellectual thinking (29.6%) followed by perceptions towards growth and development (25.8%), ability to memorize events (18.7%), and ability to critically evaluate (13.5%), and the least number of respondents (12.4%) noted that cognitive psychology relates to the ability to learn.

Table 38.4 Beliefs about clinical psychology aspects on national development

Beliefs about clinical psychology aspects on national development	Frequency	Percentage (%)
Psychological wellbeing	108	28.5
Individual behavioral traits	88	23.2
Ability to manage stress	71	18.7
Ability to manage emotions	112	29.6
Total	**379**	**100**

Source: Survey (2023)

Table 38.5 Aspects of national development

	Frequency	Percentage (%)
Handling of growth in urban areas	62	16.4
Eradication of poverty	119	31.4
Improved literacy levels	113	29.8
Increased agricultural production	85	22.4
Total	**379**	**100**

Source: Survey (2023)

The study sought to establish the effect of clinical psychology on national development, and focus was first put on the aspects of clinical psychology, and the results are presented in Table 38.4.

The results in Table 38.4 show that clinical psychology is largely associated with the ability to manage emotions (29.6%), followed by psychological wellbeing (28.5%), then individual behavioral traits (23.2%), and the least number of respondents (18.7%) noted that clinical psychology is associated with Ability to manage stress.

The study sought to establish the effect of social psychology on national development, and focus was first put on the aspects of social psychology, and the results are presented in Fig. 38.2.

The results in Fig. 38.2 show that most of the study participants (38%) revealed that social psychology is associated with social influence followed by social thinking (32%) and then 30% for social behavior. The results clearly show that the different aspects of social psychology such as social thinking help people to have deep thoughts about their lives and how best to achieve personal development, which in the long run has an impact on national development.

The study established the aspects of national development, and the results are presented in Table 38.5.

Based on the results in Table 38.5, most respondents (31.4%) showed that national development is much associated with the eradication of poverty, followed by improved literacy levels (29.8%), then increased agricultural production (22.4%), and the least number (16.4%) noted that national development relates to effective handling of growth in urban areas.

Table 38.6 Regression analysis

Model summary

Model	R	R square	Adjusted R square	Std. error of the estimate
	0.698[a]	0.686	0.654	0.10214

[a]Predictors: (Constant), cognitive psychology, clinical psychology, social psychology

Table 38.7 ANOVA

ANOVA

	Sum of squares	Df.	Mean square	F	Sig.
Regression	76.204	3	28.031	73.261	0.002
Residual	71.051	376	0.413		
Total	147.255	379			

Dependent variable: National development
Predictors: (Constant), cognitive psychology, clinical psychology, social psychology

Table 38.8 Coefficients

Coefficients

Model beliefs about different psychological approaches on national development	Unstandardized coefficients		Standardized coefficients	T	Sig.
	B	Std. error	Beta		
(Constant)	0.588	0.126		1.941	0.027
Cognitive psychology	0.168	0.054	0.321	1.124	0.024
Clinical psychology	0.424	0.072	0.162	0.817	0.001
Social psychology	0.126	0.141	0.034	0.817	0.012

National development
Predictors: Cognitive psychology, clinical psychology, social psychology

38.4.3 Regression Analysis

The belief about the efficacy of psychology on national development was established using regression analysis as presented in the subsequent tables (Table 38.6).

National development is the dependent variable. The dependent variable and independent variable are regressed, yielding an R^2 value of 0.673. This shows that cognitive psychology, clinical psychology, and social psychology account for 68.6% of national development. Additionally, the regression findings show that none of the study's independent variables had any impact on 31.4% of the changes (Table 38.7).

The F-statistic of 71.421 at prob. (Sig) = 0.014 conducted at 5% level of significance means that there is a significant linear relationship that exists between the independent variables (beliefs about cognitive psychology, clinical psychology, social psychology) and the dependent variable (national development) as a whole (Table 38.8).

The results in the table above confirm that the participants believe the influence of psychology on national developmental was measured in terms of beliefs about the role of cognitive psychology, clinical psychology, and social psychology aspects since $p < 0.05$.

38.4.3.1 Hypotheses Testing

Since the significance level of 0.024 is less than 0.05%, we confirm that the participants believe that Cognitive psychology has an influence on national development. Therefore, we accept hypothesis H1 that Cognitive psychology has an effect on national development.

Also there is a relationship between belief of clinical psychology aspects and national development since the significance level of 0.001 is less than 0.05%. We, therefore, accept H2 that the different aspects of clinical psychology have a significant influence on national development.

Since the significance level of 0.024 is less than 0.05%, we confirm that aspects of social psychology, especially social thinking and social behavior, have a great influence on national development. Therefore, we accept hypothesis H3 that social psychology positively affects national development.

38.5 Discussion

The notion that psychology is a multidimensional term that incorporates the improvement of all facets of human existence and, as a consequence, is too complicated to be described by single indices has gained increasing acceptance in recent years. Psychology is becoming more widely recognized as an important element of human development leading to national development. Owing to the limited empirical research in Greece, this study examined how the different aspects of cognitive, clinical, and social psychology influence overall national development in Greece. It was established that the different aspects of psychology, particularly cognitive, social, and clinical psychology, have an influence on national development. Clinical psychologists' activities and efforts, for instance, might be perceived as helping patients learn to better adapt to and deal with various life circumstances, even while the social environment may be the source of their mental illness (Bandawe, 2010; Moghaddam et al., 2013). Thus, clinical psychology focuses on societal stability and adaption and has a propensity to back the status quo in terms of political position. The formation of a distinct third world indigenous psychology that aims to employ psychological knowledge to support all-around political, social, and economic development, however, is generative psychology, which is of more importance. Make significant fundamental changes and lineup changes (Guiso et al., 2020; Pritchett, 2022). By examining the psychological effects of unemployment and teaching the jobless, or training the unemployed to obtain job chances and interview skills, modulative psychology, for instance, aims to assist these individuals (Prado-Abril et al., 2019). Social psychology, in contrast, is linked to psychological processes connected to the large-scale societal changes that cause unemployment (Vassilopoulos & Malikiosi-Loizos, 2016). In other words, whether psychological theories (fear, anxiety, cognitive constraints, problem-solving, decision-making, misinterpretation of reality (misunderstanding)) support the idea that a certain degree of unemployment is required to retain a competitive position (Kalogiannidis et al., 2022a, b, c, d; Dupuy & Neset, 2018; Purdy, 2013).

Human development based on different psychology aspects in Greece is increasingly seen as essential to national development in Greece, hence psychologists may contribute significantly to the discussion of national development. Social psychologists concentrate on social issues including drug misuse, crime, racism, domestic violence, public health, bullying, and hostility that have a significant impact on both individual wellbeing and the wellbeing of society as a whole (Balasundaram & Avulakunta, 2021). Such activities associated with social psychology have greatly helped to shape nations like Greece since they have a deep impact on the behavioral traits of people, which in the long run shapes the dynamics of the economy and development of the nation. Behavioral economists stick to ideas like utility, aversions, and preferences, but social psychologists may use other attitudes, motives, and actions. Developmental psychology enables us to comprehend how and why people change through time as they learn, develop, and adapt. Learn about developmental psychology's key applications and how psychologists utilize it. For instance, research provides light on how individuals develop attitudes toward others and, when these attitudes are negative—as in the case of prejudice, for instance—offers guidance on how to alter them (Artelaris, 2022).

National development necessitates the capacity to strike a balance between the human mind's volume and the velocity of change in the human environment (Hanitio & Perkins, 2017; Purdy, 2013). In order to build mental space health and increase both the quantity and quality of life as a result of the interaction between these two spaces, the human civic-cultural mind must evolve (Seifzadeh, 2013; Kalogiannidis et al., 2022a, b, c, d). So, in order to create a rich and successful society before undergoing economic change, it is essential to psychologically design each member of that society on a mental, psychological, cultural, and social level (Zymelman, 1973). Psychological modernization, also known as psychological renewal, is the process of altering one's levels of values, cognitive preferences, personality traits, etc. through exposure to things like urban life, formal education, media exposure, and employment in contemporary businesses (Carr & Maclachlan, 1998). Additionally, it results in actions that reflect the social, political, and economic progress of a society (Pritchett, 2022). In order to create a rich and successful society before reforming the economy, it is vital to psychologically design each member of that society on a mental, psychological, cultural, and social level. As a result, and in fact, as a requirement for it, psychological growth comes before economic progress. Naturally, it is necessary to train evolved people in order to produce a developed society. Until there is no aiming, planning, or expenditure for the evolved human person, material progress will be incomplete (Odedoyin, 2019).

It is obvious that kindergarten and school should be the starting point for this level of mental growth (Pezirkianidis & Stalikas, 2020).

38.6 Conclusion and Recommendation

This study assessed the beliefs about the role played by psychology in national development. It was revealed that social psychology most especially social thinking and social behavior, have a great influence on national development. Given that human development is increasingly seen as essential to national development, psychologists may contribute significantly to the discussion of national development. Lack of a suitable theory to explain change is a significant flaw in the psychological literature on country development. It is clear that the different aspects of clinical, social and cognitive psychology can have a very fundamental impact in the nature of human development and consequently on national development in Greece. Owing to Greece's strong psychology foundation, it has achieved a significant improvement in the level of human development which has greatly influenced the overall national development. If psychology is to continue having an impact on national development in Greece, it must work with other social sciences to address societal problems and achieve social development. The psychology of the twenty-first century must advance significantly in all areas, including those that are still being explored today as well as those that were first begun but subsequently dropped. The psychology of human rights and self-assertion, for example, as well as social change and intergenerational bonds, terrorism and communal violence, caste discrimination, caste violence, and untouchability, gender discrimination, violence against women, and rape, are other important topics that psychologists need to address. In order to enhance national development, psychology is essential. If we are willing to take significant disciplinary action, its effectiveness will only be realized. This kind of reaction necessitates a shift in perspective and a reexamination of the theories, techniques, and practices of Western psychology in particular, as well as a greater understanding, acceptance, and use of other various indigenous psychologies. Others have nothing to say about the capitalistic Western growth of psychology. Modernity is characterized by conflicts between democratic and hegemonic forms of globalization. The marginalized groups will resurge, and indigenous people will fight back. Localist, ethno-nationalist, pan-nationalist, regionalist, ecological, feminist, and religious movements are only a few of the many ways opposition is expressing itself today. Placement of psychologists and psychologies in their proper local and global settings is necessary under a new paradigm of psychology. New disciplines such as population psychology, psychology of health, and psychology of peace need to be strengthened. Furthermore, it is important to note that strong ties exist between the requirement for competent regional analysis and public policy. One of the top governmental initiatives in recent years in various nations moving toward more focused public policy interventions has been the enhancement of human development, which greatly relates to psychology. For European nations such as Greece, this is more crucial than ever since it has an influence on economic growth and development. In this approach, policymakers may utilize the study's results to better understand and enhance the national development process and how it is influenced by the different aspects of psychology. The current study findings serve as both instruments for assessing the role played by psychology in enhancing national development and the efficacy of focusing on the different fields of psychology by the government of Greece and any other governments.

38.6.1 Areas for Future Research

The current research focused on how psychology influences national development, with emphasis on cognitive, social, and clinical aspects of psychology. It is however important to evaluate the psychological barriers of national development. This can help to establish the areas that need to be focused on by psychological experts in order to enhance national development.

References

Abdolmalaki, S. (2022). Investigating the role of psychology in national development. *International Journal of Economics and Management Studies, 9*(1), 43–52. https://doi.org/10.14445/23939125/ijems-v9i1p108

Artelaris, P. (2022). A development index for the Greek regions. *Quality & Quantity, 56*(3), 1261–1281. https://doi.org/10.1007/s11135-021-01175-x

Balasundaram, P., & Avulakunta, I. D. (2021). *Human growth and development.* https://www.ncbi.nlm.nih.gov/books/NBK567767/

Bandawe, C. (2010). A brief history of social psychology and its contribution to health in Malawi. *Malawi Medical Journal, 22*(2), 34–37. https://doi.org/10.4314/mmj.v22i2.58788

Bruno, L. (2019). National development Strategy 2. *Journal of Chemical Information and Modeling, 53*(9), 1689–1699.

Carr, S. C., & Maclachlan, M. (1998). Psychology in developing countries: Reassessing its impact. *Psychology and Developing Societies, 10*(1), 1–20. https://doi.org/10.1177/097133369801000101

Cefai, C., Bartolo, P. A., Cavioni, V., & Downes, P. (2018). Strengthening social and emotional education as a core curricular area across the EU: A review of the international evidence. In *NESET II report* (Issue February). https://doi.org/10.2766/664439

Chatzitheodoridis, F., & Kontogeorgos, A. (2020). Exploring of a small-scale tourism product under economic instability: The case of a Greek rural border area. *Economies, 8*(3), 52.

Chatzitheodoridis, F., Melfou, K., Kontogeorgos, A., & Kalogiannidis, S. (2023). Exploring key aspects of an integrated sustainable urban development strategy in Greece: The case of Thessaloniki City. *Smart Cities, 6*(1), 19–39. MDPI AG. Retrieved from https://doi.org/10.3390/smartcities6010002

Doyle, M. S. (2014). *Counseling psychology: From industrial societies to sustainable development* (Vol. I). EOLSS.

Dupuy, K., & Neset, S. (2018). The cognitive psychology of corruption—Micro-level explanations for unethical behaviour. *U4 Anti-Corruption Resource Center, 2*, 31.

Gomes, W. B., & Fradkin, C. (2015). Historical notes on psychology in Brazil: The creation, growth and sustenance of postgraduate education. *Psicologia: Reflexao e Critica, 28*, 2–13. https://doi.org/10.1590/1678-7153.2015284002

Guiso, L., Herrera, H., Morelli, M., & Sonno, T. (2020). *Economic insecurity and the demand of populism in Europe* (CEPR Discussion Paper, pp. 1–51).

Griffin, S. D., & McConnell, D. (2001). Australian occupational therapy practice in acute care settings. *Occupational Therapy International, 8*(3), 184–197

Hanitio, F., & Perkins, D. D. (2017). Predicting the emergence of community psychology and community development in 91 countries with brief case studies of Chile and Ghana. *American Journal of Community Psychology, 59*(1–2), 200–218. https://doi.org/10.1002/ajcp.12127

Hertzman, C., & Melton, G. B. (2010). *Framework for the social determinants of early child development 20 young children's rights 28*, March 2011, pp. 1–34.

Ibrahim, R. H., & Ibrahim, F. B. (2018). WeCARE intervention program: An online multi-level international program for promoting well-being and resilience in the school community during unsettling times. *Education, 1*(2), 53–59. https://pdfs.semanticscholar.org/6592/a6eb28e6db4e302f17c47eb2c9a017bd6cf5.pdf

Joossens, E., Manca, A. R., & Zec, S. (2022). *Measuring and understanding individual resilience across the EU*. EUR 31264 EN, Publications Office of the European Union. https://doi.org/10.2760/434622

Kalantonis, P., Schoina, S., & Kallandranis, C. (2021). The impact of corporate governance on earnings management: Evidence from Greek listed firms. *Corporate Ownership and Control, 18*(2), 140–153.

Kalfas, D., Kalogiannidis, S., Chatzitheodoridis, F., & Toska, E. (2023). Urbanization and land use planning for achieving the sustainable development goals (SDGs): A case study of Greece. *Urban Science, 7*(2), 43. https://doi.org/10.3390/urbansci7020043

Kalogiannidis, S., Kontsas, S., Konteos, G., & Chatzitheodoridis, F. (2022a). Investigation of the redesigning process of the development identity of a local government regional unit (city): A case study of Kozani regional unit in Greece. In N. Tsounis & A. Vlachvei (Eds.), *Advances in quantitative economic research* (ICOAE 2021. Springer proceedings in business and economics). Springer. https://doi.org/10.1007/978-3-030-98179-2_20

Kalogiannidis, S., Loizou, E., Kalfas, D., & Chatzitheodoridis, F. (2022b). Local and regional management approaches for the redesign of local development: A case study of Greece. *Administrative Sciences, 12*, 69. https://doi.org/10.3390/admsci12020069

Kalogiannidis, S., Loizou, E., Melfou, K., & Papaevangelou, O. (2022c). Assessing relationship between entrepreneurship education and business growth. In P. Sklias, P. Polychronidou, A. Karasavvoglou, V. Pistikou, & N. Apostolopoulos (Eds.), *Business development and economic governance in Southeastern Europe* (Springer proceedings in business and economics). Springer. https://doi.org/10.1007/978-3-031-05351-1_10,183-194

Kalogiannidis, S., Savvidou, S., Papaevangelou, O., & Pakaki, F. (2022d). Role of management in optimising the quality of education in educational organisations. In N. Tsounis & A. Vlachvei (Eds.), *Advances in quantitative economic research* (ICOAE 2021. Springer proceedings in business and economics). Springer. https://doi.org/10.1007/978-3-030-98179-2_21

Kornegay, E. N. (2014, February). *The relationship between economic development and mental health: Nigeria, a case study*.

Krejcie, R. V., & Morgan, D. W. (1970). Determining sample size for research activities. *Educational and psychological measurement, 30*(3), 607–610.

LEG Training Workshops. (2013, August). *Understanding national development processes, processes, frameworks and models*.

Miller, H. P. (2023). *Theories of developmental psychology* (6th ed.). Worth Publishers. ISBN-978-1429278980.

Minibas-poussard, J. (2018). *Psychological variables involved in belief regarding the economy: A comparative study in Greece and Turkey*. International Association for Research in Economic Psychology XXIV Annual Colloquium, Belgirate, Italy, July 1999.

Moghaddam, F. M., Bianchi, C., Daniels, K., Apter, M. J., & Harre, R. (2013). Psychology and national development. *Psychology, Development and Social Policy in India, 2*(1999), 41–57. https://doi.org/10.1007/978-81-322-1003-0_3

Nezlek, J. B. (2020). Social psychological perspectives on human development. In T. Homada (Ed.), *Encyclopedia of life support systems*. UNESCO, Eolss Publishers.

Nick, B., & Angus, G. (2005). *Cognitive psychology.*. Oxford University Press.

Nicolene, J. (2023). *The theory and practice of Christian psychology in Europe*. Cambridge Scholars Publishing.

Noh Bin Amit, & Rafidah Aga Mohd Jaladin. (2007). The importance of psychological development for Malaysian students in facing vision 2020. *Masalah Pendidikan, 30*(2), 117–127. http://myais.fsktm.um.edu.my/4785/

Nordhaus, W. D. (2004, April). *The views expressed herein are those of the author(s) and not necessarily those of the National Bureau of Economic Research.* ©2004 by William D. Nordhaus. All rights reserved. Short sections of text, not to exceed two paragraphs, may be quoted without exp. Science.

Odedoyin, S. O. (2019). On the psychological foundations of economic development. *Theoretical and Practical Research in the Economic Fields, 10*(1), 60. https://doi.org/10.14505/tpref.v10.1(19).07

Oladipo, S. (2010). Psychological empowerment and development. *Edo Journal of Counselling, 2*(1), 119–126. https://doi.org/10.4314/ejc.v2i1.52661

Patitsa, C. D., Sahinidis, A. G., Tsaknis, P. A., & Giannakouli, V. (2021). Big five personality traits and students' satisfaction with synchronous online academic learning (SOAL). *Corporate Business Strategy Review, 2*(2), 8–16.

Patitsa, C. D., Sotiropoulou, K., Giannakouli, V., Sahinidis, A. G., & Tsaknis, P. A. (2022). The influence of personality on compliance with Covid-19 public health protection measures: The role of prosocial behavior. *Journal of Governance and Regulation/Volume, 11*(4), 136.

Pezirkianidis, C., & Stalikas, A. (2020). Introduction—Latest developments in positive psychology: The case of Greece. *Psychology: The Journal of the Hellenic Psychological Society, 25*(1), 01. https://doi.org/10.12681/psy_hps.25328

Pickren, W., & Rutherford, A. (2010). *Modern psychology in context*. Wiley.

Prado-Abril, J., Sánchez-Reales, S., Gimeno-Peón, A., & Aldaz-Armendáriz, J. A. (2019). Clinical psychology in Spain: History, regulation and future challenges. *Clinical Psychology in Europe, 1*(4). https://doi.org/10.32872/cpe.v1i4.38158

Pritchett, L. (2022). National development delivers: And how! And how? *Economic Modelling, 107*, 1–48. https://doi.org/10.1016/j.econmod.2021.105717

Purdy, E. R. (2013). Family and consumer sciences. *Encyclopedia of Women in Today's World*. https://doi.org/10.4135/9781412995962.n272

Qatar Government. (2014, July 1–19). *National development planning and implementation: Human development, sustainable development and national well-being.*

Reyes, G. E. (2001). Four main theories of development: Modernization, dependency, word-system, and globalization. *Revista Crítica de Ciencias Sociales y Jurídicas, 04*(1), 2.

Rosa Maria, P., Fiammetta, G., & Sonia, G. (2015, March). *For a clinical psychology of development. The competence to construct contexts as the outcome of intervention.*

Ruchi, T. (2022). *Clinical psychology, nature, development and activities of clinical psychologist* (Mapsy 202).

Sánchez, F., De Filippo, D., Blanco, A., & Lascurain, M. L. (2022). Contribution of social psychology research to the sustainable development goals (SDGs). Bibliometric and content analysis of Spanish publications. *Spanish Journal of Psychology, 25*(3), e22. https://doi.org/10.1017/SJP.2022.18

Seifzadeh, S. A. Pouya, The Role of Corporate Controls, Size, and Corporate Headquarters in the Effect of Corporate-Level Strategy on Business-Level Strategy and Business-Level Performance (2013). *Electronic Thesis and Dissertation Repository*, 1341. https://ir.lib.uwo.ca/etd/1341

Selzam, Howard, Ethics and Progress (New Values in the Revolutionary World), translated by Majid Madadi, Tehran: Third Edition (2008)

Siegler, R. S. (1976). Three aspects of cognitive development. *Cognitive Psychology, 8*(4), 481–520. https://doi.org/10.1016/0010-0285(76)90016-5

Sinha, N. C. (1986). Studies on plant type of certain forage crops. *Journal of agronomy and crop science, 156*(4), 285–288. https://doi.org/10.1111/j.1439-037X.1986.tb00039.x

Spolaore, E. (2012). *Spolaore & Wacziarg 2012 deep roots of economic development* (CESifo Working Paper Series No. 3837, pp. 66).

Statista. (2023). *Human development index score of Greece from 1990 to 2021*. Available on https://www.statista.com/statistics/880411/human-development-index-of-greece/

Tatarko, A. N., Mironova, A. A., Gari, A., & van de Vijver, F. J. R. (2020). The relationship between human values and acceptability of corruption in Russia and Greece. *Psychology in Russia: State of the Art, 13*(3), 79–95. https://doi.org/10.11621/pir.2020.06

United, T., & Commission, N. (2012, April). *Recommendations submitted by: Psychology NGOs accredited at the United Nations 1*.

Van Vlaenderen, H. (2001). Psychology in developing countries: People-centred development and local knowledge. *PINS (Psychology in Society), 27*, 88–108.

Vassilopoulos, S. P., & Malikiosi-Loizos, M. (2016). Counselling psychology research in Greece. *The European Journal of Counselling Psychology, 4*(1), 1–3. https://doi.org/10.5964/ejcop.v4i1.121

Wagemans, J. (2004). Cognitive psychology. *Encyclopedia of Social Measurement, November 2015*, 351–359. https://doi.org/10.1016/B0-12-369398-5/00480-1

Zymelman, M. (1973). *Financing and efficiency in education: Reference for administration and policy making* (p. 322). Harvard University Press.

Chapter 39
Heterogenous Consumption Responses and Wealth Inequality over the Business Cycle

Rachel Forshaw

Abstract Recent research has highlighted the importance of heterogeneity in the marginal propensity to consume (MPC) out of transitory income shocks for the efficacy of monetary and fiscal policy. However, work on estimating the distribution of MPCs remains scant and typically assumes that an individual's MPC remains constant over time. Using the US Panel Study of Income Dynamics (PSID), I calibrate a model of microeconomic wealth and discount rate heterogeneity with aggregate shocks over the Great Recession of 2008, a historical 'upper bound' in terms of the dynamics of the wealth distribution in recessionary times. Using a reduced-form model, I estimate the degree of heterogeneity in MPCs both over the population and over the business cycle and show that a state-invariant MPC distribution is irreconcilable with empirical changes in the wealth distribution.

Keywords Business cycles · Heterogeneous agents · Consumption · Income shocks

39.1 Introduction

The standard model of inequality with business cycles, the Krusell and Smith (1998) model (henceforth, KS), is becoming an increasingly important tool in the macroeconomist's toolkit. Its popularity is only set to grow given that the barriers to entry to this literature are rapidly falling. Historically, a significant barrier has been one of computation. However, recent software developments obviate the need for a computer science degree in order to solve such models.[1] These new

---

[1] See, for example, Phact by Ahn et al. (2018) and Hark by Carroll (2006).

R. Forshaw (✉)
Heriot-Watt University, Edinburgh, UK
e-mail: r.forshaw@hw.ac.uk

applications allow the economist to solve this class of models with only the level of computational savviness needed to operate such widespread applications as Dynare. The second barrier to entry has been the 'so what?' objection. KS showed that, rather than keeping track of the whole distribution of wealth holdings, agents were able to forecast prices with very high precision by only tracking the mean, a finding they term *approximate aggregation*. The corollary to this finding is that macroeconomic aggregates are incredibly similar to those generated by representative agent models. This second barrier is also falling, with a number of recent papers violating the approximate aggregation result and finding that microeconomic heterogeneity can matter significantly for macro, and allowing the study of distributional implications of economic policies across households.[2] Given that these models are becoming increasingly popular, we should care about how well they accord with empirical evidence. Since the original paper's release, a number of additions to the KS model have increased its empirical realism in terms of the degree of wealth inequality seen in the data (see, for example, Krueger et al., 2016, De Nardi & Fella, 2017, and Carroll et al., 2017)). However, this literature uses cross-sectional micro data at a point in time to discipline the cross section of the model. The major contribution of this research is to instead focus on micro-level panel data capturing the distributional dynamics over time.

It is already well documented that the KS model does a poor job of fitting the cross-sectional wealth distribution in its benchmark form.[3] An increasingly popular method for better fitting the empirical facts of the cross-sectional wealth distribution in this period is the addition of heterogeneous time preferences. It is backed by growing microeconomic evidence of such heterogeneity in the rate of time discount (Lawrance, 1991; Warner & Pleeter, 2001). I calibrate this version of the KS model, which I will call the KS-β-Dist model, to US Panel Survey of Income Dynamics (PSID) data and examine its business cycle characteristics, focusing in particular on its predictions for the marginal propensity to consume (MPC). I focus on MPCs as I establish that variation in the MPC both over the distribution and over the cycle leads to a failure of approximate aggregation. As such, they are the pathway by which microeconomic heterogeneity matters for macroeconomic aggregates. Using the reduced-form model of Blundell et al. (2008) on the same panel data, I confirm that the KS β-Dist provides a good approximation to the cross-sectional wealth distribution in accordance with the previous literature and, new to this research, the income-poor part of the distribution of cross-sectional MPCs. However, I then repeat this calibration exercise for data during the expansion period leading up to the Great Recession of 2008 and its immediate aftermath. The choice of the 2008 recession is deliberate: It was unprecedented in the postwar period for its severity and duration. It also had large-reaching influences on consumption and the wealth distribution in the USA. Bricker et al. (2012) find that over the period of 2007–2010, median net worth fell 38.8% in real terms, and the Survey of Consumer Finances also documents

---

[2] See Ahn et al. (2018) for an overview of this literature.

[3] See Krusell and Smith (1998), Krueger and Perri (2005), and De Nardi and Fella (2017).

that net worth decreased considerably relative to income; the median net worth-to-income ratio declined from 8.5 in 2007 to 5.6 in 2010. De Nardi et al. (2011) detail that it took almost 12 quarters for total real personal consumption expenditures to return to the previous peak in 2007 Q4. It therefore represents a historical 'upper bound' in terms of the dynamics of the wealth distribution in recessionary times and therefore makes the results generalisable to other recessionary periods. In order to fit the dynamics of the wealth distribution in the KS framework, I show that we must modify preference parameters significantly, with large implications for the cross-sectional variation of MPCs. Such variation is ruled out on the basis of my reduced-form evidence.

The chapter is organised as follows: Sects. 39.2 and 39.3 describe the KS structural model and the addition of heterogenous discount factors. Section 39.4 explains the importance of marginal propensities to consume and where the approximate aggregation result fails. Section 39.5 describes the dynamics of the KS β-Dist. Sections 39.6 and 39.7 take these dynamics to the data, describing the methodology of the reduced-form estimation of MPCs across the distribution. Section 39.8 discusses the results in the context of the structural model, and Sect. 39.9 concludes.

39.2 The Krusell Smith Model

KS consider an economy in which there is a continuum of infinitely lived agents of measure one. Time is discrete, $t = (0, 1, 2, \ldots)$, and each agent has preferences over flows of consuming the single consumption good, c, that can be described by

$$\sum_{t=0}^{\infty} \beta^t U(c_t)$$

with constant relative risk aversion (CRRA) utility:

$$U(c) = \lim_{i \to \sigma} \frac{c^{1-i} - 1}{1 - i}.$$

Because leisure is not valued, agents spend all of their time—each is endowed with one unit—working when employed. Idiosyncratic risk is introduced through a stochastic shock to labour input:

$$e_i \in E = \begin{cases} 1 & \text{for } i = g, \text{ 'employed'}; \\ 0 & \text{for } i = b, \text{ 'unemployed'}. \end{cases}$$

Aggregate labour L combines with aggregate capital K to make production good Y according to the Cobb–Douglas production function $Y = zK^\alpha L^{1-\alpha}$, where $\alpha \in$

[0, 1] and z is the aggregate state of the economy, which feeds through the model as a shock which can take two values:

$$z_i \in Z = \begin{cases} 1 + \delta_z & \text{for } i = g, \text{ 'expansion'}; \\ 1 - \delta_z & \text{for } i = b, \text{ 'recession'}, \end{cases}$$

where δ_z is a calibration parameter. KS assume that the aggregate state, z, and the idiosyncratic shock, e, follow a first-order Markov process with the transition matrices π_z and $\pi_{e,e'|z,z'}$, respectively. Following the standard notation a prime signifies the next period's realisation, so that $\pi_{z,z'}$ is the probability that the aggregate state transitions to z' next period from this period's realisation is z. $\pi_{e',z'|e,z}$ is the probability that next period's idiosyncratic shock is e' and that the aggregate shock is z' given that this period's employment realisation is e and the aggregate shock is z. There are no markets for insurance against uncertainty, so agents may only undertake a form of self-insurance by investing in a single-asset capital, which is restricted to take values $k \in \kappa = [0, \infty)$.

Individual Agent's Problem

An individual agent's optimisation problem is the following:

$$V(k, e, z, \Gamma) = \max_{c \in \mathbb{R}^+, \, k' \in \kappa} \left\{ U(c) + \beta \sum_{z' \in Z} \sum_{e' \in E} \pi_{e'z'|e,z} V(k', e', z', \Gamma') \right\} \tag{39.1a}$$

subject to

$$k(1 + r(K, L, z) - \delta) + [(1 - \tau)\bar{l}e + \mu(1 - e)]w(K, L, z) - c = k' \tag{39.1b}$$

$$\Gamma' = G(\Gamma, z, z') \tag{39.1c}$$

$$k' \geq 0 \tag{39.1d}$$

where $r(\cdot)$ is the real interest rate and $w(\cdot)$ the wage rate, δ is the constant rate at which capital depreciates, $\bar{l}$ is an individual's time endowment, μ is unemployment insurance as a percentage of the wage rate, τ is a tax on labour income, and Γ is the measure of agents over wealth and employment status. Equation (39.1a) is a standard Bellman equation. Budget constraint (39.1b) states that the future individual capital stock is composed of today's capital, compounded by the depreciation-adjusted rental price of capital, $r(K, L, z) - \delta$, the labour income $(1-\tau)\bar{l}w(K, L, z)$ when an agent is employed, or $\mu w(K, L, z)$ if an agent is unemployed, less today's consumption. (39.1c) is the forecasting rule for the future distribution of Γ and for the aggregate state variable. Agents care about the next period's distribution because it determines future prices. Finally, (39.1d) is the borrowing constraint, which restricts the next period's capital choice to be positive.

Government

The only role of government in the model is to tax labour income to fund the payment of unemployment insurance; they run a balanced budget each period. This means that

$$\underbrace{w(K,L,z)\tau \bar{l} L}_{\text{government income}} = \underbrace{w(K,L,z)\mu(1-L)}_{\text{government expenditure}},$$

which implies that the tax rate is

$$\tau = \frac{\mu(1-L)}{\bar{l}L},$$

where L is the total employed labour and $(1-L)$ the unemployment rate.

Firm's Problem

Factor prices follow from the competitive firm's optimisation problem, as in the standard representative agent model:

MPL $= \frac{\partial Y}{\partial L} = (1-\alpha)z(K/L)^\alpha = w(K,L,z)$;
MPK $= \frac{\partial Y}{\partial K} = \alpha z(K/L)^{\alpha-1} = r(K,L,z)$, where the last equalities hold due to competitive markets and

$$K = \int_A k' \, d\Gamma \tag{39.2}$$

$$L = \int_A e \, d\Gamma, \tag{39.3}$$

where $A = \kappa \times E$ is the type space of agents over capital holdings and employment status. The associated measurable space is $M = (A, \mathcal{B}(A))$, where $\mathcal{B}(A) = \mathcal{B}(\kappa) \times \mathcal{P}(E)$ is the Borel σ-algebra of A and $\mathcal{P}(E)$ is the power set of E. The set of all measures on M is $\mathcal{M}$, and we shall require that Γ is an element of $\mathcal{M}$.

39.2.1 Recursive Competitive Rational Expectations Equilibrium

The KS recursive competitive equilibrium can be defined in the following way:

Definition 1 Recursive competitive rational expectations equilibrium
A recursive competitive rational expectations equilibrium consists of:

(i) A value function: $V^*(k, e, z, \Gamma) : A \times Z \times \mathcal{M} \to \mathbb{R}$, which solves the individual's optimisation problem (39.1a), with the associated optimal decision rules for capital and consumption:

$$g_{k'}(k, e, z, \Gamma) : A \times Z \times \mathcal{M} \to \mathbb{R}, \quad g_{k'}(k, e, z, \Gamma) = k'^*$$
$$g_{c'}(k, e, z, \Gamma) : A \times Z \times \mathcal{M} \to \mathbb{R}, \quad g_{c'}(k, e, z, \Gamma) = c'^*.$$

(ii) Pricing functions:

$$w^*(K, L, z) : \mathcal{M} \times Z \to \mathbb{R}, \quad w^*(K, L, z) = (1 - \alpha) z (K/L)^\alpha$$
$$r^*(K, L, z) : \mathcal{M} \times Z \to \mathbb{R}, \quad r^*(K, L, z) = \alpha z (K/L)^{\alpha - 1}$$

which solve the firm's optimisation problem.

(iii) An equilibrium transition function:
$G^*(\Gamma, z, z') : Z \times Z \times \mathcal{M} \to \mathcal{M}, \quad G^*(\Gamma, z, z') = \Gamma'$,
which is consistent with the law of motion for Γ implied by individual decision rules, $g_{k'}(\cdot)$, $g_{c'}(\cdot)$, and the Markov process $\pi_{e',z'|e,z}$.

39.3 Improving the Distributional Fit (β-Dist)

The addition of heterogenous discount factors to improve the fit of the wealth distribution goes back to Krusell and Smith (1998) in which they added the assumption of a stochastic discount factor, $\tilde{\beta}$, which can take values $\{0.9858, 0.9894, 0.9930\}$. $\tilde{\beta}$ follows a three-state Markov chain which generates an invariant distribution for discount factors that is symmetric around its mean. KS gave the intuition that this was a way of modelling overlapping generations with different levels of patience— it in fact creates three types of agents (impatient, baseline, and patient). I use the specification from Castañeda et al., (2003) because it is much quicker to solve, and so is more often used in the literature. The major difference between this and the stochastic discount factor model is that agents' discount parameters do not change over time, as such the model generates much less mobility in the wealth distribution. Specifically, they choose time preference parameters to be distributed uniformly in the population between $\grave{\beta} \pm \nabla$ to fit the proportion of wealth w held by richest 20, 40, 60, and 80%, i.e.,

$$\{\grave{\beta}, \nabla\} = \underset{\beta, \nabla}{\operatorname{argmin}} \left(\sum_{i=20,40,60,80} (w_i(\beta, \nabla) - w_i)^2 \right)^{1/2}. \tag{39.4}$$

Using a distribution of discount factors helps to better fit the skewness of the empirical distribution as it attenuates the precautionary saving motive for agents with smaller discount factors to generate a larger mass at the lower end of the distribution. In a sense, they become myopic to likelihood of hitting the borrowing constraint. It also fits the upper parts of the distribution by heightening the desire

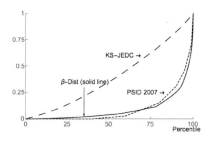
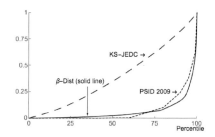

Fig. 39.1 Wealth distributions for Krusell–Smith (KS-JEDC) vs. β distribution, calibrated to 2007 (left) and 2009 (right) PSID data

to save for agents with higher discount factors. It is not only a useful device for better fitting the empirical distribution but also backed by empirical evidence of heterogeneity in discount factors. In a study of military drawdown payments, Warner and Pleeter (2001) find discount factors between 0.76 and 1.0 when military personnel were given the choice between a lump-sum payment and annuity. In order to best fit the minimisation problem of Eq. (39.4), I find that a much smaller variation in $\grave{\beta}$ of $\nabla = 0.01$ is sufficient to fit the empirical distribution. This much smaller variance is likely due to coarse fitting points, in accordance with the literature I use only four datapoints and do not fit the maximum or minimum (0 or 100%) quantiles.[4]

Figure 39.1 shows Lorenz curves generated from solving for the $\grave{\beta}$s and ∇s which solve equation (39.4) for PSID waves 2007 (i.e., pre-recession) and 2009 (recession data). The dashed line labelled KS-JEDC is the benchmark KS model. The solid line labelled β-Dist is the KS model with the addition of heterogeneous discount factors. Clearly, a relatively small variation in discount factors can dramatically improve the fit to the empirical wealth distribution. The baseline KS model exhibits very little wealth inequality, while the β-Dist models capture the pre-recession and recession data closely.

39.4 Why Are MPCs So Important?

Before exploring the KS model's predictions for the cross-sectional distribution of MPCs and the dynamics over the cycle, it is worthwhile emphasising why this research puts such emphasis on them. For this, it is important to consider when approximate aggregation holds and when it does not. Consider the following simple example. Without individual or aggregate uncertainty in the KS model, if agents had linear consumption policies, each individual i having the same intercept ϕ_0 and

---

[4] To fit the distribution more closely is a small modification to the algorithm. The contradiction in business cycle dynamics still exists in this case.

constant marginal propensity to save ϕ_1, the individual policy function would take the form:

$$k'_i = \phi_0 + \phi_1 k_i.$$

Then aggregation is easy:

$$K' = \phi_0 + \phi_1 K.$$

Because we are working with probability space and normalise the total labour supply to equal one, the first moment is equal to total asset holding, K. We can *exactly* aggregate all of the individual policy functions, and the first moment of the wealth distribution is the only statistic we need to perfectly forecast capital stock tomorrow.

Approximate aggregation holds in the standard KS model because the vast majority of agents act approximately in this manner, having near-linear savings functions and constant marginal propensities to save. Only a few that are constrained have very low zero marginal propensity to save out of income, but they are too small in number to affect the aggregate result dramatically. Figure 39.2 plots the individual capital policy functions for the baseline KS economy. Though functions exhibit nonlinearity for the poorest agents, there are very few agents in this region and low amounts of redistribution to this area.

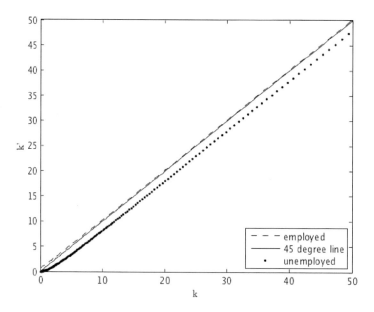

Fig. 39.2 This period's individual capital (k) plotted against next period's capital choice (k') for aggregate capital = 39 and good aggregate state

With the addition of heterogeneous βs, approximate aggregation still holds. To see why, it is useful to examine the consumption function c', which can be recovered using the savings policy and the budget constraint. Defining individual income as $m_i = w[(1-\tau))\bar{l}e_i + \mu(1-e_i)] + (1+r-\delta)k_i$, if the consumption function at the individual level were:

$$c'_i = \tilde{\phi}_0(z, \Gamma)E(m_i) + \tilde{\phi}_1(z, \Gamma)E(m_i \ln(m_i)) + \tilde{\phi}_2(z, \Gamma)E(m_i\beta_j).$$

then running a regression on the macro data generated by this economy would result in estimating:

$$c'_i = \tilde{\phi}_0(z, \Gamma)E(m_i) + \tilde{\phi}_1\pi_1(z, \Gamma)E(m_i) \ln E(m_i) + \tilde{\phi}_2\pi_2(z, \Gamma)E(m_i)E(\beta_j),$$

where:

$$\pi_1 = \frac{E(m_i \ln(m_i))}{E(m_i) \ln E(m_i)}$$

and:

$$\pi_2 = \frac{E(m_i\beta_j)}{E(m_i)E(\beta_j)}.$$

The regression coefficients recovered from the micro-level regression will only differ from the coefficients obtained by a regression on the corresponding macro aggregates if π_1 and π_2 vary highly over the cycle. They both capture how the ϕ coefficients are adjusted if individual consumption is evaluated at its average determinants. π_1 measures the degree of inequality in the economy, since $E(m_i \ln m_i)$ captures entropy. π_2 measures the fraction of income held by heterogenous sub-population $E(m_i\beta_j)$ relative to the size of that sub-population $E(\beta_j)$. Since neither varies significantly over the cycle in the KS β-Dist, the approximate aggregation result holds.

39.5 Dynamics of the KS β-Dist MPCs

Table 39.1 shows how the addition of heterogenous discount factors to the benchmark KS model accomplishes a better fit to the wealth distribution: by creating much greater variation in the marginal propensity to consume over the cross section. In the 2007 calibration, the poorest agents[5] consume over 30% of a shock to income; this figure decreases as income levels increase, with the richest consuming 15%.

---

[5] I report the MPCs for annual income quintile, and a very similar pattern of dispersion exists when looking in terms of wealth quintiles.

Table 39.1 Marginal propensity to consume over the business cycle—2006 and 2008 calibrations compared

Model	Krusell–Smith (KS): β-Dist						
	2007 calibration				2009 calibration		
Scenario	Baseline	Recession	Expansion		Baseline	Recession	Expansion
Overall average	0.25	0.27	0.24		0.35	0.37	0.33
By income quintile							
Q1	0.33	0.39	0.26		0.51	0.58	0.43
Q2	0.2	0.2	0.2		0.34	0.34	0.33
Q3	0.2	0.21	0.2		0.32	0.33	0.32
Q4	0.19	0.19	0.18		0.3	0.3	0.29
Q5	0.15	0.16	0.15		0.25	0.26	0.24
By employment status							
Employed	0.22	0.23	0.22		0.31	0.31	0.31
Unemployed	0.58	0.6	0.56		0.73	0.74	0.72
Time preference parameters[a]							
$\hat{\beta}$		0.9837				0.9787	
∇		0.00108				0.0172	
PSID 2007 % of wealth held by the richest	20%	40%	60%	80%	20%	40%	60%	80%
	80.6	95.1	99.9	100.8	85.5	97.3	100.8	101.3
PSID 2009 % of wealth held by the richest							

Notes: Annual MPC is calculated by $1 - (1 - \text{quarterly MPC})^4$. The scenarios are calculated for the β-Dist models calibrated to the net worth distributions described. For the KS aggregate shocks, the results are obtained by running the simulation over 1,000 periods, and the scenarios are defined as 'Recessions/Expansions': bad/good realisation of the aggregate state

[a] *Discount factors are uniformly distributed over the interval* $[\hat{\beta} - \nabla, \hat{\beta} + \nabla]$

High MPCs are concentrated in unemployed agents, who consume nearly 60% of an income shock in the 2007 calibration, compared to just over 20% for employed agents. In the 2009 calibration, the dispersion in marginal propensity to consume is much greater. The poorest agents consume over 50% of a shock to income, with the richest increasing their share to 25%. Both employed and unemployed agents increase their MPC compared to the 2007 calibration by around 10% points, with unemployed agents consuming over 70% of the income shock.

Table 39.1 also shows a contradiction of the model including heterogeneous discount factors. When looking the dispersion of the MPC across the distribution's internal business cycle dynamics (comparing columns 'Recession' and 'Expansion' within a calibration), it is clear to see that in both the 2007 and 2009 calibrations, the MPCs vary very little over the cycle. In the 2007 calibration, the aggregate marginal propensity to consume increases from 0.25 to 0.27 in a recession and falls to 0.24 in an expansion. Similarly, the 2009 calibration increases from an MPC of 0.35–0.37 in a recession and falls to 0.33 in an expansion. However, the implied difference in MPC given the wealth distributions *across* the calibrations is 10% points higher in the recession sample than the pre-recession sample. To make this point more clearly, Fig. 39.3 plots these MPC values within and across calibrations. While a recession within a calibration increases the MPC for the very poorest quintile significantly, the rest of the distribution barely changes. In contrast, to fit the wealth distributions across the calibrations requires a shift in the MPCs and therefore individual policy functions, for the whole of the distribution. The within-calibration MPC changes are consistent with a greater mass of agents becoming closer to the borrowing constraint. The across-calibration MPCs suggest that preferences across the distribution have fundamentally changed, or something else has occurred in the Great Recession to shift individual policy functions that the model is not capturing.[6]

Is it plausible that consumption functions could have shifted during the Great Recession? According to the logic of the KS-β-Dist model, the determinants that could plausibly generate a shift in cross-sectional MPCs are (1) an increase in the variance of income shocks, manifesting as a shift in the consumption function and (2) borrowing constraints becoming tighter during recessions. Point (1) is described extensively in Carroll et al. (2014) in a calibrated incomplete-markets, heterogeneous agents model. They consider two types of income shocks: permanent (highly persistent shocks) and transitory ones. Decomposing income into these two components is a standard way of thinking about income shocks in the literature and goes back to Friedman (1957). Carroll et al. (2014) show that increases in the variance of permanent shocks do not have a significant effect on the consumption function—this stands to reason, since recessions are temporary, there

---

[6] Note that these results are obtained without making any special assumptions about the nature of the Great Recession in terms of its severity or duration, i.e., it uses the calibration parameters of KS. Krueger et al. (2016) explore calibrating the KS model aggregate shocks to the frequency of observed severe recessions—defined as historical periods where unemployment exceeded 9% for at least one quarter and remains above 7% thereafter. Employing such a calibration does not change the qualitative result.

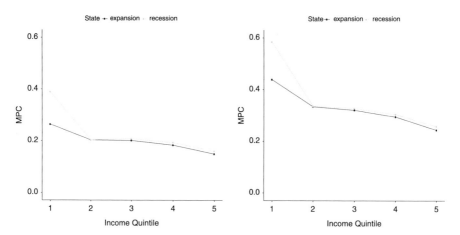

Fig. 39.3 MPC at the income quintiles generated from 2007 calibration in recession (left) and 2009 calibration in expansion (right). Annual MPC is calculated by $1 - (1-\text{quarterly MPC})^4$. Calculated for the β-Dist models calibrated to the net worth distribution for a given year. The results are obtained by running the simulation over 1,000 periods. Recession/Expansion MPCs are defined as averaging over bad/good realisations of the aggregate state

is little correlation between permanent shocks and aggregate uncertainty. However, an increase in the variance in transitory shock affects the consumption function significantly, by shifting it upward and steepening the function for the poorest households and also manifesting as a larger aggregate MPC. There is certainly a large literature on the deleterious effects of recessions on labour markets; see, for example, Elsby et al. (2010) on the Great Recession. Moreover, Guvenen et al. (2014) find that the left-skewness of income shocks is countercyclical.

For point (2), there is ample evidence that borrowing constraints are tighter during periods of falling economic activity. Particularly in financial crises, the sharp drop in lending can worsen and prolong economic downturns (Bernanke & Gertler, 1989; Kiyotaki & Moore, 1997). Ludvigson (1999) finds that predictable growth in consumer credit is significantly related to consumption growth in the macroeconomic time series. Gross (1994) estimates using bankruptcy data that MPC out of liquid funds is 20–30% higher during the Great Recession. However, as I show in the Appendix, in order to fit the proportion of households with negative wealth, the standard incomplete markets model actually implies a *decrease* (i.e., loosening) of the borrowing constraint over the Great Recession. While this mechanism certainly deserves to be explored, because the current study is concerned with reconciling the incomplete market heterogenous agent model with empirical evidence, I leave it to future research.

The focus of the following section is on point (1). I do this by estimating the marginal propensity to consume out of transitory income over the cross section of income and the business cycle while controlling for point (2), borrowing constraint changes.

39.6 Reduced-Form Estimates of the MPC

In the first-stage regressions, detailed in Sect. 39.7, I estimate the predictable elements of consumption and income changes in order to leave only permanent and transitory shocks in the residual for the second-stage regressions which recover the MPC. For this first stage, I use data from the Panel Study of Income Dynamics public use dataset, a nationally representative longitudinal survey of US households which is completed biennially. I combine it with PSID wealth supplements which provides detailed data on wealth and assets. For the pre-recession and recession periods (2003–2007 and 2009–2013), I joined each adjacent year by finding those households that had the same household head. In other words, in order to increase the sample size, I only require the households to be the same within the periods, but they can differ across the periods. The Appendix repeats the analysis with a smaller, balanced panel over 2003–2013 and finds very similar results. The additional criteria for inclusion in the sample include having a household head between the 22–65 and non-blank data not only for consumption and income but also for all demographic and other control variables. In this section, I detail the properties of the dependent and independent variables for the first-state regression.

It is important to note that the PSID is known to undersample the wealthiest 1–2% (Pfeffer et al., 2016), so I use the weights and strata information provided. The design of the PSID is a complex survey; therefore working with unweighted PSID data would violate the assumption that observations are i.i.d., since the complex survey design creates data with correlations between observations and unequal sampling probabilities. It is also a top-coded survey for purposes of anonymity, and I drop these observations since the true values are unknown. This is innocuous since the very top of the income and wealth distributions have so little mass; they do not matter for aggregate MPC.

39.6.1 Consumption Data in the PSID

Since its release, consumption data in the PSID is starting to become much more widely used in research, notably (Blundell et al., 2016). However, its introduction has been gradual, with extra expenditure categories added over time. Figure 39.4 shows the amounts calculated including food, transport, childcard, healthcare, education, and housing (consumption). In the 2004 survey, vacations, recreations, and clothing were added to the survey (consumption plus). There is some difference in the consumption amounts including and excluding the extra categories, both in levels and in co-movement with the cycle. Unfortunately, because the method of estimating marginal propensities requires a minimum of three time periods (see Sect. 39.7 below), I use consumption rather than consumption plus in the

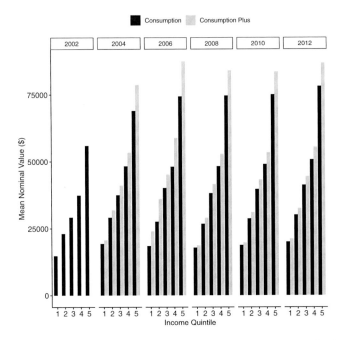

Fig. 39.4 Mean consumption in the PSID by income quintile. Consumption = food + transport + childcare + healthcare + education + housing; Consumption Plus = consumption + vacations + recreation + clothing

Table 39.2 Mean consumption comparison

Year	$\bar{c}_{i,t}^{CEX}$	$\bar{c}_{i,t}$	$\bar{c}_{i,t}^{PLUS}$
2002	40,677	28,573	NA
2004	43,395	35,612	39,559
2006	48,400	38,870	43,112
2008	50,486	37,816	41,837
2010	48,109	37,890	41,502
2012	51,442	38,213	41,878

$\bar{c}^{CEX}$ is mean consumption available from the CEX
$\bar{c}_t$ is the corresponding estimate in the PSID data
$\bar{c}_t^{PLUS}$ is mean PSID consumption plus extra expenditure categories, the author's calculations

estimations. I drop observations with negative consumption values, around 0.01% of the sample per year.[7]

Table 39.2 compares the mean values of consumption and consumption plus to the corresponding values reported from the Consumer Expenditure Survey (CEX).

---

[7] Negative consumption values come from imputed consumption values from the PSID, which uses a linear regression to predict missing consumption values.

Clearly, the PSID means are smaller relative to the CEX means, even when including the additional expenditure categories. It is likely that, even with extra consumption categories, because the PSID coverage is not as extensive as the CEX, it is underestimating consumption. It is also possible that the mean values are lower because the PSID is known to undersample the richest households. However, the dynamics of consumption over the Great Recession are very similar in both the CEX and the PSID.

39.6.2 Measuring After-Tax Income

The PSID reports total taxable income of the household in the preceding year to the survey, i.e., $y_{it} + T_t$ where T is a lump sum tax. However, for the purposes of understanding consumption and saving responses to income changes, I calculate after-tax income. It is important to use after-tax income because changes in taxation could change consumption responses. To do this, I use the TAXSIM program from NBER, which estimates the tax lump-sum given details of income, family composition and deductions. I use the method outlined in Butrica and Burkhauser (1997) by adapting code from Kimberlin et al. (2014) to include 2013 data. Clearly, it is very important that after-tax income is well measured, so Table 39.3 compares average (mean) after-tax income estimated from the CEX versus the corresponding quantity estimated from the PSID using TAXSIM.

The PSID values, although larger, are closer to CEX estimates in this case, likely because the PSID covers more income categories, though it could also be due to an underestimate of taxes in the TAXSIM programme. However, the dynamics over the sample are again similar in both surveys.

Table 39.3 After-tax income comparison

Year	$\bar{y}_t^{CEX}$	$\bar{y}_t^{alt}$
2002	46,934	53,858
2004	52,287	61,565
2006	58,101	65,033
2008	61,774	62,466
2010	60,712	62,766
2012	63,370	67,629

$\bar{y}^{CEX}$ is mean after-tax income available from the CEX

$\bar{y}_t$ is the corresponding estimate in the PSID data using

TAXSIM from the NBER, the author's calculations

39.6.3 Explanatory Variables for Predictable Consumption/Income

39.6.3.1 Demographic and Economic Variables

Demographic controls are all taken to be the values of the household head (which in the PSID are overwhelmingly male). Controls include a dummy for year of birth and dummies for education which takes three levels: up to high school education (low), college educated (medium), or some postgraduate (high). I control for employment status which can take values employed, unemployed, retired, or inactive. Also included are race dummies (taking values white, black, and other) and continuous variables for family size and the number of kids in the family unit. I include dummies for whether the family has extra income coming from those outside the household, extra dependents outside the family unit, and categorical dummies for region: North East, Midwest, South, and West. Finally, I include controls for the total net wealth level in thousands of dollars.

39.6.3.2 Controls for the Borrowing Constraint

Following Kaplan and Violante (2014) I distinguish two types of household: poor hand-to-mouth (P-HtM) and wealthy hand-to-mouth (W-HtM) which, due to a lack of liquid assets on hand, can come up against binding borrowing constraints. Poor hand-to-mouth households are defined as being at the credit limit when their illiquid wealth holdings and liquid wealth holdings are not positive, and their cash-on-hand and available credit is less than half their yearly income, i.e.,

$$a_{it} \leq 0, \quad m_{it} \leq 0 \quad \text{and} \quad m_{it} \leq y_{it}/2 - \underline{m}_{it},$$

where a_{it} is holdings of illiquid wealth by household i in period t, m_{it} is average balances of liquid wealth over period t, y_{it} is the total household income, and $\underline{m}_{it}$ is the household's credit limit.

Wealthy hand-to-mouth households are defined similarly, with the key difference being that they own positive illiquid assets, i.e.,

$$a_{it} > 0, \quad m_{it} \leq 0 \quad \text{and} \quad m_{it} \leq y_{it}/2 - \underline{m}_{it}.$$

In the PSID, illiquid wealth is calculated as the sum of home equity, other real estate equity, private annuities, and other assets. Liquid wealth is the sum of checking and saving accounts, money market funds, certificates of deposits, savings bonds, treasury bills, and stocks net of liquid debt which includes all debt other than mortgage debt. Figures 39.5 and 39.6 show the fraction of Poor HtM and Wealthy HtM households in the PSID, and the fractions are consistent with those reported by Kaplan and Violante (2014). The fraction of wealthy hand-

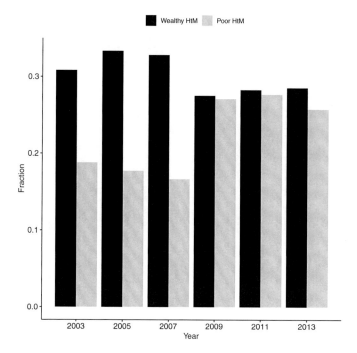

Fig. 39.5 Fraction of poor hand-to-mouth (P-HtM) and wealthy hand-to-mouth (W-HtM) consumers in the PSID by year, the author's calculations

to-mouth households falls over the Great Recession, while the fraction of poor rises. Interestingly, calculated for the quintiles of income, the fraction of P-HtM exhibits a strong negative relationship, while the fraction of W-HtM is an inverted U-shape in each year. The fractions within a given quintile for the wealthy hand-to-mouth are relatively stable over the Great Recession, while the fraction of P-HtM in the poorest income quintiles rises markedly. This is suggestive evidence that borrowing constraints became more likely to bind for the very poorest hand-to-mouth households during the recession, with less of a noticeable effect for the wealthy hand-to-mouth. To control for binding borrowing constraints in the consumption and income regressions, I use a dummy variable for Poor and Wealthy HtM households, equal to 1 when a household falls into the respective categories and 0 otherwise.

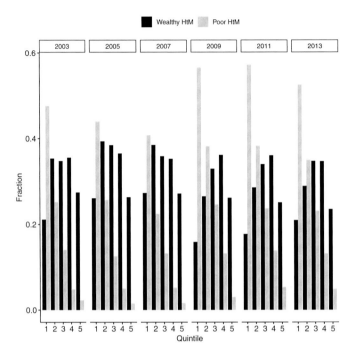

Fig. 39.6 Fraction of poor hand-to-mouth (P-HtM) and wealthy hand-to-mouth (W-HtM) consumers in the PSID by year and quintile, the author's calculations

39.7 Method

39.7.1 Estimating the Marginal Propensity to Consume

Following Blundell et al. (2008) and Kaplan et al. (2014), assume income follows the process:

$$\log Y_{i,t} = \mathbf{Z}'_{it}\mathbf{\Phi}_t + P_{i,t} + \epsilon_{i,t}, \tag{39.5}$$

where i is an individual at time t, Y is income, $\mathbf{Z}$ is a set of observable income characteristics, $P_{i,t} = P_{i,t-1} + \xi_{i,t}$ is a martingale permanent income process with i.i.d. shock ξ, and ϵ is an i.i.d. transitory income shock. Blundell et al. (2008) show that such a specification provides a good approximation to the solution of a life cycle optimisation problem where agents have CRRA utility.

By estimating equation (39.5) and recovering the first-differenced residuals, I obtain unexplained income growth:

$$\Delta \widehat{y_{i,t}} = \xi_{i,t} + \Delta \epsilon_{i,t},$$

where $\widehat{y_{i,t}} = \log Y_{i,t} - \mathbf{Z}'_{it}\hat{\mathbf{\Phi}}_t$.

Consumption is assumed to be subject to the same processes but with loading factors (marginal propensities) on permanent and transitory income shocks $\psi^P_{i,t}$ and $\psi^T_{i,t}$, giving unexplained growth as

$$\Delta \widehat{c_{i,t}} = \psi^P_{i,t} \xi_{i,t} + \psi^T_{i,t} \Delta \epsilon_{i,t},$$

where $\Delta \widehat{c_{i,t}}$ is estimated first-differenced consumption residuals $\widehat{c_{i,t}} = \log Y_{i,t} - \mathbf{Z}'_{it} \hat{\mathbf{\Psi}}_t$.

The covariance restriction necessary for the identification of the marginal propensity to save from transitory income shocks is that individuals have no foresight about future shocks, i.e., $\text{cov}(\Delta c_{i,t}, \epsilon_{i,t+1}) = \text{cov}(\Delta c_{i,t}, \xi_{i,t+1}) = 0$.

The true marginal propensity to consume out of a transitory shock is given by

$$\text{MPC}_t = \frac{\text{cov}(\Delta c_{i,t}, \epsilon_{i,t})}{\text{var}(\epsilon_{i,t})},$$

which, using the covariance restrictions, can be estimated consistently via an instrumental variable regression of $\Delta \widehat{c_{it}}$ on $\Delta \widehat{y_{i,t}}$ instrumented by $\Delta \widehat{y_{i,t+1}}$:

$$\widehat{\text{MPC}_t} = \frac{\text{cov}(\Delta \widehat{c_{i,t}}, \Delta \widehat{y_{i,t+1}})}{\text{cov}(\Delta \widehat{y_{i,t}}, \Delta \widehat{y_{i,t+1}})}. \tag{39.6}$$

By using this methodology on a panel simulated from an incomplete insurance model in which they can compare estimated and true values, Kaplan and Violante (2010) show that this method works well for estimating transitory shocks and is not biased in the presence of binding borrowing constraints. The estimation requires three periods of data for consumption: $t-1, t, t+1$, so I drop households with fewer than three consecutive years of observations in each of the two time periods. To get an estimate of the marginal propensity to consume across the distribution, I estimate equation (39.6) for the income quintiles at the beginning of the pre-recession and recession sample period (2003 and 2009).

39.8 Results

In this section I begin with a summary of the first-stage regression output, the result of estimating the income process in Eq. (39.5), and the corresponding consumption equation. I then discuss the second-stage regression results that use the residuals from the first-stage estimation to estimate the marginal propensity to consume. I first discuss the results over the entire distribution for the pre-recession and recession periods and then show the estimates over the income quintiles.

Table 39.4 details the results of the first-stage regressions to extract the predictable parts of consumption and income. Though a means to estimating the marginal propensity to consume, these results merit inspection in their own right. Year dummies show time growth in consumption and income which is greater prior to the Great Recession. As we might expect, income levels are greater by approximately 6 and 17% for the medium and high educated, respectively, relative to the low educated. This greater income level does not transfer fully into consumption, which is greater by approximately 3 and 10% for the same groups. Being a race other than white is associated with lower income and consumption levels, while the family size increases both. More kids in the household are associated with lower consumption and income levels, as is being unemployed, retired, or inactive. Comparing the pre-recession and recession periods by employment status, the penalty to consumption and income increases for all non-employment in the recession period. Being in a region that is not the North East is associated with a consumption and income penalty of between 2 and 5%, but this does not seem to change dramatically with the business cycle. Both poor hand-to-mouth households (those with cash on hand and available credit at less than half their yearly income and a negative illiquid net worth position) and wealthy hand-to-mouth households (those with cash on hand and available credit at less than half their yearly income but a positive illiquid net worth position) see a penalty to consumption and income. Those that are P-HtM have lower consumption levels of approximately 7% relative to non-HtM households and lower income levels of 12%. Meanwhile, the associated reduction for W-HtM households is not significant from zero for consumption but associated with 5% lower income levels. This is suggestive evidence that borrowing constraints are more likely to be binding for P-HtM, since it is associated with lower consumption.

Table 39.5 details the results of the instrumental variable regression estimating the marginal propensities to consume across the whole distribution over the pre-recession and recession periods—giving an estimate of the aggregate MPC. The findings for the marginal propensity to consume are in line with other empirical evidence, suggesting that the MPC out of transitory income is nonzero, a result that is significant at the 1% level. The results suggest that on average, households consumed 10% of a transitory income shock over the pre-recession period 2003–2007, and this increased to 16% in the recession period, 2009–2013. The difference in the estimated MPCs is also significant at 1% over the pre-recession and recession periods. Note that the R^2 statistics in these regressions are much lower than those of the first-stage regressions in Table 39.4. We should expect this by construction since we are running a regression on residuals. Indeed, classical theory would predict an R^2 of zero, although we have known since at least Hall (1978) that there is a predictive relationship, albeit much lower than the relationship to changes in permanent income.

Turning to the estimates over the income distribution, Tables 39.6 and 39.7 report the regression output over the pre-recession and recession periods which Fig. 39.7

Table 39.4 First-stage regressions

	$\log(\widehat{c_{it}})$		$\log(\widehat{y_{it}})$	
	2002–2006	2008–2012	2002–2006	2008–2012
	(1)	(2)	(3)	(4)
Year = 2004	0.053[a]		0.029[a]	
	(0.002)		(0.003)	
Year = 2006	0.077[a]		0.051[a]	
	(0.004)		(0.003)	
Year = 2010		0.007[b]		0.006
		(0.002)		(0.003)
Year = 2012		0.017[a]		0.025[a]
		(0.002)		(0.004)
Education = Medium	0.034[a]	0.038[a]	0.063[a]	0.063[a]
	(0.006)	(0.006)	(0.008)	(0.009)
Education = High	0.105[a]	0.109[a]	0.167[a]	0.175[a]
	(0.006)	(0.007)	(0.010)	(0.010)
Race = Black	−0.045[a]	−0.037[a]	−0.069[a]	−0.068[a]
	(0.007)	(0.007)	(0.008)	(0.007)
Race = Other	−0.009	−0.004	−0.047[b]	−0.053[b]
	(0.014)	(0.009)	(0.014)	(0.015)
Family size	0.069[a]	0.084[a]	0.091[a]	0.108[a]
	(0.004)	(0.004)	(0.005)	(0.005)
Number of kids	−0.047[a]	−0.058[a]	−0.071[a]	−0.081[a]
	(0.004)	(0.004)	(0.005)	(0.006)
Status = Unemployed	−0.028[c]	−0.058[a]	−0.082[b]	−0.107[a]
	(0.011)	(0.009)	(0.019)	(0.017)
Status = Retired	−0.055[a]	−0.075[a]	−0.089[a]	−0.106[a]
	(0.006)	(0.005)	(0.010)	(0.008)
Status = Inactive	−0.061[a]	−0.097[a]	−0.121[a]	−0.152[a]
	(0.007)	(0.007)	(0.010)	(0.011)
Extra family income	0.012[c]	0.003	0.027[b]	0.027[b]
	(0.005)	(0.007)	(0.007)	(0.008)
Region = Midwest	−0.043[a]	−0.053[a]	−0.036[b]	−0.053[b]
	(0.008)	(0.010)	(0.011)	(0.012)
Region = South	−0.027[b]	−0.033[b]	−0.032[c]	−0.038[b]
	(0.009)	(0.010)	(0.013)	(0.012)
Region = West	−0.022[c]	−0.042[a]	−0.037[b]	−0.050[a]
	(0.008)	(0.009)	(0.009)	(0.010)
Kids outside family unit	0.025[b]	0.023[a]	0.059[a]	0.062[a]
	(0.006)	(0.005)	(0.012)	(0.008)
Poor-HtM	−0.078[a]	−0.061[a]	−0.128[a]	−0.122[a]
	(0.006)	(0.006)	(0.008)	(0.009)

(continued)

Table 39.4 (continued)

	$\log(\widehat{c_{it}})$		$\log(\widehat{y_{it}})$	
	2002–2006	2008–2012	2002–2006	2008–2012
	(1)	(2)	(3)	(4)
Rich-HtM	−0.005	−0.012	−0.053[a]	−0.056[a]
	(0.005)	(0.006)	(0.007)	(0.008)
Total wealth ($1000s)	0.0002[b]	0.0004[c]	0.001[b]	0.001[b]
	(0.0001)	(0.0001)	(0.0001)	(0.0002)
Constant	11.383[a]	11.668[a]	11.731[a]	11.693[a]
	(0.015)	(0.022)	(0.022)	(0.052)
Year of birth	Yes	Yes	Yes	Yes
R^2	0.4	0.45	0.43	0.51
N	13,281	14,820	13,281	14,820

Survey-weighted generalised least squares regression for the years 2003, 2005, and 2007 (columns 1 and 3) and 2009, 2011, and 2013 (columns 2 and 4) in the PSID
[a] Significant at the 1% level
[b] Significant at the 5% level
[c] Significant at the 10% level

Table 39.5 Estimates of the marginal propensity to consume (MPC)

	MPC	
	03–07	09–13
	0.1***	0.162***
	(0.027)	(0.029)
R^2	0.052	0.075
N	4535	5160

Estimated on the whole sample of the income distribution on PSID data. Pre-recession: 2003–2007 and recession: 2009–2013. Standard errors in parentheses. * $p < 0.10$, ** $p < 0.05$, *** $p < 0.01$

shows graphically. On the left of Fig. 39.7, the MPC is downward sloping, implying an upward-sloping consumption function. The very poorest quintile consumes between 20 and 40% of a transitory income shock, and this reduces down to a value that is not significantly different to 0% for the highest income quintiles. Note that we see a downward sloping relationship between MPC and income despite controlling for borrowing constrained households, a factor that is known to generate such a relationship. R^2 values are surprisingly high for the first, second, and third quintiles but drop to near zero—as would be predicted by the permanent income hypothesis—for the richest two quintiles. This suggests that there is certainly an important role for heterogeneous preferences in matching the MPC over the distribution of income—with poorer households acting as hand-to-mouth consumers and richer

Table 39.6 IV regression: $\Delta c_{i,t}$ 2003–2007 for income quintiles

	$\widehat{\Delta c_{i,t}}$				
	(1)	(2)	(3)	(4)	(5)
$\widehat{\Delta y_{i,t}}$	0.321[a]	0.275[a]	0.135[b]	0.048	0.014
	(0.059)	(0.065)	(0.057)	(0.063)	(0.056)
N	879	882	878	881	856
R^2	0.258	0.154	0.073	0.019	0.006
Residual Std. Error	0.078 (df = 877)	0.091 (df = 880)	0.103 (df = 876)	0.116 (df = 879)	0.140 (df = 854)

Instrumental variable regression of $\widehat{\Delta c_t}$ on $\widehat{\Delta y_t}$ instrumented by $\widehat{\Delta y_{t+1}}$ for the income quintiles, 2003–2007
[a] Significant at the 1% level
[b] Significant at the 5% level

Table 39.7 IV regression: $\Delta c_{i,t}$ 2008–2012 for income quintiles

	$\Delta \widehat{c_{i,t}}$				
	(1)	(2)	(3)	(4)	(5)
$\Delta \widehat{y_{i,t}}$	0.338[a]	0.300[a]	0.179[b]	0.154[c]	0.017
	(0.054)	(0.065)	(0.087)	(0.079)	(0.057)
R^2	0.175	0.127	0.091	0.072	0.008
Residual Std. Error	0.088 (df = 982)	0.098 (df = 982)	0.114 (df = 979)	0.118 (df = 976)	0.136 (df = 958)

Instrumental variable regression of $\Delta \widehat{c_t}$ on $\Delta \widehat{y_t}$ instrumented by $\Delta \widehat{y_{t+1}}$ for the income quintiles, 2009–2013

[a] Significant at the 1% level
[b] Significant at the 5% level
[c] Significant at the 10% level

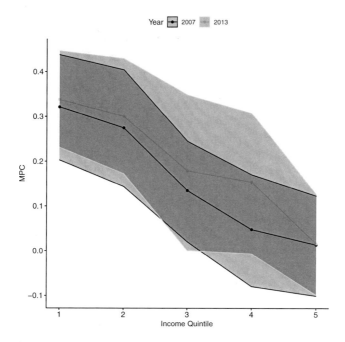

Fig. 39.7 Estimated marginal propensity to consume by income quintile and time period: pre-recession period (2003–2007) and recession period (2009–2013)

households as consumption smoothers. Indeed, the point estimates for some of the distribution in the pre-recession sample are remarkably similar to the KS β-Dist generated 2007 MPCs. Comparing Table 39.1 with the reduced-form estimates, we see that the poorest quintiles both consume approximately 30% of their transitory income and Q2 and Q3 consume 20% in the KS β-Dist model and 28 and 13%, respectively, in the estimates. There is a stark difference however, in the upper end of the distribution—KS β-Dist calibration generates MPCs of 19 and 15%, whereas the estimation does not find coefficients significantly different from zero.

Lastly, we see that the estimates of the MPCs are noisily estimated and, although point estimates are close together, we cannot completely rule in or out the possibility that the consumption function shifted over the Great Recession. However, we certainly can rule out the 2009 calibration values of the KS β-Dist for MPCs—which generated MPCs for the poorest of over 50%, declining to 25% for the income-rich. At all points, the generated MPCs exceed the estimated MPCs beyond the confidence intervals of the estimation.

39.9 Conclusion

In this chapter, I explored the distributional dynamics of the standard incomplete-markets, heterogenous agent model known as the Krusell–Smith model. Since software developments in the field allow these types of models to be applied in policy questions much more readily and particularly in questions where the distribution matters, it is incumbent on economists to make sure that these dynamics are realistic. I estimated the marginal propensity to consume out of transitory income over the pre-recession and recession periods and over the quintiles of the distribution. I provided evidence that the MPC varies greatly over the distribution of income, with income-poor households consuming around 20–40% of a transitory income shock and income-rich households consuming none. As Krusell and Smith themselves point out, while it fits the income-poor end of the distribution reasonably well at a point in time, the Krusell–Smith model does not capture the richer end of the distribution. Moreover, changing the dispersion of heterogeneous preferences to fit the dynamics of the wealth distribution implies a shift in the consumption function and distribution of MPCs which is at odds with the data. The magnitude of the shift in the consumption implied by a standard incomplete-markets, heterogeneous agent model that is calibrated to the wealth distribution in the pre-recession and recession periods is far too high to be consistent with the evidence presented in this chapter. Therefore, the analysis of the distributional implications of economic policies with such models could result in predictions far at odds from true values. Future research should focus on bridging this gap.

Acknowledgments Thanks to Carlos Carillo-Tudela, Jonathan Thomas, Mike Elsby, Ludo Visschers, and participants of the Scottish Economic Society Annual Conference (2020) for their helpful comments. An earlier version of this research constituted part of my PhD thesis and so received funding from the University of Edinburgh School of Economics.

Appendix 1

I consider a second modification to the benchmark KS model which implies a contradiction when compared to PSID data. This modification to the benchmark model is the lowering of the borrowing constraint. To my knowledge, no other paper has considered this modification—probably because it is trivial—in terms of the solution it simply shifts the distribution by a constant and has no effects on the dynamics.[8] However, I consider it firstly because a significant proportion of

---

[8] Not to mention, it takes a long time to solve—one iteration of the Carroll et al. (2017) Mathematica code takes around 8 hours on my MacBook Pro 2013 laptop with 2.6 GHz processor and 8 GB RAM; I rewrote the algorithm based on Maliar et al. (2010) code in Matlab R2016b to get a total running time of 24 hours for all iterations of the borrowing constraint.

39 Heterogenous Consumption Responses and Wealth Inequality over the... 693

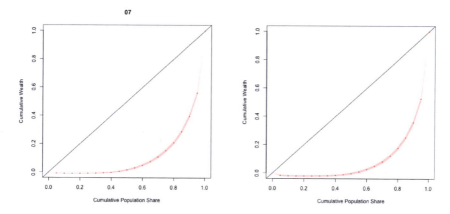

Fig. 39.8 Lorenz curves estimated from the PSID 2007 (left) and 2009 (right). Red bands are survey-weighted confidence intervals

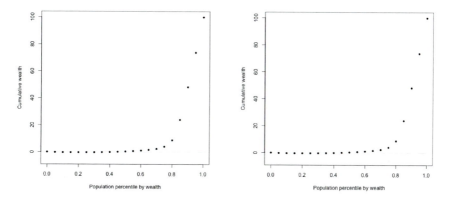

Fig. 39.9 Lorenz curves generated from 2006 calibration with BC = −3.3 in good aggregate state (left) and bad aggregate state (right)

individuals in the PSID hold zero or negative net wealth: 12.7% in 2006 and 16.1% in 2008. Secondly, I will show that changing the borrowing constraint implies a contradiction with empirical evidence that finds that credit constraints are higher in recessions than in normal economic times. To fit the evidence of significant holdings of zero or negative wealth, I add an outer loop to the algorithm which solves the model, which uses the 2006 β-Dist calibration and lowers the budget constraint by 0.1 until the gap between the model-generated percentage of agents holding negative wealth is within $\epsilon = 0.01$ of the 2006 empirical figure. Because the algorithm fits the percentage of people with negative wealth, rather than the cumulative wealth held, it does not do a great job of improving the fit of the empirical Lorenz curves—compare Fig. 39.8, the empirical Lorenz curve estimated from the PSID, and the KS β-Dist model generated, Fig. 39.9. In the data, both the fraction of individuals

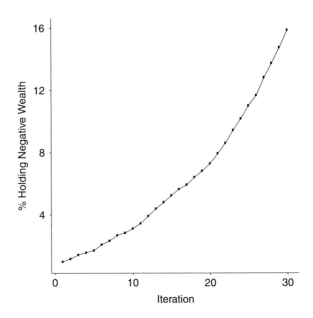

Fig. 39.10 Percent holding negative wealth by iteration through borrowing constraints. KS β-Dist model iterated through negative borrowing constraints. Each iteration is the solution to the model which, starting at zero, lowers the borrowing constraint by 0.1

holding negative wealth and the amounts of negative wealth increase substantially in the recession relative to the pre-recession estimation. Figure 39.9 shows the Lorenz curve in the good and bad aggregate state within the 2007 calibration; neither the fraction of agents holding negative wealth nor the amounts of negative wealth held change significantly in the dynamics over the cycle (which should not be surprising, given that this modification does not change the dynamics of the β-Dist model).

What is surprising is the implications for the borrowing constraint over the cycle. I find that the borrowing constraint that fits the percentage of negative wealth holdings in 2006 is −3.3. Figure 39.10 plots the percentage of the population holding negative wealth for the β-Dist model solved with progressively looser borrowing constraints, lowered by 0.1 on each iteration. The relationship between the fraction holding negative wealth and the borrowing constraint is positive and convex. This implies that, in order to better fit the greater mass of agents holding zero or negative wealth in the 2008 recession, it implies that the borrowing constraint has to be *looser*, i.e., that agents can borrow more, not less, in a recession.

Appendix 2

This appendix contains the first- and second-stage regressions in the main text repeated on a balanced panel. In other words, while the main text allowed different households over the pre-recession and recession periods, this appendix keeps only households that have non-missing data for the full 2003–2013 period. The estimated equations are the same, and the results are qualitatively identical and quantitatively very similar. The only major difference is in the sample size and, as a result, the precision of the estimates (Fig. 39.11, Tables 39.8, 39.9 and 39.10).

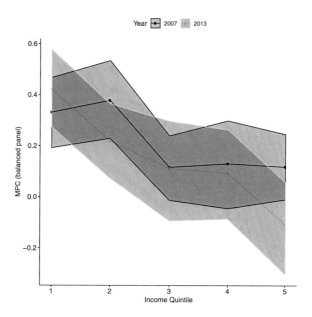

Fig. 39.11 Estimated marginal propensity to consume by income quintile and time, balanced panel: 2003–2013

Table 39.8 IV regression: $\Delta c_{i,t}$, 2003–2007 for income quintiles (balanced panel)

	$\Delta \widehat{c_{i,t}}$				
	(1)	(2)	(3)	(4)	(5)
$\Delta \widehat{y_{i,t}}$	0.255[a]	0.350[a]	0.099	0.099	0.052
	(0.074)	(0.087)	(0.069)	(0.085)	(0.073)
N	553	556	555	555	539
R^2	0.223	0.171	0.059	0.042	0.021
Residual std. error	0.082 (df = 551)	0.093 (df = 554)	0.101 (df = 553)	0.111 (df = 553)	0.132 (df = 537)

Instrumental variable regression of $\Delta \widehat{c_t}$ on $\Delta \widehat{y_t}$ instrumented by $\Delta \widehat{y_{t+1}}$ for the income quintiles, 2003–2007

[a] Significant at the 1% level

Table 39.9 IV regression: $\Delta c_{i,t}$, 2008–2012 for Income Quintiles (balanced panel)

	$\Delta \widehat{c_{i,t}}$				
	(1)	(2)	(3)	(4)	(5)
$\Delta \widehat{y_{i,t}}$	0.450[a]	0.302[a]	0.157	0.105	−0.077
	(0.078)	(0.075)	(0.100)	(0.084)	(0.084)
N	556	554	554	553	543
R^2	0.196	0.077	0.105	0.054	−0.064
Residual Std. Error	0.091 (df = 554)	0.100 (df = 552)	0.118 (df = 552)	0.124 (df = 551)	0.144 (df = 541)

Instrumental variable regression of $\Delta \widehat{c_i}$ on $\Delta \widehat{y_i}$ instrumented by $\Delta \widehat{y_{i,t+1}}$ for the income quintiles, 2008–2012

[a] Significant at the 1% level

Table 39.10 First-stage regressions

	$\log(\widehat{c_{it}})$		$\log(\widehat{y_{it}})$	
	2003–2007	2009–2013	2003–2007	2009–2013
	(1)	(2)	(3)	(4)
Year = 2004	0.056[a]		0.035[a]	
	(0.003)		(0.006)	
Year = 2006	0.082[a]		0.059[a]	
	(0.005)		(0.005)	
Year = 2010		0.006[c]		0.002
		(0.003)		(0.004)
Year = 2012		0.015[b]		0.022[b]
		(0.003)		(0.006)
Education = Medium	0.038[a]	0.037[b]	0.070[a]	0.068[a]
	(0.007)	(0.009)	(0.011)	(0.013)
Education = High	0.111[a]	0.116[a]	0.168[a]	0.191[a]
	(0.007)	(0.010)	(0.012)	(0.014)
Race = Black	−0.047[a]	−0.038[b]	−0.073[a]	−0.067[a]
	(0.010)	(0.010)	(0.011)	(0.011)
Race = Other	−0.009	−0.015	−0.053[c]	−0.076[b]
	(0.022)	(0.012)	(0.024)	(0.018)
Family size	0.068[a]	0.087[a]	0.091[a]	0.108[a]
	(0.006)	(0.005)	(0.006)	(0.006)
Number of kids	−0.045[a]	−0.062[a]	−0.073[a]	−0.080[a]
	(0.006)	(0.007)	(0.008)	(0.008)
Status = Unemployed	−0.074[b]	−0.056[a]	−0.129[b]	−0.108[a]
	(0.020)	(0.010)	(0.031)	(0.019)
Status = Retired	−0.059[a]	−0.081[a]	−0.102[a]	−0.118[a]
	(0.009)	(0.007)	(0.011)	(0.011)
Status = Inactive	−0.069[a]	−0.098[a]	−0.130[a]	−0.153[a]
	(0.011)	(0.009)	(0.011)	(0.015)
Extra family income	0.017[c]	0.003	0.031[b]	0.028[c]
	(0.007)	(0.009)	(0.008)	(0.010)
Region = Midwest	−0.043[b]	−0.055[a]	−0.041[c]	−0.059[b]
	(0.013)	(0.012)	(0.015)	(0.014)
Region = South	−0.025	−0.037[b]	−0.031	−0.043[c]
	(0.015)	(0.013)	(0.020)	(0.017)
Region = West	−0.018	−0.048[b]	−0.034[c]	−0.059[b]
	(0.014)	(0.012)	(0.013)	(0.013)
Kids outside family unit	0.022[c]	0.034[a]	0.058[b]	0.070[a]
	(0.009)	(0.005)	(0.015)	(0.010)
Poor-HtM	−0.081[a]	−0.064[a]	−0.136[a]	−0.130[a]
	(0.007)	(0.009)	(0.011)	(0.014)

(continued)

Table 39.10 (continued)

	$\log(\widehat{c_{it}})$		$\log(\widehat{y_{it}})$	
	2003–2007	2009–2013	2003–2007	2009–2013
	(1)	(2)	(3)	(4)
Rich-HtM	−0.012	−0.013	−0.066[a]	−0.064[a]
	(0.006)	(0.008)	(0.009)	(0.012)
Total wealth ($1000s)	0.0002[c]	0.0003[c]	0.0005[c]	0.001[b]
	(0.0001)	(0.0001)	(0.0002)	(0.0002)
Constant	11.615[a]	11.659[a]	11.723[a]	11.666[a]
	(0.044)	(0.035)	(0.070)	(0.079)
Year of birth	Yes	Yes	Yes	Yes
N	8,373	8,373	8,373	8,373

Survey-weighted generalised least squares regression for the years 2003, 2005, 2007, 2009, 2011, and 2013 (columns 2 and 4) in the PSID balanced panel
[a] Significant at the 1% level
[b] Significant at the 5% level
[c] Significant at the 10% level

References

Ahn, S., Kaplan, G., Moll, B., Winberry, T., & Wolf, C. (2018). When inequality matters for macro and macro matters for inequality. *NBER Macroeconomics Annual, 32*(1), 1–75.

Bernanke, B., & Gertler, M. (1989). Agency costs, net worth, and business fluctuations. *The American Economic Review, 79*(1), 14–31.

Blundell, R., Pistaferri, L., & Preston, I. (2008). Consumption inequality and partial insurance. *American Economic Review, 98*(5), 1887–1921.

Blundell, R., Pistaferri, L., & Saporta-Eksten, I. (2016). Consumption inequality and family labor supply. *American Economic Review, 106*(2), 387–435.

Bricker, J., Kennickell, A. B., Moore, K. B., & Sabelhaus, J. (2012). Changes in U.S. family finances from 2007 to 2010: Evidence from the Survey of consumer finances. *Federal Reserve Bulletin, 100*, 1–80.

Butrica, B., & Burkhauser, R. (1997). Estimating federal income tax burdens for panel study of income dynamics (PSID) families using the national bureau of economic research TAXSIM model. *Working Paper 12*, Syracuse University.

Carroll, C., Slacalek, J., Tokuoka, K., & White, M. N. (2017). The distribution of wealth and the marginal propensity to consume. *Quantitative Economics, 8*(3), 977–1020.

Carroll, C. D. (2006). The method of endogenous gridpoints for solving dynamic stochastic optimization problems. *Economics Letters, 91*(3), 312–320.

Carroll, C. D., Slacalek, J., & Tokuoka, K. (2014). The distribution of wealth and the MPC: Implications of new European data. *The American Economic Review, 104*(5), 107–111.

Castañeda, A., Giménez, J. D., & Rull, J. V. R. (2003). Accounting for the U.S. earnings and wealth inequality. *Journal of Political Economy, 111*(4), 818–857.

De Nardi, M., & Fella, G. (2017). Saving and wealth inequality. *Review of Economic Dynamics, 26*, 280–300.

De Nardi, M., French, E., & Benson, D. (2011). Consumption and the great recession. *Working Paper 17688*, National Bureau of Economic Research.

Elsby, M., Hobijn, B., & Sahin, A. (2010). The labor market in the great recession. *Brookings Papers on Economic Activity, 41*(1 (Spring)), 1–69.

Friedman, M. (1957). *A theory of the consumption function*. National Bureau of Economic Research, Inc.

Gross, D. B. (1994). The investment and financing decisions of liquidity constrained firms.***

Guvenen, F., Ozkan, S., & Song, J. (2014). The nature of countercyclical income risk. *Journal of Political Economy, 122*(3), 621–660.

Hall, R. E. (1978). Stochastic implications of the life cycle-permanent income hypothesis: Theory and evidence. *Journal of Political Economy, 86*(6), 971–87.

Kaplan, G., & Violante, G. L. (2010). How much consumption insurance beyond self-insurance? *American Economic Journal: Macroeconomics, 2*(4), 53–87.

Kaplan, G., & Violante, G. L. (2014). A model of the consumption response to fiscal stimulus payments. *Econometrica, 82*(4), 1199–1239.

Kaplan, G., Violante, G. L., & Weidner, J. (2014). The wealthy hand-to-mouth. *Working Paper 20073*, National Bureau of Economic Research.

Kimberlin, S., Kim, J., & Shaefer, H. L. (2014). *An updated method for calculating income and payroll taxes from psid data using the NBER's TAXSIM, for PSID survey years 1999 through 2011*. Manuscript, University of Michigan.

Kiyotaki, N., & Moore, J. (1997). Credit cycles. *Journal of Political Economy, 105*(2), 211–248.

Krueger, D., Mitman, K., & Perri, F. (2016). *Macroeconomics and household heterogeneity*. Handbook of Macroeconomics (Vol. 2, pp. 843–921). Elsevier.

Krueger, D., & Perri, F. (2005). Understanding consumption smoothing: Evidence from the U.S. consumer expenditure data. *Journal of the European Economic Association, 3*(2–3), 340–349.

Krusell, P., & Smith, Jr., A. A. (1998). Income and wealth heterogeneity in the macroeconomy. *Journal of Political Economy, 106*(5), 867–896.

Lawrance, E. C. (1991). Poverty and the rate of time preference: Evidence from panel data. *Journal of Political Economy, 99*(1), 54–77.

Ludvigson, S. (1999). Consumption and credit: A model of time-varying liquidity constraints. *The Review of Economics and Statistics, 81*(3), 434–447.

Maliar, L., Maliar, S., & Valli, F. (2010). Solving the incomplete markets model with aggregate uncertainty using the Krusell-Smith algorithm. *Journal of Economic Dynamics and Control, 34*(1), 42–49.

Pfeffer, F., Schoeni, R., Kennickell, A., & Andreski, P. (2016). Measuring wealth and wealth inequality: Comparing two US surveys. *Journal of Economic and Social Measurement, 41*(2), 103–120.

Warner, J. T., & Pleeter, S. (2001). The personal discount rate: Evidence from military downsizing programs. *American Economic Review, 91*(1), 33–53.

Chapter 40
Consumer Behavior When Buying Clothes in Slovakia in the Context of Environmentally Responsible Trends

Simona Bartošová, Zdenka Musová, and Zlatica Fulajtárová

Abstract The issue of sustainability and responsibility in the clothing industry is currently significant because this industry is one of the most polluting industries in the world. This chapter aims to investigate consumer behavior when buying clothes in Slovakia and the use of the new environmentally responsible trends in this area. This chapter presents the selected results of the primary research carried out in November and December 2022 through a structured online questionnaire on a sample of 743 respondents. Several mathematical and statistical tests were used to evaluate the collected primary data—Friedman's test, chi-square test of independence, Mann–Whitney test, Spearman's correlation coefficient, and Wilcoxon's test. The results show that most respondents buy clothes in fashion or retail chains by default. Respondents are most influenced by price, design/color, and high-quality/sustainable material when buying clothes. The most frequently used environmentally responsible trend is second-hand, which is used by half of the respondents. Other investigated trends are less known and used. The most durability/sustainability and quality of the materials used, which is stated by more than 60% of respondents.

Keywords Responsible consumer behavior · Sustainable clothing industry · Sustainable shopping

40.1 Introduction

The clothing industry is currently one of the most resource-intensive and environmentally polluting industries (Riba et al., 2020). Globally, the clothing industry alone uses more than 60% of the total use of textiles (Modak, 2021). For this global industry, it is crucial to constantly update the product offering to meet the

---

S. Bartošová (✉) · Z. Musová · Z. Fulajtárová
Faculty of Economics, Matej Bel University, Banska Bystrica, Slovakia
e-mail: sbartosova@umb.sk

© The Author(s), under exclusive license to Springer Nature Switzerland AG 2024
N. Tsounis, A. Vlachvei (eds.), *Applied Economic Research and Trends*, Springer Proceedings in Business and Economics,
https://doi.org/10.1007/978-3-031-49105-4_40

changing demands of consumers, and at the same time, businesses could maintain their competitiveness (Musová et al., 2021b). There are many cheap and trendy clothes on the world market, which are examples of either low-end (quality) ideas from high-end culture or celebrity ideas at relatively affordable prices to dampen the demand of low-income consumers. This phenomenon is indicated by Chen et al. (2021) as "fast fashion." Many well-known fast fashion brands, such as H&M or Zara, produce clothes that are quickly replenished, both in brick-and-mortar and in online stores, and at the same time, consumers quickly throw these clothes into the trash baskets for various reasons, which may be the out-of-date trendy clothing or rapid wear of clothing.

The current linear system, where a product is produced, purchased, used, and then thrown away, is not sustainable. It is crucial to look for other ways of production and sale that will be more environmentally friendly. Trends in the purchase of clothing and shoes are emerging on the market, which can significantly contribute to achieving long-term sustainability as well as creating a cycle guided by the principles of a circular economy. The new economic model is accompanied by fundamental changes that significantly affect the purchasing habits of consumers. In addition, the clothing industry is an example of how consumers can be offered various circular solutions that respond to current trends in the environmental field.

In the mentioned context, the aim is to investigate consumer behavior when buying clothes in Slovakia and the use of the new environmentally responsible trends in this area. After defining the theoretical starting points of the issue, the research methodology is described in the next part of the article. In the third part, selected relevant research results are presented (in the context of the aim of this chapter), which are then confronted in the Discussion section with the results of other, so far, research in the subject area. In conclusion, the most significant results and recommendations for further research have been summarized. We see the benefit of contribution as a good starting point even for further research, since the issue of consumer behavior when buying environmentally responsible clothes is just lightly researched in Slovakia. We carried out basic exploratory research on the issue of purchasing environmentally responsible clothes/textile products because this topic is not sufficiently elaborated/researched in the conditions of Slovakia. The results will be the starting point for a further, more detailed investigation of the issue and a possible/planned comparison of the behavior of Slovak consumers with consumers in other countries.

40.2 Literature Review

The clothing industry (in the literature sometimes also referred to by alternative terms such as the textile or fashion industry) is one of the industries with the biggest negative impact on the environment. However, it also has enormous potential for the implementation of the principles of the circular economy in the practice of businesses and consumer behavior. As stated by Henninger et al., up to 95% of the products of the textile and clothing industry could be put back into circulation—by re-wearing, recycling, or repairing.

Over the past two decades, the textile industry (which also includes clothing production) has doubled its production, and the average global annual consumption of textiles has almost doubled (from 7 to 13 kg per person) (Souchet, 2019). At present, the world produces approximately 80 billion new garments per year (Firth, 2016). In the textile production process in China, only 85% of the fabric is used on average, and the remaining 15% is thrown away. Other textile materials (including mainly chemical materials, which further include various synthetic fibers and man-made fibers) are thrown away. However, these materials are very difficult to decompose in nature. Therefore, they can only be regenerated or burned. Globally, the conversion of recycled textiles into new textiles is at a very low level. According to recent data (Chen et al., 2021; Modak, 2021), less than 1% of the material used for textile production is recycled/converted into new textiles. However, due to insufficient conversion of recycled textiles into new textiles, considerable landfill costs arise. Although some countries have high collection rates for reuse and recycling (for example, Germany, which collects up to 75% of textiles (Morlet et al., 2017)), a large part of the collected textiles in such countries is exported to low- and middle-income countries, which do not have their collection infrastructure, leading to a system of creating landfills (Watson et al., 2016). The whole system is like delegating responsibility to an incompetent society, which is again just another environmental problem (Chen et al., 2021).

Since few companies can ignore public pressure demanding a more ecological approach, new environmental business models are emerging for this reason. In the study, INCIEN (2020) presented environmental business models in the context of the sustainable clothing industry, in which a new product—cloth—is not sold, but an existing product that has already been purchased and used in a certain way is used. These new business models include (1) the sale of re-designed clothing, (2) clothing repair and modification services, (3) clothing rental, (4) clothing swaps, (5) fashion style consulting, and (6) extension use of products—slow fashion and capsule wardrobe. Another current trend in the clothing industry is "zero waste," which is translated as living without waste. It is the process of producing products that leave no excess material for waste (Paras et al., 2019), thus reducing the number of waste materials from the manufacturing process that often end up in landfills and subsequently contribute to the planet's pollution (Chen et al., 2018). Approximately, only 15–20% of discarded clothes are collected in Europe. The rest of the textiles used to make clothes end up in landfills (Sandin & Peters, 2018) because it is less expensive for businesses to dispose of unnecessary clothes. This is where the space is created for new designers who care about sustainability. In addition to the trend of clothing brands designing garments in such a way as to utilize every centimeter of fabric, thus eliminating waste, there is also an influx of designers sourcing waste textiles directly from factories, which they then use to create new and unique garments (Kasavan et al., 2021). This trend, called "Upcycling," is also used by various clothing companies and global clothing designers.

These new business models require active cooperation and involvement of businesses and consumers in the circular economy (CE). As stated by Musová and Drugdová, the mentioned trends can significantly contribute to achieving sustainability and creating a cycle that works according to CE principles when purchasing clothes. However, to build trust in this new system, businesses must provide consumers with enough information and present positive examples from practice.

Not only businesses but also consumers are increasingly aware of the ecological degradation caused by the materials used to manufacture clothing products. Currently, a growing phenomenon is the increasing interest of consumers in nature protection. Many consumers strive to be environmentally responsible and emphasize their environmental requirements when making purchases. Environmental global trends in the textile industry, which either directly or indirectly affect consumers around the world, are also significant factors.

Consumer behavior tends to be influenced by various factors, which can be of external or internal nature, or even situational influences. In addition, it is only up to the individual decision of the consumer, which factors will be influenced, or which factors are important to him (Steffek, 2018). Therefore, the consumer's interest in the environment, or the effort to protect nature, does not always have to be transferred to the consumer's purchasing behavior. Research by Jastrzebska generally points to the fact that, although Polish consumers are aware of the importance of sustainable consumption, this is not always reflected in their behavior. In addition, there is a significant difference between what consumers declare and how they behave.

In Slovakia, responsible shopping behavior was generally examined by various authors (Klapilová Krbová, 2016; Holotová et al., 2020; Mitríková et al., 2021), and shopping behavior when purchasing sports equipment and accessories was investigated by Bajza (2021). However, the issue of sustainable shopping in the clothing industry is lightly explored. Environmental awareness was examined by Baculáková and Čiefová (2021). Koszewska et al. (2017) used comparative analysis to investigate sustainable consumption and production for the textile and clothing sector in the Visegrad region (which also includes Slovakia). Nahalkova et al. (2022) dealt with a specific period during the pandemic, during which they investigated the impact of COVID-19 on sustainability and changing consumer behavior in the textile Industry. Steffek investigated a specific sustainable trend—slow fashion, in which she focused on the factors of the proliferation of slow fashion.

Environmentally responsible purchasing in Slovakia was investigated also by Musová et al. (2018). The results showed that environmental factors are not that important for consumers, despite negative developments in the environment. Studies (Musová et al., 2018) show that the price of the product is one of the factors that can have a significant impact on the purchase of an environmentally responsible product. Gburová et al. describe consumers as more sophisticated and price sensitive. Sustainability is often associated with a high price, and consumers mostly reckon only on the short-term household budget when making decisions about the purchase. Moreover, demand and price are inversely proportional: the higher the price, the lower the demand. Therefore, price perception significantly influences the consumer's decision to purchase a product.

40.3 Methodology

This chapter examines consumer behavior when buying clothes in Slovakia and the use of the new environmentally responsible trends in this area. Overall, trends in a certain way (directly or indirectly) affect consumers and their purchasing behavior. That also applies to the clothing industry, which is the focus of this chapter. Therefore, it is crucial to examine whether and what impact the selected environmental global trends in the clothing industry have on consumers. In addition, how consumers perceive these trends and how often they use them. It is also crucial to identify the significant factors that influence the consumer to buy products (clothes and shoes) that are environmentally friendly.

Following the aim of this chapter, we formulate the following research questions (RQ) and hypotheses (H):

RQ1: How do consumers perceive new environmental global trends in the clothing industry, and how often do they use them?

In the first research question, we will focus on the selected environmental global trends in the sale/purchase of clothing (in the clothing industry) and their consumer perception. We follow the research of Musova et al., from which it follows that younger consumers turn out to be more sensitive to social and environmental issues/problems, and their purchase is influenced by the principles of sustainability and the circular economy. In addition, future key consumers (Generation Z) are characterized by higher environmental awareness and the purchase of ecological products. In the mentioned contexts, we will test the correlation between the positive perception of the given trends and the age of the consumer.

H1: We assume that younger consumers perceive environmental global trends in the clothing industry more positively than older consumers.

A positive perception of trends does not necessarily mean the actual use of responsible procedures when purchasing clothes by consumers. We will examine which of the mentioned new trends are used by consumers, and whether their responsible purchasing behavior in this area is repeated or is only an occasional, unusual phenomenon. We will focus on the behavior of consumers in different age categories, as well as the frequency of responsible clothing shopping.

H2: We assume that half of the consumers use environmental global trends in the clothing industry at least 3 times a year.

H3: We assume that younger consumers use environmental global trends in the clothing industry more often than other consumers.

RQ2: What factors influence the consumer to buy environmentally friendly clothes?

Each consumer is specific and approaches the purchase of products in different ways. Consumer behavior is constantly evolving. It is rather complicated and determined by several factors. We assume that consumers buy a sustainable product precisely because of its properties (the product is made of high-quality sustainable material). However, according to studies (Musová et al., 2018), we cannot ignore the significant impact of price on the purchase of such a product. Following research question RQ2, we establish and test hypotheses (H4) and (H5).

H4: We assume that the high-quality sustainable material from which the product is made has the greatest influence on the consumer when purchasing environmentally friendly clothing.

H5: We assume that a product's price is one of the most strongly influencing factors influencing consumers when purchasing an environmentally friendly textile product.

To fulfill the goals of this chapter, we conducted two types of research, namely secondary data analysis and primary quantitative consumer research. When preparing the literature review, we focused on examining the starting points of the issue by applying several standard scientific research methods. We conducted primary quantitative consumer research in November and December 2022. As a tool, we used an online Google questionnaire and distributed it through social networks such as Facebook and Gmail.

The questionnaire consisted of 24 questions in four sections. The first section was focused on general attitudes toward issues of environmental protection. The second section focused on purchasing clothing products. The third section linked the clothing industry and the environment. The last part of the questionnaire was used to find out selected sociodemographic data about the respondents. We used different types of questions during the construction of the questionnaire, especially closed questions (answers with one or more answer options) and Likert scale questions. The data obtained from the questionnaire were processed using Excel software, tested using the IBM SPSS Statistics program, and subsequently analyzed.

In total, 743 respondents participated in the questionnaire survey. The basic sample consisted of all inhabitants in Slovakia aged 18 to 65. The research sample follows the structure of the Slovak population. To achieve the representativeness of the research quota sampling in terms of gender and age was chosen. The representativeness of the sample according to gender and age through the chi-square test in IBM SPSS Statistics was verified with the significance level $\alpha = 0.05$ (Table 40.1).

In the research sample, 393 (52.89%) were women, and 350 (47.11%) were men. The structure of the sample by age was as follows: Generation Z (18–26 years)—112 (15.08%) respondents, Generation Y (27–42 years)—240 (32.30%) respondents, Generation X (43–57 years)—286 (38.49%) respondents, and the Baby Boomers generation (58–65 years)—105 (14.13%) respondents.

Table 40.1 Results of test on representativeness of research sample

Gender	Observed N	Expected N	Residual
Man	350	371,8	−21,8
Woman	393	371,2	21,8
Total	743		
	Test statistics		Gender
Chi-square			2,558[a]
Df			1
Asymp. Sig.			**0,110**
Age	**Observed N**	**Expected N**	**Residual**
58–65 years	105	105,5	−0,5
43–57 years	286	276,4	9,6
27–42 years	240	249,6	−9,6
18–26 years	112	111,5	0,5
Total	743		
	Test statistics		Age
Chi-square			,712[b]
Df			3
Asymp. Sig.			**0,870**

[a]0 cells (0,0%) have expected frequencies less than 5. The minimum expected cell frequency is 371,2
[b]0 cells (0,0%) have expected frequencies less than 5. The minimum expected cell frequency is 105,5

40.4 Empirical Results and Discussion

40.4.1 *Consumer Behavior when Purchasing Clothing Products*

In this chapter, we evaluate only selected questions from the questionnaire related to the purchase of clothing and focus on the use of new environmentally responsible trends in the clothing industry. We chose current trends that were the subject of our interest based on studies, e.g., INCIEN (2020), Kasavan et al. (2021), and Paras et al. (2019).

In the first part of the questionnaire, we focused on investigating consumer behavior when purchasing textile products.

In the first question, we examined the frequency of purchase of selected clothing products. From the answers of the respondents, shown in Graph 40.1, we note that consumers buy t-shirts/shirts/dresses quite often (up to several times a year). Less frequent purchases were for other types of clothing. A positive finding was the numerous responses of respondents for all product groups that they buy clothes only when they need them (damaged clothes, worn out, etc.). Only a few respondents are influenced by the ever-changing fashion in the clothing industry, e.g., 27 respondents (3.6%) said that they buy a t-shirt/shirt/dress every time the fashion changesalways with a new collection. We present the complete results in Graph 40.1.

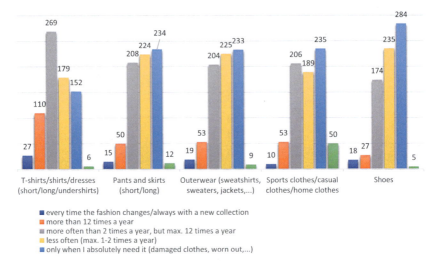

Graph 40.1 How often do you buy the following products?

As the survey further shows, the respondents usually buy clothes and shoes in fashion chains. That applies similarly to most product groups (from 540 to 554 respondents). Other frequently used places of purchase were chain stores, followed by second-hand shops. Only a few respondents buy clothes in boutiques with prestigious clothes or buy clothes from domestic manufacturers.

Various factors influence the respondents to buy clothes. Our research revealed several factors that significantly influence the respondents. The first and most important factor is the price of the product, as many as 605 respondents (81.43%) indicated this option. Followingly, a product design was marked by 68.10% of respondents, and high-quality/sustainable product material is important for 55.85% of respondents. The fourth and fifth factors were also linked to the price of the product, namely a discount from the price, which was indicated by 53.5% of respondents, and a favorable post-season sale of 39.43%. Unfortunately, only 108 (14.53%) respondents mentioned the impact on the environment, and 10.5% of the respondents cared about the country of origin.

40.4.2 New Environmentally Responsible Trends in Purchasing Clothing

Subsequently, we reconnoitered how the respondents perceive environmentally responsible global trends when buying clothes. From the results, we can conclude that the respondents perceive second-hand shopping (47%), slow fashion (45%), and the production of ethical products (42%) most positively. Just 37.1% of respondents perceive the purchase of clothing from recycled materials positively, and 42.3% of respondents perceive such a purchase rather positively. We recorded the most negative responses when renting clothes. Up to 51.55% of respondents perceive it negatively, and 19.7% rather negatively. This was followed by patchwork, which is perceived negatively by up to 40.2% of respondents and 12.5% of respondents rather negatively. However, overall, we can state a positive and rather positive perception in the case of the majority of monitored environmental trends in the clothing industry.

The results support previous research by Musová and Drugdová. They found that more than half of Slovak consumers were unaware of new environmentally responsible global trends. Among the most famous were slow fashion and swap. The research also confirmed the willingness of consumers to buy textile products in this way.

One of the reasons for short knowledge of trends and their neutral or negative perception can be a lack of information and a lack of promotion by businesses. Among other things, Grebozs-Kwawczyk and Siuda state these reasons in their studies. In a broader context, the lack of interest and awareness of consumers is cited as one of the obstacles to the transition to a circular economy by Kirchherr et al. Musová et al. (2021a) stated in their research that 62% of respondents lacked awareness of responsible activities on the part of companies. The above implies the need to change the communication strategy and more explicit support for consumers in the transition to circular models.

As part of the first hypothesis, we assumed a relationship between the consumer's age and the perception of new environmental global trends when buying clothes and shoes. To test the relationship, we used the Mann–Whitney test and Spearman's correlation coefficient at the significance level $\alpha < 0.05$. The test shows that the positive perception of the trends "buying second-hand" and "patchwork" does not depend on the age of the consumer (Appendix 1, p-values are 0.06 and 0.139). For other environmental global trends, only a weak, indirect dependence was confirmed. That means the younger the consumers are, the more positively they perceive environmental trends. Several studies (Kusá & Grešková, 2016) have already indicated that consumers of younger generations (Y and Z) are characterized by higher environmental responsibility and a higher willingness to buy environmental products, which, in our opinion, can lead to a positive perception of environmental responsible trends in the purchase of textile products.

In the questionnaire, we also investigated the use of new environmentally responsible trends in the clothing industry when purchasing clothing. We present the complete results in Graphs 40.2 and 40.3.

From the answers, it follows that in all examined types of environmentally responsible clothing shopping, the option of not using prevailed (Graphs 40.2 and 40.3). Only a few respondents use clothing rental, SWAP, upcycling, or patchwork. It may also be related to insufficient knowledge of the mentioned trends, which resulted from the research of Musova et al. (2021a) and Musova and Drugdova. Renting clothes, selling clothes for leasing, or upcycling were among the less well-known environmentally responsible trends, and the willingness to acquire clothes through these concepts was rather negative. The low interest in clothing rental/leasing was also confirmed by the study by Tu and Hu, who found that up to 45% of respondents had not encountered clothing rentals or had not heard of this concept. Therefore, they don't even have the motivation to try it. Paco et al. (2020) also confirmed a low awareness of sustainable clothing.

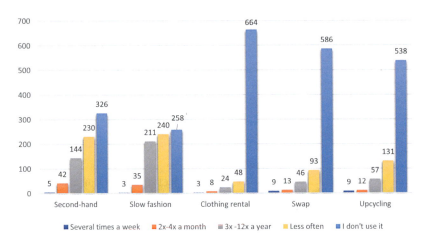

Graph 40.2 Using new environmentally responsible trends when purchasing clothing (part 1)

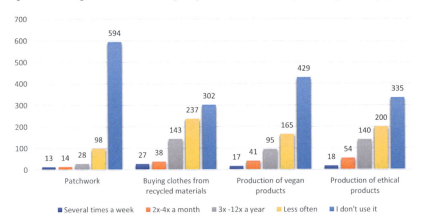

Graph 40.3 Using new environmentally responsible trends when purchasing clothing (part 2)

However, in the case of some trends, we also noticed positive developments. Overall, 421 (56%) respondents use second-hand shopping, although only 47 respondents buy this way more often and regularly (several times a week or 2 × −4× a month). In addition, 43 respondents (19%) buy clothes from recycled materials 3 to 12 times a year. Respondents also use slow fashion regularly—2–4 times a month for 35 respondents and 3–12 times a year for up to 211 respondents (28.2%).

Since most of the respondents perceive new environmental global trends when buying/acquiring clothes and shoes positively, or rather positively, we assumed that half of the respondents would use them at least 3 times a year (H2). For testing, we used a non-parametric binomial test (Appendix 2). The results of the test show that half of the consumers use most of the investigated current trends at least 3 times a year, except for upcycling and patchwork, which are used less. Based on the above, we can only partially confirm H2.

Table 40.2 Factors affecting the purchase of an environmentally friendly clothing product

Factor	Number of respondents	% of respondents
Durability/sustainability/quality of materials used	**442**	59,5%
The price	**400**	53,8%
My interest in the environment	210	28,3%
People around me (family, friends, and acquaintances)	171	23,0%
Social/cultural influences	90	12,1%
I don't buy such products	84	11,3%
Nobody/nothing	63	8,5%
Influencers/celebrities / my idol	51	6,9%
Other (design, advertising, veganism, availability of stores, material composition)	8	1,08%

To test the third hypothesis (H3: We assume that younger consumers use environmental global trends in the textile industry more often than other consumers), we used Spearman's correlation coefficient (Appendix 3). We cannot confirm our assumption from the test results for only eight trends. The test confirmed only the case of the "production of ethical products."

In the research, we also investigated various factors that influence respondents when purchasing environmentally friendly clothing products. All the responses are recorded in Table 40.2.

The most important factor influencing the purchase of an environmentally friendly textile product is the durability/sustainability and quality of the materials used (for up to 442 respondents, 59.5%). The importance of the price of sustainable products was confirmed again. Environmentally friendly products affect up to 53.8% of the respondents. We confirmed the price importance in the mentioned contexts by the Friedman and the Wilcoxon Signed Ranks test, which we used to verify the validity of H5. The importance of price also confirms studies by Jalil and Shaharuddin (2019), Chang and Watchravesringkan (2018), and Ižoldová and Fajdová (2019). On the other hand, the usually higher price of sustainable clothing products is often one of the barriers to their purchase. This is also confirmed by the research of Gubíniová et al., in which she stated that in several European countries (Belgium, France, the Netherlands, Germany, Portugal, and Spain), the price or consumption expenditure is the most often mentioned obstacle when deciding to buy sustainable products and services on the customer side. In addition to the higher price, the reason may also be consumers' lack of confidence in their quality, as they state in their research. The research of Wang et al. (2022) showed that consumers show a more positive attitude toward products that have been certified by third parties. Certified third-party sustainability labels increase the credibility of products from a consumer perspective and provide an opportunity to understand brands' commitment to sustainability.

Although approximately two-thirds of consumers in all countries are concerned with environmental impact, their interest is not always reflected in their purchasing behavior. In our survey, interest in the environment affects the purchasing behavior of only 210 respondents. According to Safitri, some consumers consider other factors when purchasing these products, such as image, store location, additional services, and product quality.

Regarding the factors that influence the purchase of environmentally friendly textile products, we tested two hypotheses H4 and H5. We used the Friedman and the Wilcoxon Signed Ranks test. Tests have confirmed that the product features (durability/sustainability/quality of materials used) most influence consumers when purchasing environmentally friendly clothing. The second most significant factor is the price of the product (Appendix 5).

Subsequently, we investigated the interrelationship of the use of environmental global trends in the acquisition of clothing with the demographic data of the respondents. We used Spearman's correlation coefficient at the significance level $\alpha < 0.05$ to test the relationship. From the results, we can state that we have not confirmed the dependences in the age and education of the respondents, and in the other demographic data, weak dependences have been confirmed only in some trends, e.g., women more often use second-hand shopping and the production of ethical products. Rausch et al. (2021) found that women generally show a higher degree of affection for environmental trends and buy environmentally friendly products in larger measures than men.

Research by Steffe (2018) showed that the environmentally responsible concept of slow fashion is significantly influenced by internal factors that represent individual attitudes, interest in health, or interest in the state of the environment. Therefore, in our research, we also focused on other factors that could influence the realization of the purchase of environmentally responsible trends. To test the relationship, we again used Spearman's correlation coefficient at the significance level $\alpha < 0.05$. The results of the test show that respondents who are interested in the environment use it more often: buying second-hand, upcycling, patchwork, buying recycled clothes, buying ethical products, or buying vegan products (Appendix 4).

We also found that respondents influenced by the product's price more often use slow fashion, clothing rental, upcycling, and patchwork. According to the research of Grazzini et al. (2021), there is a dependence between price and gender, with women having a higher tendency to consider the products' price. These findings were also confirmed by the research of Wang et al. (2022), who investigated the purchase of sustainable outdoor clothing. Results with respondents influenced by Influencers on social networks were also interesting. These respondents more often swap clothes, shop second-hand, and buy vegan products, but also use upcycling more often.

40.5 Conclusion

Each consumer is specific and approaches the satisfaction of their needs in different ways. He/She is influenced by a whole range of different factors. Recently, under the influence of negative developments in the environment, as well as higher information, education, and demanding consumers, shopping for clothes is also changing. In the mentioned contexts, this chapter focused on consumer behavior in this area with a focus on the use of new, environmentally responsible trends.

Sustainable clothing production and new trends reflecting the principles of circular economy are coming to the attention of consumers. Based on secondary data analysis, current trends were identified, which were the subject of our investigation, and their consumer perception and practical use.

However, in Slovak conditions, despite the positive perception of individual trends, only a small part of consumers use them. The best results are achieved when shopping second-hand. Consumers pay less attention to renting clothes, upcycling, and patchwork, which may be related to ignorance or lack of information about these responsible ways of procuring clothes.

Durability, sustainability, and the quality of the materials used are the dominant influencing factors when shopping for environmentally friendly clothes. Only slightly fewer respondents consider the price the most significant factor, which is also confirmed by several domestic and foreign studies. In the case of products with an environmental dimension, the usually higher price can also be one of the barriers to purchase.

The issue of consumer behavior when buying environmentally responsible clothes is slightly researched in Slovakia. Therefore, the contribution of this article may be perceived as a good starting point for further research into this issue. For a further, more detailed examination of the issue, various specifics of environmentally responsible purchasing of textile products and clothing, as well as a possible comparison of the behavior of Slovak consumers with consumers in other countries. Research results are relevant for business entities, which are based on the characteristics of different consumer segments with specific needs and wishes (also in sustainability and circularity). They can more precisely target their environmentally responsible offers to these requirements. Moreover, businesses that deal with sustainable fashion can further use the information obtained for marketing purposes and promote sustainable fashion more intensively.

However, the results could also be relevant for consumers who are interested in responsible shopping. Consumers can also help with this situation. Although it is undoubtedly difficult, they can, e.g., appeal to businesses to become environmentally conscious.

At this stage, this chapter was focused only on selected contexts of the issue regarding the age differences of the respondents. In future investigations, we will also expand our attention to the influence of other socioeconomic characteristics on the perception and use of new environmentally responsible procedures when buying clothes.

Acknowledgments This chapter has been supported by the Scientific Grant Agency of Slovak Republic under project VEGA No. 1/0479/23 "Research of circular behavior in the context of STP marketing model."

Appendices

Appendix 1

H1

Correlations

			AGE	OT8a	OT8b	OT8c	OT8d	OT8e	OT8f	OT8g	OT8h	OT8i
Spearman's rho	AGE	Correlation coefficient	1000	−,072*	−,195**	−,146**	−,228**	−,177**	−,049	−,114**	−,134**	−,160**
		Sig. (2-tailed)		0,049	0,000	0,000	0,000	0,000	0,187	0,002	0,000	0,000
		N	743	743	739	738	739	741	739	742	740	741

*. Correlation is significant at the 0.05 level (2-tailed).
**. Correlation is significant at the 0.01 level (2-tailed).

Explanations		
OT8a	Second-hand
OT8b	Slow fashion
OT8c	Clothing rental
OT8d	Swap
OT8e	Upcycling
OT8f	Patchwork
OT8g	Buying clothes from recycled materials
OT8h	Production of vegan products
OT8i	Production of ethical products

```
NPAR TESTS
/M-W= OT8a OT8b OT8c OT8d OT8e OT8f OT8g OT8h OT8i BY
OT16_2sk(1 2)
/MISSING ANALYSIS
/METHOD= MC CIN(99) SAMPLES(10000).
```

Mann-Whitney test

Ranks

	N	Mean rank	Sum of ranks
OT16_2sk			

OT8a	1,0	391	382,61	149,600,00
	2,0	352	360,22	126,796,00
	Total	743		
OT8b	1,0	388	405,39	157,289,50
	2,0	351	330,88	116,140,50
	Total	739		
OT8c	1,0	387	397,44	153,810,50
	2,0	351	338,69	118,880,50
	Total	738		
OT8d	1,0	388	411,84	159,795,50
	2,0	351	323,75	113,634,50
	Total	739		
OT8e	1,0	390	401,32	156,515,50
	2,0	351	337,31	118,395,50
	Total	741		
OT8f	1,0	389	378,11	147,084,00
	2,0	350	360,99	126,346,00
	Total	739		
OT8g	1,0	390	391,05	152,508,50
	2,0	352	349,84	123,144,50
	Total	742		
OT8h	1,0	388	393,16	152,546,50
	2,0	352	345,52	121,623,50
	Total	740		
OT8i	1,0	390	397,97	155,208,00
	2,0	351	341,03	119,703,00
	Total	741		

(continued)

Test statistics

			OT8a	OT8b	OT8c	OT8d	OT8e	OT8f	OT8g	OT8h	OT8i
Mann–Whitney U			64,668.000	54,364.500	57,104.500	51,858.500	56,619.500	64,921.000	61,016.500	59,495.500	57,927.000
Wilcoxon W			126,796.000	116,140.500	118,880.500	113,634.500	118,395.500	126,346.000	123,144.500	121,623.500	119,703.000
Z			−1542	−5056	−4047	−5863	−4273	−1143	−2802	−3161	−3837
Asymp. Sig. (2-tailed)			0,123	0,000	0,000	0,000	0,000	0,253	0,005	0,002	0,000
Monte Carlo sig. (2-tailed)	Sig.		,120[b]	,000[b]	,000[b]	,000[b]	,000[b]	,259[b]	,004[b]	,002[b]	<,001[b]
	99% confidence interval	Lower bound	0,112	0,000	0,000	0,000	0,000	0,247	0,003	0,001	0,000
		Upper bound	0,128	0,000	0,000	0,000	0,000	0,270	0,006	0,003	0,001
Monte Carlo sig. (1-tailed)	Sig.		,062[b]	,000[b]	,000[b]	,000[b]	,000[b]	,129[b]	,002[b]	<,001[b]	,000[b]
	99% confidence interval	Lower bound	0,055	0,000	0,000	0,000	0,000	0,120	0,001	0,000	0,000
		Upper bound	0,068	0,000	0,000	0,000	0,000	0,137	0,003	0,002	0,000

[a]Grouping Variable: OT16_2sk
[b]Based on 10,000 sampled tables with starting seed 2,000,000

Appendix 2

(H2)

Binomial test

		Category	N	Observed prop.	Test prop.	Exact sig. (2-tailed)
OT9a	Group 1	0,0	227	0,53	0,50	0,174
	Group 2	1,0	198	0,47		
	Total		425	1,00		
OT9b	Group 1	0,0	241	0,49	0,50	0,821
	Group 2	1,0	247	0,51		
	Total		488	1,00		
OT9c	Group 1	1,0	38	0,45	0,50	0,386
	Group 2	0,0	47	0,55		
	Total		85	1,00		
OT9d	Group 1	0,0	90	0,56	0,50	0,133
	Group 2	1,0	70	0,44		
	Total		160	1,00		
OT9e	Group 1	0,0	128	0,61	0,50	0,002
	Group 2	1,0	82	0,39		
	Total		210	1,00		
OT9f	Group 1	0,0	95	0,62	0,50	0,005
	Group 2	1,0	59	0,38		
	Total		154	1,00		
OT9g	Group 1	0,0	233	0,52	0,50	0,319
	Group 2	1,0	211	0,48		
	Total		444	1,00		

(continued)

OT9h	Group 1	0,0	163	0,52	0,50	0,573
	Group 2	1,0	152	0,48		
	Total		315	1,00		
OT9ik	Group 1	0,0	197	0,48	0,50	0,430
	Group 2	1,0	214	0,52		
	Total		411	1,00		

Question 9:	How often do you use new environmental trends when you need to buy clothes and accessories?
OT9a	Second-hand
OT9b	Slow fashion
OT9c	Clothing rental
OT9d	Swap
OT9e	Upcycling
OT9f	Patchwork
OT9g	Buying clothes from recycled materials
OT9h	Production of vegan products
OT9i	Production of ethical products

Appendix 3

(H3) Nonparametric Correlations

Correlations

		AGE	OT9a	OT9b	OT9c	OT9d	OT9e	OT9f	OT9g	OT9h	OT9i
Spearman's rho	AGE	Correlation coefficient	1000	−0,075	−0,004	0,198	−0,095	−0,104	−0,153	−0,060	−0,074	−0,096
		Sig. (2-tailed)		0,121	0,934	0,069	0,234	0,134	0,058	0,209	0,192	0,051
		N	743	425	488	85	160	210	154	444	315	411

*Correlation is significant at the 0.05 level (2-tailed)
*Correlation is significant at the 0.01 level (2-tailed)

Appendix 4

Nonparametric Correlations

		OT9a	OT9b	OT9c	OT9d	OT9e	OT9f	OT9g	OT9h	OT9i
Spearman's rho	My interest in the environment — Correlation coefficient	,167**	0,059	−0,039	0,020	,178**	,163*	,198**	,143*	,260**
	Sig. (2-tailed)	0,001	0,196	0,722	0,797	0,010	0,043	0,000	0,011	0,000
	N	425	488	85	160	210	154	444	315	411
	Malleability/ sustainability/ quality of materials used — Correlation coefficient	0,028	0,013	−,298**	−0,132	−0,046	−0,079	,146**	0,008	,184**
	Sig. (2-tailed)	0,571	0,778	0,006	0,095	0,506	0,333	0,002	0,887	0,000
	N	425	488	85	160	210	154	444	315	411
	Social/cultural influences — Correlation coefficient	0,076	0,059	0,065	0,045	0,034	,193*	0,053	0,108	0,013
	Sig. (2-tailed)	0,116	0,194	0,556	0,571	0,624	0,017	0,265	0,056	0,799
	N	425	488	85	160	210	154	444	315	411
	People around me (family, friends and acquaintances) — Correlation coefficient	,151**	0,031	−0,061	0,076	0,110	0,083	0,007	−0,046	0,021
	Sig. (2-tailed)	0,002	0,494	0,582	0,342	0,111	0,308	0,887	0,412	0,669
	N	425	488	85	160	210	154	444	315	411

Influencers/celebrities / my idol	Correlation coefficient	,110*	0,060	0,016	,164*	,156*	0,122	0,070	,123*	0,089
	Sig. (2-tailed)	0,024	0,184	0,882	0,038	0,023	0,132	0,139	0,029	0,072
	N	425	488	85	160	210	154	444	315	411
Price	Correlation coefficient	0,046	,091*	−,225*	−0,105	−,168*	−,168*	−0,025	−0,070	−0,059
	Sig. (2-tailed)	0,342	0,044	0,039	0,188	0,015	0,037	0,602	0,217	0,233
	N	425	488	85	160	210	154	444	315	411
Nobody/nothing	Correlation coefficient	−0,044	−0,021	0,110	0,067	0,109	0,107	0,029	0,062	−0,018
	Sig. (2-tailed)	0,371	0,640	0,315	0,402	0,114	0,187	0,543	0,274	0,714
	N	425	488	85	160	210	154	444	315	411
I don't buy such products	Correlation coefficient	−0,057	−0,075	0,089	−0,033	−0,067	−0,140	−0,080	−,138*	−,156**
	Sig. (2-tailed)	0,241	0,097	0,419	0,678	0,337	0,084	0,093	0,014	0,002
	N	425	488	85	160	210	154	444	315	411

Appendix 5

Question 10:	When buying an environmentally friendly textile product, I am very influenced by:
OT10a	My interest in the environment
OT10b	Malleability/sustainability/ quality of materials used
OT10c	Social/cultural influences
OT10d	People around me (family, friends, and acquaintances)
OT10e	Influencers/celebrities / my idol
OT10f	The price
OT10g	Nobody/nothing
OT10h	I don't buy such products
OT10i	My interest in the environment

Friedman test

Ranks

	Mean rank
OT10a	4,63
OT10b	5,88
OT10c	3,97
OT10d	4,40
OT10e	3,75
OT10f	5,65
OT10g	3,81
OT10h	3,91

Test statistics

N	743
Chi-square	1130,389
Df	7
Asymp. Sig.	0,000

a. Friedman test

```
NPAR TESTS
  /WILCOXON=OT10b OT10f OT10a OT10d OT10c OT10h OT10g WITH OT10f OT10a OT10d OT10c OT10h OT10g
  OT10e (PAIRED)
  /MISSING ANALYSIS.
```

NPar tests

Wilcoxon signed ranks test

Ranks

		N	Mean rank	Sum of ranks
OT10f – OT10b	Negative ranks	172[a]	150,50	25,886,00
	Positive ranks	128[b]	150,50	19,264,00
	Ties	443[c]		
	Total	743		
OT10a – OT10f	Negative ranks	311[d]	217,00	67,487,00
	Positive ranks	122[e]	217,00	26,474,00
	Ties	310[f]		
	Total	743		

(continued)

OT10d – OT10a	Negative ranks	164[g]	143,50	23,534,00
	Positive ranks	122[h]	143,50	17,507,00
	Ties	457[i]		
	Total	743		
OT10c – OT10d	Negative ranks	135[j]	95,00	12,825,00
	Positive ranks	54[k]	95,00	5130,00
	Ties	554[l]		
	Total	743		
OT10h – OT10c	Negative ranks	94[m]	89,50	8413,00
	Positive ranks	84[n]	89,50	7518,00
	Ties	565[o]		
	Total	743		
OT10g – OT10h	Negative ranks	69[p]	59,50	4105,50
	Positive ranks	49[q]	59,50	2915,50
	Ties	625[r]		
	Total	743		
OT10e – OT10g	Negative ranks	63[s]	58,50	3685,50
	Positive ranks	53[t]	58,50	3100,50
	Ties	627[u]		
	Total	743		

a. OT10f < OT10b
b. OT10f > OT10b
c. OT10f = OT10b
d. OT10a < OT10f
e. OT10a > OT10f
f. OT10a = OT10f
g. OT10d < OT10a
h. OT10d > OT10a
i. OT10d = OT10a
j. OT10c < OT10d
k. OT10c > OT10d
l. OT10c = OT10d
m. OT10h < OT10c
n. OT10h > OT10c
o. OT10h = OT10c
p. OT10g < OT10h
q. OT10g > OT10h
r. OT10g = OT10h
s. OT10e < OT10g
t. OT10e > OT10g
u. OT10e = OT10g

Test statistics

	OT10f – OT10b	OT10a – OT10f	OT10d – OT10a	OT10c – OT10d	OT10h – OT10c	OT10g – OT10h	OT10e – OT10g
Z	−2540[b]	−9083[b]	−2484[b]	−5892[b]	−,750[b]	−1841[b]	−,928[b]
Asymp. Sig. (2-tailed)	0,011	0,000	0,013	0,000	0,454	0,066	0,353

[a]Wilcoxon Signed Ranks Test
[b]Based on positive ranks

References

Bajza, F. (2021). Analýza spotrebiteľského správania respondentov pri nákupe športového vybavenia a doplnkov. *Pošta, telekomunikácie a elektronický obchod, 16*(2), 1–7. https://doi.org/10.26552/pte.C.2021.2.1

Chang, H. J., & Watchravesringkan, K. (2018). Who are sustainably minded apparel shoppers? An investigation of the influencing factors of sustainable apparel consumption. *International Journal of Retail & Distribution Management, 46*(2), 148–162. https://doi.org/10.1108/IJRDM-10-2016-0176

Chen, C.-C., et al. (2018). Relationship between fine particulate air pollution exposure and human adult life expectancy in Taiwan. *Journal of Toxicology and Environmental Health, 82*(14), 826–832. https://doi.org/10.1080/15287394.2019.1658386

Chen, X., et al. (2021). Circular economy and sustainability of the clothing and textile industry. *Materials Circular Economy, 3*(12), 9. https://doi.org/10.1007/s42824-021-00026-2

Čiefová, K. B. M. (2021). Environmentálne povedomie študentov Ekonomickej uni-verzity v Bratislave. *Jazyk v kultúre–kultúra v jazyku, 7*, 9–20.

Firth, L. (2016). *The true cost*. cit. 2022-04-26 Available on: https://truecostmovie.com/learn-more/environmental-impact/.

Grazzini, L., et al. (2021). Solving the puzzle of sustainable fashion consumption: The role of consumers' implicit attitudes and perceived warmth. *Journal of Cleaner Production, 287*(125579), 125579. https://doi.org/10.1016/j.jclepro.2020.125579

Holotová, M., Nagyová, Ľ., & HOLOTA, T. (2020). The impact of environmental responsibility on changing consumer behaviour–sustainable market in Slovakia. *Economics & Sociology, 13*(3), 84–96.

Inštitút Cirkulárnej EkonomIKY. (2020). *Textilný a odevný priemysel. Problémy a riešenia. Platforma rozvojových organizácií—Ambrela v spolupráci s Inštitútom cirkulárnej ekonomiky*. Bratislava. 2020. 84 s., ISBN 978-80-973650-1-1.

Ižoldová D., & Fajdová, M. (2019). Slow fashion—revolúcia v nákupnom správaní? In *Študentská vedecká aktivita 2019*, Zborník prác, Ekonomická fakulta, Univerzita Mateja Bela v Banskej Bystrici (p. 25). ISBN 978-80-557-1540-7.

Jalil, M. H., & Shaharuddin, S. S. (2019). Consumer purchase behavior of eco-fashion clothes as a trend to reduce clothing waste. *International Journal of Innovative Technology and Exploring Engineering, 8*(12), 4224–4233. https://doi.org/10.35940/ijitee.L2693.1081219

Kasavan, S., et al. (2021). Global trends of textile waste research from 2005 to 2020 using bibliometric analysis. *Environmental Science and Pollution Research, 28*(33), 44780–44794. https://doi.org/10.1007/s11356-021-15303-5

Koszewska, M., et al. (2017). Comparative analysis of sustainable consumption and production in Visegrad region-conclusions for textile and clothing sector. *IOP Conference Series: Materials Science and Engineering, 254*(20), 202003.

Krbová, P. K. (2016). The shopping behaviourGenerationtion Y: A comparison of The Czech Republic and Slovakia. *Acta Universitatis Agriculturae et Silviculturae Mendelianae Brunensis, 64*(2), 617–626.

Kusá, A., & Grešková, P. (2016). *Marketingová komunikácia v kontexte hodnôt a nákupného správania generácie 50+*. UCM.

Mitríková, J., et al. (2021). *Current shopping trends in Slovakia*.

Modak, P. (2021). *Practising circular economy*. CRC Press, Taylor & Francis Group. ISBN 9780367619572.

Morlet, A. et al. (2017). *A new textile economy: redesigning fashion's future. Ellen MacArthur Foundation*. cit. 2021-04-05 Available on: https://www.ellenmacarthurfoundation

Musová, Z., et al. (2018). Environmentally responsible purchasing in Slovakia. *Economics and Sociology, 1*(4), 289–305. https://doi.org/10.14254/2071-789X.2018/11-4/19

Musova, Z., et al. (2021a). Environmentally responsible behaviour of consumers: Evidence from Slovakia. *Economics and Sociology, 14*(1), 178–198. https://doi.org/10.14254/2071-789X.2021/14-1/12

Musova, Z., et al. (2021b). Správanie spotrebiteľov generácie Z v kontexte princípov kruhovej ekonomiky. Aplikácia princípov kruhovej ekonomiky na Slovensku. In Z. Musová & B. Bystrica (Eds.), *Zborník vedeckých prác II z projektu VEGA 1/0705/19* (Vol. 2021, pp. 147–159). Ekonomická fakulta Univerzity Mateja Bela v Banskej Bystrici. ISBN 978-80-557-1920-7.

Paco, A., et al. (2020). Fostering sustainable consumer behaviour regarding clothing: Assessing trends on purchases, recycling, and disposal. *Textile Research Journal, 91*(3–4), 373–384. https://doi.org/10.1177/0040517520944524

Paras, M. K., et al. (2019). A Romanian case study of clothes and accessories upcycling. *Industria Textil, 70*(3), 285–290. https://doi.org/10.35530/IT.070.03.1500

Rausch, T. M., et al. (2021). Does sustainability matter to consumers? Assessing the importance of online shop and apparel product attributes. *Journal of Retailing and Consumer Services, 63*(102681), 102681. https://doi.org/10.1016/j.jretconser.2021.102681

Riba, J. R., et al. (2020). Circular economy of post-consumer textile waste: Classification through infrared spectroscopy. *Journal of Cleaner Production, 272*(123011), 123011. https://doi.org/10.1016/j.jclepro.2020.123011

Sandin, G., & Peters, G. M. (2018). Environmental impact of textile reuse and recycling–a review. *Journal of Cleaner Production, 184*, 353. https://doi.org/10.1016/j.jclepro.2018.02.266

Souchet, F. (2019). *Fashion has a huge waste problem. Here's how it can change.* World Economic Forum. cit. 2022-04-24 Available on: https://www.weforum.org.

Steffek, V. (2018). Faktory proliferácie slow fashion. *Journal of Global Science, 3*(3), 2453.

Wang, L., et al. (2022). Preferred product attributes for sustainable outdoor apparel: A conjoint analysis approach. *Sustainable Production and Consumption, 39*, 657–671. https://doi.org/10.1016/j.spc.2021.11.011

Watson, D., et al. (2016). *Exports of Nordic used textiles: fate, benefits, and impacts.* cit. 2022-04-30 Available on: http://norden.diva-portal.org/smash/record.JSF?pid=diva2%3A1057017&dswid=10

Chapter 41
Impact of Gender Diversity Boards on Financial Health SMEs

Mário Papík and Lenka Papíková

Abstract This chapter analyzes the impact of gender diversity on the financial health of small- and medium-sized enterprises (SMEs). Financial statements of 1178 joint-stock companies, specifically 351 medium-sized enterprises and 827 small enterprises, were analyzed during the COVID-19 pandemic for 2020 and the prior year. Several logistic regression models were developed separately for small- and medium-sized enterprises. These models are described by pseudo R-squared, Akaike information criterion, Bayesian information criterion, variance inflation factor, and area under the curve. The results were cross-validated by stratified tenfold cross-validation, and they show a negative relationship and also a U-shape between gender diversity boards and the probability of SME bankruptcy. Older companies, companies with lower levels of debt, companies with larger numbers of employees, and companies with smaller volumes of tangible assets also have a lower probability of bankruptcy. Based on the results, it can be assumed that the gender diversity board by shareholders also makes sense for SMEs. Moreover, in SMEs, board members have a much stronger position. Thus, there is a significant assumption that the influence of women on the board of such companies could be more significant than in the case of large companies.

Keywords Gender diversity · SME · Bankruptcy prediction · Financial health · Altman model · COVID-19

41.1 Introduction

The new EU directive (EU 2022/2381) on gender balance on corporate boards of the European Parliament proposes to increase the share of women as nonexecutive directors to 40% by 2026 or to increase this share among all directors to 33%

M. Papík (✉) · L. Papíková
Faculty of Management, Comenius University, Bratislava, Slovakia

© The Author(s), under exclusive license to Springer Nature Switzerland AG 2024
N. Tsounis, A. Vlachvei (eds.), *Applied Economic Research and Trends*, Springer Proceedings in Business and Economics,
https://doi.org/10.1007/978-3-031-49105-4_41

(European Parliament, 2022). Despite the positive trend in the last years, even in developed countries this proportional limit of women in managerial and executive positions is far from being achieved. In 2021, women held an average of 29% of board seats in developed countries, whilst in 2017 it was only 20%. The situation in developing countries is even worse, where women make up 15% of the boards, although in 2017 their representation in boards was only slightly above 10% (MSCI, 2021).

However, according to several authors (Martín-Ugedo & Antonio, 2014; Cho et al., 2021; Elsayed et al., 2022; Garcia & Herrero, 2021), gender-diverse boards contribute to better financial management of companies. According to these authors, companies with diverse boards achieve higher performance and face a lower probability of bankruptcy. Women on the board thus contribute with their unique point of view to better strategic decisions, from which the entire company benefits. In addition, companies managed by women have a significantly higher rate of investment in innovation and support for corporate social responsibility (Rao & Titl, 2016). This is because women on the boards are significantly more oriented toward the satisfaction of employees and customers. However, women on the boards avoid activities threatening the company's reputational risk and are associated with corruption cases to a lower extent (Chen et al. 2019). All these attributes contribute to the fact that the company becomes stable and achieves above-average profits for its shareholders.

Appointing women, however, to boards is not enough. They should be given an equal voice and equal opportunities to contribute to the board's decision-making. If female representation on the board is up to 20%, they can only influence events in the company to a very small extent (Kanter, 1977). Therefore, authors such as Joeck et al. (2013) or Tampakoudis et al. (2022) showed that initially the participation of women reduces the company's performance, but when the critical mass is exceeded (30% or three females on the board out of ten members), women have a positive influence on the company's activities, which is reflected in the improvement of financial performance.

However, most of these findings of recent studies conducted research for large publicly listed companies. This chapter therefore analyzes the impact of a gender-diverse board on the financial health of small- and medium-sized enterprises (SMEs). This study has tested multiple regression models separately for small- and medium-sized enterprises. Since the existing studies assume a U-shape relationship with the performance of companies, this study therefore worked with the percentage representation of women on the board (linear relationship) along with the Blau index for the gender-diverse board (quadratic relationship). The novelty of this study lies in the fact that previous research only very rarely analyzed the influence of the board on SMEs. In addition, this is one of the very few studies dealing with gender diversity in boards from Slovakia, which can provide interesting results since women on the boards in the CEE region are still underrepresented in boards.

This chapter is divided into five sections. The first section is the introduction, and the second section includes a literature review. Methodology is included in the third section, and the fourth section includes the result. The last section describes the concluding remarks of this manuscript.

41.2 Literature Review

According to the existing studies focused mainly on listed companies, companies with gender-diverse boards have lower debt levels. For example, Adusei and Obeng (2019), on a sample of 441 global microfinance institutions, showed that increasing board gender diversity leads to decreased company leverage, making it more averse to bankruptcy risk. Similarly, García and Herrero (2021), on a sample of 1416 EU companies, found that increasing gender board diversity is negatively related to leverage, cost of debt, and debt maturity. The lower level of company debt then makes it easier to obtain other financial sources, either through loans from banks or on the capital markets, in the event of an unfavorable development of the company's financial health.

Nam and An (2021), on a sample of 581 nonfinancial companies listed on the Korean Stock Exchange over the period 2009–2017, showed that although corporate social responsibility reduces the probability of bankruptcy, gender-diverse board does not have such an effect. According to these authors, this was caused mainly by the low proportion of women on the company board. Similarly, Maj (2017) did not identify any relationship between gender diversity on a board and financial performance due to the lower representation of women on the board. Unlike Nam and An (2021) and Maj (2017), Cho et al. (2021) showed, on a sample of Chinese-listed manufacturing companies, that companies with more gender-diverse executives have a lower probability of bankruptcy. In addition, this probability was strengthened if these directors had achieved higher education. Lee and Thong (2022) showed that the company's performance positively depends on the gender diversity of its board. Moreover, this relationship is higher in countries with stronger property rights, securities law regulation, stronger economic empowerment of women, and during the COVID-19 crisis.

From the perspective of SMEs, several authors such as Dang et al. (2018), Espinosa-Méndez and Correa (2022), Martin-Ugedo and Vera (2014) showed the existence of a positive relationship between the percentage of women on the board of directors and the corporate performance of SMEs. Dang et al. (2018) analyzed French-listed SMEs from 2010 to 2014. Martin-Ugedo and Minguez-Vera (2014) analyzed Spanish SMEs for the period starting from 2003 to 2008. Their results showed a positive effect of women among board members on the performance of SMEs. In addition, these studies examined both the linear relationship and the quadratic forms using the Blau or Shannon index. The influence of these three variables on the return of assets was confirmed in each study. Similarly, Wu et al. (2017), on 469 Chinese-listed SMEs from 2011 to 2013, showed that female participation on the board significantly contributes to the growth performance of SMEs. Moreover, according to these authors, this relationship is an inverted U-shape.

Similarly, Inostroza and Espinosa-Méndez (2022) and Espinosa-Méndez and Correa (2022) surveyed 185, respectively, 188 SMEs in Chile to analyze the personal characteristics of CEOs. These studies showed that relationship exists between

CEO gender and performance. However, various sociodemographic characteristics (e.g., age and marital status) do not influence the company's performance. In the past, Weber and Geneste (2014) conducted a similar questionnaire study on a sample of 375 SME owners. Their research showed that although female-owned businesses in their sample were smaller on average, women were more satisfied with their business and lifestyle than men. Arzubiaga et al. (2018) identified the relationship between entrepreneurial orientation and performance in a sample of 230 Spanish SMEs, which were primarily family-owned. The identified relationship is stronger in companies with lower family involvement and higher gender diversity on the board.

41.3 Research Methodology

41.3.1 Data Sample

The financial statements of 1178 joint-stock companies, specifically 351 medium-sized companies and 827 small companies, from 2019 to 2020 were collected (Finstat, 2023). The size of companies was classified according to the European Union recommendation 2003/361. Those companies identified as small enterprises had up to 49 employees and turnover of up to 10 million EUR or value of total assets up to 10 million EUR. Medium-sized enterprises had up to 249 employees and turnover of up to 50 million EUR or value of total assets up to 43 million EUR.

The revised Z''-score was used as the dependent variable in this study. Altman (1983) developed the Z''-score for application in privately owned joint-stock companies since the original Altman model (1968) was originally developed for publicly listed manufacturing companies. The revised Z''-score achieved an accuracy of around 75% in repeated tests on an international sample of companies (Altman et al., 2017). The Z''-score has the following form (41.1):

$$Z'' - \text{score} = 6.56 \times 1 + 3.26 \times 2 + 6.72 \times 3 + 1.05 \times 4 \tag{41.1}$$

where x_1 is the ratio of working capital to total assets, x_2 is the ratio of retained earnings to total assets, x_3 is the ratio of EBIT to total assets, and x_4 is the book value of equity to total liabilities. If the value of the Z''-score is less than 1.1, the company is identified as bankrupt and assigned a value of 1. Otherwise, the enterprise was assigned a value of 0.

Gender diversity in the board (expressed as a percentage of females on the board) and the calculated Blau index of this variable (which quantifies diversity as variety) were used as the main independent variables. The Blau index is calculated according to the following form (41.2):

$$\text{Blau index} = 1 - \sum_{i=1}^{k} p_i^2 \qquad (41.2)$$

where k is the number of groups (two in this study: men and women), and p_i expresses the probability of occurrence in the given group. The calculated Blau index has a quadratic shape with a maximum value of 0.5. This index was used as an extension to the percentage of females on the board because some studies argue that the influence of GDB on the probability of bankruptcy is U-shaped or inverse U-shaped for company performance (Joeck et al., 2013; Wu et al., 2017).

Variables describing the characteristics of a company were chosen as control variables, such as the natural logarithm of the age of the company, the natural logarithm of total assets value, relative year-on-year sales growth, the ratio of bank loans to total assets, and the ratio of tangible assets to total assets. From the corporate characteristics point of view, the number of employees and board members was also determined. These variables were used as additional explanatory variables in the tested regression models.

41.3.2 Statistical Methods

Several logistic regression models were tested in this study. In this study, logistic regression estimates the probability that a sample contains a bankrupting company (separately for small-sized enterprises and separately for medium-sized enterprises). Logistic regression model (41.3) has the following form:

$$P(Y=1|X) = \left(1 + e^{-(\beta_1 x_1 + \cdots + \beta_k x_k + \cdots + \beta_n x_n + \varepsilon)}\right)^{-1} \qquad (41.3)$$

where $P(Y = 1 | X)$ is the probability that the company is bankrupt according to the revised Altman's model. Variable x_k (whilst k varies from 1 to n) corresponds to eight independent variables. Seven of the independent variables correspond to company characteristics, and one variable corresponds to only one of the gender-diverse variables—either the percentage of females on the board or the Blau index (Blau, 1977). Coefficient β represents the estimated coefficients for independent variables, which were estimated by using maximum-likelihood estimation. Variable ε corresponds to an error in predicting (Field et al., 2012).

Developed logistic regression models were described by pseudo R-squared, Akaike information criterion (AIC), and Bayesian information (BIC). Multi-collinearity has been detected by a variance inflation factor (VIF). The influence of gender diversity variables on the model was tested through analysis of variance (ANOVA). The predictive abilities of the models were verified through the area under the curve (AUC) and cross-validated tenfold for both models—with or without the gender diversity variable.

41.4 Results of Analysis

As already mentioned, the financial data of 1178 companies were collected. The distribution of these companies into individual sectors is shown in Table 41.1. As seen in Table 41.1, Altman's Z″-score identified the largest occurrence of companies at risk of bankruptcy in the finance (83%) and tourism and gastronomy (73%) sectors. While tourism and gastronomy are a natural culmination of the COVID-19 pandemic, the results for the finance sector could be caused by sector-related lower values of the book value of equity to total liabilities since companies in the finance sector are significantly more in debt than companies in the other sectors. On the other hand, among sectors such as wholesale or IT, the Altman Z''-score identified in the bankruptcy zone only up to 16% of the companies.

Table 41.2 contains correlation matrix for independent variables analyzed in this study. Most correlation coefficients are lower than 0.4 in absolute value, which represents a weak correlation. The highest values of the correlation coefficient were reached between variables, the number of employees, and total assets (0.45) and the

Table 41.1 Sample distribution

Sector	Total	Default rate	Sector	Total	Default rate
Advertising	10	50%	Intermediary activity	16	50%
Agriculture and forestry	83	59%	Law, consulting, and accounting	43	44%
Automobile industry	3	67%	Media, publishing, and culture	20	60%
Clothing and footwear	3	0%	Metalworking and metallurgy	27	37%
Construction	159	26%	Production—Other	12	8%
Dev. And civil engineering	49	20%	Real estate	85	62%
Education	5	60%	Research and development	30	37%
Electrical engineering	19	21%	Retail	13	46%
Energy and mining	96	46%	Sales and main. Of vehicles	20	5%
Engineering	28	46%	Service	35	31%
Finance	23	83%	Telecommunications	10	30%
Food processing industry	42	43%	Tourism and gastronomy	40	73%
Gambling	1	0%	Transportation and logistics	33	30%
Health care	45	40%	Waste management	18	33%
Chemistry and plastics	19	21%	Wholesale	86	16%
Information technology	99	14%	Wood and paper	10	10%

Source: Own calculation in RStudio

Table 41.2 Correlation matrix

	Age	Assets	Growth	Loans	Number of employees	Tangible	Female board (%)	Female board (BI)
ASSETS	0.23							
GROWTH	−0.12	−0.03						
LOANS	−0.01	0.27	−0.02					
NUMBER EMPLOYEES	0.37	0.45	−0.06	0.04				
TANGIBLE	0.07	0.24	−0.03	0.26	0.07			
FEMALE_BOARD (%)	0.01	−0.11	−0.01	−0.01	−0.02	0.03		
FEMALE BOARD (BI)	0.09	0.00	−0.01	0.01	0.06	0.07	0.59	
NUMBER_BOARD	0.25	0.33	−0.01	0.04	0.31	0.16	−0.07	0.08

Source: Own calculation in RStudio

Table 41.3 Regression model for females on the board (linear function)

	Small				Medium			
	Coeff.	Z-value	Pr(>|z|)	Sign.	Coeff.	Z-value	Pr(>|z|)	Sign.
Intercept	2.68	2.52	0.012	*	3.23	1.26	0.206	
Age	−0.38	−3.24	0.001	**	−0.48	−1.98	0.048	*
Assets	0.03	0.74	0.458		0.06	0.77	0.440	
Growth	0.04	1.96	0.050	*	−0.69	−1.92	0.055	
Loans	2.42	5.45	0.000	***	1.72	2.65	0.008	**
Employees	−0.20	−3.25	0.001	**	−0.12	−0.41	0.683	
Tangible	1.56	6.77	0.000	***	1.58	4.45	0.000	***
Female board (%)	−0.69	−2.31	0.021	*	−0.98	−1.91	0.056	
Board	−0.08	−1.21	0.227		−0.15	−1.80	0.072	
Deviance	1218.85				602.17			
pseudo R2	0.12				0.09			
VIF mean	1.26				1.22			
AIC	1242.85				626.17			
BIC	1301.77				676.23			
ANOVA	0.02	*			0.10			
AUC	0.72				0.69			
AUC without gender	0.72				0.69			

Source: Own calculation in RStudio

number of employees and the age of the company (0.37). Based on the correlation matrix, it can be assumed that larger SMEs in the data sample (in terms of value of total assets) have more employees. A similar relationship also applies to the age of the company, i.e., longer established companies have more employees. The above indicates that some companies develop in time also from the number of employees point of view, not just from the financial growth point of view. These correlations are, however, moderate or weaker correlations.

The absolute highest value of the correlation coefficient was achieved between the female representation on the board and the Blau index (0.59). This is understandable, however, since one variable is derived from the other. Therefore, these two variables were not combined within the framework of one developed model and, thus, the potential occurrence of multicollinearity was avoided.

Results of the regression model using the proportion of women on the board as an explanatory variable are shown in Table 41.3. For small- and medium-sized enterprises, the proportion of women on the board reduces the probability of bankruptcy, but for medium-sized enterprises these differences are not statistically significant. At the same time, younger companies, companies with higher levels of debt and companies with a higher proportion of tangible assets have a higher probability of bankruptcy. For small companies, those with higher sales growth and fewer employees were also more likely to face bankruptcy.

Similar findings were also observed by the second regression model shown in Table 41.4. This model worked with the Blau index (U-shaped function) to

Table 41.4 Regression model for Blau index (U-shaped function)

	Small				Medium			
	Coeff.	Z-value	Pr(>|z|)	Sign.	Coeff.	Z-value	Pr(>|z|)	Sign.
Intercept	1.97	1.72	0.09		9.48	3.99	0.00	***
Age	−0.24	−1.96	0.05	*	−0.97	−4.14	0.00	***
Assets	−0.01	−0.11	0.91		0.09	1.08	0.28	
Growth	0.03	1.61	0.11		−0.45	−1.35	0.18	
Loans	2.84	5.81	0.00	***	1.91	3.18	0.00	**
Employees	−0.27	−3.99	0.00	***	−0.65	−2.03	0.04	*
Tangible	1.70	7.20	0.00	***	1.40	3.87	0.00	***
Female board (BI)	−0.98	−2.02	0.04	*	−1.30	−2.02	0.04	*
Board	−0.13	−1.77	0.08		−0.01	−0.09	0.93	
Deviance	1207.44				564.90			
pseudo R2	0.14				0.12			
VIF mean	1.31				1.32			
AIC	1231.44				588.90			
BIC	1290.46				638.53			
ANOVA	0.09				0.09			
AUC	0.72				0.69			
AUC without gender	0.72				0.69			

Source: Own calculation in RStudio

represent women on the board. For the Blau index, greater diversity reduces the probability of bankruptcy. In this case, small- and medium-sized enterprises' results were statistically significant. Similarly to the previous models, older companies, companies with lower levels of debt, companies with more significant numbers of employees, and companies with smaller volumes of physical assets face a lower probability of bankruptcy. Again, these findings are valid for both small- and medium-sized enterprises.

For both models, the ROC is between 69% and 72%, whilst small enterprises consistently achieved slightly higher values of AUC. When comparing models with gender diversity features and without gender diversity, it can be concluded that the gender diversity variable had almost no effect on the AUC of the developed models. The models remained unchanged after rounding to whole numbers. Despite the statistical significance of gender diversity features, these variables did not improve the performance of developed prediction models. Even when comparing the developed models through ANOVA, with one exception, no statistically significant differences were identified between the developed models without and with the gender diversity variables. In addition, all developed models had very low multicollinearity, with values lower than three and the average VIF values at a maximum of 1.32.

41.5 Conclusions

This chapter analyzes the impact of gender diversity on the financial health of small- and medium-sized enterprises. Financial statements of 1178 joint-stock companies in Slovakia were collected and analyzed. The results show a negative relationship and a U-shape between gender diversity board and the probability of SME bankruptcy. The resulting relationship was confirmed for both variables, the proportion of women to the total number of board members (linear relationship) and the corresponding Blau index (U-shaped relationship). Furthermore, the true inverse U-shape was confirmed for small- and medium-sized enterprises.

Based on the findings of this paper, it can be observed that the management of gender diversity boards by shareholders proves beneficial for SMEs. Moreover, in SMEs, board members have a much stronger voice. Thus, there is a significant assumption that the influence of women on the board of such companies could be more significant than in larger companies. Especially in countries such as Slovakia, where women are still significantly underrepresented in management functions, their involvement in the management process can drive further economic growth. However, a prerequisite for such involvement is a sufficient number of qualified women with adequate experience. The above can be significantly influenced by the new legislation, which, in addition to introducing the much-discussed quotas, can reconfigure the education system to contribute to greater inclusiveness of women in the business environment. The whole society would then benefit from such a change.

The limitation of this study is in its research period of the COVID-19 pandemic. The COVID-19 pandemic hit sectors unevenly, which is also reflected in the higher share of potentially bankrupting companies, e.g., in the tourism and gastronomy sectors. Different impacts of the pandemic in each sector could have caused women to engage significantly more in sectors not affected to such an extent by the COVID-19 pandemic. Therefore, future research should focus on small- and medium-sized enterprises, as research in this area is undersized. Further future analysis should also focus on how the COVID-19 pandemic has caused structural changes in gender diversity.

Acknowledgments This manuscript was funded by VEGA 1/0393/21 titled Impact Analysis of Restrictive Measures and Government Aid Associated with Coronavirus on Financial Health of Small- and Medium-Sized Enterprises in Slovakia.

References

Adusei, M., & Obeng, E. Y. T. (2019). Board gender diversity and the capital structure of microfinance institutions: A global analysis. *The Quarterly Review of Economics and Finance, 71*, 258–269.

Altman, E. I. (1968). Financial ratios, discriminant analysis and the prediction of corporate bankruptcy. *The Journal of Finance, 23*, 589–609. https://doi.org/10.2307/2978933

Altman, E. I. (1983). *Corporate financial distress. A complete guide to predicting, avoiding, and dealing with bankruptcy*. Wiley Interscience/Wiley.

Altman, E. I., Iwanicz-Drozdowska, M., Laitinen, E. K., & Suvas, A. (2017). Financial distress prediction in an international context: A review and empirical analysis of Altman's Z-score model. *Journal of International Financial Management & Accounting, 28*(2), 131–171.

Arzubiaga, U., Iturralde, T., Maseda, A., & Kotlar, J. (2018). Entrepreneurial orientation and firm performance in family SMEs: The moderating effects of family, women, and strategic involvement in the board of directors. *International Entrepreneurship and Management Journal, 14*, 217–244. https://doi.org/10.1007/s11365-017-0473-4

Blau, P. M. (1977). *Inequality and heterogeneity*. Free Press.

Chen, L. H., Gramlich, J., & Houser, K. A. (2019). Context sensitive links the effects of board gender diversity on a firm's risk strategies. *Accounting and Finance., 59*(2), 991–1031. https://doi.org/10.1111/acfi.12283

Cho, E., Okafor, C., Ujah, N., & Zhang, L. (2021). Executives' gender-diversity, education, and firm's bankruptcy risk: Evidence from China. *Journal of Behavioral and Experimental Finance., 30*, 100500. https://doi.org/10.1016/j.jbef.2021.100500

Dang, R., Houanti, L., Ammari, A., & Lê, N. T. (2018). Is there a 'business case' for board gender diversity within French listed SMEs. *Applied Economics Letters., 25*(14), 980–983. https://doi.org/10.1080/13504851.2017.1390308

Elsayed, M., Elshandidy, T., & Ahmed, Y. (2022). Corporate failure in the UK: An examination of corporate governance reforms. *International Review of Financial Analysis., 82*, 102165. https://doi.org/10.1016/j.irfa.2022.102165

Espinosa-Méndez, C., & Correa, A. I. (2022). Gender and financial performance in SMEs in emerging economies. *Gender in Management: An International Journal, 37*(5), 603–618. https://doi.org/10.1108/GM-03-2020-0071

European Parliament. (2022). *Directive (EU) 2022/2381 on improving the gender balance among directors of listed companies and related measures*.

Field, A., Miles, J., & Field, Z. (2012). *Discovering statistics using R*. United Kingdom. SAGE.

Finstat. (2023). *Dataset of financial statements*. Retrieved from https://finstat.sk/datasety-na-stiahnutie January, 24, 2023.

Garcia, C. J., & Herrero, B. (2021). Female directors, capital structure, and financial distress. *Journal of Business Research, 136*, 592–601. https://doi.org/10.1016/j.jbusres.2021.07.061

Inostroza, M. A., & Espinosa-Mendez, C. (2022). The influence of the personality traits and sociodemographic CEO characteristics on performance of SMEs: Evidence from Chile. *Academia Revista Latinoamericana de Administración, 35*(4), 435–457. https://doi.org/10.1108/ARLA-08-2021-0163

Joecks, J., Pull, K., & Vetter, K. (2013). Gender diversity in the boardroom and firm performance: What exactly constitutes a "critical mass?". *Journal of Business Ethics, 118*, 61–72. https://doi.org/10.1007/s10551-012-1553-6

Kanter, R. (1977). *Men and women of the organization*. Basic Books.

Lee, K. W., & Thong, T. Y. (2022). Board gender diversity, firm performance and corporate financial distress risk: International evidence from tourism industry. *Equality, Diversity and Inclusion, 2*(4), 530–550. https://doi.org/10.1108/EDI-11-2021-0283

Maj, J. (2017). Women on boards: Does gender composition affect financial results of companies? In *Innovation management, entrepreneurship and sustainability (IMES 2017)* (pp. 529–539). IMES.

Martín-Ugedo, J. F., & Minguez-Vera, A. (2014). Firm performance and women on the board: Evidence from Spanish small and medium-sized enterprises. *Feminist Economics, 20*(3), 136–162. https://doi.org/10.1080/13545701.2014.895404

MSCI. (2021). *Women in boards—Progress report*. Retrieved from https://www.msci.com/documents/10199/093d46d8-982b-6466-74c9-2629d2c0229a

Nam, H. J., & An, Y. (2021). The effect of corporate social responsibility and board gender diversity on bankruptcy: Evidence from Korea. *Asian Academy of Management Journal, 26*(2), 53–74. https://doi.org/10.21315/aamj2021.26.2.3

Rao, K., & Titl, C. (2016). Board composition and corporate social responsibility: The role of diversity, gender, strategy and decision making. *Journal of Business Ethics, 138*, 327–347. https://doi.org/10.1007/s10551-015-2613-5

Tampakoudis, I., Nerantzidis, M., Eweje, G., & Leventis, S. (2022). The impact of gender diversity on shareholder wealth: Evidence from European bank M&A. *Journal of Financial Stability., 60*, 101020. https://doi.org/10.1016/j.jfs.2022.101020

Weber, C. P., & Geneste, L. (2014). Exploring gender-related perceptions of SME success. *International Journal of Gender and Entrepreneurship, 6*(1), 15–27. https://doi.org/10.1108/IJGE-04-2013-0038

Wu, P., Yao, X., & Muhammad, S. (2017). The effect of female participation in top management teams on the growth performance of small and medium-sized enterprises (SMEs). *Asia Pacific Journal of Innovation and Entrepreneurship; Bingley, 11*(1), 108–119. https://doi.org/10.1108/APJIE-04-2017-015

Chapter 42
Sustainable Banking Practice: The Role of Environmental, Social, and Governance Factors

Imlak Shaikh, Ashutosh Dash, Amit Kumar Gupta, and Manoj Kumar Srivastava

Abstract Sustainability has transcended beyond a mere slogan in the banking sector and has emerged as a pivotal concept that will steer the trajectory of the industry in the forthcoming years. This research has specifically selected the preeminent banks in India, Europe, and the United States of America. Notably, the ESG score for Indian banks is relatively lower in comparison with the average ESG disclosure score for European and American banks. It is noteworthy that the ESG-Control Group-Variable exhibits an unfavorable association with the operational performance of the firm, as indicated by the ROA metric, while a favorable correlation exists between the Control-Group-Variable and Governance-Group-Variable. Furthermore, the ESG-Control Group-Variable demonstrates an adverse relationship with the ROE metric, while a positive relationship exists between the Control-Group-Variable and Governance-Group-Variable. Overall, the ESG-Group-Variable displays a negative relationship with the financial indicators, indicating that companies expending more on ESG activities face a setback in their financial performance metrics. One plausible justification for this phenomenon is that companies are directing funds from more economically lucrative activities toward ESG initiatives, resulting in short-term profits. Country-level analysis reveals that India is the only region displaying a positive relationship between the ESG-Group-Variable and the financial indicators. This could be attributed to the fact that in India, ESG activities are often a by-product of CSR initiatives.

Keywords Sustainable banking · Environmental · Social · Governance · Firm performance

---

I. Shaikh (✉) · A. Dash · A. K. Gupta · M. K. Srivastava
Management Development Institute Gurgaon, Gurugram, Haryana, India
e-mail: imlak.shaikh@mdi.ac.in; ashutosh@mdi.ac.in; amitkgupta@mdi.ac.in; mks@mdi.ac.in

© The Author(s), under exclusive license to Springer Nature Switzerland AG 2024
N. Tsounis, A. Vlachvei (eds.), *Applied Economic Research and Trends*, Springer Proceedings in Business and Economics,
https://doi.org/10.1007/978-3-031-49105-4_42

42.1 Introduction

Sustainability is just not a slogan anymore in the banking business. It has become a key concept that will shape the direction of the banking industry in the coming years. The different aspects of sustainable banking are environmental, social, and governance (ESG). In the current scenario, sustainability initiatives by the banks primarily revolve around "environmental" and "social" considerations, though the "governance" aspect has not been considered by most of the banks. Banks today must do more than just endorse the green initiatives in promotions. In the current scenario, they must show that they can meet the guidelines and strict standards to meet the climate risk reporting standards. Banks are important and emerging as an important component in reaching the UN's Sustainable Development Goals (SDGs). Customers, stakeholders, workers, and policy controllers are looking forward to a bigger assurance of ESG priorities and are putting pressure on banks to show the desired results (Jeucken, 2001). With the increased pressure coming from all sides, the banking sector has reached a green inflection point (Porter, 1991).

Banks that have a vision for the future and are able to execute their sustainability agendas faster will get the first-mover advantage and will have enhanced performance and profitability (Weber & Remer, 2011). Through empirical work, we have tried to study and understand the relationship between the various ESG parameters and the financial performance of the various banks worldwide. For the purpose of this study, we have chosen the most prominent banks (according to asset size) in India, Europe, and the United States of America (Jeucken, 2001). The intent is to understand how various banks' investments in the ESG space have impacted their financial performance. We have studied the relationship by studying the descriptive variables and then using regression analysis.

42.2 Review of Earlier Studies

There have been numerous scholarly works that have examined the correlation between sustainability practices and financial performance. Walley and Whitehead (1994) and Hamilton (1995) have found that sustainability practices lead to increased operational expenditures and capital expenditures. However, scholars such as Porter (1991), Flammer (2015), and Makni et al. (2009) have discovered that sustainability disclosures can benefit all stakeholders and eventually result in favorable accounting profitability. Nevertheless, certain studies, including Hamilton (1995), Khanna and Damon (1999), and Konar and Cohen (2001), have demonstrated a negative impact of sustainability practices on financial performance. Hence, the aforementioned early studies have offered conflicting evidence on the effects of sustainability practices, which necessitates further statistical analysis of the relationship between sustainability and firm performance in the banking context. In the following paragraph, we present recent studies that examine the relationship between sustainability practices and financial performance. Hence, to better understand the various sustainability practices in the banking industry, we referred to various prominent studies on the topic of banking, sustainability development, and financial inclusion across various regions.

Green (1989) contended that banks are responsible for various stakeholders, including the government, customers, shareholders, staff, and the community. An organization's enduring prosperity and standing are influenced by its history and its perception of ethical principles. Moreover, the company's commitment to ethical conduct is evaluated when confronted with intricate and conflicting issues. Hitt et al. (1998) in their empirical posited that the achievement of organizational prosperity in the twenty-first century would be contingent upon the exercise of strategic leadership, the cultivation of dynamic core competencies, the nurturing of human capital, the effective utilization of novel manufacturing techniques, and the implementation of innovative organizational structures and culture. Consequently, there is a pressing need to reassess the obligations of financial institutions to ensure that the vicissitudes of the twenty-first century are managed with efficacy.

Jeucken (2001) conducted a comparative analysis of three distinct world regions, namely Europe, North America, and Oceania, during the period spanning from 1998 to 2000. The analysis was primarily based on examining banks' environmental and annual reports. Hence, this study aimed to identify and highlight significant differences pertaining to sustainable banking across various regions, countries, and banks. The study's findings indicate that banks have adopted a defensive stance on environmental issues, promoting sustainable development. Burgess and Pande (2005) conducted a research paper wherein they examined the impact of a large-scale state-led bank branch expansion program on rural poverty in India during the period spanning from 1977 to 1990. Employing deviations and regression analysis, the authors discovered that the expansion of branches into previously unbanked rural areas in India resulted in a significant reduction in rural poverty.

Dogarawa (2006) articulated the expectation for banks to conduct their operations with ethical considerations at the forefront. This expectation encompasses adherence to principles such as integrity, impartiality, reliability, transparency, social responsibility, and the prevention of money laundering. The overarching aim is to safeguard the interests and rights of numerous depositors, foster stability and trust in the financial markets, and facilitate economic development. Amaeshi et al. (2007) investigated the contradictory implications of financial exclusion for financial institutions in developing nations. Firstly, as a socioeconomic factor, it negatively affects firm profitability. Secondly, as a strategic source, it can mitigate potential risks of suboptimal regulatory policies aimed at combating financial exclusion. The authors contended that financial institutions in developing economies have the potential to alleviate poverty and social exclusion and bridge a gap in sustainable finance discourse by curbing financial exclusion. Chaudhuri (2007) conducted an investigation into the ethical considerations within business communication in the service industry, with a particular focus on the banking sector.

San Jose and Retolaza (2008) examined the fundamental distinctions between ethical banking and other funding organizations, such as banks, saving entities, and credit cooperatives. The authors proposed a metric known as the "Radical Affinity Index," which enables a comparison of the classification of banking groups. This index is mainly focused on the responsibility of lenders in relation to the ultimate use of funds, thereby providing a clear contrast among the funding organizations. Weber (2010) posited in his scholarly work that financial institutions that integrate principles of sustainability and accountability into their business model, products, and operations are deemed socially responsible. With their significant influence and responsibility, banks must contribute to government initiatives to significantly reduce carbon emissions. One noteworthy manifestation of the bank's involvement in sustainable development practices is through the implementation of "Green Banking." Weber and Remer (2011) expounded on social banking as a form of value-focused banking that prioritizes a positive social and ecological impact while ensuring its economic viability. This type of banking appeals to clients seeking secure and prudent options for depositing their funds, prompting conventional banks to consider adopting a more socially oriented approach to banking. Therefore, the next section discusses the data and descriptive analysis of sustainable banking and validates the above literature.

42.3 Data and Variable Description

In this study, we consider the ESG scores of banking companies across the world. ESG score is a data-driven quantitative measure of a corporation's environmental, social, and governance performance that investors use to evaluate performance across a range of financially material, business-relevant, and industry-specific key issues to assess company activities relative to industry peers. Table 42.1 describes the variable under consideration. Intercorrelation was also found between all the variables of ESG score, Governance, and Control. These variables showed a high correlation among themselves, and they were normalized on a scale of 10. The data were collected for 20 banks across the world for 11 years from 2011 to 2021. This gave us a cross-sectional time-series panel data. Twenty top from India, Europe and the USA were chosen for the purpose of this study. These banks comprise the biggest banks in these three regions in terms of total assets. This stage involved making the necessary changes to the data set to allow comparison and establish relationships between the various parameters. As the data involved parameters which had different scales, the first step involved normalization, which led to the conversion of all the values to a scale of 10. Once this step was complete, the parameters were grouped into three Group-Variables, namely ESG, Control, and Governance. The Group and their constituents are defined in Table 42.2. After creating Groups, an average of the values of each parameter to determine a score that was to be used as a representative value of the particular group.

Table 42.1 Variable description

Dependent variable		
Name of variable	Definition/description	Bloomberg field
ROA	% return on asset	RETURN_ON_ASSET
TOBINQ	Economic measure of firm performance	TOBIN_Q_RATIO
ROE	% return on equity	OPER_ROE
Independent and control variables		
Name of variable	Definition/description	Bloomberg field
ESGCOMP	Dummy variable IF yes = 1 Otherwise = 0	ESG_LINKED_COMPENSATION_FOR_BRD
INDP	% of independent directors	PCT_INDEPENDENT_DIRECTORS
GRI	Dummy variable IF YES = 1 Otherwise = 0	GRI_COMPLIANCE
BRDSIZE		BOARD_SIZE
WOMEN	% of women on board	PCT_WOMEN_ON_BOARD
CEODUL	Dummy variable IF YES = 1 Otherwise = 0	CEO_DUALITY
BRDMEET	% of attendance in board meeting	BOARD_MEETING_ATTENDANCE_PCT
NONEXEBRD	% of nonexecutive directors on board	PCT_OF_NON_EXEC_DIR_ON_BRD
BRDMEETYR	# meeting per year in board	BOARD_MEETINGS_PER_YR
CEOPAY		TOT_SAL_&_BNS_AW_TO_CEO_&_EQUIV
Total salary to executive		TOT_SALARIES_PAID_TO_EXECUTIVES
TOTALEMP	Total employees in org.	NUM_OF_EMPLOYEES
WOMEMP	Total women employees	PCT_WOMEN_EMPLOYEES

(continued)

Table 42.1 (continued)

CSRSUST	Dummy variable IF YES = 1 Otherwise = 0	CSR_SUSTAINABILITY_COMMITTEE
NWT	Number of times net worth	NET_WORTH_GROWTH
TOTSALES	Total sales	SALES_REV_TURN
SALGWT	% sales growth	SALES_GROWTH
NETINM	Total net income	NET_INCOME
NETPRF	% net profit margin	PROF_MARGIN
EBITDA		EBITDA
EPSGWT	% EPS growth	EPS_GROWTH
FCF	Free cash flow	CF_FREE_CASH_FLOW
CR	Current ratio (X)	CUR_RATIO
DTE	Debt-to-equity ratio (X)	TOT_DEBT_TO_TOT_EQY
TOTALAST	Total assets	BS_TOT_ASSET
INTGBL	Total intangible assets	BS_DISCLOSED_INTANGIBLES
CAPEXP	Total capital expenditure	CF_CAP_EXPEND_PRPTY_ADD
TEQT	Total equity	TOTAL_EQUITY
AGE	Age of firm	You need to calculate

Source: Authors' calculation

Table 42.2 Description of the Group-Variables

ESG-Group-Variable	Control-Group-Variable	Governance-Group-Variable
ENVIRON_DISCLOSURE_SCORE	BOARD_MEETING_ATTENDANCE_PCT	BS_DISCLOSED_INTANGIBLES
ESG_DISCLOSURE_SCORE	BOARD_MEETINGS_PER_YR	BS_TOT_ASSET
GOVNCE_DISCLOSURE_SCORE	BOARD_SIZE	CF_CAP_EXPEND_PRPTY_ADD
SOCIAL_DISCLOSURE_SCORE	CEO_DUALITY	CF_FREE_CASH_FLOW
	ESG_LINKED_COMPENSATION_FOR_BRD	CSR_SUSTAINABILITY_COMMITTEE
	GRI_COMPLIANCE	CUR_RATIO
	PCT_INDEPENDENT_DIRECTORS	EBITDA
	PCT_OF_NON_EXEC_DIR_ON_BRD	EPS_GROWTH
	PCT_WOMEN_ON_BOARD	NET_INCOME
	TOT_SAL_&_BNS_AW_TO_CEO_&_EQUIV	NET_WORTH_GROWTH
	TOT_SALARIES_PAID_TO_EXECUTIVES	NUM_OF_EMPLOYEES
		PCT_WOMEN_EMPLOYEES
		PROF_MARGIN
		SALES_GROWTH
		SALES_REV_TURN
		TOT_DEBT_TO_TOT_EQY
		TOTAL_EQUITY

Source: Authors' calculation

42.4 Descriptive Analysis

Descriptive statistics were computed for the dataset based on the aforementioned parameters and temporal scope. It has been noted that significant trends pertaining to ESG can be discerned from Fig. 42.1 and Tables 42.3 and 42.4. Notably, the mean ESG score for Indian Banks is comparatively lower than the average ESG disclosure score for European and United States banks. The ESG disclosure score of Indian banks is the lowest among the sample of banks taken for the purpose of analysis. The mean ROE of the companies is 10.96, which is below the average benchmark of 15–20. The ROA is 0.56, which is considered good for a bank and hence is an indicator that the chosen sample is a cohort of good asset-utilizing banks.

42.5 Empirical Results

In an effort to comprehend the correlation between the performance variables and the remaining parameters, a regression analysis was performed. The objective was to examine multiple hypotheses and ascertain which Group-Variables, along with their fundamental components, were noteworthy in forecasting the financial performance of the banks.

H1: There exists no substantial correlation between the Group-Variables of (ESG, Control, and Governance) and operational performance (ROA).

H2: There exists no noteworthy correlation between the Group-Variables encompassing Environmental, Social, and Governance (ESG), Control, and Governance, and the financial performance metric of return on equity (ROE).

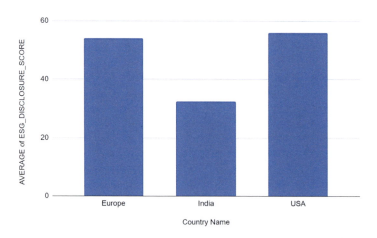

Fig. 42.1 ESG score across the countries. (Source: Authors' calculation)

Table 42.3 Average ESG score across banks

Bank name	Average ESG disclosure score
Banco Santander	53.25
Bank of America Corp	67.00
Bank of Baroda	23.07
Barclays PLC	52.91
BNP Paribas	54.55
Citigroup	61.61
Credit Agricole SA	46.64
Deutsche Bank	45.00
HDFC Bank	47.31
HSBC holdings	55.45
ICICI Bank	34.91
ING group NV	52.24
Intesa Sanpaolo SpA	70.14
JP Morgan chase	51.77
Lloyds Bank	55.02
Punjab national bank	26.95
Societe Generale SA	56.20
State Bank of India	30.36
US Bancorp	44.60
Wells Fargo & company	55.29
All	**49.21**

Source: Authors' calculation

Table 42.4 Descriptive statistics

Parameter	TOBIN_Q_RATIO	ROE	ROA
Mean	1.02	10.96	0.57
Standard error	0	0.56	0.04
Median	0.99	11	0.46
Mode	0.97	3.59	
Standard deviation	0.07	8.65	0.6
Kurtosis	8.65	2.52	0.65
Skewness	2.87	−0.5	0.1
Range	0.44	62.15	3.54
Minimum	0.93	−29.45	−1.6
Maximum	1.37	32.7	1.94
Sum	244.14	2630.86	135.92
Numbers	240	240	240

Source: Authors' calculation

H3: There is no significant relationship between the Group-Variables of (ESG, Control, and Governance) and market performance (Tobin's Q).

Looking at the above Table 42.5, column (1), it is observed that the ESG-Control Group-Variable has a negative relationship with the operational performance of the firm (ROA), whereas there is a positive relationship with the Control-Group-

Table 42.5 Panel OLS

Dependent variable	ROA (1)		ROE (2)		Tobin's Q (3)	
Regressors	Coefficient	p-value (t-stat)	Coefficient	p-value (t-stat)	Coefficient	p-value (t-stat)
Constant	0.4300**	0.010	9.7800***	0.000	1.0900***	0.000
ESG-group-variable	−0.1300***	0.000	−2.2100***	0.000	−0.0010	0.750
Control-group-variable	0.2000***	0.000	3.1100***	0.000	−0.0005	0.910
Governance-group-variable	0.0700*	0.090	1.1700***	0.049	−0.0100**	0.020
Adjusted R-square	0.13		0.17		0.15	
p-value (F-statistic)	0.000***		0.000***		0.008***	

Source: Authors' calculation
Significant at ***1%; **5%; *10%

Variable and Governance-Group-Variable. The first two relationships are significant at 99% confidence, while Governance-Group-Variable is significant at 90% confidence. R-squared of the model is 13%, which means that this model explains the 13% variance in ROA explained by the three Group-Variables. Looking at column (2), it is observed that the ESG-Control Group-Variable has a negative relationship with the firm's financial performance (ROE). In contrast, there is a positive relationship between the Control-Group-Variable and Governance-Group-Variable. The independent variables are significant at 99% level of confidence. R-squared of the model is 17%, which means that this model explains the 17% variance in ROE explained by the three Group-Variables. Looking at the above column (3), it is observed that the ESG-Control Group-Variable has a negative relationship with the financial performance of the firm (ROE), whereas there is a positive relationship between the Control-Group-Variable and Governance-Group-Variable. The independent variables are significant at 99% level of confidence. R-squared of the model is 15%, which means that this model explains the 15% variance in Tobin's Q. Based on the observations of the first three hypotheses, it can be stated as follows: (i) there exists a negative correlation between the variable ESG-Control Group and the three performance metrics, namely ROA, ROE, and Tobin's Q; (ii) the Control-Group-Variable is positively correlated with ROA/ROE, yet it exhibits a slightly negative correlation with the Tobin's Q parameter; (iii) the Governance-Group-Variable exhibits a positive correlation with ROA and ROE while exhibiting a negative correlation with Tobin's Q parameter.

42.6 Robustness Check: Regression Results of Financial Parameters—Region Wise

Based on the values presented in Table 42.6, it can be posited that the Indian Bank Group exhibits a positive correlation between ROA and Tobin's Q and the ESG-Group-Variable, Control-Group-Variable, and Governance-Group-Variable. Meanwhile, the ROE parameter displays a negative association with ESG-Group-Variable but a positive relationship with Control-Group-Variable and Governance-Group-Variable. The goodness-of-fit results for ROA, ROE, and Tobin's Q indicate a 40%, 43%, and 35% success rate, respectively. This showcases that the model is a good fit and that the independent variables sufficiently explain the variance in the dependent variable. Based on the aforementioned data, it can be observed that the ESG-Group-Variable exhibits a negative relationship to all financial performance metrics for the European banks under consideration. However, the other independent variables, such as Control-Group-Variable and Governance-Group-Variable, display positive relationships with the financial parameters. The R values for ROE, ROA, and Tobin's Q are 28%, 31%, and 10%, respectively. This signifies that while our model explains the variance in ROE and ROA to an appropriate extent, it is insufficient in explaining the variation in Tobin's Q to a satisfactory level.

Table 42.6 Robustness check

Parameter	Coefficient	p-value (t-stat)	Coefficient	p-value (t-stat)	Coefficient	p-value (t-stat)
India	ROA		ROE		Tobin's Q	
Constant	−1.32***	0.000	−19.62***	0.000	0.82***	0.000
ESG-group-variable	0.01	0.88	−2.15**	0.03	0.04***	0.000
Control-group-variable	0.72***	0.000	13.92***	0.000	0.02	0.38
Governance-group-variable	0.22*	0.070	4.56	0.02	0.01	0.523
Adjusted R-square	0.40		0.43		0.35	
p-value (F-statistic)	0.000***		0.000***		0.000***	
Europe	ROA		ROE		Tobin's Q	
Constant	−0.58**	0.010	−2.72	0.430	1.01***	0.000
ESG-group-variable	0.04	0.110	0.43	0.270	0.002	0.470
Control-group-variable	0.15***	0.000	2.65***	0.000	0.006	0.220
Governance-group-variable	0.03	0.360	0.11	0.850	0.005**	0.010
Adjusted R-square	0.28		0.31		0.10	
p-value (F-statistic)	0.000***		0.000		0.000	
USA	ROA		ROE		Tobin's Q	
Constant	1.25**	0.02	20.81	0	1.15***	0.000
ESG-group-variable	−0.22***	0.000	−3.81	0	−0.02***	0.000
Control-group-variable	0.06	0.390	1.22	0.11	−0.01	0.380
Governance-group-variable	0.17*	0.060	2.44	0.02	0.01	0.210
Adjusted R-square	0.35		0.53		0.33	
p-value (F-statistic)	0.000***		0.000***		0.000***	

Source: Authors' calculation
Significant at ***1%; **5%; *10%

Based on the findings presented in Table 42.6 for the USA, it can be concluded that the ESG-Group-Variable exhibits a negative relationship with all three financial performance indicators of ROE, ROA, and Tobin's Q. The Control-Group-Variable exhibits a negative relationship with ROE but a positive relationship with ROA and Tobin's Q. In contrast, the Governance-Group-Variable exhibits a positive relationship with all three financial indicators. The adjusted R-square value for all models is 35%, 53%, and 33%, respectively. This showcases that the models are a good fit and that the variance in the independent variable explains the variance of the dependent variables to a great extent.

42.7 Discussion

This study intends to study the relationship between the financial indicators with the ESG, Control, and Governance variables. Through statistical analysis, the following can be inferred.

Overall, the ESG-Group-Variable has a negative relationship with the financial indicators. This means that companies that spend more on ESG activities suffer in their financial performance metrics. One possible explanation for this phenomenon is that companies are diverting money from more financially lucrative activities toward ESG initiatives and are forging some small-term profits due to the same. Moreover, customers and other stakeholders will take time to understand and become aware of the various activities being undertaken by such companies and hence fail to reward the companies. It can be assumed that customers will take cognizance of such activities, leading to higher financial returns in the long run. The ESG-Group-Variable relationship is also significant in both ROA and ROE, showing that company's operational efficiency and asset efficiency are affected by its ESG activities. This makes logical sense as companies will have to divert funds, assets, and money efforts from their normal activities and this could hamper productivity and returns in the small run as ESG activities very seldom give immediate results.

The variable designated as the Control-Group-Variable exhibits a favorable correlation with both ROA and ROE, while conversely demonstrating a detrimental correlation with Tobin's Q variable. The positive relationship between ROE and ROA makes sense as the constituent parameters are indicators of the financial performance and profitability of the firm. Hence, firms that have higher profitability and better income numbers are bound to have better ROA and ROE metrics.

The Governance-Control Group-Variable represents the discipline with which it operates and reports its performance. It can be believed to be a proxy of the honesty and clarity with which the company conducts its day-to-day operations. Hence, it is logical to see that it has a positive relationship with the ROA and ROE metrics of the firm and is significant for all three parameters at 90% confidence level.

Through the country-level analysis of these relationships, it can be observed that India is the only region which has a positive relationship between ESG-Group-Variable and the financial indicators. It can be argued that in India most ESG activities are a by-product of CSR activities. These activities while being helpful to society are also means for banks to increase their awareness and spread financial inclusion. Hence, these activities are also beneficial to the financial metrics of firms. However, compared to the US and European banks, the ESG activities are not additives to the bottom-line numbers, and moreover, the banks would be more profitable in the short run had they not been committing to such activities. However, the banks continue to embark on such activities for the long-term benefit of society. The Control-Group-Variable has a positive relationship across all three regions for the ROE and ROA financial indicators. This shows that companies that have healthy numbers pertaining to EBITDA, free cash flow, and debt-to-equity ratio have better financial performance indicators as both metrics point toward efficient utilization of resources.

42.8 Conclusion and Managerial Implication for the Management Accountant

A first look might give the impression that a management accountant does not have much to do with implementing sustainable practices. Still, if looked into deeply, one can easily say that nowadays emission of greenhouse gasses also has a cost and that brings in the management accountant. They have the required skills needed to cater to changing regulatory and market demands. A management accountant will build processes to collect new types of data, which will help in decision-making, reduce waste, and increase efficiency by studying ongoing projects and doing sustainability-driven capital budgeting for long-term investments in plant and equipment. All these can help an organization reduce its carbon footprint. The research we did about our topic at hand—"Sustainable practices in Banking" gave us an insight into the importance of ESG score as a parameter for an organization's sustainability. The practices mentioned above by a management accountant can significantly enhance the ESG score of an organization.

We can reject the null hypothesis that posits the absence of a significant relationship between the Group-Variables and operational performance (ROA). With 99% confidence, it can be concluded that there is no noteworthy correlation between the ESG-Group-Variable and Control-Group-Variable with the return on assets (ROA). However, a significant correlation does exist between the Governance-Group-Variable and ROA at a 90% confidence level. The null hypothesis that posits no significant relationship between the Group-Variables and financial performance (ROE) can be rejected. There is no significant relationship between ROE and ESG-Group-Variable and Control-Group-Variable at a 99% confidence level, and a significant relationship exists between Governance-Group-Variable and ROE at a 95% confidence level. We are unable to dismiss the null hypothesis, which posits the absence of a substantial correlation between the Group-Variables and Tobin's Q at the 90%, 95%, and 99% confidence levels.

The pivotal role of management accounting in the banking industry lies in its ability to foster sustainable practices. This is achieved by providing decision-makers with comprehensive financial and nonfinancial data, empowering them to make informed choices that effectively balance economic, social, and environmental objectives. The promotion of sustainable practices in banking is intricately linked to the role played by management accounting. (i) Measuring and reporting sustainability performance: Management accounting helps banks track and report their sustainability performance, including their carbon footprint, resource use, and waste generation. (ii) Cost-benefit analysis: Management accounting helps banks conduct a cost-benefit analysis to determine sustainability initiatives' economic viability and allocate resources effectively. (iii) Risk management: Management accounting helps banks assess and manage the risks associated with sustainability, including regulatory and reputational risks. Support for decision-making: Management accounting provides decision-makers with the information they need to make informed decisions about sustainability, including financial and nonfinancial metrics and benchmarking. (iv) Encouraging innovation: Management accounting helps banks develop and implement new sustainability initiatives, such as green products and services, to improve their sustainability performance continuously.

References

Amaeshi, K. M., Ezeoha, A. E., Adi, B. C., & Nwafor, M. (2007). Financial exclusion and strategic corporate social responsibility: A missing link in sustainable finance discourse. In *Research Paper Series* No. 49–2007 I CCSR Research Paper Series—I SSN 1479–5124.

Burgess, R., & Pande, R. (2005). Do rural banks matter? Evidence from the Indian social banking experiment. *American Economic Review, 95*(3), 780–795. https://doi.org/10.1257/0002828054201242

Chaudhuri, T. (2007). A study of ethics in business communication in the service industry with emphasis on banking industry. *SSRN*. https://doi.org/10.2139/ssrn.1672202

Dogarawa, A. B. (2006). An examination of ethical dilemmas in the Nigerian banking sector. In *SSRN*. https://doi.org/10.2139/ssrn.1621054

Flammer, C. (2015). Does corporate social responsibility lead to superior financial performance? A regression discontinuity approach. *Management Science, 61*(11), 2549–2568. https://doi.org/10.1287/mnsc.2014.2038

Green, C. F. (1989). Business ethics in banking. *Journal of Business Ethics, 8*, 631–634. https://doi.org/10.1007/BF00383031

Hamilton, J. T. (1995). Pollution as news: Media and stock market reactions to the toxics release inventory data. *Journal of Environmental Economics and Management, 28*(1), 98–113. https://doi.org/10.1006/jeem.1995.1007

Hitt, M. A., Keats, B. W., & DeMarie, S. M. (1998). Navigating in the new competitive landscape: Building strategic flexibility and competitive advantage in the 21st century. *Academy of Management Perspectives, 12*(4), 22–42. https://journals.aom.org/doi/abs/10.5465/ame.1998.1333922

Jeucken, M. (2001). *Sustainable finance and banking: The financial sector and the future of the planet*. Earthscan Publications.

Khanna, M., & Damon, L. A. (1999). EPA's voluntary 33/50 program: Impact on toxic releases and economic performance of firms. *Journal of Environmental Economics and Management, 37*(1), 1–25. https://doi.org/10.1006/jeem.1998.1057

Konar, S., & Cohen, M. A. (2001). Does the market value environmental performance? *Review of Economics and Statistics, 83*(2), 281–289. https://doi.org/10.1162/00346530151143815

Makni, R., Francoeur, C., & Bellavanc, F. (2009). Causality between corporate social performance and financial performance: Evidence from Canadian firms. *Journal of Business Ethics, 89*(3), 409. https://doi.org/10.1007/s10551-008-0007-7

Porter, M. E. (1991). America's green strategy. *Scientific American, 264*(4), 168.

San Jose, L., & Retolaza, J. L. (2008). Information transparency as a differentiation factor of ethical banking in Europe: A radical affinity index approach. *The IUP Journal of Bank Management, 7*(3), 7–22.

Walley, N., & Whitehead, B. (1994). *It's not easy being green. The earth scan reader in business and the environment.* Universities Press.

Weber, O. (2010). Social banking: Products and services. In *SSRN*. https://doi.org/10.2139/ssrn.1621822

Weber, O., & Remer, S. (2011). *Social banks and the future of sustainable finance* (Vol. 64). Taylor & Francis.

Chapter 43
Corporate Social Responsibility as a Swap for Reducing Firm Risk: Evidence from Stock Market Reaction to FDI Announcements

Mei Liu and Qing-Ping Ma

Abstract Previous studies propose that corporate social responsibility (CSR) activities have insurance- or option-like property in corporate risk management, protecting shareholder value against downward changes caused by negative events. This study tests these proposals by examining (1) the relationship between CSR performance and firm risk around foreign direct investment (FDI) announcements and (2) the impact of CSR performance on increases in shareholder value caused by positive events and decreases in shareholder value caused by negative events. Using a sample of 20,275 FDI deals by 2488 firms from 48 home countries investing in 121 host countries during 2003–2014, we find that firms with high CSR performance have significantly lower volatility in their cumulative returns around FDI announcements. This risk reduction is driven principally by social CSR and secondarily by corporate governance CSR. Environmental CSR appears to have only a minor role. CSR activities not only mitigate decreases in shareholder value caused by negative events but also attenuate increases in shareholder value caused by positive events. Our present results suggest that CSR activities have a swap-like property, which exchanges riskier assets for less risky ones, rather than an insurance- or option-like property for reducing firm risk.

Keywords Corporate social responsibility · Foreign direct investment · Shareholder value · Abnormal return · Return volatility

M. Liu
Department of Finance and Trade, NingboTech University, Ningbo, Zhejiang, China

Q.-P. Ma (✉)
Department of Finance, Accounting and Economics, Nottingham University Business School China, University of Nottingham Ningbo China, Ningbo, Zhejiang, China
e-mail: qing-ping.ma@nottingham.edu.cn

43.1 Introduction

Corporate social responsibility (CSR) has become an important part of corporate management strategy, especially for multinational enterprises (MNEs). Generally speaking, there are two opposite views on CSR: the stakeholder value maximization view and the shareholder expense view (Deng et al., 2013). While the former considers that stakeholders of high CSR firms are more likely to make an effort to contribute resources to their firm's long-term profitability and efficiency (Freeman et al., 2004), the latter suggests that CSR activities are beneficial to other stakeholders at the expense of shareholders (Barnea & Rubin, 2010). Despite the growing importance of CSR in corporate strategy, research on the relationship between CSR and firm performance has presented mixed evidence. While several studies support the stakeholder value maximization view (Becchetti et al., 2012; Flammer, 2013, 2015; Edmans, 2011; Deng et al., 2013), there are also studies that support the shareholder expense view (Barnea & Rubin, 2010; Marsat & Williams, 2013; Krügerm, 2015). Some studies find no significant impact of CSR news or activities on shareholder value (Clacher & Hagendorff, 2012; Liu et al., 2020).

Instead of examining whether CSR activities increase or decrease shareholder value, another line of research focuses on the risk management role of CSR. Godfrey (2005) argues that CSR provides insurance-like protection for a firm's relationship-based intangible assets, and this protection contributes to shareholder wealth. Husted (2005) considers CSR a real option against downside business risk. Many empirical studies have also shown that there is a negative relationship between a firm's CSR performance and its systematic risk (beta) or overall risk (McGuire et al., 1988; Orlitzky & Benjamin, 2001; Oikonomou et al., 2012; Salama et al., 2011; Jo & Na, 2012). Since such studies may incur the endogeneity issue and have difficulty in identifying the causality between high CSR performance and low firm risk (Krüger, 2015; Waddock & Graves, 1997), the event study method has been used to investigate the role of CSR in corporate risk management (Schnietz & Epstein, 2005; Godfreyet al., 2009).

Event studies attempt to address the causality issue by using preevent data to estimate parameters and then evaluating the unexpected outcome with the estimated parameters and postevent data (Lertwachara & Cochran, 2007; Morck & Yeung, 1992; Aybar & Ficici, 2009; Stoker et al., 2019). Using an event study, Schnietz and Epstein (2005) examine investor reaction to the 1999 Seattle World Trade Organization (WTO) failure and find that a reputation for social responsibility protects firms from stock declines associated with that crisis. Examining 178 negative legal/regulatory actions against firms, Godfrey et al. (2009) show that institutional CSR mitigates decreases in shareholder value caused by these negative events. They argue that CSR activity has an insurance-like property that will temper stakeholders' negative judgments and sanctions toward firms when suffering a negative event. These studies demonstrate a role for CSR in preserving rather than creating value for shareholders (Godfrey, 2005; Schnietz & Epstein, 2005; Godfrey et al., 2009; Husted, 2005).

To further elucidate whether and how CSR activities might contribute to corporate risk management, we examine the relationship between CSR performance and the stock market reaction to FDI announcements. Using a sample of 20,275 FDIs announced by firms originating from 48 home countries during 2003–2014, we find that (1) high CSR performance has a negative impact on the variance/volatility of cumulative returns following and around FDI announcements; (2) social CSR is the main driver of this impact; and (3) CSR not only mitigates decreases in shareholder value caused by negative events, but also attenuates increases in shareholder value caused by positive events. Our present results suggest that CSR engagement reduces firm risk, and CSR activities provide swap-like protection for shareholder value (Hull, 2012). Our study contributes to several strands of literature.

First, to our knowledge, this is the first large sample event study using FDI announcements to link CSR to firm risk. Previous event studies use mostly negative events that are closely related to CSR in relatively small samples (Schnietz & Epstein, 2005; Godfrey et al., 2009). Using a much larger sample and FDI announcements as events, this study may provide some new insights into the role of CSR and FDI decision-making by MNEs. Moreover, since FDIs are mostly unanticipated events, using FDI announcements can potentially mitigate the reverse causality problem present in previous studies on the relationship between CSR and corporate risk (McGuire et al., 1988; Orlitzky & Benjamin, 2001; Oikonomou et al., 2012; Salama et al., 2011; Jo & Na, 2012). Morck and Yeung (1992), Lertwachara and Cochran (2007), and Stoker et al. (2019) think that event studies can address the causality issue.

Second, this study undertakes a comprehensive investigation into which pillars of CSR drive the effect of overall CSR. Previous event studies tend to examine the impact of overall CSR and some categories of CSR activities on certain event-induced market reactions (Godfrey et al., 2009; Schnietz & Epstein, 2005) or the direct impact of CSR events on shareholder value (Krüger, 2015; Clacher & Hagendorff, 2012; Flammer, 2013). By examining the impacts of environmental, social, and corporate governance CSR on FDI announcement-induced market reactions, we find that social CSR is the most important pillar in managing firm risk, and corporate governance CSR has a weaker influence. In contrast, environmental CSR only has a minor role.

Third, this study investigates the impact of CSR on shareholder value both when FDI announcements cause negative abnormal returns and when they cause positive abnormal returns. Previous event studies have mainly focused on negative events (Schnietz & Epstein, 2005; Godfrey et al., 2009). Understanding whether a management strategy/practice hinders increases in shareholder value in a positive business environment has important practical implications, because shareholders and managers prefer strategies that promote increases in shareholder value caused by a positive business environment, while mitigating decreases in shareholder value caused by an adverse business environment. We find that CSR activities not only mitigate decreases in shareholder value caused by negative events, but also attenuate increases in shareholder value caused by positive events. This result suggests that CSR activities have a swap-like property, and firms with high CSR performance suit more risk-averse investors.

This chapter is organized as follows. The next section provides background on the relationships between CSR engagement and firm risk and between FDI and shareholder value; introduces our theoretical models on CSR and risk management; and develops our hypotheses. The third section describes the data, sample, and methodology. The fourth section presents the empirical findings. The final section discusses and concludes the study.

43.2 Background, Theory, and Hypothesis Development

43.2.1 CSR and Firm Risk

Many studies have linked CSR activities with share return risk and firm risk management. McGuire et al., (1988) find that CSR measures are significantly correlated with systematic risk (Beta) and total risk of share returns. In a meta-analytic review of 18 previous studies, Orlitzky and Benjamin (2001) show that corporate social performance (CSP) is negatively correlated with measures of market risk. Oikonomou et al. (2012) find that CSR is negatively but weakly related to systematic firm risk. Using UK panel data between 1994 and 2006, Salama et al. (2011) demonstrate that a company's community and environmental responsibility performance is inversely related to its systematic market risk. Jo and Na (2012) find that CSR engagement of firms in controversial industry sectors negatively affects firm risk, both overall risk and systematic risk.

The aforementioned studies have not provided detailed mechanisms for CSR to reduce firm risk, nor have they determined the causality between high CSR performance and low firm risk. Event studies by Schnietz and Epstein (2005) and Godfrey et al. (2009) provide a mechanism for CSR activities to protect shareholder value. Godfrey (2005) proposes that corporate philanthropy can generate positive moral capital among communities and stakeholders, which provides shareholders with insurance-like protection for shareholder wealth. Husted (2005) argues that CSR is a real option to protect the firm from downside business risk, and it should be negatively correlated with the firm's *ex ante* downside business risk. Godfrey et al. (2009) further suggest that the insurance-like property of CSR activity reduces the impact of negative events on shareholder value and show empirically that institutional CSR activities protect shareholder value against negative events. While these studies have deepened our understanding of CSR in terms of risk management, the events used in them are closely related to CSR per se (i.e., existing CSR activities prevent the impact of negative CSR events), which may limit their finding's generalization. Moreover, how CSR activities impact changes in shareholder value caused by positive events has rarely been examined. These gaps in our knowledge call for more research on the relationship between CSR engagement and firm risk.

43.2.2 FDI and Shareholder Value

As one of the most important corporate investment decisions for a firm, FDI certainly has an impact on the firm's financial performance. Many studies show that FDI announcements are associated with positive abnormal returns for MNEs on average. Examining stock price reactions to international acquisitions, Doukas and Travlos (1988) find that bidding firms experience significant positive abnormal returns at the announcement of cross-border acquisitions. The returns are larger when firms expand into new industries and new geographic markets. Chari et al. (2010) show that developed market acquirers, on average, experience positive abnormal returns of 1.16% over a three-day event window. Emerging market acquirers taking over firms in emerging markets also appear to have significant positive abnormal returns. Using stock market price reactions to 425 cross-border acquisitions by Indian firms, Gubbi et al. (2010) also find that international acquisitions by emerging market acquirers create value for emerging economy firms. The value creation effect is more pronounced when the target firms are located in advanced economic and institutional environments, as those markets carry stronger complementarity to the existing capabilities of emerging economy firms.

FDI creates value because it can bring several advantages to the firms making them. Firstly, it facilitates the internalization of tangible and intangible resources that are difficult to trade through market transactions (Gubbi et al., 2010). Secondly, it enables a firm to realize economies of scale and scope (Caves, 1996). Thirdly, it enables the firms to exploit their ownership advantages in the international market and get access to the host country-specific advantages (Dunning, 1998). Fourthly, the firms can spread risks over different countries and reduce fluctuations (Kim et al., 1993). Fifthly, it may enhance a firm's knowledge base, capabilities, and competitiveness through experiential learning (Barkema & Vermeulen, 1998; Delios & Henisz, 2000). Therefore, FDI can be an important strategy for value creation for firms.

However, FDI may also present substantial costs to the firms. Foreign firms are usually at a disadvantageous position compared to local firms because of their liability of foreignness, which reduces foreign firms' competitiveness and hampers firms from investing abroad (Hymer, 1976; Zaheer, 1995). They face more challenges in a new foreign operation in such matters as staffing and establishing internal and external networks (Lu & Beamish, 2004). The coordination difficulties, information asymmetry, and agency costs between headquarters and foreign subsidiaries for MNEs are more severe than those between headquarters and divisional managers in multidivisional firms (Denis et al., 2002). Aybar and Ficici (2009) show that more than half of the cross-border acquisitions by emerging market multinationals lead to value destruction. Other studies also find a U shape, S shape, inverted U shape relation, or no relation between FDI and shareholder value (e.g., Lu & Beamish, 2004; Contractor et al., 2003).

The diverse results are understandable given that each firm making an FDI decision is unique, and each FDI project faces almost a unique set of investment conditions and environment. As asserted by the efficient market hypothesis (EMH), whose weak forms are supported by empirical studies, the market will take into account all the (public) information available in pricing assets (Malkiel, 2003). The mixed market responses to FDI announcements show that the market/investors take more information in pricing the firms than the announcements. If EMH is valid, price decreases following an announcement can be attributed to that the market/investors view the FDI announcement as a negative event after taking all the information into consideration; price increases following an announcement can be attributed to that the market/investors view the FDI announcement as a positive event after taking all the information into consideration.

This study assumes that EMH is valid in the sense that arbitrage opportunities for riskless gains either do not exist or do not persist (Malkiel, 2003). Based on EMH, we consider an FDI announcement to be a negative event if the firm's share price falls following the announcement and to be a positive event if the firm's share price increases following the announcement. Ben-David et al. (2020) show that the announcement period return is not informative of future long-run performance, which actually supports EMH and using announcement period return to evaluate the impact of the announcement. Announcement period return is not informative of future long-run performance, because (1) after an FDI announcement, the business environment (as well as the political environment) continues to evolve, and many more events might occur over the long run, and (2) current pricing has used all the available information. Therefore, it is appropriate to use the announcement period return to evaluate the impact of the announcement (Aybar & Ficici, 2009; Morck & Yeung, 1992; Lertwachara & Cochran, 2007).

43.2.3 A Theoretical Model for a Swap-Like Role of CSR

According to legitimacy theory, the expectations of society at large have to be fulfilled by the organization, not merely the owners' or investors' requirements. There appears to be an implicit social contract between a business organization and its respective societies (Deegan 2006). Only when these expectations are met, does society allow the organization to continue its operations and ensure its survival (An et al., 2011). Thus, organizations continually attempt to ensure that they are perceived as functioning within the bond and norms of society. Adopting CSR activities can be one of the firm's strategies to legitimize its operations within a society (Deegan, 2002).

Drawing on legitimacy theory, we propose that a firm creates value for both its shareholders and society at large, and it needs inputs from society (social resource) and shareholders (capital and labor costs) for its business operation (Fig. 43.1). The social resource includes but is not limited to patronage, support, goodwill, convenience, etc., provided by society. Variations in social resource input contribute to the volatility in the firm's profitability, hence the firm risk. Drawing on stakeholder theory, we call the society at large the social stakeholders.

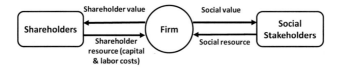

Fig. 43.1 Relationship between a firm and its social stakeholders or its shareholders. Firms create value for both their shareholders and their social stakeholders and need resources from their social stakeholders and their shareholders

CSR engagement represents an implicit contract between the firm and the social stakeholders to exchange social value from the former for social resource input from the latter. In this implicit contractual relationship, if a firm returns more social value to society when it has a good run with bumper profits, it could cut down or stop paying social value to society when it has a bad run or faces financial difficulties, while the social stakeholders supply a stable input of social resource regardless of whether the firm has a good run or a bad run.

Swaps in finance are contracts between two counterparties for the more risk-averse party to exchange risky financial products for less risky financial products from the less risk-averse party (Hull, 2012). Therefore, CSR is a swap-like tool for ensuring a stable input of social resources from social stakeholders to preserve shareholder value and reduce volatility in the firm's profitability. The level of a firm's CSR activities depends on the more volatile components of the value it creates. When it has a good run, it increases its CSR activities; when it has a bad run, it reduces its CSR activities. The social stakeholders receive more social value when the firm has a good run and receive less social value when the firm has a bad run. The relationship between the level of a firm's CSR activities and its business performance amounts to that the firm exchanges riskier value in the form of CSR engagement for a stable input of social resources from the social stakeholders.

Since obtaining a stable input of social resources is an objective of CSR activities, it is important for a firm to let consumers and other social stakeholders be aware of its CSR activities (Servaes & Tamayo, 2013). A firm's unnoticed engagement in CSR activities might decrease shareholder value because of its failure to gain social resources, as shown by Servaes and Tamayo (2013) that with low consumer awareness CSR has an insignificant or negative influence on firm value. The implicit contract between a firm and its social stakeholders is built on trust; hence, the effort of a firm with a poor prior reputation as a corporate citizen to regain social resources through more CSR activities may increase its costs and decrease its value before it regains the trust and social resource from social stakeholders. In such a scenario, high consumer awareness may remind social stakeholders of the prior poor reputation of the firm and prolong the memory of consumers and other social stakeholders about the firm's misbehaviors, leading to a negative relationship between CSR and firm value (Servaes & Tamayo, 2013).

43.2.4 Hypothesis Development

In financial economics, volatility is a commonly used measure of risk (Hull, 2012). Since Schnietz and Epstein (2005) and Godfrey et al. (2009) have shown that CSR activities provide insurance-like protection against downward changes in shareholder value caused by negative events, we expect that CSR activities would reduce firm risk measured as share return volatility. A swap-like property of CSR will also reduce share return volatility by attenuating both decreases in shareholder value caused by negative events and increases caused by positive events. Following these arguments, we propose our first hypothesis.

Hypothesis 1. There is a negative relation between firms' CSR performance and their stock return volatilities around FDI announcements.

CSR performance includes many aspects of corporate policies and practices. The three most widely used CSR components (pillars) are environmental, social, and corporate governance (ESG) (Dorfleitner et al., 2015). Since each pillar measures a distinct aspect of CSR performance, we test Hypothesis 1 with the three pillars and the overall CSR.

When investors believe an FDI project will decrease shareholder value after assessing all the available information, the stock market will react negatively to the FDI announcement. The insurance-, option-, or swap-like property of CSR implies that superior CSR performance will mitigate decreases in shareholder value caused by negative events. Following these arguments, we propose our second hypothesis.

Hypothesis 2: There is a positive relation between a firm's CSR performance and its stock price reaction to FDI announcement, when the abnormal return is negative.

An insurance- or option-like property of CSR will have no impact on increases in shareholder value caused by positive events, or at least will not attenuate such increases in shareholder value. If CSR activities have a swap-like property in reducing firm risk, high CSR performance will attenuate increases in shareholder value caused by positive events. Following these arguments, we propose our third hypothesis.

Hypothesis 3: There is a negative relation between a firm's CSR performance and its stock price reaction to FDI announcement, when the abnormal return is positive.

If Hypothesis 3 is rejected, CSR activities have an insurance- or option-like property to protect shareholder value against the impact of negative events. If it is not rejected, CSR activities are likely to have a swap-like property.

43.3 Data, Sample, and Methodology

43.3.1 Data on CSR Measures

We retrieve a firm's CSR performance from the Thomson Reuters ASSET4 database (Braam & Peeters, 2018), which includes 226 key CSR performance indicators under 18 categories and within four pillars: (1) environmental performance, (2) social performance, (3) corporate governance, and (4) economic performance. Based on CSR measure modeling and performance indicator weighting, every firm within the ASSET4 dataset is scored from zero to one for each pillar. An overall CSR ranking score captures a balanced view of the firm's performance in all four areas, while a pillar ranking score indicates a firm's performance in each category. We examine the impact of overall CSR performance and its three pillars, environmental performance, social performance, and corporate governance.

43.3.2 Sample Selection and Stock Return Data

The original sample is sourced from the SDC Platinum. Except for Greenfield investment, it consists of all types of FDI deals (partial acquisition, full acquisition, joint venture, and strategic alliance) that were recorded by SDC Platinum between 2003 and 2014 and completed by firms with available CSR data in the ASSET4 database. Initially, there were 31,437 FDIs. To eliminate the influence of confounding events, we follow Ellis et al. (2017) to exclude a deal from the sample if it was involved in multiple FDIs within a five-day window surrounding the announcement of the deal. This results in 25,943 deals. Over 400 deals were announced on Saturday and Sunday. As stock prices on weekends are not available, we use the nearby Friday as day zero in our event study. We further exclude deals that do not have stock return data available during the estimation window or have zero returns for over 100 days in the estimation period (Hue & Porter, 2006; Rapp et al., 2011). The stock return data are collected from DataStream. There are 24,880 deals left in the sample. Moreover, we delete deals that do not have firm- or country-level data available. The final sample includes 20,275 deals.

43.3.3 Methodology

We use event study methodology, which has become a standard tool in evaluating the stock price reaction to a specific event (Aybar & Ficici, 2009). It helps researchers to conclude whether an event has a positive or negative impact on shareholder wealth.

To estimate stock price reactions across countries and make the abnormal returns comparable across countries, we use the world market index rather than the national market index to calculate the abnormal returns (Ellis et al., 2017).[1] Since the market reaction to FDI announcements may be delayed in some countries and may spread over several days, we use six different event windows rather than the standard three-day window to estimate the cumulative abnormal return (CAR), to give enough time for the market to incorporate the announcement information (Ellis et al., 2017) and to examine the early responses. The FDI announcement date is defined as day zero.

We use the market model to identify normal and abnormal returns as follows:

$$R_{it} = \alpha_i + \beta_i \times R_{mt} + \varepsilon_{it} \tag{43.1}$$

where R_{it} is the return of firm i on day t, R_{mt} is the stock market return on day t, and α_i and β_i are the parameters to be estimated over an estimation window. ε_{it} is an error term for firm i on day t. Under the assumption of linearity and normality of returns, $E(\varepsilon_{it}) = 0$ and $V(\varepsilon_{it}) = \sigma_i^2$. Returns are calculated by $(P_t - P_{t-1})/P_{t-1} \times 100$, where P_t is the return index at time t and P_{t-1} is the index at time $t-1$.[2] All the analyses are based on dollar returns (Ellis et al., 2017). We estimate the above model using 205 trading days of return data, ending six trading days prior to the announcement, and use OLS regressions to estimate the market model.

We obtain the daily abnormal returns (AR) by

$$AR_{it} = R_{it} - (\alpha_i + \beta_i \times R_{mt}) \tag{43.2}$$

where AR_{it} is the abnormal return of firm i on day t, R_{it} is the actual return of firm i on day t, and $(\alpha_i + \beta_i * R_{mt})$ is the predicted normal return. Daily abnormal returns are computed for each day t for each firm i within the event window.

Daily abnormal stock returns are cumulated to obtain CAR. For each event window (T_1, T_2), we calculate CAR as

$$CAR_i = \sum_{t=T_1}^{T_2} AR_{it} \tag{43.3}$$

where T_1 and T_2 indicate the lower and upper bounds of the event window. We examine six event windows: (−1, 1), (−2, 2), (−5, 5), (0, 1), (0, 2), and (0, 5). Obviously, daily abnormal returns are predicted residuals in Eq. (43.1), and two, three, five, six, and eleven-day CARs are the predicted residuals for two, three, five, six, and eleven-day cumulative returns, respectively. Finally, all CARs are winsorized at the 1% and 99% levels to remove outliers (Alexandridis et al., 2010) and expressed in percentage. The abnormal return and CAR are actually residuals and cumulated residuals from the estimated return function, Eq. (43.1).

---

[1] We also used the individual country market indices to calculate the abnormal returns and find similar results.

[2] We also calculated the continuous return, defined by log (P_t/P_{t-1}). There is not much difference between the discrete return and the continuous return.

The expectation of CAR squared (SQ_CAR) is the variance of cumulative returns. We regress SQ_CAR on CSR performance and control variables to estimate the impact of CSR on the variance/volatility of share return. Regressing cross-sectional squared residuals on independent variables to estimate the influence of independent variables on the variance of the error term is commonly used in econometrics (Hill et al., 2018).

To test Hypothesis 1, the main regression model is specified as

$$SQ\_CAR = \alpha + \beta_0 CSR + \beta_1 X + \beta_2 Y + \gamma \sum (\text{Year } FE) + \theta \sum (\text{Sector } FE) + \varphi \sum (\text{Region } FE) + \varepsilon \quad (43.4)$$

CSR is the variable of interest, and overall CSR or one of the three pillars, environmental, social, or corporate governance CSR, is substituted into the regression equation to estimate their impacts. X is the set of firm-level control variables, including firm size, leverage, cash flow, market-to-book ratio (M/B), research and development (R&D),[3] and tangible resources. Y denotes country-level control variables, including home country GDP per capita, host country market openness, host country ores and metals, and host country unemployment rate.[4] These variables have been widely used in FDI studies. They are described in more detail in Appendix. We also include year, sector, and region-fixed effects (FEs) to eliminate possible confounding effects caused by unobservable common time-variant, industry-specific, or region-specific factors. All the independent variables are measured one year prior to the announcement. Standard errors are clustered by firm identifier. Robust standard errors are used to address the potential heteroscedasticity. The variance inflation factor (VIF) is undertaken to ensure no severe multicollinearity problem.

To compare the relative impacts of individual pillars, we estimate the following regression model:

$$SQ\_CAR = \alpha + \beta_{01} \text{environCSR} + \beta_{02} \text{socialCSR} + \beta_{03} \text{CGCSR} + \beta_1 X + \beta_2 Y + \gamma \sum (\text{Year } FE) + \theta \sum (\text{Sector } FE) + \varphi \sum (\text{Region } FE) + \varepsilon \quad (43.5)$$

In Eq. (43.5), environCSR stands for environmental CSR, socialCSR for social CSR, and CGCSR for corporate governance CSR.

To test Hypotheses 2 and 3, the regression models are specified as

---

[3] The results are robust in all of the analyses if we exclude R&D.
[4] Excluding all the country-level control variables does not affect the impact of CSR significantly, nor does including deal-type dummies, suggesting that our model and results are robust.

$$\text{PositiveCAR} = \alpha + \beta_0 CSR + \beta_1 X + \beta_2 Y + \gamma \sum (\text{Year } FE)$$
$$+ \theta \sum (\text{Sector } FE) + \varphi \sum (\text{Region } FE) + \varepsilon \quad (43.6)$$

$$\text{NegativeCAR} = \alpha + \beta_0 CSR + \beta_1 X + \beta_2 Y + \gamma \sum (\text{Year } FE)$$
$$+ \theta \sum (\text{Sector } FE) + \varphi \sum (\text{Region } FE) + \varepsilon \quad (43.7)$$

In Eqs. (43.6) and (43.7), PositiveCAR and NegativeCAR are positive and negative CARs, respectively.

43.4 Results

43.4.1 Descriptive Statistics

Summary statistics for the sample variables are presented in Table 43.1. All six CAR measures have positive means, and their medians are around zero. A multivariate analysis by regressing CARs on firm CSR performance and other control variables produces the same results as those by Liu et al. (2020), i.e., CSR performances do not have a significant effect on FDI announcement returns (data not shown).

43.4.2 Overall CSR on SQ_CAR (Hypothesis 1)

When SQ_CAR is regressed on overall CSR performance and other control variables, as shown in Table 43.2, CSR has a very significant negative influence on SQ_CAR across all six models ($p \leq 0.001$). Hence, we accept Hypothesis 1. CSR activities reduce stock return volatility. Among the control variables, the log of total assets has a very significant negative influence on SQ_CAR across all six models ($p = 0.000$). R&D has very significant positive influences on SQ_CAR in models 1 ($p = 0.003$), 2 ($p = 0.000$), 3 ($p = 0.003$), and 4 ($p = 0.006$) and significant positive influences in models 5 ($p = 0.011$) and 6 ($p = 0.019$). Cash flow has very significant negative influences on SQ_CAR in models 1 ($p = 0.003$), 2 ($p = 0.005$), 3 ($p = 0.003$), and 5 ($p = 0.006$) and a significant negative influence in model 6 ($p = 0.045$). The log of home country GDP per capita has very significant negative influences on SQ_CAR through all models. Host country market openness has a significant negative influence on SQ_CAR in model 6 ($p = 0.014$) and a weakly significant negative influence in model 5 ($p = 0.068$).

Table 43.1 Summary statistics

Variable	N	Mean	Median	Std. dev	Min	Max
Dependent variable						
CAR (−1, 1)	20,275	0.16	0.03	3.08	−9.44	11.48
CAR (−2, 2)	20,275	0.17	0.03	3.84	−11.58	14.05
CAR (−5, 5)	20,275	0.14	0.02	5.48	−16.65	18.33
CAR (0, 1)	20,275	0.15	0.01	2.66	−8.22	10.42
CAR (0, 2)	20,275	0.17	0.02	3.14	−9.63	11.99
CAR (0, 5)	20,275	0.14	−0.00	4.22	−13.13	15.41
Variable of interest						
Overall CSR	20,275	0.68	0.78	0.28	0.03	0.99
Environmental CSR	20,269	0.67	0.77	0.29	0.04	0.99
Social CSR	20,269	0.66	0.80	0.31	0.08	0.97
Corporate governance CSR	20,269	0.59	0.67	0.27	0.01	0.98
Control variable						
Log of total assets	20,275	9.96	9.74	2.01	4.74	14.61
R&D	20,275	0.02	0.00	0.04	0.00	0.21
Leverage	20,275	0.25	0.23	0.15	0.00	0.65
M/B	20,275	2.70	2.07	2.25	0.27	14.60
Tangible resources	20,275	0.20	0.14	0.20	0.00	0.86
Cash flow	20,275	0.09	0.08	0.06	−0.04	0.32
Log of home country GDP per capita	20,275	10.65	10.7	0.44	7.06	11.61
Host country market openness	20,275	0.69	0.56	0.61	0.00	4.55
Host country ores and metals exports	20,275	5.63	3.49	8.06	0.00	75.01
Host country unemployment rate	20,275	6.97	6.30	3.44	0.00	31.80

Notes: The appendix provides definitions and data sources for all variables

43.4.3 Environmental, Social, and Corporate Governance CSR on SQ_CAR

When SQ_CAR is regressed on environmental CSR performance and other control variables, as shown in Table 43.3, environmental CSR has a weakly significant negative influence on SQ_CAR only in model 4 ($p = 0.052$). This result suggests that the environmental pillar of CSR is not the main driver in the effect of overall CSR. The estimates for control variables are similar to those in regressions on overall CSR.

When SQ_CAR is regressed on social CSR performance and other control variables, social CSR has a very significant negative influence in models 1 ($p = 0.008$), 3 ($p = 0.004$), 4 ($p = 0.000$), 5 ($p = 0.001$), and 6 ($p = 0.000$) and a significant negative influence on SQ_CAR in model 2 ($p = 0.019$) (Table 43.4). This suggests that the social pillar of CSR is one of the main drivers in the effect of overall CSR. The estimates for control variables are also similar to those in the regressions on overall CSR.

Table 43.2 Regressions of SQ_CAR on CSR surrounding FDI announcements (Hypothesis 1)

Variable	(1) SQ_CAR (−1, 1)	(2) SQ_CAR (−2, 2)	(3) SQ_CAR (−5, 5)	(4) SQ_CAR (0, 1)	(5) SQ_CAR (0, 2)	(6) SQ_CAR (0, 5)
Overall CSR	−3.173	−4.024	−7.832	−3.223	−3.656	−6.329
	(0.000)	(0.001)	(0.000)	(0.000)	(0.000)	(0.000)
Log of total assets	−1.075	−1.618	−2.505	−0.918	−1.242	−1.868
	(0.000)	(0.000)	(0.000)	(0.000)	(0.000)	(0.000)
R&D	15.424	27.876	41.840	11.431	13.868	21.231
	(0.003)	(0.000)	(0.003)	(0.006)	(0.011)	(0.019)
Leverage	0.439	0.093	0.012	0.572	−0.467	0.572
	(0.752)	(0.962)	(0.997)	(0.588)	(0.738)	(0.811)
M/B	−0.004	−0.039	−0.106	−0.048	0.009	−0.159
	(0.967)	(0.792)	(0.698)	(0.560)	(0.938)	(0.385)
Tangible resources	−0.492	−0.523	−2.570	0.001	−0.444	−0.959
	(0.673)	(0.771)	(0.407)	(0.999)	(0.731)	(0.652)
Cash flow	−13.163	−19.216	−37.322	−5.931	−13.281	−16.570
	(0.003)	(0.005)	(0.003)	(0.106)	(0.006)	(0.045)
Log of home country GDP per capita	−1.174	−1.978	−4.200	−1.202	−1.725	−2.963
	(0.012)	(0.005)	(0.001)	(0.001)	(0.001)	(0.001)
Host country market openness	0.013	−0.076	−0.724	0.014	−0.440	−1.022
	(0.956)	(0.833)	(0.284)	(0.941)	(0.068)	(0.014)
Host country ores and metals exports	0.022	0.011	−0.026	0.001	−0.017	−0.051
	(0.246)	(0.683)	(0.615)	(0.972)	(0.344)	(0.122)
Host country unemployment rate	0.009	0.013	−0.073	−0.034	−0.017	−0.080
	(0.825)	(0.835)	(0.485)	(0.272)	(0.659)	(0.236)
Constant	34.269	54.417	106.492	31.091	44.554	73.220
	(0.000)	(0.000)	(0.000)	(0.000)	(0.000)	(0.000)

Industry, year, and region fixed effect	Yes	Yes	Yes	Yes	Yes	Yes
Observations	20,275	20,275	20,275	20,275	20,275	20,275
F	21.40	23.01	23.32	21.17	21.88	21.96
R-squared	0.056	0.062	0.064	0.056	0.057	0.059

Notes: This table reports results from regressing the variance of cumulative returns (SQ_CAR) on overall corporate social responsibility (CSR) performance. The appendix provides definitions and data sources for all variables. P-values based on robust standard errors adjusted for clustering by the firm are in parentheses

Table 43.3 Regressions of SQ_CAR on environmental CSR surrounding FDI announcements

Variable	(1) SQ_CAR (−1, 1)	(2) SQ_CAR (−2, 2)	(3) SQ_CAR (−5, 5)	(4) SQ_CAR (0, 1)	(5) SQ_CAR (0, 2)	(6) SQ_CAR (0, 5)
Environmental CSR	−0.859	−0.471	−2.739	−1.136	−0.881	−1.474
	(0.246)	(0.660)	(0.179)	(0.052)	(0.249)	(0.263)
Log of total assets	−1.290	−1.956	−2.975	−1.109	−1.501	−2.318
	(0.000)	(0.000)	(0.000)	(0.000)	(0.000)	(0.000)
R&D	15.314	27.318	42.309	11.348	13.649	21.068
	(0.004)	(0.000)	(0.003)	(0.006)	(0.012)	(0.020)
Leverage	0.675	0.411	0.733	0.791	−0.198	1.200
	(0.629)	(0.833)	(0.845)	(0.459)	(0.888)	(0.618)
M/B	−0.015	−0.051	−0.097	−0.060	−0.001	−0.146
	(0.878)	(0.732)	(0.724)	(0.464)	(0.990)	(0.433)
Tangible resources	−0.545	−0.648	−2.477	−0.012	−0.500	−1.057
	(0.644)	(0.722)	(0.433)	(0.990)	(0.704)	(0.626)
Cash flow	−14.673	−21.420	−41.823	−7.430	−15.168	−20.983
	(0.001)	(0.002)	(0.001)	(0.041)	(0.002)	(0.012)
Log of home country GDP per capita	−1.219	−2.049	−4.251	−1.245	−1.780	−3.153
	(0.009)	(0.003)	(0.001)	(0.001)	(0.000)	(0.000)
Host country market openness	0.031	−0.047	−0.669	0.033	−0.414	−0.971
	(0.897)	(0.895)	(0.323)	(0.862)	(0.085)	(0.019)
Host country ores and metals exports	0.020	0.007	−0.031	−0.001	−0.020	−0.056
	(0.288)	(0.780)	(0.553)	(0.939)	(0.280)	(0.091)
Host country unemployment rate	0.011	0.013	−0.073	−0.031	−0.015	−0.071
	(0.779)	(0.824)	(0.484)	(0.321)	(0.703)	(0.293)
Constant	35.254	56.029	108.053	31.977	45.743	76.254
	(0.000)	(0.000)	(0.000)	(0.000)	(0.000)	(0.000)

Industry, year, and region fixed effect	Yes	Yes	Yes	Yes	Yes	Yes
Observations	20,275	20,275	20,275	20,275	20,275	20,275
F	21.37	22.83	23.11	21.05	21.77	21.43
R-squared	0.055	0.061	0.063	0.054	0.056	0.057

Notes: This table reports results from regressing the variance of cumulative returns (SQ_CAR) on environmental corporate social responsibility (CSR) performance. The appendix provides definitions and data sources for all variables. P-values based on robust standard errors adjusted for clustering by the firm are in parentheses

Table 43.4 Regressions of SQ_CAR on social CSR surrounding FDI announcements

Variable	(1) SQ_CAR (−1, 1)	(2) SQ_CAR (−2, 2)	(3) SQ_CAR (−5, 5)	(4) SQ_CAR (0, 1)	(5) SQ_CAR (0, 2)	(6) SQ_CAR (0, 5)
Social CSR	−2.108	−2.733	−6.092	−2.502	−2.663	−5.161
	(0.008)	(0.019)	(0.004)	(0.000)	(0.001)	(0.000)
Log of total assets	−1.177	−1.743	−2.673	−0.986	−1.337	−1.976
	(0.000)	(0.000)	(0.000)	(0.000)	(0.000)	(0.000)
R&D	15.466	27.772	42.529	11.485	13.922	21.620
	(0.003)	(0.000)	(0.003)	(0.006)	(0.010)	(0.016)
Leverage	0.661	0.354	0.618	0.776	−0.228	1.100
	(0.635)	(0.856)	(0.869)	(0.464)	(0.870)	(0.645)
M/B	−0.011	−0.045	−0.084	−0.055	0.004	−0.135
	(0.911)	(0.765)	(0.760)	(0.502)	(0.970)	(0.468)
Tangible resources	−0.630	−0.639	−2.735	−0.134	−0.568	−1.125
	(0.592)	(0.724)	(0.383)	(0.889)	(0.663)	(0.601)
Cash flow	−14.048	−20.414	−40.004	−6.717	−14.316	−19.222
	(0.002)	(0.003)	(0.002)	(0.065)	(0.003)	(0.021)
Log of home country GDP per capita	−1.269	−2.086	−4.401	−1.308	−1.834	−3.249
	(0.007)	(0.003)	(0.001)	(0.000)	(0.000)	(0.000)
Host country market openness	0.022	−0.063	−0.699	0.024	−0.426	−1.000
	(0.925)	(0.861)	(0.300)	(0.900)	(0.076)	(0.016)
Host country ores and metals exports	0.021	0.008	−0.029	−0.000	−0.019	−0.054
	(0.273)	(0.748)	(0.580)	(0.978)	(0.301)	(0.103)
Host country unemployment rate	0.010	0.013	−0.070	−0.031	−0.016	−0.071
	(0.789)	(0.831)	(0.499)	(0.313)	(0.691)	(0.298)

Constant	35.581	55.968	109.140	32.446	46.004	76.581
	(0.000)	(0.000)	(0.000)	(0.000)	(0.000)	(0.000)
Industry, year, and region fixed effect	Yes	Yes	Yes	Yes	Yes	Yes
Observations	20,275	20,275	20,275	20,275	20,275	20,275
F	21.37	23.12	23.22	21.14	21.83	21.86
R-squared	0.055	0.062	0.064	0.055	0.057	0.058

Notes: This table reports results from regressing the variance of cumulative returns (SQ_CAR) on social corporate social responsibility (CSR) performance. The appendix provides definitions and data sources for all variables. P-values based on robust standard errors adjusted for clustering by the firm are in parentheses

When SQ_CAR is regressed on corporate governance CSR performance and other control variables, the negative influence of corporate governance CSR on SQ_CAR is weakly significant in model 1 ($p = 0.091$), significant in models 4 ($p = 0.021$) and 5 ($p = 0.036$), and very significant in model 6 ($p = 0.008$) (Table 43.5). The estimates for control variables are similar to those with regressions on overall CSR.

When SQ_CAR is regressed on the three pillars of CSR and other control variables, there is a weakly significant positive influence of environmental CSR on SQ_CAR in model 6 ($p = 0.051$). Social CSR has a significant negative influence on SQ_CAR in models 1 ($p = 0.019$), 2 ($p = 0.011$), and 3 ($p = 0.017$) and a very significant negative impact on SQ_CAR in models 4 ($p = 0.001$), 5 ($p = 0.003$), and 6 ($p = 0.000$). Corporate governance CSR has a weakly significant negative influence only in model 6 ($p = 0.095$) (Table 43.6). These results show that social CSR is the main contributor to the effects of overall CSR. The estimates for control variables are similar to those with regression on overall CSR.

43.4.4 Overall CSR and Negative CAR (Hypothesis 2)

When negative CAR is regressed on overall CSR performance and other control variables, overall CSR has a significant positive influence on CAR in model 1 ($p = 0.035$) and a very significant positive influence on CAR in models 2–6 ($p = 0.001$ in model 4 and $p = 0.000$ in the rest models) (Table 43.7). Therefore, we accept Hypothesis 2; CSR mitigates decreases in shareholder value caused by negative events. In contrast with regressions on SQ_CAR, the log of total assets has a very significant positive influence on CAR in all models ($p = 0.000$). R&D has a very significant negative influence on CAR in models 1 ($p = 0.000$), 2 ($p = 0.001$), 3 ($p = 0.003$), 4 ($p = 0.000$), and 5 ($p = 0.001$) and a weakly significant negative impact on CAR in model 6 ($p = 0.093$). Tangible resources have a weakly significant negative influence on CSR in model 4 ($p = 0.095$). Cash flow has a very significant positive influence on CAR in models 1 ($p = 0.000$), 2 ($p = 0.001$), 3 ($p = 0.000$), 4 ($p = 0.001$), and 5 ($p = 0.000$) and a significant positive influence in model 6 ($p = 0.012$). Log of home country GDP per capita has a significant positive influence on CAR in model 1 ($p = 0.018$), a weakly significant influence in model 2 ($p = 0.094$), and a very significant impact in models 3 ($p = 0.000$), 4 ($p = 0.006$), 5 ($p = 0.008$), and 6 ($p = 0.000$). Host country market openness has a significant positive influence on CAR in models 3 ($p = 0.049$) and 6 ($p = 0.035$).

43.4.5 Overall CSR and Positive CAR (Hypothesis 3)

When positive CAR is regressed on overall CSR performance and other control variables, overall CSR has a weakly significant negative influence on CAR in model

Table 43.5 Regressions of SQ_CAR on corporate governance CSR surrounding FDI announcements

Variable	(1) SQ_CAR (−1, 1)	(2) SQ_CAR (−2, 2)	(3) SQ_CAR (−5, 5)	(4) SQ_CAR (0, 1)	(5) SQ_CAR (0, 2)	(6) SQ_CAR (0, 5)
Corporate governance CSR	−1.367	−1.422	−3.283	−1.479	−1.818	−3.859
	(0.091)	(0.232)	(0.148)	(0.021)	(0.036)	(0.008)
Log of total assets	−1.327	−1.952	−3.132	−1.170	−1.524	−2.326
	(0.000)	(0.000)	(0.000)	(0.000)	(0.000)	(0.000)
R&D	15.010	27.168	41.317	10.938	13.347	20.582
	(0.004)	(0.000)	(0.004)	(0.008)	(0.014)	(0.022)
Leverage	0.671	0.376	0.736	0.792	−0.220	1.137
	(0.631)	(0.847)	(0.844)	(0.457)	(0.875)	(0.634)
M/B	−0.008	−0.042	−0.079	−0.051	0.009	−0.123
	(0.940)	(0.778)	(0.777)	(0.533)	(0.934)	(0.512)
Tangible resources	−0.750	−0.783	−3.099	−0.273	−0.724	−1.458
	(0.523)	(0.664)	(0.322)	(0.775)	(0.576)	(0.495)
Cash flow	−14.725	−21.343	−42.137	−7.545	−15.158	−20.845
	(0.001)	(0.002)	(0.001)	(0.039)	(0.002)	(0.012)
Log of home country GDP per capita	−1.201	−2.012	−4.232	−1.233	−1.744	−3.063
	(0.010)	(0.004)	(0.001)	(0.001)	(0.000)	(0.000)
Host country market openness	0.035	−0.045	−0.653	0.040	−0.410	−0.964
	(0.882)	(0.900)	(0.334)	(0.836)	(0.088)	(0.020)
Host country ores and metals exports	0.020	0.008	−0.031	−0.001	−0.019	−0.055
	(0.284)	(0.769)	(0.555)	(0.945)	(0.289)	(0.096)
Host country unemployment rate	0.010	0.012	−0.075	−0.032	−0.016	−0.075
	(0.802)	(0.839)	(0.469)	(0.303)	(0.675)	(0.272)

(continued)

Table 43.5 (continued)

Variable	(1) SQ_CAR (−1, 1)	(2) SQ_CAR (−2, 2)	(3) SQ_CAR (−5, 5)	(4) SQ_CAR (0, 1)	(5) SQ_CAR (0, 2)	(6) SQ_CAR (0, 5)
Constant	35.510	55.975	109.145	32.402	45.889	76.275
	(0.000)	(0.000)	(0.000)	(0.000)	(0.000)	(0.000)
Industry, year, and region fixed effect	Yes	Yes	Yes	Yes	Yes	Yes
Observations	20,275	20,275	20,275	20,275	20,275	20,275
F	21.36	22.83	23.10	21.00	21.79	21.43
R-squared	0.055	0.061	0.063	0.054	0.056	0.058

Notes: This table reports results from regressing the variance of cumulative returns (SQ_CAR) on corporate governance corporate social responsibility (CSR) performance. The appendix provides definitions and data sources for all variables. P-values based on robust standard errors adjusted for clustering by the firm are in parentheses

Table 43.6 Regressions of SQ_CAR on the three pillars of CSR surrounding FDI announcements

Variable	(1) SQ_CAR (−1, 1)	(2) SQ_CAR (−2, 2)	(3) SQ_CAR (−5, 5)	(4) SQ_CAR (0, 1)	(5) SQ_CAR (0, 2)	(6) SQ_CAR (0, 5)
Environmental CSR	0.823	2.140	1.980	0.765	1.399	3.208
	(0.373)	(0.114)	(0.457)	(0.280)	(0.145)	(0.051)
Social CSR	−2.392	−3.929	−6.929	−2.757	−3.218	−6.439
	(0.019)	(0.011)	(0.017)	(0.001)	(0.003)	(0.000)
Corporate governance	−0.779	−0.675	−1.418	−0.748	−1.109	−2.534
	(0.358)	(0.592)	(0.554)	(0.262)	(0.221)	(0.095)
Log of total assets	−1.204	−1.821	−2.742	−1.012	−1.385	−2.087
	(0.000)	(0.000)	(0.000)	(0.000)	(0.000)	(0.000)
R&D	15.229	27.227	41.982	11.262	13.529	20.720
	(0.004)	(0.000)	(0.003)	(0.007)	(0.013)	(0.020)
Leverage	0.666	0.408	0.643	0.779	−0.213	1.134
	(0.632)	(0.833)	(0.863)	(0.460)	(0.878)	(0.632)
M/B	−0.006	−0.039	−0.075	−0.050	0.011	−0.118
	(0.950)	(0.793)	(0.786)	(0.542)	(0.920)	(0.526)
Tangible resources	−0.798	−1.016	−3.121	−0.292	−0.845	−1.760
	(0.502)	(0.577)	(0.324)	(0.763)	(0.520)	(0.416)
Cash flow	−14.056	−20.449	−40.029	−6.725	−14.332	−19.261
	(0.002)	(0.003)	(0.002)	(0.065)	(0.003)	(0.021)
Log of home country GDP per capita	−1.273	−2.155	−4.432	−1.311	−1.851	−3.288
	(0.006)	(0.002)	(0.001)	(0.000)	(0.000)	(0.000)
Host country market openness	0.025	−0.057	−0.693	0.027	−0.422	−0.990
	(0.915)	(0.873)	(0.305)	(0.889)	(0.079)	(0.017)
Host country ores and metals exports	0.021	0.008	−0.029	−0.000	−0.019	−0.053
	(0.271)	(0.750)	(0.581)	(0.984)	(0.305)	(0.105)

(continued)

Table 43.6 (continued)

Variable	(1) SQ_CAR (−1, 1)	(2) SQ_CAR (−2, 2)	(3) SQ_CAR (−5, 5)	(4) SQ_CAR (0, 1)	(5) SQ_CAR (0, 2)	(6) SQ_CAR (0, 5)
Host country unemployment rate	0.010	0.012	−0.072	−0.032	−0.017	−0.073
	(0.802)	(0.840)	(0.491)	(0.303)	(0.673)	(0.283)
Constant	35.930	57.189	110.086	32.765	46.648	78.059
	(0.000)	(0.000)	(0.000)	(0.000)	(0.000)	(0.000)
Industry, year, and region fixed effect	Yes	Yes	Yes	Yes	Yes	Yes
Observations	20,275	20,275	20,275	20,275	20,275	20,275
F	20.24	22.21	21.97	20.08	20.68	20.77
R-squared	0.055	0.062	0.064	0.055	0.055	0.062

Notes: This table reports results from regressing the variance of cumulative returns (SQ_CAR) on environmental, social, and corporate social responsibility (CSR) performances. The appendix provides definitions and data sources for all variables. P-values based on robust standard errors adjusted for clustering by the firm are in parentheses

43 Corporate Social Responsibility as a Swap for Reducing Firm Risk...

Table 43.7 Regressions of negative CAR on CSR surrounding FDI announcements (Hypothesis 2)

Variable	(1) CAR (−1,1)	(2) CAR (−2, 2)	(3) CAR (−5, 5)	(4) CAR (0, 1)	(5) CAR (0, 2)	(6) CAR (0, 5)
Overall CSR	0.212	0.451	0.696	0.282	0.350	0.616
	(0.035)	(0.000)	(0.000)	(0.001)	(0.000)	(0.000)
Log of total assets	0.089	0.095	0.124	0.073	0.077	0.089
	(0.000)	(0.000)	(0.000)	(0.000)	(0.000)	(0.000)
R&D	−2.429	−2.750	−3.514	−2.146	−2.021	−1.401
	(0.000)	(0.001)	(0.003)	(0.000)	(0.001)	(0.093)
Leverage	−0.120	0.035	−0.103	−0.174	0.018	0.223
	(0.483)	(0.864)	(0.733)	(0.221)	(0.913)	(0.352)
M/B	−0.008	−0.021	−0.007	−0.005	−0.018	−0.009
	(0.534)	(0.186)	(0.758)	(0.642)	(0.136)	(0.603)
Tangible resources	−0.133	−0.208	−0.001	−0.230	−0.208	−0.166
	(0.379)	(0.278)	(0.996)	(0.095)	(0.187)	(0.451)
Cash flow	2.121	2.229	3.586	1.506	2.019	1.983
	(0.000)	(0.001)	(0.000)	(0.001)	(0.000)	(0.012)
Log of home country GDP per capita	0.153	0.124	0.427	0.152	0.166	0.349
	(0.018)	(0.094)	(0.000)	(0.006)	(0.008)	(0.000)
Host country market openness	0.005	0.025	0.117	0.015	0.041	0.089
	(0.889)	(0.568)	(0.049)	(0.596)	(0.206)	(0.035)
Host country ores and metals exports	−0.002	−0.002	0.001	−0.001	−0.000	0.004
	(0.412)	(0.474)	(0.796)	(0.700)	(0.900)	(0.307)
Host country unemployment rate	−0.005	0.002	0.010	0.005	−0.002	0.000
	(0.388)	(0.789)	(0.322)	(0.369)	(0.681)	(0.974)

(continued)

Table 43.7 (continued)

Variable	(1) CAR (−1,1)	(2) CAR (−2, 2)	(3) CAR (−5, 5)	(4) CAR (0, 1)	(5) CAR (0, 2)	(6) CAR (0, 5)
Constant	−4.715	−5.316	−10.461	−4.318	−4.972	−8.158
	(0.000)	(0.000)	(0.000)	(0.000)	(0.000)	(0.000)
Industry, year, and region fixed effect	Yes	Yes	Yes	Yes	Yes	Yes
Observations	10,021	10,032	10,116	10,089	10,060	10,148
F	15.90	19.60	17.95	17.46	19.35	15.67
R-squared	0.067	0.077	0.076	0.075	0.078	0.072

Notes: This table reports results from regressing negative cumulative abnormal returns (CAR) on overall corporate social responsibility (CSR) performances. The appendix provides definitions and data sources for all variables. P-values based on robust standard errors adjusted for clustering by the firm are in parentheses

2 ($p = 0.050$), a significant negative influence in model 3 ($p = 0.032$), and a very significant negative influence in models 1 and 4 ($p = 0.000$) and 5 and 6 ($p = 0.001$) (Table 43.8). We accept Hypothesis 3. These results indicate that CSR attenuates increases in shareholder value caused by positive events. Log of total assets has a very significant negative influence on CAR across the six models ($p = 0.000$). R&D has a significant positive influence in models 1 ($p = 0.045$), 2 ($p = 0.019$), 3 ($p = 0.014$), 4 ($p = 0.039$), and 6 ($p = 0.012$). Market-to-book value has a significant negative influence on CAR in models 2 ($p = 0.020$) and 6 ($p = 0.039$) and a weakly significant negative influence in model 5 ($p = 0.074$). Cash flow has a weakly significant negative influence on CAR in models 1 ($p = 0.059$) and 2 ($p = 0.082$). Log of home country GDP per capita has a weakly significant negative influence on CAR in models 1 ($p = 0.089$) and 6 ($p = 0.096$) and a very significant negative impact in models 2 ($p = 0.000$), 4 ($p = 0.008$), and 5 ($p = 0.007$).

43.5 Discussion and Conclusion

Several theoretical studies have emphasized the role of CSR in corporate risk management and proposed some mechanisms through which CSR activities mitigate the impacts of negative events on shareholder value (Kytle & Ruggie, 2005; Godfrey, 2005; Gardberg & Fombrun, 2006; Husted, 2005). Many previous studies have also investigated the relationship between CSR performance and shareholder value empirically and usually found a negative relationship between them (McGuire et al., 1988; Orlitzky & Benjamin, 2001; Oikonomou et al., 2012; Salama et al., 2011; Jo & Na, 2012). In these empirical studies, stock return volatility and its covariance with the market return are used to measure overall and systematic risks, respectively. Return variance and its square root standard deviation (i.e., volatility) play an important role in financial economics for pricing financial assets. When the relationship between two variables is examined with observations over a long period, there are often concerns about the ambiguous causality between changes in the two variables (Krüger, 2015; Waddock & Graves, 1997). The present study uses an event study method to investigate the relationship between CSR performance and the variance of cumulative abnormal return around FDI announcements, which might alleviate such concerns (Morck & Yeung, 1992; Lertwachara & Cochran, 2007; Stoker et al., 2019). We find that CSR performance significantly negatively affects the variance of cumulative returns. Our finding suggests that high CSR performance may affect asset pricing and portfolio composition chosen by investors by reducing the variance of stock returns.

Our present study also addresses the issue concerning which pillar of CSR is the main driver in this risk-reducing role. Our results show that social CSR is the most important factor in the effects of overall CSR, while corporate governance CSR also has some noticeable contributions. Environmental CSR appears to play only a minor role. One explanation for the present results may be that social and governance dimensions of CSR are more visible to investors/social stakeholders and

Table 43.8 Regressions of positive CAR on CSR surrounding FDI announcements (Hypothesis 3)

Variable	(1) CAR (−1,1)	(2) CAR (−2, 2)	(3) CAR (−5, 5)	(4) CAR (0, 1)	(5) CAR (0, 2)	(6) CAR (0, 5)
Overall CSR	−0.483	−0.294	−0.423	−0.531	−0.470	−0.535
	(0.000)	(0.050)	(0.032)	(0.000)	(0.001)	(0.001)
Log of total assets	−0.176	−0.220	−0.256	−0.171	−0.203	−0.242
	(0.000)	(0.000)	(0.000)	(0.000)	(0.000)	(0.000)
R&D	1.472	2.101	3.055	1.402	1.175	2.668
	(0.045)	(0.019)	(0.014)	(0.039)	(0.140)	(0.012)
Leverage	−0.082	−0.007	−0.011	−0.058	−0.075	0.249
	(0.709)	(0.977)	(0.973)	(0.761)	(0.735)	(0.376)
M/B	−0.015	−0.042	−0.033	−0.022	−0.029	−0.041
	(0.293)	(0.020)	(0.196)	(0.117)	(0.074)	(0.039)
Tangible resources	−0.219	−0.332	−0.330	−0.068	−0.211	−0.125
	(0.220)	(0.139)	(0.231)	(0.669)	(0.259)	(0.597)
Cash flow	−1.209	−1.362	−1.341	−0.499	−1.020	−1.177
	(0.059)	(0.082)	(0.225)	(0.424)	(0.133)	(0.166)
Log of home country GDP per capita	−0.115	−0.293	−0.143	−0.165	−0.201	−0.167
	(0.089)	(0.000)	(0.223)	(0.008)	(0.007)	(0.096)
Host country market openness	−0.016	−0.012	−0.025	−0.004	−0.056	−0.068
	(0.672)	(0.797)	(0.704)	(0.913)	(0.160)	(0.216)
Host country ores and metals exports	0.002	−0.000	−0.004	0.000	−0.004	−0.005
	(0.408)	(0.901)	(0.396)	(0.974)	(0.246)	(0.247)
Host country unemployment rate	−0.002	0.005	0.003	−0.006	−0.004	−0.008
	(0.764)	(0.548)	(0.763)	(0.307)	(0.528)	(0.351)

Constant	5.719	8.534	8.689	5.820	7.191	7.848
	(0.000)	(0.000)	(0.000)	(0.000)	(0.000)	(0.000)
Industry, year, and region fixed effect	Yes	Yes	Yes	Yes	Yes	Yes
Observations	10,254	10,243	10,159	10,186	10,215	10,127
F	16.89	18.43	17.39	16.69	17.85	18.92
R-squared	0.074	0.075	0.073	0.074	0.074	0.074

Notes: This table reports results from regressing positive cumulative abnormal returns (CAR) on overall corporate social responsibility (CSR) performances. The appendix provides definitions and data sources for all variables. P-values based on robust standard errors adjusted for clustering by the firm are in parentheses more relevant to their current interests, thus having stronger risk-reducing effects than the environmental dimension (Chollet & Sandwidi, 2018). Our findings are generally consistent with previous studies. For example, firm-specific and total risks are mainly explained by social and governance CSR in Chollet and Sandwidi (2018). Qiu et al. (2016) find that social rather than environmental disclosures matter to investors, and the link is driven by higher expected growth rates in the cash flows of the company. Miralles-Quirós and Miralles-Quirós (2018) find that the market positively and significantly values a firm's social and corporate governance practices in sensitive industries.

There are also some studies with different findings from our current study on the role of individual pillars. Both Flammer (2013) and Krüger (2015) find that environmental CSR news significantly affects firms' stock prices. Salama et al. (2011) demonstrate that a company's environmental performance is inversely related to its systematic financial risk. Limkriangkrai et al. (2017) show that firms with low environment ratings and high governance ratings tend to raise less debt, while social ratings have no impact on corporate financing decisions. The differences might arise from different methods and research designs employed. While CSR performance in our study is a quantitative variable, CSR news used by Flammer (2013) and Krüger (2015) is a qualitative variable. The significant influence of environmental CSR in the findings by Salama et al. (2011) might have endogeneity and reverse causality issues (Waddock & Graves, 1997; Krüger, 2015).

How do CSR activities reduce firm risk? Godfrey (2005) proposes that positive moral capital among communities and stakeholders generated by corporate philanthropy provides shareholders with insurance-like protection against negative events. Husted (2005) has argued that CSR is a real option to protect the firm from downside business risk. Godfrey et al. (2009) think that CSR will temper stakeholders' negative judgments and sanctions toward firms when they suffer a negative event. Our present finding that high CSR performance also attenuates increases in shareholder value caused by positive events suggests that CSR activities have a swap-like property rather than an insurance- or option-like property. Drawing on legitimacy theory and stakeholder theory, we propose a new framework involving the firm, its shareholders, and social stakeholders to explain the swap-like property of CSR. According to our new framework, CSR activities are an implicit contract between a firm and its social stakeholders, through which the firm exchanges riskier (social) value for a stable input of social resources from social stakeholders. Therefore, firms have better CSR performance when they are less financially constrained (Hong et al., 2012).

The present results of control variables are also noteworthy. Log of total assets, R&D, and cash flow are most influential on SQ_CAR and CAR. Log of total assets has a very significant negative impact on SQ_CAR, positive impact on negative CAR, and negative impact on positive CAR, which is the same pattern as the influence of CSR performance on SQ_CAR and CAR. There are two explanations for this phenomenon. One is that the log of total assets acts through CSR, i.e., larger firms practice more CSR. The other is that log of total assets acts independently. Drawing on Newton's law of motion, we propose that a firm has inertia, which is proportional to the firm's total assets (i.e., total assets correspond to mass in Newtonian mechanics). Because of inertia, positive or negative events will cause smaller changes in the shareholder value of large firms. As larger firms may practice environmental CSR more than smaller firms as well, the lack of effects by environmental CSR suggests that at least some impacts of social and governance CSR on firm risk are independent of firm size. The significant effects of overall CSR, social CSR, and corporate governance CSR with the inclusion of firm-level control variables also support their direct roles rather than acting indirectly via firm size.

R&D has a significant positive effect on SQ_CAR, a negative effect on negative CAR, and a positive effect on positive CAR, suggesting that R&D increases firm risk. This is understandable because large R&D expenditure might cause over-optimistic expectations of return growth, and failure of R&D projects often leads to overreaction to correct the initial overvaluation of firms with large R&D expenditure. Since large firms tend to have large cash flow, the finding that cash flow has a significant negative effect on SQ_CAR and a positive effect on negative CAR also implies that large firms have lower volatility in shareholder value than small firms. The impact of cash flow on positive CAR is much weaker than that on negative CAR, which indicates that investors are less concerned with a firm's cash flow when positive events occur.

Log of home country GDP per capita has a significant negative impact on SQ_CAR, positive impact on negative CAR, and negative impact on positive CAR, which may suggest that mature financial systems in more developed economies can reduce firm risk. Countries with high GDP per capita tend to have more mature financial systems. Similar to the effect of cash flow, the impact of the log of home country GDP per capita on positive CAR is much weaker than that on negative CAR, indicating that a mature financial system is better at mitigating decreases caused by negative events than at attenuating increases caused by positive events.

In conclusion, CSR performance has a negative impact on stock return volatility. High CSR performance is associated with lower variance in stock returns around FDI announcements. Poor CSR performance is associated with higher variance in stock returns. The impact of overall CSR performance is driven principally by social CSR and secondarily by corporate governance CSR. Environmental CSR appears to play only a minor role. High CSR performance not only mitigates decreases in shareholder value caused by negative events but also attenuates increases in shareholder value caused by positive events. Therefore, CSR has a swap-like property in corporate risk management.

Acknowledgments This research did not receive any specific grant from funding agencies in the public, commercial, or not-for-profit sectors. The authors have no conflicts of interest to declare that are relevant to the content of this article.

This research does not involve human participants, animals, or biological materials. Informed consent is not applicable.

A.1 Appendix: Variable Descriptions and Data Source

Variable	Description	Data source
Dependent variable		
CAR (−1, 1)	Cumulative abnormal return from day −1 to day 1, expressed in percentage	Own calculation
CAR (−2, 2)	Cumulative abnormal return from day −2 to day 2, expressed in percentage	Own calculation
CAR (−5, 5)	Cumulative abnormal return from day −5 to day −5, expressed in percentage	Own calculation
CAR (0, 1)	Cumulative abnormal return from day 0 to day 1, expressed in percentage	Own calculation
CAR (0, 2)	Cumulative abnormal return from day 0 to day 2, expressed in percentage	Own calculation
CAR (0, 5)	Cumulative abnormal return from day 0 to day 5, expressed in percentage	Own calculation
Independent variable		
Variable of interest		
Overall CSR	Overall ESG performance score	ASSET4
Environmental CSR	Environmental CSR performance score	ASSET4
Social CSR	Social CSR performance score	ASSET4
Corporate governance CSR	Corporate governance CSR performance score	ASSET4
Control variable		
Total assets	Book value of assets in billion US dollars (WC07230)	Worldscope
R&D	Research and development expenses divided by net sales or revenues (WC01201/WC01001)	Worldscope
Leverage	Sum of long- and short-term debt divided by the book value of an asset (WC03255/WC02999)	Worldscope

(continued)

Variable	Description	Data source
M/B	Market value of equity divided by the book value of equity (WC02999-WC03255)/(WC03501)	Worldscope
Tangible resources	Property, plant, and equipment divided by net sales or revenues (WC02501/WC01001)	Worldscope
Cash flow	Cash flow divided by book value of assets (WC04201/WC02999)	Worldscope
Log of home country GDP per capita	The natural logarithm of country's real GDP per capita in US $	World development indicators (WDI)
Host country market openness	Country's imports and exports divided by GDP	WDI
Host country ores and metals exports	Country's ores and metals exports divided by merchandise exports, expressed in percentage	WDI
Host country unemployment rate	The unemployment rate of the country, expressed in percentage	WDI

References

Alexandridis, G., Petmezas, D., & Travlos, N. G. (2010). Gains from mergers and acquisitions around the world: New evidence. *Financial Management, 39*(4), 1671–1695.

An, Y., Davey, H., & Eggleton, I. R. C. (2011). Towards a comprehensive theoretical framework for voluntary IC disclosure. *Journal of Intellectual Capital, 12*(4), 571–586.

Aybar, B., & Ficici, A. (2009). Cross-border acquisitions and firm value: An analysis of emerging-market multinationals. *Journal of International Business Studies, 40*(8), 1317–1338.

Barkema, H. G., & Vermeulen, F. (1998). International expansion through start up or acquisition: A learning perspective. *Academy of Management Journal, 41*(1), 7–26.

Barnea, A., & Rubin, A. (2010). Corporate social responsibility as a conflict between shareholders. *Journal of Business Ethics, 97*(1), 71–86. https://doi.org/10.1007/s10551-010-0496-z

Becchetti, L., Ciciretti, R., Hasan, I., & Kobeissi, N. (2012). Corporate social responsibility and shareholder's value. *Journal of Business Research, 65*(11), 1628–1635.

Ben-David, I., Bhattacharya, U. & Jacobsen, S. E. (2020). *Do announcement returns contain information about value creation?* Fisher College of Business Working Paper (2020-3) (p. 018).

Braam, G., & Peeters, R. (2018). Corporate sustainability performance and assurance on sustainability reports: Diffusion of accounting practices in the realm of sustainable development. *Corporate Social Responsibility and Environmental Management, 25*(2), 164–181.

Caves, R. E. (1996). *Multinational enterprise and economic analysis*. Cambridge University Press.

Chari, A., Ouimet, P. P., & Tesar, L. L. (2010). The value of control in emerging markets. *Review of Financial Studies, 23*(4), 1741–1770.

Chollet, P., & Sandwidi, B. W. (2018). CSR engagement and financial risk: A virtuous circle? International evidence. *Global Finance Journal, 38*, 65–81.

Clacher, I., & Hagendorff, J. (2012). Do announcements about corporate social responsibility create or destroy shareholder wealth? Evidence from the UK. *Journal of Business Ethics, 106*(3), 253–266.

Contractor, F. J., Kundu, S. K., & Hsu, C.-C. (2003). A three-stage theory of international expansion: The link between multinationality and performance in the service sector. *Journal of International Business Studies, 33*(1), 48–60.

Deegan, C. (2002). The legitimising effect of social and environmental disclosures–a theoretical foundation. *Accounting, Auditing & Accountability Journal, 15*(3), 282–311.

Deegan, C. (2006). Legitimacy theory. In Z. Hoque (Ed.), *Methodological issues in accounting research: Theories, methods and issues* (pp. 161–181). Spiramus Press.

Delios, A., & Henisz, W. J. (2000). Japanese Firms' Investment strategies in emerging economies. *Academy of Management Journal, 43*(3), 305–323. https://doi.org/10.2307/1556397

Deng, X., Kang, J., & Low, B. S. (2013). Corporate social responsibility and stakeholder value maximization: Evidence from mergers. *Journal of Financial Economics, 110*(1), 87–109.

Denis, D. J., Denis, D. K., & Yost, K. (2002). Global diversification, industrial diversification, and firm value. *The Journal of Finance, 57*(5), 1951–1979.

Dorfleitner, G., Halbritter, G., & Nguyen, M. (2015). Measuring the level and risk of corporate responsibility – An empirical comparison of different ESG rating approaches. *Journal of Asset Management, 16*(7), 17.

Doukas, J., & Travlos, N. G. (1988). The effect of corporate multinationalism on Shareholders' wealth: Evidence from international acquisitions. *The Journal of Finance, 43*(5), 1161–1175.

Dunning, J. H. (1998). Location and the multinational Enterprise: A neglected factor? *Journal of International Business Studies, 29*(1), 45–66. https://doi.org/10.2307/155587

Edmans, A. (2011). Does the stock market fully value intangibles? Employee satisfaction and equity prices. *Journal of Financial Economics, 101*(3), 621–640.

Ellis, J. A., Moeller, S. B., Schlingemann, F. P., & Stulz, R. M. (2017). Portable country governance and cross-border acquisitions. *Journal of International Business Studies, 48*(2), 148–173. https://doi.org/10.1057/s41267-016-0029-9

Flammer, C. (2013). Corporate social responsibility and shareholder reaction: The environmental awareness of investors. *Academy of Management Journal, 56*(3), 758–781.

Flammer, C. (2015). Does corporate social responsibility Lead to superior financial performance? A regression discontinuity approach. *Management Science, 61*(11), 2549–2568.

Freeman, R. E., Wicks, A. C., & Parmar, B. (2004). Stakeholder theory and "the corporate objective revisited". *Organization Science, 15*(3), 364–369.

Gardberg, N. A., & Fombrun, C. J. (2006). Corporate citizenship: Creating intangible assets across institutional environments. *Academy of Management Review, 31*(2), 329–346.

Godfrey, P. C. (2005). The relationship between corporate philanthropy and shareholder wealth: A risk management perspective. *Academy of Management Review, 30*(4), 777–798.

Godfrey, P. C., Merrill, C. B., & Hansen, J. M. (2009). The relationship between corporate social responsibility and shareholder value: An empirical test of the risk management hypothesis. *Strategic Management Journal, 30*(4), 425–445.

Gubbi, R., Sathyajit, S. P., Aulakh, S. R., Sarkar, B. M., & Chittoor, R. (2010). Do international acquisitions by emerging-economy firms create shareholder value? The case of Indian firms. *Journal of International Business Studies, 41*(3), 397–418. https://doi.org/10.1057/jibs.2009.47

Hill, R. C., Griffiths, W. E., & Lim, G. C. (2018). *Principles of econometrics*. Wiley.

Hong, H. G., Kubik, J. D., & Scheinkman, J. (2012). Financial constraints on corporate goodness. In *SSRN*. https://ssrn.com/abstract=1734164

Hull, J. C. (2012). *Options, futures, and other derivatives*. Pearson.

Husted, B. W. (2005). Risk management, real options, corporate social responsibility. *Journal of Business Ethics, 60*(2), 175–183.

Hymer, S. H. (1976). *The international operations of national firms: A study of direct foreign investment* (p. 1960). MIT Press. Original edition.

Ince, O. S., & Burt Porter, R. (2006). Individual equity return data from Thomson Datastream: Handle with care! *Journal of Financial Research, 29*(4), 463–479.

Jo, H., & Na, H. (2012). Does CSR reduce firm risk? Evidence from controversial industry sectors. *Journal of Business Ethics, 110*(4), 441–456.

Kim, W. C., Hwang, P., & Burgers, W. P. (1993). Multinationals' diversification and the risk-return trade-off. *Strategic Management Journal, 14*(4), 275–286.

Krüger, P. (2015). Corporate goodness and shareholder wealth. *Journal of Financial Economics, 115*(2), 304–329.

Kytle, B. & Ruggie, J. G.. (2005). *Corporate social responsibility as risk management: A model for multinationals*. Harvard University Corporate Social Responsibility Initiative Working Papers, No. 10, Cambridge, MA.

Lertwachara, K., & Cochran, J. J. (2007). An event study of the economic impact of professional sport franchises on local US economies. *Journal of Sports Economics, 8*(3), 244–254.

Limkriangkrai, M., Koh, S. K., & Durand, R. B. (2017). Environmental, social, and governance (ESG) profiles, stock returns, and financial policy: Australian evidence. *International Review of Finance, 17*(3), 461–471.

Liu, M., Marshall, A. P., & McColgan, P. (2020). Corporate social responsibility, foreign direct investment, and shareholder value. In *SSRN*. https://ssrn.com/abstract=3576213

Lu, J. W., & Beamish, P. W. (2004). International diversification and firm performance: The S-curve hypothesis. *The Academy of Management Journal, 47*(4), 598–609.

Malkiel, B. G. (2003). The efficient market hypothesis and its critics. *Journal of Economic Perspectives, 17*(1), 59–82.

Marsat, S., & Williams, B. (2013). CSR and market valuation: International evidence. *Bankers, Markets & Investors, 123*, 29–42.

McGuire, J. B., Sundgren, A., & Schneeweis, T. (1988). Corporate social responsibility and firm financial performance. *Academy of Management Journal, 31*(4), 854–872.

Miralles-Quirós, M. M., Miralles-Quirós, J. L. V. G., & Miguel, L. (2018). The value relevance of environmental, social, and governance performance: The Brazilian case. *Sustainability, 10*(3), 574.

Morck, R., & Yeung, B. (1992). Internalization: An event study test. *Journal of International Economics, 33*(1-2), 41–56.

Oikonomou, I., Brooks, C., & Pavelin, S. (2012). The impact of corporate social performance on financial risk and utility: A longitudinal analysis. *Financial Management, 41*(2), 483–515.

Orlitzky, M., & Benjamin, J. D. (2001). Corporate social performance and firm risk: A meta-analytic review. *Business & Society, 40*(4), 369–396.

Qiu, Y., Shaukat, A., & Tharyan, R. (2016). Environmental and social disclosures: Link with corporate financial performance. *The British Accounting Review, 48*(1), 102–116.

Rapp, M. S., Schellong, D., Schmidt, M., & Wolff, M. (2011). Considering the shareholder perspective: Value-based management systems and stock market performance. *Review of Managerial Science, 5*(2), 171–194. https://doi.org/10.1007/s11846-010-0056-z

Salama, A., Anderson, K., & Toms, J. S. (2011). Does community and environmental responsibility affect firm risk? Evidence from UK panel data 1994–2006. *Business Ethics: A European Review, 20*(2), 192–204.

Schnietz, K. E., & Epstein, M. J. (2005). Exploring the financial value of a reputation for corporate social responsibility during a crisis. *Corporate Reputation Review, 7*(4), 327–345.

Servaes, H., & Tamayo, A. (2013). The impact of corporate social responsibility on firm value: The role of customer awareness. *Management Science, 59*(5), 1045–1061.

Stoker, J. I., Garretsen, H., & Soudis, D. (2019). Tightening the leash after a threat: A multi-level event study on leadership behavior following the financial crisis. *The Leadership Quarterly, 30*(2), 199–214.

Waddock, S. A., & Graves, S. B. (1997). The corporate social performance – Financial performance link. *Strategic Management Journal, 18*(4), 303–319.

Zaheer, S. (1995). Overcoming the liability of foreignness. *Academy of Management Journal, 38*(2), 341–363. https://doi.org/10.2307/256683

Chapter 44
The Impact of Housing Market Policy on House Prices in China

Mei Liu and Qing-Ping Ma

Abstract The phenomenal growth of the housing industry in China has been accompanied by the rapid rise in house prices in the past two decades. Governments at different levels have issued various housing policies to moderate the house price increase and prevent bubbles in the housing market. This study investigates whether and how housing market policies influence house prices as policymakers intend, using monthly time-series data of house prices, policy variables, and control variables between 2004 and 2022. The policy variables include monetary, land, tax, and down payment-related policies. The regression analysis shows that suppressive housing market policies have a significant negative impact on house prices; suppressive monetary, land, and tax-related policies also individually have a significant negative impact on house prices. There are several delays between the implementation of a housing market policy and the appearance of a significant impact. The time trend represents the expectation of continuing house price increases in the past two decades and appears to be the most crucial driver. The present findings indicate that housing market policy tools have significant impacts on house prices and can be effectively used to prevent bubbles in the housing market in China.

Keywords House price · Time trend · Monetary policy · Land price · Tax policy · Down payment

---

M. Liu (✉)
Department of International Economics and Trade, NingboTech University, Ningbo, Zhejiang, China

Q.-P. Ma
Department of Finance, Accounting and Economics, Nottingham University Business School China, The University of Nottingham Ningbo China, Ningbo, Zhejiang, China
e-mail: qing-ping.ma@nottingham.edu.cn

© The Author(s), under exclusive license to Springer Nature Switzerland AG 2024
N. Tsounis, A. Vlachvei (eds.), *Applied Economic Research and Trends*, Springer Proceedings in Business and Economics,
https://doi.org/10.1007/978-3-031-49105-4_44

44.1 Introduction

Since the urban housing system reform in 1998, which abolished welfare housing distribution and encouraged people to become homeowners, the housing industry has gradually become one of the most critical sectors in China's economy. It accounts for around one-sixth of China's GDP, one-quarter of total fixed asset investment, 14% of total urban employment, and approximately 20% of bank loans in the past decade, becoming one of the main drivers of China's economic growth (International Monetary Fund, 2014). China's housing industry has successfully addressed the severe housing shortage that triggered housing reform. By 2018, China's per capita living space for urban citizens reached 39 square meters, exceeding that of many developed countries (National Bureau of Statistics of China, 2019). Accompanying the successful development of the Chinese housing industry is the rapid increase in house prices; China's average house price has quadrupled between 2000 and 2018. With the rapid price increase, real estate companies had been the most profitable before the current downturn. Many large companies that have operated successfully in other industries moved into the housing industry because of the enormous profits. The phenomenal increase in house prices in China has attracted many researchers to investigate the causes of this price increase, the determinants of house prices in China, and whether price bubbles exist in China's housing market, given the continuous price appreciation (e.g., Ahuja et al., 2010; Dreger & Zhang, 2013).

Land price is one determinant of house prices, and its price increase has been an important cause of house price increases. Du et al. (2011) have investigated the relationship between Chinese urban housing and land markets using panel data sets collected from Beijing, Shanghai, Tianjin, and Chongqing and found a long-run equilibrium between them. Unlike most countries, local governments are the ultimate owners of land and the only land suppliers, controlling the quantity, structure, and timing of land supply (Du et al., 2011; Zhang et al., 2013). The rapid development of the housing industry and the high demand for residential housing have enabled local governments to make land sales a key source of their fiscal revenue. According to Ahuja et al. (2010), land sales accounted for as much as 30% of government revenue in 2009. To enhance transparency and competition on land demand, the central government initiated a market-oriented tender/auction/listing method for developers to acquire land in 2002, which was fully implemented on August 31, 2004, for all land resources. Since the higher the house price, the higher the land price, and the higher the fiscal revenue of local governments from land sales, local governments have a strong incentive to support a booming housing market in their jurisdiction and encourage state-owned enterprises (SOEs) to bid for land for housing development (Luo et al., 2022). With their financial strength and fund-raising ability, the participation of SOEs raises the overall land price in the market and house prices dramatically (Wen & Goodman, 2013; Du et al., 2011).

Many researchers try to explain China's house prices with economic fundamentals. Hu et al. (2006) show that economic fundamentals, such as personal income growth and interest rate changes, drive house prices in China. Li and Chand (2013) also demonstrate that income level is one of the primary determinants of house prices. Li and Chand (2013) have examined annual data from 29 provinces from 1998 to 2009 and shown that incomes, construction costs, impending marriages, user costs, and land prices are the primary determinants of house prices. Wu et al. (2015) show that factors from the demand side, such as amenities, income, and the user cost of housing capital, have been pulling up house prices. Wang et al. (2017) also show that the proportion of renters, floating population, wage level, land cost, the housing market, and city service level positively affect house prices. However, Yu (2010) finds that house prices have deviated from economic fundamentals since the government started macrocontrol of the real estate market. There is no stable relationship between house prices and economic fundamentals in China.

Multiple factors influence house prices, and many of them are often colinear, which may make their impact insignificant in a regression analysis. Liu and Ma (2021) have investigated the impacts of 30 macroeconomic and social variables, from both the supply and demand sides, on house prices in 31 municipalities, provinces, and autonomous regions in China from 2000 to 2018. They find that land prices, loans of real estate developers, per capita savings, and the proportion of people with a college or above educational degree significantly drive house prices. In contrast, the number of unemployed people have a significant negative impact. The impact of other variables is insignificant because they are colinear with other variables or do not influence house prices. Zhang et al. (2012) examine the impact of 16 variables on house prices and find that monetary variables, such as mortgage rate, broad money supply, producer price, and real effective exchange rate, primarily determine Chinese house prices. In their study, the real economic variables such as land price, personal disposable income, GDP, imports, exports, and other factors such as the stock index are not independently significant.

A key factor that has driven up house prices in China in the past two decades is the expectation of continuing house price increases. Ma (2010) argues that the main driving force of the soaring house price is people's expectation that house prices will continue to increase, which Wen and Goodman (2013) have similar findings. Bhatt and Kishor (2022) also find that expectations, measured by past house price growth, are associated with house price booms in 18 developed countries. Due to the shortage of investment tools in China and the expectation of continuing house price increases in the past two decades, households tend to devote most of their wealth to housing for consumption and investment. China has the world's highest homeownership rate of 88% (Economist Intelligence Unit, 2011); China's urban residential property market is estimated to be 130 trillion CNY as of the end of 2019 (Lu et al., 2021). Because housing assets now constitute the largest single source of Chinese household wealth, a sharp drop in house prices would significantly damage the real economy. If this happens, China may need many years to recover from the shock, just as other countries have experienced (Malpezzi & Wachter, 2005; Jannsen, 2009).

Since the rapid increase in house prices raises concerns about house price bubbles, whether bubbles exist in the Chinese housing market has been investigated by many researchers at different time points in the past two decades. Ahuja et al. (2010) found that house prices were not significantly overvalued in China during the first half of 2010. Still, there might be bubbles in the mass-market segments of Shanghai and Shenzhen and the luxury segments of Beijing and Nanjing. Wu et al. (2012) and Ren et al. (2012) find no conclusive evidence of a housing bubble in China but raise great concern about the overvaluation of house prices. Using dataset for 35 major Chinese cities from 1998 to 2009, Dreger and Zhang (2013) concluded that there was a bubble that was about 25% higher than the equilibrium value implied by the fundamentals by the end of 2009, and the bubble was huge in the south-eastern coastal cities and special economic zones. Fang et al. (2015) show that the rampant run-up in house prices and speculation present significant challenges to China's economy and regulators. Liu et al. (2017) examine time-series data for the four largest cities in China and find that bubbles drive house prices to stand high. Based on their finding, Liu and Ma (2021) conclude that house prices were not significantly overvalued in China by the end of 2014.

The collapse of debt-laden housing bubbles is the leading cause of many financial crises (Reinhart & Rogoff, 2009), and housing bubbles fueled by credit booms are the most dangerous and costly (Jordà et al., 2015). Monetary policies such as low interest rates and easy credit cause bubbles and bursts (Almeida et al., 2006; Mian & Sufi, 2009), and financial intermediaries contribute to housing bubbles (Cheng et al., 2014). A recent example is the 2007–2009 financial crisis, which some call the Great Recession. The finding by Glaeser et al. (2017) that housing bubbles often occur when government intervention is minimal might argue for government intervention in the property market.

The Chinese government was aware of the risk carried by a credit-fueled housing market boom, and it started intervention soon after the rapid rise of house prices following the issuance of a *Notice on Promoting Sustained and Healthy Development of Real Estate Market* in August 2003 by the State Council, China's central government. The Notice identifies the real estate industry as a pillar of the national economy and advocates commercial housing to replace affordable housing as the mainstay of construction. In October 2004, the People's Bank of China (PBOC), China's central bank, raised deposit and loan interest rates to prevent overheating the economy. In March 2005, PBOC raised housing loan interest rates to slow the pace of house price increases. In the following years, the central and local governments and PBOC have heavily interfered in the housing market through various regulations to control the pace of house price increases, curb speculations, or prevent bubbles. Their policy tools include the rise in the minimum down payment ratio; a cap on the loan-to-value ratio; higher mortgage rates for the second house; taxes on capital gains; and credit rationing for real estate developers, home purchase restriction, etc. Under the house purchase restriction policy, which is decentralized in that cities can decide whether or not to adopt this policy on their own, only investors who have local household registration (hukou) or those with work records in their cities for specific consecutive years are qualified to purchase new homes (Deng et al., 2011). The overall policy objective is to prevent house prices from rising excessively fast rather than preventing house prices from increasing. When there are signs of a decrease in house prices, the government will reverse the suppressive policies to support or stimulate house prices like what happened from October 2008 to May 2009.

Although the determinants of Chinese house prices and whether bubbles exist in China's housing market have been widely researched over the past 20 years, among the various influencing factors, the impact of housing market policy on house prices has been mostly absent from the literature. There are a few studies investigating the effects of the house purchase restriction policy on house prices and sales in the markets of Beijing, Shanghai, and Guangzhou (Sun et al., 2017; Du & Zhang, 2013; Jia et al., 2017), but they all lack a systematic analysis of the impact of the policy. Using detailed city-level quarterly panel data for 2008–2013, Cao et al. (2018) employ the two-step difference-in-differences (DID) approach to systematically analyze the house purchase restriction policy's effect on the housing market and capture heterogeneous market responses to the policy across cities. They discover a temporary decrease in house prices and a sharp plunge in the transaction volume of new homes following the house purchase restriction policy implementation, which is consistent with the policy motivation of curbing speculative demand in the housing market. Lu et al. (2021) use the structural model to analyze the impact of the house purchase restriction policy on house prices in Beijing, Shanghai, Guangzhou, Hangzhou, and Wuhan and find that following the implementation of home purchase restrictions, overall housing demand in most cities becomes weaker and less price elastic. The lack of studies investigating the impact of other policy tools on the housing market is noteworthy, especially at times experiencing colossal uncertainty.

The aim of the present study was to examine whether and how housing market policy tools influence house prices in China as policymakers intend them to do, with monthly data between 2004 and 2022. Here, housing market policy means the measures the Chinese government and central bank take to regulate house prices. Since the trend of house price changes in the past two decades has been increasing, government interventions have been primarily suppressive. The stimulus policies are usually the reversal of the suppressive policies. Therefore, in the present study, we focus on the impact of suppressive policies. We look at four types of policy tools: monetary, land, tax, and down payment-related policies. We also collect data on land prices, loans of real estate developers, per capita income of urban residents, the proportion of people with a college or above educational degree, and the number of unemployed people as control variables. We find that house price suppressive policies generally negatively impact house prices, as predicted by the regression models. House prices have a very significant time trend, which reflects the impact of the expectation of continuing house price increases. It takes several months for the suppressive policies to show their effects on house prices.

This study contributes to the current literature in three aspects. First, we have developed a house price model that incorporates housing market policy tools and time trends into the model, enabling us to examine the impact of housing policies on house prices. The effects of these policy tools have not been well investigated in the previous literature. Second, we have examined the dynamic process of housing policies impacting house prices. The present study finds that it takes several months for a policy decision to show its effects on house prices. Third, this study shows that the time trend, which represents people's expectations of future house prices based on past growth, has a stronger impact than the economic variables that co-determine house prices.

The rest of the chapter is arranged as follows. The next section introduces data and methods used in this study, followed by results in Sect. 44.3. Section 44.4 discusses our findings. Section 44.5 concludes.

44.2 Data and Methods

44.2.1 Data

To perform the empirical analysis, we construct a time-series data file for 2004–2022. Monthly data are retrieved from the National Bureau of Statistics (NBS) and the EPS data platform. The variables we used are:

House Price. House price denotes the nominal average selling price of commercial residential buildings. As the NBS does not monthly report house prices, we use the commercial residential building sales amount divided by sales area to compute the house price.

Housing Policy. We manually collected the housing market-related policies over the past 18 years (206 months) and categorized them into four types: monetary, land, tax, and down payment-related policies. For a given month, if the government issued a policy targeting suppressing the increase in national house prices, we denote the corresponding policy variable as one. Otherwise, it takes a value of 0. We then aggregated the four categorical variables into an overall policy variable. It would take a value of 1 if any individual policies targeting suppressing the house prices were issued that month and zero otherwise. The reason to pool the four price-suppressing policies into one overall policy variable is to examine whether they share a common property in suppressing house price increases. We provide an example of housing market policies that curb house prices in Table 44.1.[1]

The policies are collected from various web sources. The monetary policies are mainly from the PBOC and China Banking Regulatory Commission. The State Council and various departments, including the Ministry of Land and Resources and the National Development and Reform Commission, issue land policies. The tax policies are mainly issued by the State Administration of Taxation and the Ministry of Housing and Urban-Rural Development. The State Council and PBOC mainly issue the down payment policies, but they mainly provide guidelines on the minimum down payment ratio. The local government can improve the down payment ratio if needed.

---

[1] Due to the list of the relevant housing policies is too long, we therefore give examples for each category. The full list is available on request.

Table 44.1 Examples of policies that may curb house price

Variable	Month	Examples
Monetary policy	Oct 2004	The central bank announced an increase in deposit and loan interest rates
	Mar 2005	The central bank raised the interest rate of housing loans
	Apr 2006	The housing loan interest rate was raised again
	Aug 2006	The central bank adjusted the benchmark interest rate of financial institutions' RMB deposits and loans by 0.27 percentage points
	Mar 2007	The central bank raised the benchmark interest rate for deposits and loans
	...	...
Land policy	Mar 2005	The general Office of the State Council issued the document "notice on practically stabilizing house prices." one of the rules is to increase the land supply of ordinary commercial housing and economic housing
	June 2008	The development period of commercial residential buildings should not exceed 3 years
	Jan 2010	Ministry of Land and Resources: For the application of residential land, the proportion of land for affordable housing, low-rent housing, and medium and low price, small- and medium-sized ordinary commercial housing in overall residential land shall not be less than 70%
	...	...
Tax policy	Oct 2005	State Administration of Taxation announced that personal tax shall be paid when individuals buy or sell second-hand houses
	Jul 2006	Personal income tax should be paid for second-hand housing transfers nationwide
	June 2008	State Administration of Taxation: Individual income tax is required for enterprises to purchase real estate for individuals
	May 2009	The Ministry of Finance, the state Administration of Taxation, the National Development and reform commission, and the Ministry of Construction would be responsible for studying the introduction of property tax in 2009
	...	...
Down payment policy	Mar 2005	The down payment ratio of personal housing loans was raised from 20% to 30%
	Sep 2007	The down payment ratio for the second set of housing should not be less than 50%
	Jan 2010	Strictly manage the second set of housing loans, and the down payment shall not be less than 40%
	...	...

We restrict our policy on the state level and consider the influence of state-level housing policies on the overall house prices in China. Local governments' housing policies may also greatly impact house prices. The heterogeneity of local house prices, such as the home purchase restriction policies, has attracted some scholars' attention in recent years (e.g., Cao et al., 2018).

Control Variables: We follow Liu and Ma (2021) and add the following variables as control variables: the proportion of the population with a college or above educational degree (Education), land price in CNY, domestic loan of real estate developers in the unit of 10,000 CNY (Loan), and unemployment population in the unit of 10,000 people (Unemployment), which is a better explanatory variable than the unemployment rate in that empirical study. We also add urban households' per capita disposable income in CNY (Income). These variables have been demonstrated as essential determinants of house price by previous studies (e.g., Shen et al., 2005; Caoet al., 2018; Liu & Ma, 2021).

44.2.2 Method of Estimation

We hypothesize that house price-suppressive policies have negative impacts on house prices and regress house prices on housing policy and other control variables. Since our sample is comprised of monthly data from January 2004 to October 2022 and the augmented Dickey-Fuller unit-root test indicates that house price, land price, education, loan, and income are all trend stationary, we add a time trend in the regression model. Our regression model is shown by Eq. 44.1:

$$\text{Housing Price}_t = \alpha + \beta * \text{POLICY}_t + r * \text{CONTROL}_t + \delta * t + \varepsilon_t \quad (44.1)$$

where Housing Price$_t$ is China's average house price at month t. We have five policy-related variables. We will test them one by one. We will also test the lagging effect of the policies.

44.2.3 Validity and Robustness Tests

Ordinary least squares (OLS) estimation assumes homoscedasticity and no autocorrelation in the error term. Heteroscedasticity is tested by the Breusch-Pagan test and autocorrelation by the Breusch-Godfrey LM test. Nonstationary time series may lead to spurious regression if they are not cointegrated. Stationarity is examined by the augmented Dickey-Fuller unit-root test. Remedial measures will be taken if the above tests reveal any validity problems.

44.3 Results

44.3.1 Summary Statistics

We report the summary statistics of all variables in Table 44.2. Since NBS reports disposable income and unemployment-related data seasonally and demographic

44 The Impact of Housing Market Policy on House Prices in China

Table 44.2 Summary statistics

Variable	N	Mean	St. dev	Min	Max
House price	186	5932.28	2141.59	2581.96	10,448.29
Land price	186	2834.81	1928.18	543.6	8891.90
Loan	186	9146.69	6441.61	694.54	26,675.94
Income	186	6224.85	2769.54	2175.76	11,691.00
Unemployment	186	920.23	68.58	810.00	1160.00
Education	186	0.10	0.03	0.06	0.15
Overall policy	186	0.25	0.44	0	1
Monetary policy	186	0.12	0.32	0	1
Land policy	186	0.12	0.33	0	1
Tax policy	186	0.11	0.31	0	1
Down payment policy	186	0.03	0.16	0	1

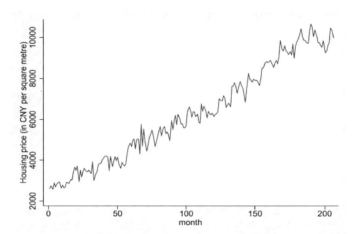

Fig. 44.1 China's average house price between 2004 and 2022. (Data source: National Bureau of Statistics)

data annually, we made a monthly adjustment to three control variables: Income, Unemployment, and Education.

The mean house price is 5932.28 CNY per square meter. The minimum house price was in April 2004, and the maximum was in August 2020. Although there are fluctuations from time to time, the overall house price has an increasing trend over time (as shown in Fig. 44.1). The mean land price is 2834.81 CNY per square meter, which is 47.79% of house price, indicating that land cost is a large component in estimating house prices. Urban residents' per capita disposal income has also increased a lot, from an average of 2175.76 CNY per person in the second quarter of 2004 to 11,691.00 CNY in the first quarter of 2020. Although the admission rate to higher education has increased a lot, the average proportion of people with a college or above educational degree in the population is only 10%.

Regarding housing policies, the government issued administrative orders to curb house price increases over one-fourth of the sample periods. Among the four types of policies, the monetary policy and land policy have the highest frequency (12% of the sample periods), followed by tax policy (11% of the sample periods). The down payment policies were announced much fewer than the other policies. This may be because local governments use this policy more frequently than the central government.

44.3.2 Effects of the Overall Housing Policy on House Prices

The augmented Dickey-Fuller unit-root test indicates that house price, land price, education, loan, and income are all stationary (with drift and time trend) except unemployment. After taking the first difference of unemployment, it becomes stationary. Therefore, we use the first difference of unemployment in the following regression models. Since the Breusch-Godfrey LM test reports the presence of serial correlation of OLS and the Breusch-Pagan test shows the existence of heteroscedasticity, we use Newey-West corrected standard errors. Assuming housing policies may have lagging effects on the house price (depending on whether the policy has been expected), we use both the original policy variable and policy variable lagged by 1–11 months. The results of regressing house prices on aggregate housing policy and other control variables are reported in Table 44.3.

The policy variable does not have a significant impact on house prices (Model 1). We also notice that it is insignificant when lagged by two, three, four, and six months but becomes negatively significant when lagged by five, seven, eight, nine, ten, and eleven months, respectively. This confirms our assumption that housing policies have lagged effects. It may take several months for the public to absorb the complete information and change their decision and actions based on the new information. Since the results of the 12 models presented in Table 44.3 are highly similar (except that Policy variables are lagged by different months), we will use Model 6 as an example for an economic interpretation. L5. Policy has a coefficient of -0.012 ($P < 0.05$), indicating that when the government issues a policy to curb the house price, the house price will decrease by 120CNY per square meter on average 5 months later. Land price is significantly and positively related to the house price across all models ($P < 0.01$). When the land price increases by 1 CNY per square meter, the house price will increase by 0.242 CNY per square meter in Model 6. Loan has significantly negative coefficients across all models ($P < 0.01$). When the loan of estate developers increases by 10,000 CNY, the house price will decrease by 610 CNY per square meter in Model 6. Income has a significantly negative effect on the house price ($P < 0.05$ or $P < 0.1$). When the urban resident's per capita disposable income increases by 1 CNY per person, the house price will decrease by 0.121 CNY per square meter. The time trend variable, Time, is always positive and significant, indicating that house prices will continue to go up as time goes on.

Table 44.3 Regression of house prices on housing policy and other variables

Variables	(1)	(2)	(3)	(4)	(5)	(6)	(7)	(8)	(9)	(10)	(11)	(12)
Land price	0.273***	0.268***	0.267***	0.263***	0.251***	0.242***	0.246***	0.223***	0.216***	0.213***	0.210***	0.202***
	(5.24)	(5.19)	(5.11)	(5.06)	(4.71)	(4.53)	(4.57)	(4.23)	(4.10)	(4.09)	(3.84)	(3.73)
Loan	−0.061***	−0.060***	−0.061***	−0.061***	−0.061***	−0.061***	−0.061***	−0.058***	−0.059***	−0.058***	−0.059***	−0.059***
	(−6.73)	(−6.68)	(−6.78)	(−6.76)	(−6.75)	(−6.61)	(−6.69)	(−6.31)	(−6.33)	(−6.37)	(−6.73)	(−7.23)
Education	−0.507	−0.492	−0.559	−0.616	−0.737	−0.868	−0.873	−1.142*	−1.278*	−1.320*	−1.364*	−1.426**
	(−0.80)	(−0.78)	(−0.87)	(−0.94)	(−1.12)	(−1.32)	(−1.30)	(−1.76)	(−1.94)	(−1.91)	(−1.90)	(−1.98)
Unemployment	−0.000	−0.000	−0.000	−0.000	−0.000	−0.000	−0.000	−0.000	−0.000	−0.000	−0.000	−0.000
	(−0.59)	(−0.59)	(−0.61)	(−0.72)	(−0.71)	(−0.68)	(−0.67)	(−0.51)	(−0.58)	(−0.54)	(−0.72)	(−0.70)
Income	−0.099*	−0.097*	−0.104*	−0.103*	−0.114**	−0.121**	−0.114**	−0.113**	−0.112**	−0.104*	−0.114**	−0.112**
	(−1.79)	(−1.75)	(−1.88)	(−1.85)	(−2.07)	(−2.21)	(−2.04)	(−2.08)	(−2.09)	(−1.92)	(−2.06)	(−2.05)
Time	0.004***	0.004***	0.004***	0.005***	0.005***	0.005***	0.005***	0.005***	0.005***	0.005***	0.005***	0.005***
	(8.40)	(8.36)	(8.35)	(8.22)	(8.53)	(8.85)	(8.47)	(9.06)	(9.22)	(8.78)	(8.57)	(8.46)
Policy	0.006											
	(1.03)											
L1. Policy		0.005										
		(0.81)										
L2. Policy			0.005									
			(0.84)									
L3. Policy				0.003								
				(0.49)								

(continued)

Table 44.3 (continued)

Variables	(1)	(2)	(3)	(4)	(5)	(6)	(7)	(8)	(9)	(10)	(11)	(12)
L4. Policy					−0.004							
					(−0.72)							
L5. Policy						−0.012**						
						(−2.17)						
L6. Policy							−0.001					
							(−0.21)					
L7. Policy								−0.014**				
								(−2.51)				
L8. Policy									−0.016***			
									(−2.65)			
L9. Policy										−0.018***		
										(−3.42)		
L10. Policy											−0.016***	
											(−2.94)	
L11. Policy												−0.017***
												(−3.33)
Constant	0.269***	0.269***	0.272***	0.275***	0.283***	0.293***	0.286***	0.302***	0.307***	0.308***	0.310***	0.312***
	(8.86)	(8.81)	(8.83)	(8.78)	(8.97)	(9.40)	(9.19)	(9.91)	(9.90)	(9.43)	(9.24)	(9.29)
F	662.65	661.86	648.24	635.17	645.67	664.34	639.16	676.05	710.25	667.16	614.53	582.99
Observations	186	186	185	184	183	182	181	180	179	178	177	176

Note: t-statistics in parentheses
***p < 0.01, **p < 0.05, *p < 0.1. Unemployment is in first difference

Since Income and Loan have significant negative impacts, inconsistent with the findings by Liu and Ma (2021), we hypothesize that their significant positive impacts in the previous study are absorbed by Time. Their significant negative influences arise because their existence in the regression model can reduce the regression residuals. Removing Income from the regression models based on this hypothesis has almost no effect on the regression estimates except that Land price becomes weakly significant (P < 0.1) in models 1–4 and insignificant in models 5–12. Further removing Loan from the regression models has almost no influence on the regression estimates except that Land price becomes insignificant in all models. Further removing Unemployment, which is insignificant all along, from the regression models also has almost no influence on the regression estimates (details of the above regression results are not reported here to avoid repetition). As shown in Table 44.4, further removing Land price from the regression models also has almost no influence on the regression estimates except for L4. Policy becomes weakly significant ($P < 0.1$). The results in Table 44.4 show that house prices in China in the past two decades are determined by the expectation of continuing price increases (represented by the time trend) and housing policies. Changes in other variables also reflect this expectation.

44.3.3 *Effects of Monetary Policy on House Prices*

We replace the overall housing policy with monetary policy to test the individual policy effect. Since the results for control variables are highly similar to those of Table 44.3, we do not report them in the remaining regression tables. We also stop reporting insignificant models to reduce repetition. Results are shown in Table 44.5. It shows that when house prices are regressed on monetary policy and other control variables, the policy is negatively significant only when lagging the policy variable by seven-, eight-, nine-, or ten-month periods.

44.3.4 *Effects of Land Policy on House Prices*

When regressing house prices on land policies and other control variables, the land policy has a significant negative effect on the house price when lagged by nine-, ten-, and eleven-month periods (Table 44.6).

44.3.5 *Effects of Tax Policy on House Prices*

When regressing house prices on tax-related policies and other control variables, the tax policy has a significant positive effect on the house price when lagged by

Table 44.4 Regression of house prices on housing policy and time

Variables	(1)	(2)	(3)	(4)	(5)	(6)	(7)	(8)	(9)	(10)	(11)	(12)
Time	0.004***	0.004***	0.004***	0.004***	0.004***	0.004***	0.004***	0.004***	0.004***	0.004***	0.004***	0.004***
	(60.81)	(59.61)	(59.28)	(59.97)	(61.44)	(62.17)	(61.71)	(62.87)	(62.61)	(60.58)	(59.42)	(58.12)
Policy	−0.006											
	(−0.79)											
L1. Policy		−0.002										
		(−0.27)										
L2. Policy			−0.003									
			(−0.48)									
L3. Policy				−0.004								
				(−0.60)								
L4. Policy					−0.010*							
					(−1.69)							
L5. Policy						−0.015**						
						(−2.52)						
L6. Policy							−0.008					
							(−1.29)					
L7. Policy								−0.021***				
								(−3.56)				
L8. Policy									−0.022***			
									(−3.38)			
L9. Policy										−0.023***		
										(−3.91)		
L10. Policy											−0.022***	
											(−3.38)	

											-0.022***
L11.Policy											(−3.34)
Constant	0.227***	0.225***	0.225***	0.224***	0.226***	0.228***	0.224***	0.228***	0.228***	0.229***	0.228***	0.228***
	(32.89)	(30.81)	(30.16)	(30.96)	(32.35)	(34.49)	(33.60)	(35.76)	(35.98)	(33.21)	(32.91)	(31.71)
F	1942	1913	1913	1872	1911	1934	1905	1979	1960	1854	1777	1700
Observations	206	205	204	203	202	201	200	199	198	197	196	195

Note: t-statistics in parentheses
*** p < 0.01, ** p < 0.05, * p < 0.1

Table 44.5 Regression of house prices on monetary policy and other control variables

Variables	(1)	(2)	(3)	(4)
L7. Monetary policy	−0.016**			
	(−2.21)			
L8. Monetary policy		−0.021**		
		(−2.32)		
L9. Monetary policy			−0.022***	
			(−2.86)	
L10. Monetary policy				−0.015**
				(−2.43)
Constant	0.302***	0.310***	0.309***	0.307***
	(10.10)	(10.41)	(9.86)	(9.54)
Control variables	Yes	Yes	Yes	Yes
Time trend	Yes	Yes	Yes	Yes
Observations	180	179	178	177
F	647.4	667.9	641.8	591.1

Note: t-statistics in parentheses
** $p < 0.01$, ** $p < 0.05$, * $p < 0.1$

Table 44.6 Regression of house prices on land policy and other control variables

Variables	(1)	(2)	(3)
L9. Land policy	−0.016**		
	(−2.58)		
L10. Land policy		−0.016**	
		(−2.20)	
L11. Land policy			−0.020***
			(−3.11)
Constant	0.295***	0.295***	0.295***
	(8.89)	(8.77)	(8.58)
Control variables	Yes	Yes	Yes
Time trend	Yes	Yes	Yes
Observations	178	177	176
F	618.0	599.1	590.4

Note: t-statistics in parentheses
**$p < 0.01$, **$p < 0.05$, *$p < 0.1$

1 month (Model 1 of Table 44.7), but a significant negative effect when lagged by nine-, ten-, and eleven-month periods (models 2, 3, and 4 in Table 44.7). The results of Model 1 contradict our prediction. However, this can be explained as a consequence of reversed causality; high house prices lead to the implementation of a tax-increasing policy such that they are significantly correlated even after lagging by one period. It takes time for a suppressive housing policy to impact house prices.

Table 44.7 Regression of house prices on tax policy and other control variables

Variables	(1)	(2)	(3)	(4)
L1. Tax policy	0.013**			
	(2.02)			
L7. Tax policy		−0.017**		
		(−2.23)		
L9. Tax policy			−0.016**	
			(−2.55)	
L11. Tax policy				−0.013**
				(−1.98)
Constant	0.271***	0.291***	0.294***	0.298***
	(9.01)	(8.90)	(8.84)	(8.73)
Control variables	Yes	Yes	Yes	Yes
Time trend	Yes	Yes	Yes	Yes
Observations	186	180	178	176
F	671.5	643.3	617.3	563.9

Note: t-statistics in parentheses
** $p < 0.01$, ** $p < 0.05$, * $p < 0.1$

Table 44.8 Regression of house prices on down payment and other control variables

Variables	(1)
L2. Down payment	0.016*
	(1.90)
Constant	0.273***
	(8.84)
Control variables	Yes
Time trend	Yes
Observations	185
F	657.1

Note: t-statistics in parentheses
** $p < 0.01$, ** $p < 0.05$, * $p < 0.1$

44.3.6 Effects of Down Payment Policy on House Prices

When regressing house prices on down payment policies and other control variables, the down payment policy has a weakly significant and positive effect on house prices when lagged by 2 months (Model 1 of Table 44.8), but no effect on other periods. The result of Model 1 contradicts our prediction. This might also be explained as a consequence of reversed causality; high house prices lead to the implementation of a down payment-increasing policy such that they are significantly correlated even after lagging by two periods.

44.4 Discussion

The present finding that suppressive housing market policies have significant negative impacts on house prices confirms our working hypothesis, indicating that these policies can be effective in controlling house price increases. Therefore, the continuing house price increase in the past two decades is due to neither the government's lack of policy tools nor the ineffectiveness of these policy tools. Instead, it is because the policy objective is to have a sustainable moderate house price increase and local governments' incentive to have a booming housing market that enables more fiscal revenue through land sales (Luo et al., 2022). Moreover, with the highest homeownership rate of 88% in the world (Economist Intelligence Unit, 2011), the political and economic risk of a house price decrease is probably much higher than that of a house price increase; hence, governments at all levels in China have a much higher tolerance to a house price increase than to a house price decrease. In contrast, the central government would respond rapidly to signals of a reduction in house prices. Local governments usually would stop any plans of housing developers who want to promote sales by reducing the price. These policy practices by governments make people believe that house prices would not decrease, something like the "Greenspan put" for the US stock market before the 2007–2008 financial crisis (Miller et al., 2002).

The present study shows a strong time trend in determining house prices. We consider the time trend as a consequence of the persistent expectation of continuing house price increase, which has been the most important driving force of China's booming housing market and the continuing house price increase in the past two decades. This result confirms the earlier findings by Ma (2010). This expectation is probably based on both the past house price changes and a belief in the "Greenspan put"-like policy behavior of governments at all levels in China. The impact of this expectation encompasses the negative impact of one variable and the positive impact of three out of four variables identified by Liu and Ma (2021). The positive effects of land price are also largely absorbed by the time trend, since removing the insignificant or negatively significant variables would make land price insignificant. The robust impact of the time trend on house price is probably partially underlaid by the expectation dependence of the land price and loan to real estate developers, etc. When house prices are expected to increase, the land price will also be bid up; developers will borrow more, and banks will be willing to lend more.

The time trend represents the expectation of continuing house price increases, which is likely to include the expectation of inflation as a component. Although Kuang and Liu (2015) show that inflation has a significant positive impact on house prices in 35 major cities in China, the house price index increased much faster than inflation in the period investigated. Liu and Ma (2021) find that when the proportion of the population with a college or above educational degree (Education), land price, domestic loan of real estate developers (Loan), and unemployment population are included as explanatory variables, inflation has no significant impact on house prices. Therefore, the expectation of continuing house price increases is not equal to the expectation of inflation, and the time trend of house prices during the past decades is not a manifestation of inflation.

In the present study, not only the housing market policy as a whole but also three out of the four policy types individually have significant impacts on house prices, suggesting that these three policy tools are individually effective and might be effectively used on their own. It is unclear why an increase in down payments does not significantly impact house prices. One possibility is that the study has not included sufficient observations in terms of the down payment policy. Another possibility is that the increase in the required down payment is not large enough to have a significant impact. In this study, the policy variables are treated as dummies, which cannot reflect the quantitative aspect of housing market policy. All these four policy tools are quantitative, and their impacts depend on the size of the change. A small increase in the down payment percentage may have no significant impact. Furthermore, different policies may have different scales of impact. Aggregating different policies and integrating them into a dummy variable may ignore their individual effects. The quantitative relationship between the value of a policy tool and house prices may also be worth investigating.

The present findings demonstrate the importance of using dynamic models, especially in evaluating the effects of policy shocks. When a policy is announced, it takes time to have its full impact. In the present study, it takes 9 months (lags) for a land policy to become significant in its impact, and it takes 7 months (lags) for monetary policies and tax policies to become significant in their intended effects. If we only examined the contemporary impacts, we would not find the right impacts of these policies; or worse, we might discover a wrong impact in the opposite direction. In dynamic models, we also need to choose the suitable duration of one period in the time series. In our pilot study, we tested yearly data and failed to identify significant impacts of these policies because yearly data lack a sufficient temporal resolution.

The present results also demonstrate the need to be aware of endogeneity and reverse causality issues in evaluating the impacts of a policy. Since stimulus policies tend to be implemented when the targeted indicator is low and suppressive policies tend to be executed when the targeted indicator is high, if we regress the targeted indicator on the contemporary suppressive policy variable, the most likely outcome is a positive impact. This might be what happened with the tax policy, which has a significant positive effect on house prices when lagged by one period. In contrast, it has a significant negative impact when lagged by seven periods.

In recent years, the impacts of the house purchase restriction policy have attracted the attention of many researchers. Cao et al. (2018) find that the policy has a limited impact on house prices but a pronounced effect in reducing trading volume; the duration of the policy's impact is short-lived, averaging four quarters. Lu et al. (2021) report that the house purchase restriction policy makes the housing demand in most cities weaker. We have not studied the house purchase restriction policy. The policies we have investigated in this paper focus only on the state level. The house purchase restriction policy is decentralized; whether it will be implemented is decided by local governments based on their local conditions (Deng et al., 2011).

Since local governments have also issued other policies to suppress or promote their local housing markets, which sometimes may play a larger role than a state-level policy in their local markets, these policies are not included in the current study. A complete understanding of the impacts of government policies requires research on both the state and local levels.

Our present findings have important policy implications. Firstly, policy tools such as monetary, land, and tax policies are significant in negatively impacting house prices; therefore, governments and the central bank can use these tools to effectively prevent bubbles in the housing market in China. Secondly, the time trend or the expectation of continuing price increases is the most important driver of the house price increases; to prevent bubbles in the housing market, the most effective approach is to manage expectations of future house prices, and governments should act early to avoid an overoptimistic expectation in society. Thirdly, there is a delay between the implementation of a policy and its maximum impact; governments need to carefully choose the timing of a new policy to avoid implementing a massive suppressive policy when the rise has reached its maximum or an enormous stimulus policy when the decline has reached its bottom.

44.5 Conclusions

The present study finds that suppressive housing policies significantly negatively impact house prices in China. Among the four types of housing market policy investigated, monetary, land, and tax policies all individually have a significant negative impact on house prices. Therefore, housing market policy tools have significant impacts on house prices and can be used to prevent bubbles in the housing market. There is a several-period delay between the implementation of a policy and appearance of significant impacts; so, policy implementation needs to have the right timing. There is a strong time trend in the determination of house prices in China, which reflects the expectation of continuing house price increases in the past two decades. The time trend encompasses the impacts of most economic and social variables that may contribute to the determination of house prices in China and might exert its influence through time-dependent changes in those economic and social variables.

References

Ahuja, A., Cheung, L., Han, G., Porter, N., & Zhang, W.. (2010). *Are house prices rising too fast in China?* IMF working papers (pp. 1–31).

Almeida, H., Campello, M., & Liu, C. (2006). The financial accelerator: Evidence from international housing markets. *Review of Finance, 10*(3), 1–32.

Bhatt, V., & Kundan Kishor, N. (2022). Role of credit and expectations in house price dynamics. *Finance Research Letters, 50*, 103203.

Cao, X., Huang, B., & Lai, R. N. (2018). *The impact of exogenous demand shock on the housing market: Evidence from the home purchase restriction policy in the People's Republic of China.* ADBI Working Paper.

Cheng, I.-H., Raina, S., & Xiong, W. (2014). Wall street and the housing bubble. *American Economic Review, 104*(9), 2797–2829.

Deng, L., Shen, Q., & Wang, L. (2011). The emerging housing policy framework in China. *Journal of Planning Literature, 26*(2), 168–183.

Dreger, C., & Zhang, Y. (2013). Is there a bubble in the Chinese housing market? *Urban Policy and Research, 31*(1), 27–39.

Du, H., Ma, Y., & An, Y. (2011). The impact of land policy on the relation between housing and land prices: Evidence from China. *The Quarterly Review of Economics and Finance, 51*(1), 19–27.

Economist Intelligence Unit. (2011). *Building Rome in a day: The sustainability of China's housing Boom.*

Fang, H., Quanlin, G., Xiong, W., & Zhou, L.-A. (2015). Demystifying the Chinese housing boom. *NBER Macroeconomics Annual, 30*(1), 105–166.

Glaeser, E. L., Huang, W., Ma, Y., & Shleifer, A. (2017). A real estate boom with Chinese characteristics. *Journal of Economic Perspectives, 31*(1), 93–116.

Hu, J., Liangjun, S., & Jiang, W. (2006). The rise in house prices in China: Bubbles or fundamentals? *Economics Bulletin, 3*(7), 1–8.

International Monetary Fund. (2014). *Country report no. 14/235—People's Republic of China: 2014.* International Monetary Fund.

Nils, J. (2009). *National and international business cycle effects of housing crises.* Kiel working paper.

Jia, S., Wang, Y., & Fan, G.-Z. (2017). Home-Purchase Limits and Housing Prices: Evidence from China. *The Journal of Real Estate Finance and Economics, 56*, 386.

Jordà, Ò., Schularick, M., & Taylor, A. M. (2015). Leveraged Bubbles. *Journal of Monetary Economics, 76*(Supplement), S1–S20.

Kuang, W., & Liu, P. (2015). Inflation and house prices: Theory and evidence from 35 major cities in China. *International Real Estate Review, 18*(1), 217–240.

Li, Q., & Chand, S. (2013). House prices and market fundamentals in urban China. *Habitat International, 40*, 148–153.

Liu, M., & Ma, Q.-P. (2021). Determinants of house prices in China: A panel corrected regression approach. *The Annals of Regional Science, 67*, 47–72. https://doi.org/10.1007/s00168-020-01040-z

Liu, R., Hui, E. C.-m., Lv, J., & Chen, Y. (2017). What drives housing markets: Fundamentals or bubbles? *The Journal of Real Estate Finance and Economics, 55*(4), 395–415. https://doi.org/10.1007/s11146-016-9565-0

Lu, Z., Zhang, S., & Hong, J. (2021). "Title." Staff Working Paper, Ottawa.

Luo, Y., Wang, X., & Wang, L. (2022). The influence of China's local fiscal revenue targets on house Price growth. *Housing Policy Debate, 33*(3), 699–723. https://doi.org/10.1080/10511482.2021.2010117

Ma, Q.-P. (2010). Housing market in China's growth recovery and house price determination. In *21st CEA (UK) and 2nd CEA (Europe) Annual Conference Global Economic Recovery: The Role of China and Other Emerging Economies.* IEEE.

Malpezzi, S., & Wachter, S. (2005). The role of speculation in real estate cycles. *Journal of Real Estate Literature, 13*(2), 141–164.

Mian, A., & Sufi, A. (2009). The consequences of mortgage credit expansion: Evidence from the US mortgage default crisis. *The Quarterly Journal of Economics, 124*(4), 1449–1496.

Miller, M., Weller, P., & Zhang, L. (2002). Moral hazard and the US stock market: Analysing the "Greenspan put". *The Economic Journal, 112*(March), C178–C186.

National Bureau of Statistics of China. (2019). *Sustained and rapid development of construction industry and significant improvement of Urban and rural appearance – Report No. 10 on economic and social development achievements for the 70th anniversary of the founding of new China.* National Bureau of Statistics of China.

Reinhart, C. M., & Rogoff, K. (2009). *This time is different: Eight centuries of financial folly.* Princeton University Press.

Ren, Y., Xiong, C., & Yuan, Y. (2012). House Price bubbles in China. *China Economic Review, 23*(4), 786–800.

Shen, Y., Hui, E. C.-m., & Liu, H. (2005). Housing price bubbles in Beijing and Shanghai. *Management Decision, 43*(4), 611–627.

Sun, W., Zheng, S., Geltner, D., & Wang, R. (2017). The housing market effects of local home purchase restrictions: Evidence from Beijing. *Journal of Real Estate Finance and Economics, 55*(3), 288–312.

Wang, Y., Wang, S., Li, G., Zhang, H., Jin, L., Yongxian, S., & Kangmin, W. (2017). Identifying the determinants of housing prices in China using spatial regression and the geographical detector technique. *Applied Geography, 79*, 26–36. https://doi.org/10.1016/j.apgeog.2016.12.003

Wen, H., & Goodman, A. C. (2013). Relationship between urban land price and housing price: Evidence from 21 provincial capitals in China. *Habitat International, 40*, 9–17. https://doi.org/10.1016/j.habitatint.2013.01.004

Wu, J., Gyourko, J., & Deng, Y. (2012). Evaluating conditions in major Chinese housing markets. *Regional Science and Urban Economics, 42*(3), 531–543.

Wu, G. L., Feng, Q., & Li, P. (2015). Does local governments' budget deficit push up housing prices in China? *China Economic Review, 35*, 183–196. https://doi.org/10.1016/j.chieco.2014.08.007

Yu, H. (2010). China's house price: Affected by economic fundamentals or real estate policy? *Frontiers of Economics in China, 5*(1), 25–51.

Zhang, Y., Hua, X., & Zhao, L. (2012). Exploring determinants of housing prices: A case study of Chinese experience in 1999–2010. *Economic Modelling, 29*(6), 2349–2361.

Zhang, D., Cheng, W., & Ng, Y.-K. (2013). Increasing returns, land use controls and housing prices in China. *Economic Modelling, 31*, 789–795. https://doi.org/10.1016/j.econmod.2013.01.034

Chapter 45
Changes in the Use of Employee Training Methods in Slovakia in the Context of the COVID-19 Pandemic: A Quantitative and Qualitative Perspective

Jozef Ďurian, Lukas Smerek, and Ivana Simockova

Abstract Human resources-related costs are the issue of cost cutting in any crisis. Especially the costs of employees' training and development are the subject of effectivity improvement decision of a company. The reaction of companies to the pandemic situation in employee training and development is the focus of the study. The aim of this study was to identify methods that were used in employee education before and after the COVID-19 pandemic. We assume that companies took action to be effective in training and development even under the pandemic impact. The study is based on a comparison of data between 2018 and 2023. According to sample conformity, we identify the differences in primary data gathered by questionnaire. Survey results proved that the number of enterprises implementing training increased after the pandemic. This is a positive reaction to the pandemic challenge with a strong impact on employees' overall performance and satisfaction. We discovered that there were no changes in the order of use of these methods over the examined years. The same online learning methods (self-learning, e-learning, and video recordings) were used most frequently in both 2018 and 2023. Also, the use of the most frequent offline learning methods in Slovak companies is lower after the pandemic than before the pandemic.

Keywords Employee training and development · Online training · Offline training · Training methods · COVID pandemic impact

J. Ďurian (✉) · L. Smerek · I. Simockova
Department of Corporate Economics and Management, Matej Bel University, Bystrica, Slovakia
e-mail: jozef.durian@umb.sk

© The Author(s), under exclusive license to Springer Nature Switzerland AG 2024
N. Tsounis, A. Vlachvei (eds.), *Applied Economic Research and Trends*, Springer Proceedings in Business and Economics,
https://doi.org/10.1007/978-3-031-49105-4_45

45.1 Introduction

The importance of employee training in human resource (HR) management is unquestionable. The focus of this HR process is on the person, the result of his/her activity, potential, and the added value he or she can bring. According to several authors (Savov & Skočdopole, 2019; Hitka et al., 2021; Kucharčíková et al., 2023), it is clear that human capital, or human resource management itself, can be considered as a competitive advantage of a company. The level of human capital can be raised, whether through formal education or various forms of education and training at the workplace (Cárachová, 2019). For this reason, every employer should pay attention to their employees, support them, and enable them to develop their potential. As Dachner et al. (2021) stated, it is necessary that individuals are motivated to learn and that the company provides the necessary resources to enable them to do so.

The last few years have been marked by COVID-19, which has greatly affected the functioning of the entire world. It has affected all areas and activities including employee training. Firstly, in addition to other methods of education, the actual meeting of employees in the workplace during working hours or work meetings has been significantly impacted by COVID-19. For jobs that allowed home-office employees started to work directly from their homes. Individual conferences and meetings also moved online and were conducted through various platforms such as MS Teams or Zoom. Since this era lasted for an extended period of time, virtual teams of staff members eventually began to emerge, which had both benefits and drawbacks. For example, virtual teams had the advantage of bringing together employees from different countries who may never have met before. However, disadvantages included the various time zones, which made it challenging to communicate with all personnel at a predetermined time, the absence of personal contact and maintaining relationships.

45.2 Employee Training and Development

Employee adaptation, which comes before training, and talent management, which emphasizes the promotion of human potential and its proper management, are two activities found in human resource management that come after the development of people and the promotion of their potential. This is because, in the modern business world, it is the talented individuals who create the competitive advantage of the company through their activities and can make substantial changes (Savov & Skočdopole, 2019). This whole sequence of activities starts when the person first begins working, since they have to go through numerous parts of training as required by various regulations and laws. As stated by Katanikova et al. (2019) and Malik (2022), in addition to focusing on the development of skills related to job tasks, it is crucial to identify, but most importantly to be able to retain talented employees in the company. By supporting talented employees and developing their potential, individuals are able to contribute to increasing the value of the company and improving various work processes or generating ideas, which in turn leads to increased competitiveness of the company as a whole. This means that having the right human capital is imperative if a company wants to succeed in a competitive environment (Alruwaili, 2018). With regard to retaining not only talented but all employees, a company must consider their needs and provide an environment in which those demands are met. However, a large group of employees cannot be influenced by various forms of compensation or the accomplishment of organizational objectives because their aim is to learn and grow because they want to, i.e., for their benefit (Vnoučková, 2013). Support in this context is mainly understood as the provision of continuous learning or the opportunity to acquire new skills and knowledge.

Employee training is part of the human resource management system, as one of the many activities found in any company and is essential to its existence. Training is an activity to improve the ability and improve performance of employees or members in carrying out their duties by increasing skills, knowledge, abilities, attitudes, and behaviors related to work (McCrie & Lee, 2022). Every training attended by employees raises the existence of good performance by employees who take part in the training because employees get the skills, abilities, and knowledge of their needs to carry out their work (Rivaldo & Nabella, 2023). Each training activity that an employee completes should be translated in the workplace into a specific output that has some added value to the company, for example, in the form of increased labor productivity, improved workflow or increased profitability of the company.

Taking into account the time factor, according to several authors (Kravčáková & Bernátová, 2020; Suleimanová et al., 2019), it is evident that educational activities are time-bound, meaning that they begin at one time and cease at another. We tend to agree with this viewpoint since learning focuses on improving an employee's effectiveness in their current role. However, it is essential for the further development of employees, which is future-oriented and prepares the employee for more complex and demanding tasks, also taking into consideration his or her personal growth. The main difference between training and employee development was also pointed out by Suleimanová et al. (2019), who believed that training focuses on employees with unsatisfactory job performance in the positions they currently hold, while development focuses its attention on employees who perform above standard job performance. Among others, Yusuf et al. (2022) argued that employee development should also focus more on future advancement than only the current needs of the company or its employees. This implies that while development is long term, employee training is short term in nature. Employee training is a form of lifelong learning that allows each person to supplement, broaden, and deepen the knowledge already obtained and also retrain or pursue their hobbies. At the same time, continuous human resources development is key to achieving not only corporate but also country economic and social development goals and objectives (Fernando, 2015).

Table 45.1 Methods of training and development of employees

On-the-job methods	Off-the-job methods
Instructing	Lectures
Coaching	Seminars
Mentoring	Case studies
Counselling	Workshops
Assisting	Brainstorming
Task assignment	Simulations
Cross-training program	Role-playing
Work meetings	Diagnostic training programs
Demonstrating	E-learning
Shadowing	Self-studies
Consulting	Development centers
Job rotation	Video recordings
	Serious games

45.2.1 Methods of Employee Training

Certain methods need to be used in the implementation of employee training. These should be appropriately chosen individually for each employee, taking into account the nature of the work he or she is or will be doing, as well as his or her existing skills and abilities. According to several authors (Vaverčáková & Hromková, 2018; Huang, 2020; Hebron, 2020), employee training methods are divided into two basic groups, namely on-the-job methods and off-the-job methods, with the individual methods from these groups clearly demonstrated in Table 45.1.

In the case of off-the-job methods, employees do not have to be physically present at the workplace but can be located in other areas, which has the advantage of eliminating factors such as stress, frustration or the hustle of everyday work. The main disadvantage of these methods is that the focus is more on the transfer of theoretical knowledge and erases contact with various tools or aids that could be part of the work process and will be used by the employee in the performance of his/her work. The second group of methods is used directly in the workplace, allowing employees to produce real outputs directly in the performance of their work. These methods allow the use of existing work tools, aids, or other equipment that the employee will realistically handle in the future, which will greatly facilitate the employee's work (Vasanthi & Basariya, 2019).

45.2.2 The Impact of COVID-19 on Employee Learning and Development

The COVID-19 pandemic has presented a significant challenge for managers working in various industries to think about incorporating new management techniques and technology tools in this unstable and changing world. Dvouletý (2021) argued that there may not have been a significant decline in business activity after the end of 2020. On the contrary, this research suggests that activity has increased to a higher level than in 2019. However, human resource management practices, including management itself, are other activities in a company that were affected by COVID-19 (Stachova et al., 2020; Tomcikova et al., 2021). Remote work, creating virtual teams, and knowledge management are some of the many practices that most companies adopt as concepts to keep companies running smoothly (Carnevale & Hatak, 2020). A major change is the popularization of e-learning as a training method and the growing interest in personalized lectures, courses, and modules. The demand for e-learning is also reported by companies that have never used it before (Mikołajczyk, 2021). According to Blanár (2021), most companies have responded to the corona crisis by changing education from face-to-face to distance learning, i.e., the aforementioned e-learning. Similarly, Ribbers and Waring (2015) argued that in a rapidly changing world, Internet connectivity is a necessary development for any trainer, mentor or instructor. In addition, Rahmadi et al. (2021) argued that transferring the aforementioned methods to the online space is one of the solutions during the COVID-19 pandemic. However, on the other hand, not all companies were able to implement online teaching courses or training. According to Tomcikova (2021), those companies that could not afford to switch to online training programs were forced to either reduce the number of training programs or not implement the training at all. All other missing training and development methods can be replaced by self-study as employees are not receiving enough support from companies. Intrinsic motivation plays a key role in this.

Other mechanisms that have been affected by the pandemic include coaching, mentoring, and job instruction training, which are classified as methods at work. Due to the need for personal contact between the employee being educated and the person educating them and the fact that employees have not been able to stay in the workplace, there has been a slight decline in the use of these methods (Smerek, 2022). Despite this, most methods have been moved to the online space. However, the quality of education through the aforementioned methods was lower compared to the implementation of educational activities in a face-to-face form, if only because of the lack of personal contact, technical equipment, etc. For instance, taking coaching interviews as an example of these methods, although they could have been conducted online, they also faced a number of obstacles, including poor technical equipment, a slow Internet connection, and many more. Furthermore, on-the-job coaching loses its relevance to an even greater extent in this case.

On the other hand, there are plenty of people who are much more comfortable in a home-office environment. Even though the days of lockdowns and forbidden mass gatherings are gone, most businesses have not backed away from the option of working remotely from home. Mikołajczyk (2021) argued that video conferences, online meetings, training sessions or webinars conducted in an online space will now become a regular part of our lives. For this reason, it is necessary to find ways to efficiently implement the above activities and make the most of them in the field of competitive advantage. First of all, one of the factors that can positively influence the level of online learning is the accessibility to all employees individually, regardless of where they are or the time in which they want to carry out a certain learning activity (Thilagaraj & Rengaraj, 2021). Therefore, employees will not be forced to disrupt their personal or work schedules but will participate in the training or other learning activities when it is most convenient for them.

45.3 Research Methodology

The aim of this study is to identify which of the methods in employee education were used before and after the COVID-19 pandemic. We assume that online education currently dominates companies as a trend for effective education during the pandemic period. Based on the available literature (primarily Carnavale & Hatak, 2020; Mikołajczyk, 2021; Blanár, 2021; Rahmadi et al., 2021; Tomčíková, 2021), we formulated research hypotheses.

H1: The number of companies implementing employee training has decreased since the pandemic.
H2: The use of the most common online learning methods in Slovak companies is higher after the pandemic than before the pandemic.
H3: The use of the most frequent offline learning methods in Slovak companies is lower after the pandemic than before the pandemic.

Data collection to test the formulated hypotheses was carried out using two questionnaire surveys. The first one was conducted before the COVID-19 pandemic in the first half of 2018, and 381 companies participated. The second was conducted after the COVID-19 pandemic in the first half of 2023, and 356 companies participated. The questionnaire contained extra questions as they were part of a long-term research project. For this study, besides the identification questions of the respondents (companies), the questions that were relevant were whether training is carried out in the companies and what methods are used for training. To evaluate the results of the questionnaire survey, we used the chi-square goodness-of-fit test as we tested the distribution of categorical variables. The goodness-of-fit is a measure of how well a statistical model fits a set of observations. It tests the null hypothesis H0: The variables have the same distribution as in 2018, against the alternative hypothesis HA: The variables do not have the same distribution as in 2018 (Turney, 2022). Testing was conducted at a significance level of $\alpha = 0.05$ using Microsoft SPSS software. In 2023, we implemented quota sampling to ensure the similarity of the samples under study. The structure of the study samples and their comparison are shown in Tables 45.1, 45.2 and 45.3.

Based on the results of the chi-square goodness-of-fit test, we argue that the samples of companies we studied in 2018 and 2023 are not significantly different in terms of the structure of the number of employees ($\chi^2 = 5.517$, p-value $= 0.138$) or terms of sectoral affiliation ($\chi^2 = 0.465$, p-value $= 0.495$).

Table 45.2 Size structure of research samples

			Number of employees				
			<10	10–49	50–249	≥250	Total
Year	2018	Count	87	110	120	64	381
		Expected count	85.8	119.4	107.0	68.8	381.0
		%	22.8%	28.9%	31.5%	16.8%	100.0%
		Adjusted resid.	0.2	−1.5	2.1	−0.9	
	2023	Count	79	121	87	69	356
		Expected count	80.2	111.6	100.0	64.2	356.0
		%	22.2%	34.0%	24.4%	19.4%	100.0%
		Adjusted resid.	−0.2	1.5	−2.1	0.9	
Total		Count	166	231	207	133	737
		Expected count	166.0	231.0	207.0	133.0	737.0
		%	22.5%	31.3%	28.1%	18.0%	100.0%

	Value	Df	Asymp. Sig. (2-sided)
Pearson's chi-square	5.517[a]	3	0.138
Likelihood ratio	5.533	3	0.137
Linear-by-linear association	0.027	1	0.869
No. of valid cases	737		

[a]0 cells (0,0%) have an expected count of less than 5. The minimum expected count is 64,24

Table 45.3 Sectoral structure of research samples

			Sector		
			Private	Public	Total
Year	2018	Count	337	44	381
		Expected count	334.0	47.0	381.0
		%	88.5%	11.5%	100.0%
		Adjusted residual	0.7	−0.7	
	2023	Count	309	47	356
		Expected count	312.0	44.0	356.0
		%	86.8%	13.2%	100.0%
		Adjusted residual	−0.7	0.7	
Total		Count	646	91	737
		Expected count	646.0	91.0	737.0
		%	87.7%	12.3%	100.0%

	Value	Df	Asymp. Sig. (2-sided)
Pearson's chi-square	0.465[a]	1	0.495
Continuity correction	0.325	1	0.569
Likelihood ratio	0.465	1	0.495
Linear-by-linear association	0.464	1	0.496
No. of valid cases	737		

[a]0 cells (0,0%) have an expected count of less than 5. The minimum expected count is 43.96

45.4 Results and Discussion

Firstly, we focused on examining the impact of the COVID-19 pandemic on the number of companies that implement employee training. We hypothesize that the number of companies conducting training activities decreased after the pandemic. Thus, we aimed to determine whether there is a statistically significant difference between the expected and actual number of companies that engage in training activities. We used Pearson's chi-square test to establish whether there is a statistically significant relationship between the variables. The hypothesis is that if the number of companies conducting training declined after the pandemic, the expected frequency should be lower than the actual frequency. Conversely, if the number of companies increased, the expected frequency should be higher than the actual one. The results of this study will have the potential to provide valuable information on the evolution of educational activities in the corporate environment during the pandemic and their impact on business strategies and practices (Table 45.4).

Based on the results, we can evaluate Hypothesis H1 that the number of companies implementing employee training decreased after the pandemic. We concluded that the actual number of companies that implement employee training is 318, which is higher than the expected number of 305.8 companies. This increase is statistically significant as Pearson's chi-square test value was 3.931 with a p-value of 0.047. A p-value of less than 0.05 allows us to reject the null hypothesis and accept the alternative hypothesis that the number of companies implementing training increased after the pandemic. Such results suggest that the pandemic may have had

Table 45.4 Comparison of the implementation of employee training and development in Slovak companies before and after the COVID-19 pandemic

			Employee training		Total
			No	Yes	
Year	2018	Count	66	315	381
		Expected count	53.8	327.2	381.0
		Adjusted residual	2.6	−2.6	
	2023	Count	38	318	356
		Expected count	50.2	305.8	356.0
		Adjusted residual	−2.6	2.6	
Total		Count	104	633	737
		Expected count	104.0	633.0	737.0
		Value	Df	Asymp. Sig. (2-sided)	
Pearson's chi-square		3.931[a]	1	0.047	
Likelihood ratio		3.958	1	0.047	
Linear-by-linear association		3.926	1	0.048	
No. of valid cases		743			

[a]0 cells (0,0%) have an expected count of less than 5. The minimum expected count is 53.59

a positive effect on companies' efforts to train their employees. The increase in the number of companies implementing training practices can be interpreted as their effort to accommodate the new challenges and needs arising from the postpandemic reality. These results may have important implications for the strategic decisions of companies and indicate their commitment to developing employees' potential and increasing their productivity once companies resume their regular operations.

We then compared the most commonly used online and offline learning methods in businesses in 2018 and 2023. We discovered that there were no changes in the order of use of these methods over this period. The same three online learning methods were used most frequently in both 2018 and 2023, the 2 years studied. Online self-learning, e-learning, and video recordings remained the preferred methods of online learning for employees in companies. These methods offer flexibility and the ability to access learning content regardless of location and time. Similarly, we observed continuity in offline learning methods in both years. Lectures, job instruction training and coaching remained the most commonly used offline learning methods. These methods provide direct interaction between lecturers and employees and are often used in group activities and discussions. The question remains whether there has been a change in the frequency of their use. Again, we use the chi-square test of goodness-of-fit.

To test the second hypothesis, we focused on analyzing the use of online self-education by employees in companies and compared the data between 2018 and 2023. In the hypothesis, we assessed and compared the shifts in this employee training method over the time period of the pandemic and postpandemic years. Online self-education is seen as an important tool for employees in their attempt to improve their knowledge and skills, so we decided to examine how this usage has evolved over time. Based on the data collected, we used Pearson's chi-square goodness-of-fit test to see if the predicted change had indeed occurred (Table 45.5).

In 2018, we recorded a total of 197 businesses that used online self-education. The expected number for this year was set at 174.2. Comparing these values, we obtained an adjusted residual value of 3.4. In 2023, we observed a decrease in the use of online self-education, where we found a count of 140 companies that used it. The expected frequency for this year was set at 162.8. Comparing these values, we obtained an adjusted residual value of −3.4. The results of Pearson's chi-squared test showed a value of 11.366 with a p-value of 0.001. These values indicate a statistically significant difference in the use of online self-education between 2018 and 2023 in the companies. In 2018, we observed a higher rate of use of online self-education, while in 2023, we observed a decrease in the number of companies that used it (Table 45.6).

E-learning as one of the online learning methods was not among the dominant ones in 2018, we observed its use in the case of 73 companies and the expected count was set up at 114,8. Comparing these values, we obtained an adjusted residual value of −6.7. In 2023, we observed an increase in the use of e-learning to more than double (149 companies). The expected frequency for that year was set at 107.2. Comparing these values, we obtained an adjusted residual value of 6.7. The results of Pearson's chi-squared test showed a value of 45.030 with a p-value of 0.000. The

Table 45.5 Comparison of the use of online self-education in Slovak companies before and after the COVID-19 pandemic

			Self-education		
			No	Yes	Total
Year	2018	Count	184	197	381
		Expected count	206.8	174.2	381.0
		Adjusted residual	−3.4	3.4	
	2023	Count	216	140	356
		Expected count	193.2	162.8	356.0
		Adjusted residual	3.4	−3.4	
Total		Count	400	337	737
		Expected count	400.0	337.0	737.0
		Value	Df	Asymp. Sig. (2-sided)	
Pearson's chi-square	11.366[a]	1	0.001
Likelihood ratio	11.402	1	0.001
Linear-by-linear association	11.351	1	0.001
No. of valid cases	737		

[a]0 cells (0,0%) have an expected count of less than 5. The minimum expected count is 162.78

Table 45.6 Comparison of the use of e-learning in Slovak companies before and after the COVID-19 pandemic

			E-learning		
			No	Yes	Total
Year	2018	Count	308	73	381
		Expected count	266.2	114.8	381.0
		Adjusted residual	6.7	−6.7	
	2023	Count	207	149	356
		Expected count	248.8	107.2	356.0
		Adjusted residual	−6.7	6.7	
Total		Count	515	222	737
		Expected count	515.0	222.0	737.0
		Value	Df	Asymp. Sig. (2-sided)	
Pearson's chi-square	45.030[a]	1	0.000
Likelihood ratio	45.640	1	0.000
Linear-by-linear association	44.968	1	0.000
No. of valid cases	737		

[a]0 cells (0,0%) have an expected count of less than 5. The minimum expected count is 107.23

results show that there is a statistically significant difference in the use of e-learning between 2018 and 2023 in the companies under study. We observed a higher rate of e-learning use in 2023 compared to 2018 (Table 45.7).

In 2018, we recorded a total of 34 businesses using video recordings. The expected frequency for this year was set at 52.2. Comparing these values, we obtained an adjusted residual value of −3.9. In 2023, we observed an increase

Table 45.7 Comparison of the use of video recordings in Slovak companies before and after the COVID-19 pandemic

			Video recordings		Total
			No	Yes	
Rok	2018	Count	347	34	381
		Expected count	328,8	52.2	381.0
		Adjusted residual	3.9	−3.9	
	2023	Count	289	67	356
		Expected count	307.2	48.8	356.0
		Adjusted residual	−3.9	3.9	
Total		Count	636	101	737
		Expected count	636.0	101.0	737.0
		Value	Df	Asymp. Sig. (2-sided)	
Pearson's chi-square		15.241[a]	1	0.000	
Likelihood ratio		15.431	1	0.000	
Linear-by-linear association		15.220	1	0.000	
No. of valid cases		737			

[a]0 cells (0,0%) have an expected count of less than 5. The minimum expected count is 48.79

in the use of video recordings, where we found a number of 67 businesses that used them. The expected frequency for this year was set at 48.8. Comparing these values, we obtained an adjusted residual value of 3.9. The results of Pearson's chi-squared test showed a value of 15.241 with a *p*-value of 0.000. These values indicate a statistically significant difference in the use of video recordings in companies between 2018 and 2023. In 2018, we observed a lower rate of use of video recordings, while in 2023, we observed an increase in the number of companies that used it (Table 45.8).

Lecture as one of the offline learning methods was used by 232 companies in 2018. The expected frequency for this year was set at 213.0. Comparing these values, we obtained an adjusted residual value of 2.8. In 2023, we observed a decrease in the use of lectures, where we found a count of 180 companies. The expected frequency for this year was set at 199. Comparing these values, we obtained an adjusted residual value of −2.8. The results of Pearson's chi-squared test showed a value of 7.967 with a *p*-value of 0.005. These values indicate a statistically significant difference in the use of lectures by companies between 2018 and 2023. In 2018, we observed a higher rate of lecture use, while in 2023, we observed a decrease in the number of businesses that used it (Table 45.9).

In 2018, we recorded a total of 186 businesses using job instruction training. The expected number for this year was set at 171.1. Comparing these values, we obtained an adjusted residual value of 2.2. In 2023, we observed a decrease in the use of job instruction training where we found a number of 145 businesses that used it. The expected frequency for this year was set at 159.9. Comparing these values, we obtained an adjusted residual value of −2.2. The results of Pearson's chi-square test showed a value of 4.867 with a *p*-value of 0.027. These values indicate a statistically

Table 45.8 Comparison of the use of lectures in Slovak companies before and after the COVID-19 pandemic

			Lectures		
			No	Yes	Total
Year	2018	Count	149	232	381
		Expected count	168.0	213.0	381.0
		Adjusted residual	−2.8	2.8	
	2023	Count	176	180	356
		Expected count	157.0	199.0	356.0
		Adjusted residual	2.8	−2.8	
Total		Count	325	412	737
		Expected count	325.0	412.0	737.0
		Value	Df	Asymp. Sig. (2-sided)	
Pearson's chi-square	7.967[a]	1	0.005
Likelihood ratio	7.978	1	0.005
Linear-by-linear association	7.957	1	0.005
No. of valid cases	737		

[a]0 cells (0,0%) have an expected count of less than 5. The minimum expected count is 156.99

Table 45.9 Comparison of the use of job instruction training in Slovak companies before and after the COVID-19 pandemic

			Job instruction training		
			No	Yes	Total
Year	2018	Count	195	186	381
		Expected count	209.9	171.1	381.0
		Adjusted residual	−2.2	2.2	
	2023	Count	211	145	356
		Expected count	196.1	159.9	356.0
		Adjusted residual	2.2	−2.2	
Total		Count	406	331	737
		Expected count	406.0	331.0	737.0
		Value	df	Asymp. Sig. (2-sided)	
Pearson's chi-square	4.867[a]	1	0.027
Likelihood ratio	4.874	1	0.027
Linear-by-linear association	4.860	1	0.027
No. of valid cases	737		

[a]0 cells (0,0%) have an expected count of less than 5. The minimum expected count is 159.89

significant difference in the use of online job instruction training between 2018 and 2023 in businesses. In 2018, we observed a higher rate of use of job instruction training, while in 2023, we observed a decrease in the number of companies that used it (Table 45.10).

In 2018, we recorded a total of 121 businesses that used the offline learning method of coaching. The expected frequency for this year was set at 104.9 When

Table 45.10 Comparison of the use of coaching in Slovak companies before and after the COVID-19 pandemic

			Coaching No	Coaching Yes	Total
Year	2018	Count	260	121	381
		Expected count	276.1	104.9	381.0
		Adjusted residual	−2.6	2.6	
	2023	Count	274	82	356
		Expected count	257.9	98.1	356.0
		Adjusted residual	2.6	−2.6	
Total		Count	534	203	737
		Expected count	534.0	203.0	737.0

	Value	Df	Asymp. Sig. (2-sided)
Pearson's chi-square	7.020[a]	1	0.008
Likelihood ratio	7.058	1	0.008
Linear-by-linear association	7.010	1	0.008
No. of valid cases	737		

[a]0 cells (0,0%) have an expected count of less than 5. The minimum expected count is 98.06

comparing these values, we obtained an adjusted residual value of 2.6. In 2023, we observed a decrease in the use of coaching where we found a count of 82 companies that used coaching. The expected frequency for this year was set at 98.1. Comparing these values, we obtained an adjusted residual value of −2.6. The results of Pearson's chi-squared test showed a value of 7.020 with a p-value of 0.008. These values indicate a statistically significant difference in the use of coaching between 2018 and 2023 in the companies. In 2018, we observed a higher rate of coaching usage, while in 2023, we observed a decrease in the number of companies that used coaching.

Based on the results of the statistical survey, we rejected hypothesis H2, according to which the use of the most frequent online learning methods in Slovak companies after the pandemic is higher than before the pandemic. Comparing 2018 and 2023, it is evident that there has been an increase in the use of e-learning and video recordings as online learning methods. Self-education has seen a decline, while e-learning is used more frequently by businesses in 2023. The number has more than doubled compared to 2018. According to Blanár (2021), this was a natural occurrence. Furthermore, he also claimed that most companies have responded to the corona crisis by changing their training from face-to-face to distance learning, i.e., the aforementioned e-learning. Together with Mikolajczyk (2021), we agreed that the increase in the use of e-learning is extensive even in the case of companies that did not use it before the corona crisis. As Tomčíková (2021) stated, the transition to the online environment was a prerequisite for survival and almost 2 years the only option for employee training in companies in Slovakia. The results of our analysis point to an important fact, also highlighted by Rahmadi et al. (2021), namely that not all companies were able to implement employee training in an online environment.

In addition, several issues including a lack of employee engagement hinder the effective delivery of online corporate training (Alfqiri et al., 2022).

Hypothesis H3, according to which the use of the most frequent offline learning methods in Slovak companies is lower after the pandemic than before the pandemic, was confirmed. The decrease was confirmed in the use of the most frequently used offline learning methods (lecture, job instruction training and coaching). The separate use of offline and online learning methods, typical of the precorona crisis period, is now a relic, and employees are now positively perceiving the use of combined methods. Almohammadi et al. (2023) claimed that the majority of their respondents (coming from Saudi university employees) are satisfied with the transition to mixed methods and actively utilize them.

45.5 Conclusion

Corona crisis introduced a hugely disruptive force into human resource management, and education and development were not an exception. However, employee training as one of the most important processes of the HRM was not stopped by the corona crisis, the period presented an opportunity to invest in human capital. We consider it to be a long-term competitive advantage of individual companies, which is directly proportional to the implemented educational activities and, according to several authors, also to investments in human capital development. The qualitative and quantitative research has shown the importance of individual methods of education in the conditions of the Slovak Republic. The aim of the article was to investigate the use of the most frequently used methods of employee education before and after the COVID-19 pandemic and to determine whether online education is still dominant in companies after the end of the COVID-19 pandemic. We consider the fact that we rejected hypothesis H1, according to which the number of companies that implement employee training decreased after the pandemic, to be positive. The increase in the number of companies that implement employee training reflects a strategic approach to human resource management. The results of the analysis confirm that the position of employee training and development in the various strategic documents of companies has its justification and relevance for practical use. The results of the research show that during the corona crisis, there was an increase in learning and development practices in companies. This increase was caused by a partial transition to the online space, and the use of online learning methods remains relevant even after the crisis has passed in 2023. One of the most frequent online learning methods, e-learning, and the use of video recordings have distinctively increased, while online self-learning has subsided. The isolated use of offline learning methods is now a rarity, as confirmed by the survey results. Employees' needs and preferences in learning methods must be taken into account in the activities implemented. Studies by foreign authors prove that the combination of learning methods is crucial for the final effect of the learning process. The needs and preferences of employees in the process of training and development in the conditions of the Slovak Republic represent an opportunity for further research, and their subsequent comparison with the preferences of companies will contribute to talent retention.

References

Alfaqiri, A. S., Noor, S. F., & Sahari, N. (2022). Framework for gamification of online training platforms for employee engagement enhancement. *International Journal of Interactive Mobile Technologies, 16*, 159–175. https://doi.org/10.3991/ijim.v16i06.28485

Almohammadi, S., Panatik, S. A., & Sayyd, S. M. (2023). Employees' satisfaction with online learning and transfer of training during Covid-19 in Saudi universities. *Social Science Journal in Res Militaris, 12*(4), 2363–2370. ISSN 22656294.

Alruwaili, N. F. (2018). Talent management and talent building in upgrading employee performance. *European Journal of Sustainable Development, 7*, 98–106. https://doi.org/10.14207/ejsd.2018.v7n1p98

Blanár, F. (2021). *Dopad pandémie ochorenia COVID-19 na oblasť d'alšieho vzdelávania na Slovensku*. Centrum vedecko-technických informácií SR. Available via https://www.cvtisr.sk/buxus/docs/VS/DALV/2021/COVID19_dopad_na_DVZ_v_SR_final.pdf

Cárachová, M. (2019). Selected aspects of employee training. In *ICERI2019 proceedings* (pp. 10035–10044). https://doi.org/10.21125/iceri.2019.2460

Carnevale, J. B., & Hatak, I. (2020). Employee adjustment and Well-being in the era of COVID-19: Implications for human resource management. *Journal of Business Research, 116*, 183–187. https://doi.org/10.1016/j.jbusres.2020.05.037

Dachner, A. M., Ellingson, J. E., Noe, R. A., & Saxton, B. M. (2021). The future of employee development. *Human Resource Management Review, 31*(2), 100732. https://doi.org/10.1016/j.hrmr.2019.100732

Dvouletý, O. (2021). A first Year's impact of the pandemic on the Czech entrepreneurial activity. *Foresight and STI Governance, 15*, 52–60. https://doi.org/10.17323/2500-2597.2021.4.52.60

Fernando, S. (2015, March). *Vocational education and training with individuals entrepreneurship skills development, under the framework of effective public policies in order to achieving national development objectives together with eliminating the poverty in the long run*. Presented at the 8th annual poverty and social protection conference.

Hebron, D. E. (2020). On-the-job training (OJT) practices of select colleges and universities in Quezon City, Philippines: An assessment. In *Proceedings of ADVED 2020- 6th international conference on advances in education*. https://doi.org/10.47696/adved.202063

Hitka, M., Štarchoň, P., Lorincová, S., & Caha, Z. (2021). Education as a key in career building. *Journal of Business Economics and Management, 22*, 1065–1083. https://doi.org/10.3846/jbem.2021.15399

Huang, W. R. (2020). Job training satisfaction, job satisfaction, and job performance. In *Career development and job satisfaction*. https://doi.org/10.5772/intechopen.89117

Kataniková, R., Kapsdorferová, Z., Švikruhová, P., & Grman, P. (2019). *Rozvoj talentov v organizácii. In Talent manažment ako súčasť rozvoja ľudských zdrojov v moderných podnikoch, jeho prínosy a nedostatky* (pp. 54–62). Slovenská Poľnohospodárska Univerzita. ISBN 978-80-552-2130-4.

Kravčáková, G., & Bernátová, D. (2020). *Manažment ľudských zdrojov*. ŠafárikPress.

Kucharčíková, A., Mičiak, M., Tokarčíková, E., & Štaffenová, N. (2023). The investments in human capital within the human capital management and the impact on the enterprise's performance. *Sustainability, 15*, 5015. https://doi.org/10.3390/su15065015

Malik, A. (2022). *Strategic human resource management and employment relations*. Springer.

McCrie, R., & Lee, S. (2022). Training and development for high performance. In *Security operations management*. https://doi.org/10.1016/B978-0-12-822371-0.00004-9

Mikołajczyk, K. (2021). Changes in the approach to employee development in organisations as a result of the COVID-19 pandemic. *European Journal of Training and Development, 46*, 544–562. https://doi.org/10.1108/EJTD-12-2020-0171

Rahmadi, M. H., Riyadi, S. S., Mintarti, S., Suharto, R. B., & Setini, M. (2021). Effect of E-coaching and learning styles on the performance training participants. *Webology, 18*, 1002–1014.

Ribbers, A., & Waring, A. (2015). *E-coaching: Theory and practice for a new online approach to coaching*. Routledge.

Rivaldo, Y., & Nabella, S. D. (2023). Employee performance: Education, training, experience and work discipline. *Quality – Access to Success, 24*, 182–188. https://doi.org/10.47750/QAS/24.193.20

Savov, R., & Skočdopole, P. (2019). *Strategické riadenie ľudských zdrojov: Talent manažment. Talent manažment ako súčasť rozvoja ľudských zdrojov v moderných podnikoch, jeho prínosy a nedostatky* (pp. 18–23). Slovenská poľnohospodárska univerzita. ISBN 978-80-552-2130-4.

Smerek L (2022) Changes in employee training and development in Slovakia during the COVID-19 pandemic. In Madzík, P., Askarnia, M. Conference proceedings from international scientific conference. Springer.

Stachová, K., Stacho, Z., Raišienė, A. G., & Baroková, A. (2020). Human resource management trends in Slovakia. *Journal of International Studies, 13*, 320–331.

Suleimanová, J. H., Wojčák, E., & Poláková, M. (2019). *Vzdelávanie a rozvoj zamestnancov*. Elfa s.r.o.

Thilagaraj, A., & Rengaraj, S. (2021). Training and development in a post-Covid-19 workplace: A short history of the advancement of preparation and development. *Utkal Historical Research Journal, 34*, 77–80.

Tomčíková, Ľ. (2021). Dopady globálnej pandemickej krízy covid-19 na oblasť riadenia ľudských zdrojov a manažment talentov. *Journal of Global Science, 6*, 1–7.

Tomčíková, L., Svetozarovová, N., Cocuľová, J., & Daňková, Z. (2021). The impact of the global Covid-19 pandemic on the selected practices of human resources management in the relationship to the performance of tourism companies. *Geojournal of Tourism and Geosites, 35*, 525–530. https://doi.org/10.30892/gtg.35233-680

Turney, S. (2022). *Chi-square goodness of fit test | Formula, guide & examples*. Scribbr. https://www.scribbr.com/statistics/chi-square-goodness-of-fit/. Accessed 15 May 2023.

Vasanthi, S., & Basariya, S. R. (2019). On the job training implementation and its benefits. *International Journal of Research and Analytical Reviews, 6*, 210–215.

Vaverčáková, M., & hromková, M. (2018). *Riadenie ľudských zdrojov*. Fakulta zdravotníctva a sociálnej práce Trnavskej univerzity v Trnave. 79 s. ISBN 978-80-568-0135-2.

Vnoučková, L. (2013). Employee learning and development in organisations. *Journal of Efficiency and Responsibility in Education and Science, 6*, 180–189.

Yusuf Iis, E., Wahyuddin, W., Thoyib, A., Nur Ilham, R., & Sinta, I. (2022). The effect of career development and work environment on employee performance with work motivation as intervening variable at the office of agriculture and livestock in ACEH. *International Journal of Economic, Business, Accounting, Agriculture Management and Sharia Administration (IJEBAS), 2*, 227–236. https://doi.org/10.54443/ijebas.v2i2.191

Chapter 46
Centralized Governance in Decentralized Autonomous Organizations

Ivan Sedliačik and Kamil Ščerba

Abstract Blockchain and cryptography enable secure collaboration in a digital environment without the need for a central institution. The study deals with decentralized autonomous organizations (DAOs) and their risks. The goal of the study was to identify legal, regulatory, and manipulation risks. In literature review, we cover the basic characteristics of centralization and decentralization based on blockchain technology, smart contracts, decentralized finance, and the functioning of decentralized autonomous organizations (DAOs). We examine sample of 20 selected DAOs that comprise 65.7% of the total treasury value from the point of view of possible regulatory, legal, and manipulation risks. Our findings show a paradox in great concentration of voting power in decentralized organizations. Manipulation risks arise from token ownership concentration, where a small number of participants can influence voting outcomes. These findings emphasize the need for addressing governance and regulatory aspects of DAOs to ensure transparency, fairness, and decentralization. In our qualitative research, we apply the praxeological approach of the Austrian school of economics with a priori approach, axiom, and deductive logic.

Keywords Decentralized autonomous organizations · Blockchain · Risk · Governance

JEL Codes O16, G30, L20

I. Sedliačik (✉) · K. Ščerba
Department of Finance and Accounting, Faculty of Economics, Matej Bel University in Banská Bystrica, Banská Bystrica, Slovakia
e-mail: ivan.sedliacik@umb.sk; kamil.scerba@umb.sk

© The Author(s), under exclusive license to Springer Nature Switzerland AG 2024
N. Tsounis, A. Vlachvei (eds.), *Applied Economic Research and Trends*, Springer Proceedings in Business and Economics,
https://doi.org/10.1007/978-3-031-49105-4_46

46.1 Introduction

Decentralized ledger technology and blockchain's original purpose was to provide a secure environment for collaboration without the need of the middleman. Central authorities act as approvers of transactions and pose a risk of "single point of failure." In response to this, autonomous decentralized organizations (DAOs) seem to provide partial solutions to eliminate risks of management misconduct, fraudulent behavior, or technical failures.

DAOs might eliminate risk of single point of failure when they are in operation; however, they are still vulnerable to risks at the design phase. As each DAO is a code or smart contract designed by computer programmers, it is the result of human design. Thus, it is possible for DAO initiators to secure control stake in DAO, enabling them to manage all further decisions.

As current academic literature focuses mainly on technological advances and use cases of DAO, there is limited focus on socioeconomic aspects, including governance risks in the form of potential manipulation.

In this article, we aimed to assess the benefits of decentralized autonomous organizations and identify potential risks, challenges, and limits. The structure of this study starts with the introduction of the topic, which is followed by literature review, methodology, results, and discussion and ends with conclusions.

46.2 Literature Review

Our theoretical framework comprises two parts. Firstly, we focus on blockchain and decentralized finance as ecosystem that enables secure and tamper-proof collaboration across worldwide communities on various use. Secondly, we elaborate on the characteristics of decentralized autonomous organizations in the context of their organizational structure, decision-making, and potential risks.

In our society today, centralized systems dominate over decentralized ones. Governments, companies, or nongovernmental organizations rely on centralized structures at governance, decision-taking, and generally collaboration. In particular, finance is the industry where trust is delegated to central authorities, which act as bookkeepers and validators. Nevertheless, computer and software-based technologies brought development in various areas, including finance.

Descriptions of the fundamentals of a decentralized blockchain system and the most valued cryptocurrency Bitcoin can be found in Nakamoto (2008). Esposito et al. (2021) described blockchain as a distributed ledger technology where cryptographic techniques and consensus algorithms are utilized to achieve features like decentralization, traceability, immutability, anonymity, transparency, and security. Hosp (2018) saw blockchain as a distributed ledger technology that is open, borderless, secure, and transparent. Yaga et al. (2018) further characterized blockchain as a digital ledger of cryptographically signed transactions, which are registered in grouped blocks that are cryptographically linked with the previous ones. After each added block, older blocks become more difficult to modify and thus create resistance against unauthorized manipulation. All blocks are encrypted, and once closed, the contents of the block are permanently sealed, and any attempt to change the block will alert everyone on the network. Blockchain technology provides accessible and verifiable data control over a distributed or decentralized environment to every participating node (i.e., computer involved in the network) in a fast and convenient way. Though blockchain technology is mostly associated with the financial industry (Narayanan et al., 2016), it can be also applied to other industries such as health care (Taghreed, 2019). As blockchain is relatively infant technology, there are many concerns such as security, privacy, efficiency, scalability, energy consumption, interoperability, or regulatory concerns, yet to be thoroughly investigated for its mass adoption (Shrimali & Patel, 2022).

Blockchain technology reduces transaction costs, expands transaction scope, and empowers peer-to-peer transactions, thus creating a new paradigm for decentralized business models. Chen and Bellavitis (2020) stated that this new paradigm has led to the emergence of decentralized finance, which leverages blockchain technology to create an alternative financial system that can be more decentralized, innovative, interoperable, borderless, and transparent. The programmability and composability of cryptocurrencies currently support decentralized, blockchain-based markets and services, known as decentralized finance. Protocols allow for market making, collateralized lending, derivatives, asset management, and other services. There are also several risks of cryptocurrency exposure. As traditional finance industry is heavily regulated, similarly a decentralized finance ecosystem is subject to regulatory schemes and thus bears regulatory risks. Technological security represents another risk (Narayanan et al., 2016). According to Kerr et al. (2023), there were multiple cases of hacks or security breaches of cryptocurrency exchanges. There have been a number of high-profile fraud cases associated with cryptocurrencies, such as the FTX scandal in late 2022, thereby making fraud a real concern to current and potential future investors.

A smart contract is executable code that runs on top of the blockchain to facilitate, execute, and enforce an agreement between untrusted parties without the involvement of a trusted third party (Alharby & Van Moorsel, 2017). According to De Filipi et al. (2021), smart contracts work automatically and thus eliminate the need for intermediaries and other third parties. They do not need manual intervention and perform actions immediately. These smart contracts, by virtue of being placed on the blockchain, are also transparent, so anyone can verify their functionality, but cannot change, manipulate, or modify them without authorization. There are certain concerns about security vulnerabilities of smart contracts (Mense & Fletscher, 2018).

Smart contracts are used in decentralized autonomous organizations (DAOs), which are blockchain-based systems that enable people to coordinate and govern themselves mediated by a set of self-executing rules deployed on a public blockchain, and whose governance is decentralized (Hassan & De Filippi, 2021). Though early DAOs showed serious technological flaws (Mehar et al., 2020), DAO maximalists advocate many use cases, even debating necessity of the state's role as a central point of coordination in society (Atzori, 2015). This trust-free concept is now applicable beyond digital currencies, in the form of smart contracts securing decentralized autonomous organizations (DAOs) or corporations in which various management functions are automated by code instead of humans (Frizzo-Barker et al., 2020). El Faqir et al. (2020) considered DAO as an Internet-native entity with no central management, which is regulated by a set of automatically enforceable rules on a public blockchain, and whose goal is to take a life of its own and incentives people to achieve a shared common mission.

Santana & Albareda (2022) described DAO functioning through token economy principles, as it requires the development of a governance token based on cryptocurrency investment. DAO participants receive these tokens that allow ownership and governance, including voting rights in the community according to the share of their token holdings, and use tokens to adopt DAO's internal activities, e.g., propose changes or new actions.

46.3 Methodology

The main aim of this study was to examine DAO governance token ownership concentration, in order to identify potential risks of manipulation or fraudulent behavior. We formulated the following research question: Does the distribution of DAO governance tokens pose a risk of manipulation? We shall identify, analyze, and compare the most valued DAOs in terms of their total treasury holdings. The subject of the research is DAO governance token distribution, and the object of the research is potential risks of manipulation and regulatory/legal risks. In our qualitative research, we applied the praxeological approach of the Austrian school of economics (Degutis, 2011). Additionally, we used a different set of complementary methods, such as induction, deduction, analysis, synthesis, comparison, or abstraction. Emphasis is placed on the literary, historical-logical, content-critical, and content-causal method. In assessing the correctness or incorrectness of the economic theorem, we proceed from a priori approach (reason without the help of experience), axiom, and deductive logic. In this approach, empirical knowledge is used only as an illustrative supplement to the praxeological analysis, and therefore, it is not necessary to evaluate data using mathematical-statistical methods and verify or falsify the conclusions based on experience. The work is mostly of a qualitative research nature.

46.4 Results and Discussion

In the following part of the work, our analysis will focus on individual types of DAOs, their mutual comparison based on specific characteristics, and identification of the risks of DAO participation, while defining the most fundamental threats.

Currently, there are 12.763 DAOs (DeepDao.io, 2023) representing numerous types of focus and mission. Total treasury holdings market capitalization of these DAOs is over 21 billion USD. For the purposes of this research, 20 specific DAOs were selected from different areas of their operation based on their mission. They comprise treasury market capitalization value of 13.8 billion USD, which represents approximately 65.7% of the total DAO treasury.

46.4.1 DAO's Regulatory and Legal Risks

Unlike centralized organizations, which undertake compliance responsibility, decentralized systems including DAOs are less or nonregulated. Therefore, it is more difficult for authorities to target a potential threat, since there is often no legal entity to represent. DAOs most often deal with the following risks:

- Manipulation risks.
- Regulatory and legal risks.
- Cyber attacks.

Our work is focused on the identification of the first two risks that usually represent the greatest potential threat to the users of DAOs.

When creating a DAO, the legal entity of the entire organization is taken into account. Since these organizations involve participants (governance token holders) who are pseudonymous people from all over the world, it is difficult to attribute a legal and regulatory adjustment based on a demographic basis. The very act of coding and making an organization available to the public does not automatically make it a legal entity, so it is necessary for developers to set a certain legal framework in advance. Currently, there are so-called unwrapped and wrapped DAOs. Unwrapped DAOs are not protected by limited liability, and therefore, without legal form, each token holder assumes personal responsibility for the operation of the entire DAO. Wrapped DAOs take the form of limited liability companies that provide sufficient security thanks to smart contracts and treasury. Also, based on this, they can create legal contracts with third parties. However, some jurisdictions consider DAOs as software or technology. If a token holder wants to join a DAO, it should consider the risks related to the area of operation defined by the DAO and consider the legal implications of the country and continent in which it is located.

46.4.2 DAO's Manipulation Risks

Presumably, one of the greatest risks with DAOs is potential manipulation issues. If each member has the right to vote based on the number of tokens, users with the majority of tokens can influence the entire vote if ownership is concentrated. In the

Table 46.1 Token ownership concentration in terms of number of addresses, own elaboration according to Coinmarketcap.com and DeepDAO.io as of May 21, 2023

Token	Number of total addresses	Treasury market capitalization (bil. USD)	Top 10 addresses	Top 20 addresses	Top 50 addresses	Top 100 addresses
ARB	3247	4,0	67,88%	74,32%	82,08%	87,29%
BIT	24, 292	2,5	89,67%	95,55%	98,98%	**99,62%**
UNI	369, 926	2,2	52,10%	61,10%	74,36%	84,41%
MATIC	609, 161	1,0	69,36%	75,18%	80,29%	85,71%
GNO	17, 823	0,8	92,05%	95,42%	97,62%	98,67%
ENS	64, 521	0,7	81,44%	83,94%	87,49%	90,02%
DYDX	40, 860	0,7	62,99%	72,81%	84,46%	92,84%
LDO	35, 215	0,3	50,77%	62,47%	76,51%	86,60%
STG	28, 134	0,2	92,89%	95,58%	97,68%	98,58%
FRAX	7727	0,2	87,51%	92,20%	96,90%	98,87%
ANT	14, 599	0,2	72,65%	81,35%	88,08%	91,96%
OHM	7988	0,2	95,89%	96,67%	97,48%	98,05%
CRV	78, 432	0,1	80,64%	87,18%	91,87%	94,57%
FEI	3844	0,1	91,07%	96,81%	98,98%	99,62%
RAD	6689	0,1	75,17%	84,91%	93,02%	97,43%
AAVE	160, 560	0,1	58,07%	67,65%	77,40%	82,90%
DXD	1358	0,1	**97,12%**	**98,19%**	99,05%	99,60%
UMA	20, 510	0,1	79,28%	88,88%	95,63%	98,26%
GAL	15, 337	0,1	82,47%	90,60%	95,76%	98,52%
MANA	321, 326	0,1	**44,22%**	**51,98%**	**64,29%**	**72,84%**
BTC	47, 700, 277	520,1	5,37%	7,42%	10,77%	13,55%

Source: CoinMarketCap (2023)

case of specific DAOs, a few participants from a large pool of users are enough to make up 50% of the total voting power. We compared the token ownership of 20 selected DAOs and Bitcoin cryptocurrency, which served as a benchmark (Table 46.1).

DAOs are governed by democratic voting, where a majority of participants must agree to the proposal. According to our findings, decision-making in 19 out of 20 selected sample DAOs is performed by less than ten participants, while total participation is in the thousands. The most democratic DAO is Decentraland DAO (MANA); on the contrary, DXdao (DXD) has the absolute highest concentration of power among the first top owners.

It is very surprising that in a community where there are several thousand individuals, only a few individuals can push through a proposal. This fact is against the whole concept of decentralization, which is based on democratic decision-making and the absence of authority. We assume that participation concentration with governance tokens might refer to the existence of selfish and malicious actors that intentionally design smart contracts in the initial token distribution.

46.5 Conclusion

In conclusion, our analysis revealed several major findings regarding DAOs. There are currently 12,763 DAOs representing various types of focus and mission, with a total treasury market capitalization exceeding 21 billion USD. The study focused on 20 specific DAOs, which accounted for approximately 65,7% of the total DAO treasury, with a combined market capitalization of 13,8 billion USD.

DAOs pose regulatory and legal risks due to their decentralized nature. Establishing a legal framework for DAOs is challenging due to the involvement of pseudonymous individuals from around the world. There are "unwrapped" and "wrapped" DAOs, with the latter providing greater legal protection through limited liability and the ability to create contracts with third parties.

Manipulation risks are a significant concern with DAOs. Token ownership concentration can lead to a few participants having a substantial influence on voting outcomes. In some cases, a small number of individuals can hold a majority of the voting power, contradicting the principles of decentralization and democratic decision-making.

The study compared token ownership concentration in 20 selected DAOs and Bitcoin cryptocurrency. It found that in many DAOs, a significant percentage of token ownership is concentrated among a small number of addresses, indicating a high level of centralization of power. The Decentraland DAO (MANA) was identified as the most democratic DAO among the sample, with decision-making involving a larger number of participants. In contrast, DXdao (DXD) exhibited the highest concentration of power among its top owners. The concentration of decision-making power in a few individuals within a community of thousands goes against the principle of decentralization and raises concerns about the presence of selfish and malicious actors.

Overall, the research highlights the regulatory and legal challenges faced by DAOs, as well as the risks associated with concentration of power and potential manipulation. These findings emphasize the need for careful consideration of legal frameworks, governance structures, and distribution mechanisms to ensure the integrity and democratic functioning of DAOs. The paper enhances academic literature with new approach to risks that DAO's represent.

Acknowledgments This study was supported by the Scientific Grant Agency of Slovak Republic under project VEGA No. 1/0579/21 "Research on Determinants and Paradigms of Financial Management in the context of the COVID-19 Pandemic." The authors would like to express their gratitude to the Scientific Grant Agency of the Ministry of Education, Science, Research, and Sport of the Slovak Republic for financial support of this research and publication.

References

Alharby, M., & Van Moorsel, A. (2017). *Blockchain-based smart contracts: A systematic mapping study*. arXiv preprint arXiv:1710.06372.

Atzori, M. (2015). *Blockchain technology and decentralized governance: Is the state still necessary?* Available at SSRN: https://ssrn.com/abstract=2709713 or https://doi.org/10.2139/ssrn.2709713

Chen, Y., & Bellavitis, C. (2020). Blockchain disruption and decentralized finance: The rise of decentralized business models. *Journal of Business Venturing Insights, 13*, e00151.

CoinMarketCap. (2023, May 20). *Today's cryptocurrency prices by market cap*. Retrieved from https://coinmarketcap.com/

De Filippi, P., Wray, C., & Sileno, G. (2021). Smart contracts. *Internet Policy Review, 10*(2). https://doi.org/10.14763/2021.2.1549

DeepDao.io. (2023, May 20). *Organisations*. Retrieved from https://deepdao.io/organizations

Degutis, A. (2011). Economics as praxeology: Philosophical foundations of the 'Austrian School of Economics'. *Logos-Vilnius, 69*, 6–20.

El Faqir, Y., Arroyo, J., & Hassan, S. (2020). *An overview of decentralized autonomous organizations on the blockchain*. Paper presented at the ACM international conference proceeding series. https://doi.org/10.1145/3412569.341257.

Esposito, C., Ficco, M., & Gupta, B. B. (2021). Blockchain-based authentication and authorization for smart city applications. *Information Processing & Management, 58*(2), 102468. https://doi.org/10.1016/j.ipm.2020.102468

Frizzo-Barker, J., Chow-White, P. A., Adams, P. R., Mentanko, J., Ha, D., & Green, S. (2020). Blockchain as a disruptive technology for business: A systematic review. *International Journal of Information Management, 51*, 0268–4012. https://doi.org/10.1016/j.ijinfomgt.2019.10.014

Hassan, S., & De Filippi, P. (2021). Decentralized autonomous organization. *Internet Policy Review, 10*(2), 1–10. https://doi.org/10.14763/2021.2.1556

Hosp, J. (2018). *Kryptomeny*. TATRAN. ISBN 978-80-222-0945-8.

Kerr, D. S., Loveland, K. A., Smith, K. T., & Smith, L. M. (2023). Cryptocurrency risks, fraud cases, and financial performance. *Risks, 11*(3), 51. https://doi.org/10.3390/risks11030051

Mehar, M. I., Shier, C. L., Giambattista, A., Gong, E., Fletcher, G., Sanayhie, R., & Laskowski, M. (2020). Understanding a revolutionary and flawed grand experiment in blockchain: The DAO attack. In *Research anthology on blockchain technology in business, healthcare, education, and government* (pp. 1253–1266). IGI Global. https://doi.org/10.4018/978-1-7998-5351-0.ch069

Mense, A., Fletcher, A. (2018). Security vulnerabilities in Ethereum smart contracts. IEEE. ISBN 978-1450364799.

Nakamoto, S. (2008, October 31). *Bitcoin: A peer-to-peer electronic cash system*. Retrieved from https://bitcoin.org/bitcoin.pdf

Narayanan, A., Bonneau, J., Felten, E., Miller, A., & Goldfelder, S. (2016). Bitcoin and Cryptocurrency Technologies: A Comprehensive Introduction. Princeton, NJ: Princeton University Press

Santana, C., & Albareda, L. (2022). Blockchain and the emergence of decentralized autonomous organizations (DAOs): An integrative model and research agenda. *Technological Forecasting and Social Change, 182*, 121806. https://doi.org/10.1016/j.techfore.2022.121806

Shrimali, B., & Patel, H. (2022). Blockchain state-of-the-art: Architecture, use cases, consensus, challenges and opportunities. *Journal of King Saud University—Computer and Information Sciences, 34*(9), 6793–6807. ISSN 1319-1578.

Taghreed, J. (2019). Blockchain technologies: Opportunities for solving real-world problems in healthcare and biomedical sciences. *Acta Informatica Medica, 27*(4), 284–291. https://doi.org/10.5455/aim.2019.27.284-291

Yaga, D., et al. (2018). *Blockchain technology overview*. National Institute of Standards and Technology Internal Report. ISBN 978-1984263148. https://nvlpubs.nist.gov/nistpubs/ir/2018/NIST.IR.8202.pdf

Chapter 47
Do Consumers Seek Terroir Elements When Choosing a Wine? Insight from Four Generational Cohorts

Spyridon Mamalis, Irene (Eirini) Kamenidou, Aikaterini Karampatea, Elisavet Bouloumpasi, and Adriana Skendi

Abstract Consumers' wine purchasing decision is complex since wines carry a plethora of attributes associated with them, varying from intrinsic to extrinsic cues. Among the extrinsic cues that wines project to market their brand and by extension its winery and area of origin is the concept of wine terroir and its elements. This research provides the first results of ongoing research that deals with what wine consumers in a retail setting seek for, when choosing a wine. It provides insight from four generational cohorts and explores, if, among these components ($N = 44$), elements of wine terroir are included. Data were collected online, and a sample of 366 valid responses were gathered. Results revealed that on a seven-point Likert scale, no item had a mean score > 6.00, while six items (out of 44) were sought by cohorts when choosing a wine. These characteristics are "taste," "smell," "aroma," "price," "clarity and color of wine," and "authenticity." Factor analysis of the 44 items extracted three factors, namely "Wine terroir," "Core wine elements," and "Wine communication terroir." Segmentation analysis extracted three distinctive groups of wine consumers, the "Wine terroirists," the "Sensory-driven consumers," and the "Apathetic wine consumers." Upon segments, the findings are discussed and recommendations for wineries are presented.

Keywords Wine terroir · Generational cohorts · Consumer behavior · Wine marketing · Segmentation

JEL codes M30 · M31 · M39

S. Mamalis (✉) · I. (Eirini) Kamenidou
Department of Management Science and Technology, School of Business and Economics, International Hellenic University, Kavala, Greece
e-mail: mamalis@mst.ihu.gr; rkam@mst.ihu.gr

A. Karampatea · E. Bouloumpasi · A. Skendi
Department of Agricultural Biotechnology and Oenology, International Hellenic University, Drama, Greece
e-mail: katerina_karampatea@yahoo.gr; elisboul@abo.ihu.gr; andrianaskendi@hotmail.com

© The Author(s), under exclusive license to Springer Nature Switzerland AG 2024
N. Tsounis, A. Vlachvei (eds.), *Applied Economic Research and Trends*, Springer Proceedings in Business and Economics,
https://doi.org/10.1007/978-3-031-49105-4_47

47.1 Introduction

Fierce competition between wine brands and wineries, alongside consumers' changes in preferences, product concerns, and regulations, resulted in significant changes in the wine market (Giacomarra et al., 2020; Vrontis et al., 2011) demanding from wineries to align their marketing with consumer preferences (Giacomarra et al., 2020). Within this logic and having in mind that consumers consider wines from a specific country, area, or place superior to other wines from a different country, area, or place, wineries reinforce the link of territory to the wine product (Makrides et al., 2020) and through "wine terroir" differentiating their wines from the competitive ones.

The International Organization of Vine and Wine (OIV, 2010) defines vitivinicultural "terroir" as follows: "Vitivinicultural 'terroir' is a concept that refers to an area in which collective knowledge of the interactions between the identifiable physical and biological environment and applied vitivinicultural practices develops, providing distinctive characteristics for the products originating from that area. 'Terroir' includes specific soil, topography, climate, landscape characteristics, and biodiversity features" (OIV, 2010). Today, wineries use extensively the concept of terroir and its components for differentiation and marketing of their wines. In order to communicate effectively with their target customers on the different aspects of their wine terroir, consumers must be seeking the elements that the winery and its terroir are communicating.

Therefore, the aim of this research is to explore what are the wine attributes that consumers seek when they are interested in choosing a wine and if elements of terroir are among them. Besides the main aim of the research, wine consumers are additionally segmented by the wine elements they are looking for. In order to complete this aim, it draws data from Greece, a country that has a long history and is ranked 19th in the world in wine production (OIV, 2023).

This work makes a theoretical contribution to academia by providing insight from the consumers' standpoint, specifically, about what wine elements the Greek consumers seek in a retail setting and thus empirically offers information that wineries can build upon their marketing communication for their wines.

This chapter is organized as follows. First, the literature review on terroir and the methodology and results of the data analysis are presented. Then, the results are discussed and marketing implications are highlighted.

47.2 Literature Review

Wine terroir is not a new concept, and a search in https://scholar.google.com/ reveals that published work referring to wine terroir goes back to the 1800s (e.g., Loua, 1875), using the French phrase "goût de terroir." Today, more than 29,000 articles refer to wine terroir studying different elements that shape it. These articles mainly fall into several main categories, such as the importance, measurement, or mapping of the natural components of terroir (such as soil) and their interaction (e.g., Hoff et al., 2010; White, 2020), analyses of the concept of wine terroir and the elements that shape it (Cross et al., 2011; Moran, 2001; Patterson & Buechsenstein, 2018; Spielmann & Gélinas-Chebat, 2012; Van Leeuwen & Seguin, 2006; Vaudour, 2002), wine terroir and tourist destination, winescape (e.g., Capitello et al., 2021b; Kastenholz et al., 2021; Marlowe & Lee, 2018), and wine terroir and marketing in general (Camanzi et al., 2017; Castelló, 2021; Charters, 2010). Also, there are a significant number of articles that deal with wine terroir and consumer behavior associated with geographical identification schemes/L'appellation d'origine (Espejel & Fandos, 2009; Schäufele & Hamm, 2017; Skuras & Vakrou, 2002).

Definitions of wine terroir fall into two broad groups, the one that refers to the physical and natural environment of the winery (e.g., Dubos, 1984; Laville, 1993) and the other that includes the human factor added to the physical and natural environment. Regarding the human factor, different approaches exist, such as the approach of solely humans' impact on wine production, for example, selecting the grape varieties, while other approaches include the sociocultural, historical, and communicative factors (e.g., Barham, 2003; Capitello et al., 2021a; Castelló, 2021; Charters et al., 2017; Patterson & Buechsenstein, 2018; Vaudour, 2002).

Moreover, researchers point out that wine terroir is a complex construct, incorporating many elements that also interact with each other (Van Leeuwen et al., 2010), analyzing the integrated facets of wine terroir (Moran, 2001; Patterson & Buechsenstein, 2018; Vaudour, 2002).

Elements of wine terroir have been studied extensively, but usually without the connection to the concept of wine terroir, for example studies examining consumers' willingness to pay for Protected Designation of Origin (PDO), Protected Geographical Indication (PGI), and Traditional Specialty Guaranteed (TSG) wines (e.g., Espejel et al., 2011; Espejel & Fandos, 2009; Ribeiro & Santos, 2007).

As to articles that deal with wine terroir and segmentation, a search on https://scholar.google.com (eighth of May 2023), with the terms "wine terroir," "research," "consumer," and "segmentation" yielded 71 articles, while adding the term "generational cohort" one item was returned of segmentation of the generation Y consumers and terroir elements and wine selection (Capitello et al., 2021a).

Though, using the search items, "wine terroir," "research," "consumer," and "generation Z," four articles were reported. For the terms "wine terroir," "research," "consumer," and "generation Y," 11 articles were returned. Regarding the terms "wine terroir," "research," "consumer," and "generation X," seven articles were returned, and as to the terms, "wine terroir," "research," "consumer," and "Baby Boomers" returned nine articles. However, a closer investigation reveals that only the abovementioned article (Capitello et al., 2021a) deals with generational cohorts per se, and the others have a vague reference to cohorts or terroir in the text or the reference section.

Capitello et al. (2021a) examined the wine-related terroir and sustainability behaviors of Generation Y ($N = 982$; Italy). They precisely examined "preferences for two sets of attributes which are playing a growing role in wine consumer choice: sustainability-related attributes (represented by a carbon reduction label) and origin-related attributes (specified through visual and textual expression of terroir cues)." They used a discrete choice experiment (DCE) that included a carbon-related claim (C-RC) and various elements of terroir. By estimating with a latent class model Generation Y's willingness to pay and grouping participants, they found seven groups, namely the LC1: "Young females seeking new, original, terroir wines"; LC2: "Young males driven by the traditional aspects of wine production"; LC3: "Young consumers aspiring to luxury terroir wines"; LC4: "Young consumers looking for information on terroir"; LC5: "Young consumers interested in different expressions of terroir"; LC6: "Young consumers seeking institutional representations of terroir"; and LC7: "Young males, price-sensitive and interested (but with low WTP) in the carbon claim, and terroir information."

47.3 Materials and Methods

Forty-four items related to wine elements that consumers might look for when selecting a wine in a retail setting were rated on a seven-point Likert scale. Items were adopted from an extensive literature review on consumer behavior, wine choice, and wine terroir (e.g., Capitello et al., 2021a; Castelló, 2021; Charters et al., 2017; Moran, 2001; Patterson & Buechsenstein, 2018; Vaudour, 2002). The items selected were validated by qualitative research with 12 participants, who were asked to report the elements of a wine that they seek in a retail setting. In a small-scale pilot test with 135 participants, all wine consumers (excluded from this sample) tested the comprehension and understanding of the questionnaire and its functionality. The questionnaire was distributed online to adult wine consumers (age 18+). A total of 366 valid questionnaires were obtained and analyzed with the SPSS ver. 28 statistical program. Data analysis included descriptive statistics, i.e., frequencies, percentages, and mean scores (MS). Additionally, it incorporated factor and reliability analysis, cluster analysis, and chi-square tests.

47.4 Results

47.4.1 Sample Profile

Male subjects (59.0%) were overrepresented compared with female subjects (41.0%), and the sample's age ranged from 18 to 76. Participants were grouped into four Greek generational cohorts, i.e., the Baby Boomers born between 1946 and 1964 (Schewe & Meredith, 2004); Generation X, consisting of people born between 1965 and 1977 (Schewe & Meredith, 2004); Generation Y (or millennials according to many scholars) who were born between 1978 and 1994 (Williams &

Page, 2011); and Generation Z, i.e., people born from 1995 to 2009 (O'Neill, 2010). These periods were adopted due to life-changing events that affected Greece and those entering adulthood. Also, participants were married IN majority (50.5%) or single (41.8%), while a small percentage (7.7%) were either divorced or widowed. The area of residence for the majority was the city (63.9%), and 36.1% resided in rural or semi-rural areas. As to education level, two main categories stood out, the participants with secondary education (44.1%) and those with at least a university degree (46.2%), while 10.7% had postsecondary education. Regarding the occupation of the participants, most were people with a monthly salary (58.7%), followed by dependent on others (22.7%), and businesspeople (16.4%). Only a very small percentage (2.2%) were blue-collar workers. Lastly, with reference to net monthly family income in euros, up to 1000.00€ was reported by 35.2% of the sample, while 38.0% reported an income of 1000,01–2000,00€, and 26.8% had a net family monthly income of more than 2000,00 €.

47.4.2 Cohorts Wine Consumption Behavior

The majority of the sample (42.1%) drinks wine 1–3 times per month, while a large percentage (30.1%) drink wine 1–3 times per week. Also, 8.2% drink wine 4–6 times a week, 4.3% daily, and, lastly, 0.3% more than once per day. Additionally, 15.0% drink wine on special occasions. Consumers considered that they have very limited (31.4%), limited/some (38.0%), or no knowledge (7.1%) about wines and (23.5%) considered that they have advanced or expertise knowledge.

47.4.3 Wine Characteristics That Cohorts Seek from a Wine

Participants were presented with 44 items on a seven-point Likert scale and were requested to indicate how much they agreed with each item as an element that they looked for when choosing a wine in a retail setting. For each item/element, its mean score (MS) was calculated, which revealed that answers fit in the range of 3.63–5.86 on the Likert scale. For the total sample (Table 47.1), no item had MS > 6.00, while six items were rated with MS > 5.00 and five were rated with MS < 4.00, while the rest 33 were rated with MS: 4.00–4.99. The highest-rated item was "taste" (MS = 5.86), followed by "smell" (MS = 5.59), "aroma" (MS = 5.52), "price" (MS = 5.48), "clarity and color of wine" (MS = 5.24), and "authenticity" (MS = 5.02). In contrast, the three wine elements that consumers seek least are "landscape architecture" (MS = 3.63), "production ritual" (MS = 3.82), and "producer history" (MS = 3.91). Referring to wine terroir elements, only "authenticity" (MS = 5.02) was rated with an MS > 5.00. Table 47.1 illustrates the elements of a wine that cohorts choose, which were rated with MS ≥ 5.00 on the seven-point Likert scale. Gen Z, Gen X, Gen Y, and BB stands for each generational

Table 47.1 Wine elements that cohorts seek when choosing a wine in mean scores per cohort and total sample (MS ≥ 5.00)

Elements of a wine that cohorts seek when choosing a wine (MS ≥ 5.00)	Gen Z	Gen X	Gen Y	BB	TS
Taste	6.02	5.91	5.73	5.77	5.86
Smell	5.62	5.65	5.65	5.35	5.59
Aroma	5.42	5.51	5.54	5.65	5.52
Price	5.48	5.44	5.55	5.42	5.48
Clarity and color of wine	5.33	5.07	5.37	5.16	5.24
Authenticity	5.02	5.01	5.13	5.23	5.02
Matching food	5.02	–	–	5.03	–
Organic wine	–	5.01	5.04	–	–

Source: The authors

cohort, i.e., the cohorts generation Z, generation x, generation Y, and Baby Boomers. Lastly, TS stands for the total sample.

47.4.4 Factor Analysis of Wine Elements

To identify the key variables that wine consumers look for when selecting a wine, exploratory factor analysis (EFA) was conducted using principal component analysis with varimax rotation. By using this factor model, it was possible to reduce the 44 items to a smaller set of variables and to continue with other data analyses. Through EFA, 12 items were dropped either because their loadings on the factor were smaller than 0.4 or because the same item was loaded on more than one factor. EFA extracted three constructs/dimensions (KMO = 0.962; BTS = 11,615,283; df = 496; sign = 0.000) accounting for 70.2% of the total variance (Table 47.2). Table 47.2 presents the total variance (TV) explained by each factor (second column), the number of items that each factor has (third column), the loading range of the items on the factor (fourth factor), the reliability of each factor measured with Cronbach a (fifth column), and the mean score of the factor (MFS; last column of Table 47.2).

The first factor explains 40.2% of the variance and is named "Wine terroir." This dimension contains 21 items that are associated with the wine terroir literature, containing elements of the core terroir or natural terroir elements (such as "landscape architecture" and "climate"), the human terroir (such as "grape varieties" and "method and means of storage"), and the sociocultural-historical terroir (such as "historical aspects of the region in the cultivation of grapes and the production of wine" and "Cultural identity of a wine-producing region"). Loadings of items on the factor range from 0.588 to 0.855 and have MFS = 4.29 (Std = 1.48).

The second factor accounts for 15.7% of the variance and is called "Core wine elements" because the items that it incorporates deal with the wine attributes itself

Table 47.2 Factor analysis results of the 44 items studied referring to wine elements that consumers seek when choosing a wine

Name of factor	% of TV	No. of items	Loading range	Cronbach a of factor	MFS (std)
Wine terroir	40.2	21	0.588–0.855	0.976	4.29 (1.48)
Core wine elements	15.7	6	0.643–0.856	0.897	5.46 (1.29)
Wine communication terroir	14.3	5	0.673–804	0.919	4.50 (1.51)

Source: The authors

that the consumers identify when drinking the product (i.e., intrinsic cues). This dimension has six (6) elements that consumers seek and is associated directly toward the wine itself as a final-total product, such as "aroma," "clarity and color of wine," and "taste." Loadings of items on the factor range from 0.643 to 0.897 and have MFS = 5.46 (Std = 1.29).

The third factor accounts for 14.2% of the variance and identifies the marketing communication elements that wineries implement to differentiate their wines from competitors. It incorporates five (5) elements of marketing communication of the wine, such as wine label design, package, and brand name. The loadings on the factor range from 0.673 to 0.804 and have the MFS = 4.50 (std = 1.51). This dimension is named "Wine communication terroir."

47.4.5 Segmentation Analysis

Using the MFS of the produced dimensions, first, a hierarchical cluster analysis (Ward's method) was performed to determine the number of clusters identified and the estimate of their centroids (Everitt, 1993). Subsequently, K-means cluster analysis was made use of, and the probable solution was checked and compared with other solutions obtained from different subsets of data (McIntyre & Blashfield, 1980). Furthermore, several numbers of clusters were observed, taking into account that the final extracted clusters should have a practical and physical meaning (Everitt, 1993). Moreover, the results from the ANOVA test exposed that the three dimensions contributed to the differentiation of the final clusters (Saunders, 1994). Therefore, the three resultant segments differed significantly (Table 47.3).

Additionally, the chi-square tests were utilized to explore socioeconomic and demographic characteristics (gender, marital status, generational cohort, area of residence, education, and income) of the clusters and illustrate if differences between clusters based on these characteristics exist. As to derived differences between clusters and socioeconomic and demographic characteristics of participants, only

Table 47.3 Clusters of wine elements that cohorts seek when choosing a wine

Dimensions of selected wine attributes	Cluster I N = 172	Cluster II N = 142	Cluster III N = 52	F	Sig.
Wine terroir	5,51	3,64	2,05	487,729	,000
Core wine elements	6,18	5,35	3,41	188,122	,000
Wine communication terroir	5,58	4,10	2,01	338,396	,000

Source: The authors

in one case statistically significant differences were observed, i.e., from the "area of residence" demographic characteristic ($\chi^2 = 9.585$, $df = 4$; $p = 0.047$).

Cluster I was assigned the name "Wine terroirists." This segment covers 47.0% of the participants and has the highest MFS for all dimensions as compared to the other segments. Therefore, this segment is the most demanding (compared to) of all the segments. They first seek the core wine elements, such as taste, color, and aroma, but they also seek for the wine communication terroir elements and the wine terroir elements when choosing a wine. This segment is comprised mainly of males, generation X participants, living in cities but having the highest percentage of participants living in villages compared to the other segments, and with a moderate family income (1000.01–2000.00€). They also have at least a university degree, with limited knowledge on wines, and have no knowledge of the term wine terroir.

Cluster II covers 38.8% of the participants and is named the "Sensory-driven consumers." This segment seeks the core wine attributes and is indifferent in seeking the rest of the dimensions of the wines, i.e., the wine terroir dimension and the wine terroir communication dimension. This segment is comprised mainly of males, with generation X and generation Y having the highest similar percentage (28.5% and 29.1%, respectively) and living in the city (but also having the highest percentage of participants living in towns compared to the other segments). This segment also encompasses participants with a moderate family income (1000.01–2000.00€), having at least a university degree and with the highest percentage of participants considering that they have advanced knowledge of wines. Lastly, this segment has the highest percentage compared to the rest of the knowledgeable people of the term wine terroir.

Cluster 3 covers 14.2% of the total sample and is named "Apathetic wine consumers," in the sense that all their MFS <3.50 and do not seek any of these dimensions when choosing a wine. This segment consists mainly of men, members of the generation Y cohort, living in the city, with a university (at least) degree, and family net monthly income of 600.01–1000.00€. This segment has the highest percentage of participants living in the city and the lowest income compared to all segments with about half of the sample having a net monthly income up to 1000.00€. This group considers themselves as having very limited or no knowledge of wines, with no member stating that they have advanced or expertise knowledge. Lastly, about three-quarters of the members have no knowledge of the term wine terroir.

47.5 Discussion and Implications

Self-assessment of knowledge about wine revealed that the majority of the sample had no or very limited and limited/some knowledge (76.5%), clearly indicating that consumer education about wines is needed. Previous research has emphasized that there is a need to inform and train consumers about wine and wine attributes (Alonso, 2014; Kalazić et al., 2010; McGarry Wolf & Higgins, 2017; Tzimitra-Kalogianni et al., 1999). Also, Bruwer et al. (2017) studied (among others) if product (wine) knowledge affects product choice cue and found that it has a "positive impact on intrinsic product cue utilization" (p. 830).

Additionally, 44 elements associated with wines' intrinsic and extrinsic cues were presented to participants and was requested from them to point out, which ones they seek for when choosing a wine, no element was rated with a MS > 6.00 and five were rated with a MS > 5.00. The ones that had MS > 5.00 were "taste," "smell," "aroma," "price," "clarity and color of wine," and "authenticity." Three out of the five have to do with the product characteristics itself, while the other two have to do with the "attached to the product's characteristics" in the sense that price may vary, and authenticity of the wine refers to a marketing element of the wine product.

These results are not directly comparable to other studies since they did not use the same variables but can be partially associated to. For example, MacDonald et al. (2013) explored the "relative importance of driver and choice factors in wine consumption behavior" and how generational cohorts affect drivers of wine consumption and wine choice features. They found that taste was considered the most important. This is in line with our findings. Other factors that were considered as important were price, brand, region, variety of grapes, and aroma. Comparing these results to our study, the aroma and price factor were also cues that consumers seek when choosing a wine, while the rest were not. Cho et al. (2014) explored ($N = 457$; USA) the importance of 12 wine attributes in wine purchasing, i.e., taste, aroma, color, quality, region, grape varietal, wine type, brand, aging, price, label, and medal/award/rating. They found that the sensory-related wine characteristics (i.e., "taste," "aroma," and "color") were considered the most important by consumers. These are directly in line with the findings of our study.

Factor analysis on the 44 wine elements resulted in a three-dimensional model. The three dimensions (wine terroir, core wine elements, and wine communication terroir) were cluster analyzed to explore the number of consumer groups with the same behavior and what elements of wine they are interested in. Three clusters arose, namely the "Wine terroirists," the "Sensory-driven consumers," and the "Apathetic wine consumers." These results cannot be directly compared with other studies due to the variables included in each dimension, as well as the nature of the analysis. Therefore, the comparisons made are with extreme caution. For example, Koksal (2019) and Seyedimany and Koksal (2022) considered each cohort as a segment and then proceeded to explore generational cohort differences. Our study preceded with segmentation analysis and then sought which cohorts are the dominant ones in each segment. De Magistris et al. (2011), in investigating the Millennial cohort preferences for wine attributes in the New World" (USA) and the "Old World" (Spain) identified five consumer segments in terms of the importance attached to different wine attributes: "Traditionalists," "Wine seekers," "Label fans," "Insecure," and "Price conscious." They also found that Spanish Millennials are primarily interested in the country of origin and secondarily in the food with which the wine goes, while the US Millennials are interested in the taste experience and secondly in its price. As noted above, these can be partially compared to our study. For example, the country of origin is incorporated in the "wine terroir" dimension and is not investigated by itself. Price on the other hand was dropped as a variable due to double loading on factors. Capitello et al. (2021a) explored generation Y's ($N = 982$; Italy) wine-related terroir and sustainability behavior using a DCE that includes a C-RC and different dimensions of terroir and through the estimation of a latent class model in willingness to pay found seven consumer segments. Even though this research deals with generational cohort segmentation, it is outside the aim and objective of our study since our study does not examine willingness to pay nor does it include C-RC.

Although these research findings are preliminary results of ongoing study, they demonstrate the need to educate Greek generational cohorts about wine, wine characteristics, and wine terroir. If wineries acknowledge that they will differentiate from competitors on elements of terroir, then there is a need to invest in educating their potential customers through different means, either through social media, which is less costly, up to excursions to their wineries with sensory tests and winemaking seminars, which highlight the importance of wine terroir.

47.6 Conclusion, Limitations, and Directions for Further Research

The contribution of this empirical study to existing research is that it sheds light on the terroir elements that consumers looked for when choosing a wine, in terms of the multiconstruct of wine terroir and the behavior of Greek consumers, where there is a lack of research. In realizing this research, a number of unavoidable limitations were faced. Firstly, this is ongoing research, and therefore, results may or may not change. Also, criteria for participating were stated a priori, such as being a wine consumer and having access to the Internet, thus implementing a nonprobability sampling procedure. Therefore, the above limitation restricts any generalizability of results. Another issue is that the study only included one country with specific variables measured, while additional variables could be needed for exploring elements of wine terroir. These limitations can be used as driving factors for future research on this topic.

Acknowledgments-Funding This research was cofinanced by the European Regional Development Fund of the European Union and Greek national funds through the Operational Program Competitiveness, Entrepreneurship, and Innovation, under the call Research-Create-Innovate (project code: T2EΔK-02974 Drama terroir).

Ethical Approval "There are no ethical issues involved in the processing of the questionnaire data used in the study. The necessary consent has been obtained by the persons involved, and the anonymity of the participants has been secured. All procedures performed in studies involving human participants were in accordance with the ethical standards of the International Hellenic University research committee and with the 1964 Helsinki Declaration and its later amendments or comparable ethical standards."

References

Alonso, A. D. (2014). Wine cellar experiences in the Southeastern United States: Educating the winery visitor on Muscadine wines. *Journal of Foodservice Business Research, 17*(1), 1–18. https://doi.org/10.1080/15378020.2014.886903

Barham, E. (2003). Translating terroir: The global challenge of French AOC labeling. *Journal of Rural Studies, 19*(1), 127–138. https://doi.org/10.1016/S0743-0167(02)00052-9

Bruwer, J., Chrysochou, P., & Lesschaeve, I. (2017). Consumer involvement and knowledge influence on wine choice cue utilisation. *British Food Journal, 119*(4), 830–844. https://doi.org/10.1108/BFJ-08-2016-0360

Camanzi, L., Grazia, C., Héraud, E. G., & Malorgio, G. (2017). Quality differentiation in the Italian wine industry: Terroir-based vs. brand-based strategies. *International Journal of Globalisation and Small Business, 9*(2/3), 86. https://doi.org/10.1504/IJGSB.2017.088920

Capitello, R., Agnoli, L., Charters, S., & Begalli, D. (2021a). Labelling environmental and terroir attributes: Young Italian consumers' wine preferences. *Journal of Cleaner Production, 304*, 126991. https://doi.org/10.1016/j.jclepro.2021.126991

Capitello, R., Sidali, K. L., & Schamel, G. (2021b). Wine terroir commitment in the development of a wine destination. *Cornell Hospitality Quarterly, 62*(3), 313–323.

Castelló, E. (2021). The will for terroir: A communicative approach. *Journal of Rural Studies, 86*, 386–397. https://doi.org/10.1016/j.jrurstud.2021.06.007

Charters, S. (2010, February). Marketing terroir: A conceptual approach. In *Proceedings of the 5th International Academy of Wine Business Research Conference, Auckland, New Zealand* (pp. 8–10). Academy of Wine Business Research in the Publisher. http://academyofwinebusiness.com/wp-content/uploads/2010/04/Charters-Marketing-terroir.pdf

Charters, S., Spielmann, N., & Babin, B. J. (2017). The nature and value of terroir products. *European Journal of Marketing, 51*(4), 748–771. https://doi.org/10.1108/EJM-06-2015-0330

Cho, M., Bonn, M. A., & Kang, S. (2014). Wine attributes, perceived risk and online wine repurchase intention: The cross-level interaction effects of website quality. *International Journal of Hospitality Management, 43*, 108–120. https://doi.org/10.1016/j.ijhm.2014.09.002

Cross, R., Plantinga, A. J., & Stavins, R. N. (2011). What is the value of terroir? *American Economic Review, 101*(3), 152–156. https://doi.org/10.1257/aer.101.3.152

De Magistris, T., Groot, E., Gracia, A., & Miguel Albisu, L. (2011). Do millennial generation's wine preferences of the "New World" differ from the "Old World"? A pilot study. *International Journal of Wine Business Research, 23*(2), 145–160. https://doi.org/10.1108/17511061111143007

Dubos, J. (1984). Importance of "terroir" as a factor of the qualitative differentiation of wines climate, soil; agronomical, psychosociological and economic aspects. *Bulletin de l'OIV (France)*.

Espejel, J., & Fandos, C. (2009). Wine marketing strategies in Spain: A structural equation approach to consumer response to protected designations of origin (PDOs). *International Journal of Wine Business Research, 21*(3), 267–288. https://doi.org/10.1108/17511060910985980

Espejel, J., Fandos, C., & Flavián, C. (2011). Antecedents of consumer commitment to a PDO wine: An empirical analysis of Spanish consumers. *Journal of Wine Research, 22*(3), 205–225. https://doi.org/10.1080/09571264.2011.622516

Everitt, B. (1993). *Cluster analysis* (3rd ed.). Wiley.

Giacomarra, M., Galati, A., Crescimanno, M., & Vrontis, D. (2020). Geographical cues: Evidences from new and Old World countries' wine consumers. *British Food Journal, 122*(4), 1252–1267. https://doi.org/10.1108/BFJ-08-2019-0580

Hoff, R., Ducati, J. R., & Bergmann, M. (2010, December). Geologic and geomorphologic features applied for identification of wine terroir unit by digital image processing, spectroradiometric and GIS techniques in Encruzilhada do Sul, RS, Brazil. In *International Terroir Congress* (Vol. 8, pp. 44–49). IVES Conference Series. International Viticulture and Enology Society (IVES). https://ives-openscience.eu/ives-conference-series/

Kalazić, Z., Šimić, M., & Horvat, J. (2010). Wine market segmentation in continental Croatia. *Journal of Food Product Marketing, 16*(3), 325–335.

Kastenholz, E., Cunha, D., Eletxigerra, A., Carvalho, M., & Silva, I. (2021). Exploring wine terroir experiences: A social media analysis. In A. Abreu, D. Liberato, E. A. González, & J. C. Garcia Ojeda (Eds.), *Advances in tourism, technology and systems* (Vol. 209, pp. 401–420). Springer. https://doi.org/10.1007/978-981-33-4260-6_35

Koksal, M. H. (2019). Differences among baby boomers, generation X, millennials, and generation Z wine consumers in Lebanon: Some perspectives. *International Journal of Wine Business Research, 31*(3), 456–472. https://doi.org/10.1108/IJWBR-09-2018-0047

Laville, P. (1993). Unités de terroir naturel et terroir. Une distinction nécessaire pour redonner plus de cohérence au système d'appellation d'origine. *Bulletin OIV, 745*(746), 227–251.

Loua, T. (1875). Aperçu statistique sur les vignobles européens. *Journal de La Société Française de Statistique, 16*, 23–28.

MacDonald, J. B., Saliba, A. J., & Bruwer, J. (2013). Wine choice and drivers of consumption explored in relation to generational cohorts and methodology. *Journal of Retailing and Consumer Services, 20*(3), 349–357. https://doi.org/10.1016/j.jretconser.2013.01.013

Makrides, A., Vrontis, D., & Christofi, M. (2020). The gold rush of digital marketing: Assessing prospects of building brand awareness overseas. *Business Perspectives and Research, 8*(1), 4–20. https://doi.org/10.1177/2278533719860016

Marlowe, B., & Lee, S. (2018). Conceptualizing terroir wine tourism. *Tourism Review International, 22*(2), 143–151. https://doi.org/10.3727/154427218X15319286372298

McGarry Wolf, M., & Higgins, L. M. (2017). Segmenting the sustainable wine consumer. *Journal of Food Distribution Research, 48*(856–2018–3086), 109–110.

McIntyre, R. M., & Blashfield, R. K. (1980). A nearest-centroid technique for evaluating the minimum-variance clustering procedure. *Multivariate Behavioral Research, 15*(2), 225–238. https://doi.org/10.1207/s15327906mbr1502_7

Moran, W. (2001). Terroir – The human factor. *Australian and New Zealand Wine Industry Journal, 16*(2), 32–51.

O'Neill, M. (2010). Generational preferences: A glimpse into the future office. *Knoll Workplace Research, 10*.

OIV. (2010). *Definition of vitivinicultural "Terroir". Resolution OIV/VITI 333/2010*. https://www.oiv.int/public/medias/379/viti-2010-1-en.pdf

OIV. (2023). *Country statistics*. https://www.oiv.int/what-we-do/country-report?oiv

Patterson, T., & Buechsenstein, J. (2018). *Wine and place: A terroir reader*. University of California Press.

Ribeiro, J. C., & Santos, J. F. (2007). *Consumer perception of Portuguese quality wine and the region-of-origin effect*. 47th Congress of the European Regional Science Association.

Saunders, J. (1994). Cluster analysis. *Journal of Marketing Management, 10*(1–3), 13–28. https://doi.org/10.1080/0267257X.1994.9964257

Schäufele, I., & Hamm, U. (2017). Consumers' perceptions, preferences and willingness-to-pay for wine with sustainability characteristics: A review. *Journal of Cleaner Production, 147*, 379–394. https://doi.org/10.1016/j.jclepro.2017.01.118

Schewe, C. D., & Meredith, G. (2004). Segmenting global markets by generational cohorts: Determining motivations by age. *Journal of Consumer Behaviour, 4*(1), 51–63. https://doi.org/10.1002/cb.157

Seyedimany, A., & Koksal, M. H. (2022). Segmentation of Turkish wine consumers based on generational cohorts: An exploratory study. *Sustainability, 14*(5), 3031. https://doi.org/10.3390/su14053031

Skuras, D., & Vakrou, A. (2002). Consumers' willingness to pay for origin labelled wine: A Greek case study. *British Food Journal, 104*(11), 898–912. https://doi.org/10.1108/00070700210454622

Spielmann, N., & Gélinas-Chebat, C. (2012). Terroir? That's not how I would describe it. *International Journal of Wine Business Research, 24*(4), 254–270.

Tzimitra-Kalogianni, I., Papadaki-Klavdianou, A., Alexaki, A., & Tsakiridou, E. (1999). Wine routes in northern Greece: Consumer perceptions. *British Food Journal, 101*(11), 884–892. https://doi.org/10.1108/00070709910301391

Van Leeuwen, C., & Seguin, G. (2006). The concept of terroir in viticulture. *Journal of Wine Research, 17*(1), 1–10.

Van Leeuwen, C., Roby, J.-P., Pernet, D., & Bois, B. (2010). Methodology of soil-based zoning for viticultural terroirs. *Bulletin de l'OIV, 83*(947), 13.

Vaudour, E. (2002). The quality of grapes and wine in relation to geography: Notions of terroir at various scales. *Journal of Wine Research, 13*(2), 117–141. https://doi.org/10.1080/0957126022000017981

Vrontis, D., Thrassou, A., & Czinkota, M. R. (2011). Wine marketing: A framework for consumer-centred planning. *Journal of Brand Management, 18*(4–5), 245–263. https://doi.org/10.1057/bm.2010.39

White, R. E. (2020). The value of soil knowledge in understanding wine terroir. *Frontiers in Environmental Science, 8*, 12. https://doi.org/10.3389/fenvs.2020.00012

Williams, K., & Page, R. (2011). Marketing to the generations. *Journal of Behavioral Studies in Business, 3*, 1–17.

Chapter 48
Recreational Uses of the Protected Natural Ecosystem of Grammos in the Region of Western Macedonia

Katerina Melfou, Georgia Koutouzidou, Dimitrios Kalfas, Stergios Loudovaris, and Ioannis A. Giantsis

Abstract Researching mountain destinations can be an exciting endeavor, as these locations often offer stunning natural landscapes, outdoor activities, and unique cultural experiences. The forest ecosystems in Greece form the backbone of mountain excursions and the natural environment, playing an important role in the biological balance and survival of animal species and human beings. The attempt to evaluate the benefits provided by the forest ecosystems, specifically the Grammos area in the Region of Western Macedonia, through goods and services (usually unquantifiable, such as oxygen, recreation, and protection from dangerous weather phenomena) is a quantification of natural capital. This chapter attempts to link the characteristics of visitors to the area and nature with sustainable development, analyzing the attractiveness factors of the mountainous complex of Grammos, while at the same time investigating the perspective of sustainable tourism development through the development of recreational uses that take place within the study area, an area known for its natural beauty but also for its historical and cultural richness.

Keywords Mountain tourism · Grammos · Nature 2000 · Visitor profile · Protected areas · Sustainable tourism

48.1 Introduction

Ecosystems, which are complex and dynamic systems of interactions and interdependencies between the biological community and habitats, provide us with material goods and services that cannot be obtained from other sources and are called ecosystem services. These extend from the provision of raw materials, climate regulation,

---

K. Melfou (✉) · G. Koutouzidou · D. Kalfas · S. Loudovaris · I. A. Giantsis
Department of Agriculture, School of Agricultural Sciences, University of Western Macedonia, Florina, Greece
e-mail: kmelfou@uowm.gr

© The Author(s), under exclusive license to Springer Nature Switzerland AG 2024
N. Tsounis, A. Vlachvei (eds.), *Applied Economic Research and Trends*, Springer Proceedings in Business and Economics,
https://doi.org/10.1007/978-3-031-49105-4_48

and biodiversity conservation, to cultural and recreational services related to esthetic enjoyment and tourism. These services are essentially the interface between the natural and human domain on which human welfare depends (Costanza et al., 2014; Burkhard, 2017). Mountain areas are characterized by rare biodiversity, ecosystem diversity, and a multitude of cultural and historical values that classify them as important tourist destinations (Romeo et al., 2021). Several mountainous regions, taking advantage of appropriate development opportunities and policy choices, have managed to initiate structural changes enabling their socioeconomic transformation (Kalfas et al., 2021; Melfou et al., 2022).

The article by Choe et al. (2017) surveyed visitors to the Bukhansan National Park in Korea with study variables including sociodemographics, travel behavior, motivation, and satisfaction with park features, services, and facilities. In addition, they presented ways to improve visitor satisfaction and preservation of natural, cultural, and historical resources in Bukhansan National Park and other national parks in Korea. In the work of Needham et al. (2004), the impact of recreation and tourism on mountain resorts has focused on tourism development and management, service quality and winter visitor characteristics, and the environmental impacts of recreation development. D. Lee and J.H. Lee's (2017) study explores visitors' intention to conserve natural landscapes based on the relationship with their place attachment to the National Park landscape. Results suggest that National Park managers should focus on increasing visit satisfaction based on how visitors are emotionally connected to the places they visit in order to enhance visitors' landscape conservation intentions in national parks. Research by Tretiakova et al. (2019) analyzes the attitudes and habits of visitors to the Taganay National Park (NP) in the South Urals in Russia and found a strong positive perception of overall experiences of visiting the place. Bhatt and Pickering's (2022) work focused on obtaining data and information regarding all those elements that would ensure positive experiences for visitors in the Annapurna Conservation Area of Nepal while protecting the area's natural and cultural values. Local land managers, governments, nongovernmental organizations, and tourism operators need information about who is traveling where and when in these protected areas.

Such information is required for all destinations that provide a variety of ecosystem services Tsitsoni (2015). The municipality of the Region of Western Macedonia in Greece has been classified as mountainous and is such a case. Its area extends to 618.46 km^2, and its remaining inhabitants amount to 2188, highlighting the demographic problem that still exists in this mountainous area. Within the administrative boundaries of Nestorio are the forest ecosystems of the Grammos mountain range, which are rich in rare biodiversity and have been declared protected areas (Natura 2000 network, Nature Monuments, Game Reserves, and Important Bird Areas). They constitute a unique mosaic of picturesque landscapes and habitats where important historical events in contemporary Greek history took place and local mountain cultural communities developed.

The area of the survey is a mountainous terrain, characterized mainly by steep and moderate slopes. The highest peak of Grammos reaches an altitude of 2520 m with the peaks Skirtsi (2444 m), Kiafa (2395 m), Pano Arrena (2196 m), and Kato

Arrena (2158 m) defining a relatively undisturbed area, with extensive forests and alpine meadows lying above the forested areas. The terrains with relatively gentle slopes are few and are located around the municipality of Nestorio, which in the past were cultivated in their entirety. Today, however, only a small part is cultivated to meet the family needs of the remaining inhabitants.

On the northern slopes of Mount Grammos are the sources of the Aliakmonas River. Its upper estuary up to Nestorio is characterized by steep gorges, both of the main river and of its torrents and tributaries. The dense vegetation of the area is a habitat for rare wildlife species (brown bear, deer, wild boar, wolf, otter, and wild goat) and endangered bird species (woodpecker, golden eagle, and Egyptian vulture). Among them, particular geomorphological features are highlighted which are particularly rare in the country and should be protected in order to be preserved and promoted, such as:

- The Aliakmonas gorge, with its steep and almost vertical slopes, and the spectacular gorge at Kotyli, which reaches a height of 300 m and offers impressive views
- The alpine lakes, which are permanent water bodies and natural breeding sites for amphibians
- The extensive alpine meadows of Grammos with their rich flora
- Permanent flow waterfalls in the "Kefalovryso" of Pefkoftos or temporary flow in Tsouka of Agia Anna
- The riparian parts of Aliakmon near Nestorio with the huge rocks that rise above the area where every year the music festival known as the "River party" is held
- The area of Pefkos Grammos in which there are extensive mixed deciduous and coniferous forests and many broad-leaved trees with a sporadic appearance, which make up a healthy forest ecosystem and an exquisite landscape with a variety of impressive colors, especially during the autumn months

The existing land uses in the area are related to forestry, agriculture, livestock, and tourism. Livestock farming follows two main patterns: the small agro-pastoral farms of a mixed type, usually on a family scale, and large extensive livestock units, including both mobile units (sheep, cattle, and goats) for summer grazing and large permanent units (mainly sheep and goats). The extensive areas of mountainous, subalpine, and alpine pastures developed in the altitudinal zones of the Grammos area provide a summer livelihood for transhumant livestock farmers. The pastures are valuable not only for the grazing matter they produce but also for their contribution to the customs and culture of the region.

Forestry is the dominant land use in the forests and woodlands of the municipality of Nestorio. The black pine and beech forests that occupy the main part of the Grammos mountain range are characterized by a high productive potential, which corresponds to approximately 4% of the total timber stock of the country. In the oak forests located in the lower parts of the Aliakmonas catchment area, forestry is mainly practiced for the production of firewood. Additional land uses and activities carried out in the area include recreational hunting (except in Wildlife Refuges and no-hunting areas), recreational fishing, and ecotourism.

Fig. 48.1 Natura 2000 site boundaries. (Source: https://natura2000.eea.europa.eu/)

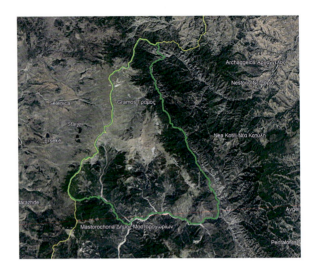

In order to implement the necessary protection and management measures aimed at the conservation, protection, and enhancement of the above endangered and important biodiversity, an area of 34,357.03 ha of the mountain complex of Grammos has been included in the Natura 2000 network under the name "Peaks of Mount Grammos" and code GR 1320002 as a Special Conservation Area (SCA) and Special Protection Area (SPA).

Part of the Natura 2000 network area is the spatial object of the survey and belongs administratively to the municipality of Nestorio in the municipality of Kastoria (Fig. 48.1), while the remaining part belongs administratively to the municipality of Konitsa in the municipality of Ioannina.

In Greece, many of the ecosystems of mountainous regions such as Grammos are protected areas and the development of alternative forms of tourism in these areas may negatively affect their services. Nevertheless, with appropriate management, these areas can be integrated into a wider ecological, economic, and social environment. A key prerequisite for this is the existence of a strategic development plan Loudovaris (2022); Rickly (2018).

A strategic development plan for mountain regions usually involves addressing the unique challenges and opportunities these regions present. It is therefore of particular interest to establish mechanisms to monitor and evaluate the progress of the strategic plan, including regular assessments of key indicators and feedback from stakeholders. For this reason, investigation and evaluation, as well as feedback from visitors to the area, are deemed necessary Kalfas et al. (2013).

The aim of this study was to identify the factors that contribute to the attractiveness of the mountain complex of Grammos, which is a protected area, and to investigate the profile of tourists and day visitors. The prospect of sustainable tourism development through the evolution of recreational uses that take place within the boundaries of the protected area, toward the development of alternative forms of mountain tourism, is also being explored. The main concern is that such tourism development should be defined by clear and distinct boundaries to protect and enhance the natural, historical, and cultural wealth of the area. The research methodology is described in the next section, followed by the presentation of results and concluding remarks.

48.2 Research Methodology

Creating a system to monitor and assess the impact of tourism on the environment and local communities requires the collection of data, which will be used to ensure a sustainable and beneficial long-term tourism strategy. The approach applied in this chapter consists mainly of two steps. Data are analyzed using descriptive statistics, and statistical significance is examined using the chi-square test.

The study was based on a primary sample survey, which was carried out in the protected natural ecosystems of Mount Grammos within the administrative boundaries of the municipality of Nestorio, in the prefecture of Kastoria, with the help of questionnaires designed and distributed in printed and Google Forms. The total number of questionnaires analyzed (paper and online) was 216, and their collection started in June 2022 and was completed at the end of August 2022.

The number of observations in the sample are important for the results to have some degree of reliability. The sample size was based on the following formula:

$$n = \frac{N \times (zs)^2}{Nd^2 + (zs)^2}$$

where

N = the total population of visitors
z = the confidence level
s = the standard deviation of the sample
d = desired precision (which is equal to half of the confidence interval) (Siardos, 2005)

The sample size and the fact that it includes visitors' views on the same type of ecosystem satisfy the requirements for this empirical application without imposing any limitations.

The collected data through the primary survey were statistically analyzed using SPSS software, through the test of independence (chi-square test). The chi-square test (χ^2 test) belongs to a family of tests based on a series of assumptions and is frequently used in the statistical analysis of experimental data (Bolboacă et al., 2011). The chi-square tests are statistical tests used to determine whether there is a significant association or dependence between two categorical variables. In particular, this includes looking at visitor statistics, development patterns, emerging markets, and factors affecting visitor numbers, such as threats to forest ecosystems or changes in visitor economic conditions. An effect size measurement for the chi-square test of independence was then performed with Cramér's V, indicating an effect size measurement for the chi-square test of independence. It measures how strongly two categorical fields are connected (Kiefer, 1959).

Several key aspects were taken into account when conducting the survey of visitors to the mountain destination of Grammos. The main aspects considered in this survey were geographical characteristics, outdoor activities, infrastructure and services supporting visitors, environmental issues under pressure and threats, demographics, and visitor preferences, as well as tourism trends and market analysis for specific destinations. By examining these points and conducting thorough research with primary data, a comprehensive understanding of a particular mountain destination and its attractiveness to visitors was achieved. This knowledge will assist in developing strategies for destination marketing, product development, and improving the overall visitor experience.

48.3 Results and Discussion

The data of the questionnaires were analyzed, and the description and clarification of the profile of the visitors and the assessment of the degree of satisfaction of their expectations emerged. In addition, an analysis of the attractiveness and tourism development factors of the area was carried out, as well as an assessment of the pressures and threats faced by natural ecosystems in Grammos. Finally, a test of independence was performed, which showed the dependence between the respondents' sociodemographic and income profiles with the individual opinions of the questionnaires.

From the total sample of 216 respondents, 118 are men and 98 are women. The highest observed rates of ages are the middle age (45–60 years) with a percentage of 39%, followed by the age between 31 and 44 years with 37% and the youngest age group (19–30 years) with 14%. The percentage of the sample of visitors with a higher education reaches 80%, of which 28% have attended postgraduate study programs.

Regarding employment, 48% are employees of the wider public sector, followed by those employed in the private sector with a percentage of 37% and pensioners with a percentage of 6%. It is important to mention that 31% of the survey participants have monthly individual incomes of up to €1000, 47% from €1000 to 1500, and 15% from €1500 to 2000, while 7% earn more than €2000 per month. Finally, regarding the distribution of the annual family income, 74% of the respondents have an annual family income of 10,000 to 35,000 euros and 12% up to 10,000 euros, while 14% have an annual family income of over 35,000 euros.

The vast majority of visitors (96%) used a car to reach their destination, and in 68% of the cars, the number of passengers were more than two, while in 43% of them there was a passenger under the age of 18. The independence test indicated that there is a dependence between the use of the particular means of transport and the sociodemographic profiles, such as work ($X^2_{(16,5\%)} = 0.00$) and number of children

($X^2_{(2,5\%)} = 0.012$), as well as income profiles of the respondents, personal income ($X^2_{(12,5\%)} = 0.00$), and annual family income ($X^2_{(63,5\%)} = 0.00$). Likewise, there is a dependence between respondents' income figures and the category (cubic meters) of their cars.

The responses of most of the sample, 63%, stated that they were determined to make an excursion to another mountainous area with similar characteristics in the event that it would not be possible for them to visit the natural ecosystems of Grammos. For 60% of the respondents, friends/acquaintances/relatives were the source of information they trusted to choose the area of Grammos as a leisure destination, while 25% of the visitors were informed from the Internet, 10% from newspapers and magazines of various subjects, 3% from radio or television, and just 1% from travel agencies.

In the effort to assess the factors of attractiveness and tourism development, the natural environment (forests, flora, fauna, and wetlands) at a rate of 41% and the mountainous character of the area at a rate of 24% collected the most answers for the attractiveness factors of Grammos. It was followed by the National Reconciliation Park with a percentage of 17%, which functions as a center of memory and research of the Civil War, highlighting the historical and ecological wealth of the area, while 12% of the visitors chose the four-day music festival "River Party of Nestorius" on the banks of the Aliakmon's, which is organized on the first weekend of August and is a cultural institution for the municipality of Nestorio. It is worth mentioning that the characterization of Grammos as a nature protection area of the "Natura 2000" network was a selection criterion for only 6% of visitors when the corresponding percentage estimated by research in other areas of the "Natura 2000" network is 21% (BIO Intelligence Service, 2011). The opinions regarding the selection elements that played a decisive role in the touristic choice of Grammos, during the investigation, revealed that it depends on the family situation of the interviewees, specifically the existence of children ($X^2_{(24,5\%)} = 0.039$), as well as the annual family income ($X^2_{(72,5\%)} = 0.00$).

Regarding the evaluation of the degree of satisfaction of their expectations, 48% of the sample stated that they were satisfied with the condition of the road network, while the image of nature and landscapes compensated almost all visitors (99%). The independence test showed that there is a dependent relationship between the two above characteristics related to the satisfaction of visitors with the area of Grammos and their socioeconomic characteristics regarding work and annual family income. In addition, the cleanliness and organization of the mountain settlements and the quality of catering and local cuisine were, respectively, evaluated positively by 69% and 66% of the sample, while with regard to the services provided in the accommodation and shops and the behavior of the residents, the employees, or entrepreneurs, 84% of respondents declared themselves fully satisfied (Table 48.1).

Regarding the assessment of pressures and threats faced by the protected area of Mount Grammos, the risk of forest fires was assessed as the most serious risk to the forest ecosystems as 43% of respondents ranked it as "very high" and 33% as "high." The results indicate that there is a statistically significant

Table 48.1 Satisfaction of visitors from the wider area of Grammos

As to:	Very good %	Very good RF[a]	Good %	Good RF[a]	Average %	Average RF[a]	Bad %	Bad RF[a]	Very bad %	Very bad RF[a]	Don't know/don't answer %	Don't know/don't answer RF[a]
Road network condition	11	23	37	79	40	87	8	18	3	6	1	2
Landscapes/nature	91	197	8	17	0	1	0	0	0	0	0	1
Cleanliness/organization	21	45	48	105	26	56	3	7	1	3	0	1
Local gastronomy	26	55	40	86	23	49	7	16	1	3	2	5
Service/behavior/hospitality	43	91	41	87	11	24	1	2	1	2	2	5
Services/quality of accommodation	19	41	41	90	19	42	1	3	2	4	17	36

[a]*RF* response frequency, % the percentage of responses

association between the visitors having children and threats of forest fires (p-value = 0.042 < 0.05) at 5% level of significance. However, there was no significant dependence between any other threats and risks and the family situation of the visitors. Nevertheless, the reduction of cultivated land, the absence of grazing in mountainous areas, the abandonment of the countryside, and the climate crisis are responsible for frequent and high-intensity fires that have serious effects on natural ecosystems and human communities.

This is followed by illegal logging, which was assessed as a "very high" threat by 38% and as "high" by 38% of respondents. Illegal logging by residents of the neighboring country and the mountainous settlements, the economic crisis of recent years, combined with the recent energy crisis and the profound profit in the firewood trade, create conditions capable of exacerbating the phenomenon, for which immediate action is required.

Poaching was ranked third in terms of severity, as 21% of visitors rated it as a "very high" threat, 36% as a "high" threat, and 36% as a "moderate" threat. Poaching occurs in the research area as in other regions of mountainous Greece. Large mammals, especially the most vulnerable and legally protected species such as the wild goat, deer, and bear, as well as partridge and hare, are under considerable pressure from this illegal activity.

Overgrazing pressure was assessed as "very high" by 7% and as "high" by 24%. Grazing has been recognized as an important ecological factor for grassland ecosystems, which determines the succession of vegetation, the diversity of plant species, and consequently the natural landscape while significantly improving the food quality of wild avians (Dong et al., 2020; Gosnell et al., 2020; Ren et al., 2016; Savory & Butterfield, 2016).

Additional environmental impacts on natural ecosystems are caused by organized or nonorganized recreational activities that take place in them (Barros & Pickering, 2015; IPCC – Intergovernmental Panel on Climate Change, 2022; Taylor & Komissarov, 2019). In addition, the inability to integrate remote areas into integrated waste management systems often leads to informal waste disposal methods, which are harmful to human health and the environment (Alfthan et al., 2016). Although the ecotourism activities in Grammos are in a relatively mild form, it is possible to cause negative impacts on the ecosystems as they include a wide range of small and unique habitats particularly sensitive to the changes caused by human activity. According to the results of the survey, the ecotourism flow is a "moderate threat" for 44% of the sample, while 8% and 6% assessed the threat as "high" or "very high." Accordingly, the threat posed by waste accumulation was assessed as "very high" by 17%, as "high" by 24%, and as "moderate" by 42% (Table 48.2).

Furthermore, very interesting are the results, which show that there is a statistically significant dependence between visitors' age and days of stay (p-value = 0.042 < 0.05) at 5% level of significance. There is also a significant dependence between age and an excursion to another area with similar characteristics (p-value = 0.030 < 0.05).

The answers show that 63% of the sample took a one-day trip. When asked about the amount they spent or will spend on food, snacks, coffee, soft drinks,

Table 48.2 Major pressures—threats faced by the forest ecosystems of Grammos

As to:	Very high %	RF[a]	High %	RF[a]	Moderate %	RF[a]	Low %	RF[a]	Very low %	RF[a]
Fires	43	92	33	71	16	34	5	10	3	6
Illegal logging	38	81	38	82	16	35	7	15	1	2
Poaching	21	44	36	76	36	77	5	11	2	5
Overgrazing	7	15	24	50	42	88	18	38	10	21
Trash accumulation	17	35	24	51	40	85	13	28	5	11
Large number of visitors	6	12	8	17	44	93	24	51	18	38
Uncontrollable mushroom collection	8	17	22	45	37	78	19	40	14	29
Illegal harvesting of tea	24	51	29	61	28	59	11	23	8	16
Illegal harvesting of protected species (primroses)	23	49	21	45	33	70	13	27	9	19

[a]RF response frequency, % the percentage of responses

or beverages per person, the vast majority (95%) answered that they spent or will spend more than €5 per person, which demonstrates the willingness of visitors to stay in their destination area for several hours and to accompany their presence there with a meal or snack in local shops of health interest. Similarly, for the part of the sample that made a multi-day trip, the corresponding percentage of daily expenditure becomes 97%. Of the respondents, 17% chose hotel amenities and services for their accommodation, 23% preferred free camping, 29% stayed in the homes of friends or relatives, and 31% stayed in hostels. Regarding the cost of a night's stay, 59% spent up to €50, 24% up to €80, 14% up to €110, and 3% over €110.

Analyzing further the research data, it is found that a visitor spends on average 54 ± 23 euros for accommodation per day and on average 22 ± 10 euros per day for meals and beverages, which indicates that there is a large variability in the amount that the visitors spent for accommodation and meals and beverages, too. Interesting differences are observed between the visitors if they are separated in terms of their place of residence, from where they started their visit to the area of Grammos (Table 48.3). Analyzing the visitors in two categories, those who made an excursion from Kastoria and those staying in other areas, litigations were found regarding the amounts they allocated for accommodation and food and beverages. A visitor, who resides in the same prefecture and specifically in Kastoria, spends on average 47 ± 23 euros per day for accommodation and on average 18 ± 9 euros per day for meals and beverages. The results of visitors from other areas outside the prefecture indicate that an expense on average 57 ± 22 euros per day is incurred for accommodation per day and on average 24 ± 10 euros per day for meals and beverages. The results can be justified due to the relationships between people from nearby areas and also the possibility of frequent visits from the Kastoria area.

Comparing these two categories of visitors, not only was there a difference in the amounts spent, but also there were differences according to their financial status. In

Table 48.3 Averages and standard deviations in euros

	Visitors		Visitors of prefecture Kastoria		Visitors of other areas	
As to:	Averages	St. Dev.	Averages	St. Dev.	Averages	St. Dev.
Accommodation	54	±23	47	±23	57	±22
Meals and beverages	22	±10	18	±9	24	±10

particular, there is also a significant dependence between the annual family incomes of the respondents and the data on the basis of which they chose the area. It is noteworthy that for the visitors who are not from the area of Kastoria, there is no interaction with any of the threats that the Grammos ecosystem receives.

With the dangers and threats faced by the mountainous ecosystem of Grammos, it seems that the inhabitants of the prefecture are more critical. Great is their interest in the dangers of fires, poaching, and illegal gathering of primroses. They seem to be more concerned about the dangers of fires, poaching, and illegal primrose gathering. The results indicate the correlation that exists regarding the risks and the average annual income of the respondents. More specifically, there is a statistically significant association between the visitor's average annual income and the dangers and threats of the area (p-value = 0.00 < 0.05) at 5% level of significance. However, there was no significant dependence between any threats and risks and the average annual income of the visitors of other prefectures.

In addition, by making this separation it is found that the attraction of visitors from other areas can be achieved by shaping and promoting activities, such as organized hikes, mountain biking, and guided tours of the National Reconciliation Park, while the residents of the surrounding area, probably because they know the area and make escapades in it more often, showed interest in the development of organized excursions and the creation of organized camping, as well as various environmental education programs. Consequently, in both categories, it appears that there is an interest in the development and protection of the area, but the activities chosen are different for each of them.

These results are confirmed by observing the correlations made by separating our sample, based on the visitors' permanent residence area. In particular, 76% of the respondents who live outside the prefectures of Western Macedonia visited the region to go hiking, while the other activities that attracted their interest were less compared to visitors from the surrounding regions. Coming to strengthen this observation is the existence of a statistically significant correlation between visitors from areas outside Western Macedonia and the activities they took part in during their visit to the wider area of Grammos (p-value = 0.001 < 0.05) at a 5% level of significance.

In more detail, the correlation between the visitors of Grammos, who come from prefectures of Western Macedonia, and the purpose of the visit (p-value = 0.019), the way they learned about the area (p-value = 0.047), and the activities they choose indicates that there is the possibility for targeted actions to develop the tourism strategy and increase the number of visitors coming from the area. Accordingly, in order to achieve the development of the tourism strategy for visitors, who come from distant areas, it is necessary to develop the accommodation in the area, upgrade the existing accommodation, and, in addition, it must remain a relatively economic destination (p-value <0.001).

Along the way, a magnitude method was performed, using Cramér's V, to find possible interdependencies between visiting factors of Grammos. In particular, interactions were found to a large extent between the following factors: (1) money spent and times of visitation (0.837); (2) monthly individual income and local gastronomy (0.979); (3) annual family income and accommodation cleanliness (0.999); (4) family situation and visited areas (Kastoria 0.892, Florina 0.960, Nymphaeum 0.991, and Prespes 0.977), which indicates that there is room to increase the interest of visitors, especially those who belong to the group of people with families; and (5) the level of satisfaction of the local gastronomy and the surrounding visit areas (especially Florina 0.942 and Nymphaeum 0.963).

There were not any dependencies at all between the individual monthly income and the visited areas (Kastoria 0.097, Florina 0.021, Nymphaeum 0.054, and Prespes 0.001), the level of knowledge/education, and the activities in another area (0.099). The coefficient regarding the level of education and the visit ratio of the area remains similar at 0.135, which indicates that they have no correlation.

48.4 Conclusions

The research carried out aimed to provide information about the area of Grammos, in order to assess the degree of satisfaction of its visitors' expectations, the analysis of the attractiveness and tourist development factors of the area, and the assessment of pressures and threats faced by its natural ecosystems.

In carrying out the research conducted with visitors to the mountain destination of Grammos, several key aspects were taken into account, such as demographics and visitor preferences that determine tourism trends and are included in the market analysis of this destination.

By examining these points and conducting thorough research with primary data, a comprehensive understanding of the specific mountain destination and its visitor appeal was achieved. This knowledge will assist in developing strategies for destination marketing, product development, and improving the overall visitor experience.

References

Alfthan, B., Semernya, L., Ramola, A., Adler, C., Peñaranda, L. F., Andresen, M., Rucevska, I., Jurek, M., Schoolmeester, T., Baker, E., Hauer, W., & Memon, M. (2016). *Waste management outlook for mountain regions – Sources and solutions*. Nairobi, Arendal and Vienna. www.unep.org, www.grida.no, www.iswa.org

Barros, A., & Pickering, C. M. (2015). Impacts of experimental trampling by hikers and pack animals on a high-altitude alpine sedge meadow in the Andes. *Plant Ecology and Diversity, 8*, 265–276. https://doi.org/10.1080/17550874.2014.893592

Bhatt, P., & Pickering, C. M. (2022). Spatial and temporal patterns of visitation in the Annapurna conservation area, Nepal. *International Mountain Society, Mountain Research and Development, 42*(3), R16–R24. https://www.jstor.org/stable/10.2307/48695006

BIO Intelligence Service. (2011). *Estimating the economic value of the benefits provided by the tourism/recreation and employment supported by Natura 2000*. Final Report prepared for European Commission – DG Environment.

Bolboacă, S. D., Jäntschi, L., Sestraş, A. F., Sestraş, R. E., & Pamfil, D. C. (2011). Pearson-fisher chi-square statistic revisited. *Information, 2011*(2), 528–545. https://doi.org/10.3390/info2030528

Burkhard, B., & Maes, J. (Eds.). (2017). *Mapping ecosystem services* (p. 374). Pensoft Publishers.

Choe, Y., Schuett, M. A., & Sim, K. W. (2017). An analysis of first-time and repeat visitors to Korean national parks from 2007 and 2013. *Journal of Mountain Science, 14*(12). https://doi.org/10.1007/s11629-017-4387-y

Costanza, R., de Groot, R. S., Sutton, P., van der Ploeg, S., Anderson, S. J., Kubiszewski, I., Farber, S., & Turner, R. K. (2014). Changes in the global value of ecosystem services. *Global Environmental Change, 26*, 152–158.

Dong, S., Shang, Z., Gao, J., & Boone, R. B. (2020). Enhancing sustainability of grassland ecosystems through ecological restoration and grazing management in an era of climate change on Qinghai-Tibetan plateau. *Agriculture, Ecosystems and Environment, 287*, 106684. https://doi.org/10.1016/j.agee.2019.106684

Gosnell, H., Grimm, K., & Goldstein, B. E. (2020). A half century of holistic management: What does the evidence reveal? *Agriculture and Human Values, 37*, 849–867. https://doi.org/10.1007/s10460-020-10016-w

IPCC – Intergovernmental Panel on Climate Change. (2022). High mountain areas. In Intergovernmental Panel on Climate Change (IPCC) [Ed.]. In *The ocean and cryosphere in a changing climate: Special report of the intergovernmental panel on climate change* (pp. 131–202). Cambridge University Press.

Kalfas, D., Tyrselis, X., Grigoriadis, N., & Matsinos, Y. (2013). Sustainable management of local resources regarding mountainous regions. The case of Nymfaio in Florina, Greece. *Journal of Environmental Protection and Ecology, 14*, 655–663.

Kalfas, D. G., Zagkas, D. T., Dragozi, E. I., & Melfou, K. (2021). An approach of landsenses ecology and landsenseology in Greece. *International Journal of Sustainable Development & World Ecology, 28*(8), 677–692. https://doi.org/10.1080/13504509.2021.1920061

Kiefer, J. (1959). K-Sample Analogues of the Kolmogorov-Smirnov and Cramer-V. Mises Tests, *The Annals of Mathematical Statistics, 30*(2), 420–447.

Lee, D., & Lee, J. H. (2017). A structural relationship between place attachment and intention to conserve landscapes – A case study of Harz National Park in Germany. *Journal of Mountain Science, 14*(5). https://doi.org/10.1007/s11629-017-4366-3

Loudovaris, S. (2022). *Recreational uses of the protected natural ecosystem of Grammos of the municipality of Nestori* (p. 130). University of Western Macedonia. (In Greek).

Melfou, K., Kalfas, D., Chatzitheodoridis, F., Kalogiannidis, S., Loizou, E., & Toska, E. (2022). Comparison of approaches for determining grazing capacity in forest Rangelands: The case of Pisoderion Forest Florina-Greece. *Environmental Sciences Proceedings, 22*, 68. https://doi.org/10.3390/IECF2022-13055

Needham, D. M., Wood, J., & B C., Rollins B. R. (2004). Understanding summer visitors and their experiences at the Whistler mountain Ski area. *Mountain Research and Development, 24*(3), 234–242.

Ren, Y., Lü, Y., & Fu, B. (2016). Quantifying the impacts of grassland restoration on biodiversity and ecosystem services in China: A meta-analysis. *Ecological Engineering, 95*, 542–550. https://doi.org/10.1016/j.ecoleng.2016.06.082

Rickly, M. J. (2018). Tourism geographies and the place of authenticity. *Tourism Geographies, 20*(4), 733–736. https://doi.org/10.1080/14616688.2018.1477169

Romeo, R., Russo, L., Parisi, F., Notarianni, M., Manuelli, S., Carvao, S., & UNWTO. (2021). *Mountain tourism – Towards a more sustainable path*. FAO.

Savory, A., & Butterfield, J. (2016). *Holistic management, third edition: A commonsense revolution to restore our environment* (p. 532). Third. Island Press.

Siardos, G. (2005). *Sociological research methodology, 2nd edition improved and supplemented*. Ziti. (In Greek).

Taylor, S., & Komissarov, V. (2019). *Sustainable mountaineering tourism on Lenin Peak, Kyrgyzstan: Current issues and potential solutions*. In ATRA – Adventure Tourism Research Association [Ed.] 7th ATRA International Adventure Conference. ATRA – Adventure Tourism Research Association, Laggan, Gatehouse of Fleet. http://researchrepository.napier.ac.uk/Output/1932257

Tretiakova, T. N., Brankov, J., Petrović, M. D., Syromiatnikova, Y. A., Radovanović, M. M., & Mikhailovich Yakovlev, A. (2019). Tourism and natural environment in the NP Taganay (Russia) – Habits and perceptions of the visitors. *Geojournal of Tourism and Geosites, 25*(2), 595–608. https://doi.org/10.30892/gtg.25225-383

Tsitsoni, T. (2015). *Protected areas as a driver of sustainable development at local and National Level*. In Hellenic Forestry Society [Ed.] The Contribution of Modern Forestry and Protected Areas to Sustainable Development. Hellenic Forestry Society, Argostoli Kefalonia, October 4–7. (In Greek).

Chapter 49
National and Regional Disparities: How Recovering?

Anna Maria Bagnasco, Viviana Clavenna, and Federica Fortunato

Abstract Italy is the only OECD country in which, during the period 2000–2019, two gaps have grown simultaneously: the one dictated by territorial disparities between the north and the south, measured in terms of GDP per capita, and the one related to the aggregate growth deficit relative to other countries. In this chapter, we consider the quality of the institutional context as a key factor in affecting the growth and development gaps between economies and, within them, between different regions.

By comparing economic data and indicators regarding the quality of government and social cohesion, we try to understand if there is a link between economic and social characteristics in different regions and the quality and effectiveness of governance. The idea is that institutional shortcomings are decisive in explaining the modest results recorded by our country in the last few decades. Understanding and addressing this factor could be essential for promoting balanced development and reducing regional disparities within the country.

Keywords Public efficiency · Regional gaps · Quality government · Social cohesion · Public policies · Next-generation EU

JEL Classifications H50, H70, H80, J24, O43, R11

49.1 Introduction

During the period of 2000–2019, Italy stands out among OECD countries as the only one where two gaps have grown simultaneously. Firstly, Italy has experienced the

A. M. Bagnasco (✉) · V. Clavenna · F. Fortunato
Department of Business, Law, Economics and Consumer Behaviour, IULM University, Milan, Italy
e-mail: annamaria.bagnasco@iulm.it

strongest aggregate growth deficit compared to other countries, further exacerbating its lag behind more advanced nations and the rest of Europe.

Secondly, there is a significant disparity between the northern and southern regions of Italy, measured in terms of GDP per capita, and this territorial discrepancy has widened over time.

The financial crisis of 2008–2009 and the subsequent sovereign debt crisis of 2011–2013 have played a substantial role in Italy's decline and its widening gap with other economies. The challenges faced by Italy in terms of economic growth and catching up with other countries have become more pronounced in recent decades.[1]

All components of aggregate demand declined more markedly in the South; the fall in GDP during the double crisis was associated in particular with the drastic drop in investment. Even during the phase of slight recovery in southern GDP recorded from 2015 onward, investment remained well below pre-crisis levels, while in the Centre-North, the restart of the economy was favored by a recovery in the accumulation process. This divergence is particularly evident for private investment, which fell more in the South than in the rest of the country (Accetturo et al., 2022a). With regard to the public component, on the other hand, the drop was sharp and of similar magnitude in both areas, reflecting above all the negative contribution of local governments (Bardozzetti et al., 2022). However, given the greater dependence of the South on public demand, and the delays in its endowment of infrastructural capital (Bucci et al., 2021), the impact on economic activity was more significant for the southern regions. Finally, with regard to the regional trends within the Mezzogiorno, the negative dynamics of GDP showed limited territorial heterogeneity. The unfavourable performance of the Mezzogiorno, in absolute and relative terms, can be explained by a combination of several factors of a global, national, and local nature. First, it can be observed that the widening of territorial income gaps since the global financial crisis is a phenomenon common to other advanced countries (Iammarino et al., 2019; Viesti, 2019).

Compared to the other less-developed regions of Europe, the negative peculiarity of the Mezzogiorno is, however, its characterization as a region in difficulty within a country, Italy, which as a whole has been characterized over the last quarter of a century by economic trends that are markedly worse than those of other European states.

In 2022, the Bank of Italy published a research project dedicated to the southern economy (Accetturo et al., 2022b). Compared to the previous research project on the same topic (Cannari & Franco, 2010), the analyses show a somewhat more worrying picture, as the gaps have widened, and the southern issue has become even more clearly part of a broader national issue. Ten years later, the problems of the Mezzogiorno remain largely unresolved. It is necessary to ask to what extent this is the result of inadequate public policies, both place-based (i.e. specifically

---

[1] Overall, the loss of output between 2007 and 2019 was 2% in the Centre-North and 10% in the Mezzogiorno (Accetturo et al., 2022).

dedicated to the development of the South) and national policies with differentiated effects on the territory.

The public operator influences the activities of economic actors in various ways, by setting the rules and procedures for authorizing the exercise of activities and for their regular performance, by modifying the environmental context (e.g. in terms of infrastructure or control of the territory) in which the activity is conducted, and by supporting financially, in some cases, the investments of enterprises. The performance of public administrations is therefore an important factor that contributes to determining the competitiveness of the territory on which the public action takes place. Strengthening the capacity of the administration can therefore be a decisive factor for development.

The issue of the Public Administration as a key factor in determining the development (or delay) of the territories is complex and multifaceted because it concerns not only management and administration but also politicians. The literature of *political economy* and *public choice* show that politicians do not always behave in such a way as to maximize the collective welfare.[2]

In their study, Presson and Tabellini (2002) highlight a fundamental divergence in goals between politicians and citizens. Politicians typically prioritize goals such as reelection and maximizing consensus, whereas citizens are more concerned with the welfare of their families and communities. This fundamental misalignment of objectives can lead to inefficiencies in the management of public spending.

Shortcomings in the institutional environment not only directly affect the growth potential of the local economic system but also influence the ability to efficiently deliver and adequately design public goods and policies. The relevance of the institutional environment well emerges in the work of Borge et al. (2008),[3] where the cohesive government majorities and high levels of democratic participation increase efficiency.

Understanding and addressing institutional shortcomings is essential for promoting balanced development and reducing regional disparities within the country. This factor could therefore be decisive in explaining the modest results recorded by our country in the last decades.

In focusing on the question of how rather than how much is spent, this work refers to the strand of studies on the quality of public administration, which has recently been the subject of growing interest on the part of economists and policy makers. In this strand of literature, the term quality has come to encompass many meanings that refer to the multiple aspects through which the institutional context can foster, or at least not hinder, long-term economic growth. Among others, we cite transparency, simplification, governance, responsibility, and control as the most

---

[2] The relationship between citizens and the political class is, in some respects, comparable to that of principal agent, with the consequent risks of opportunism and moral hazard.

[3] The authors construct an aggregate index of public administration efficiency for approximately 400 Norwegian provinces in 2001–2005. It includes six types of services: elderly care, primary and secondary education, kindergarten, day care, welfare services, and basic medical care.

relevant characteristics for a good quality of the institutional context (Accetturo et al., 2022b; IMF, 2015).

Any policy, even one that is theoretically sound and capable of correctly choosing objectives and methods, can be thwarted by the way in which these choices are implemented. Implementation difficulties are part of the more general issue of quality of public administration and policy governance.

The aim of this chapter is to understand if the institutional context and the quality of administration, with the connected mechanisms of expenditure management, play any role in explaining the regional gaps.

The issue is particularly current because of the great amount of European resources assigned to our country for the recovery of the economy after the covid-19 era: without changes, it will be difficult to fully exploit the potential contribution of investment to the growth of the economy. In this work, we adopt a multidimensional perspective, by examining the relationship between economic performance indicators and other measures of well-being in the different regions (European Quality of Government and Social Cohesion Indexes).

We hope that this approach allows for a more comprehensive evaluation of regional development and can suggest policies and interventions aimed at enhancing overall well-being in different regions.

This chapter is organized as follows. In Sect. 50.2, we review the related literature; in Sect. 50.3, we describe data, methodology, and results; and in Sect. 50.4, we conclude.

49.2 Literature Review

Economic theory has in recent years attached increasing importance to the role that national or sub-national institutions play in fostering economic development.[4]

Various studies show that the Mezzogiorno lags behind in the quantity and, especially, in the quality of the supply of essential services such as justice, health, education, security, and in local public services (Accetturo et al., 2022b; Arpaia et al., 2009; Giordano et al., 2009). These differences are rooted in the past but also depend on current administrative capacities and the socio-institutional context in which the policies operate.

Different international works (de Jong et al., 2017; IMF, 2015; Gupta et al., 2014; Chakraborty and Dabla-Norris, 2009), document that both the quality of the institutional context in which economic activity takes place and the action of the public administration can significantly affect the growth and development gaps between economies and, within them, between different regions. In Italy, Ferro et al.

---

[4] In contrast to the neoclassical model, with the development of endogenous growth theory in the late 1980s and new theories of regional growth (Krugman, 1991), arguments emerged in favor of a specific role attributable to national institutions in general and local institutions.

in the late 1990s (1998 and 1999) signaled the Italian public administration as one of the crucial elements of the country's poor economic performance.

Also, in the policy debate on the gap between the South and the Centre North, this factor has always been considered among the most relevant (Cannari & Franco, 2010).

Numerous empirical works have highlighted how the action, efficiency, administrative capacity, and governmental institutions can have direct effects on the increase in per capita income and are able to explain the persistence of growth differentials both between nations (Hall & Jones, 1999; Knack & Keefer, 1997) and between regions within the same country (Caroleo & Coppola, 2005). The view of public administration as a key factor in determining the development (or backwardness) of territories is widely shared also by the studies of the most important international economic organizations (IMF, 2015; World Bank, 2020).

According to some studies at the European level (Becker et al., 2013; Rodríguez-Pose & Garcilazo, 2015), the quantity of resources deployed alone cannot be regarded as a sufficient condition for the success of public policies: the institutional quality at the local level seems to be one of the main drivers of the effectiveness of territorial policies.

Our work is in line with the institutionalist literature of growth (Hall & Jones, 1999; Acemoglu et al., 2005): what is particularly relevant is a concept of institutional context in a broad sense, encompassing both political and economic dimensions, as well as formal and informal aspects (such as conventions, social cohesion, and widespread rules of conduct).

From a policy perspective, our work fits with the body of studies that suggests that the link between investment and development outcomes depends critically on the quality and efficiency of public capital: this points out that is essential to go beyond discussions of spending levels and addressing issues of the broad institutional framework underpinning the provision of investment (IMF, 2015).

In Italy, starting with Putnam's study (1993), which noted huge differences in the functioning of the administrative machine in the 20 Italian regions, revealing widespread inefficiencies in the Mezzogiorno, many studies have analyzed the performance gaps in public spending between the Mezzogiorno and the rest of Italy.

The link between public policies and local institutional quality emerges in the work of Barone and Mocetti (2014), who examine the economic effect of public intervention following the earthquakes in Friuli (in the North, 1976) and Irpinia (in the South, 1980). Their work uses the synthetic control method, comparing the GDP per capita of the affected area with that of a combination of a group of regions, tending to belong to the same macro-area, not affected by the earthquake. The results of the study indicate that, in both cases, in the years immediately following the earthquake, the trend in GDP per capita benefited from the expansionary effect of the large flow of funds linked to the emergency and reconstruction. In the long term, on the contrary, the effects were opposite: after 20 years the GDP per capita in Friuli-Venezia Giulia was 23% higher than that of the control group; in Irpinia it was 12% lower. One potential explanation of these differences between the two areas can depend on the different initial conditions before the earthquake in terms of the quality of institutions: lower than the national average in Irpinia, higher in Friuli.

Regarding more recent years, similar evidence emerges from the study by Barone et al. (2017).[5]

Their results suggest that the implemented program's impact in the regions of Southern Italy was only partially effective; moreover, the impact differed considerably between regions and objectives, particularly in connection with the different local institutional quality.

Baltrunaite et al. (2021), based on data from the Open-Anac database of the National Anti-Corruption Authority and the Public Administrations Database of the Ministry of Economy and Finance, analyse the completion times of public works in Italy in the period 2012–2020. The results indicate that with the same characteristics of the work and the contracting administration, the public works managed by the administrations of the South show generally longer completion times, i.e., entrusting and execution[6] (Accetturo, 2022a).

The high heterogeneity observed in Italy thus signals the existence of local factors that play a relevant role in determining the quality of the institutional context and the effectiveness of public policies (Becker et al., 2013).

In this chapter, we adopt a multidimensional perspective by crossing economic data with quality government perception and social cohesion indexes. This perspective strives to enhance our comprehension of how various variables interact and influence each other, thereby providing a more comprehensive framework for conducting further research and taking effective action.

This is in line with the literature that, starting from the work of Stiglitz et al. (2009), emphasizes that growth and well-being can no longer be thought of according to economic criteria but must be considered in a way that defines the intersection, place by place, of different inequalities as well as social dimensions.

49.3 Data, Methodology, and Results

Our work starts with a cluster analysis using distinctive economic data to establish if there is a significant similar or different pattern among the Italian regions. Results are in line with expectations, confirming the economic heterogeneity between the north and the south of the country. After that, we compare economic data and cluster results with indicators regarding quality of government and social cohesion: the aim

---

[5] The study is on the effectiveness of the program named 'Service Objectives', set up by the Italian government and implemented in the regions of Southern Italy with the aim of encouraging local authorities to achieve specific targets for the provision of public services in the fields of education, services for children and the elderly, waste management, and water supply.

[6] On average almost 700 days, more than 25% longer than in the rest of the country.

is to understand if there is a link between economic and social characteristics in different regions and the quality and effectiveness of governance.

49.3.1 Economic Indexes and Cluster Analysis

To establish if there are significant similar or different patterns among the singular Italian regions, a cluster analysis has been used with distinctive economic data. The indexes used, extracted by ISTAT (2020), are GDP per capita at market prices, value added per person employed, value added per hour worked, final consumption per capita, compensation for employees per hour worked, added value per inhabitant, and households' disposable income per inhabitant. Data were processed using IBM SPSS version: 28.0.1.9.

These data have been standardized to eliminate scale factors that could be disrupted the algorithm and saved as new variables called Z scores. The k-means cluster analysis with normalized scores—as shown in Table 49.1—has been reached with two iterations, and two natural clusters have been identified (Table 49.2).

From the following ANOVA table (Table 49.3), it is inferred that every variable has a maximum significance (<0.001) as shown from Fisher's test. The highest influence is linked to "value added per hour worked" (81.916), which is one of the most important measures to analyse the productivity of an economic system and one of the most used indicators of the economic growth. The lowest influence is "final consumption per capita" (21.906).

In line with expectations, the clustering split Italy into two parts (Fig. 49.1): a clear separation emerges between the northern regions,[7] with two regions from the

Table 49.1 Iteration history

	Change in cluster centers	
Iteration	1	2
1	1.497	2.342
2	0.000	0.000

[a]Convergence achieved due to no or small change in cluster centers. The maximum absolute coordinate change for any center is 0.000. The current iteration is 2. The minimum distance between initial centers is 8.178

Table 49.2 Number of cases in each cluster

Cluster	1	10.000
	2	10.000
Valid		20.000
Missing		0.000

---

[7] Valle d'Aosta, Piemonte, Liguria, Lombardia, Veneto, Trentino Alto Adige (Provincia Autonoma di Bolzano and Provincia Autonoma di Trento), Friuli Venezia Giulia, Emilia Romagna.

Table 49.3 ANOVA

	Cluster Mean square	df	Error Mean square	df	F	Sig.
Z scores_GDP per capita at market prices	14.707	1	0.239	18	61.659	<0.001
Z scores_Value added per person employed	15.249	1	0.208	18	73.174	<0.001
Z scores_Value added per hour worked	15.577	1	0.190	18	81.916	<0.001
Z scores_ Final consumption per capita	10.430	1	0.476	18	21.906	<0.001
Z scores_ Compensation for employees per hour worked	15.069	1	0.218	18	68.997	<0.001
Z scores_ Added value per inhabitant	14.567	1	0.246	18	59.152	<0.001
Z scores_ Households' disposable income per inhabitant	14.973	1	0.224	18	66.918	<0.001

center-west of the country, Lazio and Toscana, and all the other center and southern regions.[8]

For every variable considered, in cluster 1, the medium value is below the average and in cluster 2 is over the average, with quite specular scores for the final cluster centers. As indicated by the ANOVA results in Table 49.3, the value added per hour worked is highest in the final center, suggesting a higher productivity of regions in cluster 2.

Consumption per person is the score with the fewest differences between the two clusters.

The next chart (Fig. 49.2) displays values for different variables across regions.

Most variables exhibit a clear pattern of belonging to specific clusters for each region, except for households' disposable income per inhabitant in the Marche region, which stands out as an outlier. Notably, Trentino Alto Adige consistently shows the highest Z-scores for most variables, indicating relatively higher values compared to other regions, while Calabria consistently exhibits the lowest Z-scores, indicating relatively lower values.

A particularly interesting observation can be made regarding final consumption data. Valle d'Aosta stands out with a substantial deviation from the average values,

---

[8] Umbria, Marche, Abruzzo, Molise, Puglia, Basilicata, Calabria, Sicilia, and Sardegna.

49 National and Regional Disparities: How Recovering? 875

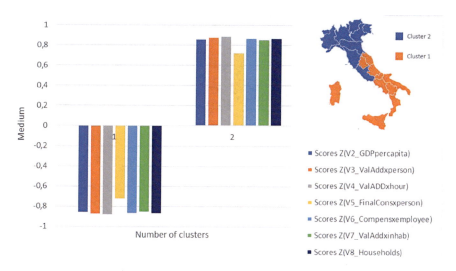

Fig. 49.1 Cluster description

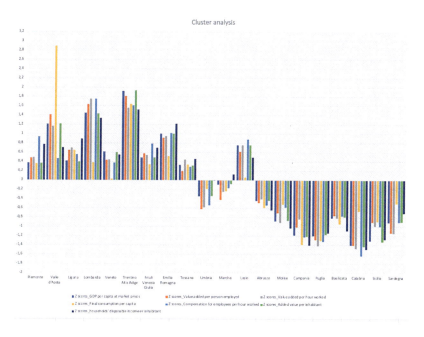

Fig. 49.2 Cluster analysis

suggesting that it has the highest level of consumption among the regions in Italy. On the other hand, Lazio and Veneto are closest to the average values, indicating a more moderate level of consumption compared to other regions.

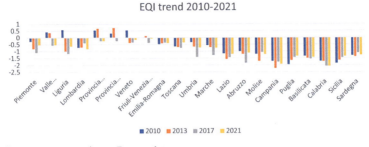

Fig. 49.3 EQI in Italian regions 2017–2021. (Source: Our reprocessing on Eurostat data)

49.3.2 The European Quality of Government Index

With the aim of reaching a more comprehensive evaluation of regional development, we take into consideration an additional indicator: the *European Quality of Government Index*. By analyzing the rankings of Italian regions in relation to this index, we establish correlations with GDP growth and the irregular rate of labor. This multidimensional perspective enhances our understanding of the interplay among different variables and provides a broader framework for further research and action.

The European Quality of Government Index (EQI)[9] collects the average citizen's perceptions and experiences with corruption, quality, and impartiality of three public services: health, education, and policing. As written in the European Commission report, it describes the informal practices of formal institutions. Considering the EU average value of zero, positive indexes are those with values above the EU average, while negative indexes have values below.

As shown in Fig. 49.3, comparing the EQI data from 2017 to 2021, it is observed that most regions in Italy have negative values. This indicates that the average citizen's perceptions and experiences with corruption, quality, and impartiality of public services have generally worsened during this period. Similarly, when analyzing the EQI values for all regions over the past ten years, it is evident that the regions with positive scores were unable to maintain those values consistently, and their recent scores have declined.

Among the various indicators that comprise the EQI, impartiality, which measures the impartiality of institutions exercising government authority, emerges as the most significant. This implies that the perception of impartiality in governance has deteriorated in Italy over the specified period.

---

[9] For European Quality of Government Index, data used are from EU Urban and Regional Development of European Commission. Territorial division is based on Eurostat NUTS (Nomenclature des Unités territoriales statistiques), in particular the hierarchical level NUTS2 that considers regional sub-units, such as Trentino Alto Adige, separated into Provincia Autonoma di Trento and Provincia Autonoma di Bolzano.

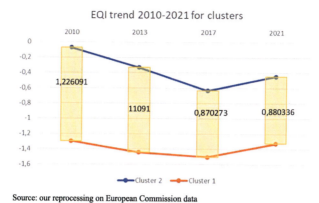

Fig. 49.4 EQI trend between 2010 and 2021. (Source: Our reprocessing on European Commission data)

These findings highlight the importance of addressing issues related to corruption, quality, and impartiality of public services to improve the overall governance and well-being in Italy. Enhancing impartiality in the functioning of institutions can contribute to restoring trust and confidence among citizens and fostering a more favorable environment for growth and development.

It is interesting to note that after a declining trend, several regions in the northern part of Italy have experienced an improvement in their perception of the EQI in 2021. However, Lombardia stands out as an exception, as it has witnessed a negative increase of 0.42 points in its EQI score. This deterioration in perception may be attributed to the challenges and difficulties associated with the COVID-19 pandemic. Lombardia was one of the regions most affected by the pandemic, particularly during the initial stages, and it also recorded a high number of fatalities.

Observing the trend of the EQI values from 2010 to 2021 (Fig. 49.4), it is noteworthy that even the southern regions of Italy consistently maintain the highest negative values. These regions have also demonstrated considerable variability in their scores over the years, with some of them experiencing notable positive variations in 2021. The reasons behind this positive variation may vary, but it could be attributed to specific efforts or improvements made in certain aspects of governance and public service delivery in those regions. Italy has made notable progress in recent years in terms of its positioning in international rankings: in the Corruption Perceptions Index, calculated every year on 180 countries by Transparency International,[10] Italy has, during the last two years, improved 11 positions on the global ranking. This reflects the country's efforts toward economic and social development. However, it is important to acknowledge that despite

---

[10] https://www.transparency.org/en/cpi/2022

this progress, Italy's overall position still lags significantly behind other European countries.

When comparing the EQI trends from 2010 to 2021 for the two clusters (Fig. 49.4), there are noticeable differences and similarities. One prominent observation is the consistent proximity between the two trends, with a difference of approximately one point throughout the years. This distance, although it decreased from 2010 to 2017, has increased again in 2021.

Both clusters exhibit a similar pattern of worsening until 2017, followed by an improvement in 2021. However, this improvement seems to be less significant for cluster 1 compared to cluster 2. According to the European Commission report, this pattern can be partially explained by a significant decline in the rate of corruption, which has positively impacted the EQI scores. However, the other indicators show negligible changes over the years.

Overall, while there are similarities in the general trend of improvement in EQI scores from 2017 to 2021, there are also notable differences between the two clusters, suggesting variations in the perception and experiences of corruption and quality of public services across regions.

The territorial gaps in institutional quality within Italy seem to be more pronounced compared to other major countries, most European, such as France, Germany, Spain, and the United Kingdom. These countries also experience significant internal economic disparities. However, the differences in institutional quality within Italy appear to be even higher (Albanese & Gentili, 2021).

Additionally, when comparing Italy's average institutional quality and public action to other countries on an international scale, Italy tends to have lower scores. This observation is based on the average of the WGI indicators (Worldwide Governance Indicators)[11] for the EU28 countries during the period of 2010–2017.

Figure 49.5 illustrates this comparison, highlighting Italy's lower average institutional quality in relation to other European Union countries during the specified timeframe.

The EQI index has been found to be correlated with GDP per capita. The linear regression analysis between these variables, with a correlation index of 0.79, reveals a distinct division between two clusters. Cluster 2 comprises regions with a GDP per capita higher than the center-south regions in Cluster 1.

It is interesting to note that despite their higher GDP per capita and a larger population, regions such as Lazio and Lombardia have lower EQI levels compared to some center-south regions. This suggests that the complexity of administering these densely populated and economically significant regions may pose challenges in maintaining high levels of perceived corruption, quality, and impartiality in public services. The influx of large funds may create an environment where the oversight and monitoring of resource allocation become more complex. This is in line with the literature (De Angelis et al., 2018) that shows that the availability of substantial

---

[11] The WGI indicators assess various dimensions of governance and institutional quality and are normalized on a scale of 0–100.

Fig. 49.5 Institutional quality indicators at national level (2010, 2017). (Source: Albanese and Gentili (2021)) The indicators considered are the following: *cce* control of corruption, *gee* government effectiveness, *pve* political stability and absence of violence, *rle* rule of law, *rqe* regulatory quality, *vae* voice and accountability

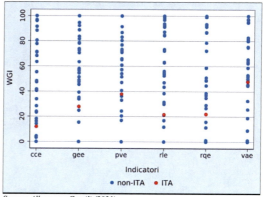

Source: Albanese e Gentili (2021)

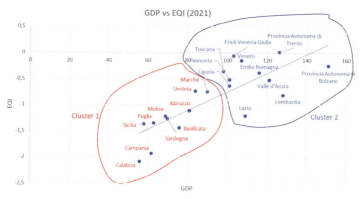

Source: our reprocessing on Istat and European Commission data, 2022

Fig. 49.6 GDP vs EQI, 2021. (Source: our reprocessing on Istat and European Commission data, 2022)

financial resources can indeed present challenges in terms of accountability among local administrators and the potential for opportunistic behavior (Fig. 49.6).

In addition, with the aim of investigating if any connection emerges, we consider the relationship between the rate of irregularity in labor[12] and the EQI. We chose the rate of irregularity in labor as a possible *proxy* for the trust that employers and employees have in the regulatory system.

The main drivers behind irregular labor can be grouped into economic and administrative motivators. Undeclared work provides individuals with the opportunity to maximize the income of their enterprise while avoiding taxes and other financial obligations. By operating in the informal sector, individuals can potentially

---

[12] The rate of irregularity in labor, as measured by ISTAT 2021, indicates the proportion of individuals working without a regular employment contract per 100 employed individuals.

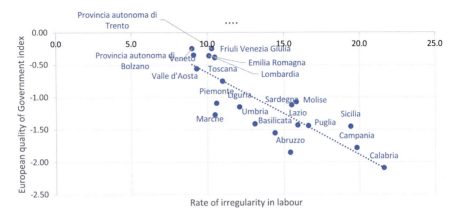

Fig. 49.7 Rate of irregularity vs EQI, 2021. (Source: Our reprocessing on Istat and European Commission data)

retain more of their earnings and reduce the burden of contributions. The administrative reasons can relate to the greater flexibility and simplicity of a not formal contract (EEPO, 2016).

The economic consequence is that lower revenues lead to lower levels of services, higher taxation for those who pay regularly, and therefore lower economic growth in the short and medium terms.

The linear regression between the EQI index and the rate of irregularity in labor shows a high value of correlation.

As shown in Fig. 49.7, areas such as Provincia Autonoma di Bolzano (9) and Veneto (9.1) have the lowest rates of irregular workers, while Calabria (21.6) and Campania (19.8) have the highest rates of irregular workers. It is noteworthy that the regions with the highest rates of irregularity also tend to have the lowest EQI scores, indicating a negative correlation (0.84) between the two variables. These regions are predominantly located in the center-south of Italy: according to the European Employment Policies Observatory (EEPO, 2016) report, in some areas, mainly in Southern Italy, there exists a cultural acceptance of the informal economy, and undeclared work is sometimes perceived as a form of reciprocal assistance between employers and employees. This cultural tolerance toward undeclared work creates an environment where it can thrive and be sustained.

In this scenario, it is challenging to determine the dependent variable because there may be a reciprocal relationship between the two factors, creating a negative feedback loop. A low EQI score may lead individuals to engage in informal practices, seeking to navigate the system outside legal boundaries. Conversely, labor irregularity can contribute to economic and social issues, ultimately resulting in a lower EQI score.

Multiple studies (Accetturo et al., 2022a; Cappariello & Zizza, 2009) have consistently demonstrated that individuals with higher levels of education are more likely to secure regular employment. In the context of Italy, the southern regions, which experience a high prevalence of irregular employment, also face challenges in terms of human capital development. There is a notable delay in the production of human capital in these regions, and they struggle to retain highly skilled young individuals within their territories.[13] High unemployment and irregularity rates indeed encourage emigration and reduce the labor attractiveness of the southern regions, contributing to the demographic decline of the area and the shrinking of the southern production base, undermining long-term growth potential.

49.3.3 The Social Cohesion and Inclusion Index

We consider social cohesion as another index useful for the comparison of various characteristics across different regions. It provides insights into the level of inclusiveness, equality, and overall well-being within a given population.

The Observatory for Social Cohesion and Inclusion (OCIS)[14] defines social cohesion as a concept encompassing individual orientations, behaviors, and institutional outcomes that aim to reduce inequalities and disadvantages within a specific population.

Social cohesion encompasses factors such as political participation, economic opportunities, gender equality, cultural integration, social inclusion, non-discrimination, and environmental sustainability.[15] These indicators encompass different aspects of society and aim to provide a comprehensive understanding of social cohesion within a region.

By analyzing social cohesion indicators, policymakers and researchers can gain a better understanding of the strengths and weaknesses of different regions, identify

---

[13] In comparison with other industrialized economies, Italy is characterized by the presence of a large undeclared sector, much more extensive in the South. This dualism clashes with the substantial homogeneity, at least de jure, of the regulatory framework and of the tax regulations, considered in the literature to be one of the main factors capable of explaining the differences between countries in the diffusion rates of the informal sector.

[14] https://osservatoriocoesionesociale.eu/

[15] The politics indicator focuses on the participation and engagement of individuals in political processes, reflecting the level of trust and involvement in governance. The society indicator assesses social relationships, community engagement, and social capital within the region. The economy indicator examines factors such as employment rates, income distribution, and economic opportunities, shedding light on the economic dimensions of social cohesion. Gender equality is another important component, measuring the degree of gender equity and equal opportunities for individuals. The culture indicator considers cultural diversity, social integration, and access to cultural resources and activities. Social inclusion and non-discrimination indicator evaluates the extent to which all members of society are included and treated fairly, regardless of their background or characteristics. Finally, the environment indicator assesses the state of the environment and sustainable practices, reflecting the importance of ecological factors in promoting social cohesion.

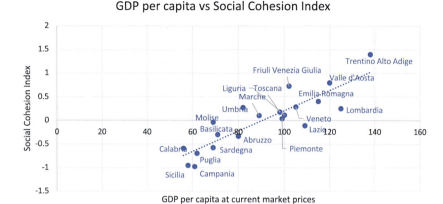

Fig. 49.8 GDP per capita vs social cohesion index, 2021. (Source: our reprocessing on Istat and OCIS data)

areas that require attention and improvement, and develop strategies to foster social cohesion and inclusive development.

The linear regression between the EQI index and the rate of irregularity in labor shows a high value of correlation (Fig. 49.8).

Interestingly, the social cohesion index (SCI) shows a strong correlation with GDP per capita, with a correlation coefficient of 0.87. Data on the social cohesion index appear to reflect the regional geographical order of Italy: the most cohesive regions are found in the North and Central North, while the level of cohesion drops as we move toward the southern regions. Additionally, regions with a lower GDP per capita tend to have lower scores on the social cohesion index.

These findings suggest that there is a relationship between economic development, as measured by GDP per capita, and social cohesion. Higher levels of economic prosperity in certain regions may contribute to better outcomes in terms of social cohesion indicators. However, it is important to note that social cohesion is a multifaceted concept that encompasses various dimensions beyond economic factors, and addressing disparities and promoting social cohesion requires a comprehensive approach that goes beyond income considerations. Relevant for the issue is the work of Accetturo et al. (2014): the authors show that the disbursement of EU funds negatively influenced the degree of civic sense and social cooperation in the most deprived areas. Their work investigates the extent to which the presence of public transfers to the most disadvantaged areas and the efficiency in the use of these funds influence the cultural values and social capital of a given locality.[16]

---

[16] The concepts of social capital and social cohesion are closely interconnected. Berger-Schmitt (2000) sees social capital as one of the two key elements of social cohesion, namely: 'the reduction of disparities, inequalities, and social exclusion', and 'the strengthening of social relations,

The findings suggest that the presence of EU transfers has a negative effect on the level of general trust and cooperation among individuals. The study highlights that the loss of social capital is linked to the prevalence of distortions in the allocation and utilization of funds. In other words, when there are more available transfers and the management of public goods and services financed by cohesion policies is less efficient, the likelihood of distortions in fund usage increases, leading to a decline in social capital.

The research also employs a theoretical model to analyze the behavioral implications of transfers on individuals. It underscores the importance of efficient and effective utilization of funds to prevent the erosion of social capital. The study emphasizes that the negative impact on social cooperation arises from the presence of inefficiencies and mismanagement in the distribution and utilization of EU funds.

This aspect is further explored in De Angelis et al. (2018), who analyze the relationship between public transfers and the incidence of crimes against public administration (PA) at the local level. The possibility of benefiting from large financial resources from national or supranational sources can in fact reduce the degree of accountability of local administrators and incentivize opportunistic behavior. Using data on the European structural funds allocated to the Mezzogiorno in the 2007–2013 cycle, authors indicate the existence of a positive correlation between the amount of European funds and the number of crimes against the PA recorded in the destination municipality. In particular, a 10% increase in transfers would be associated with a 0.4% increase in crimes.

In our opinion, social cohesion can also be linked to the issue of *tax fairness*. The MEF report (2021) shows how the degree of tax and social security contribution evasion is higher in the southern regions. In particular, the "tax gap" (defined as the difference between theoretical revenue and actual revenue calculated at a basic or standard rate) is significantly higher in the South both for income and consumption taxation, also in line with the higher incidence of the unobserved economy.

The examined indicators in the work consistently suggest poorer performance in the southern regions, albeit with some variations: the first relevant piece of information to grasp is that the strong regional economic gaps in the country are also found in terms of EQI and social cohesion.

The work does not aim to determine whether this lower quality is the cause or consequence of the underdeveloped socio-economic environment in which these regions operate. However, it is our belief that the economic growth of the Mezzogiorno cannot be detached from the need to improve the performance of public institutions and establish a "good government" characterized by efficiency and effectiveness. Such improvements are crucial prerequisites for any development efforts.

---

interactions and ties' (Berger-Schmitt, 2000: 3). The second element contains aspects such as social relations that are traditionally linked to social capital.

49.4 Conclusions

It is worth noting that the quality of public action, as summarized by the EQI in the paper, is closely associated not only with higher levels of GDP per capita but also with other not economic well-being indicators such as social cohesion, public capital, and fiscal loyalty. The combination of a high incidence of irregular employment and limited human capital development poses significant obstacles to the economic growth and development of the southern regions.

Although the positioning of the southern regions in the analyzed rankings is, on a national level, overall, systematically unflattering, it cannot be ignored that the northern regions also perform below average in the European context. This makes the competitiveness deficit a national issue. No Italian region, for any of the indicators considered, records values significantly above the European average. The result is the image of a country that is excluded from the core of Europe. The problem of modest growth in the Mezzogiorno is a problem largely connected with the weakness of the Italian environment.

The literature on the territorial disparities has shown that the heterogeneity of the results of public action is not fully explained by observable factors, including primarily financial resources, and that elements attributable to organizational factors also play a role: an adequate level of local institutional quality can be considered an essential precondition for well-functioning public policies.

About recent years, the perception of the low quality of regional policies in Italy remains widespread. It manifests itself in the main limitations highlighted by the public debate: the delays and deficits in the programming phase; the low speed of implementation, especially connected to bureaucratic slowness and the weight of lead times; the excessive emphasis on transfers and incentives, which have often proved ineffective, especially with reference to those distributed according to discretionary practices; the high fragmentation in objectives and interventions.

One aspect that is less highlighted, however, is how inefficient use of public funds and institutional quality deficits can reinforce each other, thus triggering a vicious circle. We think that this situation could become ever more a dangerous reality in our country if the national system of rules will not change, taking the direction of transparency, control, and responsibility. Politics must play the fundamental role but all of us, as citizens, must work and push in this direction through active participation, cooperation, and respect for the common goods.

The work by Accetturo et al. (2014) shed light on the complex relationship between EU transfers, cultural values, and social capital in deprived areas. Their work underscores the significance of proper management and efficient utilization of funds to mitigate the potential negative consequences and preserve social cohesion in beneficiary regions.

These considerations are particularly relevant at a time when Italy benefits from many resources under the Next Generation EU. The recovery and resilience facility (RRF) provides an opportunity for the country to rethink public action with potential benefits for the country strengthening the leading role of the state and outlining a results-oriented approach.

It cannot be ignored that transferring resources to disadvantaged areas could be detrimental if this encourages rent-seeking and increases the payoff of deviant behavior (such as corruption).

Our work considered only few indicators and cannot be considered conclusive. Nevertheless, we think that the process to cross quantitative and qualitative data can suggest relevant relationships, useful in the direction to address policies and rules.

We note that, despite the widespread acknowledgement that improving the efficiency and effectiveness of public administrations' actions contributes to making a local system more competitive, there is a substantial lack of disaggregated data at regional level capable of highlighting the different levels of development and competitive capacity of public administrations. The need for indicators in this area is particularly felt since it is only from a comparative analysis of the actions of the various administrations that it is possible to understand what the "best practices" are and study their impact on local economic realities.

References

Acemoglu, D., Johnson, S., & Robinson, J. (2005). Chapter 06: Institutions as a fundamental cause of long-run growth. In *Handbook of Economic Growth X* (vol. 1, Part A, pp 385–472). From Elsevier.

Accetturo A., Albanese, G., Ballatore, R. M., Ropele, T., & Sestito, P. (2022a). *I divari territoriali in Italia tra crisi economiche, ripresa ed emergenza sanitaria.* [Territorial gaps in Italy between economic crises, recovery, and health emergency] Banca d'Italia, Questioni di Economia e Finanza, n. 685. [Online] Available from https://www.bancaditalia.it/pubblicazioni/qef/2022-0685/index.html?dotcache=refresh. Accessed 20 May 2023

Accetturo, A., Albanese, G., & Torrini, R. (2022b). *Il divario nord-sud: sviluppo economico e intervento pubblico.* [The North-South divide: economic development and public intervention] Banca d'Italia. [online] Available from https://www.bancaditalia.it/pubblicazioni/collana-seminari-convegni/2022-0025/n-25_mezzogiorno.pdf. Accessed 20 May 2023

Accetturo, A., de Blasio, G., & Ricci, L. (2014). A tale of an unwanted outcome: Transfers and local endowments of trust and cooperation. *Journal of Economic Behavior & Organization, 102,* 74–89.

Albanese, G., & Gentili, E. (2021). Indicatori territoriali di qualità delle istituzioni: un aggiornamento. [Territorial quality indicators of institutions: an update]. *Regional economy, 5*(Q3), 43–58.

Arpaia, C. M., Doronzo, R. & Ferro, P. (2009). *Informatizzazione, trasparenza contabile e competitività della Pubblica amministrazione: un'analisi a livello regionale.* [Computerisation, accounting transparency and competitiveness of the public administration: an analysis at the regional level] [online] Available from https://www.bancaditalia.it/pubblicazioni/qef/2009-0048/QEF_48.pdf?language_id=1. Accessed 20 May 2023

Baltrunaite A., Orlando, T., & Rovigatti, G. (2021). *La realizzazione dei lavori pubblici in Italia: fattori istituzionali e caratteristiche regionali.* [The implementation of public works in Italy: institutional factors and regional characteristics] Banca d'Italia, Questioni di Economia e Finanza, n. 659. [online] Available from https://www.bancaditalia.it/pubblicazioni/qef/20210659/index.html?com.dotmarketing.htmlpage.language=102. Accessed 20 May 2023

Bardozzetti A., Chiades, P., Mancini, A. L., Mengotto, V., & Ziglio, G. (2022). *Criticità e prospettive della finanza comunale nel Mezzogiorno alla vigilia del Covid-19.* [Critical issues and perspectives of municipal finance in the South on the eve of the Covid-19] Banca d'Italia, Questioni di Economia e Finanza. [Online] Available from https://www.bancaditalia.it/pubblicazioni/qef/2022-0708/index.html. Accessed 20 May 2023

Barone G., de Blasio G., D'Ignazio A., & Salvati A. (2017). *Incentives to local public service provision: An evaluation of Italy's Obiettivi di Servizio*. Bank of Italy occasional papers N. 388. [Online] Available from https://www.bancaditalia.it/pubblicazioni/qef/2017-0388/index.html?language_id=1. Accessed 20 May 2023

Barone, G., & Mocetti, S. (2014). Natural disasters, growth and institutions: A tale of two earthquakes. *Journal of Urban Economics, 84*, 52–66.

Becker, S. O., Egger, P. H., & von Ehrlich, M. (2013). Absorptive capacity and the growth and investment effects of regional transfers: A regression discontinuity design with heterogeneous treatment effects. *American Economic Journal: Economic Policy, 5*, 29–77.

Berger-Schmitt, R. (2000). *Social cohesion as an aspect of the quality of societies: Concept and measurement*. EuReporting Working Paper No. 14, Centre for Survey Research and Methodology (ZUMA), Mannheim.

Borge, L. E., Falch, T., & Tvomo, P. (2008). Public sector efficiency: The roles of political and budgetary institutions, fiscal capacity, and democratic participation. *Public Choice, 136*, 475–495.

Bucci M., Gennari, E. G., Ivaldi, Messina, G. & Moller, L. (2021). *I divari infrastrutturali in Italia: una misurazione caso per caso*. [Infrastructural gaps in Italy: a case-by-case measurement] Banca d'Italia, Questioni di Economia e Finanza, n. 635. [Online] Available from https://www.bancaditalia.it/pubblicazioni/qef/2021-0635/index.html. Accessed 20 May 2023

Cannari L., & Franco, D. (2010). *Il Mezzogiorno e la politica economica dell'Italia*. [The south and the economic policy of Italy] Banca d'Italia, Seminari e Convegni, n. 4. [Online] Available from https://www.bancaditalia.it/dotAsset/261c5662-0cf4-47cd-9fa0-2d0162ce03ea.pdf. Accessed 20 May 2023

Caroleo, F., & Coppola, G. (2005). *The impact of the institutions on regional unemployment disparities*. Università di Salerno, discussion paper no. 98. CELPE Discussion Papers 98, CELPE – Centre of Labour Economics and Economic Policy, University of Salerno. [Online]. Available from https://www3.unisa.it/uploads/2551/98_dp.pdf. Accessed 20 May 2023

Cappariello, R., & Zizza, R. (2009). *Dropping the books and working off the books*. Banca d'Italia, [Online] Available from https://www.bancaditalia.it/pubblicazioni/temidiscussione/2009/20090702/en_tema_702.pdf?language_id=1. Accessed 20 May 2023.

Chakraborty, S., & Dabla-Norris, E. (2009). The quality of public investment. *IMF Working Papers, 2009*(154).

de Jong, J., Ferdinandusse, M., Vetlov, I., & Funda, J. (2017). *The effect of public investment in Europe: A model-based assessment*. No 2021, Working Paper Series from European Central Bank. [online] Available at: https://www.ecb.europa.eu/pub/pdf/scpwps/ecbwp2021.en.pdf. Accessed 14 June 2023.

De Angelis, I., de Blasio G. & Rizzica L. (2018). *On the unintended effects of public transfers: Evidence from EU funding to southern Italy*. Bank of Italy working papers N. 1180. [Online] Available from https://www.bancaditalia.it/pubblicazioni/temi-discussione/2018/2018-1180/index.html?com.dotmarketing.htmlpage.language=1. Accessed 20 May 2023

European Employment Policies Observatory (EEPO, 2016). European Platform tackling undeclared work Member State Factsheets and Synthesis Report. Available from https://www.uiltucs.it/wp-content/uploads/2016/11/Study-UDW-in-MS-Factsheets-and-synthesis.pdf. Accessed 20 May 2023

Ferro P., Momigliano S., & Salvemini G. (1998). Sistemi imprenditoriali, pubblica amministrazione e competitività. [Entrepreneurial systems, public administration and competitiveness.] in *I controlli delle gestioni pubbliche*. [The controls of public management] Banca d'Italia, Roma.

Ferro, P., Lo Faso, S., & Salvemini, G. (1999). L'azione della pubblica amministrazione per la competitività internazionale in presenza di vincoli di finanza pubblica. [The action of the public administration for international competitiveness in the presence of public finance constraints] in

Concorrenza fiscale in un'economia internazionale integrata. [Tax competition in an integrated international economy] edited by Bordignon M. & Empoli D., Franco Angeli,.

Giordano, R., Tommasino, P. & Casiraghi, M. (2009). *Le determinanti dell'efficienza del settore pubblico: il ruolo della cultura e delle istituzioni.* [The determinants of public sector efficiency: the role of culture and institutions] [Online] Available from https://www.bancaditalia.it/pubblicazioni/collanaseminariconvegni/20090002/2_volume_mezzogiorno.pdf. Accessed 20 May 2023

Gupta, S., Kangur, A., Papageorgiou, & Wane, A. (2014). Efficiency-Adjusted Public Capital and Growth. *World Economic Development, 57*(C), 164–78.

Hall, R., & Jones, C. (1999). Why do some countries produce so much more output than others? *The Quarterly Journal of Economics, 114*, 83–116.

Iammarino, S., Rodriguez-Pose, A., & Storper, M. (2019). Regional inequality in Europe: Evidence, theory and policy implications. *Journal of Economic Geography, 19*, 273–298.

IMF, (2015). *Making Public Investment more efficient.* [online] Available from https://www.imf.org/external/np/pp/eng/2015/061115.pdf. Accessed 20 May 2023

Knack, S., & Keefer, P. (1997). Does social capital have an economic payoff? A cross-country investigation. *The Quarterly Journal of Economics, 112*(4), 1251–88.

Krugman, P. (1991). Increasing returns and economic geography. *Journal of Political Economy, 99*, 183–199.

Presson, T., & Tabellini, G. (2002). Political economics and public finance. *Handbook of Public Economics, 3*, 1549–1659.

Rodríguez-Pose, A., & Garcilazo, E. (2015). Quality of government and the returns of investment: Examining the impact of cohesion expenditure in European regions. *Regional Studies, 49*(8), 1274–1290.

Stiglitz, J., Sen, A., & Fitoussi, J.P. (2009). The measurement of economic performance and social progress revisited: Reflections and overview. *Sciences Po publications* 2009–33, Sciences Po.

Viesti, G. (2019). *Centri e periferie. Europa, Italia, Mezzogiorno dal XX al XXI secolo.* [Centers and peripheries. Europe, Italy, Southern Italy from the 20th to the 21st century] Laterza.

World Bank. (2020). *Doing business in Italia.* [Online] Available from https://subnational.doingbusiness.org/content/dam/doingBusiness/media/Subnational/DB2020-SNDB-ITL-Report-Italian.pdf. Accessed 20 May 2023

Chapter 50
The Impact of Insurance Needs Satisfaction on Consumers' Purchase and Repurchase Intention

Dimitrios Karnachoritis and Irene Samanta

Abstract The purpose of this research was to examine the impact of insurance needs satisfaction on consumer's purchase intention and repurchase intention. The satisfaction of needs touches the core of private insurance as well as the core of marketing. Specifically, this research examines whether needs satisfaction is a factor that affects the formation of the purchase intention and repurchase intention variables. In order to examine all the above, a qualitative research was held in inductive manner, under the research philosophy of phenomenology via depth interviews. Depth interviews were conducted in June of 2022 out of five professionals of the Greek insurance market. The thorough analysis of primary data and coding of the findings with interdisciplinary approach combined with the subjectivity and reflexivity of the researcher contributed to the completion of the construction of the theory. The correct coverage of the needs affects the fulfillment satisfaction of the customer's insurance needs, and as a sequence, the needs satisfaction (*needSat*) affects the purchase intention as well as the repurchase intention.

Keywords Purchase intention · Repurchase intention · Customer satisfaction · Needs satisfaction · (needSat) · Insurance needs · Relationship marketing · Consumer behavior · Decision-making

50.1 Introduction

The insurance industry is one of the three main financial markets, along with the banking and stock exchange industry, which is called upon to compensate financial losses in accidental and not ordinary damaging events (Tajudeen et al.,

---

D. Karnachoritis (✉) · I. Samanta
Department of Business Administration, School of Administrative, Economics and Social Sciences, University of West Attica, Aigaleo, Greece
e-mail: dkarnachoritis@uniwa.gr

© The Author(s), under exclusive license to Springer Nature Switzerland AG 2024
N. Tsounis, A. Vlachvei (eds.), *Applied Economic Research and Trends*, Springer Proceedings in Business and Economics,
https://doi.org/10.1007/978-3-031-49105-4_50

889

2009). The institution of insurance is based on the minimization of losses and the sharing of risk (Treerattanapun, 2011). Preventing and forestalling economic disasters contributes to the development of the national economy index.

Despite the socioeconomic nature of insurance and the benefits it offers, it is treated by many consumers as a product of secondary importance (Treerattanapun, 2011). There are many consumers who, although they believe that insurance is an important product, do not have an insurance policy (Kunreuther & Pauly, 2005). Insurance as an institution shows downward trends in the Greek Market, while the GDP from insurance activities barely reaches 2.63%, when the European Market fluctuates at 7.43% (Hellenic Association of Insurance Companies, 2022).

Understanding consumer's behavior toward insurance products and identifying those factors that contribute to the development of the institution of insurance is of crucial importance. For a more complete understanding of consumer behavior, it is important to correctly identify consumer's real needs. Recognizing and identifying the consumer's needs is the key success factor (Karnachoritis & Samanta, 2020). The prioritization of consumer's insurance needs can contribute to the improvement of insurance market and at the same time, growth of insurance operations and GDP index (Karnachoritis & Samanta, 2020).

The purpose of this research was to examine the consumer's insurance needs satisfaction fulfillment correlated to purchase intention and repurchase intention. The satisfaction of needs touches the core of private insurance as well as the core of marketing. Specifically, this research examines whether needs satisfaction is a factor that affects the formation of the purchase intention and repurchase intention variables.

In this way, it will be examined whether needs satisfaction (needSat) as a variable affects the above concepts as well as the effect on the institution of insurance which consequently contributes, either microeconomically and macroeconomically, to the development of insurance companies and to the development of the national economic indexes.

50.2 Literature Review

The Greek insurance industry is divided into private insurance and social insurance. Each of them has a lead role in the social and economic contribution to society. Social insurance is provided by public social insurance operators, has a redistributive nature, and only concerns the insurance of persons. Private insurance is provided by private insurance companies, has capital nature, and concerns the insurance of persons, things, and liabilities.

Private insurance is a main lever of the Greek economy and growth. It is an important statute both for the direct and indirect results it offers. It stably remains, one of the main investors in Greece with investments amounting to €17.4 billion. At the same time, insurance industry constitutes a significant factor against unemployment, since it employs 9700 insurance employees in addition to the 20,000 insurance intermediaries where they operate in the industry (Hellenic Association of Insurance Companies, 2018).

In the Greek insurance market, there are 50 insurance companies active (Hellenic Association of Insurance Companies, 2022) of which, 33 nonlife companies, five exclusively life, and 12 mixed. The above market consists of 30 SA insurance companies, 17 branches of foreign companies, and three mutual insurance cooperatives.

A steady decrease in the number of insurance companies compared to the last few years is observed, where 5 years ago amounted to 57 insurance companies and 61 companies 6 years ago (Hellenic Association of Insurance Companies, 2016).

50.2.1 Insurance Needs Satisfaction (NeedSat)

The insurance market and insurance products have particularities, which differ from traditional retail products as well as other financial products (Nogueira & Oliveira, 2003; Prymostka, 2018).

In insurance and financial products, customers are faced with increased and more complex needs that cannot be met by themselves than in other products (Chung-Herrera, 2007).

According to Zahorik and Rust (1992), variable "satisfaction" is a main variable both in the purchasing behavior equations and in the subsequent reactions and actions of the consumer (Trasorras et al., 2009).

When insurance needs satisfaction is fully achieved, i.e., complete coverage of the customer's needs, there is a stronger purchase intention and repurchase intention. In contrast, in cases where the customer's needs have not been adequately met, there is a withdrawal from the insurance product. As a consequence, in cases where the customer's needs have not been sufficiently met, the customer does not purchase new products apart from the mandatory coverage (Karnachoritis & Samanta, 2020).

Differences appear in how the insured feels and behaves when he feels that his needs have been properly assessed compared to when they have not been properly assessed or partially assessed (Karnachoritis & Samanta, 2020).

Customers feel more calm and less insecure when during the assessment and analysis, their needs have been fully and correctly assessed. Therefore, they feel calm and complete, knowing that they have chosen the ideal product for them according to a correct evaluation of their needs (Karnachoritis & Samanta, 2020).

During the sale process, customer's needs often do not match the proposed offer or the product that is being purchased. The same happens with insurance products as well, with the result that customer's insurance needs are not covered (Strandvik et al., 2012; Vlassis, 1997).

Trying to achieve complete coverage of insurance needs, Karnachoritis and Samanta (2020) proposed the Hierarchy of Insurance Needs Model or otherwise the Pyramid of Insurance Needs which concerns the organized and systematic process of identifying insurance needs for their optimal analysis and evaluation.

The inseparable relationship of danger based on the size of the risk is what determines the Hierarchy of Insurance Needs. In addition, the importance of the risk stems from the damage it can cause (Karnachoritis & Samanta, 2020).

Hence, the most important risk is the risk of loss of human life, and according to the Hierarchy of the Pyramid, the next risk is total incapacitation, partial incapacitation, and temporary incapacitation. The Hierarchy continues with the health insurances that can be covered by both private and social insurance (Karnachoritis & Samanta, 2020).

In the general insurance classes, the most important risks are considered passive risks such as liability, followed by catastrophic active risks and finally other active risks (Karnachoritis & Samanta, 2020).

The Hierarchy of Insurance Needs Model or otherwise the Pyramid of Insurance Needs based on the international classes of insurance is an international tool able to recognize and identify customer's insurance needs minimizing financial losses caused by accidental and not ordinary damaging events (Karnachoritis & Samanta, 2020).

50.2.2 Gaining Commitment Through the Relationship Marketing Philosophy

Every agreement's goal is "the closing" of the sale or as it is called, the completion of an insurance relationship, when we have to deal with insurance products. Levitt (1983) said that the relationship between seller and buyer always ends when a sale is made. How we manage this relationship is critical to its continuation (Trasorras et al., 2009).

One of the early approaches of Relationship Marketing is that of Hammarkvist et al., (1982) which says that Relationship Marketing is all those activities by the business that are needed to build, maintain, and develop customer relationships (Gummesson, 1987), while according to Berry and Parasuraman (1991), RM deals with attracting, developing, and maintaining customer relationships. Jackson's (1985) version differs in that he considers that relationships should be continuing and profitable (Harker, 1999).

Cravens and Piercy (1994) emphasize the management of ongoing business relationships and collaboration, as well as understanding the relationships of the two parties, customer and supplier (Gummesson, 1994), while Evans and Laskin (1996) present a process in which a firm builds long-term alliances with both potential and existing customers so that both the buyer and the seller work toward a common direction having a set of specific goals. Matthyssens and Van den Bulte (1994) state that RM does not just aim at direct transactions but is based on building, supporting, and exploring relationships.

Cant and Van Heerden (2004) schematically describe the RM process as a process with four distinct stages. Each stage is closely interdependent with the others. This means that both parties either the seller or the customer can complete a stage but, if needed, can return to it.

Focusing on the customer, according to Cant and Van Heerden (2004), the four stages of RM are as follows:

- Analyze Needs
- Present Product Benefits
- Gain Commitment
- Service

Gaining Commitment or otherwise the conclusion of the insurance policy is not a specific moment during the insurance sale. Essentially, the Gaining Commitment of the sale of a product can be done at all stages of an insurance presentation, since there is always the possibility that the prospective customer will be excited by a special feature of the product and immediately accept the offer of the program (Samanta & Karnachoritis, 2020).

Schematically, the Gaining Commitment process follows the organized presentation of the intermediary's insurance proposal. In this step, the insurance intermediary must be sure that the customer has completely understood the product he is promoting and its benefits, asking him his opinion about everything he presented to him.

Gaining Commitment or completing the sale is a process that requires training and skills, as well as proper preparation. The seller's incomplete preparation is a key reason for the client to reject the proposal. At this stage, the client may present obstacles (Toman et al., 2017) and objections, which are usually due to:

- Incomplete information
- Need for confirmation
- The fact that he is not fully convinced of the product/service
- The fact that he has not understood the benefits
- The fact that the product does not excite the customer

Customer objections are essentially the reasons for rejection by the customer, and handling them correctly is what leads to a successful sale. Customer objections are usually about the price of the product, their own financial situation, and the need to extend the Gaining Commitment to decide or think about it further (Samanta & Karnachoritis, 2020). Further reasons for rejection are the obstacles encountered by the consumer during the purchase process which the seller must have foreseen in order to eliminate them (Toman et al., 2017).

The preparation of alternative offers beyond the basic proposed program during the presentation is deemed necessary in order to avoid rejection of the product and the conclusion of the insurance policy (Toman et al., 2017).

What finalizes the sale of the product and formalizes the commitment of the agreement is the written conclusion of the agreement that leads to the absolute acceptance of the insurance program by the customer.

At the moment of acceptance of the application, the insurance intermediary carefully ensures that the coverage of the risk undertaken is recorded, thus essentially completing the commitment of the agreement (Cant & Van Heerden, 2004).

Therefore, as supported by Grönroos (1990) in order to build and create relationships, you need promises, which you must fulfill so that these relationships can be maintained. Furthermore, the strengthening of relationships and their long maintenance stems from new promises and correspondingly their fulfillment.

50.2.3 Purchase Intention

Purchase intention constitutes a variable of consumer behavior, and the main aim is to understand the factors that form it. Of critical importance is Ajzen and Fishbein's (1977) theory of Reasoned Action, which asserts that there are two driving forces when it comes to a person's action: behavioral beliefs and normative beliefs.

The psychological factors that influence behavioral intentions are elusive. There is no consensus on the variables that tend to influence them (Cronin et al., 2000; Pauluzzo & Geretto, 2017; Zhao et al., 2012).

The consumer's intention to act in a certain way, according to Ajzen (1991), is influenced and shaped by the consequences that this decision is expected to have on the individual (Ajzen, 1991; Walsh et al., 2012). Behavioral intentions are a representation of a future action that is likely to be performed (Bandura, 2001).

According to Bandura (2001), actions and intentions are completely different and are done at different times. For this reason, Bandura believes that intentions create motivations that influence the final future action. It is considered that purchase intention is a key and powerful factor in the final purchase decision (Walsh et al., 2012).

Bandura (2001) continues by stating that the result of an action is not characteristic of the action itself but its consequence. With the above, he wants to emphasize that possible actions/decisions had, as their initial purpose, a specific result but are likely to bring about a different result than the desired one. It is possible for them to bring about not only an unexpected but even an undesirable result, despite the opposite original intention.

Behavioral intentions and how the customer thinks or acts are also, as mainly reported in the literature, clearly shaped by the culture of each country (Craig & Douglas, 2006; De Mooij & Hofstede, 2002; Hong & Lee, 2012; Knight, 1999; Laroche, 2009).

The purchase intention variable is also influenced by several other factors where, as the researchers report, some of them are encountered more often (Ferreira et al., 2015; Fraering & Minor, 2013; Pauluzzo & Geretto, 2017; Piha & Avlonitis, 2015; Zeithaml, 1988). Some main factors of the purchase intention variable can be considered the "Perceived Quality," the "Brand," and the "Attitudes" (Choi & Coughlan, 2006; Walsh et al., 2012).

Purchase intention follows both perceived quality and satisfaction, which tend to correlate more generally with behavioral intentions (Molinari et al., 2008; Storbacka et al., 1994).

Walsh et al.'s (2012) research confirms that consumers' quality perceptions are more powerful than the antecedent variables of purchase intention. As a consequence, enterprises should emphasize in quality issues clearly and not defy this factor, giving importance to higher quality and more reliable "materials" and "benefits" (Walsh et al., 2012).

Also, according to Zeithaml (1988), the purchase intention and the purchase decision follow the variable value (value) (Molinari et al., 2008).

Zeithaml et al. (1996) agree with the above, who consider that consumer intentions are positively or negatively affected by the level of commitment of the consumer to the company, with the fact that the more the commitment increases, the more the frequency of purchase increases as well, or consciously spends more on the product/service that is interested (Tsoukatos & Rand, 2006).

Purchase intentions are stronger when consumer feels that he is "connected" with a brand (Walsh et al., 2012). Purchase decision is affected by the brand, where the consumer assumes that the product is as valuable as he thinks his brand is (Andersen, 2005; Walsh et al., 2012).

Holt (2006) states that famous brands provide indicative privileges to consumers, making them more acceptable in social life, and at the same time are interactive in relation to the product (Holt, 2006; Walsh et al., 2012).

Researches have shown that the purchasing decision is affected by product's reliability, brand name, and reputation, as well as quality, which are "functional benefits" of the brand, and when such benefits are perceived, purchase intention is more possible and stronger, since the attitude toward the product is also stronger (Walsh et al., 2012).

According to Wangenheim (2005), purchase intention is affected, such as the purchase decision, by "Word of Mouth" (WoM), which is considered a strong influence factor since, apart from the above, it is associated with attitudes and preferences (Molinari et al., 2008).

Additionally, according to Lee and Hwan (2005), purchase intention, for the financial industry, is influenced by the variable customer satisfaction (Tsoukatos & Rand, 2006) which has the result of affecting the profitability of the business.

Thereafter the exploration of insurance needs, the insurance intermediary, is called upon to design the consumer's insurance coverage package in order to assume the risk and cover the customer's insurance needs. At this stage, it is chosen which of the consumer's needs will be met. It is therefore important to examine the extent to which *needs satisfaction*, in the Relationship Marketing stage of Gaining Commitment/Covering Risk and Need-Satisfaction, affects *purchase intention*.

In this context, the following research hypotheses are developed:

H1: To investigate whether in the stage of Relationship Marketing: Gaining Commitment/Covering Risk and Need-Satisfaction, variable *needs satisfaction (needSat)*, affects *purchase intention*.

50.2.4 Repurchase Intention

Repurchase intention is defined as the autonomous judgment of whether to repurchase a service or product from the same provider (Hellier et al., 2003). Among the main affective factors of repurchase intention variable are the value variable, satisfaction, loyalty, and customer expectations.

On the other hand, as cross-selling or cross-buying, we define the process of buying separate products, different from each other, but from the same supplier or provider (Hong & Lee, 2012; Verhoef et al., 2001).

The above topic has not been extensively researched in the financial product market, something that strengthens the relationship between the client and the organization and builds a prosperous future (Hong & Lee, 2012; Kumar et al., 2008; Ngobo, 2004; Verhoef et al., 2001; Verhoef & Donkers, 2005).

Various researchers define satisfaction as well as consumer's attitude as the main factors in forming repurchase intention. If we consider attitude as a preacquisition factor, the sequence goes as follows: satisfaction – attitudes – repurchase intention. Repurchase intention usually depends on a general evaluation of the service and the supplier, based on experiences from multiple transactions with the supplier (Samanta & Karnachoritis, 2020).

According to Hellier et al. (2003), there are researches on repurchase intention that focus on key preexisting variables (Storbacka et al., 1994), while others consider the single event of repurchase as a critical factor of interaction or relationship between variables (Bitner, 1990). Accordingly, other researchers such as Mittal and Kamakura (2001) consider the predicted reliability of repurchase intention as a substitute for repurchase behavior.

The research of Trasorras et al. (2009) defined that although we consider satisfaction as the main and dominant variable affecting repurchase intention, the value variable contributes to repurchase intention but less than satisfaction. However, the same does not apply, when the loyalty variable combined with the value variable which in combination, turns value into a stronger influence on repurchase intention than satisfaction (Trasorras et al., 2009).

In the insurance market, loyalty as a behavioral factor is reflected through the intention to either maintain or renew existing services or insurance policies and through the intention to purchase new products from the same provider (Tsoukatos & Rand, 2006).

Customer loyalty can be considered the extent to which the customer shows repurchase intentions and behaviors or when repurchases a specific product/brand/service/business. This behavior is considered calculable if it occurs in recent periods of time and is measured in proportion to the customer's overall trading habits in corresponding products or services (Hellier et al., 2003). On the contrary, in the case of cross-selling or cross-buying, we do not examine either the periodicity or the transaction time (Reinartz et al., 2008).

Loyalty is linked to repurchase intention, which is strongly supported by the research of Trasorras et al. (2009). They also state that loyalty has different levels of measurement as well as satisfaction.

High or true loyalty shields consumers by making them resistant to competing offers. Customers who have strong positive attitudinal ties with the brand or business show a high degree of loyalty and repurchase (Trasorras et al., 2009).

Low and limited loyalty customers have also lower repetitive purchases, allowing competition and pricing to affect them (Trasorras et al., 2009).

Trasorras et al.'s (2009) research presents loyalty as the most powerful and important variable for repurchase intention. The combination of loyalty with value increases the influence on repurchase intention (Trasorras et al., 2009).

Hellier et al. (2003), however, argue that past loyalty is not directly related to customer satisfaction or current brand preference. The main affective factor of brand preference is perceived value with customer satisfaction. Also, brand preference is an intervening factor between satisfaction and repurchase intention.

In order to maintain customer satisfaction and to ensure a profitable and sustainable entrepreneurship, it is required the organized development and the maintenance of mutually rewarding relationships with customers achieved through the total integration of information and management systems for quality, support, service, business strategy, and organizational mission (Bennett, 1996).

Researches held by Dawkins and Reicheld (1990) show that the higher the retention rate is, the higher the customer value becomes (net present value of the customer) (Ahmad & Buttle, 2002).

The main concern of companies should be targeting the management of the customer's value variable and correspondingly the repurchase relationship for a long-term increase in business and revenue (Trasorras et al., 2009).

Satisfaction and value are vital variables for repurchase (Trasorras et al., 2009). Satisfaction appears to have various stages and levels that tend to influence repurchase intention accordingly (Trasorras et al., 2009).

The feeling insurance needs satisfaction is affected by the correct identification and evaluation of the needs. Consequently, needs satisfaction (*needSat*) is a factor that shapes and contributes to the creation of purchase intention, repurchase intention, and retention. The feeling insurance needs satisfaction varies depending on whether the client's needs are identified/assessed fully, partially, or not at all (Karnachoritis & Samanta, 2020).

In this context, the following research hypotheses are developed:

H2: To examine whether in the stage of Relationship Marketing: Gaining Commitment/Covering Risk and Need-Satisfaction, variable *needs satisfaction (needSat)*, affects *repurchase intention*.

50.3 Methodology

The purpose of the research was to investigate consumer's insurance needs satisfaction in relation to purchase intention and repurchase intention. The satisfaction of needs touches the core of private insurance as well as the core of marketing science, further to examine whether needs satisfaction is a factor that contributes to the formation of the variables purchase intention and repurchase.

In order to examine all the above, a qualitative research was held in inductive manner, under the research philosophy of phenomenology. Phenomenology philosophy deals with subjectivity and in this way investigates and examines reality and truth. The aim of phenomenology is the phenomenon itself and its essence to emerge through research and observation (Chalikias, 2015).

Primary data were collected via in-depth interviews. Depth interviews were conducted in June of 2022 out of five professionals of the Greek insurance market.

The thorough analysis of primary data and coding of the findings with an interdisciplinary approach combined with the subjectivity and reflexivity of the researcher contributed to the completion of the construction of the theory.

The selected sample of the qualitative research is judged to be qualitatively representative. In the present research, purposive sampling was chosen as sample method in which sampling is performed based on specific criteria (to share an experience – usually homogeneous).

In the research, the respondents who took part in the in-depth interviews are experienced and specialized executives of the insurance market, that is, executives of insurance companies and a free network of sellers/brokers. Five executives participated in the research with the criterion of being able to know and have an opinion on the highly specialized subject being investigated. Job position, experience, and education on insurance matters were basic criteria.

They are not differentiated by gender or age. The five executives of the insurance market who participated in the research consisted of three executives of insurance companies and two executives of the free market.

50.4 Results

From the analysis of the interviews and after their line-by-line coding, the following thematic subsections emerged:

The Hypothesis H1 concerns:

H1: To investigate whether in the stage of Relationship Marketing: Gaining Commitment/Covering Risk and Need-Satisfaction, variable *needs satisfaction (needSat)*, affects *purchase intention*.

- *Customer criteria for purchasing insurance products*
- *Meeting needs and customer satisfaction*

50.4.1 Customer Criteria for Purchasing Insurance Products

- Customers proceed to purchase an insurance product mainly through the participatory sales process, i.e., depending on whether customers themselves participate in the selection of the appropriate product and not when the insurance intermediary proposes a product that serves or suits him and his company better.

Pathmarajah (1991) also refers to the above process, who states that in the sales process, the seller and the buyer must participate together, resulting in a strong personal, professional, and mutually profitable relationship over time.

- Also, the customer buys when he perceives, understands what is proposed to him, and desires the proposed product.

The above is also supported by Bennett (1996), who states that the salesperson seeks to establish long-term, committed, trusting, and cooperative relationships with customers, characterized by honesty, genuine interest in delivering high-quality products and services, responsiveness to customer suggestions, fair treatment, and the willingness to sacrifice long-term advantages for long-term gain.

- An additional important factor has the customer's financial profile. The customer proceeds with a purchase when he feels that his choice will not put him on an "adventure" that he cannot fulfill financially in the future.

As Karnachoritis and Samanta (2020) mention, insurance needs vary and change in relation to the client's income and financial dynamics.

- Another basic purchase criterion is the fulfillment of the purpose of the insurance, i.e., for the customer to know that he will be compensated in any case.

50.4.2 Meeting Needs and Customer Satisfaction

- There is a difference in how the customer feels if their needs are properly met or not properly met. When the needs are properly met, customer feels that any harm that befalls him will be properly compensated.

The above is also supported by Karnachoritis and Samanta (2020) who state that being insured means properly meeting and covering the needs I have.

- A client who has not fully met or covered his needs does not feel calm and safe because he worries about the uncertain future and how he will cope with it.

The Hypothesis H2 concerns:

H2: To examine whether in the stage of Relationship Marketing: Gaining Commitment/Covering Risk and Need-Satisfaction, variable *needs satisfaction (needSat)*, affects *repurchase intention*.

- *Meeting needs and insurance policy renewal*
- *Meeting needs and new purchases of insurance products*
- *Customer criteria for repurchase insurance products*

50.4.3 Meeting Needs and Insurance Policy Renewal

- Customers who have not met their needs do not renew insurance policies because they feel insecure. Those who have not met their needs renew only out of obligation as in compulsory car insurance.
- On the contrary, customers who have covered their needs fully, realize the risk and renew their coverage. Customers who have their needs fully covered feel confident and feel that whatever happens, the loss will be repaired and they will be able to continue their work and their life without interruption.
- A "wrong" sale (incorrect coverage) results in policy cancellations as well as nonrenewal of the insurance policy. The above happens when the needs that the insured seeks to cover do not coincide with the insurance plan that has finally been designed and obtained.

According to Porrini (2017), insurance companies and insurance intermediaries need to continue improving their services and product distribution methods to keep meeting customer demands and expectations.

- If needs are properly met, the customer will retain his insurance product and will remain connected with the company. On the contrary, when he obtains a different insurance product than the one he expected, he will cancel it by searching again for the solution he is looking for.

Tzanis (2012) states that the insurance intermediary analyzes and searches for the ideal products/coverages for the customer by analyzing and understanding their real needs in order to satisfy them (Karnachoritis & Samanta, 2020).

- As long as the insurance process has been done correctly even in the event of a possible change or damage, the intention to cancel is smaller.

Ranaweera and Praghu (2003) state that there is a strong belief that the more satisfied customers are, the greater their retention will be (Trasorras et al., 2009). The key to survival in businesses and organizations is the retention of satisfied both external and internal customers (Fecikova, 2004).

50.4.4 Meeting Needs and New Purchases of Insurance Products

- Customers who have fully covered their needs proceed to repurchase and acquire new products. These customers, when their needs change, will add additional coverage by repurchasing.

Porrini (2017) states that the distribution of insurance products is driven by changes in customer needs.

- A customer who is satisfied with the insurance product he has already chosen has a greater intention to proceed with the purchase or repurchase of additional coverage for a new need that arises.
- Customers who have not properly and fully covered their needs do not proceed to purchase new products but only cover mandatory coverages.

The above is also explained by the position of Prymostka (2018) where she states that mostly consumers tend to renew mainly mandatory products based on the price.

50.4.5 Customers Criteria for Repurchase Insurance Products

- When customer need has been properly assessed, customers proceed to renewal of insurance policies. If customers are compensated properly, they tend to gain confidence toward the insurance idea and proceed to repurchase. When they trust the intermediary, they proceed to repurchase.

Suppliers strive to build and strengthen relationships with their customers. They move from trying to maximize profits on each individual transaction to establishing a solid, reliable, and above all, lasting relationship with the people they serve (Bennett, 1996).

- Customers proceed to purchase a new product when a new need is presented to them or when a need is differentiated. When there is support and service for every change in their needs and possible risks, they proceed to repurchase.

Consumer insurance needs do not remain constant, but continuously change (Karnachoritis & Samanta, 2020; Vlassis, 1997). These alterations are due to various factors such as the family life cycle such as any other change that the consumer experiences during his life (Karnachoritis & Samanta, 2020).

- Consumers also proceed to purchase when there is regular contact with the intermediary and have updated information and briefing about new coverage and new products.

Gummesson (1994) emphasizes that a long-term interactive relationship between supplier and customer results in long-term gain.

50.5 Discussion

The difficulty of professional relationships arises from the oversupply of competition to the consumer, the more complete information of consumers but also from the attitudes, perceptions, and personality that the consumer has formed in the market. So, in addition to the question of how to acquire a customer, there is the question of the vital importance of how to maintain a long-term relationship with him. The seller/insurance broker develops a personal and long-term relationship with the buyer, aiming to satisfy his needs in the best possible way by exploring, understanding, and analyzing them.

The main goal of the insurance intermediary is not simply to deliver the insurance policy but to understand the problems and needs of consumers by providing a solution with his specialized services and also with support after the sale is completed.

The insurance intermediary should aim at the integrated fulfillment of all of his and his organization's promises, the development of commitment and trust, and the establishment of personal contacts and bonds between him and the client. He should aim for participation and empathy for the other side. Cooperation with customers and participative selling is a criterion for customers to purchase insurance products. It therefore helps to improve the productivity, efficiency, and effectiveness of the insurance intermediary's tasks.

Designing, developing, and fostering a relationship climate that promotes dialogue between the insurance intermediary and its clients helps the insured to understand the products but also helps to build confidence in the provider's capabilities as well as developing mutual respect for the concerns of each party. When the customer understands and comprehends the insurance product that is proposed to him and believes that he will be compensated, he proceeds with the purchase process if it is something he is interested in and if it is a package that he is able to repay now and in the future.

As the findings showed, customers who feel that their needs have been fully and properly met consequently feel that any damages that may occur in the future will be properly compensated, strengthening their purchase intention. On the contrary, those who feel that they did not fully cover their needs feel insecure about the uncertain future, as a result of which they do not renew their existing insurance policies.

The results also showed that needs satisfaction (needSat) affects purchase intention as well as repurchase intention.

There is a difference in how a customer feels when his needs are properly met and partially met, or when he was not insured based on his needs because his needs were not assessed at all. The feeling of satisfaction of the customer's needs is affected when his needs are fully and correctly met.

A satisfied customer intends to purchase or repurchase additional coverage for a new need that arises. Customers who have fully met their needs have a greater intention to repurchase and acquire new products.

Conversely, customers who have not met their needs do not renew their insurance policies because they have not been satisfied. Customers who have not properly and fully covered their needs do not proceed to purchase new products but only cover mandatory coverage.

Apart from the direct benefit of coverage for the consumer, this practical application has multiple economic and social implications. If consumers are able to meet their needs better than they do, it will create a sense of satisfaction that will enhance both the insurance idea and the insurance industry. Indirect consequences could be the increase of employment as well as the reduction of insecurity both at the individual and commercial levels.

By achieving consumer's needs satisfaction, real and targeted coverage of needs, purchase and repurchase intention, and retention are created as a result.

50.6 Conclusion

This study investigates consumer's insurance needs satisfaction correlated to purchase intention and repurchase intention. The satisfaction of needs touches the core of private insurance as well as the core of marketing. Specifically, it examines whether needs satisfaction is a factor that affects the formation of the purchase intention and repurchase intention variables.

Insured client wants to participate in the insurance process and understand what their insurance policy is about. They are willing to buy an insurance product when they can pay it back as well as when they feel that all their insurance needs are properly covered where they consequently feel that they will be compensated if needed. Those who do not fully meet their needs feel insecure, worrying about the uncertain future.

The findings show that when the insurance needs are not properly covered, the cancellation of the insurance policies is caused by customers who are seeking again for the solution that were looking for. When their insurance needs are satisfied and covered, they are also willing to renew their insurance policies as well as add new coverages. The above intention is strengthened when they feel that there is trust toward the insurance intermediary, continuous information, and proper service.

The results revealed that the correct coverage of the needs affects the satisfaction of the customer's insurance needs, and as a sequence, the needs satisfaction (needSat) affects the purchase intention as well as the repurchase intention.

References

Ahmad, R., & Buttle, F. (2002). Customer retention management: A reflection of theory and practice. *Marketing Intelligence & Planning, 20*(3), 149–161. https://doi.org/10.1108/02634500210428003

Ajzen, I. (1991). The theory of planned behaviour. *Organizational Behavior and Human Decision Processes, 50*(2), 79–211. https://doi.org/10.1016/0749-5978(91)90020-T

Ajzen, I., & Fishbein, M. (1977). Attitude-behavior relations: A theoretical analysis and review of empirical research. *Psychological Bulletin 1977, 84*(5), 8–918.

Andersen, P. H. (2005). Relationship marketing and brand involvement of professionals through web-enhanced brand communities: The case of Coloplast. *Industrial Marketing Management, 34*(1), 39–51. https://doi.org/10.1016/j.indmarman.2004.07.002

Bandura, A. (2001). Social cognitive theory: An agentic perspective. *Annual Review of Psychology, 52*, 1–26.
Bennett, R. (1996). Relationship formation and governance in consumer markets: Transactional analysis versus the behaviourist approach. *Journal o Marketing Management, 12*(12), 417–436.
Berry, L. L., & Parasuraman, A. (1991). *Marketing services: Competing through quality*. The Free Press.
Bitner, M. J. (1990). Evaluating service encounters: The effects of physical surroundings and employee responses. *Journal of Marketing, 54*(4), 69–82. https://doi.org/10.2307/1251871
Cant, M. C., & Van Heerden, C. H. (2004). *Personal selling*. Juta & Co LTD.
Chalikias, M. (2015). *Research methodology and introduction to statistic data analysis via IBM SPSS STATISTICS*. Athens: SEAB Publication. Greek Edition: Χαλικιάς, Μ. (2015). Μεθοδολογία Έρευνας και Εισαγωγή στην Στατιστική Ανάλυση Δεδομένων με το IBM SPSS STATISTICS. Αθήνα: Εκδόσεις ΣΕΑΒ.
Choi, S. C., & Coughlan, T. A. (2006). Private label positioning: Quality versus feature differentiation from the national brand. *Journal of Retailing, 82*(2), 79–93. https://doi.org/10.1016/j.jretai.2006.02.005
Chung-Herrera, B. G. (2007). Customers' psychological needs in different service industries. *Journal of Services Marketing, 21*(4), 263–269. https://doi.org/10.1108/08876040710758568
Craig, C. S., & Douglas, S. P. (2006). Beyond national culture: Implications of cultural dynamics for consumer research. *International Marketing Review, 23*(3), 322–342. https://doi.org/10.1108/02651330610670479
Cravens, W. D., & Piercy, F. N. (1994). Relationship marketing and collaborative networks in service organizations. *International Journal of Service Industry Management, 5*(5), 39–53. https://doi.org/10.1108/09564239410074376
Cronin, J. J., Brady, K. M., & Hult, G. T. (2000). Assessing the effects of quality, value, and customer satisfaction on consumer behavioral intentions in service environments. *Journal of Retailing, 76*(2), 193–218. https://doi.org/10.1016/S0022-4359(00)00028-2
Dawkins, P. M., & Reichheld, E. F. (1990). Customer retention as a competitive weapon. *Directors & Board Summer*, 42–47.
De Mooij, M., & Hofstede, G. (2002). Convergence and divergence in consumer behavior: Implications for international retailing. *Journal of Retailing, 78*(1), 61–69. https://doi.org/10.1016/S0022-4359(01)00067-7
Evans, J. R., & Laskin, R. L. (1996). The relationship marketing process. *Industrial Marketing Management, 23*(2), 439–452.
Fecikova, I. (2004). An index method for measurement of customer satisfaction. *The TQM Magazine, 16*(1), 57–66. https://doi.org/10.1108/09544780410511498
Ferreira, A. F. F., Jalali, S. M., Meidute-Kavaliauskiene, I., & Viana, A. C. P. B. (2015). A metacognitive decision making based-framework for bank customer loyalty measurement and management. *Technological and Economic Development of Economy, 21*(2), 280–300. https://doi.org/10.3846/20294913.2014.981764
Fraering, M., & Minor, S. M. (2013). Beyond loyalty: Customer satisfaction, loyalty, and fortitude. *Journal of Services Marketing, 27*(4), 334–344. https://doi.org/10.1108/08876041311330807
Grönroos, C. (1990). The marketing strategy continuum: Towards a marketing concept for the 1990s. *Management Decision, 29*(1), 7–13.
Gummesson, E. (1987). The new marketing-developing long-term interactive relationships. *Long Range Planning, 20*(4), 10–20. https://doi.org/10.1016/0024-6301(87)90151-8
Gummesson, E. (1994). Making relationship marketing operational. *International Journal of Service Industry Management, 5*(5), 5–20. https://doi.org/10.1108/09564239410074349
Hammarkvist, K. O., Hakansson, H., & Mattsson, L. (1982). *Marketing for Competitiveness*. Liber.
Harker, M. J. (1999). Relationship marketing defined? An examination of current relationship marketing definitions. *Marketing Intelligence & Planning, 17*(1), 13–20. https://doi.org/10.1108/02634509910253768
Hellenic Association of Insurance Companies. (2016). *Annual Statistic Report Private Insurance in Greece*. HAIC.

Hellenic Association of Insurance Companies. (2018). *Annual Statistic Report Private Insurance in Greece*. HAIC.

Hellenic Association of Insurance Companies. (2022). *Annual Statistic Report Private Insurance in Greece*. HAIC.

Hellier, K. P., Geursen, M. G., Carr, A. R., & Rickard, A. J. (2003). Customer repurchase intention: A general structural equation model. *European Journal of Marketing, 37*(11/12), 1762–1800. https://doi.org/10.1108/03090560310495456

Holt, B. D. (2006). Toward a sociology of branding. *Journal of Consumer Culture, 6*(3), 299–302. https://doi.org/10.1177/1469540506068680

Hong, J.-K., & Lee, Y.-I. (2012). Determinants of cross-buying intentions in banking services in collectivistic culture. *International Journal of Bank Marketing, 30*(5), 328–358. https://doi.org/10.1108/02652321211247408

Jackson, B. B. (1985). Build customer relationships that last. *Harvard Business Review, 63, November/December*, 120–128.

Karnachoritis, D., & Samanta, I. (2020). Building consumers insurance needs satisfaction through a structured hierarchy model. *International Journal of Economics, Business and Management Research, 4*(11), 1–19.

Knight, G. (1999). International services marketing: Review of research, 1980?1998. *Journal of Services Marketing, 13*(4/5), 347–360. https://doi.org/10.1108/08876049910282619

Kumar, V., George, M., & Pancras, J. (2008). Cross-buying in retailing: Drivers and consequences. *Journal of Retailing, 84*(1), 15–27. https://doi.org/10.1016/j.jretai.2008.01.007

Kunreuther, H., & Pauly, M. (2005). Insurance decision-making and market behavior. *Foundation and Trends in Microeconomics, 1*(2), 63–127.

Laroche, M. (2009). Impact of culture on marketing strategy: Introduction to the special issue. *Journal of Business Research, 62*(10), 921–923. https://doi.org/10.1016/j.jbusres.2008.10.013

Lee, M. C., & Hwan, I. S. (2005). Relationships among service quality, customer satisfaction and profitability in the Taiwanese banking industry. *International Journal of Management, 22*(4), 635–648.

Levitt, T. (1983). "After the sale is over..." Harvard business review. *September–October*, 1–8.

Matthyssens, P., & Van Den, B. C. (1994). Getting closer and nicer: Partnerships in the supply chain. *Long Range Planning, 27*(1), 72–83. https://doi.org/10.1016/0024-6301(94)90008-6

Mittal, V., & Kamakura, W. A. (2001). Satisfaction, repurchase intent, and repurchase behavior: Investigating the moderating effect of customers characteristics. *Journal of Marketing Research, 38*(1), 131–142.

Molinari, K. L., Abratt, R., & Dion, P. (2008). Satisfaction, quality and value and effects on repurchase and positive word of mouth behavioral intentions in a B2B services context. *Journal of Services Marketing, 22*(5), 363–373. https://doi.org/10.1108/08876040810889139

Ngobo, P. V. (2004). Drivers of customers' cross buying intentions. *European Journal of Marketing, 38*(9/10), 1129–1157. https://doi.org/10.1108/03090560410548906

Nogueira, L., & Oliveira, E. (2003). A multi-agent system for e-insurance brokering. In *Agent technologies, infrastructures, tools, and applications for E-services: NODe 2002 Agent-Related Workshops Erfurt, Germany.*, October 7–10, 2002 Revised Papers 4 (pp. 263–282). Springer.

Pathmarajah, A. (1991). Creativity in relationship marketing. *The Singapore Marketer, 1*(1), 14–17.

Pauluzzo, R., & Geretto, E. F. (2017). Evaluating customers' behavioral intentions in less significant financial institutions. *International Journal of Bank Marketing, 35*(4), 714–732. https://doi.org/10.1108/IJBM-06-2016-0078

Piha, P. L., & Avlonitis, J. G. (2015). Customer defection in retail banking: Attitudinal and behavioural consequences of failed service quality. *Journal of Service Theory and Practice, 25*(3), 304–326. https://doi.org/10.1108/JSTP-04-2014-0080

Porrini, D. (2017). Regulating big data effects in the European insurance market. *Insurance Markets and Companies, 8*(1), 6–15. https://doi.org/10.21511/ins.08(1).2017.01

Prymostka, O. (2018). Life insurance companies marketing strategy in the digital world. *Insurance Markets and Companies, 9*(1), 66–73.

Ranaweera, C., & Prabhu, J. (2003). On the relative importance of customer satisfaction and trust as determinants of customer retention and positive word-of-mouth. *Journal of Targeting, Measurement and Analysis for Marketing, 12*(1), 82–89. https://doi.org/10.1057/palgrave.jt.5740100

Reinartz, W., Thomas, J., & Bascoul, G. (2008). Investigating cross-buying and customer loyalty. *Journal of Interactive Marketing, 22*(1), 5–20. https://doi.org/10.1002/dir.20103

Samanta, I., & Karnachoritis, D. (2020). *Sales management: Strategic approach* (1st ed.). Benou Publication. ISBN 978-960-359-164-1. *(Σαμαντά, Ε., & Καρναχωρίτης, Δ. (2020). Διοίκηση Πωλήσεων: Στρατηγική Προσέγγιση (1η Εκδ). Αθήνα: Εκδόσεις Μπένου.*, ISBN 978-960-359-164-1).

Storbacka, K., Strandvik, T., & Gronroos, C. (1994). Managing customer relationships for profit: The dynamics of relationship quality. *International Journal of Service Industry Management, 5*(5), 21–38. https://doi.org/10.1108/09564239410074358

Strandvik, T., Holmlund, M., & Edvardsson, B. (2012). Customer needing: A challenge for the seller offering. *Journal of Business & Industrial Marketing, 27*(2), 132–141. https://doi.org/10.1108/08858621211196994

Tajudeen, O. Y., Ayantunji, G., & Dallah, H. (2009). Attitudes of Nigerians towards insurance services: An empirical study. *African Journal of Accounting, Economics, Finance and Banking Research, 4*(4).

Toman, N., Adamson, B., & Gomez, C. (2017). The new sales imperative. *Harvard Business Review, 95*(2), 188–125.

Trasorras, R., Weinstein, A., & Abratt, R. (2009). Value, satisfaction, loyalty and retention in professional services. *Marketing Intelligence & Planning, 27*(5), 615–632. https://doi.org/10.1108/02634500910977854

Treerattanapun, A. (2011). The impact of culture on non-life insurance consumption. *Wharton Research Scholars, 78*.

Tsoukatos, E., & Rand, K. G. (2006). Path analysis of perceived service quality, satisfaction and loyalty in Greek insurance. *Managing Service Quality: An International Journal, 16*(5), 501–519. https://doi.org/10.1108/09604520610686746

Tzanis, S. (2012). *Direct insurance the determinants of success*. University of St. Gallen.

Verhoef, P., & Donkers, B. (2005). The effect of acquisition channels on customer loyalty and cross-buying. *Journal of Interactive Marketing, 19*(2), 31–43. https://doi.org/10.1002/dir.20033

Verhoef, P., Franses, P. H., & Hoekstra, J. (2001). The impact of satisfaction and payment equity on cross-buying: A dynamic model for multi service provider. *Journal of Retailing, 77*(3), 359–378. https://doi.org/10.1016/S0022-4359(01)00052-5

Vlassis, G. (1997). *Life Insurance Salesman*. Interbooks Publications.

Walsh, G., Shiu, E., & Hassan, M. L. (2012). Investigating the drivers of consumer intention to buy manufacturer brands. *Journal of Product & Brand Management, 21*(5), 328–340. https://doi.org/10.1108/10610421211253623

Wangenheim, F. V. (2005). Postswitching negative word of mouth. *Journal of Service Research, 8*(1), 67–78.

Zahorik, A. J., & Rust, R. T. (1992). Modeling the impact of service quality on profitability: A review. *Advances in Services Marketing and Management, 1*(1), 247–276.

Zeithaml, A. V. (1988). Consumer perceptions of price, quality and value: A means-end model and synthesis of evidence. *Journal of Marketing, 52*(July), 2–22. http://www.jstor.org/stable/1251446

Zeithaml, A. V., Berry, L. L., & Parasuraman, A. (1996). The behavioral consequences of service quality. *Journal of Marketing, 60*(2), 31–46.

Zhao, L., Lu, Y., Zhang, L., & Chau, Y. K. P. (2012). Assessing the effects of service quality and justice on customer satisfaction and the continuance intention of mobile value-added services: An empirical test of a multidimensional model. *Decision Support Systems, 52*(3), 645–656.

Chapter 51
Factors Determining Business Eco-Innovation Activities: A Case of Slovak SMEs

Miroslava Vinczeová, Ladislav Klement, and Vladimíra Klementová

Abstract The purpose of the chapter is to identify and assess the importance of motives and barriers to eco-innovations among small- and medium-sized Slovak enterprises. The authors expect that the size of the company could be an important factor, influencing the different perceptions of motives and barriers to eco-innovation activities among small- and medium-sized enterprises (SMEs). The chapter analyzes empirical data on barriers and motives to eco-innovation. The research sample consisted of randomly selected small- and medium-sized enterprises in Slovakia. The structure of the sample was representative of the population according to the size of the respondents. The analysis was carried out on a total of 487 SMEs in Slovakia that completed the electronic questionnaire within the period from December 2022 to April 2023. The authors subjected the answers obtained to the analysis of the importance of individual barriers and motives of eco-innovations, while separately assessing the order of the factors of eco-innovations considering the size groups of enterprises. The results obtained from the study conducted brought some conclusions similar to those of other studies from selected countries of the European Union. However, we identified barriers that were specifically highly rated among SMEs in Slovakia.

Keywords Eco-innovation · Barriers · Motives · SMEs

51.1 Introduction

The world is currently facing serious environmental, social, and economic challenges that are bringing constant and often turbulent changes to the business environment. Humanity absolutely must embark on a path of sustainable development without compromising the ability to meet the needs of future generations.

M. Vinczeová · L. Klement (✉) · V. Klementová
Faculty of Economics, Matej Bel University in Banská Bystrica, Banská Bystrica, Slovakia
e-mail: ladislav.klement@umb.sk

Thus, sustainable development is becoming the imperative of today. To maintain or strengthen their competitiveness, companies are forced to become socially responsible and respond to these changes in an appropriate and flexible manner. Their long-term vision and strategy must take into account the need to contribute to stable and sustainable economic growth in the long term, while ensuring environmental protection. Eco-innovation is one of the effective tools for eliminating the negative environmental impacts of economic activity and can make a significant contribution to the sustainable development of both the corporate sector and the economy as a whole. The research stream to date indicates that the design, implementation, and dissemination of ecological innovations enabling to reduce the consumption of natural resources, raw materials, and harmful emissions while improving the working conditions of people appear to be a very effective instrument combining environmental protection with the sustainable development of businesses (Carfora et al., 2022). Green innovation, as Aboelmaged and Gharib (2019) refer to the eco-innovation, includes new processes, equipment, systems, practices, products, and methods that can create business value by minimizing negative impacts on the environment and promoting sustainable goals. Porter and van der Linde (1995) define eco-innovation as a change in economic activities improving both the economic performance and the environmental performance of the society, according to a win-win situation from both the economic and environmental perspectives.

A better understanding of eco-innovation requires a deeper and more thorough investigation and identification of the factors that largely influence the decision to undertake eco-innovation and its implementation in enterprises. In Slovakia, as in many other countries, SMEs represent an important business segment that influences the country's eco-innovation performance. As the adoption of eco-innovations in SMEs is still underexplored (Carfora et al., 2022) and this is particularly true for the literature dealing with research on the factors affecting eco-innovation activities in this segment of enterprises, we have decided to fill this knowledge gap and to address this issue in more detail in this chapter.

The chapter is structured as follows. Section 52.2 presents the theoretical background of the research on factors affecting eco-innovation activities in businesses. Subsequently, we describe the methodology used to collect and analyze data about eco-innovation barriers in Sect. 52.3. We present the results of the research in Sect. 52.4 and discuss the findings in Sect. 52.5. Finally, the conclusions along with the limitations constraining our study are presented in Sect. 52.6.

51.2 Theoretical Background and Review of the Literature

The aim of an economy has traditionally been linked to efficient resource allocation. However, the real economic systems are complex and involve many actors other than government and businesses, including social groups and individuals. All these actors create, protect, and destroy social values, cooperate, or compete with each other. The complexity of this social process of resource allocation, with its possibilities and limitations, determines the interactions between the economy and the environment (Spash, 2017). In an economy dependent on the use of nonrenewable resources, issues of sustainability have been at the forefront for a quite long period. Today, it is unequivocal that the traditional mode of production and consumption is destructive and not sustainable anymore, and we have to look for ways to do things differently. Therefore, businesses that want to offer value to their customers and maintain long-term relationships in the new environment must look for new or improved solutions that are more sustainable (Tan & Cha, 2021). The need for an ecological transformation inspires the pursuit of new technologies and innovative ways of functioning economic systems. Eco-innovations are one of the key instruments in mitigating and preventing environmental damage caused by economic activities and, at the same time, one of the main drivers of successful transformation toward a more circular and sustainable future (Horbach & Reif, 2018). De Jesus et al. (2017) consider them crucial for developing new business models, new more competitive technologies, and new institutional structures allowing for environmental benefits reflected in a more efficient resource allocation and consumption, thus also bringing economic benefits. Eco-innovation is any form of innovation that results in or aims at significant and demonstrable progress toward the goal of sustainable development, through reducing impacts on the environment, improving resilience to environmental pressures, or achieving a more efficient and responsible use of natural resources (European Commission, 2011). Klewitz and Hansen (2014) talk about eco-innovation (such as eco-design and cleaner production) and refer to sustainability-oriented innovation, which is the integration of ecological and social aspects into products, processes, and organizational structures.

Like all innovations, eco-innovation represents a new or fundamentally improved solution for products and services or the introduction of a new method in the production or organization of business processes. What distinguishes ecological innovations from other types of innovation is precisely the fact that they result in benefits in the economic and the environmental field (Lesáková et al., 2021). Environmental benefits include a reduction in the use of natural resources and a reduction in the release of harmful substances per unit of production throughout the life cycle. Ecological innovations result in higher resource productivity, lower greenhouse gas emissions, and reduced waste generation. Ecological innovations produce positive externalities during their creation and implementation, both in the phase of the introduction of the innovation and in the phase of its expansion on the market. Positive side effects appear in the market penetration phase due to lower external costs compared to competing goods and services in the market. The literature calls this feature the problem of double externalities. The problem of double externalities reduces the motivation of companies to invest in ecological innovations, and therefore, the innovation policy of the state should be properly coordinated with the environmental policy in order to contribute to reducing the costs of technological, institutional, and social innovations, especially in the phase of research and development, as well as the introduction of the innovation on the market. At least in the innovation diffusion phase, environmental policy should be responsible for ensuring that competing nonenvironmental products or services are burdened with the external costs they cause (e.g., in the form of taxes), because otherwise, the competition between ecological and environmentally harmful innovations is distorted and ecological innovations are disadvantaged.

The study of factors that influence business innovation activity has been attracting increasing attention in both academia and business practice. The literature offers different classifications of the factors that influence these activities. Many authors divide the factors of the enterprise's innovation activity into external and internal ones, with external factors being those of the external business environment and internal factors being those that are determined by the internal environment of the enterprise. The definition of external factors is closely related to the definition of the external business environment, including economic and political conditions and prerequisites for the development of business activities. The external economic environment can be divided into several areas. Some authors distinguish three of its components, namely the broader business environment (i.e., the macroenvironment), the sectoral environment (i.e., competition), and the operational environment of the enterprise. However, the prevailing approach in the literature is to include the first two of the above components in an external business environment and to ignore the last one. Variables belonging to the broader business environment, that is, the macroenvironment, do not act selectively, but affect all enterprises. The frameworks used to analyze external factors that can impact businesses can be taken from the PEST (also PESTE, PESTLE) analysis that identifies the political, economic, sociocultural, technological, legal, and environmental factors. Their identification may then help businesses develop effective strategies to respond to them (Moro-Visconti, 2022). As some authors argue (see, e.g., Lesáková et al., 2017), these factors can also be perceived as important external factors influencing the innovation activity of enterprises. The objective of industry or competitive environment analysis is to reveal the factors that influence the situation in the industry and may become a source of potential opportunities or threats. The range of internal factors that determine innovative business activities is very wide. Several authors (e.g., Bessant & Tidd, 2015; Kiefer et al., 2018; Jové-Llopis et al., 2018) characterize them in a very similar way and usually consider them as technological capabilities, shared vision, leadership, the will to innovate, appropriate organizational structure, qualified human resources, training and staff development, availability of financial resources, an innovative environment, and a corporate culture that promotes innovation and collaboration with external partners.

The knowledge of and understanding of the nature of eco-innovations and the factors and determinants that influence them are important for all actors in any economy. Eco-innovation research is still considered a relatively young field. Thus, even though the number of publications devoted to this line of research, especially in the last decade, are very large, the meaning and practical implications of eco-innovations remain insufficiently unfolded and questionable (Colombo et al., 2019). This also applies to factors that affect eco-innovation activities in businesses. The literature on them in transition countries is relatively scarce. When studying eco-innovations, we can rely on the above classifications, as the main

51 Factors Determining Business Eco-Innovation Activities: A Case of Slovak SMEs

Table 51.1 Drivers of eco-innovation activities

Supply side	Technological and management capabilities
	Collaboration with research institutions
	Access to external information and knowledge
	Size
	Material and energy prices
Demand side	Market share
	Social and environmental consciousness and market demand for green products
Institutional and political influences	Environmental policy
	Institutional structure

Source: Lesáková et al. (2021), Triguero et al. (2013), Horbach (2008)

determinants discussed in theoretical studies of environmental innovations are largely based on general innovations (García-Pozo et al., 2019). A growing number of studies investigating the determinants affecting eco-innovations have recently paid special attention to the knowledge and understanding of the drivers and barriers to their implementation. The drivers for implementing eco-innovations represent the motives or reasons and readiness of the business to carry out eco-innovation activities. Adopting the approach of Lesáková et al. (2021), Triguero et al. (2013), or Horbach (2008), the drivers of eco-innovations can be classified into three groups including supply-side factors, demand-side factors, and institutional and political influences. An overview is given in Table 51.1.

Some other authors divide drivers into motives and incentives. Motives could be understood as factors that could be found inside or outside a person and activate goal-oriented behavior (Solomon et al., 2006). Intrinsic motives are very strong and persuasive characteristics of human behavior. This behavior occurs naturally and represents doing of activity for its own inherent satisfaction rather than for some consequence. They do not need external stimulation to be activated. Extrinsic motives relate to an activity that is done in order to attain some separable outcome (Ryan & Deci, 2000). Bhaduri and Kumar (2011) found that pure extrinsic forms of motivation drive only a fraction of individual innovative behavior. SME entrepreneurs are mainly motivated by intrinsic motivation or by a combination of intrinsic and extrinsic motivations.

Incentives affect entrepreneurs to innovate in two ways: first, by lowering the barriers for innovating and, secondly, by stimulating the motives that drive an entrepreneur to invest in eco-innovations (Madrid-Guijarro et al., 2009). Examples of tangible incentives that may stimulate the entrepreneurs to innovate include financial subsidies, attaining resources, and access to technology. Intangible incentives might include knowledge and emotional support. Research has proven that tangible incentives (such as financial subsidies) are more effective than indirect aid (fairs, network events, advice) in the diffusion of innovation (Tolkamp, 2012).

Barriers to eco-innovation are factors that affect the eco-innovation efforts of enterprises in a negative way, thus hindering their development and adoption. The high heterogeneity of the environment in which today's SMEs operate is not very conducive to the introduction of innovation in these enterprises (Ciambotti & Palazzi, 2015). Accompanied by frequent and turbulent changes in the external environment, which these enterprises must face more and more often, they suffer from many problems and barriers on the way to the implementation of innovations. Carfora et al. (2022) include mainly difficulties related to the qualitative and quantitative rationing of credit, the weak presence of networking economies with research institutions or corporations penalizing the ability to learn, and the weak social capital. Del Brio and Junquera (2003) named insufficient business resources, whether financial, human, or technical, the lack of information, knowledge, special expertise, focus on short-term objectives, lack of management skills, risk aversion, or inadequate relations with the business external stakeholders. Many studies suggest that the lack of financial resources and skilled personnel is among the most frequent barriers to eco-innovations (Arranz et al., 2019; Marin & Marzucchi, 2015; Ociepa-Kubicka & Pachura, 2017; Segarra-Oña et al., 2015). Urbaniec (2015) argues that the lack of capital is even more significant in the new EU member states than in the old ones. When examining the drivers and barriers to eco-innovations in developing countries, Aloise and Macke (2017) find that the biggest barrier to eco-innovation in emerging countries is the absence of a consolidated innovation model including the lack of support and incentives, bureaucracy of processes, lack of governance, lack of planning and coordinated actions among companies, government agencies and academia, and lack of consistency among basic research, applied research, and markets. Díaz-García, González-Moreno, and Sáez-Martínez, argue that there are specific obstacles – competitive advantages based on low labor costs, deficient environmental and industrial policies, and the lack of awareness related to potential productivity increases stimulated by eco-innovations – deterring eco-innovation endeavors in transition economies. Horbach emphasizes the need to analyze the process in Eastern European EU member states, for which even country-level studies are not readily available.

In line with the above classifications of factors influencing innovation activities of enterprises, the drivers and barriers to eco-innovation can also be classified as external and internal. Hinojosa (2022) presents a summary of the drivers and barriers to eco-innovation, also broken down into external and internal, as listed in Table 51.2.

Drivers and barriers to eco-innovation, their incidence, and intensity vary between different countries and sectors (Urbaniec, 2015).

51.3 Research Methodology

The purpose of the chapter is to identify and assess the importance of motives and barriers to eco-innovations among small- and medium-sized Slovak enterprises.

Table 51.2 Classification of drivers and barriers to eco-innovations

External drivers
Cooperation agreements
Environmental regulations
Public financial support
Access to external information sources (such as customers and suppliers)
Internal drivers
R&D investment
Long-term cost savings
Better corporate image
Employee training for innovation activities
Implementation of quality and environmental systems
Access to new markets
External barriers
Market uncertainty
Long investment payback periods
Internal barriers
Lack of financial resources
Lack of qualified human resources
Lack of technological competence

Table 51.3 Structure of the research sample

Respondents	Frequency
Microenterprise	465
Small enterprise	17
Medium enterprise	5
Total	487

The research sample (respondents) was randomly selected, and we used an online questionnaire to collect responses. In total, we received 672 responses from companies in the Slovak Republic.

The questionnaires were distributed and collected from December 2022 to April 2023. We rejected 186 questionnaires due to missing responses or untrustworthy information. To ensure the representativeness of the sample, we randomly selected respondents in the following structure (Table 51.3).

We selected respondents according to size (measured by the number of employees), while we did not consider regional location or affiliation to the sector of the economy. We verified the representativeness of the research sample through the Chi-square goodness-of-fit test, based on the structure of the population in the Slovak Republic (*p*-value equal to 0.08). Since our research has been oriented toward small- and medium-sized enterprises, we excluded large companies from the population. It is worth noting the slightly atypical structure of the population, since, unlike the EU average, the share of small and medium enterprises in the Slovak economy was up to 99.5%, with the dominance of microenterprises and small enterprises.

Based on the purpose of the chapter, we set the following research hypotheses:

- H1: The order of motives for eco-innovations is not dependent on the SME's size categories.
- H2: The order of barriers to eco-innovations is not dependent on the SME's size categories.

We tested the normality of the distribution of responses for barriers and motives with the Shapiro-Wilk test. Since the normality of the distribution was not confirmed, we continued with nonparametric tests. We verified the independence between the size groups of enterprises and the obtained assessment of barriers using the Spearman correlation test. The Spearman correlation test confirmed that both barriers and motives are independent (at 0.05 level of confidence) of the size of respondents. For the purpose of the chapter, we used the mean values of importance for particular barriers and motives to describe the importance of barriers and motives in SMEs size groups.

Then, we tested the order of importance of all barriers and all motives for eco-innovations separately, disregarding size groups of enterprises. For this purpose, we used the Friedman test. The order of barriers and motives was consequently tested on population by using the Wilcoxon Signed-Ranks test.

51.4 Results and Conceptual Framework

The respondents evaluated the motives for the implementation of eco-innovation in SMEs on the Likert scale from 1 to 5, with 1 representing the least important motive; 5, the most important one. Table 51.4 presents the perception of the motives assessed by the mean within each size category of the respondents.

As can be seen in Table 51.4, both micro- and small-sized enterprises were most motivated to pursue eco-innovations by the opportunity to save costs and the need to reduce energy consumption. Medium-sized enterprises were most motivated by the need to support demand for products and services and the business's strategy driven by their own belief in the need for eco-innovations, followed by the motives involving image or brand improvement, the need to reduce consumables and raw material consumption, and the need to reduce energy consumption. Quite consistently across the three size categories of businesses surveyed, the initiative of trade associations emerged as the least motivating factor.

Similarly, to identify the main barriers to eco-innovations in Slovak SMEs, we asked respondents to rate potential barriers on a Likert scale from 1 to 5, with 1 being the least important barrier and 5 being the most important one. The mean values of the barriers in each category of business size are shown in Table 51.5.

The table shows that a high level of bureaucracy was the most serious barrier to eco-innovations in Slovak small- and medium-sized enterprises and the second most serious barrier in microenterprises. The high cost of implementing eco-innovations was also among the biggest barriers in all three size categories of

Table 51.4 Motives of eco-innovations in Slovak SMEs (mean values)

Motives	Micro	Small	Medium
Saving of costs	4.38	4.76	4.00
Support of demand for products/services	3.82	4.00	4.60
Customer pressure on eco-features of products and services	3.05	2.41	3.60
The opportunity to collaborate with another company/institution	3.01	2.82	3.20
Business's strategy – Own belief in the need for eco-innovations	3.71	3.65	4.60
EU regulations and initiatives (e.g., certification and labeling of green products)	3.17	3.18	3.00
Slovak legislation – New policies, regulations, and rules that require the introduction of eco-innovations	3.24	3.41	3.20
Financial and nonfinancial state aid	3.48	3.53	3.40
Improvement of the image or brand	3.85	3.65	4.40
Growing competition in the market	3.44	3.41	4.20
The initiative by trade/interest associations	2.71	2.12	2.60
The need to reduce consumables and raw material consumption in the production	3.61	4.12	4.40
The need to reduce energy consumption in a business	4.14	4.47	4.40
Efforts to reduce the business dependence on resources (particularly on nonrenewable ones)	3.66	3.53	3.60

enterprises surveyed. Microenterprises perceived it as the most significant barrier, small enterprises considered it the second most significant barrier, and for medium-sized enterprises, it meant the third most significant barrier. The limited access of enterprises to capital, both internal and external, also belonged to the more significant barriers to eco-innovations. In all three size categories, the lack of financial resources was ranked among the top five most serious barriers. On the contrary, the least significant barriers were the lack of cooperation with research institutions and universities (microenterprises), the lack of cooperation with other companies (small companies), and the lack of willingness of business management to innovate (medium-sized companies).

The Wilcoxon test confirmed (at 0.05 level of confidence) the following order of the most important motives for the Slovak population of SMEs disregarding the size of respondents: (1) saving of costs, (2) the need to reduce energy consumption in a company, and (3) support of the demand for products/services and improvement of the image or brand. As the least important motive was identified: the initiative to eco-innovate by trade associations.

The Wilcoxon test confirmed (at 0.05 level of confidence) the following barriers as the most important for SMEs in Slovakia (regardless of the size of SMEs): (1) the high cost of eco-innovations and the high level of bureaucracy, (2) lack of internal financial sources, and (3) difficult access to external sources of funding for eco-innovations. The least important were the barriers: lack of cooperation with research institutions and universities and the lack of cooperation with other businesses.

Table 51.5 Barriers to eco-innovations in Slovak SMEs (mean value)

Barriers	Micro	Small	Medium
Lack of internal financial sources	4.00	4.24	4.00
Difficult access to external sources of funding for eco-innovations	3.94	4.29	4.00
The high cost of eco-innovations	4.16	4.35	4.20
Lack of qualified staff to create or implement eco-innovations	3.51	3.59	3.60
Lack of willingness of business's management to innovate	3.07	2.82	2.00
Lack of cooperation with other businesses	2.93	2.59	3.40
Lack of cooperation with research institutions and universities	2.91	2.82	3.40
Insufficient state policy to support innovative activities of businesses	3.66	3.59	3.80
The high level of bureaucracy (when drawing financial support, dealing with various permits, etc.)	4.14	4.47	4.60
Lack of awareness of the benefits of eco-innovations in a business	3.54	3.65	4.00
Uncertain returns on investments in eco-innovations or a too-long payback period	3.76	3.88	3.40
Limited access to external sources of information and knowledge on eco-innovations	3.53	3.53	4.20
Lack of support services (from state institutions) necessary for the introduction of eco-innovations in a business	3.77	4.00	4.40
Uncertain customer demand for eco-innovations in the current market	3.34	3.18	3.80
Existing technical and technological constraints in the economy (e.g., outdated technical infrastructure)	3.50	3.41	3.40
Existing legal restrictions in a country	3.30	2.82	3.00
Macroeconomic uncertainties (COVID-19, war in Ukraine, inflation, etc.)	3.70	3.35	3.80

51.5 Discussion

The results of our research, based on the questionnaire survey carried out on the sample of Slovak SMEs, allowed us to assess the main factors determining the implementation of eco-innovation activities in these enterprises, leaning toward their definition in the form of motives and barriers. The list of factors determining eco-innovation presented in the econometric studies published so far is very extensive, with individual studies often differing considerably from each other and the penetration of commonly reported factors being relatively small (del Río et al., 2016). Therefore, for the purpose of our research, we have chosen to examine the factors that are most relevant in our geopolitical context.

The desire to reduce costs in Slovak SMEs was particularly prevalent as a driver of eco-innovations among micro- and small enterprises, with small enterprises perceiving it as a motive more strongly (with an average value of 4.76 out of 5 on the Likert scale) than microenterprises (value of 4.38 out of 5). The same result was confirmed by the research on Polish SMEs conducted in 2017, which also identified cost reduction as the main motivation to undertake environmentally beneficial activities (Wielgórka & Szczepaniak, 2019). The strong influence of cost savings as a motivator has also been shown to be statistically significant in some other studies (e.g., Horbach et al., 2012; Kesidou & Demirel, 2012). It should be added that cost saving is not a distinctive feature of eco-innovation but is often seen as one of the main drivers of innovation in general (del Río et al., 2016). Interestingly, while in Slovak micro- and small enterprises, cost saving was clearly the most important motive driving eco-innovations, in medium-sized enterprises this motive was roughly in the middle of the overall ranking of motives. Slovak micro- and small enterprises considered the need to reduce energy consumption as the second most important motive for eco-innovation. Again, this motive was perceived somewhat more strongly by small businesses than by microbusinesses. We assume that this result is also related to the current energy crisis, which has brought a substantial increase in energy prices. Medium-sized enterprises also considered this motivation important. Together with the improvement of the image or brand and the need to reduce consumables and raw material consumption with a Likert scale value of 4.40 out of 5, they ranked it right behind the most important factors motivating their eco-innovation activities, including the support of demand for their products and services and the business strategy embodying the belief in the need for eco-innovations, both with a Likert scale value of 4.60. Different forms of market and nonmarket pressures were often reported as one of the most significant motives of eco-innovation (del Río Gonzáles, 2009). This supports our findings, as the need to support the demand for products or services has been shown to be the most significant for medium-sized enterprises, while in micro- and small enterprises, it was the fourth most important motive. Contrary to our results, we found conflicting evidence in the literature on the significance of demand pull. While it has been demonstrated as a key driver of eco-innovations in Germany (Rehfeld, 2007) and Belgium (Veugelers, 2012), in the United Kingdom (Horbach et al., 2012), its relevance has not been confirmed. We are now seeing consumer demand for green products and services increasing with stronger support and stricter regulation at both the national and the EU levels, and the incentive for businesses to pursue eco-innovation can be expected to grow significantly in this context as well. The increasing competition in the market (also one of the market pressures) was not ranked as a top driver for eco-innovation by the surveyed enterprises and was even considered less important by micro- and small enterprises. Management commitment to environmental issues reflecting their belief in the need for eco-innovations was confirmed as a highly relevant driver also by some other authors (see, e.g., Cainelli & Mazzanti, 2013). As can be seen in Table 51.4, these motives were also in the top ranks of importance in micro- and small enterprises, differing slightly only in the ranking determined by the average values on the Likert scale.

Previous literature shows that particular high costs and insufficient funds are relevant barriers to eco-innovations (Arranz et al., 2019; Cuerva et al., 2014; García-Granero et al., 2020). Our research has shown similar results. The high cost of eco-innovation proved to be the most significant barrier in Slovak microenterprises (4.16 out of 5 on the Likert scale), as the second most significant barrier in small enterprises (4.35 out of 5) and the third most significant barrier in medium-sized enterprises (4.20 out of 5). The lack of internal sources of capital and the difficult access to external sources of finance were also significant barriers, especially in small and medium-sized Slovak enterprises. The lack of funds was also one of the most frequent barriers in Greece, Cyprus, Malta, Spain, Hungary, Poland, Bulgaria, and Romania (Ociepa-Kubicka & Pachura, 2017). Urbaniec (2015) confirmed the lack of funding as a very significant barrier to the absorption of eco-innovations in European SMEs. Both Slovak micro- and small enterprises ranked the lack of internal and external capital in the top four barriers; however, we do not see it among the most significant barriers to eco-innovations in medium-sized enterprises (they are fifth and sixth in the ranking of barriers). It can be assumed that the stronger financial position and more favorable financial structure of medium-sized enterprises open more opportunities for raising appropriate funds to finance eco-innovations compared to micro and small enterprises. Looking at the Likert scale score, the lack of access to capital appears to be a slightly more acute problem in small enterprises (difficult access to external sources of finance scored 4.29 out of 5, lack of internal capital 4.24 out of 5) than in medium-sized enterprises with a Likert scale score oscillating around 4. Although the lack of capital in medium-sized enterprises did not feature high on the list, it was nevertheless perceived as a barrier quite strongly, with an average Likert scale score of 4 out of 5. In contrast to the abovementioned results of other authors, the high level of bureaucracy appears to be the most significant barrier in Slovak SMEs, which was the biggest obstacle by both small enterprises (rating 4.47 out of 5) and medium-sized enterprises (rating 4.60 out of 5). Microenterprises identified it as the second largest barrier. This result is not so surprising because excessive bureaucracy in Slovakia has long been criticized by many institutions as a significant obstacle hindering the development of entrepreneurship. We assume that the respondents mentioned a high level of bureaucracy at least in connection with the possibility of getting support funds from the state and from European funds for their eco-innovations. Closely related to high bureaucracy was another significant and denounced limiting factor in the Slovak Republic, the lack of services supporting eco-innovations provided by the state. Medium-sized enterprises even considered it as the second most significant barrier with a score of 4.40 out of 5. Micro and small enterprises also ranked it among the top five significant barriers. Similar results have been reached by several other authors, including some of those mentioned above, who cite the lack of government incentives and agencies involved in the support of business eco-innovations, as well as the absence of a consolidated and systematic approach on the part of the state, as significant barriers. Although nowadays the need for cooperation between enterprises and research institutions, universities, or other enterprises and entities, e.g., within clusters, is increasingly coming to the forefront and its importance in the implementation of eco-innovations is confirmed by several studies (e.g., Aloise & Macke, 2017; Triguero et al., 2013), our research revealed that Slovak SMEs did not perceive the lack of such cooperative relationships as a strong barrier.

51.6 Conclusions, Limitations, and Directions for Future Research

Eco-innovations represent a huge potential in strategic planning and sustainable development, especially for SMEs, which play an increasingly important role within industrial sectors and are considered the so-called backbone of the economy due to their abundance. Due to the relative immaturity of the market, especially SMEs involved in eco-innovations with a perceived high business risk have a difficult access to financing. There is a need for further support for businesses with an emphasis on SMEs, which will contribute to improving investment readiness, creating networking opportunities, and supporting the building of market confidence in eco-innovation.

Based on the results of the empirical research, it can be concluded that the strength of the motives and barriers to eco-innovations analyzed among small- and medium-sized enterprises in Slovakia is not dependent on the size of the enterprises. However, according to the mean value of motives' importance within the sample of respondents, it can be observed that the smaller the company the more important the effort to achieve better cost efficiency was, and on the contrary, with the increasing size of the respondents, the benefits of eco-innovation in the form of goodwill and a positive image were more important motives to the respondents. It is interesting to note that SMEs in Slovakia perceive pressure from customers who demand the introduction of eco-innovative products and services, but do not consider it as a strongly significant motive.

The results of our investigation of barriers to eco-innovation activity confirmed that the most significant barrier for surveyed micro- and small enterprises was the high cost of the eco-innovation. Another barrier in the sequence was the related unavailability of financial resources that would enable a wider application of eco-innovations. On the other hand, among medium-sized enterprises, the first two most significant barriers were associated with the efficiency and scope of services provided by the state in this area. It can be concluded that if we want to intensify the level of eco-innovative activity among SMEs in Slovakia, it is necessary to financially stimulate the procurement of modern eco-innovative technologies (not necessarily with direct financial assistance, but also with assistance in the form of tax relief) in the group of micro- and small businesses. Similarly, it is important to simplify and make transparent the conditions for entrepreneurship to obtain the necessary information and support from the state institutions on the part of all enterprises in Slovakia.

The limit of our investigation and the interpretation of the results are the facts that the results were valid at the time of obtaining information from the respondents. The results must be seen in connection with the exceptional situation in the world and especially in Europe, when individual countries, companies, and especially SMEs react very sensitively to an unprecedented COVID-19 pandemic, high rates of inflation (the Slovak Republic had in 2022 one of the highest inflation rates in the EU), and still ongoing military conflict in Ukraine. The related energy crisis and strong restrictions on the supply side of raw materials, energy, and technologies used in the areas of eco-innovations influenced the perception of barriers and the importance of some drivers to eco-innovation activities among Slovak SMEs.

As the increased sensitivity of small- and medium-sized enterprises to changes in their surroundings is the characteristic feature of SMEs, we believe that it would be interesting to investigate the influence of selected external economic factors on the eco-innovative behavior (barriers and motives of eco-innovation) of SMEs in Slovakia and to compare future results with current ones. As we could not confirm the dependence between the barriers/motives and the size group of SMEs in our survey, it would be interesting to explore if there is any dependence of barriers and motives with the share of foreign capital.

Acknowledgments This article is a result of the research project VEGA 1/0036/21 "Determinants of the eco-innovation activity of enterprises in the context of changes in the external economic environment," funded by the Scientific Grant Agency of the Ministry of Education, Science, Research, and Sport of the Slovak Republic.

References

Aboelmaged, M., & Gharib, H. (2019). Absorptive capacity and green innovation adoption in SMEs: The mediating effects of sustainable organisational capabilities. *Journal of Cleaner Production, 220*, 853–863. https://doi.org/10.1016/j.jclepro.2019.02.150

Aloise, P. G., & Macke, J. (2017). Eco-innovations in developing countries: The case of Manaus Free Trade Zone (Brazil). *Journal of Cleaner Production, 168*, 30–38. https://doi.org/10.1016/j.jclepro.2017.08.212

Arranz, N., Arroyabe, M. F., Molina-García, A., & Fernandez de Arroyabe, J. C. (2019). Incentives and inhibiting factors of eco-innovation in the Spanish firms. *Journal of Cleaner Production, 220*, 167–176.

Bessant, J., & Tidd, J. (2015). *Innovation and entrepreneurship*. John Wiley & Sons.

Bhaduri, S., & Kumar, H. (2011). Extrinsic and intrinsic motivations to innovate: Tracing the motivation of grassroot innovators in India. *Mind and Society, 10*(1), 27–25.

Cainelli, G., & Mazzanti, M. (2013). Environmental innovations in services: Manufacturing–services integration and policy transmissions. *Research Policy, 42*(2013), 1595–1604. https://doi.org/10.1016/j.respol.2013.05.010

Carfora, A., Passaro, R., Scandurra, G., & Thomas, A. (2022). Do determinants of eco-innovations vary? An investigation of innovative SMEs through a quantile regression approach. *Journal of Cleaner Production, 370*, 133475. https://doi.org/10.1016/j.jclepro.2022.133475

Ciambotti, M., & Palazzi, F. (2015). Social capital and SMEs: An exploratory case study. *Journal of International Business and Economics, 15*(2), 53–64. https://doi.org/10.18374/JIBE-15-2.4

Colombo, L. A., Pansera, M., & Owen, R. (2019). The discourse of eco-innovation in the European Union: An analysis of the eco-innovation action plan and horizon 2020. *Journal of Cleaner Production, 214*, 653–665. https://doi.org/10.1016/j.jclepro.2018.12.150

Cuerva, M. C., Triguero-Cano, Á., & Córcoles, D. (2014). Drivers of green and non-green innovation: Empirical evidence in low-tech SMEs. *Journal of Cleaner Production, 68*(2014), 104–113. https://doi.org/10.1016/j.jclepro.2013.10.049

de Jesus, A., Antunes, P., Santos, R., & Mendonça, S. (2017). Eco-innovation in the transition to a circular economy: An analytical literature review. *Journal of Cleaner Production, 172*, 1999–2018. https://doi.org/10.1016/j.jclepro.2017.11.111

del Brío, J. Á., & Junquera, B. (2003). A review of the literature in environmental innovation management in SMEs: Implications for public policies. *Technovation, 23*, 939–948.

del Río Gonzáles, P. (2009). The empirical analysis of the determinants for environmental technological change: A research agenda. *Ecological Economics, 68*(3), 861–878. https://doi.org/10.1016/j.ecolecon.2008.07.004

del Río, P., Peñasco, C., & Romero-Jordán, D. (2016). What drives eco-innovators? A critical review of the empirical literature based on econometric methods. *Journal of Cleaner Production, 112*(2016), 2158–2170. https://doi.org/10.1016/j.jclepro.2015.09.009

European Commission. (2011). Communication from the Commission to the European Parliament the Council, the European Economic and Social Committee and the Committee of the Regions. *Innovation for the Sustainable Future – the Eco-innovation Action Plan (Eco-AP)*. https://eur-lex.europa.eu/legal-content/EN/ALL/?uri=celex%3A52011DC0899. Accessed 19 April 2023

García-Granero, E. M., Piedra-Muñoz, L., & Galdeano-Gómez, E. (2020). Multidimensional assessment of eco-innovation implementation: Evidence from Spanish agri-food sector. *International Journal of Environmental Research and Public Health, 17*(4), 1432. https://doi.org/10.3390/ijerph17041432

García-Pozo, A., Campos-Soria, J. A., Santos, M. C., & Santos, J. A. C. (2019). Determinants of environmental innovations: New evidence at the sector level. *Journal of Scientific & Industrial Research, 78*, 76–80.

Hinojosa, K. (2022). Determinants of eco-innovation in the change towards a circular economy: An empirical analysis of Spanish firms. *Journal of Innovation Economics & Management, 39*, 105–139. https://doi.org/10.3917/jie.pr1.0119

Horbach, J. (2008). Determinants of environmental innovation – New evidence from German panel data sources. *Research Policy, 37*, 163–173.

Horbach, J., Rammer, C., & Rennings, K. (2012). Determinants of eco-innovations by type of environmental impact – The role of regulatory push/pull, technology push and market pull. *Ecological Economics, 78*, 112–122. https://doi.org/10.1016/j.ecolecon.2012.04.005

Horbach, J., & Reif, C. (2018). New developments in eco-innovation research: Aim of the book and overview of the different chapters. In J. Horbach & C. Reif (Eds.), *New developments in eco-innovation research* (pp. 1–11). Springer.

Jové-Llopis, E., & Segarra-Blasco, A. (2018). *Eco-innovation strategies: A panel data analysis of Spanish manufacturing firms*. Business Strategy and the Environment. https://doi.org/10.1002/bse.2063

Kesidou, E., & Demirel, P. (2012). On the drivers of eco-innovations: Empirical evidence from the UK. *Research Policy, 41*(5), 862–870. https://doi.org/10.1016/j.respol.2012.01.005

Kiefer, C. P., González, P. D. R., & Carillo-Hermosilla, J. (2018). Drivers and barriers of eco-innovation types for sustainable transitions: A quantitative perspective. *Business Strategy and the Environment*. https://doi.org/10.1002/bse.2246

Klewitz, J., & Hansen, E. G. (2014). Sustainability-oriented innovation of SMEs: A systematic review. *Journal of Cleaner Production, 65*, 57–75. https://doi.org/10.1016/j.jclepro.2013.07.017

Lesáková, Ľ., Gundová, P., Hvolková, L., Klement, L., Klementová, V., Kovaľová, M., & Vinczeová, M. (2017). *Inovácie v činnosti malých a stredných podnikov v Slovenskej republike [Innovations in business activities of small and medium-sized enterprises in the Slovak Republic]*. Belianum.

Lesáková, Ľ., Klement, L., Klementová, V., & Vinczeová, M. (2021). *Ekologické inovácie a udržateľný rozvoj malých a stredných podnikov [Eco-innovations and sustainable development of SMEs in the Slova Republic]*. Belianum.

Madrid-Guijarro, A., & Garcia, D. (2009). Barriers to innovation among Spanish manufacturing SMEs. *Journal of Small Business and Management, 47*(4), 465–488.

Marin, G., & Marzucchi, A. (2015). SMEs and barriers to eco-innovation in the EU: Exploring different firm profiles. *Journal of Evolutionary Economics, 25*, 671–705.

Moro-Visconti, R. (2022). *Augmented corporate valuation. From digital networking to ESG compliance*. Springer. https://link.springer.com/book/10.1007/978-3-030-97117-5. Accessed 10 April 2023

Ociepa-Kubicka, A., & Pachura, P. (2017). Eco-innovations in the functioning of companies. *Environmental Research, 156*, 284–290.

Porter, M. E., & van der Linde, C. (1995). Toward a new conception of the environment-competitiveness relationship. *Journal of Economic Perspectives, 9*(4), 97–118.

Rehfeld, K. M., Rennings, K., & Ziegler, A. (2007). Integrated product policy and environmental product innovations: An empirical analysis. *Ecological Economics, 61*(1), 91–100. https://doi.org/10.1016/j.ecolecon.2006.02.003

Ryan, R. M., & Deci, E. L. (2000). Intrinsic and extrinsic motivations: Classic definitions and new directions. *Contemporary Educational Psychology, 25*(1), 54–67.

Segarra-Oña, M. V., Peiró-Signes, A., & Cervelló-Royo, R. (2015). A framework to move forward on the path to eco-innovation in the construction industry: Implications to improve firms´ sustainable orientation. *Science and Engineering Ethics, 21*, 1469–1484. https://doi.org/10.1007/s11948-014-9620-2

Solomon, M., & Barmossy, G. (2006). *Motivation, values, and involvement. Consumer Behaviour: A European perspective* (pp. 89–136). Pearson Education Limited.

Spash, C. L. (2017). Social ecological economics. In C. L. Spash (Ed.), *Routledge handbook of ecological economics* (pp. 3–16). Routledge.

Tan, J., & Cha, V. (2021). Innovation for circular economy. In *An introduction to circular economy* (pp. 369–395). Springer Nature Singapore.

Tolkamp, J. W. (2012). *Motives, incentives and barriers for sustainable innovations*. Holland.

Triguero, A., Moreno-Mondéjar, L., & Davia, M. A. (2013). Drivers of different types of eco-innovation in European SMES. *Ecological Economics, 92*, 25–33. https://doi.org/10.1016/j.ecolecon.2013.04.009

Urbaniec, M. (2015). Towards sustainable development through eco-innovations: Drivers and barriers in Poland. *Economics and Sociology, 8*, 179–190. https://doi.org/10.14254/2071-789X.2015/8-4/13

Veugelers, R. (2012). Which policy instruments to induce clean innovating? *Research Policy, 41*(10), 1770–1778. https://doi.org/10.1016/j.respol.2012.06.012

Wielgórka, D., & Szczepaniak, W. (2019). Eco-innovation of enterprises operating in Poland against the background of EU countries. *Global Journal of Environmental Science and Management, 5*(51), 113–121.

ID="N" />
# Chapter 52
# The Impact of COVID-19 and Lockdowns on Media: The Greek Case

Athanasios Papathanasopoulos

Abstract The COVID-19 pandemic has significantly altered worldwide media consumption trends. The goal of this study is to determine how much the pandemic influenced media consumption in Greece and to investigate if the pandemic played a crucial role in the rise of streaming services. Quantitative data from various sources were analyzed as part of the approach. According to the data, TV was the most popular medium at the beginning of the pandemic and social restriction measures. However, following the end of the second lockdown in Greece, streaming platform usage accelerated, with 48% of all respondents reporting weekly usage. Additionally, a sizable portion of the Greek audience claimed that they never used traditional media outlets, such as newspapers and television, indicating a shift in media consumption from traditional to digital. This study aims to shed light on how Greece's media consumption habits changed because of the COVID-19 outbreak and the rising popularity of streaming services.

Keywords COVID-19 · Lockdowns · Media consumption · Greece · OTT platforms · Streaming

52.1 Introduction

The COVID-19 pandemic has impacted all aspects of society and economy. The media sector was one of the most affected by the implementation of widespread lockdowns and social distancing measures (Croucher & Diers-Lawson, 2023). For instance, traditional media channels such as movie theaters and live events have

---

A. Papathanasopoulos (✉)
Department of Informatics and Telecommunications, National and Kapodistrian University of Athens, Athens, Greece
e-mail: athpapat@di.uoa.gr

© The Author(s), under exclusive license to Springer Nature Switzerland AG 2024
N. Tsounis, A. Vlachvei (eds.), *Applied Economic Research and Trends*, Springer Proceedings in Business and Economics,
https://doi.org/10.1007/978-3-031-49105-4_52

been disrupted or even suspended entirely. In response to these challenges, media companies have had to adjust quickly to the new reality, seeking alternative ways to reach audiences and remain relevant in an ever-changing landscape. As a result, the pandemic has accelerated the shift toward digital media and streaming platforms, as people turn to online sources for news, entertainment, and social connection.

In the UK, in April 2020, individuals devoted a substantial amount of time to consuming television and online video content, spending an average of six hours and 25 min per day, which amounts to almost 45 h per week. This represents a notable increase of 31% from the previous year (OfCom, 2020). Moreover, people spent more time watching TV news about COVID-19 and updates from health organizations. The living room became a hub for families to congregate and socialize, as social media played a vital role in keeping people connected during lockdowns and restrictions when physical gatherings were not feasible (Johnson, 2020).

During lockdowns, an increasing number of individuals turned to streaming platforms for entertainment, resulting in a surge in their subscription numbers (Daily Mail, 2020; Napchi, 2022). In 2020, due to COVID-19 restrictions and the closure of movie theaters, box office revenues were estimated at 30 billion US dollars, a notable decrease from the previous years (42.3 billion US dollars). In contrast, the popularity of streaming platforms such as Netflix has skyrocketed, with Netflix surpassing 200 million subscribers and Disney+ reaching 100 million subscribers, despite its recent introduction to the streaming market (Dayal, 2022).

In Greece, the government made significant efforts to effectively manage the COVID-19 pandemic crisis by implementing early and strict measures, including a lockdown, like in other countries. This led Greeks to become more accustomed to using digital devices and services. However, the situation for the media was somewhat different. Despite emerging from a decade-long fiscal crisis during which they suffered major losses in advertising revenue, the media had to cope with the consequences of the COVID-19 pandemic. Like in other countries, the pandemic had a significant impact on the lives of most Greeks, as well as on their media behavior.

This study aims to provide insights into how the COVID-19 pandemic has impacted media consumption in Greece. At the same time, we review how pandemic of COVID-19, and lockdowns accelerated the digitalization of media and streaming consumption. It is hypothesized that the pandemic may have accelerated the shift toward digital media and streaming platforms in Greece, as has been observed globally. To test this hypothesis, data from various sources will be utilized. By analyzing several data sources, we aim to gain a comprehensive understanding of the impact that lockdowns and COVID-19 have had on the Greek media landscape and to what extent they have influenced the population's adoption of digital media and streaming platforms.

52.2 Literature Review

52.2.1 The Global Impact of COVID-19 on Media and Streaming Services

The COVID-19 virus, which led to a global pandemic and necessitated social distancing and quarantine measures, has resulted in significant changes in people's behaviors and lifestyles from 2020 until the end of 2021 (Carey et al., 2022). This has also impacted the way media content is consumed. In the United States, it is estimated that during the first week of the pandemic in March 2020, TV viewing increased by 18% (Gupta & Singharia, 2021). Similarly, in India, there was a 38% increase in TV viewing during the lockdown period compared to the pre-COVID era (Gupta & Singharia, 2021). According to a study conducted across 17 European countries on media consumption during the COVID-19 pandemic, Europeans demonstrated an increased preference for digital media and television over other forms of media. While newspapers and radio maintained their prepandemic numbers in some cases, there was a slight decrease in others. In contrast, TV viewing rates increased, as did the usage of news websites (Van Aelst et al., 2021).

In effect, the media journalism sector was among the hardest hit by the pandemic. However, during this period, there was a significant increase in online news consumption (Nielsen, 2020). News became a vital source of information for citizens, with television being the primary source. In fact, 82% of users consider TV news to be the most reliable source of pandemic-related information. Citizens relied on both linear and cable TV for news consumption, with a 96% increase in the frequency of citizens receiving information from this source. Social media platforms, which experienced a 49% increase in traffic, were considered suitable by 87% of the public for obtaining information, while print or digital versions of newspapers were considered suitable by 93% of the public (Casero-Ripolles, 2020).

Newspapers, which were on a downward trend since 2008, experienced a decrease in circulation during the pandemic, but at the same time, their digital versions increased. For example, the *New York Times* gained approximately 600,000 online subscribers in the first quarter of 2020. In general, it is estimated that the COVID-19 pandemic resulted in an 18% increase in online subscriptions, compared to 10% in 2019. Nevertheless, newspapers were hit hard by the pandemic, with a 13% decline in sales, and possibly even 20% in central and eastern European countries. However, some Western countries saw a small increase of around 2% in online subscriptions. This trend indicates that the pandemic has accelerated the shift toward digital media and online subscriptions, especially in the newspaper industry. It remains to be seen whether this trend will continue postpandemic (Economist Impact, 2022; Nicolaou & Barker, 2020).

During the pandemic, citizens turned to digital media. It is widely known that people increasingly used social media platforms to socialize and share information about the pandemic news (Carey et al., 2022). In fact, international and national health organizations, governments, and the global community used social media to communicate directly with the public (Zhou & Zheng, 2022). The pandemic led to a significant shift toward digital platforms in many aspects of life. More people began working remotely, using digital media for work and socializing, and the economy shifted toward online marketplaces (Seekins, 2020). Furthermore, the deployment of 5G networks in some countries was accelerated due to the pandemic (McKinsey & Company, 2020). Finally, there was a significant increase in so-called digital nomads during the pandemic, with the number of them in America alone increasing by almost 50% in 2020 compared to 2019 (MBO Partners, 2020).

Furthermore, the pandemic significantly limited citizens' entertainment options, especially in the movie theater industry. However, this led to the growth of other sectors, such as over-the-top (OTT) platforms that provide streaming content. These platforms, including Netflix, Amazon Prime, and Disney+, experienced a surge in their subscribers, especially among younger audiences, during the pandemic (Gupta & Singharia, 2021). The primary reason for choosing these platforms, aside from the limited alternatives, was the abundance of rich and diverse international content, as well as access to informative documentaries (European Audiovisual Observatory, 2020; Navsangeet, 2022).

It is worth noting that during the pandemic, the subscriptions of streaming platforms increased significantly compared to cable TV. This can be attributed to the fact that users on these platforms have the option to navigate and choose from a multitude of content, unlike cable TV, which is often more expensive and requires payment for multiple channels, most of which may not interest the user (Sung, 2023). Moreover, streaming platforms such as Netflix follow a subscription video-on-demand (SVOD) model, where users pay a monthly fee for the service as long as they wish to continue using it. In contrast, cable TV often requires an annual or two-year subscription, which may discourage users (Cooper, 2022).

In the UK, for instance, 40% of adults increased their time spent watching online content on screens during the pandemic. This led to a doubling in the number of streaming service subscriptions, with a total of 4.6 million households subscribing to subscription video-on-demand (SVOD) platforms. OTT platforms also tried various strategies to attract new users, such as offering trial subscription packages (European Audiovisual Observatory, 2020; Ofcom, 2020). Netflix, for example, reached close to 183 million subscribers in March 2020, which is a 23% increase from the previous year. The platform also generated $709 million USD dollars in revenue during the first quarter of 2020 alone (Daily Mail, 2020). Similarly, Disney+, which debuted during the pandemic, experienced a significant increase in subscribers, reaching 50 million in the first five months of operation (New York Times, 2020). These figures demonstrate the immense popularity of OTT platforms, particularly during the pandemic, and highlight the effectiveness of their strategies to reach new users. Additionally, the revenue generated by these platforms underscores their potential as a viable business model for the entertainment industry.

52.2.2 The Greek Media in the Eve of the COVID-19

The Greek media industry has been in a state of crisis due to various factors such as a small market size and declining advertising expenditure. The fiscal crisis and austerity measures further impacted the industry (Skamnakis, 2018). The advertising spending declined by about 65% over the 2007–2016 period (Statista, 2019). Furthermore, government advertising spending was decreasing, and orders for public works were postponed. The Greek state was an important advertiser, and due to its overextended character of the public sector, it used to play an important role in the economy. This had a negative impact on media outlets, especially newspapers and magazines. The owners of TV and radio stations, as well as newspapers, could thus no longer cross-subsidize their media outlets with revenues from orders for public works (Leandros, 2010; Papathanassopoulos, 2013).

In the aftermath of the fiscal crisis, even nowadays, Greek media outlets in general and the legacy media in particular faced their most difficult period ever. Nevertheless, the print media (newspapers and magazines) suffered the most. Additionally, four major media groups collapsed – Dimosiographicos Organismos Lambraki (DOL), Pegasos, IMAKO, and Liberis Publications. A similar trend one can be seen in the case of the regional press. On a national level, more than 40 local dailies were either shut down or changed to weekly editions, while subscribers declined significantly (Skamnakis, 2018). The situation in the TV sector was not better. Two private/commercial channels – Alter in 2011 and Mega channel in 2018 – collapsed due to their financial problems. In effect, almost all TV and radio stations faced severe financial problems due to the collapse of advertising spending.

Within this context, one can also relate, to a certain extent, the closure of the public broadcaster, ERT, on June 11, 2013. Although ERT's closure was a purely politically led decision rather than one based on public broadcasters' financial problems, the then-opposition claimed that the government fired ERT's 2500 employees to prove to Greece's international lenders that it was serious about cutting the country's bloated public sector. The troika of international lenders expected 4000 jobs to go by the end of 2013 (Iosifidis & Papathanassopoulos, 2019). In one way or another, one can say that there was an optimism regarding the future of the media market. The economy had started functioning again, while the advertising expenditure was on the rise (Iosifidis & Papathanassopoulos, 2019).

52.2.3 The Impact of COVID-19 on Greek Media

The media, coming out of the recent fiscal crisis with major losses of advertising revenues, had now to face the pandemic and its side effects on media economy. On the other hand, the pandemic had, as in other countries, an impact on the lives of most Greeks and on their media consumption.

During the first weeks of the lockdown, we saw a substantial rise in TV and news consumption. More and more people tuned in, especially the news shows and the press conferences and announcements of the National Public Health Organization (eody.gov.gr). In effect, during the "lockdown," the TV total audience has considerably increased. According to Nielsen, the measurement company, in March and April 2020, TV viewing ratings were increased by 25% and by more than 60% among 4- to 17-year-olds (Ntarzanou, 2020).

During the first 3 weeks of the lockdown, the average TV viewing was skyrocketed to 8 h per day. The TV news programs of the national channels also attracted almost half of the Greek population tuned on to their frequencies. Gradually, this number of TV viewers, as noted, started (Chaimanta, 2020). Nevertheless, these findings suggest the emergence of important developments such as the resurgence of the role of so-called legacy media, especially mainstream TV channels, and the fact that citizens who usually remain far from the information have reconnected with the news provided by the legacy media and not the social media as it was the trend in the recent years, especially in Greece (Nielsen et al., 2020).

During the lockdown period, the distribution of press faced additional challenges as newsstands remained open but with reduced sales. This led to a sharper decline in newspaper sales, and radio listenership also decreased as daily commuting to work, a common time for listening to the radio, came to a halt. On the other hand, the news sites of the Greek leading news media generated a marked increase in traffic. Internet users have considerably increased their visits to newspapers apps and websites, possibly more than other European users. In effect, during COVID-19, the average daily time spent online by every Internet user has remarkably increased (+50% from February to mid-March 2020). In the same period, the increase in mobile Internet was equally high (Papazoglou, 2020).

On the other hand, during the same period, the advertising market collapsed. According to media professionals, 80% of advertisers postponed their advertising campaigns. The fall of income from advertisements fell by 60%, leading, especially commercial media organizations, into "crisis mode" (Chaimanta, 2020). In effect, it caused major revenue losses in advertising-based media, affecting especially Sunday newspapers and private commercial TV and radio channels.

Finally, according to a study conducted by diaNeosis (Dianeosis, 2021), a Greek research and public policy institute, most Greeks were informed about COVID-19 through TV (48%), followed by Websites (25%) and social media platforms (7%). Furthermore, 3% of the total sample was informed by radio and only 1% of the population relied on newspapers. Other sources of information made up 16% of the total.

52.3 Methodology

This study analyzed quantitative data derived from multiple sources. These sources include an original study conducted by the "Laboratory of Journalism Studies and Communication Applications,[1]" in 2021. The author was part of the research team in the study, making the specific questions that have been used in this study. Permission was granted for the use of those data. The study took place from October to November 2021. The other sources are as follows: the European Commission and Directorate-General for Communication (Eurobarometer Journal 94), the Eurobarometer (Journal 93), and Statista. Those sources are employed to support the conclusions of the main one.

Access to the data collected by Statista, the European Commission Directorate-General for Communication and Eurobarometer was obtained through the National and Kapodistrian University of Athens.

The main research question is what impact the COVID-19 pandemic had on media consumption in Greece. In addition, this study aims to explore to what extent the pandemic drove the Greek audience toward streaming platforms. Furthermore, this paper aims to identify significant trends in media consumption that emerged as a result. The findings of this study are intended to contribute to a better understanding of the impact of the pandemic on the Greek media sector and to contribute to future research on this topic.

52.4 Analysis

52.4.1 Media Consumption in Greece at the Beginning of the Pandemic

A Eurobarometer survey (Eurobarometer, 2020) of 1016 respondents has taken place in the summer of 2020, after the first lockdown in Greece (March–May 2020), to examine the media consumption patterns in this period among European Countries. In Greece, as illustrated in Fig. 52.1, TV was the most popular medium during the initial stages of the pandemic, with 35% of respondents reporting frequent watching for information purposes. Additionally, websites and social media were frequently used by 23% and 20% of participants, respectively. Radio and press, on the other hand, were less commonly used, with only 15% and 7% of respondents reporting a frequent usage, respectively.

In the winter of 2020–2021, Greece experienced a second lockdown. A study conducted in this period and published in Eurobarometer (European Commission and Directorate-General for Communication, 2021), employing a total sample of 1058 respondents, revealed some interesting findings. TV was once again the most popular medium among Greeks, with 73% of respondents reporting daily usage. In this study, 14% of the total sample reported watching daily TV via the Internet.

---

[1] https://www.jourlab.media.uoa.gr

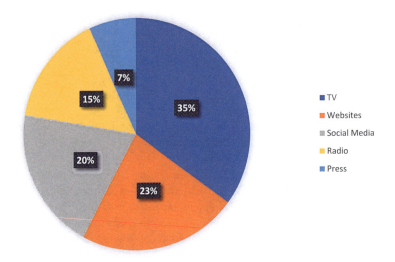

Fig. 52.1 Media consumption in the start of the pandemic (March–April 2020), in Greece. (Source: (Eurobarometer, 2020), compilation by the author)

Table 52.1 Media consumption in winter 2020–2021, in Greece

Media	Consumption				
	Daily	Weekly	Less often	Never	No access
TV	73%	16%	6%	5%	–
TV via internet	14%	17%	23%	44%	2%
Radio	42%	28%	22%	8%	–
Press	11%	23%	40%	26%	–
Social media	64%	8%	4%	21%	3%

Source: (European Commission and Directorate-General for Communication, 2021), compilation by the author

However, 44% of them reported never using TV via the Internet, indicating a preference for traditional broadcast TV.

Radio was also frequently used, with 42% of respondents reporting daily usage. On the other hand, press consumption was relatively low, with only 11% of respondents reading newspapers daily. Social media was used by 64% of respondents on a daily basis, making it the second most commonly used media channel. Nevertheless, it is important to note that 21% of the population reported never using social media. It is noteworthy that a significant percentage of the total sample reported having no access to certain media, particularly TV via the Internet (2%) and social media (3%). This could be attributed to various factors, such as the lack of access to the Internet or a preference for traditional types of media (Table 52.1).

Table 52.2 Media consumption at the end of the second lockdown (2021)

Media	Consumption			
	Daily	Weekly	Less often	Never
TV	27%	31%	18%	24%
Websites	56%	29%	9%	6%
Social media	49%	20%	13%	18%
Press	6%	16%	24%	54%
Radio	19%	26%	27%	28%
Streaming platforms	20%	28%	20%	32%

Source: (Laboratory of Journalism Studies and Communication Applications 2021), compilation by the author

52.4.2 Media Consumption in Greece at the End of 2021

After the end of the second lockdown in Greece (November 2020 to May 2021), the "Laboratory of Journalism Studies and Communication Applications" conducted a study with a total sample of 1554 respondents. The survey was conducted via the online snowball technique. A questionnaire has been distributed to various Internet users. Among the participants, 36% were male and 64% were female. In terms of age distribution, 16% were under 24 years old, 20% and 26% were aged between 25 and 34 years old and 35 and 44 years old, respectively. Additionally, 23% were between 45 and 54 years old and 15% were aged 55 and above. Regarding the respondents' level of education, 12% held a high-school degree, 11% had a diploma from a nonuniversity institution, while 36% had graduated from a university. Notably, the majority of the sample (41%) held an MSc or PhD diploma.

According to Table 52.2, 27% of the respondents reported daily usage of TV. It is noteworthy that a significant proportion of the population (24%) reported never using it. However, the consumption of TV streaming platforms is seemed to become popular in the second lockdown, giving a hit that a considerable part of, at least, Internet users are becoming news avoiders. Moreover, website and social media usage were prevalent, with 56% and 49% of respondents reporting daily usage, respectively. Press consumption became even lower, with only 6% of respondents reporting reading newspapers. Furthermore, radio consumption was also relatively low (19%). Interestingly, a significant amount of the population reported no usage of certain media, such as press (54%) and TV (24%).

Furthermore, 52% of the respondents reported to our survey that they watch movies and series more frequently at home than they did before the pandemic. In addition, 39% watched at the same frequency, while only 9% of the total sample reported a decrease in their viewership of such programs.

Based on the data presented in Fig. 52.3, it could be said that the Greeks have gradually become "digital users" since the majority of the respondents use multiple media on a weekly basis. Based on the data presented in Figs. 52.2 and 52.3, it can be observed that the majority of respondents in Greece engage with multiple media platforms on a weekly basis, particularly for consuming content such as movies and

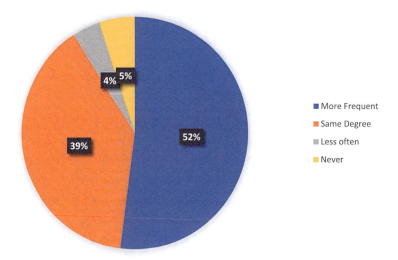

Fig. 52.2 Consumption of movie/series at the end of the second lockdown (2021) in contrast before the pandemic. (Source: (Laboratory of Journalism Studies and Communication Applications 2021), compilation by the author)

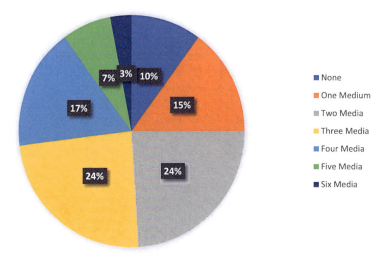

Fig. 52.3 How many media users consume in a weekly basis at the end of the second lockdown (2021). (Source: (Laboratory of Journalism Studies and Communication Applications 2021), compilation by the author)

series. Finally, the data presented in Table 52.3 show the revenue generated and how many users are subscribed to two types of video streaming platforms – transactional video on demand (TVOD) and subscription video on demand (SVOD) – from 2019

Table 52.3 Platform revenues and user bases in Greece

Platforms	Revenue in million (€)				User's subscriptions			
	2019	2020	2021	2022	2019	2020	2021	2022
TVOD	12.06	15.93	17.96	19.39	1.23	1.48	1.57	1.40
SVOD	39.27	48.02	52.84	56.22	1.46	1.66	1.74	1.55

Source: Statista (2023), compilation by the author

to 2022, in Greece. Both types of platforms have shown consistent growth in terms of revenue and user subscriptions. The revenue generated by TVOD increased from 12.06 million euros in 2019 to 19.39 million euros in 2022, while the revenue generated by SVOD increased from 39.27 million euros in 2019 to 56.22 million euros in 2022. Furthermore, the data show that the user subscriptions for both types of platforms have also increased steadily over the years. In 2019, TVOD had 1.23 million users, which increased to 1.57 million users in 2021 and then declined slightly to 1.40 million users in 2022. Similarly, SVOD had 1.46 million users in 2019, which increased to 1.74 million users in 2021 and then declined slightly to 1.55 million users in 2022.

52.5 Discussion

Based on the data presented above, certain trends can be highlighted regarding the effects of the two lockdowns on media consumption in Greece. During the first lockdown, TV reconfirmed its popularity, with the majority of respondents citing it as their primary source of information. Traditional media such as radio and newspapers had a lower impact. Additionally, news websites and social media networks reported relatively equal percentages, following closely behind TV. This trend can be attributed to the suddenness of the lockdown, which prompted the public to seek immediate and trustful information from traditional media channels, such as TV, through which they could receive real-time updates from the government or the World Health Organization.

During the second lockdown, TV continued to perform as the preferred medium, with 73% of respondents reporting daily viewership. Nevertheless, the Greek public has also begun to watch TV through the Internet, with 31% of respondents doing so at least once a week. Furthermore, 64% of respondents reported using social media daily. Although radio usage increased, the share of newspaper usage remained consistently low. Overall, these findings suggest that the pandemic has had a significant impact on media consumption patterns in Greece, with TV being the preferred one. However, the Internet is becoming a popular alternative, too. The Greek audience used to watch TV via the Internet, while social media platforms are gaining more popularity and usage.

The second lockdown in Greece (November 2020–May 2021) was the longest one in terms of duration. Media play a crucial role in entertaining citizens, apart from information. With recreational activities outside the home curtailed by social distancing measures, people turned to alternative means of entertainment. According to the provided data, 52% of respondents reported watching more films and series than before the pandemic, indicating a shift in media consumption patterns.

Although TV emerged as the primary medium during the initial lockdown and early stages of the second one, the situation changed toward the end of May 2021. More specifically, daily linear TV usage decreased from 73% to 27%. At the same time, other traditional media (press and radio) showed a declining trend, too. However, the use of websites and social media remained relatively stable. Furthermore, streaming platforms have now become a crucial part of the Greek public's media consumption habits, with almost half of the sample (48%) using them at least once per week. The study also highlights the significance of using multiple media sources during the second lockdown, with 48% of people reporting simultaneous usage of two or three media outlets per week.

The surge in the popularity of streaming platforms, as identified in this study and supported by the literature review, is further reinforced by data from Statista. The data from Statista confirms the increasing popularity of streaming services in Greece, as highlighted in the original study. As discussed in the previous chapter, there has been a significant rise in both transactional video-on-demand (TVOD) and subscription video-on-demand (SVOD) platform revenues between 2020 and 2021, surpassing prepandemic levels. This trend is also reflected in the growth of total user subscriptions. However, it is noteworthy that the lifting of restrictions in 2022 led to a decline in the number of subscriptions, despite the continued increase in revenues. This can be attributed to the fact that, after the lockdowns, people now have the opportunity to spend time outdoors and engage in a variety of activities that were previously restricted. Additionally, the reopening of cinemas and theaters may have had an impact on subscription numbers, too.

52.6 Conclusions

This study aimed to understand to what extent the COVID-19 pandemic had impacted media consumption in Greece. Data from the original study, combined with other sources, provide a comprehensive picture of Greek media consumption during the two COVID-19 lockdowns. Analysis of the data indicates that during the early stages of the pandemic, TV reconfirmed its popularity. Then TV was followed by websites and social media. People watched TV to stay informed about the developments regarding an unknown and deadly virus and the government's restrictions and responses. Gradually, in the second lockdown, TV remained the most preferred medium, but platforms such as social media and hybrid television gained momentum. Other traditional media, such as the press and radio, gradually declined in usage.

In effect, after the end of the second lockdown in May 2021, the Greek audience began to consume more content from streaming platforms. About half of the total sample reported watching more movies and series from home than before the pandemic. Additionally, 48% of the total respondents reported watching content from streaming platforms at least once a week. Furthermore, streaming platforms in Greece experienced an increase in revenues and subscriptions.

It seems that the two subsequent lockdowns, at least in the case of Greece, have affected media consumption. Greek media users seem to have abandoned reading newspapers and turned to screens. Greeks were increasingly dedicating their leisure time to watching TV shows and movies on streaming platforms. Major events such as COVID-19 and lockdowns have significantly influenced media consumption patterns. The widespread availability of broadband networks has made it easier for the Greek public to shift toward streaming platforms. Linear TV remains popular, but, as in other countries, TV screens are increasingly used for other viewership of the content emanating from TV streaming services.

This study employed data from various sources to provide a comprehensive understanding of how the Greek audience consumed media during the two lockdowns. Overall, it can be argued that although TV was the most preferred medium during the early stages of the pandemic, the Internet and various platforms such as social media and streaming platforms gained momentum and became even more popular than before. A study like this, conducted in a country with a smaller market size such as Greece, can provide valuable insights into the ways the pandemic influenced the media landscape. For future research, the author can suggest a cross-country analysis encompassing multiple European countries, to gain a broader and more comprehensive understanding of the changes that occurred in the media industry due to the impact of the pandemic.

Acknowledgments The research work was supported by the Hellenic Foundation for Research and Innovation (HFRI) under the fourth Call for HFRI PhD Fellowships (Fellowship Number: 10764).

References

Carey, J., Gallent, J. S., & Stipp, H. (2022). The COVID-19 pandemic and consumer media behavior. In G. Einav (Ed.), *Transitioning Media in a Post COVID world*. The Economics of Information, Communication, and Entertainment. Springer. https://doi.org/10.1007/978-3-030-95330-0_1

Casero-Ripolles, A. (2020). Impact of Covid-19 on the media system. Communicative and democratic consequences of news consumption during the outbreak. *El Profesional de La Información, 29*(2). https://doi.org/10.3145/epi.2020.mar.23

Chaimanta, S. (2020). How TV changed during the Covid19 era (in Greek). *Media, 2020*. https://medianalysis.net/2020/04/23/tv-stin-covid19-epohi/. Accessed 20 April 2023.

Cooper, T. (2022). *Cutting the cord: Is streaming or cable better for you?* BROADBANDNOW. https://broadbandnow.com/guides/cable-bundle-vs-streaming. Accessed 5 May 2023

Croucher, S. M., & Diers-Lawson, A. (2023). *Introduction to pandemic communication.* Pandemic Communication. Routledge.

Daily Mail. (2020). *Pandemic and chill: Netflix adds a cool 16M subscribers.* Daily Mail. https://www.dailymail.co.uk/news/article-8242803/Pandemic-chill-Netflix-adds-cool-16M-subscribers.html. Accessed 10 April 2023

Dayal, T. (2022). *How the pandemic boosted business for streaming services.* Jumpstart. https://www.jumpstartmag.com/how-the-pandemic-boosted-business-for-streaming-services/. Accessed 19 April 2023

Dianeosis. (2021). *One year pandemic: How Greeks live (in Greek).* https://www.dianeosis.org/2021/03/enas-xronos-pandimia-pws-zoyn-oi-ellines/. Accessed 19 April 2023.

Economist Impact. (2022). *Breaking news: The economic Impact of Covid-19 on the global news media industry.* Economist Impact Supported by UNESCO. https://impact.economist.com/perspectives/sites/default/files/breaking_news_the_economic_impact_of_covid-19_on_the_global_news_media_industry.pdf. Accessed 3 May 2023

Eurobarometer. (2020). *Standard Eurobarometer 93 – Summer 2020.* https://europa.eu/eurobarometer/surveys/detail/2262. Accessed 3 May 2023.

European Audiovisual Observatory. (2020). *The European Audiovisual Industry in the Time of COVID-19.* https://data.europa.eu/doi/10.2775/726029. Accessed 3 May 2023.

European Commission, and Directorate-General for Communication. (2021). *Media use in the European Union: Report, European Commission.* https://data.europa.eu/doi/10.2775/726029. Accessed 3 May 2023.

Gupta, G., & Singharia, K. (2021). Consumption of OTT media streaming in COVID-19 lockdown: Insights from PLS analysis. *Vision: The Journal of Business Perspective, 25*(1), 36–46. https://doi.org/10.1177/0972262921989118

Iosifidis, P., & Papathanassopoulos, S. (2019). Media, politics and state broadcasting in Greece. *European Journal of Communication, 34*(4), 345–359. https://doi.org/10.1177/0267323119844414

Johnson, C. (2020). *How coronavirus might have changed TV viewing habits for good – New research.* https://www.hud.ac.uk/news/2020/november/how-coronavirus-changed-tv-viewing-c-johnson/. Accessed 10 April 2023.

Leandros, N. (2010). Media concentration and systemic failures in Greece. *International Journal of Communication, 4,* 886–905.

MBO Partners. (2020). *COVID-19 and the rise of the digital nomad.* https://www.mbopartners.com/state-of-independence/2020-digital-nomads-report/. Accessed 19 April 2023.

McKinsey & Company. (2020). *Critical communications infrastructure and COVID-19: An interview with Ericsson's CEO.* August 2020. https://www.mckinsey.com/industries/technology-media-and-telecommunications/our-insights/critical-communications-infrastructure-and-covid-19-an-interview-with-ericssons-ceo. Accessed 20 April 2023.

Nakil, S. (2023). COVID-19, over-the-top services, and the future of pay television: The case of South Korea, applied economics. https://doi.org/10.1080/00036846.2023.2204214

Napchi, O. (2022). The challenge of being lazy. In G. Einav (Ed.), *Transitioning Media in a Post COVID world.* The Economics of Information, Communication, and Entertainment. Springer. https://doi.org/10.1007/978-3-030-95330-0_6

Navsangeet, S. (2022). Usage of ott platforms during covid-19 lockdown: Trends, rationale and implications. *PalArch's Journal of Archaeology of Egypt/Egyptology, 16*(7), 4212–4222.

New York Times. (2020). Disney plus racks up 50 million subscribers in 5 months. *New York Times,* https://www.nytimes.com/2020/04/08/business/disney-plus-50-million-subscribers.html. Accessed 19 April 2023.

Nicolaou, A., & Barker, A. (2020). Coronavirus rips a hole in newspapers' business models. *Financial Times.* https://www.ft.com/content/b6fdec4c-e3e7-43b9-a804-03c435de65bb?sh. June 25.

Nielsen, R. K., & Andı, N. N. S. (2020). *The COVID-19 pandemic's dramatic and unequal Impact on independent news media*. Reuters Institute Report. Accessed 20 May 2023.

Nielsen, R. K., Newman, N., Fletcher, R., & Kalogeropoulos, A. (2020). *Reuters institute digital news report 2020*. Oxford University. https://www.digitalnewsreport.org/survey/2020/. Accessed 19 April 2023

Ntarzanou, A. (2020). *Covid-19 has driven us to sofa (in Greek)*. Avgi. March 23.

Ofcom. (2020). *Lockdown leads to surge in TV screen time and streaming*. https://www.ofcom.org.uk/news-centre/2020/lockdown-leads-to-surge-in-tv-screen-time-and-streaming. August 5.

Papathanassopoulos, S. (2013). Greece: Press subsidies in turmoil. In P. C. Murschetz (Ed.), *State aid for newspapers, media business and innovation; theories, cases, actions* (pp. 237–521). Springer.

Papazoglou, N. (2020). *The Blow up of Data Consumption during the Corona Period (In Greek)*. https://www.insider.gr/tehnologia/136900/ektoxeytikan-ta-dedomena-poy-katanalosan-oi-ellines-tin-periodo-toy-koronoioy. Accessed 20 April 2023.

Seekins, R. (2020). Competition in digital markets. *InterMedia, 48*(2), 15–18.

Skamnakis, A. (2018). Accelerating a freefall? The impact of the post-2008 economic crisis on Greek media and journalism. *Journal of Greek Media & Culture, 4*(1), 9–25. https://doi.org/10.1386/jgmc.4.1.9_1

Statista. (2019). *Advertising expenditure in Greece from 2007 to 2016*. https://www.statista.com/topics/990/global-advertising-market/. Accessed 20 April 2023.

Statista. (2023). *Video Streaming (SVoD) – Greece*. https://www.statista.com/outlook/dmo/digital-media/video-on-demand/video-streaming-svod/greece. Accessed 3 May 2023.

Van Aelst, P., Toth, F., Castro, L., Štětka, V., de Vreese, C., Aalberg, T., Cardenal, A. S., et al. (2021). Does a crisis change news habits? A comparative study of the effects of COVID-19 on news media use in 17 European countries. *Digital Journalism, 9*(9), 1208–1238. https://doi.org/10.1080/21670811.2021.1943481

Zhou, S., & Zheng, X. (2022). Agenda dynamics on social media during COVID-19 pandemic: Interactions between public, media, and government agendas. *Communication Studies, 73*(3), 211–228. https://doi.org/10.1080/10510974.2022.2082504

Chapter 53
The Impact of Macroeconomic Indicators on Exchange Rates of the Visegrad Group

Kitty Klacsánová, Mária Bohdalová, and Nico Haberer

Abstract The chapter aims to examine a wide range of macroeconomic indicators as potential determinants of exchange rates for each currency of the Visegrad Group against US Dollars. In this context, the chapter presents two selected empirical exchange rate models and a new proposed model that explain the significance of differences between two economies and approaches used in exchange rate determination. The chapter employs multiple linear regression models on real-life data to test the relevance of these models in current economic conditions. Additionally, it analyses several macroeconomic factors and their effects on the end-month exchange rates of the Visegrad Group. The research pointed out the most significant economic indicators affecting the volatility of the analysed currencies during the period from 2004 to 2017. 2004 is the year when all the Visegrad Group countries joined the EU. The models of Frenkel–Bilson and Dornbusch–Frenkel yielded similar results for the Hungarian forint, Polish zloty and the euro, suggesting that the month-end exchange rate of these currencies depends on the changes of relative money supply, real GDP and long-term interest rates differentials. Overall, the best models were built for the Czech crown and the euro in terms of the greatest proportion of explained variance and low root mean square of error values. Finally, the research considered our proposed modified empirical exchange rate model. Its results support the relevance of economic complexity, and therefore it plays a key role in predicting exchange rate movements across the Visegrad Group.

Keywords Exchange rates · Currency · Visegrad Group · Macroeconomic indicator

K. Klacsánová · M. Bohdalová (✉) · N. Haberer
Comenius University in Bratislava, Faculty of Management, Bratislava, Slovak Republic
e-mail: maria.bohdalova@fm.uniba.sk

53.1 Introduction

A new perspective on exchange rate models was introduced during the Conference on Flexible Exchange Rates and Stabilization Policy (Frenkel, 1977). The authors of the new models, Frenkel and Bilson and Dornbusch and Frenkel, assumed that the relative price of money, representing the nominal exchange rate, is determined by the motivation of subjects in the economy to possess a particular currency. These models among others extend the modern monetary theory, which states that the nominal interest rate of bonds is determined by the volume of money supply and investor preferences regarding the composition of their portfolios. Additionally, these models are based on international capital flows.

In our research, we considered the following models of exchange rates, described in Clements and Frenkel (1982), Hwang (2003), Wang (2009) and Cihelková et al. (2008):

1. Flexible price monetary model established by Frenkel–Bilson. It is an equilibrium model as it assumes an immediate adjustment of markets to different shocks as well as the continuous validity of the purchasing power parity.
2. Sticky-price model introduced by Dornbusch–Frenkel. This monetary model considers the prices to be inflexible, and it includes inflation expectations.

The chapter aims to point out those macroeconomic indicators that have a major impact on the exchange rates of the Visegrad Group countries. This chapter contributes to the research in this field, by carefully investigating the influence of American economic development on the Visegrad Group's FX rates. The framework of our analysis is provided by two models, Frenkel–Bilson's and Dornbusch–Frenkel's model (Frenkel, 1983; Dornbusch, 1976a,b, 2019). The main contribution of this chapter is our proposed model that considers the level of knowledge expressed by the economic complexity index (ECI) and the level of corruption given by corruption scores (CSs).

The chapter is organized as follows. The next section introduces the used methodology. The Data and Results section employed our data and results. Finally, the Conclusion section concludes our findings.

53.2 Methodology

Our methodology is based on the monetary models of the exchange rates developed by Frenkel (1976), Frenkel (2019), Clements and Frenkel (1982), Hwang (2003) and Dornbusch (1976b). We can find a systematic comparison of the predictive accuracy of these models in Costantini et al. (2014).

This chapter uses the flexible price exchange rate model of Frenkel–Bilson described by the equation

$$\ln e = a_0 + a_1(m - m^*) + a_2(y - y^*) + a_3(r - r^*) + \varepsilon \tag{53.1}$$

and the Dornbusch–Frenkel model expressed by equation

$$\ln e = a_0 + a_1(m - m^*) + a_2(y - y^*) + a_3(r - r^*) + a_4(\pi^e - \pi^{e^*}) + \varepsilon \tag{53.2}$$

where the asterisk ∗ denotes a foreign country.

$\ln e$ represents the logarithm of the exchange rate at time t.
$m - m^*$ is the logarithm of relative money supply.
$y - y^*$ is the logarithm of relative real GDP.
$r - r^*$ represents the differences between two countries in terms of short-term interest rates.
$\pi - \pi^*$ represents the expected long-term inflation differences.

Meese and Rogoff (1983) explain that the coefficients of the Frenkel–Bilson and Dornbusch–Frenkel models acquire the following values: $a_1 = 1$ or $a_1 > 0$. Additionally, the coefficient a_4 in Frenkel–Bilson's model of flexible prices equals 0.

Contemporary economic conditions of the analysed countries are characterized by a certain level of knowledge and corruption; therefore, we decided to take into account economic complexity and corruption as the misuse of public power for private benefit in each analysed country. The index of economic complexity expresses the knowledge base of a country, which can be measured by the products and services that an economy produces. According to Hidalgo and Hausmann (2009), economic complexity is built on the concept that the production process of a particular product has to link specific expertise and consider how knowledge enables to create more complex products, which cannot be produced in simpler economies. The know-how of individuals is limited as the international division of labour is also associated with knowledge. To produce new complex products, employees from different firms should interact more.

We propose a new modified Dornbusch–Frenkel model that considers not only the original variables but also the relative corruption scores and economic complexity indexes:

$$\ln e = a_0 + a_1(m - m^*) + a_2(y - y^*) + a_3(r - r^*) + a_4(\pi^e - \pi^{e^*}) + a_5 \frac{eci}{eci^*}$$
$$+ a_6 \frac{CS}{CS^*} + \varepsilon \tag{53.3}$$

To denote the relative values and the differences of the analysed macroeconomic indicators, we employed the following variables: $M = (m - m^*)$, $Y = (y - y^*)$, $R = (r - r^*)$, $P = (\pi^e - \pi^{e^*})$, $relative_{eci} = \frac{eci}{eci^*}$, and $relative_{CS} = \frac{CS}{CS^*}$.

53.2.1 Flexible Price Monetary Model for Exchange Rates

From the monetary point of view, changes in the volume of money supply in an economy play an important role in determining exchange rates; hence the relative supply of money affects exchange rates. Currency is more valuable if there is less amount of it on the market and vice versa. According to Cheung (1996) and Pugel (2019), withdrawing a certain amount of currency from circulation tends to make the conditions for borrowing stricter, reduces the volume of money available for consumption purposes and lowers aggregate demand, gross domestic product and the prices in a country. However, the relative purchasing power parity theory suggests that a drop in the money supply by a certain percentage can strengthen that country's currency by the same percentage.

The flexible price monetary model Wang (2009) assumes that each market immediately adjusts to monetary influences, and the purchasing power parity holds continuously. On the contrary, the Dornbusch–Frenkel model does not consider the previous facts. It states that only the money and the foreign exchange rate markets are those with immediate adjustments. The adjustment is gradual in the market of goods and services, which is different from the flexible price monetary model.

The model of Frenkel–Bilson (Frenkel, 1983) explains that all prices, including those of goods and services, wages and exchange rates, are perfectly flexible in the short and the long run. This model also incorporates the effects of inflation expectation and the condition of the uncovered interest rate parity. The riskiness of domestic and foreign assets is the same if their returns are well balanced; hence, domestic and foreign assets are perfect substitutes. According to the flexible price monetary model, the actual exchange rate depends on the values of relative money supply, relative real GDP and interest rates.

Changes in the above explanatory variables have the following impacts on exchange rates:

1. The coefficient of relative money supply always equals 1, due to the neutrality of money. After an increase in the money supply, prices in the economy should also rise by the same percentage. As Civcir et al. stated in paper Civcir et al. (2003), to restore the equilibrium it would mean a depreciation of the domestic currency by the same percentage, considering that the purchasing power parity holds. On the contrary, the increase in the foreign money supply leads to an appreciation of the domestic currency.
2. An increase in the values of relative real GDP in the domestic economy influences its exchange rate, decreases the domestic prices of goods and services and strengthens the domestic currency.
3. Lastly, when domestic interest rates rise, the currency of that country weakens, and therefore $a_3 > 0$. The reason behind this is the Fisher effect (Cihelková et al., 2008).

53.2.2 Sticky-Price Model

The model examining the reasons why exchange rates exceed their long-run equilibrium compiled by Rudiger Dornbusch in (1976a; 1976b). The extremely high volatility of real exchange rates during the 1970s led to the development of this model, to determine the exchange rates more precisely. As Bitzenis and Marangos (2007) assumed, exchange rates approach their long-run equilibrium, and for a short time, they even tend to exceed this equilibrium, which is then gradually eliminated over time. Changes in interest rates, expectations and wealth usually distort the equilibrium which encourages investors to reallocate their financial assets to achieve a new equilibrium. In other words, also interpreted by Salvatore (2019), in the presence of distortion factors exchange rates continuously fluctuate to achieve their long-run equilibrium, which never occurs.

International trade of goods and services plays an important role in the process of exchange rate determination, as well as the speed of financial assets' adjustments. Their effects on exchange rates are different. An unexpected increase in the money supply of a country, combined with a decrease in its interest rates (the model assumes that the foreign interest rates remain unchanged), leads to a rapid increase in the demand for the foreign currency presented in Dornbusch (1976a) and Dornbusch (1976b). Then, investors will increase the number of foreign bonds in their portfolios, which will cause an appreciation of the foreign currency. On the other hand, as Pugel discusses in his book Pugel (2019), this leads to an immediate depreciation of the domestic currency, which will be greater than minor changes in exchange rates, happening gradually due to international trade. Certainly, the opposite situation would arise if the money supply increased and interest rates dropped in the foreign economy. Whilst in the long run, the effect of changes in the exchange rate is reflected in international trade, in the short term we can expect an immediate reaction only from the financial sector.

A decrease in money supply and a consequent increase in domestic interest rates lead to capital inflows and an appreciation of both the nominal and real domestic exchange rates. Investors based in a foreign country may suffer losses from foreign exchange transactions when their returns on investments convert back into their domestic currency. Following the argument of Bitzenis and Marangos (2007), a short-run equilibrium is reached if the expected rate of gradual depreciation is equal to the differences in interest rates between the domestic and the foreign country. In the medium run, however, domestic prices begin to shrink as a response to the decrease in the money supply. Consequently, domestic interest rates also fall, and the exchange rate then weakens slowly. Regarding the previous fact, currencies with relatively high interest rates tend to weaken in the long run.

53.3 Data and Results

In this chapter, we have analysed the impact of the economic development in the USA on the Visegrad Group countries after they became member states of the

Table 53.1 Description of models variables (source: own processing)

Variable	Description	Frequency	Unit	Source
e	End-month spot exchange rate ($USD/CZK, USD/HUF, USD/PLN, USD/EUR$)	Monthly	Value	BIS, Bank of England
m	Monetary base $M1$	Monthly	Index base 2015 = 100	OECD, NBS
r	Long-term interest rate of government bonds a 10-year maturity	Monthly	Percentage	OECD
y	Real GDP growth	Yearly	Percentage	OECD
CS	Corruption score (values between 0 and 100. Countries with lower values are more corrupt)	Yearly	Value	Transparency international
ECI	Economic complexity index	Yearly	Value	OECD

European Union in the year 2004. The Slovak Republic is one of the member states of the EU, which introduced the euro; therefore, we analysed its economy's contribution to the volatility of USD/EUR. We established regression models based on the multivariate stepwise OLS method.

We have used several influence factors, which are described in more detail along with their frequencies and sources in Table 53.1. We have analysed the data for the monetary base $M1$, interest rate and inflation every month. However, the other indicators were available only yearly or quarterly; therefore, we considered the same values in each month of a particular year. In each model, we could employ the long-term interest rates of 10-year maturity bonds.

Initially, the analyses presented in this chapter verified the empirical exchange rate models of Frenkel–Bilson and Dornbusch–Frenkel. Additionally, in the last part, the chapter gives suggestions on macroeconomic factors not considered in the previous theoretical exchange rate models, which may influence the Visegrad Group's currencies (see Sect. 53.3.2)

53.3.1 The Relevance of Monetary Exchange Rate Models Between 2004 and 2017

Results of the Frenkel–Bilson Model

The results (see Tables 53.2 and 53.3) for the flexible price model (53.1) between 2004 and 2017 support the assumptions on the dependence of exchange rates on M, Y, and R in the case of each country except in the Czech Republic. Despite the significance of the model in this country, according to our findings, the relative real GDP did not play an important role in the end-month values of the Czech

Table 53.2 Coefficients of the original exchange rate models (source: own processing)

Original model		Frenkel–Bilson					Dornbusch–Frenkel				
		A	Sig.	Tol	VIF	%change	A	Sig.	Tol	VIF	%change
USD/CZK	a_0	3.652	0	–	–	–	3.555	0	–	–	–
	M	−0.892	0	0.139	7.208	−0.884	−0.948	0	0.138	7.255	−0.939
	Y	0.670	0.058	0.143	6.970	0.669	0.567	0.087	0.143	6.999	0.565
	R	−0.059	0	0.672	1.488	−5.721	−0.074	0	0.552	1.813	−7.152
	P	–	–	–	–	–	0.028	0	0.666	1.502	2.816
USD/HUF	a_0	13.711	0	–	–	–	13.485	0	–	–	–
	M	−0.877	0	0.292	3.428	−0.869	−0.848	0	0.193	5.181	−0.840
	Y	6.456	0	0.242	4.137	6.635	6.279	0	0.157	6.384	6.447
	R	−0.012	0.044	0.634	1.577	−1.227	−0.012	0.076	0.565	1.769	−1.146
	P	–	–	–	–	–	−0.002	0.701	0.479	2.087	−0.207
USD/PLN	a_0	2.762	0	–	–	–	2.822	0	–	–	–
	M	−0.750	0	0.458	2.185	−0.743	−0.772	0	0.439	2.277	−0.765
	Y	1.153	0	0.460	2.174	1.154	1.177	0	0.450	2.223	1.178
	R	−0.026	0	0.991	1.009	−2.545	−0.042	0	0.405	2.469	−4.099
	P	–	–	–	–	–	0.012	0.065	0.394	2.538	1.249
USD/EUR	a_0	0.196	0	–	–	–	0.232	0	–	–	–
	M	−0.319	0	0.719	1.391	−0.317	−0.305	0	0.611	1.637	−0.303
	Y	0.380	0	0.762	1.313	0.379	0.414	0	0.608	1.644	0.413
	R	−0.029	0	0.914	1.095	−2.817	−0.033	0	0.504	1.984	−3.279
	P	–	–	–	–	–	0.005	0.090	0.393	2.546	0.550

Table 53.3 Summary statistics of the models (source: own processing)

		Frenkel–Bilson				Dornbusch-Franke			
		R^2	Adj. R^2	RMSE	Sig.	R^2	Adj. R^2	RMSE	Sig.
Original model	USD/CZK	0.646	0.639	0.083	0	0.69	0.682	0.078	0
	USD/HUF	0.505	0.496	0.114	0	0.506	0.494	0.114	0
	USD/PLN	0.565	0.557	0.096	0	0.574	0.563	0.095	0
	USD/EUR	0.733	0.728	0.050	0	0.737	0.731	0.049	0
Reduced model	USD/CZK	0.638	0.634	0.083	0	0.684	0.679	0.078	0
	USD/HUF	0.505	0.496	0.114	0	0.505	0.496	0.114	0
	USD/PLN	0.565	0.557	0.096	0	0.565	0.557	0.096	0
	USD/EUR	0.733	0.728	0.050	0	0.733	0.728	0.050	0

crown against US Dollars through this period. Frenkel–Bilson's model proved itself to be the most adequate for the Slovak Republic since it explained the greatest proportion of the USD/EUR variability (73.3%). The exchange rates USD/HUF, USD/PLN and USD/EUR significantly depend on the relative values of the monetary base $M1$, real GDP and interest rates. Simultaneously, based on the results only a small proportion of the forint's and zloty's variability could be explained by Frenkel–Bilson's exchange rate model, compared to that of the euro. Concerning this, it is advisable to establish a different model or include additional variables to get a better view of the USD/HUF and USD/PLN.

Furthermore, the assumptions on the model's coefficients, $a_1 = 1$, $a_2 < 0$ and $a_3 > 0$, were not confirmed in our analysis owing to the following facts:

1. According to the regression analyses, the coefficient $a_1 \neq 1$, which is against the identical movement of exchange rates and money supply. The increase of $M = (m - m^*)$ appreciates the Visegrad Group's exchange rates against US Dollars. This appreciation represents, however, only a small value. Regarding the coefficients a_1, the monetary base accounts for the lowest changes across the Visegrad Group from 2004 to 2017.
2. The increase of the relative real GDP tends for exchange rates to depreciate against US Dollars. With the increasing wealth of a domestic economy, the likewise increasing amount of investment flowing out of that country can lead to a higher money supply of the domestic currency.
3. An increase in interest rate differences results in a decrease in the values of exchange rates, appreciating the domestic currencies of the Visegrad Group. Favourable conditions on the Visegrad Group's bond market could attract investors holding US Dollars. After exchanging their dollars for one of the Visegrad Group's currencies, the dollar depreciates against these currencies.

The model established for Hungary shows that an increase in its relative real GDP causes the USD/HUF exchange rate begin to rise with the highest amount from all the four countries. Additionally, if relative real GDP increases by 1%, it is followed by an increase of USD/HUF by $100(1.01^{a_2} - 1) = 6.63\%$ on average, indicating that the Hungarian forint depreciates, and the US dollar appreciates. Regarding the findings for the Slovak Republic, greater values of relative real GDP are also linked to a depreciation of the euro against US dollars. The economic development of the Slovak Republic, therefore, contributes to the previously described depreciation with a percentage of 0.37% after a 1% increase of its relative real GDP.

The findings reveal that an increase in the differences of the interest rates by one-unit results in the smallest decrease, $100(e^{a_3} - 1) = -1.192\%$, of the mean value of USD/HUF within the four domestic currencies of the Visegrad Group. On the contrary, the Czech crown would appreciate the most, by -5.72%, if the interest rate differences of its bonds with 10-year maturities compared to the ones issued in the USA increased by 1%. For this reason, it is expectable for the Czech Republic to receive greater attractiveness from subjects holding US dollars. They would invest more in Czech bonds after converting their dollars into Czech crowns. In this context, the euro is placed second.

Results of the Dornbusch–Frenkel Model

Model 53.2 including the variables M, Y, R and P is significant for each country (see Tables 53.2 and 53.3). The p-values are smaller than the significance level of 0.05. After adding the explanatory variable P to form the Dornbusch–Frenkel model, we find similar results compared to those of the flexible price model. This was supported by the explained variance and the extent to which relative money supply and relative real GDP influence the Visegrad Group's exchange rate movements.

Despite the statistical significance of Dornbusch–Frenkel's models, not every explanatory variable has an impact on the selected exchange rates. The results pointed out that in the analysed period the assumption on inflation does not hold in the case of Hungary, Poland and Slovakia since the inflation P is not representative for the following exchange rates: USD/HUF, USD/PLN and USD/EUR. The expected change in one unit of inflation differences has a similar effect on exchange rates; therefore, with increasing inflation differences the exchange rate USD/CZK increases approximately by 2.81%. Intensifying inflation in the Czech Republic in contrast to the USA weakens the Czech crown on average by the previous 2.81%.

At the same time, as also stated in the previous regression analysis, the relative real GDP is not a momentous indicator to determine the USD/CZK exchange rate regarding Dornbusch–Frenkel's model. Furthermore, after adding the differences in the consumer price indexes between the two countries into the model, the significance increased to 0.076. This result indicates that the Dornbusch–Frenkel model did not prove the importance of interest rate R for the Hungarian forint.

The exchange rate model for Slovakia reflects the highest proportion of the variance of the USD/EUR exchange rate since $R^2 = 0.737$ and the adjusted $R^2 = 0.731$. The other three models correspond roughly to 50–68% of the variance of the USD/CZK, USD/HUF and USD/PLN.

After a one-unit growth in interest rate differences, when the values of the other explanatory variables are held constant, the Polish zloty and the euro strengthen on average by more than 3%, whilst the Czech crown appreciates by 7%. The different economic development of Poland, Slovakia and the Czech Republic compared to the United States in terms of interest rates has a significant power to deviate CZK, PLN and EUR against USD. There are two options for these three currencies to appreciate, either by increasing long-term interest rates in the domestic economy or by decreasing returns on US bonds along with steady interest rates in the Visegrad Group (domestic economies in our case). Higher interest rates attract investors who need to exchange their dollars for CZK, PLN or EUR. In the end, USD weakens against these currencies. The previous assumption is based on an initial state, which following Dornbusch is a steady state of the economy when domestic and foreign interest rates are equal.

Comparison of the Empirical Models

In each regression analysis, we find controversial results when it comes to the monetary base $M1$. An increase in its relative values ($M1/M^*$) causes that the Visegrad Group's domestic currencies appreciate through all analyses. The findings, therefore, point out that in the period from 2004 to 2017 a higher relative monetary base did not necessarily lead to a depreciation of domestic currencies in the Visegrad Group. However, it is important to state that the monetary base $M1$ involves only banknotes, coins and deposits with an immediate expiration. We would achieve different results, if we looked at the other two monetary aggregates, $M2$ and $M3$, which consider additional components to those of $M1$.

In the models built for Hungary and the Czech Republic, we can notice moderate multicollinearity in the case of the relative monetary base and relative real GDP. The values of the *VIF* statistic are between 5 and 7, and the unexplained variabilities by other explanatory variables obtain high values.

Our next step was to test the previous two models (Frenkel–Bilson and Dornbusch–Frenkel) including only significant explanatory variables (see Tables 53.3 and 53.4). We could build a better reduced model for the Czech crown from that of the flexible price model with almost the same amount of explained variability, as in the full model. Regarding the results from the stepwise regression analysis, we can affirm that the Czech currency is influenced the most by the changes in the relative monetary base, interest rate differences and inflation. Compared to the other three reduced models, this model keeps the largest proportion of variability, $R^2 = 68.4\%$.

The full models of Frenkel–Bilson showed to be the most representative for USD/EUR since each variable is significant in explaining the volatility of the previously mentioned exchange rate with low multicollinearities. For both the Hungarian and the Polish currencies, we could explain no more than 57% of the variability in the data with the two models for exchange rate determination.

It is important to evaluate the findings in the Visegrad Group from a current exchange rate regime perspective. Every country monitors its macroeconomic development in a different way assigning more weight to particular indicators.

Table 53.4 Coefficients of the reduced exchange rate models (source: own processing)

Reduced model		Frenkel–Bilson					Dornbusch–Frenkel				
		A	Sig.	Tol.	VIF	%change	A	Sig.	Tol.	VIF	%change
USD/CZK	a_0	3.039	0	–	–	–	3.036	0	–	–	–
	M	−0.624	0	0.962	1.039	−0.619	−0.723	0	0.846	1.182	−0.717
	Y	–	–	–	–	–	–	–	–	–	–
	R	−0.067	0	0.962	1.039	−6.435	−0.081	0	0.760	1.315	−7.778
	P	–	–	–	–	–	0.028	0	0.669	1.496	2.883
USD/HUF	a_0	13.711	0	–	–	–	13.711	0	–	–	–
	M	−0.877	0	0.292	3.428	−0.869	−0.877	0	0.292	3.428	−0.869
	Y	6.456	0	0.242	4.137	6.635	6.456	0	0.242	4.137	6.635
	R	−0.012	0.044	0.634	1.577	−1.227	−0.012	0.044	0.634	1.577	−1.227
	P	–	–	–	–	–	–	–	–	–	–
USD/PLN	a_0	2.762	0	–	–	–	2.762	0	–	–	–
	M	−0.750	0	0.458	2.185	−0.743	−0.750	0	0.458	2.185	−0.743
	Y	1.153	0	0.460	2.174	1.154	1.153	0	0.460	2.174	1.154
	R	−0.026	0	0.991	1.009	−2.545	−0.026	0	0.991	1.009	−2.545
	P	–	–	–	–	–	–	–	–	–	–
USD/EUR	a_0	0.196	0	–	–	–	0.196	0	–	–	–
	M	−0.319	0	0.719	1.391	−0.317	−0.319	0	0.719	1.391	−0.317
	Y	0.380	0	0.762	1.313	0.379	0.380	0	0.762	1.313	0.379
	R	−0.029	0	0.914	1.095	−2.817	−0.029	0	0.914	1.095	−2.817
	P	–	–	–	–	–	–	–	–	–	–

Simultaneously, it can intervene and guide the future development of specific indicators through monetary policy decisions. According to the IMF's de facto categorization of exchange rate regimes, after certain economic outcomes, it is possible to expect monetary policy decisions, especially those central banks that have fixed exchange rates. We can see that the biggest changes in exchange rates in terms of the Czech crown and Hungarian forint occur when long-term interest rates and relative real GDP fluctuate. In case of steep increases or decreases, we can expect interventions from the Czech central bank, since it followed through the analysed period a particular form of a fixed exchange rate regime (stabilized arrangements). Nowadays Hungary and the Czech Republic practice a managed floating exchange rate regime; hence, in case of need, they may apply interventions.

53.3.2 New Modified Dornbusch–Frenkel Model

In this part, we did alterations to the previous exchange rate models. The new model, Model 53.3, consists of the four original variables, M, Y, R and P, and two additional ones, relative economic complexity and corruption scores of the Visegrad Group and the USA.

The assumption on identical exchange rate movements with the monetary base is also not supported by the new model, meaning that in the analysed period a rise in the relative money supply did not result in depreciation of the domestic currencies in the Visegrad Group. Table 53.5 shows the estimated coefficients of our proposed Dornbusch–Frenkel model. Table 53.6 summarizes the most representative models with solely significant macroeconomic indicators. In the case of the USD/CZK, this model proved again that relative real GDP does not influence the oscillation of the Czech crown. On the contrary, inflation differences between Hungary, Poland, Slovakia and the USA do not have a significant impact on the exchange rates of the Hungarian forint, Polish zloty and euro against US dollars.

The model explained a greater proportion of variability in the data, after including the relative ECI index and corruption scores CS than the original empirical exchange rate models. We received better results for the euro as well. However, the explained variability increased only by 1% for the euro compared to 4% for the Czech crown.

Within the stepwise regression for the exchange rate USD/CZK, the relative ECI index was the first one to enter the model explaining 39.1% of the Czech exchange rate. It accounts for more than 50% of the overall explained variability in the USD/CZK. For the other countries, it is characteristic that the relative economic complexity contributes to the overall explained variability with a smaller percentage, between 2 and 8%. This economic indicator well describes the changes in exchange rates of the Visegrad Group through the period from 2004 to 2017. A one-unit increase in the relative values of the economic complexity of a country,

Table 53.5 Coefficients of the new modified Dornbusch–Frenkel model (source: own processing)

		New Dornbusch–Frenkel model				
		A	Sig.	Tol	VIF	%change
USD/CZK	a_0	3.489	0	–	–	–
	M	−0.514	0	0.875	1.143	−0.510
	Y	–	–	–	–	–
	R	−0.053	0	0.848	1.179	−5.173
	P	–	–	–	–	–
	$relative_{eci}$	−0.449	0	0.775	1.290	−36.159
	$relative_{CS}$	–	–	–	–	–
USD/HUF	a_0	14.904	0	–	–	–
	M	−0.982	0	0.261	3.834	−0.972
	Y	7.298	0	0.280	3.577	7.532
	R	–	–	–	–	–
	P	–	–	–	–	–
	$relative_{eci}$	−0.178	0.011	0.875	1.143	−16.341
	$relative_{CS}$	–	–	–	–	–
$USD/PLN1$	a_0	3.278	0	–	–	–
	M	−0.589	0	0.301	3.321	−0.585
	Y	1.177	0	0.458	2.182	1.178
	R	–	–	–	–	–
	P	–	–	–	–	–
	$relative_{eci}$	−0.839	0	0.436	2.292	−56.769
	$relative_{CS}$	–	–	–	–	–
$USD/PLN2$	a_0	7.118	0	–	–	–
	M	−0.654	0	0.294	3.397	−0.648
	Y	3.032	0	0.032	31.279	3.063
	R	–	–	–	–	–
	P	–	–	–	–	–
	$relative_{eci}$	−1.111	0	0.415	2.410	−67.062
	$relative_{CS}$	−1.622	0	0.038	26.108	−80.256
USD/EUR	a_0	0.431	0	–	–	–
	M	−0.304	0	0.672	1.488	−0.302
	Y	0.442	0	0.582	1.717	0.441
	R	−0.022	0	0.597	1.675	−2.197
	P	–	–	–	–	–
	$relative_{eci}$	−0.208	0.005	0.427	2.341	−18.820
	$relative_{CS}$	–	–	–	–	–

those that form the Visegrad Group, would appreciate the Visegrad Group's domestic currencies from 16 to 56%.

The index of economic complexity ECI considers the diversity of a country's products that it exports and the ubiquity of those products indicating in how

Table 53.6 Summary statistics of the new modified Dornbusch–Frenkel model (source: own processing)

	New Dornbusch–Frenkel model			
	R^2	Adj. R^2	RMSE	Sig.
USD/CZK	0.717	0.712	0.074	0
USD/HUF	0.512	0.503	0.113	0
$USD/PLN1$	0.576	0.568	0.095	0
$USD/PLN2$	0.666	0.658	0.084	0
USD/EUR	0.746	0.739	0.048	0

many countries it is possible to produce an identical product. Countries with more knowledge are generally more successful in producing sophisticated products and achieving higher diversification. Products that cannot be produced through a simple production process will enjoy less ubiquity; therefore, it is expected for countries with higher economic complexity to be better diversified and produce fewer products with wide ubiquity.

The values of the coefficients reveal that, when economic complexity in one of the Visegrad Groups' countries increases compared to that of the USA, the domestic currencies of the Visegrad Group strengthen their position against the US dollar. Simultaneously, it can also happen when the economic complexity in the USA declines and causes the relative economic complexity to rise. According to the previous contemplation, higher economic complexity in the Visegrad Group, which is linked to the knowledge base that subjects in the economy utilize through a production process, creates an incentive for US-based firms to set up subsidiaries or otherwise invest in these countries. Generally, the USA as an important economy wants to retain its position among the other countries of the world, including the Visegrad Group. One possible way to achieve this goal is for the USA to create more intensive cooperation with the Visegrad Group. Eventually, both parties can profit from this partnership by mutually strengthening each other's economic complexity. Nowadays, the Slovak Republic, Czech Republic, Poland and Hungary rank among the first 25 countries out of 129 evaluated ones. As of 2015, the USA is in a higher position in this ranking compared to the ranking of the Visegrad Group countries.

In exchange rate determination, corruption scores do not represent an important measure for the Czech crown, Hungarian forint and the euro. Corruption is only significant for the USD/PLN exchange rate. However, the model does not support the multicollinearity criteria of the explanatory variables. If we abstract from this circumstance, it is obvious from the values of the coefficients that favourable social conditions resulting in less corruption can be linked to an appreciation of the Polish currency. The reason behind higher corruption scores (a higher corruption score means better evaluation) followed by the Polish currency's appreciation could be the strengthening confidence and a change in investors' preferences who hold US dollars, to invest them in Poland.

53.4 Conclusion

The research aimed to point out the factors that may influence the development of exchange rates across the Visegrad Group. The analyses are based on monthly data from 2004 to 2017.

Through regression analyses, we find significant macroeconomic indicators of the Visegrad Group as well as the economy of the USA with an essential role in exchange rate determination. For the Hungarian, Polish and Slovakian currencies, the model of Frenkel–Bilson was representative because each explanatory variable was significant along with low values of multicollinearity. These three currencies depend substantially on the particular country's relative money supply, real GDP and interest rate differences. The coefficients of the model indicate that the relative real GDP has the greatest intensity. It is responsible on average for 6.63% of the depreciation of the Hungarian forint.

The assumptions of Dornbusch–Frenkel did not hold in the analysed period for the forint, zloty and euro. Overall, the analysis of the Dornbusch–Frenkel model showed that only the original assumptions of Frenkel–Bilson were met between 2004 and 2017.

The research pointed out the best model, which is the new modified Dornbusch–Frenkel model containing economic complexity and corruption in terms of explained variability and forecasting, especially of the Czech crown and the euro. The R^2 and adj. R^2 acquired the highest values besides the lowest $RMSE$ statistic. This model was established from significant variables of the theoretical models. The findings suggest that the end-month exchange rates of the four countries do not depend significantly on the degree of corruption. On the other hand, it is important to dedicate attention to economic complexity as this economic indicator influenced all four exchange rates of the Visegrad Group against US dollars. In this context, our main finding was the momentous impact of increasing relative economic complexity on currency appreciation.

Another important finding in this chapter is that the Czech crown is the only currency whose US dollar exchange rate from 2004 to 2017 was not influenced by the development of its relative real GDP. The relative money supply, interest rate and inflation differences of the Czech Republic represent the most dominant indicators affecting the USD/CZK exchange rate. A one-unit or a one-percentage change in their values caused a considerable shift of the Czech crown against US dollars. More precisely, the most significant impact on its value has a rise in the importance of interest rate differences, which are on average responsible for a 7.78% appreciation of the Czech crown. This represents the biggest impact of interest rate differences among the four countries.

Overall, the presented analyses can serve as a base for investment decisions. They offer an overview of different factors that might influence the Visegrad Group's exchange rate movements against US dollars with more or less significance. Within international trade, they can signal the need for currency risk hedging or evaluating international partnerships by considering the development of the analysed macroeconomic indicators.

Acknowledgments The first two authors kindly announce the support of the KEGA 029UKF-4/2022

References

Bitzenis, A., & Marangos, J. (2007). The monetary model of exchange rate determination: The case of Greece (1974–1994). *International Journal of Monetary Economics and Finance, 1*(1), 57–88.

Cheung, Y. W. (1996). International economics: Peter H. Lindert and Thomas A. Pugel. *The North American Journal of Economics and Finance, 7*(2), 231–232. https://ideas.repec.org/a/eee/ecofin/v7y1996i2p231-232.html

Cihelková, E., Frait, J., Varadzin, F., Mach, M., Žamberský, P. (2008). *Mezinárodní ekonomie II.* Nakladatelství CH Beck

Civcir, I., et al. (2003). The monetary model of the exchange rate under high inflation—the case of the Turkish Lira/US dollar. *Czech Journal of Economics and Finance, 53*(3–4), 113–129.

Clements, K., & Frenkel, J. (1982). *Exchange rates in the 1920's: A monetary approach.* National Bureau of Economic Research.

Costantini, M., Cuaresma, J. C., & Hlouskova, J. (2014). Can macroeconomists get rich forecasting exchange rates? *Department of Economics Working Paper Series.*

Dornbusch, R. (1976a). Capital mobility, flexible exchange rates and macroeconomic equilibrium. In *Recent issues in international monetary economics* (Vol. 2). North-Holland Amsterdam.

Dornbusch, R. (1976b). Expectations and exchange rate dynamics. *Journal of Political Economy, 84*(6), 1161–1176. http://www.jstor.org/stable/1831272

Dornbusch, R. (2019). The theory of flexible exchange rate regimes and macroeconomic policy. In *Flexible exchange rates and stabilization policy* (pp. 123–143). Routledge.

Frenkel, J. (1977). *A monetary approach to the exchange rate: Doctrinal aspects and empirical evidence* (pp. 68–92). Palgrave Macmillan.

Frenkel, J. A. (1976). A monetary approach to the exchange rate: Doctrinal aspects and empirical evidence. *The Scandinavian Journal of Economics, 78*(2), 200–224. http://www.jstor.org/stable/3439924

Frenkel, J. A. (1983). *An Introduction to Exchange Rates and International Macroeconomics* (pp. 1–18). University of Chicago Press. http://www.nber.org/chapters/c11375

Frenkel, J. A. (2019). A monetary approach to the exchange rate: doctrinal aspects and empirical evidence. In *Flexible exchange rates and stabilization policy* (pp. 68–92). Routledge.

Hidalgo, C. A., & Hausmann, R. (2009). The building blocks of economic complexity. *Proceedings of the National Academy of Sciences, 106*(26), 10570–10575.

Hwang, J. K. (2003). The Dornbusch-Frankel exchange rate model and cointegration: Evidence from the Yen-Dollar. *Journal of International Business and Economics.* Available at SSRN: https://ssrn.com/abstract=1713575

Meese, R. A., & Rogoff, K. (1983). Empirical exchange rate models of the seventies: Do they fit out of sample? *Journal of International Economics, 14*(1), 3–24. https://doi.org/10.1016/0022-1996(83)90017-X. https://www.sciencedirect.com/science/article/pii/002219968390017X

Pugel, T. A. (2019). *International economics.* McGraw Hill.

Salvatore, D. (2019). *International economics.* Wiley.

Wang, P. (2009). *The flexible price monetary model* (pp. 1–17). Springer.

Chapter 54
Working Capital Management Policy and Its Financing Across Selected Enterprises According to Size in the Czech Republic

Markéta Skupieňová

Abstract The aim of this chapter is to evaluate whether the policy of working capital management and its financing affects the profitability of enterprises divided by size in the Czech Republic and thus to find out the differences in the management of working capital across the size of enterprises. In order to fulfill the goal of this article, Granger causality and the generalized method of moments, the so-called GMM, will be used. The data sample will include data for the period 2012–2021. The analysis will include companies operating in the Czech Republic, which are divided according to size into medium-sized companies, large companies, and very large companies. The result will be to find out whether and how the management of working capital and its financing affects the profitability of enterprises according to size and whether there are differences in this connection across enterprises according to size in the Czech Republic. It was found that if medium-sized enterprises want to achieve higher profitability, they should apply a more aggressive working capital management policy and a more aggressive working capital financing policy. On the contrary, in order to increase profitability, large enterprises and very large enterprises should apply a more aggressive working capital management policy, but on the contrary, a more conservative working capital financing policy compared to medium-sized enterprises.

Keywords GMM · Granger causality · Profitability · Sales · Working capital · Working capital management policy

---

M. Skupieňová (✉)
Silesian University in Opava, School of Business Administration in Karviná, Karvina, Czech Republic
e-mail: seligova@opf.slu.cz

© The Author(s), under exclusive license to Springer Nature Switzerland AG 2024
N. Tsounis, A. Vlachvei (eds.), *Applied Economic Research and Trends*, Springer Proceedings in Business and Economics,
https://doi.org/10.1007/978-3-031-49105-4_54

54.1 Introduction

The basis of the entire Czech Republic is nonfinancial enterprises or the business sector as such. Following the financial and business characteristics, it is necessary to distinguish what type of business it is. Whether these are enterprises that can be distinguished by size (small enterprises, medium-sized enterprises, large enterprises, very large enterprises), by sector (e.g., enterprises in the manufacturing industry, the construction or service sector), by ownership (e.g., private, state, cooperative, church, foundation), according to focus and method of management (profit and nonprofit enterprises) and the like. Small- and medium-sized enterprises are an integral part of the national economy, where they are an important source of employment. In connection with large enterprises, many studies have pointed to the significant interdependence of medium and large enterprises, where the deterioration of the competitiveness of large enterprises and their possible investments will be reflected in the economic situation of medium-sized enterprises, which act as suppliers of individual goods and services. No less important is the division of enterprises by sector. The manufacturing industry participates to the highest extent in the production of capital goods and significantly influences the level of the entire economy of a given economy. It is an important segment of the economy, which is an important carrier of the development of technology, knowledge, and job opportunities. Among the key sectors of the Czech Republic is also construction, which is considered one of the important indicators of economic development. The service sector also represents a significant part of the national economy of modern economies, where service providers create approximately 60% of the gross domestic product in developed countries; moreover, this share is still growing.

The goal of each of the aforementioned businesses is mainly to generate profit. Companies can achieve higher profitability, for example, by reducing costs on the one hand or increasing revenues on the other, or their combination within a longer period of time. In order for companies to ensure their business activities, they must have a certain amount of working capital available, for which a suitable source of financing needs to be found. An important role in corporate management is played by the search for an optimal combination of own and external funding sources, without which the company would not be able to carry out its business activities. Companies are thus trying to find the optimal level of their indebtedness. Too high a level of indebtedness can reduce the profitability of the given business and lead it to bankruptcy. However, this may not always be the case and may create a financial leverage effect, where foreign capital is used in order to increase the company's profit. Likewise, working capital management is a very important area of corporate finance, especially due to its impact on liquidity, profitability, and business growth. It is therefore clear that both the working capital management policy and the sources of working capital financing can have a significant impact on the liquidity, profitability, and overall development or growth of the business. Effective management of working capital and its financing can ensure the success of a business, while their inefficient management can lead to its bankruptcy. Working capital management enables a business to obtain sufficient liquidity needed to pay payables.

Each type of business mentioned above will be characterized by a different level of working capital management and its impact on corporate profitability. On the basis of the abovementioned facts, it can be concluded that both the development of enterprises by sector and the development of enterprises by size are key for the Czech Republic. All this became the basis for determining the goal of this article.

Based on the abovementioned facts, the aim of this article is to evaluate whether the policy of working capital management and its financing affects the profitability of enterprises divided by size in the Czech Republic and thus to find out the differences in working capital management across the size of enterprises. The analysis will include companies operating in the Czech Republic, which are divided according to size into medium-sized companies, large companies, and very large companies. The result will be to find out whether and how the management of working capital and its financing affects the profitability of enterprises according to size and whether there are differences in this connection across enterprises according to size in the Czech Republic.

In order to fulfill the research goal, Granger causality and the generalized method of moments, the so-called GMM, will be used. The data sample will include data on an annual basis for the period 2012–2021, which will be drawn from the Orbis database.

The article is divided into several capitols, which are logically connected to each other. The first part of the chapter is devoted to the introduction, then the next part is focused on the literature review, which will help to clarify the issues of the investigated problem. The next part of the article is focused on data and methodology, where the analyzed data will be described in more detail, including the methods used to fulfill the research objective. The penultimate part of the article contains results and discussion, where the results found are analyzed in more detail in connection with the operation of the company. The last part is devoted to the conclusion, where the most important information resulting from this article is summarized.

54.2 Literature Review

There are many studies that have investigated the relationship between working capital (or working capital management policy) and corporate profitability. However, most of the studies were focused on countries outside of Europe. Only a few studies focused on European countries. For this reason, this article is focused on the analysis of the relationship between working capital and the profitability of enterprises in the territory of the Czech Republic. Despite these facts, the article will present at least a partial overview of the relevant literature.

Evci and Şak (2018) examined the relationship between working capital components and firm's profitability by using the data of the firms listed on the Borsa Istanbul Industry Index in Turkey. Annual data from 41 firms were used for the period 2005–2016 in the study. The working capital components and firm's profitability trade-off were examined via the fixed-effects panel regression model. The dependent variable is defined as the return on assets; independent variables are cash conversion cycle, inventory conversion period, and payables deferral period. Findings show the existence of trade-off working capital management profitability. A negative relationship exists between return on assets and payables deferral period, cash conversion cycle, the ratio of short-term financial debts to short-term debts, and the ratio of fixed assets to total assets, while return on assets is positively related to inventory conversion period and sales growth.

Korent and Orsag (2018) believe that working capital management impacts profitability and risk of a company is generally accepted and in the last 10–15 years has acquired a substantial interest. They evaluated the working capital management impact on the profitability of Croatian software companies. This impact was examined using descriptive and correlation as well as panel regression analysis for a 6-year period (2008–2013). The results show after controlling for characteristics of the company and macroeconomic conditions working capital management significantly affects the profitability of Croatian software firms. Moreover, the results imply the existence of a nonlinear, concave quadratic relationship between the net working capital and return on assets. This suggests the existence of an optimal level of net working capital that balances costs and benefits and maximizes the profitability of analyzed companies.

Yousaf et al. (2021) suppose that working capital management is one of the most important decisions for all firms. The main components of working capital management are days sales outstanding, days inventory outstanding, days payable outstanding, and cash conversion cycle. Using a sample of 332 Czech firms, they explored the effects of the main components of working capital management on firms' profitability. They used two different regression models to test the hypothesis, i.e., pooled regression and maximum likelihood estimation (MLE). The findings of the research revealed that all the components of working capital management have a negative impact on firm profitability.

Mandipa and Sibindi (2022) examined the relationship between the financial performance and working capital management practices of South African retail firms listed on the Johannesburg Stock Exchange. The study sample comprised a panel of 16 South African retail firms for the period 2010–2019. A fixed-effects estimator was employed in the analysis. The working capital management was proxied by average age of inventory (AAI), average collection period (ACP), average payment period (APP), and cash conversion cycle (CCC), while the financial performance was proxied by net operating profit margin (NOPM), return on assets (ROA), and return on equity (ROE). It was found that there is a negative relationship between average collection period and financial performance. A negative relationship between average age of inventory and financial performance measures (NOPM and ROA) was found. The average payment period was found to be negatively related to return on equity. The cash conversion cycle and net operating profit margin variables were found to be negatively related. The study concludes that working capital management practices influenced the financial performance of South African retail firms. It is recommended that South African retail firms observe prudent optimal working capital management practices, as these influence their financial performance.

Al-Shubiri (2011) investigated the relationship between aggressive and conservative working capital practices and profitability, as well as risk. The sample includes 59 industrial firms and 14 banks listed on the Amman Stock Exchange for the period of 2004–2008. The results indicate a negative relationship between profitability measures and working capital aggressiveness, investment and financing policy. Firms have negative returns if they follow an aggressive working capital policy. In general, there is no statistically significant relationship between the level of current assets and current liabilities on operating and financial risk in industrial firms. There is some statistically significant evidence to indicate a relationship between standard deviation of return on investments and working capital practices in banks.

Afza and Nazir (2008) investigated the relationship between the aggressive and conservative working capital policies for 17 industrial groups of 263 nonfinancial public limited companies listed on Karachi Stock Exchange for a period of 1998–2003. He found significant differences among their working capital investment and financing policies across different industries. Moreover, these significant differences are remarkably stable over the period of 6 years. The aggressive investment working capital policies are accompanied by aggressive working capital financing policies. Finally, it was found a negative relationship between the profitability measures of firms and the degree of aggressiveness of working capital investment and financing policies.

54.3 Data and Methodology

This part of the chapter is first focused on the description of the data used, including the number of analyzed enterprises. Subsequently, in the second part of this chapter, the methods that will be used to fulfill the goal of the article are described.

54.3.1 Data

The data sample will include annual data drawn from the global Orbis database for the period 2012–2021. The Orbis database includes data from the annual reports of companies operating not only in the Czech Republic. In addition to the Orbis database, data based on analyzes of the Ministry of Industry and Trade of the Czech Republic will be used. The analysis will include companies operating in the Czech Republic, which are divided according to size into medium-sized companies,

Table 54.1 Number of analyzed companies

Category of the companies	Number of companies
Medium-sized companies	7087
Large companies	2787
Very large companies	321

Source: Own processing

large companies, and very large companies. The result will be the determination of whether and how the management of working capital and its financing affects the profitability of enterprises according to size and whether there are differences in this context across enterprises according to size in the Czech Republic.

Within the framework of the division of enterprises into small enterprises, medium-sized enterprises, large enterprises, and very large enterprises, it is necessary to define the criteria by means of which individual enterprises will be divided into the abovementioned groups according to their size. According to the Orbis database, companies are divided by size as follows:

- Very large companies characterized by operating revenues of more than EUR 100 million, total assets of more than EUR 200 million, and the number of employees of more than 1000
- Large companies characterized by operating revenues of more than EUR 10 million, total assets of more than EUR 20 million, and the number of employees of more than 150.
- Medium-sized companies characterized by operating revenues greater than EUR 1 million, total assets greater than EUR 2 million, and the number of employees greater than 15.
- Small businesses are considered to be businesses that do not meet the criteria set for medium-sized businesses.

Table 54.1 presents the number of enterprises included in the research.

54.3.2 Methodology

Granger causality and the generalized method of moments (GMM) will be used to find out whether the policy of working capital management and its financing affects the profitability of enterprises divided by size in the Czech Republic.

Granger causality can be used to determine which variable can influence another variable. In accordance with the research, attention is focused on using the Granger causality test to find out whether the policy of working capital management and its financing affects the profitability of enterprises according to size in the Czech Republic. Granger causality works with the stationary series and lags used in cointegration analysis to determine the existence of short-term relationships between two variables. Granger causality takes into account that the past can affect the future. A variable X has a causal effect (in the Granger sense) on Y if past values of X can help explain Y. In the case of Granger causality, the goal is to reject the null hypothesis that there is no causal relationship between the variables being studied. In their study, Engle and Granger (1987) quantify Granger causality using the following equations, where Y_t and X_t represent the working capital management policy and its financing on the one hand and the profitability of enterprises on the other hand; ε_t, the error or residual component; β_0 and φ_0, the constants of the causal equations; β_{1t}, β_{2t}, φ_{1t}, and φ_{2t}, intersections with the X and Y axes.

$$\Delta Y_t = \beta_0 + \sum_{i=1}^{\sigma} \beta_{1i} \Delta Y_{t-i} + \sum_{i=1}^{\gamma} \beta_{2i} \Delta X_{t-1} + \varepsilon_{1t} \qquad (54.1)$$

$$\Delta X_t = \varphi_0 + \sum_{i=1}^{\gamma} \varphi_{1i} \Delta X_{t-i} + \sum_{i=1}^{\gamma} \varphi_{2i} \Delta Y_{t-1} + \varepsilon_{2t} \qquad (54.2)$$

The Granger causality test can only be used to determine which variable can affect another variable. However, it is not possible to determine how strong the dependence is between these variables and what the causal relationship or connection between them is, examining the relationship between the cause and its consequences within the variables analyzed by us. For this reason, the generalized method of moments (GMM) will be used to determine the causal relationship between the variables and to determine the dependence of the endogenous variable on the exogenous variables.

Using the GMM, it is possible to evaluate whether and to what extent the working capital management policy and its financing influences the profitability of enterprises divided by size. In this context, the following equation will be used, which is in accordance with Karaduman et al. (2010).

$$P_{it} = \alpha_1 + \beta_1 \times \Delta P_{it-1} + \beta_2 \times X_{1it} + \beta_3 \times X_{2it} + \cdots + \beta_n \times X_{nit} + \varepsilon_{it}, \qquad (54.3)$$

where P_{it} represents a dependent variable, which is represented by an indicator expressing the operating result of the economy before taxation to the sales of the ith company within the Czech Republic at time t, ΔP_{it-1} is an explanatory variable that represents the lagged value of PVH from the previous year, and X_{nit} in itself includes explanatory variables characterizing the working capital management policy and its financing. These can then influence the profitability of the analyzed companies. This is mainly the cash conversion cycle (CCC), net working capital on sales. In connection with the financing of working capital, the indicator of noncurrent liabilities on assets will be included in the equation. The characters α_1 and ε_{it} represent the model constant and the residual component of the model within the generalized method of moments (GMM) (Table 54.2).

Table 54.2 Description of used variables

Variable	Calculation	Variable abbreviation and its character
Profitability	Operating profit before tax/sales	P (dependent variable)
Cash conversion cycle	Average age of inventory + average collection period − average payment period	CCC (independent variable)
Working capital policy	Net working capital/sales	WCP (independent variable)
Working capital financing	Noncurrent liabilities/total assets = (short-term debt + long-term debt)/assets	WCF (independent variable)

Source: Own processing

Profitability is represented in this research through an indicator expressing the share of the operating result of the economy before taxation on sales. This indicator is sometimes referred to as the profit margin, and it expresses the percentage share of the economic result on sales of goods, products, and services (generally described as % share of profit per CZK 1 of sales). The development of the trend of the sales profitability indicator is mainly influenced by the change in price (sales margin), change in costs, amount of sales, exchange rate differences, and change in the structure of the sales assortment.

Cash conversion cycle (CCC) also known as the cash cycle expresses how many days it takes a company to convert the cash it spends on inventory back into cash by selling its product. The shorter a company's CCC, the less time it has money tied up in accounts receivable and inventory.

Working capital policy is represented by the share of net working capital on sales. This indicator is an important indicator within the working capital management policy. Many studies exploring working capital management policy take this indicator into account. The higher the value of this indicator, the more conservative working capital management policy is applied in the company. On the contrary, the lower the value of this indicator, the more the company applies a more aggressive working capital management policy.

Working capital financing is represented by an indicator showing the share of noncurrent liabilities on total assets, which is an important indicator in determining the working capital financing policy. Following the financing of working capital, we distinguish between an aggressive financial policy and a conservative financial policy. This indicator is crucial for determining the degree of financial policy. Aggressive financial policy uses, on the one hand, higher levels of short-term liabilities and, on the other hand, a smaller volume of indebtedness. If this indicator tends to decrease, the company will use a conservative financial policy within the financing of working capital.

54.4 Results and Discussion

This part includes a description of the results, including a discussion of the conclusions. As part of this analysis, Granger causality will first be used to determine which variable can influence another variable. The result should thus be to find out whether the policy of working capital management and its financing affects the profitability of enterprises according to size in the Czech Republic. Furthermore, the GMM will be used to evaluate whether and to what extent the working capital management policy and its financing influences the profitability of companies across companies by size in the Czech Republic.

54.4.1 Granger Causality Test

The Granger causality test was performed for three types of companies according to size, namely medium-sized companies, large companies, and very large companies within the Czech Republic. The results of the Granger causality test are presented in the following tables (Tables 54.3, 54.4, and 54.5). All results found were tested and proven at the 1% level of statistical significance.

Table 54.3 presents the results of the Granger causality test within medium-sized enterprises operating in the Czech Republic for the period 2012–2021. Within the framework of the relationship between the cash conversion cycle (CCC) and profitability (P), a two-way relationship was demonstrated. Within this connection, the hypothesis that the cash conversion cycle does not cause or has no effect on the development of the profitability of medium-sized enterprises in the Czech Republic

Table 54.3 Results of Granger causality test of medium-sized enterprises in the Czech Republic

Null hypothesis	F-statistic	Probability
P $\neq$ CCC	135.897	7E-30
CCC $\neq$ P	46.859	4E-20
P $\neq$ WCP	685.975	9E-55
WCP $\neq$ P	259.849	3E-10
P $\neq$ WCF	387.957	1E-30
WCF $\neq$ P	495.958	4E-155

Source: Own processing

Table 54.4 Results of Granger causality test of large enterprises in the Czech Republic

Null hypothesis	F-statistic	Probability
CCC $\neq$ P	256.978	6E-20
P $\neq$ WCP	685.433	4E-10
WCP $\neq$ P	159.963	8E-20
P $\neq$ WCF	37.749	4E-30
WCF $\neq$ P	398.266	8E-30

Source: Own processing

Table 54.5 Results of Granger causality test of very large enterprises in the Czech Republic

Null hypothesis	F-statistic	Probability
P ≠ CCC	166.537	5E-10
CCC ≠ P	250.847	7E-20
P ≠ WCP	40.948	3E-30
WCP ≠ P	495.538	8E-20
WCF ≠ P	666.362	2E-30

Source: Own processing

can be rejected and vice versa. It therefore means that within this relationship there is a causal connection between the cash conversion cycle and profitability of the analyzed companies and vice versa.

A two-way link was also demonstrated between the profitability of medium-sized enterprises and working capital policy. It was therefore proven that working capital policy has a significant impact on the level of profitability of analyzed companies. On the contrary, it was also found that the level of profitability can have an impact on the working capital policy.

As for working capital financing, the Granger causality test was used to prove a two-way relationship, where working capital financing affects the level of profitability of analyzed companies and vice versa.

Within large enterprises, the results of the Granger causality test showed only a one-sided relationship between the cash conversion cycle and profitability of large enterprises in the Czech Republic (Table 54.4). This means that the profitability of businesses will be affected to some extent by the height of the cash conversion cycle.

The results thus demonstrated a two-way link between the profitability of enterprises and the policy of working capital management and its financing. Based on the above results, it can be concluded that the policy of working capital management and also the financing of working capital influence the development of profitability of large companies in the Czech Republic and vice versa.

Regarding the resulting relationships in very large enterprises, one can see similarities with large enterprises and, to a certain extent, differences with large enterprises (Table 54.5). As part of this analysis, it was found that there are two-way links between cash conversion cycle and profitability of very large companies on the one hand and working capital policy and profitability of very large companies on the other hand.

A one-sided relationship was demonstrated only between working capital financing and profitability of analyzed companies. It is therefore evident that the profitability of businesses will depend on working capital financing.

Using the Granger causality test, we found out whether there is a link between the analyzed variables and whether any of the analyzed variables can affect the level of profitability of medium-sized enterprises, large enterprises, and very large enterprises in the Czech Republic. The GMM will be used to find out what influence or impact on the profitability this is.

Table 54.6 Results of GMM of medium-sized enterprises in the Czech Republic

Variables	CCC	WCP	WCF	J statistic
Profitability (P)	−0.4957	−3.3937	−0.1187	31.2589

Source: Own processing
Note: * statistical significance at the 1% significance level, ** statistical significance at the 5% significance level, *** statistical significance at the 10% significance level

Table 54.7 Results of GMM of large enterprises in the Czech Republic

Variables	CCC	WCP	WCF	J statistic
Profitability (P)	−0.4829	−0.7630	+0.3623	25.8354

Source: Own processing
Note: * statistical significance at the 1% significance level, ** statistical significance at the 5% significance level, *** statistical significance at the 10% significance level

Table 54.8 Results of GMM of very large enterprises in the Czech Republic

Variables	CCC	WCP	WCF	J statistic
Profitability (P)	−0.1275	−0.3639	+0.6973	42.5973

Source: Own processing
Note: * statistical significance at the 1% significance level, ** statistical significance at the 5% significance level, *** statistical significance at the 10% significance level

54.4.2 Generalized Method of Moments (GMM)

The GMM, like the Granger causality test, was used for three types of companies according to size, namely medium-sized companies, large companies, and very large companies within the Czech Republic. The results of the GMM are presented in the following tables (Tables 54.6, 54.7, and 54.8).

Using the Granger causality test, we demonstrated in the previous chapter whether the policy of working capital management and its financing can influence the development of the profitability of the abovementioned enterprises. Using the GMM, we will try to find out what the influence is. From Table 54.6, it can be concluded that the cash conversion cycle, working capital policy, and working capital financing have a negative effect on the profitability of medium-sized enterprises in the Czech Republic.

Regarding the cash conversion cycle, if the company succeeds in reducing the time, it takes for the company to convert the cash it spent on inventory back into cash by selling its products, this fact will translate into increased profitability. The more the cash conversion cycle will decrease and the shorter the cash conversion will be, the shorter the period the company will have tied up money in receivables or inventories.

Working capital policy has a negative effect on the level of profitability of companies. This means that if a more aggressive working capital management policy is applied in the company, the higher profitability the company should achieve.

If companies want to increase their profitability, they should consider taking working capital financing. The results of the GMM showed a negative effect of working capital financing on the profitability of analyzed companies. If companies reduce the volume of debt, thereby applying a more aggressive policy of financing working capital, this fact will be reflected in the growth of the profitability of companies.

Within large enterprises, it was found that the cash conversion cycle and working capital policy have a negative effect on the profitability of large enterprises. If large enterprises succeed in reducing the time during which they will be able to convert inventories and receivables into cash, this fact should be reflected in increasing profitability (Table 54.7).

Companies could also achieve higher profitability by applying a more aggressive working capital management policy. If we compare the working capital financing of medium-sized enterprises and large enterprises, we see a different impact on their profitability. While the negative impact of working capital financing would be proven for medium-sized enterprises, it was found that working capital financing positively affects the development of profitability for large enterprises. This means that if companies apply a more conservative working capital financing policy and thus increase the amount of debt, such large companies are likely to experience an increase in profitability.

The last type of enterprises analyzed by size were enterprises belonging to the category of very large enterprises. If we compare the results of very large enterprises with the results of large enterprises and medium-sized enterprises, we see similar common features with large enterprises (Table 54.8).

If very large enterprises want to increase their profitability, the managers of these enterprises should pay increased attention to reducing the cash conversion cycle, thus decreasing the time during which these enterprises will be able to convert their inventories and receivables into cash.

Managers of very large enterprises, similarly to managers of large enterprises, could achieve higher profitability by applying a more aggressive policy in the management of working capital policy.

On the contrary, within the framework of working capital financing, managers of very large enterprises should lean toward a more conservative financing policy, which could achieve higher profitability with the help of a higher volume of indebtedness.

Add why higher debt will have a positive impact on profit and will grow compared to medium-sized companies.

All the conclusions found are in accordance with the studies of, for example, Evci and Şak (2018), Yousaf et al. (2021), and Mandipa and Sibindi (2022), who demonstrated similar resulting relationships in their studies. Working capital management is a very important issue in successful business management. It is necessary to bear in mind that this working capital entails the need to finance it, which entails a certain amount of costs for businesses. The issue of collection policy is also very important, when in the case of poor monitoring in this area, the company can get into problems in connection with payment ethics or policy.

54.5 Conclusion

The aim of this chapter was to evaluate whether the policy of working capital management and its financing affects the profitability of enterprises divided by size in the Czech Republic and thus to determine differences in working capital management across the size of enterprises. In order to fulfill the goal of this article, Granger causality and the generalized method of moments, the so-called GMM, were used. The data sample included data for the period from 2012 to 2021. The analysis included companies operating in the Czech Republic, which are divided by size into medium-sized companies, large companies, and very large companies.

Using Granger causality test results within medium-sized enterprises proved that there is a relationship between cash conversion cycle and profitability and vice versa. In other words, the cash conversion cycle affects the profitability of these businesses and vice versa. Working capital policy also has an influence on the development of the profitability of the analyzed companies and vice versa. In the framework of working capital financing, a two-way link was also demonstrated in comparison with the profitability of companies. It can therefore be stated that the cash conversion cycle, working capital policy, and working capital financing can have an influence on the development of profitability and vice versa. As for large enterprises, it has been proven that the cash conversion cycle will have an impact on the level of profitability of large enterprises, but the opposite link has not been proven. Here, compared to medium-sized enterprises, a different result can be seen. Within the framework of working capital policy and working capital financing on the one hand and profitability on the other hand, two-way links were demonstrated. If we compare the results of very large enterprises with the results of medium-sized enterprises and large enterprises, a difference can be seen in the framework of working capital financing. Only a one-sided connection of working capital financing to the profitability of very large enterprises was proven. It can therefore be concluded that the choice of working capital financing influences the development of the profitability of very large enterprises. Within the framework of the cash conversion cycle and working capital policy on the one hand, and the profitability of businesses on the other hand, a two-way link was demonstrated.

Using the GMM, it was found that the cash conversion cycle, working capital policy, and working capital financing negatively affect the profitability of medium-sized enterprises in the Czech Republic. If business managers want to increase the level of profitability, they should try to reduce the time in which these businesses will be able to convert inventory and receivables into cash and choose a more aggressive working capital management policy and a more aggressive working capital financing policy. The results of the GMM of large enterprises and very large enterprises are identical. Compared to medium-sized enterprises, large enterprises and very large enterprises differ only in the context of working capital financing in terms of profitability. While a more aggressive working capital financing policy has been recommended for medium-sized enterprises in order to increase profitability, a more conservative working capital financing policy has been recommended for large and very large enterprises.

From the above results, it can be concluded that the management of working capital and its monitoring is a very important area that can have a significant impact on the profitability of the business sector. The results of this research pointed out whether and how the management of working capital and its financing affects the profitability of enterprises according to size and whether there are differences in this connection across enterprises according to size in the Czech Republic.

Acknowledgment This chapter ensued thanks to the support of the grant IGS/11/2023 "Working capital management policy and its financing across selected enterprises according to size in the Czech Republic."

References

Afza, T., & Nazir, S. M. (2008). Working capital approaches and firm's returns. *Pakistan Journal of Commerce and Social Sciences, 1*, 25–36.

Al-Shubiri, F. N. (2011). The effect of working capital practices on risk management: Evidence from Jordan. *Global Journal of Business Research, 5*(1), 39–54.

Engle, R. F., & Granger, W. C. (1987). Co-integration and error correction: Representation, estimation, and testing. *Econometrica, 55*(2), 251–276. ISSN 1468-0262. https://doi.org/10.2307/1913236

Evci, S., & Şak, N. (2018). The effect of working capital management on profitability in emerging countries: Evidence from Turkey. In *Financial management from an emerging market perspective*. IntechOpen. https://doi.org/10.5772/intechopen.70871

Karaduman, H. A., Akbas, H. E., Ozsozgun, A., & Durer, S. (2010). Effects of working capital management on profitability: The case for selected companies in the Istanbul stock exchange (2005–2008). *International Journal of Economics and Finance Studies, 2*(2), 47–54. ISSN: 1309-8055.

Korent, D., & Orsag, S. (2018). The impact of working capital management on profitability of Croatian software companies. *Zagreb International Review of Economics and Business, 21*(1), 47–66. https://doi.org/10.2478/zireb-2018-0007

Mandipa, G., & Sibindi, B. A. (2022). Financial performance and working capital management practices in the retail sector: Empirical evidence from South Africa. *Risk and Multifaceted Failures in Business Operations, 10*(3), 63. https://doi.org/10.3390/risks10030063

Yousaf, M., et al. (2021). Impact of working capital management approaches (aggressive/conservative) on the profitability and Shareholder's worth: Comparative analysis of cement and sugar industry. *Cogent Economics & Finance, 9*(1). https://doi.org/10.1080/23322039.2021.1954318

Chapter 55
Effects of Monetary Policy and the External Sector on Peru's Economic Cycles

Vony Sucaticona-Aguilar and Polan Ferro-Gonzales

Abstract This study aims to determine the effects of monetary policy and external economic activity on Peru's economic cycles during the period 2003–2019, within the framework of implementing the explicit inflation-targeting approach. It contributes as evidence of the effectiveness of this approach for making economic policy decisions. Four equations were estimated: an aggregate demand (AD) curve, an aggregate supply (AS) curve, an exchange rate dynamics equation, and the Taylor rule. The generalized method of moments (GMM) in a system was employed as the estimation method. The results indicate that the effect of the external sector was more significant than that of monetary policy on Peru's economic cycle during the analyzed period. Additionally, the hybrid nature of the aggregate supply and demand curves with a predominant forward-looking role is revealed. Finally, it is found that the monetary authority not only aims to maintain inflation within the target range but also seeks output stability.

Keywords Economic cycles · Monetary policy · New Keynesian · Generalized method of moments · Explicit inflation targets

55.1 Introduction

In Peru, the explicit inflation-targeting (EIT) framework was adopted in 2002, and starting from September 2003, the reference interest rate became the operational target, employing alternative instruments simultaneously to achieve the ultimate objective (P. Castillo et al., 2011). Regarding the implementation of this framework, there has been an excellent application of this monetary policy approach. As a result, the announced inflation targets by the Central Reserve Bank of Peru (BCRP)

V. Sucaticona-Aguilar · P. Ferro-Gonzales (✉)
Departamento Académico de la Facultad de Ingeniería Económica, Universidad Nacional del Altiplano, Puno, Perú
e-mail: polanf@unap.edu.pe

have been successfully met, at least in the initial years of its implementation. Additionally, the monetary authority has achieved greater transparency by communicating the inflation target to economic agents, along with the measures that would be implemented to achieve it, accompanied by a rationale. This transparency is facilitated through the publication of the inflation report, which is released three times a year (Melgarejo, 2006). However, at different stages, such as during the global financial crisis between 2008 and 2009, some limitations were observed. In these years, the announced ranges could not be met, resulting in an annual inflation rate of 6.65% in December 2008, 3.65% higher than the upper range of 3% announced by the BCRP. In this scenario, high rates of imported inflation were a significant factor. Additionally, within these limitations, there is also the production-inflation trade-off, as pointed out by R. Clarida et al. (1999) who argue that in the presence of inflation costs, there is a short-term *trade-off* between inflation and output variability. In other words, when monetary policy is used to reduce inflation by increasing the reference rate, there is a negative effect on output. Furthermore, as Peru is a small, open economy with dollarization, it affects the design and implementation of monetary policy, through phenomena such as balance sheet effects and the so-called pass-through effect (Hoyle, 2002), through which the exchange rate affects the domestic price level and is constantly subjected to external shocks (Salas, 2011). Additionally, P. T. Rodríguez and Kon (1998) point out that while the Peruvian economy has experienced export diversification in recent years, its structure still heavily relies on international commodity prices. Moreover, the characteristic of Peru being a small, open economy exposes it to various external fluctuations.

Therefore, the research aims to determine the effects of monetary policy and external economic activity on Peru's economic cycles. By evaluating the aggregate demand (AD), aggregate supply (AS), exchange rate behavior, and the Taylor rule, the study seeks to identify relationships through simultaneous analysis. This is done within the framework of implementing the explicit inflation-targeting approach in the Peruvian economy, contributing to demonstrating the effectiveness of this approach for making economic policy decisions.

55.2 Literature Review

This article aims to conduct a simultaneous analysis of economic agents within the framework of the Neo-Keynesian model to determine the effects of monetary policy and the external sector on the economic cycles of the Peruvian economy. Within this analysis, there are numerous studies that have found relevant relationships for this research, among which we consider the following:

Internationally, there is a study by Cano et al. (2007) that examines the relationships between intertemporal preferences, monetary policy, and the economic cycle in Colombia from an Austrian perspective. The study concludes that the economic cycle is not explained in the short term by this approach, but relationships are found in the long term.

On the other hand, García and Gonzales (2007) sought to characterize the transmission mechanisms and effectiveness of monetary policy in several countries such as Paraguay, Mexico, Bolivia, Peru, and Chile. They estimated a simple general equilibrium model from the Keynesian tradition. Among their results, they found a higher response value for Paraguay's policy decisions to inflation levels and production dynamics and a lower response for Bolivia. In all cases, it is observed that the monetary policy response is greater to inflation than to output.

Additionally, Cermeño et al. (2012) developed a macroeconomic model for a small, open economy, specifically focusing on Mexico within the Neo-Keynesian framework. They estimated four equations using the generalized method of moments (GMM) in a system. Their findings highlight that despite operating under an inflation-targeting regime, the Central Bank of Mexico prioritizes output stability over the inflation target, aiming to minimize output fluctuations around zero in relation to its potential level.

Furthermore, Gomez (2013) studies the impact of monetary policy on the economic cycle and the transmission mechanisms involved by estimating a dynamic stochastic general equilibrium (DSGE) model for the Colombian economy, considering three equations. The results highlight that increases in the policy interest rate led to a decrease in both output and inflation. Additionally, it suggests that increases in productivity result in a decrease in the unemployment level, with a greater effect if there is no informal sector.

Moreover, Alonso et al. (2013) analyzed the behavior of the US economy with regard to three variables that illustrate the Austrian Theory of Economic Cycles (ATEC). Firstly, they employ Granger causality to confirm that the U.S. cycles are Granger-caused by production, interest rates, and money. For the analysis of propagation mechanisms, they use distributed lag models. The results establish the existence of a positive effect in the early stages of the capital and time-intensive production process, resulting from an increase in the slope representing the yield curve. Additionally, they confirm the countercyclical nature of monetary policy in the behavior of aggregate industrial production.

Regarding Peru, there is the work carried out by Salas (2011) which analyzes the effects of monetary policy. The study utilizes a Neo-Keynesian model consisting of three equations, with the addition of the uncovered interest rate parity equation for an open economy. The parameters are estimated using Bayesian methods, and impulse response functions are also estimated to validate the model. The research results demonstrate that despite the presence of dollarization in the Peruvian economy, monetary policy has short-term effects. The evidence presented highlights the importance of transmission channels such as the interest rate channel, the expectations channel, and the exchange rate channel.

Furthermore, Winkelried (2013) conducts simulations of monetary policy and projections of various macroeconomic variables using a Bayesian approach. According to the results, it is concluded that large external supply shocks can have a short duration and the capacity to reverse quickly. Therefore, it is suggested that the Central Reserve Bank of Peru (BCRP) should not respond to supply shocks. Additionally, it is found that changes in the output gap due to economic growth led to inflation, influenced by variations in expectations and interest rate differentials. Moreover, frequent movements in the exchange rate are observed, which can absorb pressures of depreciation or appreciation, particularly when they are more prolonged and systematic.

Additionally, Rivas (2016) aims to describe how monetary policy influenced short-, medium-, and long-term economic cycles. Using a lagged VAR model and Granger causality, the study seeks to demonstrate that changes in monetary policy caused periods of economic booms and recessions. According to the results, the Central Reserve Bank of Peru (BCRP), through its policy direction, contributes to the formation of financial bubbles that drive economic cycles. The study finds that an increase in monetary policy has a positive influence on the production of durable goods. Furthermore, it shows that expansionary and recessionary cycles tend to be self-perpetuating.

Taking into account these research studies, the variables included in their estimations, and the foundations of the Neo-Keynesian model, this present research formulates four equations for estimation. Unlike previous studies, this estimation is conducted using the generalized method of moments, considering the condition of using variables of rational expectations. Furthermore, the estimation is carried out simultaneously, considering the interdependencies among the equations.

55.3 Neo-Keynesian Model

In recent decades, a generation of medium-scale macroeconomic models has been developed within the international research community. The International Monetary Fund (IMF), the European Central Bank (ECB), the Federal Reserve Board, and other central banks have provided theoretical foundations for strategies aimed at inflation stability, which have been adopted by the majority of central banks. As a reference, the Neo-Keynesian framework has been developed as a "scientific" approach to monetary policy, based on microeconomic foundations. It was initiated by Clarida et al. (1999), expanded upon by Woodford (2003), and further affirmed by Galí and Gertler (2007 y 2009). Taking into consideration the algebraic and explanatory developments of the latter, the following describes the evolution of this framework.

55.3.1 Assumptions of the Model

The Neo-Keynesian model is a product of a combination between the DSGE framework developed in real business cycle (RBC) models and aspects considered by classical monetary models. It is based on several assumptions, which are explained below:

- Nominal rigidity
- Monopolistic competition
- Short-term nonneutrality of monetary policy

55.3.2 Economic Agents in the Model

The economic agents involved in the development of the Neo-Keynesian framework are a representative household, firms, and the monetary authority. It is worth mentioning that the algebraic development presented below is based on the work by Galí (2009).

55.3.2.1 Representative Household

It is represented as an economic agent that maximizes the expected value of its intertemporal utility function (consumption-saving) under rational expectations (forward-looking), and it is assumed to have an infinite lifespan. The function to be maximized is represented by

$$E_0 \sum_{t=0}^{\infty} \beta^t U(C_t N_t) \tag{55.1}$$

where $C_t = \left(\int_0^1 C_t(i)^{1-\frac{1}{\varepsilon}} di\right)^{\frac{\varepsilon}{\varepsilon-1}}$. Additionally, C_t is a consumption index, and $C_t(i)$ represents the quantity of good i consumed by the household in period t, assuming the existence of two goods in the economy represented by the interval [0, 1].

Esta función de utilidad sujeta a la restricción presupuestaria del período dada por:

$$\int_0^1 P_t(i) C_t(i) di + Q_t B_t \leq B_{t-1} + W_t N_t + T_t \tag{55.2}$$

For $t = 0, 1, 2, \ldots$, where $P_t(i)$ is the price of good i, N_t is the hours of work, W_t is the nominal wage, B_t is the purchase of bonds for one period (whose price is Q_t), and y T_t is the overall income (including dividends from ownership of firms and others).

By solving the maximization problem and rewriting it in terms of the output gap, we obtain the first equation in the Neo-Keynesian approach of the IS or AD.

$$\tilde{y}_t = -\frac{1}{\sigma}\left(i_t - E_t\{\pi_{t+1}\} - r_t^n\right) + E_t\{\tilde{y}_{t+1}\} \tag{55.3}$$

55.3.2.2 Firms

The New Keynesian Phillips curve, also known as the new neoclassical synthesis, is based on price rigidities. Its derivation assumes that each firm produces a differentiated good, but all firms use the same technology. Furthermore, firms are represented by $i \in [0, 1]$. They face a production function given by

$$Y_t(i) = A_t N_t(i)^{1-\alpha} \tag{55.4}$$

where A_t is the level of technology, which is identical for each firm but evolves exogenously over time. Additionally, all firms face an identical isoelastic demand described by Eq. (55.1) and take the aggregate price level P_t and aggregate consumption index C_t.

In the optimization process, firms in period t maximize their market profits by choosing the price P_t^* to be set, which is determined by solving the following maximization problem.

$$\max_{P_t^*} \sum_{k=0}^{\infty} \theta^k E_t \left\{ Q_{t,t+k} \left(P_t^* Y_{t+k|t} - \psi_{t+k} \left(Y_{t+k|t} \right) \right) \right\} \tag{55.5}$$

where $\psi_{t+k|t} = \psi'_{t+k}\left(Y_{t+k|t}\right)$ is the nominal marginal cost in period $t + k$ or a firm that last reoptimized its price in period t and $\mathcal{M} = \frac{\epsilon}{\epsilon-1}$. Additionally, it should be noted that in the case where there is no price rigidity, i.e., when ($\theta = 0$), Eq. (55.5) is optimized subject to demand functions whose solution is combined with the optimization of the goods market to finally obtain the equation for the AS or the NKPC.

$$\pi_t = \beta\, E_t \left\{ \pi_{t+1} \right\} + \kappa\, \tilde{y}_t \tag{55.6}$$

55.3.2.3 Monetary Authority

To complement the Neo-Keynesian model, a Taylor-type monetary policy rule is considered for the Central Reserve Bank (BCRP). The rule specifies the central bank's response function and guides its decision-making process:

$$i_t = \rho + \phi_\pi \pi_t + \phi_y \tilde{y}_t + \upsilon_t \tag{55.7}$$

where ϕ_π and ϕ_y are nonnegative coefficients representing the impact on the interest rate in response to changes in inflation and output, respectively. ρ represents the intercept of the equation, ensuring the rule is consistent when inflation is at its steady-state level or zero. υ_t is a stochastic component.

In practice, this rule is often adjusted, particularly in emerging economies where there is high-interest rate inertia. This adjustment is known as "interest rate smoothing," as described by Richard Clarida et al. (1999).

$$i_t = \phi_1 i_{t-1} + (1 - \phi_1)\left[\phi_2 \bar{i}_t + \phi_3 (\pi_t - \bar{\pi}_t) + \phi_4 \tilde{y}_t\right] + \varepsilon_t^i \qquad (55.8)$$

55.3.3 Character of an Open Economy: Exchange Rate Dynamics in an Open Economy

The analysis of monetary policy and its effects in an open economy should include the behavior of the exchange rate, which is essentially based on the theory of purchasing power parity (PPP)[1] represented by the following function in levels:

$$P = eP^* \qquad (55.9)$$

Interest rates, based on the assumption of free capital mobility, are part of the uncovered interest rate parity equation: $i_t = i_t^* + E_t e_{t+k} - e_t$, where i_t is the domestic nominal interest rate, i_t^* is the international nominal interest rate, e_t is the logarithm of the exchange rate, and E_t is the expectations operator in period t.

From the combination and algebraic development of both, the following is derived:

$$= \sum_{j=1}^{J} \partial_{1j} q_{t-j} + \partial_2 \left(E_t\left[q_{t+1}\right] + \left(r_t^* - r_t\right)\right) \qquad (55.10)$$

55.4 Methods and Data

In this research, secondary data from various sources are used. Historical time series data from the Central Reserve Bank of Peru (BCRP), the Superintendence of Banking, Insurance, and the Private Pension Funds (SBS), and the Federal Reserve Bank of St. Louis are utilized. All variables have a monthly frequency and are described in Table 55.1. It is worth noting that unobservable variables such as the output gap, external output gap, inflation target rate, natural nominal interest rate, and real natural interest rate are derived using the Hodrick-Prescott filter. The research period spans from 2003 to 2019.

---

[1] This theory indicates that the value of goods is the same anywhere in the world. See (De Gregorio, 2007) p. 216.

Table 55.1 Description of variables in the model

Types of variables	Model variables		Variable descriptions
Endogenous variables	$\tilde{y}_t$	Output gap	Monthly logarithmic deviation of GDP
	π_t	Inflation	Monthly change in the logarithm of the seasonally adjusted Consumer Price Index (CPI)
	q_t	Real exchange rate	Logarithm of the multilateral real exchange rate index
	i_t	Interest rate	Logarithm of the average interbank interest rate
Exogenous variables	e_t	Nominal exchange rate	Logarithm of the monthly average of the bank exchange rate
	r_t	Real interest rate	Derived from the Fisher[a] equation definition
	g_t	Government fiscal position	Logarithm of government expenditure
	$\tilde{y}_t^*$	External production	Logarithmic difference between the gross domestic product (GDP) of the United States
	π_t^*	External inflation	Monthly change in the logarithm of the consumer price index (CPI) of the United States
	i_t^*	External nominal interest rate	LIBOR rate of the United States
	r_t^*	External real interest rate	Derived from the Fisher equation definition
	$\bar{\pi}_t$	Target inflation rate	Derived using the Hodrick-Prescott filter
	$\bar{i}_t$	Natural nominal interest rate	Derived using the Hodrick-Prescott filter
	$\bar{r}_t$	Natural real interest rate	Derived using the Hodrick-Prescott filter

[a]The definition that Fisher gives to the real interest rate

It should be noted that this research is a quantitative correlational study, as it measures the relationship between dependent and independent variables, specifically the degree of association or determination among GDP, monetary policy rate, inflation, exchange rate, and other variables analyzed within the system of equations that comprise the analysis of the research. The proposed model consists of a system of four equations, including the intertemporal IS curve or aggregate demand (optimizing behavior of households).

$$\tilde{y}_t = \beta_1 (r_t - \bar{r}_t) + \beta_2 \tilde{y}_{t-1} + \beta_3 E_t [\tilde{y}_{t+1}] + \beta_4 q_t + \beta_5 g_t + \beta_6 \tilde{y}_t^* + \varepsilon_t^{\tilde{y}}$$

The NKPC or aggregate supply (optimizing behavior of firms)

$$\pi_t = \alpha_1 \pi_{t-1} + \alpha_2 \pi_{t-2} + \alpha_3 \pi_{t-3} + \alpha_4 E_t [\pi_{t+1}] + \alpha_5 \tilde{y}_t + \alpha_6 (\Delta e_t + \pi_t^*) + \varepsilon_t^s$$

Real exchange rate equation (open economy nature)

$$q_t = \sum_{j=1}^{J} \partial_{1j} q_{t-j} + \partial_2 (E_t [q_{t+1}] + (r_t^* - r_t)) + \varepsilon_t^q, \text{ where } j = 1, 2, 3 \text{ y } 4$$

Taylor's monetary policy rule (central bank reaction function)

$$i_t = \phi_1 i_{t-1} + (1 - \phi_1) [\phi_2 \bar{i}_t + \phi_3 (\pi_t - \bar{\pi}_t) + \phi_4 \tilde{y}_t] + \varepsilon_t^i$$

It should be noted that within the AD and AS equations of the model, variables representing adaptive expectations are included (which means that economic agents base their forecasts on past behaviors and are presented in each equation as lagged variables $t - 1$ of the endogenous variable). Additionally, variables representing rational expectations are included (which assume that economic agents form their forecasts efficiently and rationally based on all available experience and information and are given by the expectation variables of the endogenous variable in $t + 1$). These equations are referred to as hybrid due to the inclusion of both components, as suggested by the literature.

The estimation method used is the generalized method of moments (GMM) in a system framework. It should be noted that for the selection of the instrument vector that allows obtaining efficient and optimal estimators, the identification problem is addressed through the selection of moment conditions.

The choice of instruments is made through the Sargan/Hansen[2] J statistic, which is compared with the chi-square distribution x_{q-p}^2, where $(q - p)$ represents the

---

[2] The Hansen''s J test of overidentification is an extension of the test proposed by Sargan, with the same null hypothesis in both cases. The difference lies in the fact that the instrumental variable estimators used in the Hansen''s test are estimated using the generalized method of moments (GMM).

overidentification restrictions. Here, "q" refers to the moment conditions given by the set of instruments $Z_t = 1, 2, 3, 4, \ldots, q$ and "p" represents the number of parameters to be estimated, denoted as "β." The optimal weighting or distance matrix is determined by minimizing the objective function $TJ_T(\beta_T)$, aiming to obtain efficient and optimal estimators. Additionally, Bayesian information, Akaike, and Hannan-Quinn criteria based on GMM, as proposed in Andrews (2007), are also employed. These criteria are as follows:

GMM-BIC: $\text{MSC}_{\text{BIC}, N}(Z_t) = J_t(Z_t) - (p - q) \ln(N)$
GMM-AIC: $\text{MSC}_{\text{AIC}, N}(Z_t) = J_t(Z_t) - 2 \times (p - q)$
GMM-HQIC: $\text{MSC}_{\text{HQIC}, N}(Z_t) = J_t(Z_t) - 2,01(p - q) \ln(\ln(N))$

where Z_t is a vector that contains p instruments, and q is the coefficient vector.

55.5 Results and Discussion

55.5.1 Selection of the Moment Conditions for the GMM Estimation

The estimation of the system is made under the generalized method of moments, and it should be noted that the effective number of observations is less than that attributed in the period of analysis, due to the fact that there are variables that are used as regressors and at the same time as instruments. The results of the analysis are shown below in Table 55.2.

Table 55.2 allows us to choose the vector of moment conditions that makes the weighting or distance matrix optimal and that guarantees that the estimated parameters are efficient; results are shown for three sets of moment conditions contained in Z_t instruments, containing three models with different instrument vectors. The results allow us to evaluate under the overidentification restrictions

Table 55.2 Selection criterion of the GMM

	System with simple Taylor rule		
System	Model I	Model II	Model III
J statistic	0,200342	0,203521	0,203558
J	39,667716	39,686595	39,286694
Chi-2(q-p)	23,6848	37,6545	40,1133
Number of moment conditions	39	50	52
No of observations	198	195	193
Number of parameters (p)	25	25	25
GMM-BIC	−34,3680	−92,1384	−102,8059
GMM-AIC	−27,7997	−49,7965	−53,7964
GMM-HQIC	−7,1992	−43,8590	−50,8364

test, where the nonrejection of the H_o allows us to infer that the instruments, the weighting matrix, and therefore the coefficients are the optimal product of the minimization of the given criterion function by Hansen's J statistic, which compared to $x^2(q - p)$ at the five percent significance level alone cannot be rejected by model 3, so this model would be the most appropriate. In a complementary way, the analysis of the GMM-BIC, AIC, and HQIC criteria is made, whose choice is given from the minimum value attributed to said test statistics. According to the results and Hansen's test of overidentification conditions, under these three criteria they reaffirm model 3 as the most appropriate, the results of which will be presented in the next part.

55.5.2 Results and Discussion of the Estimation of the New Keynesian Model Under a Simple Taylor Rule

The relationships found in the dynamics of the equations are the following:

55.5.2.1 The Intertemporal Curve IS or Aggregate Demand

The estimation of aggregate demand is presented in the first column of Table 55.3. Firstly, one of the transmission mechanisms of monetary policy is evidenced, the interest rate effect that stimulates investment, which is exposed by the coefficient corresponding to the elasticity of the output gap with the interest rate, which is negative, consistent with what economic theory indicates and with the study by Winkelried (2013), where these parameters represents the effects of monetary policy on the output gap (economic cycle), resulting from its impact on investment. Also, this coefficient is statistically significant at the 5% level. Second, the first lag and the expected value of the output gap are statistically significant and have the expected sign. This result is consistent with the literature that estimates hybrid aggregate demand equations (backward- and forward-looking) for developed and developing economies. Additionally, the magnitude of the estimated coefficients is acceptable since it shows that the formation of adaptive expectations and rational expectations by economic agents have an important effect on determining the output gap, as in Salas (2011), who also finds that future expectations are quantitatively more relevant. In addition, the results show a slight coefficient that represents the fiscal position of the government, which shows that the greater public spending of the government effectively encourages aggregate demand and therefore contributes to the amplification of the production gap. Finally, the coefficient that corresponds to external production allows us to see the effect that this produces on the output gap, which reveals the strong synchronization of the Peruvian economic cycle with the cycle abroad, specifically with that of the United States.

Table 55.3 Results of the estimation of the GMM system with a simple Taylor rule

Aggregate demand: $\tilde{y}_t$		Aggregate Supply: π_t^s		Real exchange rate: q_t		Taylor's rule: i	
β_1	−0.3142**	α_1	0.1945**	∂_{11}	0.7666**	ϕ_1	0.9488**
	(0.023)		(0.005)		(0.003)		(0.000)
β_2	0.2402**	α_2	0.1791**	∂_{12}	−0.3608**	ϕ_2	1.5699**
	(0.003)		(0.004)		(0.004)		(0.001)
β_3	0.2257**	α_3	−0.0130**	∂_{13}	0.1498**	ϕ_3	4.6279**
	(0.003)		(0.003)		(0.004)		(0.002)
β_4	0.1175**	α_4	0.3828**	∂_{14}	−0.0153**	ϕ_4	0.02961**
	(0.002)		(0.006)		(0.002)		(0.000)
β_5	0.0261**	α_5	0.0041**	∂_2	0.0046**		
	(0.000)		(0.000)		(0.000)		
β_6	1.1095**	α_6	0.0025**				
	(0.004)		(0.000)				
R^2 adjust.	0.89		0.27		0.99		0.97
S.E. regr.	0.0337		0.0015		0.0072		0.0020
Sum $\hat{u}^2$	0.2102		0.0004		0.0918		0.0008

Instruments: $\tilde{y}_{t-k}$, $(r_t - \overline{r}_t)_{t-m}$, dlg_{t-m}, $\tilde{y}_{t-m}^*$, π_{t-n}^s, $(\pi_{t-m}^* + \Delta e_{t-m}) \cdot q_{t-n}$, $E_t [q_{t+1}] + (r_t^* - r_t)_{t-m}$, i_{t-n}, $\overline{i}_t$, $(\pi_t - \overline{\pi}_t)_{t-m}$.

Residual determinant of covariance: 4.69E-19; J statistic: 0.2036

Note: ** indicates the rejection of the null hypothesis of the coefficient equal to zero at 1% of the significance level. The values in parentheses () are the standard errors, each equation includes a constant in its estimation that does not appear in the results, and they also include a constant term as an instrument. It should be considered that, $k = 1, 2, \ldots, 9$; $m = 0, 1, 2, 3$; $n = 1, 2, \ldots, 6$

According to the results, considering a simple rule of the central bank's reaction function, the effects of monetary policy on economic cycles are significant and important (coefficient of −0.31). Furthermore, given the simultaneous analysis approach of the research, monetary policy proves to be relevant through its various transmission channels. At the same time, the estimations highlight the hybrid nature of the AD curve (coefficients of 0.24 and 0.23 for the lagged and forward components, respectively), which were significant and had a substantial impact on the GDP gap during the analyzed period. Additionally, the impact of the external sector on the economic cycle, represented by the coefficients of the real exchange rate (0.12) and the external production gap (1.11), was found to be significant and therefore important in the development of the economic cycle in Peru. This highlights the synchronization of the Peruvian economic cycle with that of the U.S. economy.

55.5.2.2 NK Phillips Curve or Aggregate Supply

In the second column of Table 55.3, the estimation of the hybrid inflation equation is observed, whose results show, firstly, that the elasticities of the inertial component of inflation, considered with three lags including the backward-looking effect, given by the first three coefficients, contribute significantly to the explanation of present inflation and are statistically significant at 5%. Next, there is the coefficient that belongs to the inflation expectation (forward-looking) which, in addition to being positive and presenting a high value, is statistically significant at 5% and higher than the backward coefficient, which demonstrates the relevant and preponderant role that rational expectations play a role in Peruvian inflation; these results are consistent with Aquino (2019) who highlights the relevance of expectations even more after the 2008 crisis and Salas (2011) who finds relevant values of expectations forward in their estimate of the Phillip curve. In addition, reviewing the coefficient associated with the inflation gap, we see the slope of the CPNK that is positive and consistent with economic theory, demonstrating that when aggregate demand is dynamized, contributing to the amplification of the production gap, it generates a pressure of rise in prices and, therefore, inflation; on the other hand, the coefficient of the external sector represented by external inflation and the depreciation of the exchange rate shows us that they have had small impacts on inflation in Peru, throughout the period of analysis, despite the fact that in the years of economic crisis they had a strong impact on it, in addition to being statistically significant. It should be noted that the fit of the model is small, which includes the error term ε_t^s, which contains preference shocks, technology, and forecast errors and contains important information that explains the inflation of the Peruvian economy, containing additional variables to the margin of the New Keynesian framework.

When observing the estimation of the aggregate supply equation, the inertial nature of inflation in the Peruvian economy is highlighted (coefficients of 0.19, 0.18, and 0.013 for the lagged components). It also shows its hybrid nature, being significantly explained by both rational and adaptive expectation components.

Significant and important coefficients are found in the estimation. It is worth noting the predominance of the forward-looking component, with an estimated coefficient of 0.34. Additionally, it is determined that the impact of external inflation was small (coefficient of 0.0025) but significant in determining inflation during the analyzed period.

It is noteworthy that the model has a small adjustment, with an adjusted R-squared of only 27%. This implies that the error term, which includes preference shocks, technological shocks, and prediction errors, contains important information that explains inflation in the Peruvian economy. This suggests the presence of additional variables beyond the Neo-Keynesian framework.

55.5.2.3 Behavior of the Real Exchange Rate

The results shown in the third column of Table 55.3 demonstrate the dynamics of the real exchange rate behavior. In the study by Jaramillo and Serván (2011), as well as in the present research, a combination of purchasing power parity (PPP) and uncovered interest parity (UIP) is found to provide an excellent and consistent representation of the exchange rate dynamics for the Peruvian economy, however, in contrast to Salas (2011), who uses an equation that weighs both prospective and retrospective components of the exchange rate to explain its variations.

In the results of the present study, it can be observed that the coefficient representing the interest rate parity condition is positive and statistically significant. This relationship indicates that an increase in the national or local interest rate leads to a depreciation of the local currency in the economy, highlighting the relevance of the exchange rate channel. Additionally, the lagged values of the real exchange rate show significant and important coefficients, which contain useful information about its current value. Furthermore, these effects diminish as the lags increase. The obtained results suggest that, in line with empirical literature, while the future coefficient may not be very large, it is still significant.

According to the estimation, the dynamics of the exchange rate were determined by the monetary policy rate through the interest rate differential (coefficient of 0.0046). Additionally, it is found that lagged values of the real exchange rate determine the current value of the exchange rate, as reflected in their significant and important coefficients. Furthermore, these effects diminish as the number of lags increase (coefficients of 0.77, 0.36, 0.15, and 0.015 for lags 1, 2, 3, and 4, respectively).

55.5.2.4 Taylor Monetary Policy Rule

In the present research, a smoothed Taylor rule is estimated, similar to Salas (2011), Winkelried (2013), and Vega (2019), who also consider it to be a more realistic version of the Taylor rule for Peru due to the caution of central banks regarding changes in the policy interest rate. It is worth noting the study by G. Rodríguez et al. (2021), which estimates a smoothed Taylor rule within the DSGE framework by including the nominal exchange rate as part of the central bank's reaction function. In their estimation, the interest rate does not respond to changes in the nominal exchange rate, and the response of the interest rate to inflation is close to 2, while the response to the output gap is 1. On the other hand, Bazán (2013) estimates a simple traditional Taylor rule and finds consistent results with the theory only in the period starting from the third break in 2009.

Under a simple interest rate rule, the estimation confirms the inertial nature of interest rates in emerging economies, as mentioned in the econometric methodology section of the present research. This reflects the prudence and caution of the monetary authority when adjusting interest rates, indicating a high degree of adherence to maintaining the interest rate unchanged. Additionally, the coefficient related to the inflation gap with respect to its target is greater than one, in line with the Taylor principle. This ensures that when inflation rises and the central bank aims to discourage the economy toward its target inflation, the increase in the interest rate set by the monetary authority should be greater than the increase in inflation. As a result, the real interest rate will rise, reducing aggregate demand and causing an economic contraction that will also narrow the output gap, according to the obtained results, the coefficient of the output gap is small but significant, confirming the central bank's preference to keep inflation within its target range. However, it also reveals that deviations in production, i.e., the amplitude of the business cycle, influence the central bank's decision to adjust the interest rate.

It is determined that the central bank's reaction function shows a strong commitment to keeping the interest rate unchanged, with an estimated coefficient of 0.95. The preference of the Central Reserve Bank of Peru (BCRP) to maintain inflation within its target range is confirmed, as reflected in the coefficient of 4.62. However, the amplitude of the economic cycle also plays a relevant role in the central bank's decision to adjust the interest rate, albeit to a lesser extent, with a coefficient of 0.030.

55.6 Conclusions

There are significant and meaningful effects of monetary policy on economic cycles, as indicated by the simultaneous analysis approach in this research. These effects occur through various transmission channels, which, according to the estimated coefficient, reduce the amplitude of the output gap in response to contractionary policy. Additionally, the hybrid nature of the AD curve should be considered, as revealed by the significant and relevant coefficients of the lagged and expected production gaps.

An important aspect to highlight is the impact of the external sector on the output gap, represented by the coefficients of the real exchange rate and the external production gap. The latter has an even higher value than the monetary policy coefficient, indicating that the effect of the external sector is even greater than that of monetary policy in shaping economic cycles in Peru during the analyzed period. These results provide valuable evidence for the monetary authority's economic policy decision-making.

In the estimation of the aggregate supply equation, the inertial and hybrid nature is emphasized, with significant and important coefficients. The predominance of the forward-looking component in the estimation is notable. Additionally, it is determined that the impact of external inflation, although small, is significant in determining inflation during the analyzed period. The model has a small adjustment, suggesting that the error term, which includes preference shocks, technological shocks, and prediction errors, contains important information that explains inflation in the Peruvian economy. This implies the inclusion of additional variables beyond the Neo-Keynesian framework for future research to improve the model's predictive power in the aggregate supply equation.

The dynamics of the exchange rate were determined by the monetary policy rate through the interest rate differential. Additionally, it is found that lagged values of the real exchange rate determine the current value of the exchange rate, as reflected in their significant and important coefficients. Furthermore, these effects diminish as the number of lags increase.

Finally, regarding the central bank's reaction function, its preference to maintain inflation within its target range is confirmed. However, the amplitude of the output gap or economic cycle also plays a relevant role in the central bank's decision to adjust the interest rate.

References

Alonso, M., Bagus, P., & Ania, A. (2013). Una ilustración empírica de la teoría austriaca del ciclo económico: El caso de estados unidos, 1988–2010. *Investigacion Economica, 72*(285), 41–74. https://doi.org/10.1016/S0185-1667(13)72596-7

Andrews, D. (2007). Consistent moment selection procedures for generalized method of moments estimation. *Economics Letters, 95*(3), 380–385. https://doi.org/10.1016/j.econlet.2006.11.011

Aquino, J. C. (2019). La curva de Phillips Neokeynesiana de una economía pequeña y abierta : Especificación, quiebres estructurales y robustez. *Revista de Estudios Económicos, 59*(Diciembre), 43–59.

Bazán, W. (2013). *Análisis de la Curva de Phillips Neokeynesiana, la IS dinámica y la Regla de Taylor en un contexto de cambio estructural* [Pontificia Universidad Católica del Perú]. https://tesis.pucp.edu.pe/repositorio/bitstream/handle/20.500.12404/5117/BAZAN_WALTER_ANALISIS.pdf?sequence=1&isAllowed=y

Cano, C., Orozco, M., & Sánchez, L. (2007). Mecanismo de transmisión de las tasas de interés en colombia (2001-2007). *Cuadernos de Economia, XXVII*, 209–240. http://www.scielo.org.co/scielo.php?script=sci_arttext&pid=S0121-47722008000100008

Castillo, P., Pérez, F., & Tuesta, V. (2011). Los mecanismos de transmisión de la política monetaria en Perú. *Revista de Estudios Económicos, 63*(21), 41–63. http://www.bcrp.gob.pe/docs/Publicaciones/Revista-Estudios-Economicos/21/ree-21-castillo-perez-tuesta.pdf

Cermeño, R., Villagómez, A., & Orellana, J. (2012). Monetary policy rules in a small open economy: An application to Mexico. *Journal of Applied Economics, 15*(2), 259–286. https://doi.org/10.1016/S1514-0326(12)60012-9

Clarida, R., Galí, J., & Gertler, M. (1999). The science of Monetary Policy: A new Keynesian perspective. *Journal of Economic Literature, 37*(4), 1661–1707. https://doi.org/10.1257/jel.37.4.1661

De Gregorio, J. (2007). *Macroeconomía* (M. F. Castillo (ed.); Primera). Pearson Educación de Mexico, S.A.

Galí, J. (2009). The new Keynesian approach to monetary policy analysis: Lessons and new directions. *Journal of Monetary Economics*. https://doi.org/10.1007/978-3-642-02953-0_2

Galí, J., & Gertler, M. (2007). Macroeconomic modeling for monetary policy evaluation. *Journal of Monetary Economics, 44*, 195–222. 10.3386.

García, C., & Gonzales, W. (2007). Efectividad de la política monetaria en alguna economias latinoamericanas. *Research Papers in Economics*, 1–59. https://www.researchgate.net/publication/5115559_Efectividad_de_la_politica_monetaria_en_algunas_economias_latinoamericanas

Gomez, M. (2013). Análisis del ciclo económico en una economía con rigideces nominales y un amplio sector informal. *ELSERVIER, 31*(72), 51–66. https://doi.org/10.1016/S0120-4483(13)70004-6

Hoyle, D. (2002). *Reglas monetarias para economías parcialmente dolarizadas: Evidencia para el casi peruano* (No. 03–2001). https://www.bcrp.gob.pe/docs/Publicaciones/Documentos-de-Trabajo/2001/Documento-Trabajo-03-2001.pdf

Jaramillo, M., & Serván, S. (2011). Modelando la dinámica del tipo de cambio en el Perú: un enfoque de cointegración usando la PPP y UIP. *Superintendencia de Banca y Seguros*, 1–58. https://www.sbs.gob.pe/Portals/0/jer/rebper_2012_vol_vi/20150908_Jaramillo-Serván.pdf

Melgarejo, K. (2006). *Efectos de la adopción del esquema de metas explícitas de inflación en el Perú (2002–2006)*. https://www.bcrp.gob.pe/docs/Proyeccion-Institucional/Seminarios/Conferencia-12-2006/Paper_0612_10-Melgarejo.pdf

Rivas, P. (2016). Vista de La teoría del ciclo monetario ... los ciclos económicos.pdf. *Pensamiento Crítico, 21*, 83–92. https://doi.org/10.15381/pc.v21i1.12638

Rodríguez, P. T., & Kon, A. C. (1998). Términos de Intercambio y Ciclos Económicos: 1950–1998. *Estudios Económicos, 6*(January 2000), 10. http://www.bcrp.gob.pe/docs/Publicaciones/Revista-Estudios-Economicos/06/Estudios-Economicos-6-8.pdf

Rodríguez, G., Castillo, P., & Hasegawa, H. (2021). *Departamento de economía*. https://doi.org/10.18800/2079-8474.0504

Salas, J. (2011). Estimación bayesiana de un modelo de pequeña economía abierta con dolarización parcial. *Revista Estudios Economicos, 62*(22), 41–62. www.bcrp.gob.pe/publicaciones/revista-estudios-economicos/estudios-economicos-no-22.html

Vega, H. (2019). *Perú. ¿ Qué hará el Banco Central con su tasa de política en los próximos meses ?* (pp. 1–9). BBVA Research. https://www.bbvaresearch.com/wp-content/uploads/2019/04/Observatorio-Regla-Taylor-Peru-2019-2.pdf

Winkelried, D. (2013). Modelo de Proyección Trimestral del BCRP: Actualización y Novedades. *Revista Estudios Económicos, 26*(26), 9–60.

Woodford, M. (2003). Inflation targeting and optimal monetary policy. *Annual Economic Policy Conference, 53*. http://www.columbia.edu/~mw2230/StLFed.pdf

Chapter 56
Importance of Business Digitization: The Case of the Region of Western Macedonia, Greece

Ioannis Metsios, Vaggelis Saprikis, and Ioannis Antoniadis

Abstract The twenty-first century is an era of technological evolution, with the use of new data to demonstrate the significant increase in the use of electronic media, social media, and new technologies, as well as digital tools that these novel technologies have developed. These new technological tools offer many opportunities for businesses, making them consider their digital transformation, digitalization, and digital marketing to be extremely important. Therefore, the use of technologies and new production techniques is important to achieve interconnection and communication with clients and other business partners. Digitalization can be made possible through the use of various technologies, which will enable the digital transformation of businesses.

This research chapter focuses on investigating digitization in the four prefectures of Western Macedonia, Greece, with the aim of examining whether the business' digital development is related to the number of years of operation and the digital skills and digital literacy of the owner or the marketing executive of that business. The secondary purposes are to investigate whether the Greek SMEs can easily implement various digital marketing strategies and have achieved good levels of digital growth and whether digital literacy and knowledge depend on the region where the enterprise is located or on the place of origin of the owner of the enterprise.

Keywords Business digitization · Digital transformation · Digital marketing · Internet of Things · Viral marketing · Social media · Digital strategy

---

I. Metsios (✉) · V. Saprikis · I. Antoniadis
Department of Management Science and Technology, School of Economic Sciences, University of Western Macedonia, Koila, Kozani, Greece

© The Author(s), under exclusive license to Springer Nature Switzerland AG 2024
N. Tsounis, A. Vlachvei (eds.), *Applied Economic Research and Trends*, Springer Proceedings in Business and Economics,
https://doi.org/10.1007/978-3-031-49105-4_56

56.1 Introduction

The digital age, also known as the fourth industrial revolution, makes it clear that digital transformation dominates all public and private sectors. This makes the use of technologies and new techniques an extremely important digital strategy so that businesses can achieve interconnection and communication with their clients, as well as other businesses. Digitalization can be made possible through the use of various technologies such as the Internet of Things (IoT), Artificial Intelligence (AI), Big Data, virtual reality, and many others, which can lead to businesses' digital transformation, which is an extremely complex and demanding process. This requires the utilization of human resources as well as the correct use of technological advances and processes, as well as necessary actions (Cenamor et al., 2019).

Digital transformation has, therefore, become a reality and necessity in our times due to the health crisis of COVID-19 and the extremely difficult conditions it has brought about in the creation and operation of businesses since it has necessitated the use and exploitation of digital marketing more than it had before (Koronaki et al., 2023). Digital transformation has managed to offer a competitive advantage to a couple of businesses, as it has reshaped the way their functions and processes are used. Moreover, businesses that invested more in ICT, specifically the use of internet and managed to enter the new digitized era remain competitive and survive in the challenging business world (Hitpass & Astudillo, 2019).

56.2 Literature Review

56.2.1 Digitization Challenges

Digitalization is a test for traditional business models and provokes a challenge in adapting to new market realities, as it implies taking new risks. However, behind these risks a business takes, it must be considered that risk-taking is a necessary process for the firm to survive, but at the same time, within these risks, new opportunities arise for the business to maximize its profits. For example, the emergence of COVID-19 has forced local businesses to interconnect work structures between remote regions. Therefore, business operations can change radically as traditional hierarchical work structures are often transformed. The new forms that a business can adopt involve working from home, known as "telecommuting," or working in different locations. These new work structures do not set limits to business activity, but maybe it is the beginning of new opportunities for collaboration between firms and has the direct effect of reducing costs and commitment for firms, significantly increasing their productivity and profit at the same time (Shafer et al., 2005; Antoniadis et al., 2015).

Baden-Fuller and Morgan (2010) consider equally important the fact that digitization dramatically reduces both the transaction costs between firms and also between businesses and customers, and the costs concerning the collection of information, the control processes, and communication between different firms. This happens because businesses manage through technological means to gain direct access to a vast field of information the so-called Big Data, through which they are able to analyze the online behavior of their customers and manage to tailor their advertising and marketing habits based on personalized preferences, thereby increasing the demand for their products and reducing the costs. Digitalization also provides firms with the opportunity to diversify their portfolios in terms of production, as it allows them to move their production processes to economies that are emerging and where costs are lower, while still struggling to develop the best design to achieve user and customer contact (Teece, 2010).

Business models can determine not only how a firm's revenue is earned, but also how the firm's organization is structured. Therefore, it widens the gap between a firm's strategy and how it operates. Meanwhile, business models describe ways of creating value for a firm's customers and may generate revenue for the firm itself. Therefore, the business operating model is the way in which each firm conducts its business (Berman & Bell, 2011). As stated above, digitalization offers businesses the opportunity to alternate their production processes to economies that are emerging and where costs are lower while continuing to struggle to develop the best strategic plan for user and customer contact. On the contrary, the company does not need to spend too much money but can develop a service purchasing model only when necessary. It can implement outsourcing models that are outsourced and have to do with all types of processes that are not related to the core business of the company, which can only be made possible through digital models.

Undoubtedly, the "sharing economy" is based on the phenomenon of sharing human and natural resources, including the sharing of creation, production, and distribution, as well as trade and consumption of goods and services, carried out by different enterprises. Digital media is characterized by the development of the Internet and a large number of social platforms through which goods and services are shared. The main advantage of these models is the creation of beneficial situations for all parties, while an advantage is that every customer can access goods and services and the company can use its previously unused resources in the most efficient way (Verhoef et al., 2021).

As Reis et al. (2018) pointed out, another characteristic of the modern digital age is the fact that every product is treated and can be offered in the form of a service. In this case, the consumer does not own the product by paying a certain price but has the possibility of using the product whenever he or she wants by paying a monthly subscription. With the development of digital technology, the promotion of this type of business model has been observed to a large extent. The millennial generation has played a significant role in the adoption of this model because of its modern lifestyle.

56.2.2 Changes in the Supply Chain

Undoubtedly, due to globalization, there have been changes in customer demands and the development of information technology; therefore, it is undeniable that changes have occurred in the way businesses operate. In particular, there are huge differences in terms of the supply chain, as new technologies completely overturn the data on which the supply chain is based, resulting in the creation of digital technologies that are described as "Supply Chain 4.0" (Ghobakhloo, 2020). Supply chain 4.0 has the following characteristics, with the first and most distinctive feature being the speed of order fulfillment, particularly concerning speed codes. This means that orders are instantly fulfilled in a few hours or even in a day and based on it, new demand forecasting models such as the model called "Demand sensing" (Bursa, 2008) play an important role.

Unlike earlier times, when business sales forecasting is performed once a month and the accuracy is extremely low, models can now gather and process large amounts of data. These data include market trends, promotions being carried out, weather conditions, place of residence, and so on. Thus, businesses can be driven to produce sales forecasts, which will be updated either every day or weekly, two or three times, and its accuracy will be extremely high. Through these models, which work extremely effectively, it is made possible for the more developed businesses to be able to make it possible for them to adopt strategic shipments that are made earlier, which means that the shipment is made first and then the match is made with the specific order (Byrne, 2012). It is noteworthy that there is also greater efficiency in the supply chain if we consider that many actions that take place within the supply chain can now be performed digitally and automatically. In particular, it is possible to have digital means nowadays, which also control the warehouses where the products are present, gathering the order, leading to the minimization of errors that can occur, while simultaneously extending the opening hours of the stores, thus offering significant benefits to businesses. Thus, not only can the store operate for more hours but it also provides business with the ability to sharply reduce its operating costs through improvements made in the supply chain, warehouse network, transportation planning, etc. (Lu, 2017; Saprikis & Vlachopoulou, 2012).

Another important issue is that lost sales can be significantly reduced compared with the current situation. This is because the inventory mix can be continuously improved by limiting the inventory amount. This can greatly help the company reduce working capital, which is an extremely important objective of its operation. Another characteristic of Supply Chain 4.0 is the fact that it is characterized by agility, which is the major requirement of the modern era; until recently, companies' objective was to create large factories that could produce extremely large quantities of products, which would have the same characteristics in response to market demands during the seasons we are living through. This is the so-called "agility" property, but it is now seen more as a disadvantage than an advantage since modern-day customers, whether individuals or businesses, demand more, faster, and as personalized as possible products/services.

The adoption of Industry 4.0 principles has become crucial for businesses striving for excellence. However, implementing the concept poses significant challenges, especially for small and medium-sized enterprises (SMEs). These industries face the greatest difficulties and barriers in adopting modern technologies and methods. The introduction of innovative technologies requires a complex set of procedures, which is a weak point for SMEs lacking established models to assess their technological position. In Industry 4.0, effective business management relies on monitoring and analyzing collected data. Smart manufacturing encompasses elements such as processes, human–machine interactions, and the transition from paper-based to digital data. The main focus is on establishing digital connectivity among humans, objects, and the entire production process. Cyber-physical systems, represented by the Internet of Things, are the primary technologies in Industry 4.0. However, generating the necessary digital data for company management presents significant challenges in terms of strategy assessment, modern machinery, and process monitoring. Rauch et al. offer a model that provides SMEs with a clear understanding of Industry 4.0 concepts, helping them define their individual strategies for implementation. Liu et al. consider strategies for implementing Industry 4.0 in SMEs based on cost control and investment effects, considering factors like human capital investment and R&D investment. On the other hand, the implications of Industry 4.0 for business models should be examined using the Business Model Canvas. Key resources and value propositions are highly affected, while channels are least impacted (Klimecka-Tatar & Ingaldi, 2022).

56.2.3 Changes in Marketing

The biggest change in the sales marketing function has been the huge volume of data, which makes it extremely difficult to process. However, it is becoming possible through technology to obtain real-time data on consumer behavior. In addition, it is now a fact that firms can use tools through which they can discover, explain, and create specific patterns of consumer behavior with these data, possibly coming from the digital footprint that the consumer has and from IoT applications (Shafique et al., 2020). When specific patterns are applied, which are the result of historical data through the presence of new data, companies can predict the outcome of specific marketing actions and thus determine the potential amount of their sales. This is described by the term "predictive" marketing, which refers to marketing prediction that transforms the way businesses operate concerning the consumer audience and characteristics. Now, the focus of businesses is shifting from products and sales channels to consumers, and through various techniques, they manage to develop strategies to increase the consumer base and maintain it for as long as possible. This occurs in cases where instead of seeking customers who demonstrate a desire for a firm's products, the firm can develop products that customers may seek in the future. This process also involves anticipation of the term. Thus firms, in order to be able to increase their profitability, seek ways through which they can increase the percentage of potential customers, aiming to retain existing and potential customers for a longer period. Another important aspect that firms are trying to achieve is communication relevance performance rather than just communication (Stone et al., 2020). In conclusion, the development of digital technologies has helped businesses develop what is called "digital marketing" and, in extension, has a strong presence in areas related to social media marketing.

The COVID-19 pandemic has compelled companies, institutions, schools, and organizations from both the public and private sectors to swiftly embrace more agile and adaptable forms of digital transformation in various areas. This includes sectors such as telecommunications, on-demand food and services, virtual events, and cloud utilization. As many physical jobs shifted to remote work arrangements to prevent complete isolation, telecommunication applications have become a significant solution. It is increasingly evident that any business unable to modify its methods of delivering products and services may face severe restrictions. The events industry is reallocating budgets toward digital events and digital content. In the recent past, people used to share photos and events on social media, but now they share photos of their online meetings and enjoyable experiences from teams adapting to this new way of working. The cloud has provided the ability to securely share and collaborate on documents, access real-time analytics, and more. During the quarantine period, technology has become a necessity, and individuals or groups rely on the technological elements that work well for them. However, while many companies acknowledge the importance of digitalization, they often feel overwhelmed by the prospect of completely overhauling their digital approach and struggle with implementing the necessary transformation. At the same time, they are acutely aware that by taking no action, they run the risk of being disrupted and replaced by more digitally savvy competitors (Staboulis & Lazaridou, 2020b).

56.2.4 Digital Marketing

"Viral marketing" is a form of digital marketing that relies on the transmission of information and messages through various online websites. This dissemination is conducted by users on different websites or apps. This technique belongs to the forms of electronic digital marketing and is called "viral" marketing and has become particularly widespread in large enterprises in modern times. It is an extremely important tool to increase the promotion of products and services because companies are able to broadcast information about their products and services in a short period of time while spreading their brand name and logo to a wide number of consumers (Leskovec et al., 2007).

"Viral" marketing is a highly effective method of digital marketing that does not require a large monetary budget, by making the consumer audience the "carriers" that transmit the messages, the firm wants to share with other consumer receivers.

Thus, through messages that go viral, potential consumers come into contact with the business, specifically with the services and products it provides on a large scale. Therefore, "viral" marketing promotes business advertising with minimal effort and money. This is made possible because it is the customers themselves who transmit their experience and their criticism of the various products to their social environment and their friends, mentioning the good service and the products they have bought, transmitting positive messages that the company wishes to transmit, the well-known way of transmission by "word of mouth" (De Bruyn & Lilien, 2008; Saprikis, 2013).

"Search engine marketing," which refers to marketing through search engines, is another widespread type of digital marketing, since people nowadays are using the internet daily, searching, and receiving information on topics and issues of interest to them. The knowledge and information available on various websites are a very important part of the information received by each recipient of the messages through digital media (Vlahvei et al., 2013). Thus, users and consumers can gather an infinite amount of information through search engines, which are specific web pages that allow users to search for information that they want by sorting the web pages in order of appearance and with results that facilitate the search for information (Boughton, 2005). Therefore, search engines sort the information by listing a series of different web pages to the user, which are related to their search object, and by matching the data that the user has put in the search.

A widespread marketing technique is "mobile marketing," which is also a type of digital marketing. Its use is made possible through mobile devices, providing businesses with the possibility of communicating with users who use these mobile devices, that is, the majority of the consumer audience, achieving active and intense interaction with them. Marketing through mobile devices includes actions and activities that can add value to the products and services of businesses, helping to promote and ensure the creation of close and quality relationships between a business and potential customers using mobile devices. This type of marketing technique has seen significant development in recent times, and, in fact, many companies have placed their progress and development on this method since marketing through mobile devices enables customers to be informed directly and in a timely manner regarding products, services, and any other issue of interest (Leppäniemi et al., 2006).

Social network marketing uses social media, meaning digital media that take advantage of the growth of the Internet, facilitating the exchange of information and content and thus ensuring communication among users (Antoniadis et al., 2019). In essence, that is, social media form digital communication networks by encouraging users to exchange content and information and in this way communicate better through digital platforms, suc as Facebook, WhatsApp, Instagram, Twitter, and TikTok (Evans et al., 2021).

56.3 Research Methodology

Owners of micro and small businesses must have a guide on how to integrate digitalization, digital transformation, and digital marketing to promote their products or services. Practitioners and researchers working in this area should first focus on providing SME owners with the necessary background, allowing them to understand their importance, and then offer insights and views on how to take advantage of the potential of online media by creating a strategic approach. More specifically, digital marketing and digitalization, with all its channels and strategies, can be integrated into the owner's skills and capabilities for holistic business performance.

Although Western Macedonia is considered a region where people live by high standards, the economic crisis that erupted globally in 2008 and has deeply affected Greece since 2010 forced many SMEs to close and many others to undergo significant organizational and structural changes. Given that SMEs, that is, those employing fewer than 250 employees, constitute almost all enterprises in Greece at 99.93% (EKT, 2018), this has significantly impacted the economy, leading to a major increase in unemployment. Currently, the vast majority of the remaining SMEs are in the time being trying to survive because of the delignification process, which is an important issue in the municipality of Kozani because the region is highly dependent on the mining and use of lignite for energy production. However, delignification is required to meet EU targets to reduce greenhouse gas emissions and achieve sustainable development. The Greek government is committed to phasing out lignite use by 2028 and has accelerated the transition to renewable energy sources. In Kozani, HELPE (Hellenic Petroleum S.A.) has already started the process of delignification to reduce emissions and improve the quality of life in the area. Delignification requires a number of changes in the way energy is produced and in the economy of the region. However, the transition to renewable energy can create new employment and growth opportunities in the region.

Therefore, owing to the new perspectives, research on the adaptation of digital strategies is crucial in the area, with the following research questions and research hypotheses.

56.3.1 Aim and Research Questions

1. At what level have SMEs in Greece, especially in Western Macedonia, adopted digital strategies?
2. What are the main challenges these SMEs face in their transition to the digital era?

56.3.2 Research Cases

Certain characteristics distinguish small and medium enterprises from larger ones. The owners of SMEs are mostly managers, and the firm's success and growth are greatly influenced by the owner's characteristics, knowledge, and skills. Thus, the skills and knowledge of the owners are likely to affect SMEs to a greater extent, as most SME owners are also their managers; thus, all tasks are coordinated and often performed by the owner.

Lack of visibility is also the reason SMEs do not have the same customer approach as larger businesses. Due to a lack of time and financial resources, owners consider new types of advertising ineffective, relying mainly on word-of-mouth. In addition, without data and data analysis capabilities, they face challenges in identifying market opportunities. Thus, we hypothesized that if the business owner-manager is at a good level in terms of digital skills, this will lead to business growth and, hence, better performance (Ingaldi & Klimecka-Tatar, 2022; OECD, 2020; Staboulis & Lazaridou, 2020a, b; Andreou, 2020).

56.3.3 Research Hypotheses

The needs of the Western Macedonia region are as follows:

First Research Hypothesis
Each business' digital development is related to (a) the number of years of operation, (b) the year in which the business was launched, and (c) the digital skills and digital literacy of the owner or the marketing executive of that business (Ingaldi & Klimecka-Tatar, 2022; OECD, 2020; Staboulis & Lazaridou, 2020a, b; Andreou, 2020).

Second Research Hypothesis
Greek SMEs can easily implement various digital marketing strategies and have achieved good levels of digital growth (Staboulis & Lazaridou, 2020a, b; Andreou, 2020).

Third Research Hypothesis
Digital literacy and knowledge about (a) the available digitization solutions, (b) the processes of their installation and implementation, and (c) the potential benefits of their implementation in SMEs of Western Macedonia do not depend on the region where the enterprise is located or on the place of origin of the owner of the enterprise (Ingaldi & Klimecka-Tatar, 2022).

According to Veal (2006), there are two crucial research methods that can be applied to an abductive survey: the first is the quantitative approach, where the analysis is based on a large unbiased sample, and the second is the qualitative approach, which is based on a smaller sample but uses more descriptive data.

In the first stage, with the literature review as secondary data, the condition for primary quantitative data was met in the second stage. His research was based on an extensive literature review.

According to McMillan and Weyers (2011), questionnaires are considered more applicable when the sample is widely dispersed (as it allows the possibility to be sent via e-mail or social media) and in cases where data collection is sensitive (the questionnaire is anonymous and encourages honesty; therefore, it is more reliable). The questionnaire was then created to collect a sufficient amount of primary data and accurately review the progress of digitization in Western Macedonia. In addition, a questionnaire was created to identify the digital strategies that Greek SMEs should consider. Due to the author's motivation to collect data on the level of digitization of SMEs, it was decided that the sample of the survey would be micro, small, and medium enterprises.

56.3.4 Research Sample

The questionnaire[1] was distributed to people involved in the digital marketing of the company or the head of the digital marketing department. Noted in the subject as well as in the introductory text of the email that was sent with the questionnaire was the specification that the person who should answer the questionnaire is the person who is involved in the digital marketing of the company.

The questionnaires were sent to 200 individuals, and respondents were given 10 days to complete and return the questionnaire. When the period ended, a reminder was sent. The completed questionnaires that were returned provided 126 valid questionnaires because all the questions were declared mandatory in Google Drive Forms. The research was conducted from 25/08 to 03/09/2022.

56.4 Empirical Results

Regarding the headquarters of the company, 47 of the companies were placed in Kozani, 23 in Kastoria, 28 in Grevena, and also 28 in the region of Florina. Therefore, the sample's majority operates in the biggest city of Western Macedonia (Kozani) (see Fig. 56.1).

When examining the launching year of the 126 SMEs that participated in the survey, we observe that 78 were established in the 12-year period 1998–2010, 26 in the 12-year period 1986–1997, 21 in the 12-year period 2011–2022, and, finally, only 1 was established between 1960 and 1972 (see Fig. 56.2).

---

[1] https://docs.google.com/forms/d/e/1FAIpQLScnIsQB9F0_ZFb9Bw5KhselsxOSwrp-0B2z8N3Yz27Jhcel1g/viewform?usp=sf_link

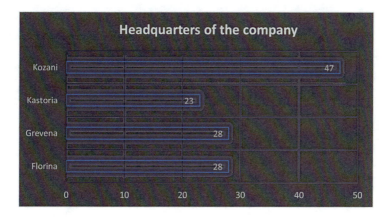

Fig. 56.1 Headquarters of the company

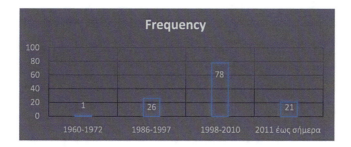

Fig. 56.2 Number of years of operation—business' launching year

Concerning the company's attitude and perception toward digital marketing, the majority (38 businesses, 30%) think that digital marketing strategies are very important, while 36 (28%) think that it is important to adopt digital marketing strategies. Twenty companies (16%) think digital marketing strategies play a crucial role in the company's well-being, and only 17 companies (13%) expressed no opinion on the matter. A minority of 15 companies (12%) believed that digital marketing strategies do not concern their businesses (see Fig. 56.3).

Concerning the use of digital tools to enhance a company's digital presence, the majority of the companies have occupied an expert to do it, and 42 of them (33.3%) expressed their lack of knowledge regarding the ways to do it. Of a vast number of companies, 25 (19.9%) do not use digital tools and only eight (a percentage lower than 1%) answered "yes" to the use of tools to enhance their digital presence (see Fig. 56.4).

The majority of the companies that participated in the study have a digital marketing plan (33 companies, 26.19%) or are in the process or thinking of making one (16 companies, 17%), which shows the importance that the companies place on the use of a digital marketing plan. Thirty-two of them (25%) were not persuaded of the importance of digital marketing plans, and 22 of them (17.5%) thought it was unimportant (see Fig. 56.5).

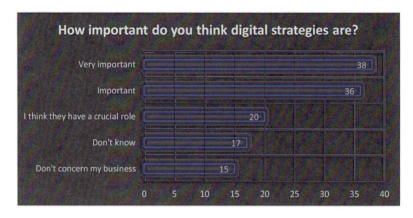

Fig. 56.3 Company's attitude and perception toward digital marketing

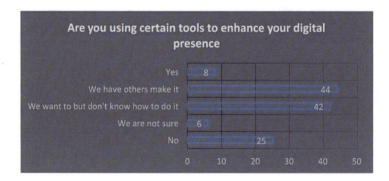

Fig. 56.4 Use of digital skills and digital marketing strategies

Fig. 56.5 Digital marketing plan application

Table 56.1 Descriptive statistics

Descriptive Statistics – Are you familiar with digitalization solutions in business	N	Mean	Std. Dev.
C1 Horizontal integration (HI) / Vertical integration (VI)	126	1,54	,797
C2 Big Data Analytics (BDA)	126	1,86	1,018
C3 Chatbots	126	1,91	1,073
C4 Network infrastructure development	126	1,63	,944
C5 Cloud Computing	126	2,13	1,117
C6 Use of AI	126	1,59	,822
C7 Use of the Internet	126	3,17	1,276
C8 Access to digital services	126	2,62	1,301
C9 Integration of digital technologies	126	2,09	1,207
C10 Touchpad	126	1,62	,818
C11 Voice control	126	1,58	,842
C12 Customize the interface	126	1,56	,908
C13 Internet of things	126	1,54	,855
C14 Multichannel	126	1,44	,825
C15 Cyber-security	126	1,75	,987
C16 Simulation	126	1,63	,865
C17 Social e-mobile	126	2,45	1,401
C18 AR/VR	126	1,56	,796
C19 AGV	126	1,42	,719

56.4.1 Digitization Solutions, Implementation, and Their Benefits

When the companies were asked whether they were aware of digitization solutions that they could implement in their businesses, it was observed that the ratings, and therefore the level of knowledge of individual digitization solutions, are very different. Some solutions are known for medium 3, high 4, and very high 5 values. In Table 56.1, the descriptive statistics are distinguished by the number of responses of the sample "N," the means "m," and the standard deviation "p."

For all 19 questions from Table 56.1, the average of the mean values computed for each question equals 1.84 with an average of standard deviation $p = 0.977$, which means that the 126 business respondents tend to have little knowledge about the digitization solutions that emerged from the literature review.

The companies could select their level of digital literacy on a Likert-type scale (from "not at all" to "very well"). Their responses showed that the companies sampled seem to be aware of specific solutions ("access to digital services," "use of internet," and "Cloud Computing") as they were the only cases that the majority of the sample selected the replies "good enough," "much," and "very much." Specifically, in the case of "use of the Internet," 26% said that they had adequate knowledge, 35% that they knew this solution well, and 13% that they knew very well about the use of the Internet. Similar percentages were found for the cases of "access to digital services" and "social e-mobile," as can be seen in Fig. 56.6.

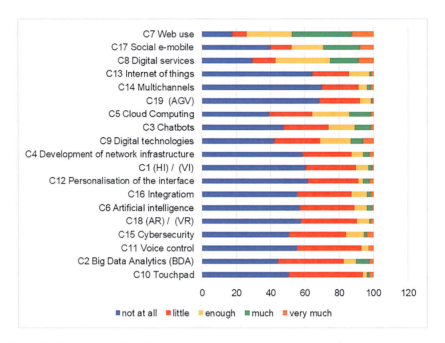

Fig. 56.6 Knowledge of digitalization solutions

Respondents reported that they have no knowledge about "Omnichannel" (multichannel enterprise execution) at a percentage of 70%, "autonomous guided vehicles" (AGV) at 68%, "Internet of Things" at 64%, "interface personalization" at 62%, "horizontal integration" and "vertical integration" at 60%, "network infrastructure deployment" at 59%, "augmented reality" (AR)/virtual reality (VR) at 58%, "artificial intelligence" at 57%, "voice control" at 56%, "simulation" at 56%, "cyber security," and "touchpad" at 51% (see Fig. 56.6).

The companies answered that they have "Little knowledge and information" about "Touchpad" at a percentage of 43%, "Big Data Analytics" at 38%, "Voice Control" at 37%, "Cybersecurity" and "Augmented Reality" (AR)/Virtual Reality (VR) at 33%, and the use of "AI and Simulation" at 32% (see Fig. 56.6), which means that businesses know that such solutions exist, but they do not know too much about them. In the case of these solutions, knowledge is slightly higher, but still low overall, but it should be taken into consideration that the survey was conducted among small- and medium-sized enterprises. Often, such companies, for various reasons, do not seek knowledge about the latest digitization solutions due to difficulties in implementing them or the high cost of their budget.

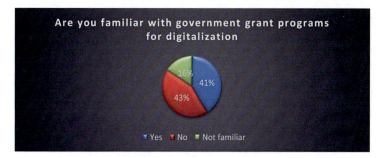

Fig. 56.7 Familiarity with government grant programs

56.4.2 Digital Transformation Actions for SMEs

Greece promotes the digital transformation of its companies by enhancing their abilities to do so, thereby offering grant programs for the digitalization of the country's companies. However, most of the companies, at a percentage of 43% aren't familiar with the government's grant programs and 16% are not familiar with the process of applying for a grant program. Only 41% are quite familiar with those governmental programs and have expressed concern for grant programs (Fig. 56.7).

First Research Hypothesis Examination

The first research hypothesis is:

H0: *Each business' digital development is related to (a) the number of years of operation, (b) the year in which the business was launched, and (c) the digital skills and digital literacy of the owner or the marketing executive of that business.*

To investigate the above hypothesis, the chi-squared statistical test of one variable of the year of commencement of operations against the correlation variables was used in order to be able to generalize the results from the sample level. The frequencies that we would theoretically expect the population to exhibit in order for the alternative hypothesis not to be true are those of a uniform distribution. The confidence level for the test is 0.05 (5%) (see Table 56.2).

Table 56.2 shows the results of the chi-squared statistical test. It becomes obvious that for the test of the relationship between the year of the start of operations of enterprises in Western Macedonia and the level of digital development of the enterprise, we can reject the null hypothesis and say that there is no significant correlation overall, but in three cases there is a statistically significant effect. The aim of the research hypothesis was to test whether the year in which the company started its activities had an effect on the philosophy that very old businesses may not adopt new digital marketing strategies and may not have gone digital yet. However, this was not the case, according to the results. However, there were three cases out of nine where there seems to be a statistically significant difference between the year

Table 56.2 Chi-square tests

Chi-Square Tests			
	Value	df	Asymptotic Significance (2-sided)
B3 How effective do you think your business's digital marketing activities are overall?	21,100[a]	12	0,049
B6 How do you approach digital marketing?	16,341[a]	12	0,176
B7 Do you use tools to track your digital activity?	17,182[a]	15	0,308
B8 How often do you study analytics tool reports?	14,160[a]	12	0,291
B10 How do you manage your website?	18,791[a]	12	0,094
B11 You believe that the articles on the know-how and trends prevailing in the market of your products	22,245[a]	12	0,035
B12 Are you implementing a content strategy?	23,402[a]	12	0,024
B13 Checking your website's Google ranking?	15,670[a]	12	0,207
B14 How are you leveraging social media in your business growth plan?	13,035[a]	12	0,366

[a]Statistically different from zero are 5% level of statistical significance

Fig. 56.8 Implementation of content strategy

of the start of operations and the opinions on "How effective do you consider your company's digital marketing activities overall," what "Do you think articles about expertise and trends in your product market," and finally if "Do you implement a content strategy?" (Fig. 56.8).

As far as the implementation of content strategy, 34% of the companies are not familiar with the term, 2% know its importance but are not familiar with the term, while 34% believe in its importance but they haven't implemented it yet. A major percentage of 18% try to use a content strategy and a percentage of 12% give a lot of credit to keywords and the use of the content strategy.

The second part of the hypothesis is whether the business level of the company's digital growth is largely determined by the digital skills and knowledge of the owner or marketing manager. From the responses and descriptive statistics (see Tables 56.1

Table 56.3 Descriptive statistics of the answers to the questions related to the second research hypothesis

Statistics	B4	B5	B6	B9	B12	B14	B16	B17	B18	M.O
N	126	126	126	126	126	126	126	126	126	
Mean	3,05	3,14	2,73	3,82	2,72	3,51	3,63	3,30	2,66	3,17
Std.Dev.	1,46	1,42	1,29	1,52	1,41	1,39	1,32	1,26	1,59	1,41
Range	4	4	4	4	4	4	4	4	4	
Min	1	1	1	1	1	1	1	1	1	
Max	5	5	5	5	5	5	5	5	5	
Sum	384	396	344	481	343	442	458	416	335	400

and 56.2, and Fig. 56.6), it is clear that business owners do not know indepth the importance of digital presence and have not yet developed the necessary digital skills.

The results are consistent with research and studies such as those by SEV (2020), OECD (2020), and Staboulis and Lazaridou (2020a, b), which describe how digital skills are related to business, their importance, and the level of digital presence of SMEs in Europe and Greece.

Second Research Hypothesis Examination
The second research hypothesis is:

H0: *Greek SMEs can easily implement various digital marketing strategies and have achieved good levels of digital growth.*

Table 56.3 shows the statistics of the group of questions in research hypothesis 2. It can be seen that the mean value is $\mu = 3.17$ with standard deviation $\sigma = 1.41$ and corresponds in most of the questions to an answer like: "*We are in thought to start implementing as it would be useful, but we do not have resources*" or "*We recognize their value but maybe later.*" These statistics show that the second research hypothesis cannot be verified and is, thus, rejected. Therefore, with relative certainty, we can say that digital marketing strategies are not so easily applicable in Greek SMEs and have not yet reached a good level of development.

Third Research Hypothesis Examination
The third research hypothesis is:

H0: *Digital literacy and knowledge about (a) the available digitization solutions, (b) the processes of their installation and implementation, and (c) the potential benefits of their implementation in SMEs of Western Macedonia do not depend on the region where the enterprise is located or on the place of origin of the owner of the enterprise.*

We applied a nonparametric test with k independent samples with the Kruskal–Wallis test criterion and with a control variable list of questions C1–C19 digitization

Table 56.4 Kruskal–Wallis test results

	C1	C2	C3	C4	C5	C6	C7	C8	C9	C10
Kruskal-Wallis H	2,136	0,504	0,383	1,87	4,737	2,193	3,595	1,458	0,488	0,758
p	0,545	0,918	0,944	0,6	0,192	0,533	0,309	0,692	0,922	0,859
	C11	C12	C13	C14	C15	C16	C17	C18	C19	D1
Kruskal-Wallis H	1,922	1,588	19,801	4,684	6,26	5,3	2,711	0,87	3,111	1,095
p	0,589	0,662	0	0,196	0,1	0,151	0,438	0,833	0,375	0,778
	D2	D3	D4	D5	D6	D7	D8	D9	D10	D11
Kruskal-Wallis H	2,777	1,735	1,587	1,359	6,286	2,85	1,698	2,232	0,743	1,459
p	0,427	0,629	0,662	0,715	0,099	0,415	0,637	0,526	0,863	0,692
	D12	D13	D14	D15	D16	D17	D18	D19	E1	E2
Kruskal-Wallis H	1,381	2,184	1,088	1,673	3,356	1,573	0,165	0,211	3,247	2,428
p	0,71	0,535	0,78	0,643	0,34	0,666	0,983	0,976	0,355	0,488
	E3	E4	E5	E6	E7	E8	E9	E10	E11	E12
Kruskal-Wallis H	0,537	1,653	2,978	2,69	6,137	7,324	7,606	2,805	1,727	4,429
p	0,911	0,647	0,395	0,442	0,105	0,062	0,055	0,423	0,631	0,219
	E13	E14	E15	E16	E17	E18	E19	E20		
Kruskal-Wallis H	2,877	5,825	7,072	6,634	5,784	5,632	4,262	8,203		
p	0,411	0,12	0,07	0,085	0,123	0,131	0,234	0,042		

solutions, D1–D19 degree of implementation of digitization solutions, and E1–E20 advantages of digitization solutions with the prefecture of origin of the company as a clustering variable with values (1) Kozani prefecture, (2) Kastoria prefecture, (3) Florina prefecture, and (4) Grevena prefecture (see Table 56.4).

We note that $p > 0.05$ is valid for most variables. Therefore, at the significance level $p = 0.05$, there are no statistically significant differences between the county of origin and the knowledge of digitization solutions by companies except for one variable C13—the Internet of Things and we can say that there are statistically significant differences between counties and digitization solutions. In the implementation of digitization solutions, there are no statistically significant differences between the county of origin and the implementation of digitization solutions as well as in the 19 variables $p > 0.05$. In the opinion on the advantages offered by digitization solutions at a 5% level of significance, there seem to be statistically significant differences in two variables E9 and E20.

Therefore, the null hypothesis can be confirmed.

56.5 Conclusions

Very old companies seem to be adopting new digital marketing strategies at a level and have partially gone digital yet, as business owners seem to comprehend the importance of digital presence in depth and have not developed the necessary digital skills. Digital marketing strategies are not easily applicable to Greek SMEs, and they have not yet reached a good level of development. This conclusion is consistent with studies in Greece and Cyprus, which show that digital marketing strategies are not easily applicable to SMEs and have not yet reached a good level of digitalization (Andreou, 2020; Semedeferis, 2022). The county of origin does not affect knowledge about digitization solutions, their implementation process, or the advantages they offer to SMEs in Western Macedonia. Overall, there appears to be a low level of knowledge among enterprises in Western Macedonia regarding digitization-related solutions. It was shown that many of the solutions are known to some extent, but the level of implementation of many of them is very low, which means that they may not meet market requirements, especially when it comes to digitization.

The results of our descriptive statistics show that digitization in SMEs in the region of Western Macedonia, Greece, is at a low rate and the main barriers to nonadoption are not only the few skills and knowledge of their owners, but also the continuous technological development, the economic crisis, and the health crisis. It is a fact that our society has just crossed the threshold of digital transformation, and in this direction, SMEs in Greece and especially in Western Macedonia are still struggling to grow, but many are also struggling to survive. What is remarkable and confirmed by this research is that small business owners are not fully or sufficiently familiar with the advantages of digital marketing and other ICT solutions, as well as the importance of its strategy.

In line with Sin and Dimitrova (2018), businesses, due to limited resources and capabilities, are often driven by unsuccessful digitalization efforts. It is emphasized that to overcome significant barriers and benefits from digital platforms, it is necessary to understand the impact on the performance of digital strategies, which are the best channels to use according to market characteristics, which is confirmed by the findings of this research.

One of the most important challenges is the digitalization of the processes that take place in SMEs, and because of the challenges of providing services and products, it is possible to provide them not only in the traditional way but also online. This gives businesses easier access to customers; however, competition in the e-services sector is particularly fierce. The service process becomes faster and the customer base becomes larger.

SMEs have few investment opportunities and, therefore, often encounter difficulties in introducing various innovations, including digitalization. However, the recent global situation related to the health and economic crisis has shown that without the digitalization of service delivery processes and digital transformation, these companies cannot survive.

This study has limitations that must be considered. The sample used in this research, 124 enterprises in the four prefectures of Western Macedonia is to a certain extent representative of the number of SMEs, but it must be acknowledged that it is a relatively small sample and there is a limitation in terms of further groupings by production sector and sector of activity.

In addition, the need to interview business and organization owners is recognized to determine whether these owners understand challenging factors, such as limited financial resources, limited skills, or knowledge about the importance of their digital presence. Finally, interviews with practitioners would highlight how to overcome these challenges in a way that would help micro businesses.

A list of solutions related to the digitization of processes and their advantages was generated based on a literature survey. It may be the case that some solutions, which may seem important to some researchers, were not included, but this was not the intended purpose.

References

Andreou, Έ. (2020). *Socioeconomic challenges on building a strong online presence. Case study small and micro businesses in Cyprus*. Open University of Cyprus.

Antoniadis, I., Tsiakiris, T., & Tsopogloy, S. (2015). Business intelligence during times of crisis: Adoption and usage of ERP systems by SMEs. *Procedia-Social and Behavioral Sciences, 175*, 299–307.

Antoniadis, I., Assimakopoulos, C., & Koukoulis, I. (2019). Attitudes of college students towards online advertisement in social networking sites: A structural equation modelling approach. *International Journal of Internet Marketing and Advertising, 13*(2), 137–154.

Baden-Fuller, C., & Morgan, M. S. (2010). Business models as models. *Long Range Planning, 43*(2–3), 156–171.

Berman, S. J., & Bell, R. (2011). Digital transformation: Creating new business models where digital meets physical. *IBM Institute for Business Value*, 1–17.

Boughton, S. B. (2005). Search engine marketing. *Perspectives in Business, 2*(1), 29–33.

Bursa, K. (2008). How to effectively manage demand with demand sensing and shaping using point of sales data. *Journal of Business Forecasting, 27*(4), 26.

Byrne, R. F. (2012). Beyond traditional time-series: Using demand sensing to improve forecasts in volatile times. *Journal of Business Forecasting, 31*(2), 13.

Cenamor, J., Parida, V., & Wincen, J. (2019). How entrepreneurial SMEs compete through digital platforms: The roles of digital platforms capability and ambidexterity. Elsevier. *Journal of Business Research, 100*, 196–206.

De Bruyn, A., & Lilien, G. L. (2008). A multi-stage model of word-of-mouth influence through viral marketing. *International Journal of Research in Marketing, 25*(3), 151–163.

ΕΚΤ, Η. Π. (2018). Εθνικό Κέντρο Τεκμηρίωσης: Μικρομεσαίες Επιχειρήσεις: καινοτομία, εξωστρέφεια, πρόσβαση στη χρηματοδότηση και δομές στήριξης τα κλειδιά για την ανάπτυξή τους, Τεύχος 110 | Δεκέμβριος 2017-Φεβρουάριος 2018. https://www.ekt.gr/el/magazines/features/21907

Evans, D., Bratton, S., & McKee, J. (2021). *Social media marketing*. AG Printing & Publishing.

Ghobakhloo, M. (2020). Industry 4.0, digitization, and opportunities for sustainability. *Journal of Cleaner Production, 252*, 119869.

Hitpass, B., & Astudillo, H. (2019). Industry 4.0 challenges for business process management and electronic-commerce. *Journal of Theoretical and Applied Electronic Commerce Research, 14*(1), I–III.

Koronaki, E., Vlachvei, A., & Panopoulos, A. (2023). Managing the online customer experience and subsequent consumer responses across the customer journey: A review and future research agenda. *Electronic Commerce Research and Applications, 58*, 101242.

Leppäniemi, M., Sinisalo, J., & Karjaluoto, H. (2006). A review of mobile marketing research. *International Journal of Mobile Marketing, 1*(1), 30–40.

Leskovec, J., Adamic, L. A., & Huberman, B. A. (2007). The dynamics of viral marketing. *ACM Transactions on the Web (TWEB), 1*(1), 5-es.

Lu, Y. (2017). Industry 4.0: A survey on technologies, applications and open research issues. *Journal of Industrial Information Integration, 6*, 1–10.

McMillan, K. And Weyers, J. (2011) How to write a dissertation and project report. Pearson Education Limited.

OECD. (2020). *Global survey on digitalization*. OECD.

Reis, J., Amorim, M., Melão, N., & Matos, P. (2018). Digital transformation: A literature review and guidelines for future research. In *World conference on information systems and technologies* (pp. 411–421). Springer.

Saprikis, V. (2013). Consumers' perceptions towards e-shopping advertisements and promotional actions in social networking sites. *International Journal of E-Adoption, 5*(4), 36–47.

Saprikis, V., & Vlachopoulou, M. (2012). Investigating factors influencing use of B2B e-marketplaces in Greek firms: The B2B e-MarketFLU Framewok. *International Journal of Business Research and Development, 4*(1), 1–24.

Semedeferis, Th. (2022). Digital transformation of the organization and management of businesses and their production process, utilizing new technological means and flexible production forms.

Shafer, S. M., Smith, H. J., & Linder, J. C. (2005). The power of business models. *Business Horizons, 48*(3), 199–207.

Shafique, K., Khawaja, B. A., Sabir, F., Qazi, S., & Mustaqim, M. (2020). Internet of things (IoT) for next-generation smart systems: A review of current challenges, future trends and prospects for emerging 5G-IoT scenarios. *IEEE Access, 8*, 23022–23040.

Sin, I., & Dimitrova, P. (2018). *Digital Marketing in Start-Ups: The role of digital marketing in acquiring and maintaining business relationships*. Available at: https://pdfs.semanticscholar.org/e92f/e10647790c1cf32c1b27e777f4a5c84fe8 37.pdf

Staboulis, M., & Lazaridou, I. (2020a). The impact of COVID-19 on economy, employment and new skills. *Journal of European Economy, 19*(3), 409–422.

Staboulis, M., & Lazaridou, I. (2020b). Non cognitive skills as the new metric in recent labor markets case study: The impact of social media in promoting and developing skills. In L. G. Chova, A. L. Martinez, & I. C. Torres (Eds.), *14th International Technology, Education and Development conference (INTED 2020). March 2–4, 2020, Valencia, Spain* (pp. 3943–3950). INTED Proceedings.

Stone, M., Aravopoulou, E., Ekinci, Y., Evans, G., Hobbs, M., Labib, A., et al. (2020). Artificial intelligence (AI) in strategic marketing decision-making: A research agenda. *The Bottom Line, 33*(2), 183–200.

Teece, D. J. (2010). Business models, business strategy and innovation. *Long Range Planning, 43*(2–3), 172–194.

Veal, A. (2006). *Research methods: A practical guide* (3rd ed.). Pearson Education Limited.

Verhoef, P. C., Broekhuizen, T., Bart, Y., Bhattacharya, A., Dong, J. Q., Fabian, N., & Haenlein, M. (2021). Digital transformation: A multidisciplinary reflection and research agenda. *Journal of Business Research, 122*, 889–901.

Vlahvei, A., Notta, O., & Grigoriou, E. (2013). Establishing a strong brand identity through a website: The case of Greek food SMEs. *Procedia Economics and Finance, 5*, 771–778.

Chapter 57
Using the Predictive Model IN05 to Assess the Business Environment in Czechia

Tomáš Pražák

Abstract Assessing the financial situation of businesses requires considering both internal factors and the external macroeconomic environment. The aim of this study is to investigate how the macroeconomic environment affects business activities by evaluating the financial health of companies in Czechia. The comprehensive model IN05 is used to evaluate companies' financial situations, taking into account the specifics of Czech companies' financial statements. The analysis focuses on the impact of key macroeconomic determinants, such as real GDP growth rates, consumer price index, industrial producer price index, nominal interest rates, and the unemployment rate. Panel regression method, called General Methods of Moments (GMM), is employed to analyze the relationships within this two-dimensional space. The research seeks to identify the macroeconomic factors that exert the most significant influence on companies' financial situation in Czechia. The study considers the national level as well as variations across economic sectors and enterprise sizes. The factors that have the strongest impact on the financial situation of companies in Czechia include interest rates or the price level.

Keywords Macroeconomic factors · Czechia · GMM · Regression analyses · Predictive model financial situation

57.1 Introduction

Since businesses are not isolated from the outside world, the assessment of the financial situation of businesses is influenced not only by the internal setup of business processes but also by the external environment. The results of the literature provide evidence of the existence of a direct influence of the macroeconomic

T. Pražák (✉)
Department of Business Economic and Management, Silesian University in Opava, School of Business Administration in Karviná, Karvina, Czechia
e-mail: prazak@opf.slu.cz

environment on the financial position of firms. The classification and predictive power of default models can be improved by adding information about the onset of an economic recession, thereby reflecting the fact that accounting data may change its content during a recession.

The financial situation of a company can be captured using multidimensional models working with criteria that are assigned specific weights. The company's situation is then expressed as a single aggregate figure, which assesses the degree of financial health of the company. The resulting aggregate index values aim to determine the financial situation of the firm in terms of value creation (creditworthiness models) or to assess the firm's ability to repay its liabilities (bankruptcy models). The models for predicting the financial situation of a firm allow a basic classification of the assessed firm into the categories of going concern or failing firms. This information is very important for business owners, investors, and other regional stakeholders.

The aim of this chapter is to determine how the macroeconomic environment of a company affects business activities on the basis of an assessment of the financial health of companies in Czechia. In order to evaluate the financial situation of companies, the article will use the comprehensive model IN05. This model reflects the specifics of Czech companies' financial statements. The analysis conducted on the impact of the strength and direction of individual macroeconomic factors on companies' financial situation during the economic cycle of 2005–2018 can provide valuable insights into management decision-making and the establishment of internal processes. The examination will focus on key macroeconomic determinants, including growth rates of real gross domestic product, consumer price index, industrial producer price index, nominal interest rates, and unemployment rate. Given the extensive amount of input data, panel regression methods are commonly employed to analyze the relationships and connections within this two-dimensional space. Consequently, the General Methods of Moments (GMM) will be utilized. The outcomes of this analysis will address the research question of which macroeconomic factors exert the most substantial influence on companies' financial situation in Czechia. The relationship among the variables will be monitored not only at the national level but also at the level of economic activity and enterprise size.

The structure of this chapter is as follows: Sect. 57.2 provides a review of the relevant literature. In Sect. 57.3, the data and methodology employed in this study are presented. The empirical estimation results are outlined in Sect. 57.4. Section 57.5 is dedicated to the discussion of these findings, while the Conclusion section presents the main conclusions and a summary of the key findings.

57.2 Literature Review

The IN05 index was created in 2005 as an updated version of the similarly constructed IN01 index. The modified version of IN05 focuses on the prediction of financial distress, but also on the ability to create value for owners. In the opinion of Kubíčková and Jindřichovská (2015), IN05 is considered by Czech economists to be the most accurate and the most suitable to be used to analyze Czech companies.

Comparisons of individual models and their ability to identify a firm in financial distress in the Czech Republic have been discussed by Machek (2014) and Čamská (2016). Machek (2014) analyzed the Kralick Quick test, Taffler bankruptcy model, IN99 and IN05 indices, and Altman's Z'score for Czech firms from 2007 to 2010. Based on the results of the individual models that predicted the financial distress of a company, he found that the most suitable models for practical use of financial distress prediction are Altman's Z'score and IN05. On the other hand, the least suitable is the Quick Kralick test. Čamská (2016) compared the predictive ability of both bankruptcy and creditworthiness models in the manufacturing industry during the global financial crisis. The bankruptcy models that achieved the highest predictive values were IN01, IN05, or Altman's Z'score. These conclusions were also confirmed by Pražák (2019) in his evaluation of the predictive ability of bankruptcy models during the period of structural changes in companies operating in the V4 countries in the period 2004–2016.

On the other hand, Misanková et al. (2017) pointed out that the predictive ability of bankruptcy models is not very high and they tested the predictive ability of bankruptcy models constructed in V4 countries (IN05 index, Poznansky bankruptcy model, and Hungarian bankruptcy model of Virag and Hajda), Altman bankruptcy model, Springate bankruptcy model, and the Taffler bankruptcy model on Slovak companies. The authors point out the different predictive powers across business sectors.

Mokhova and Zinecker (2014) examined the impact of the macroeconomic environment on the financial situation of firms. For their article, they selected firms operating in the manufacturing industry in the Czech Republic, Slovakia, Hungary, Poland, Greece, Germany, and France. The main macroeconomic factors under observation were short- and long-term interest rates, inflation, M2 monetary aggregate, level of government debt, tax revenues, unemployment rate, and year-on-year change in real GDP. The chapter uses the values of total leverage or short- and long-term indebtedness of firms as indicators of the financial situation of the firm. After conducting Pearson correlation analysis, the authors found that the impact of macroeconomic indicators on the financial position of enterprises varies from country to country and depends mainly on the structure of corporate liabilities. The high predictive value of macroeconomic factors on the financial situation of firms is also confirmed by Liou and Smith (2007). Similarly, Šimáková et al. (2019) or Plachy and Rasovec (2015) pointed out that the main macroeconomic factors that affect the development of the financial situation of a firm are gross domestic product, inflation, interest rate, or unemployment rate.

The variation of the observed relationship also depends on the size of the firm. Salman et al. (2011) used a time-series cointegration approach to evaluate the relationship between small- and medium-sized enterprise (SME) failure and macroeconomic factors for the Swedish manufacturing sector over the period 1986–2006. They found that in the long run, firm failure is negatively associated with the level of industrial activity, money supply, GDP, and the degree of economic openness, and positively associated with real wages. Angelache et al. (2014) investigated the long-run dynamic relationships between macroeconomic factors and financial situation in the Czech Republic, Hungary, Poland, and Romania. Using a vector autoregressive model, they showed a significant impact of the evolution of macroeconomic variables on the financial situation of large firms, especially during the global financial crisis in 2008 and 2009.

57.3 Data and Methodology

57.3.1 Data Description

For further analysis, due to their specificity and based on the availability of analytical materials and reports of the Ministry of Industry and Trade, the sectors of agriculture, forestry and fishing (A), and money and insurance (K) are not taken into account. The individual sectors of economic activity monitored are divided into three categories, according to the area of economic activity according to the NACE classification:

- Industry: Mining and quarrying (B), manufacturing (C), production electricity, gas, heat and air conditioning (D), and water supply; waste and remediation activities (E).
- Construction: Building and civil engineering (F).
- Services: Wholesale and retail trade; repair and maintenance of motor vehicles (G), transport and storage (H), accommodation, food, and beverage service activities (I), information and communication activities (J), real estate activities (L), professional, scientific, and technical activities (M), administrative and support service activities (N), public administration and defense; compulsory social security (O), education (P), health, and social work activities (Q), cultural, entertainment, and recreational activities (R), and other activities (S).

According to the BvD Amadeus and Orbis databases, enterprises are categorized by size as follows:

- Large: A large enterprise is characterized by operating revenues greater than EUR 10 million, total assets greater than EUR 20 million, and number of employees greater than 150.
- SME: Enterprises that do not meet the criteria set for large enterprises are considered.

Table 57.1 shows the number of enterprises that were analyzed. Companies with available data for the entire period under review were analyzed and the criterion of not operating on the stock markets was defined for selection.

Table 57.1 Number of companies under investigation

Classification	Czechia	SME	Large	Industry	Construction	Services
Number of companies	3736	1962	1774	1603	321	1823

Source: Orbis and Amadeus databases

Table 57.2 Mean values of macroeconomic variables

	GDP	UNE	CPI	PPI	IR
Czechia	2.51	6.22	2.01	0.61	3.02

Source: Eurostat database

The table provides an overview of the number of companies under investigation in Czechia, categorized based on their classification. According to the data presented, there are a total of 3736 companies being investigated in Czechia. Among them, 1962 are classified as SMEs, while 1774 are categorized as large companies. Furthermore, the table breaks down the investigations by economic classification, with 1603 companies from the industry sector, 321 from the construction sector, and 1823 from the services sector.

In the monitored period, the economic environment in the Czech Republic was negatively affected by the financial crisis in 2009 and the subsequent euro area debt crisis. A complementary negative factor until 2013 was the prolonged slow GDP growth accompanied by rising unemployment and indebtedness or a decline in output, value added, and productivity. Since 2014, economic growth in the Czech Republic has become more dynamic, with a decline in unemployment and indebtedness and a subsequent increase in output and value added.

The growing number of enterprises and their outputs are also supported by the continuously improving business environment and increasing export performance. On the other hand, however, it should be noted that the Czech Republic often experienced a decline in labor productivity during the period under review.

The Table 57.2 provides a summary of key economic indicators for Czechia. The GDP stands at 2.51, reflecting the overall value of goods and services produced. The unemployment rate is reported as 6.22%, indicating the portion of the labor force actively seeking employment. The Consumer Price Index (CPI) is recorded as 2.01, reflecting changes in the cost of living. The Producer Price Index (PPI) stands at 0.61, representing changes in the selling prices received by domestic producers. Lastly, the interest rate is reported as 3.02%, which influences borrowing costs and returns on savings and investments.

57.3.2 Methodology

The initial phase of the research involved creating a database of corporate data and selected macroeconomic factors for the V4 countries. Corporate data were sourced from databases such as Orbis or Amadeus, while macroeconomic data were obtained from available sources like Eurostat, OECD, or individual central bank databases.

The period under review was from 2005 to 2018, based on the data availability. This period provides a view of the entire business cycle. At the same time, the Covid-19 period has not been taken into account. In the second phase, bankruptcy models were developed using MS Excel. Subsequently, in the third phase of the research, regression analyses were conducted on the obtained data using the Eviews econometric program.

The modified version of IN05 focuses on the prediction of financial distress and also on the ability of the business to create value for owners. It is the IN05 model from the available literature that shows the best predictive ability due to its construction, which reflects the specifics of the corporate sector in the Czech Republic. The final form of the equation according to Růčková (2019) is as follows:

$$IN05 = 0.13X_1 + 0.04X_2 + 3.97X_3 + 0.21X_4 + 0.09X_5$$

where: X_1 = assets/foreign capital, X_2 = EBIT/interest expense, X_3 = EBIT/assets, X_4 = revenues/assets, X_5 = current assets/current liabilities.

The resulting value of X_1 captures the ratio of the firm's assets financed by external capital, thereby informing the firm about its debt burden. Conversely, indicator X_2 reflects how much interest creditors provide relative to how much the firm is able to earn. The results of indicators X_3 and X_4 show the ratio of assets that can be covered either by own profits or by earnings. Indicator X_5 informs the firm about the proportion of current assets financed through short-term external resources.

The resulting qualification of the company will be done according to the following:

IN05 > 1.6 enterprise is in a good situation.
0.9 < IN05 < 1.6 gray zone of unresolved results.
IN05 < 0.9 for bankruptcy is very likely.

After conducting bankruptcy models, the resulting values, denoted as explanatory variables (Y), are utilized in subsequent regression models. These values are represented in indexed form, indicating the real change compared to the previous value. The focus then shifts to individual macroeconomic factors, which act as explanatory variables. These factors include year-on-year changes in GDP, year-on-year changes in CPI and PPI price levels, year-on-year changes in the unemployment rate (UNE), and year-on-year changes in interest rates on new business to nonfinancial corporations (IR).

To obtain meaningful results, a two-step differenced GMM (Generalized Method of Moments) panel regression analysis is employed. Stationarity of the time and panel data is a fundamental prerequisite for its application. Stationarity implies stochastic stability within the behavior of individual data. Panel unit root tests such as the Levin, Lin, and Chu tests are commonly used to assess stationarity. Hansen (2014) deals with the application of econometric models based on the dynamic evolution of macroeconomic factors based on this formula:

$$L_{it} = \alpha_1 + \beta_1 \times \Delta L_{it-1} + \beta_2 \times X_{1it} + \beta_3 \times X_{2it} + \cdots + \beta_n \times X_{nit} + \varepsilon_{it},$$

The dependent variable, L_{it}, represents the financial situation of the i-th enterprise at time t. It is influenced by the delayed explanatory variable of the previous year, ΔL_{it-1}, and the explanatory macroeconomic variables captured in X_{nit}. The parameter β_n determines the strength and direction of the impact of each individual explanatory variable.

To ensure the reliability of the results and their explanatory power, all explanatory variables are subjected to tests for statistical significance. Additionally, it is essential to assess the overall robustness of the observed model using the Sargan/Hansen J-test (J-stat.). This test, developed by John Denis Sargan in 1958 and extended by Lars Peter Hansen in 1982, examines the model's ability to produce consistent results even with slight parameter changes.

The Sargan/Hansen J-test is crucial in evaluating the model's robustness, and the statistical significance of the test results should exceed the chosen significance level of 5%. These tests help validate the overall reliability and stability of the model's outcomes, providing confidence in its explanatory capacity and generalizability.

57.4 The Analysis of Empirical Results

Before conducting the practical analysis using the GMM model, a stationarity test was performed using the Levin, Lin, and Chu test. The results of this test indicated statistical significance, confirming the stability of the data.

Subsequently, the GMM model was applied, and the statistical significance of the results was assessed using the J-statistic. Notably, all models exhibited statistically significant results based on the J-statistic. The relationships and their corresponding statistical significance can be observed in Table 57.3.

This indicates that the relationships between the dependent variable and the explanatory variables, as captured by the GMM model, are statistically significant.

Table 57.3 Results of the GMM model

Model	GDP	CPI	PPI	UNE	IR	J-stat.
Czechia	0.0337*	−0.0675*	−0.0301*	−0.0137*	−0.0211*	53.33
SME	0.0069	−0.0362*	−0.0353*	−0.0103*	−0.0264*	71.23
Large	0.0455	−0.1218*	0.0251	−0.0105*	−0.0611*	76.00
Industry	0.0549*	−0.1489*	0.0390	−0.0135*	−0.1401*	71.63
Construction	0.0103	−0.0322*	−0.0677*	−0.0136*	−0.0601*	67.43
Services	0.0293*	−0.0846*	−0.0256*	−0.0104	−0.0230*	60.80

Source: Author's calculations
Notes: * statistical significance at 5%

Table 57.4 Evaluating the relationship between variables

Country	GDP	CPI	PPI	UNE	IR	The strongest impact	The weakest impact
Czechia	+	–	–	–	–	CPI	UNE
SME	X	–	–	–	–	CPI	UNE
Large	X	–	X	–	–	CPI	UNE
Industry	+	–	X	–	–	CPI	UNE
Construction	X	–	–	–	–	PPI	UNE
Services	+	–	–	X	–	CPI	IR

Source: Author's calculations
Notes: X mean statistical insignificant results

The inclusion of robust statistical methods and the successful passing of the stationarity test enhance the credibility and reliability of the findings.

The GMM model results, as shown in Table 57.3, reveal significant relationships between the dependent variable and the explanatory macroeconomic variables. The asterisks (*) indicate statistical significance at the 5% level. These findings provide valuable insights into the impact of GDP, CPI, PPI, UNE, and IR on the financial situation of various entities, such as Czechia, SMEs, large companies, industry, construction, and services. The J-statistic values further support the robustness of the observed models.

GDP shows a positive and statistically significant impact, indicating that higher economic growth is associated with improved financial situations for companies in these sectors. Across multiple models, CPI exhibits a negative and statistically significant impact. This suggests that higher inflation rates are generally associated with a deterioration in the financial situation of companies. The impact of PPI varies across models. While it shows a negative and statistically significant impact in the Czechia and Construction models, it is not statistically significant in the Large and Industry models. These results indicate that changes in producer prices have mixed effects on the financial situation of companies, depending on the industry or sector. In all models, except the Services model, the unemployment rate (UNE) demonstrates a negative and statistically significant impact. This implies that higher levels of unemployment are generally associated with a decline in the financial situation of companies. The interest rate (IR) has a negative and statistically significant impact in all models except the Czechia model. This suggests that higher interest rates on new business loans to nonfinancial corporations are associated with a decrease in the financial situation of companies.

The final evaluation is shown in Table 57.4. The final impact of macroeconomic variables on the financial situation of companies is described on the basis of GMM results.

On the basis of results in particular, it can be observed that in Czechia, the differences in the impact of individual factors on enterprises of different sizes and economic activities are not well-confirmed. The factor having the strongest impact on the financial situation of enterprises in the period under review was the price level, characterized in particular by the CPI. On the other hand, the factor with the weakest impact was unemployment.

The potential financial distress of enterprises was influenced by the decline in GDP. The economic situation in Czechia was negatively affected by the global financial crisis, the effects of which were particularly evident in 2009, and also by the European debt crisis in 2011. Until 2011, the financial situation of companies in Czechia followed a similar trend to the change in real GDP. The economic performance of the country and the productivity of enterprises in Czechia were stagnated. Several expansionary measures were taken to restore economic growth and business productivity. However, this dynamic GDP growth did not translate into an equally rapid improvement in the financial situation of enterprises. For this reason, it was evident that the strongest impact on the evolution of the financial situation of enterprises would come from factors other than the change in real GDP.

Thus, the factors with the strongest impact on the financial situation of enterprises in Czechia include interest rates or, in particular, the price level. The stronger impact of interest rates has been limited by long-term low interest rates supporting higher corporate investment and households.

However, the price level factor had the most significant impact. The expected relationship between the variables under study was thus confirmed, with both the CPI and PPI having a statistically negative effect. After the aforementioned financial crisis, the CPI has been within the inflation band for the whole time. Low inflation during the crisis and subdued economic growth did not mean higher demand for goods and services and household consumption. Following the improved economic situation and the monetary measures adopted by the Czech National Bank, the CPI started to rise. Only in the case of the construction sector was the PPI the strongest indicator. Thus, the increase in prices of source materials had the greatest impact on the potential financial distress of enterprises in the construction sector. With the exception of the services sector, where, as expected, the highest dependence was attributed to the CPI, the change in the PPI also had a significant impact on the industry. It is the firms operating in the industrial and construction sectors that are negatively affected by the jump in resource prices.

57.5 Conclusions

The aim of this chapter was to assess the impact of the macroeconomic environment on the financial situation of companies, focusing on the financial distress of companies operating in Czechia. Through econometric and statistical methods, the interrelationship between selected macroeconomic factors was analyzed for the period 2005–2018. This period is characterized by alternating phases of the business cycle. Based on the chosen econometric method GMM, it is possible to look at this period comprehensively and discuss the individual resulting relationships over the entire business cycle period.

According to the results, it can be concluded that the factor with the strongest impact is the CPI. This confirmed the assumption of high consumer sensitivity to price changes in services, where any demand shock would have an immediate and significant impact. The interaction between the PPI and the CPI can be also observed. The evolution of the PPI predicts the future evolution of the CPI, especially in the event of a supply shock. A nonreactive supply shock will increase input prices, especially for industrial firms and construction industries, and will thus affect PPI growth by leaps and bounds. The construction sector was particularly sensitive to changes in the producer price index, indicating the impact of rising prices of input materials. Changes in both the CPI and the producer price index showed a statistically significant negative effect, suggesting the importance of price levels for potential financial distress. Unemployment, on the other hand, had the weakest effect, suggesting that changes in the unemployment rate have less of an impact on firms' financial difficulties. The decline in gross domestic product (GDP) played a significant role in influencing the potential financial distress of firms. The financial situation of firms in Czechia followed trends in real GDP, reflecting the impact of the global financial crises. Overall, understanding the impact of macroeconomic factors such as the price level and GDP is crucial for monitoring and assessing the financial situation of enterprises in Czechia. These findings provide valuable insights for policymakers and enterprises in managing financial risks and promoting economic stability.

The main limitation of the study is the observation period, which ends in 2018. For further research, it will be necessary to ensure the timeliness of the data, where it will be necessary to monitor the influence of the pandemic and post-pandemic periods. Given the currently high CPI values in Czechia, it will be interesting to observe their expected effect on the financial situation of companies reflecting the results of this chapter. For further research, it also seems appropriate to use other methods for calculating the financial health of a company such as Economic Value Added or Altman models.

Acknowledgments Publication of this chapter was supported by the Internal Grant System of Silesian University in Opava within the project IGS 10/23 "The impact of investment expenditures on the financial situation of companies". The support is greatly acknowledged.

References

Angelache, G. V., Kralik, L. I., Acatrinei, M., & Pete, S. (2014). Influence of the EU accession process and the global crisis on the CEE stock markets: A multivariate correlation analysis. *Romanian Journal of Economic Forecasting, 17*, 35–52.

Čamská, D. (2016). Accurancy of models predicting corporate bankruptcy in a selected industry branch. *Ekonomický časopis, 64*, 353–366.

Hansen, L. P. (1982). Large sample properties of generalized method of moments estimators. *Econometrica, 50*(4), 1029–1054.

Hansen, L. P. (2014). Uncertainty outside and inside economic models. *Journal of Political Economy, 122*(5), 945–987.

Kubíčková, D., & Jindřichovská, I. (2015). *Finanční analýza a hodnocení výkonnosti firem*. C. H. Beck. ISBN 978-80-7400-538-1.

Liou, D., & Smith, M. (2007). Macroeconomic variables and financial distress. *Journal of Accounting-Business and Management, 14*, 17–31.

Machek, O. (2014). Long-term predictivity ability of bankruptcy models in the Czech Republic: Evidence from 2007-2012. *Central European Business Review, 3*, 14–17.

Misanková, M., Zvariková, K., & Kliestiková, J. (2017). Bankruptcy practice in countries of Visegrad Four. *Economics and Culture, 14*, 108–118.

Mokhova, N., & Zinecker, M. (2014). Macroeconomic factors and corporate capital structure. *Procedia – Social and Behavioral Sciences, 110*, 530–540.

Plachy, R., & Rasovec, T. (2015). Impact of economic indicators on development of capital market. *E+M Ekonomie a Management, 18*, 101–112.

Pražák, T. (2019). Financial health of small and medium sized companies in the Visegrad countries. *Financial Internet Quarterly "e-Finanse", 15*(3), 56–66.

Růčková, P. (2019). *Finanční analýza – Metody, ukazatele, využití v praxi*. Grada Publishing. ISBN 978-80-271-2028-4.

Salman, K., Friedrichs, Y., & Shukur, G. (2011). The determinants of failure of small manufacturing firms: Assessing the macroeconomic factors. *International Business Research, 4*(3), 22–32.

Šimáková, J., Stavárek, D., Pražák, T., & Ligocká, M. (2019). Macroeconomic factors and stock prices in the food and drink industry. *British Food Journal, 121*(7), 1627–1641.

Chapter 58
The WWW Factor: Understanding Generation Z's Website Preferences

Tereza Ikášová

Abstract Websites are key platforms for presenting products and companies. Nowadays, it is rather an exception when a company does not have a website. That is why it is important to make sure that the website meets all the requirements of modern times and that it is not average or below average compared to the competition. To create a great website, it is essential to have a good understanding of the behavior of website visitors and the factors that influence their interaction. This chapter focuses on finding out which factors most influence Generation Z on a website. It then explores whether these preferences differ between different demographic groups, particularly between men and women and between Generation Z and Generation Y. The factors examined are the clarity of the website, the colors used, the loading speed, the shapes used, the advertising banners, the length of the forms, and the functional elements on the website. The research is conducted through a questionnaire survey to gain a deeper understanding of what users prefer on a website. The results of this research can provide valuable information for website designers and marketers when creating and optimizing websites.

Keywords Web design · Kruskal-Wallis test · Generation Z · Colors · Website speed · Functional elements

58.1 Introduction

Websites are key platforms for showcasing products and companies. In order to create a quality website, it is essential to have a good understanding of visitors' behavior on the site. However, in their desire to create a visually appealing website, they often overlook key elements on the site that can influence conversions. Only

T. Ikášová (✉)
Department of Informatics and Mathematics, School of Business Administration in Karviná, Silesian University in Opava, Karviná, Czechia
e-mail: ikasova@opf.slu.cz

© The Author(s), under exclusive license to Springer Nature Switzerland AG 2024
N. Tsounis, A. Vlachvei (eds.), *Applied Economic Research and Trends*, Springer Proceedings in Business and Economics,
https://doi.org/10.1007/978-3-031-49105-4_58

through a deep understanding of users can a website that truly fulfills its purpose be created. This is why there is an increasingly urgent need to assess what visitors really pay attention to on the web, what is important to them, and what web designers are worrying about unnecessarily. There are many guidelines that tell web designers what a website should look like. But these are often not based on transparent foundations that describe the research methodology. At the same time, little work is done on whether this advice to designers applies to all Internet users, or whether preferences on the web change based on the gender or generation of the target audience. The factors monitored in this research are the clarity of the website, the colors used, the loading speed of the website, the shapes used, the advertising banners, the short forms, and the functional elements on the website.

The aim of this chapter was to find out which of the selected factors most influence Generation Z respondents on websites. And also to find out whether the perception of each factor on the web differs between the groups of respondents studied. Generation Z is just entering the job market, and it will be important for companies to be able to reach them correctly on their corporate website. In order to do this, it is important to first understand the preferences of Generation Z on the website. This research is conducted through a questionnaire survey. The questionnaires were chosen in order to find out what web users think about the factors. Future research is then envisaged to include whether users act in accordance with what they think about the factors. At the same time, this research is designed to be longitudinal, so the sample size will be continuously increased.

The paper is organized as follows: The Literature Review section provides a basic review of the literature on the factors of interest and the characteristics of the selected groups. The following Data and Methodology chapter contains the research questions, information on how the data were obtained, a basic description of the data, and a description of how the data were evaluated. The Results chapter contains the answers to the research questions and the findings from the implementation of the survey. This is followed by the Discussion, Conclusion, and References chapters.

58.2 Literature Review

Generations Y and Z are the dominant Internet users. They mostly use it for work and study reasons, and also for socializing. These generations, more than any other generation, are considered leaders in the use of online technology as they spend an enormous amount of time surfing and browsing the Internet (Issa & Isaias, 2016). With these generations spending so much time online, it can be more challenging for companies to reach them on their sites. That's why it's important for companies and web designers to understand generational behavior on websites in order to create competitive sites. The following are selected factors that can influence site visitors.

The perception of esthetics by website users has a significant impact on their perceived usefulness and attitudes, which can influence the corporate image of the website owner (Zhenhui et al., 2016). Website esthetics is closely related to the simplicity and clarity of a website. This is also why there is an increasing emphasis on user experience, where a website should be simple, intuitive, and effective (Donnelly, 2001).

As mentioned, the visual esthetics of the site are very important. However, the same applies to the usability of the site. It is difficult to decide which of these two aspects to pay more attention to when designing a website, as esthetics focuses on the look and feel, while usability focuses on the functionality. Moreover, it is often difficult to strike a balance between these two seemingly contradictory web design goals. (Yusof et al., 2010). Web functionality has a significant impact on the perceived usability of a website (Tandon et al., 2016). This in turn can lead to a positive user experience of the website and also to a higher number of online transactions (Tarafdar & Zhang, 2005).

The colors used in the design of websites can influence their users. According to Cyr et al. (2010), the color appeal of a website is a significant factor for trust and satisfaction with a website. Cao et al. (2021) found that web link colors can attract users' attention and increase their sense of control over the process. Colors were also addressed by Xiaoxiong et al. (2022), who examined the effect of colors on the complexity of a web page and recommended that the number of colors on a page should be less than 6. People generally prefer blue the most, among all colors (Mythili & Kiruthiga, 2022). This is because blue-colored websites require less effort in cognitive processing. When viewing such a site, there is an increase in brain structures related to the processing of pleasant and esthetic stimuli. Moss et al. (2006) found statistically significant differences between women and men on product pages. This suggests that the attractiveness of websites can be maximized if they reflect the needs and interests of their target audience. The differences between women and men, and also the intergenerational age differences, are contradicted by Mythili and Kiruthiga (2022), who found no statistically significant difference in preference for certain colors.

Research suggests that page loading speed affects web users. Speed can have a significant impact on user experience and satisfaction. A loading delay of 4 s or more can reduce page performance and affect users' intention to complete an action. If a page takes 8 s or longer to load, attitudes flatten (Galletta et al., 2004). A difference of a few hundred milliseconds can even cause a visitor to favor a site over competing sites in their selection process. (Iliev & Dimitrov, 2014). Lanza et al. (2022) found that slow web loading times negatively affect the user experience on public service portals, which can be particularly problematic in countries with poor Internet infrastructure. Slow sites cause frustration for users and force them to abandon sites, even if they find the information they are looking for. Research has shown that increasing loading times can increase immediate abandonment rates by up to 32%. Users are most sensitive to the speed of checkout subpages on e-commerce sites and least sensitive on homepage sites. (Xilogianni et al., 2022). According to Nordin et al. (2020), Generation Z students like to move quickly in the online environment because they want to get information and answers instantly from a variety of sources, often untrusted ones.

What may seem like an even bigger problem than a slow site may be when the site doesn't work. It could be that buttons, forms, or other elements are not working on the site. And logically, they prevent users from finding the information they want and completing their conversions. A failing website can negatively affect usability and user experience (Mahajan & Halfond, 2014). Users usually do not care about the reasons why a website is not working, such as site crashes, network congestion, bandwidth, or other indicators of system failure. For the online customer, quality of service means fast and predictable site response. Low quality means that the customer will not visit the site again (Torkey et al., 2007).

The curvature of object corners is another factor that deserves attention. It can be interspersed on the web in different ways. For example, the shape of buttons, the roundness of sections, etc. Sharp transitions in the outline can make people feel threatened (Bertamini et al., 2015) or can have an aggressive effect on them (Hess et al., 2013). In general, people prefer more round shapes (Leder et al., 2011; Bertamini et al., 2015). Okamura (2018) further argues that round shapes are preferred more by women compared to men.

Scientists and respondents have different views on banner ads; especially when it comes to online banners. Internet ads are annoying to users, so it's no wonder that they actively try to avoid them. They are often even the reason why people leave a website. More sophisticated users even exhibit various scanning patterns, where their eyes scan a web page casually without wasting time looking at the ad. (Rettie et al., 2003). If there is an intolerably large number of ads on a website, people perceive them as clickbait; they appear untrustworthy and often make the website look tacky (Zeng et al., 2021). In contrast, Le and Vo (2017) argue that users perceive online banner ads positively if they have high information value.

Most websites provide users with the opportunity to contact the website owner through dedicated contact pages. On these pages, users are usually asked to provide their name, email, and the content of the message (Starov et al., 2016). Forms can vary in structure and design, which is why designers try to optimize them. For example, Bargas-Avila et al. (2011) recommend using checkboxes instead of drop-down lists, as this increases the usability of the form and the satisfaction of its users—unless, of course, the number of options is too high.

58.3 Data and Methodology

The main focus of the chapter are members of Generation Z. The oldest of them are 23 years old this year, which means that they are just now starting to influence the job market. They don't know a world without the Internet and digital technology. Their behavior is also different compared to Generation Y according to the literature review. They are influenced by different factors in their customer decision-making. Thus, in the context of the topic under study, web designers also need to pay attention to the aforementioned factors when designing websites. For this reason, the first research question (RQ1) was set.

RQ1: Which factors most influence Generation Z on the web?

As mentioned in the literature review, different factors affect different groups differently. From the research cited above, it is evident that the most frequently cited differentiator is the gender of the respondents. The research alludes to the fact that corporate websites are often built thematically according to the target group that visits the corporate website. Therefore, there is a difference in the construction of a website designed for men and for women. At the same time, it is also necessary to observe the main motivation of this paper, namely, the different opinions on the importance of the elements between the different generations. For this reason, RQ2 was established.

RQ2: Do the perceptions of different factors on the web differ between the groups of respondents studied?

The research instrument was a questionnaire that included both closed and open-ended questions. Responses were rated using a five-point Likert scale, which allows to determine not only the content of the attitude but also its approximate strength. A total of 236 questionnaires were processed. This research is designed as a longitudinal study, so the sample size will be continuously increased and other forms of research will be conducted with the respondents at the same time.

Generation Z is specific in that they have grown up with social media and are technology oriented since birth. This is the reason why it is also called digital nomads (Dangmei & Singh, 2016). In the experimental design, this target group was further restricted to students above 18 years of age, which limited the age range of the respondents to 18–27 years. According to the Ministry of Education, Youth and Sports, there were a total of 250,341 students in this age range in the country in 2022, of which 140,190 were female and 110,150 were male.

In order to calculate the necessary sample size, the first step is to calculate the margin of error. This is the percentage of errors that can potentially exist in the sample. A higher value of margin of error means a lower level of confidence in the results. The following formula is used for the calculation.

$$\text{Margin of error} = Z * \frac{\sigma}{\sqrt{n}}$$

σ represents the standard deviation, n is the sample size, and z represents the confidence level, which is based on statistical tables. Subsequently, the number of individuals in the sample must be calculated. The confidence level is set at 95% and the margin of error was determined to be 10%. The number of students in the Czech Republic in the age range of 18–27 years is 250,341. The formula for calculating the sample size is as follows.

$$\text{Sample size} = Z^2 * (p) * (1 - 5)/c^2$$

Table 58.1 Descriptive statistics of respondents' gender

Sex	Frequency	Percent	Valid percent	Cumulative percent
Female	112	47,5	47,5	47,5
Male	124	52,5	52,5	100,0
Total	236	100,0	100,0	

Source: Author's description

Table 58.2 Descriptive statistics of respondent generation

Generation	Frequency	Percent	Valid percent	Cumulative percent
Generation Z	192	81,4	81,4	81,4
Generation Y	44	18,6	18,6	100,0
Total	236	100,0	100,0	

Source: Author's description

In the formula, where Z is the confidence level, p is the percentage of variability (most commonly used is 50%) and c is the margin of error; the required sample size of 97 respondents was found after its application. The distribution of respondents who were involved in the study and their gender distribution are shown in Table 58.1. A total of 236 respondents were included in the study, of which 112 were female and 124 were male. Women constituted 47.5% of the respondents and men 52.5%. The research was conducted on a fairly balanced sample of men and women.

Table 58.2 shows the distribution of respondents in the survey by generation. Of the 236 respondents, 192 (81.4%) were from Generation Z and 44 (18.6%) were from Generation Y.

Data from the questionnaire survey were analyzed using statistic software IBM SPSS. Nonparametric tests were used to determine the relationships between the variables of interest. This type of tests is applied when comparing statistical datasets where there is no normal probability distribution of the characteristics under study.

The Kruskal-Wallis test will be used to evaluate the data. This is a nonparametric statistical test that evaluates differences between three or more independently selected groups on a single, non-normally distributed continuous variable. Non-normally distributed data are suitable for the Kruskal-Wallis test. (McKight & Najab, 2010).

The nonparametric Kruskal-Wallis test was used to answer the research question, which, as Gravetter and Wallnau (2007) stated, is a more general version of the nonparametric Mann-Whitney test for more than two comparison groups. This test is applied to compare two or more independent samples of the same or different sizes. The basic principle of the Kruskal-Wallis test is that, when the null hypothesis is valid, the pooled values from all samples are so mixed that the mean ranks corresponding to the individual samples are similar. To calculate this test, we again sort all observations by size and assign ranks to each value. The computational formula of the Kruskal-Wallis test has the following structure:

$$Q = \frac{12}{n(n+1)} \sum_{i=1}^{k} \frac{T_i^2}{n_i} - 3(n+1)$$

The null hypothesis is rejected at the α significance level if the value of the test statistic Q exceeds the critical value (quantile) corresponding to the given α significance level. The Kruskal-Wallis test was used to examine the significance of the observed factors on the web within a selected group of respondents.

58.4 Results

The Results chapter is divided into two subchapters. Each of them deals with the evaluation of one of the research questions.

58.4.1 The Importance of Factors

Table 58.3 assesses the average importance of various factors on the website and is based on the answers of the respondents in the questionnaire survey. Respondents selected ratings on a scale of 1 (very important) to 5 (very unimportant), so a lower average value indicates a higher importance.

The most important, with the lowest average of 1.16, is "Web clarity". This shows that respondents consider the logical structure and clear esthetics of the site to be very important. The next significant element is "Page loading speed", with a score of 1.57. "Functionality of elements on the page" is also considered important, as shown by the average score of 1.48. Users expect the website to function properly. "Colors Used" and "Short Forms" have averages of 2.63 and 2.66, respectively, indicating that these elements are of moderate to high importance to respondents. "Shapes" and "Banner Ads" were rated as less important, with averages of 3.33 and 3.29. These elements may be less important to Generation Z users than the others.

Table 58.3 Importance of factors according to respondents

Factor	Mean
Web clarity	1,16
Colors	2,63
Page loading speed	1,57
Shapes	3,33
Advertising banners	3,29
Short forms	2,66
Functionality of elements on the page	1,48

Source: Author's description

Table 58.4 Kruskal-Wallis test by gender

	Kruskal-Wallis H	df	Asymp. Sig.
Web clarity	4,084	1	0,043
Colors	3,398	1	0,065
Page loading speed	3,158	1	0,076
Shapes	0,835	1	0,361
Advertising banners	1,053	1	0,305
Short forms	1,259	1	0,262
Functionality of elements on the page	0,092	1	0,762

Source: Author's description

58.4.2 Differences Among Selected Groups

The Kruskal-Wallis test was used to monitor selected factors in the data analysis. These are web clarity, colors, loading speed, shapes, ad banners, short forms, and functional elements. The results are available in Table 58.4.

If statistically significant relationships were identified, attention was focused on analyzing the results of individual respondents' responses by gender to these questions.

At the 5% level of significance, differences were identified for web clarity, and at the 10% level of significance, differences were identified for color and loading speed.

Table 58.5 contains respondents' choices about the importance of site clarity. A total of 236 respondents were interviewed, of which 112 were female and 124 were male. Of these, 202 respondents (104 women and 98 men) considered web clarity to be very important. This group therefore constitutes the vast majority of respondents. Total 28 respondents (4 women and 24 men) answered that clarity was important to them. This is a significantly smaller group compared to those who consider clarity to be very important. Only 4 respondents (2 women and 2 men) expressed a neutral attitude towards web clarity. None of the respondents rated the clarity of the website as unimportant. However, 2 women responded that they found the clarity of the site very unimportant. No men chose this option. These data suggest that for most respondents, site clarity is very important, with men being slightly more tolerant of less clear sites, as indicated by the higher number of men who consider clarity to be only "important".

Another factor examined was the colors on the site. The results are available in Table 58.6 where 32 respondents (24 women and 8 men) said that colors on the web were very important to them. Total 76 respondents (32 women and 44 men) said that colors were important to them. This group is more than twice as large as the group recognizing colors as very important. A total of 94 respondents (46 women and 48 men) took a neutral stance on web color. This group is the largest of the total number of respondents. Twenty-two respondents (8 women and 14 men) perceived web colors as unimportant. Twelve respondents (2 women and 10 men)

Table 58.5 Web clarity by gender

	Female	Male	Total
Very important	104	98	202
Important	4	24	28
Neutral	2	2	4
Unimportant	0	0	0
Very unimportant	2	0	2
Total	112	124	236

Source: Author's description

Table 58.6 Website colors by gender

	Female	Male	Total
Very important	48	16	64
Important	64	88	152
Neutral	92	96	188
Unimportant	16	28	44
Very unimportant	4	20	24
Total	112	124	236

Source: Author's description

Table 58.7 Web loading speed by gender

	Female	Male	Total
Very important	180	54	126
Important	28	62	90
Neutral	8	6	14
Unimportant	2	2	4
Very unimportant	2	0	2
Total	112	124	236

Source: Author's description

perceived web colors as very unimportant. The largest group of respondents has a neutral attitude towards web colors. Men seem to be a little more indifferent to colors compared to women.

The majority of respondents considered loading speed to be important. Total 126 respondents (72 women and 54 men) ranked it as very important and a further 90 respondents (28 women and 62 men) selected it as important to them. Only 14 respondents were neutral. For 4 respondents, loading the website is unimportant and for 2 respondents it is very unimportant. The data show that web loading speed is an important factor for most respondents. Men's assessment of web speed is more benevolent compared to women. The values are available in Table 58.7.

In terms of generations, only the functional elements factor came out significantly at 10%. However, this may be due to the lower number of respondents. It will be important for future research to increase this number. Even though no statistical differences emerge from the results, it can be assumed that there may be some differences in the functional elements. The specific values are available in Table 58.8.

Table 58.8 Kruskal-Wallis by generation

Factor	Kruskal-Wallis H	df	Asymp. Sig.
Web clarity	0,001	1	0,973
Colors	0,201	1	0,654
Page loading speed	0,003	1	0,957
Shapes	0,670	1	0,413
Advertising banners	1,077	1	0,299
Short forms	0,470	1	0,493
Functionality of elements on the page	2,525	1	0,089

Source: Author's description

Table 58.9 Functionality of page elements by generation

	Generation Z	Generation Y	Total
Very important	122	36	158
Important	50	6	56
Neutral	18	0	18
Unimportant	2	0	2
Very unimportant	0	2	2
Total	192	44	236

Source: Author's description

The survey includes 236 respondents in total. Of these, 192 respondents belong to Generation Z and 44 respondents belong to Generation Y.

In Generation Z, 122 respondents rated the functionality of the features as very important. Another 50 rated the functionality of the elements as important, 18 respondents had a neutral opinion, and 2 respondents rated the functionality of the elements as not important. None of the Generation Z respondents considered the functionality of the elements as very unimportant.

Generation Y included 44 respondents and therefore had a smaller representation. Of these, 36 respondents rated the functionality of the elements as very important and 6 respondents rated it as important. No Generation Y respondent had a neutral opinion or considered the functionality of the elements as not important. Two respondents in this group rated the functionality of the elements as very unimportant.

Generation Y considered functional elements to be very important, while more than 30% of Generation Z respondents did not consider clarity to be most important. An overview is available in Table 58.9.

58.5 Discussion

Generation Z is a group of people who are just entering the job market, which is why it will be an increasing priority for companies looking for employees to reach out to this group. The good news for companies is that, according to the answers to the questionnaire, the most frequently visited company websites by Generation

Z are those offering jobs or internships. Therefore, it is crucial for web designers to reflect the behavior of Generation Z when creating websites for them. A better understanding of the needs of Generation Z can be a significant advantage. In fact, it can be assumed that websites that match the preferences and priorities of Generation Z will show higher conversions with this target group.

The research study focused on identifying the key factors that influence website users. In interpreting the findings, it was found that factors such as the clarity of the website, the colors used, the loading speed, and the functionality of the elements on the website play a role in influencing users.

The findings agree in many aspects with the results of other authors' studies on this topic; in the case of web clarity with Zhenhui et al. (2016); in the case of used colors, for example, Cyr et al. (2010) and Moss et al. (2006); and for loading speed, with Galletta (2004). Functionality is also considered important by Mahajan and Halfond (2014) and Torkey et al. (2007). Similar to those studies, this study highlights the importance of the factors mentioned.

If we focus on the practical implications of this research, the findings can provide a valuable resource for web design and marketing practitioners. A detailed understanding of the aspects that most influence users on a website could help to optimize the website, leading to greater attractiveness, efficiency, and user-friendliness.

The research also highlighted differences in the perception of websites between these demographic groups. The findings suggest that perceptions of websites may differ between men and women, as well as between Generation Z and other generations.

58.6 Conclusions

The research explored the factors that influence website users. It was found that the clarity of the website, the colors used, the loading speed of the website, and the functional elements on the website have a significant impact on the user experience and can also influence conversions. The research conducted in this paper also showed that there are demographic differences in how each factor affects users. It was found that there are differences in the perception of websites between men and women, and also between Generation Z and Generation Y.

The findings could provide significant insights for website designers and marketing professionals, as understanding these factors can lead to websites that are not only visually appealing but also user-friendly and deliver the desired conversions.

It is important to highlight some of the limitations of the research conducted. The data collection methodology and sample size are factors that affect the ability to generalize conclusions. This research is designed as longitudinal research, so the sample size will be continuously increased and other forms of research will be conducted with the respondents at the same time. Another limitation of the study may be various biases where respondents indicate that something influences them when in fact it may not. For this reason, eye-tracking experiments will also be conducted with the respondents in a subsequent phase of the research. However, these experiments would not be possible without the information obtained from this presented research.

In terms of future research, our study suggests several potential areas for further exploration. It may be useful to explore other potentially important factors that influence website users. In addition, more detailed research on different age, gender, and cultural groups could be conducted to gain a deeper understanding of demographic differences.

Considering these findings, this research appears to make a further contribution to understanding how different factors influence website users and how these perceptions may be influenced by demographic characteristics.

Acknowledgments The publication of this chapter was financially supported by the Student grant competition of Silesian University in Opava SGS/23/2023 within the project: "Factors influencing conversions on the corporate website." The support is gratefully acknowledged.

References

Bargas-Avila, J. A., Brenzikofer, O., Tuch, A. N., et al. (2011). Working towards usable forms on the Worldwide Web: Optimizing multiple selection interface elements. *Advances in Human-Computer Interaction, 2011*, 1–8.

Bertamini, M., Palumbo, L., Gheorghes, T. N., & Galatsidas, M. (2015). Do observers like curvature or do they dislike angularity? *British Journal of Psychology, 107*(1), 154–178.

Cao, G., Proctor, R. W., Ding, Y., Duffy, V. G., Zhang, Y., & Zhang, X. (2021). Influences of color salience and location of website links on user performance and affective experience with a mobile web directory. *International Journal of Human–Computer Interaction, 37*(6), 547–559.

Cyr, D., Head, M., & Larios, H. (2010). Colour appeal in website design within and across cultures: A multi-method evaluation. *International Journal of Human-Computer Studies, 68*(1–2), 1–21.

Dangmei, J., & Singh, A. P. (2016). Understanding the generation Z: The future workspace. *South-Asian Journal of Multidisciplinary Studies, 3*(3), 1–5.

Donnelly, V. (2001). *Designing easy-to-use websites: a hands-on approach to structuring successful websites*. Addison-Wesley. ISBN: 0201674688.

Galletta, D. F., Raymond, H., McCoy, S., & Polak, P. (2004). Web site delays: How tolerant are users? *Journal of the Association for Information Systems, 5*(1), 1–28.

Gravetter, F. J., & Wallnau, L. B. (2007). *Statistics for the behavioral sciences* (7th ed.). Thomson Wadsworth.

Hess, U., Gryc, O., & Hareli, S. (2013). How shapes influence social judgments. *Social Cognition, 31*(1), 72–80.

Iliev, I., & Dimitrov, G. P. (2014). Front end optimization methods and their effect. In *37th international convention on information and communication technology, electronics and microelectronics (MIPRO), Opatija, Croatia 26–30 May 2014*.

Issa, T., & Isaias, P. (2016). Internet factors influencing generations Y and Z in Australia and Portugal: A practical study. *Information Processing & Management, 52*(4), 592–617.

Lanza, B., Aparecida Oliviera, M., Juk, Y., et al. (2022). Does web page loading speed matter? An analysis in the Brazilian Public Service Portals. In *DG.O 2022: The 23rd annual international conference on digital government research. Association for Computing Machinery, New York, 15–17 June 2022*.

Le, T. D., & Vo, H. (2017). Consumer attitude towards website advertising formats: a comparative study of banner, pop-up and in-line display advertisements. *International Journal of Internet Marketing and Advertising, 11*(3), 202–217.

Leder, H., Tinio, P. P. L., & Bar, M. (2011). Emotional valence modulates the preference for curved objects. *Perception, 40*(6), 649–655.

Mahajan, S., & Halfond, W. G. J. (2014). Finding HTML presentation failures using image comparison techniques. In *Proceedings of the 29th ACM/IEEE international conference on automated software engineering (ASE'14). Association for Computing Machinery, New York, NY, USA, 15–19 September 2014.*

McKight, P. E., & Najab, J. (2010). Kruskal-Wallis test. In I. B. Weiner & W. E. Craighead (Eds.), *The Corsini encyclopedia of psychology.*

Moss, G., Gunn, R., & Heller, J. (2006). Some men like it black, some women like it pink: Consumer implications of differences in male and female website design. *Journal of Consumer Behaviour, 5*(4), 328–341.

Mythili, R., & Kiruthiga, V. (2022). Scrutiny on colour psychology by utilising colour wheel to determine its effect on gen Z for website design. *International Journal of Health Sciences, 6*(S3), 2687–2700.

Nordin, H., Singh, D., & Mansor, Z. (2020). An empirical study of e-learning interface design elements for generation Z. *International Journal of Advanced Computer Science and Applications, 11*(9), 507–515.

Okamura, Y. (2018). Shape preference and the gender differences. In *Proceedings of the 5th international conference on research in behavioral and social science, Barcelona, Spain, 7 December 2018.*

Rettie, R., Robinson, H., & Jenner, B. (2003). Does internet advertising alienate users? *Kingston Business School, 2*, 1–10.

Starov, O., Gill, P., & Nikiforakis, N. (2016). Are you sure you want to contact us? In *Proceedings on privacy enhancing technologies, Darmstadt, Germany, 19–22 July 2016.*

Tandon, U., Kiran, R., & Sah, A. N. (2016). Customer satisfaction using website functionality, perceived usability and perceived usefulness towards online shopping in India. *Information Development, 32*(5), 1657–1673.

Tarafdar, M., & Zhang, J. J. (2005). Analyzing the influence of web site design parameters on web site usability. *Information Resources Management Journal (IRMJ), 18*(4), 62–80.

Torkey, F. A., Keshk, A., Hamza, T., & Ibrahim, A. (2007). A new methodology for web testing. In *2007 ITI 5th international conference on information and communications technology, Cairo, Egypt.*

Xiaoxiong, W., Jinchun, W., & Haiyan, W. (2022). The influence of color on web page complexity and color recommendation. In T. Ahram & C. Falcão (Eds.), *Usability and user experience.*

Xilogianni, C., Doukas, F. R., Drivas, I. C., & Kouis, D. (2022). Speed matters: What to prioritize in optimization for faster websites. *Analytics, 1*(2), 175–192.

Yusof, U. K., Khaw, L. K., Ch'ng, H. Y., & Neow, B. J. (2010). Balancing between usability and aesthetics of Web design. In *2010 international symposium on information technology, Kuala Lumpur, Malaysia.*

Zeng, E., Kohno, T., & Roesner, F. (2021). What makes a "Bad" Ad? User perceptions of problematic online advertising. In *Proceedings of the 2021 CHI conference on human factors in computing systems (CHI'21). Yokohama, Japan, 8–13 May 2021.*

Zhenhui, J. J., Weiquan, W., Bernard, C. Y., & Jie, Y. (2016). The determinants and impacts of aesthetics in users' first interaction with websites. *Journal of Management Information Systems, 33*(1), 229–259.

Chapter 59
Factors Affecting the Effectiveness of Email Marketing

Lola Maria Sempelidou, Giorgos Avlogiaris, and Ioannis Antoniadis

Abstract Email marketing is an effective online tool for promoting products or services, enhancing brand awareness, and increasing sales. To ensure the effectiveness of email marketing, companies must adhere to best practices, creating campaigns that are relevant and attractive to the target audience while continuously monitoring the factors that influence their success. Therefore, the objective of this study is to examine the factors that influence the effectiveness of email marketing. In a constantly changing environment, the role of marketing, in addition to promoting products, contributes to the acquisition of competitive advantage. In this study, a literature review was initially conducted, as well as a reference to previous research. This study specifically focuses on factors such as characteristics, incentives, frequency, and type of email marketing, which affect the effectiveness of email marketing. Finally, the findings indicate that factors such as the characteristics, incentives, and type of email marketing significantly affect the effectiveness of email marketing.

Keywords Email marketing · Factors · Email characteristics · Frequency · Email type

59.1 Introduction

Digital marketing is highly interactive, targets individual customers, and offers a continuous measurement of advertising results, leading to more effective ongoing campaigns (Mahmoud et al., 2019; Antoniadis et al., 2020; Hudak et al., 2017; Koronaki et al., 2023; Saprikis, 2013). The increase in the use of electronic devices, such as smartphones and tablets, has pushed users to rely more on the Internet (Miranda & d'Angelo, 2019). Many people access the Internet on a daily basis and

---

L. M. Sempelidou (✉) · G. Avlogiaris · I. Antoniadis
University of Western Macedonia, Management Science and Technology, Koila, Kozani, Greece

feel the need to be connected throughout the day, either through their email services or social networking (Kumar, 2021). Despite the fact that new technologies now pave the way for changes in digital marketing like Web 3.0 (Antoniadis et al., 2019a, b, c), email marketing still remains an integral part of digital marketing strategies worldwide (Kumar, 2021). Furthermore, email marketing has become an essential tool for businesses of all sizes to promote their products and services (Thomas et al., 2022). Email marketing has a huge global reach, with a staggering volume of over 306 billion emails sent and received every day (Thomas et al., 2022). In particular, as of 2021, 4 billion people use email for communication and marketing, a number that is projected to grow to 4.6 billion by 2025 (Hudak et al., 2017; Radicati Group, 2018–2022). Email marketing has many advantages, including cost-effectiveness, the ability to reach a wide audience, ease of personalization, and the ability to track and measure results (Fariborzi & Zahedifard, 2012; Hudak et al., 2017). However, despite the effectiveness of email marketing, it is important to mention that there are some problems with it, such as spam emails (Chittenden & Rettie, 2003; Kanich et al., 2008). Therefore, it can lead recipients to treat emails as spam, which can damage the sender's reputation and possibly lead to the email account being blocked or blacklisted (Miranda & d'Angelo, 2019). Another problem is low open rates; that is, if the subject line and content of the email are not attractive, recipients may not open the email, reducing the effectiveness of the campaign (Chaffey, 2003; Lewis, 2002). In addition, sending too many emails or sending them too often can lead to recipients getting tired of receiving them and proceeding to an unsubscribe (Baggott, 2011; Rizka et al. 2016). Moreover, the Hellenic Statistical Authority released a survey that examined the utilization of information and communication technologies within private households in 2022. The survey aimed to understand how households in Greece engage with these technologies. The results of this survey revealed that the percentage of households with home Internet access increased by 59.5% in 2022. Additionally, regarding the reasons for using the Internet, the main activity was the search for information about products and services and it concerns the 89.2% for the year 2022. Regarding e-commerce, 53.2% have made an online purchase or order of goods or services over the Internet, for personal use. Indeed, this percentage revealed a decrease compared to the previous 58.3% (2021) (National Statistical Service of Greece (NSSG), 2022). It is imperative to underscore that this research did not encompass purchases conducted via email marketing. Therefore, considering all the above peculiarities and advantages of email marketing, it is crucial to examine the Greek market. It is pertinent to highlight that relevant Greek literature and available Greek data are limited; the research specifically for the Greek market can contribute to the identification of certain characteristics and particularities that require further analysis. Understanding the specific dynamics of the Greek market can assist in comprehending factors that affect the effectiveness of email marketing and guide future research in this area.

59.2 Literature Review

There is extensive literature on the importance of email marketing as an essential tool for product promotion and business marketing strategies (Ellis-Chadwik & Doherty, 2012; Lewis, 2002; Khedkar & Khedkar, 2021; Kumar, 2021). Email marketing is generally considered an effective method of communicating with customers and a means of creating long-term trusting relationships (Jenkins, 2009; Lorente-Páramoa et al., 2020; Miranda & d'Angelo, 2019). The history of email marketing dates to the early twentieth century, when American companies began forming small databases and sending advertisements via mail (Merisavo & Raulas, 2004). According to research conducted by "The Radicati Group," email marketing is a form of direct marketing that involves sending messages to customers via email to achieve various goals, such as customer loyalty, sales growth, and brand awareness (Radicati Group, 2018–2022). With email accounts projected to grow to over 361 billion by the end of 2024, email marketing has become a popular strategy among businesses because of its ability to reach large audiences and reduce communication costs (Radicati Group, 2018–2022). In 2020, the number of daily emails sent was estimated at 306 billion, underscoring the prevalence of email marketing as a communication tool for businesses with their customers (Bawm & Nath, 2015; Radicati Group, 2018–2022).

59.2.1 Conceptual Framework and Research Hypotheses

Based on the literature review, a conceptual framework can be formed to encompass the initial hypotheses (Chaparro-Peláez et al., 2022; Feld et al., 2013; McKinsey & Company, 2014). This framework incorporates various variables that are crucial for analyzing the effectiveness of email marketing campaigns. The variables consisted of email characteristics, incentives, frequency of sending emails, and type of emails, as well as the effectiveness of email marketing measured by conversion rate, open email rate, clickthrough rate, attention retention, and unsubscribe rate. These variables have been identified as key factors for understanding the dynamics and impact of email marketing campaigns (Chaparro-Peláez et al., 2022; Namira & Wandebori, 2016) (Fig. 59.1).

Characteristics
The characteristics of an email play an important role in the engagement the recipients have with the message, in similar ways that characteristics of a post on social media and online advertisement affect their engagement (Antoniadis et al., 2019a, b, c; Iliopoulou & Vlachvei, 2022). According to research by Ruth Rettie and Lisa, which was carried out as part of the research "Email Marketing: Success Factors" (Rettie & Chittenden, 2003a, b), it is reported that marketing through email is an effective online marketing tool. The study identifies key factors such as the subject line, email length, incentives, and number of images that significantly

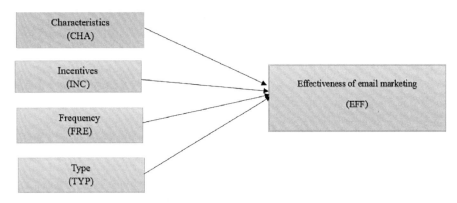

Fig. 59.1 Conceptual framework

impact the response rate of email campaigns. Additionally, the research highlights a three-stage model for effective email marketing, involving the recipient opening the email, maintaining their interest, and ultimately encouraging a response through a click-through URL link, emphasizing the importance of subject line, content, and recipient characteristics in determining the success of email marketing (Rettie & Chittenden, 2003a, b). The research of Paulo et al. (2022)), proposes a methodology to improve email open rates by enabling campaign editors to create engaging subject lines and anticipate campaign success levels (Paulo et al., 2022). Therefore, the first hypothesis is as follows.

Hypothesis 1 (H1) Email characteristics significantly affect the effectiveness of email marketing.

Incentives

The study by Hsin Hsin Chang, Hamid Rizal, and Hanudin Amin emphasizes the substantial impact of financial incentives in mitigating consumer-perceived intrusiveness in email advertising, regardless of whether it is permission-based or spamming email (Balakrishnan & Parekh, 2014; Chang et al., 2013). Incentives may include discounts, free trials, or other offers that provide value to recipients (Rettie & Chittenden, 2003a, b). The study found that incentives have a significant and positive influence on the consumer decision journey, indicating that providing attractive incentives through email marketing can effectively drive customer behavior and contribute to the success of marketing campaigns (Rettie & Chittenden, 2003a, b). By offering attractive incentives, businesses can increase the effectiveness of their email campaigns and achieve better results (Gamage, 2021). Regarding incentives, the second hypothesis of the study is formed, which claims that higher response rates are associated with more attractive incentives (Mahmoud et al., 2019; Merisavo & Raulas, 2004).

Hypothesis 2 (H2) Email incentives significantly affect the effectiveness of email marketing.

Frequency

Understanding the key success factors of email marketing communications is imperative for marketers to achieve their desired results (Kotler & Armstrong, 2009; Micheaux, 2011). According to the research of Ansari and Mela, personalized email content and design increase response rates by an average of 62%, and Bill Nussey's study highlights the importance of choosing the right time to send emails, resulting in a significant increase in revenue in some cases (Ansari & Mela, 2003; Nussey, 2009). Indeed, the study by Marko Merisavo and Mika Raulas revealed that regular contact with consumers through email marketing has positive effects on brand loyalty, as it leads to increased brand recommendations, store visits, product purchases, and positive brand attitudes (Merisavo & Raulas, 2004). Furthermore, the frequency of posts and content quality play significant roles in campaign performance (Feld et al., 2012; Kumar, 2021; Micheaux, 2011; Gamage, 2021). According to a study conducted by Julián Chaparro Peláez et al. in 2022, the research provides the value of making small, inexpensive adjustments to current practices, such as controlling email campaign frequency and utilizing technical segments and personalization techniques, to enhance email openings, recipient attention, and overall engagement (Chaparro-Peláez et al., 2022).

Hypothesis 3 (H3) Frequency significantly affects the effectiveness of email-marketing.

Email Type

The results suggest a positive and significant relationship between segmentation and the degree of attention recipients give to promotional emails (Biloša et al., 2016). This finding is consistent with practitioners' positive perceptions of personalization and current digital marketing trends that emphasize the importance of providing personalized content to improve customer experience (Chang et al., 2013; Lewis, 2002). Segmentation involves dividing the target audience into distinct subgroups based on specific characteristics, allowing marketers to tailor promotional emails to suit the preferences and interests of each subgroup (Hartemo, 2016; Kanich et al., 2008). This personalized approach is believed to capture recipients' attention, enhance their overall experience, and increase their engagement and response rates (Baggott, 2007; Biloša et al., 2016). Practitioners recognize the effectiveness of personalization in building stronger connections with customers, and current digital marketing trends highlight it as a key strategy for optimizing customer experiences and enhancing marketing outcomes (Mahmoud et al., 2019). Email marketing success increases when there is an emphasis on empowering consumers by sending relevant emails with their approval and encouraging their active participation in the communication process (Hartemo, 2016). However, further experimental studies are needed to investigate various aspects, such as the effect of email newsletter features, the role of consumer-controlled systems, and the impact of technological development on the effectiveness of email marketing (Hartemo, 2016).

Hypothesis 4 (H4) Email type significantly affects the effectiveness of email marketing.

Table 59.1 Research hypothesis

Hypothesis	Description	Path
H1	Email characteristics significantly affect the effectiveness of email marketing	CHA → EFF
H2	Email incentives affect the effectiveness of email marketing	INC → EFF
H3	Frequency significantly affects the effectiveness of email marketing.	FRE → EFF
H4	Email type significantly affects email marketing effectiveness	TYP → EFF

Regarding the current gap in the field, further research could explore the impact of emerging technologies, such as artificial intelligence and automation, on the effectiveness of email marketing (Verma et al., 2021). Finally, understanding the significance of customer preferences, behavior, and engagement in different industries and target segments could provide valuable insights to improve email marketing strategies.

59.3 Methodology

This section presents the operationalization of the research variable of the hypothesized conceptual framework, followed by the data collection and sample characteristics.

59.3.1 Functionality of Determinants

The format of the questionnaire was based on questionnaires used in similar studies and adapted appropriately to the research objectives of this study. The specific questions are aimed at better understanding the behavior of users-consumers from the whole of their online experiences by focusing on their habits and perceptions of electronic advertisements via email and how much all the above contribute or not to the purchase of the advertised products or services. The questionnaire had sixteen (16) closed questions. Table 59.2 lists the determinants of the survey. For each determinant, a multi-item scale was developed according to comprehensive information in the literature review and measured on a 5-point Likert scale (Vaggelis Saprikis et al., 2021). Four items were used to measure email marketing factors.

Table 59.2 Operationalization of research variables

Research variables	Operational definition	Sources
Characteristics (CHA)	Which of the following do you consider important and to what extent in your decision to open an email?	Shastya Rizka Namira and Harimukti Wandebori (2016). Measuring The Effectiveness Of Email Marketing toward the consumer decision journey. Journal of Business and Management, Vol. 5, No. 6, pp. 727–738.
Subject Line	The title	
E-mail Length	The length	
Images	The images	
Number of links	Links	
Emoji	Emoji	
Incentives (INC)	Which of the following incentives and to what extent can affect you in completing the purchase?	Shastya Rizka Namira and Harimukti Wandebori (2016). Measuring The Effectiveness Of Email Marketing toward the consumer decision journey. Journal of Business and Management, Vol. 5, No. 6, pp. 727–738.
Subscribe to Newsletter	Subscription to a Newsletter (Which offers a discount)	
Coupons	Discount / Offers	
Discounts	Customized emails	
Sales coupons	Sales coupons	
Frequency (FRE)	Do you consider the frequency of the messages that you receive regarding a particular email can affect your decision in	Micheaux, A.L. (2011). Managing e-mail advertising frequency from the consumer perspective. Journal of advertising, p. 47. Ansari A., Mela K.F. (2003). Customization. Journal of Marketing Research., p. 138.
	unsubscribe	
	report it as spam	

(continued)

Table 59.2 (continued)

Research variables	Operational definition	Sources
Type of email (TYP)	Which type of email do you consider more likely to respond and to what extent?	Sebastian Feld, Heiko Frenzen, Manfred Krafft, Kay Peters, Peter C. Verhoef. (2013). The effects of mailing design characteristics on direct mail campaign performance. Intern. J. of Research in Marketing, pp. 143–159.
Newsletters	Newsletter	
Personalization	Personalized email	
Welcome email	Welcome email	
Reengagement email	Reengagement email	
Effectiveness of email marketing (EFE)	When you receive an email with promotional content to what extent do you:	Ruth Rettie,Lisa Chittenden. (2003a, b). An evaluation of e-mail marketing and factors affecting response. 7 Journal of Targeting, Measurement and Analysis for Marketing, Henry Stewart Publications 1479–1862 (2003, pp. 203–217.42. Zirthang Lian Bawm, Rudra Pratap Deb Nath. (2015). A Conceptual Model for Effective Email Marketing. 17th International Conference on Computer and Information Technology (ICCIT), pp. 250–256.
Open Email	Open it	
Pay Attention to the Email	Pay attention to its content	
Conversion	Buy the promoted product	
Clickthrough	Click on the links	

59.3.2 Data Collection and Sample Characteristics

The research sample consisted of Internet users from all age groups. The questionnaire was created using Google Forms and promoted as a link via email and social media pages. The survey was conducted from September 30 to November 22, 2022, with a sample size of 317. Data analysis and processing were performed using IBM SPSS software.

In the study, 236 women and 81 men participated; in the first case, the percentage was 74.4%, and in the second case, the percentage was 25.6% of the sample. Our sample consisted of 317 participants. The 31–50 age group comprised the majority with a percentage of 75.7% ($n = 240$), followed by the age groups 18–30 with a percentage of 15.1% ($n = 48$), 51–70 with a percentage of 8.5% ($n = 27$), and 70 and over with a rate of 0.6% ($n = 2$).

59.3.3 Data Analysis

The analysis of the data was carried out using the SEM statistical technique. To be precise, data analysis was performed using the measurement and structural models. In addition, the constructs were assessed for reliability and convergent and discriminant validity (Saprikis et al., 2021). In the subsequent stage of the research, the structural model was examined to test the relationships between the theoretical determinants in terms of their strength and direction. The relationships were calculated and analyzed within the structural model framework. The overall goodness-of-fit of the model was evaluated using a combination of measures. A well-fitted model was determined by criteria such as a chi-square/df ratio less than five, comparative fit index (CFI), normed fit index (NFI), incremental fit index (IFI), and Tucker-Lewis index (TLI) values greater than 0.90. Additionally, a root mean square error of approximation (RMSEA) value less than 0.08 indicated a good fit for the model. These measures provided a comprehensive assessment of the overall goodness-of-fit of the structural model.

59.4 Results

The results section focuses on the assessment of the structural model within the SEM framework. This provides a comprehensive summary of the outcomes obtained from the analysis, offering valuable insights into the tested variable relationships and their statistical significance. This section examines the effectiveness and validity of the proposed structural model, providing a clear understanding of how variables interact and contribute to the overall theoretical framework (Table 59.3).

Table 59.3 Evaluation of model goodness-of-fit

Measures	Recommended value	Structural model
$\chi 2/df$	≤5.00	2.342
GFI	≥0.90	0.904
CFI	≥0.90	0.938
IFI	≥0.90	0.939
TLI	≥0.90	0.923
RMSEA [90%CI]	≤0.08	0.065 [0.56, 0.74]

First, the data were analyzed for reliability issues. Moreover, convergent and discriminant validity between the latent constructs were also investigated. In particular, factor analysis, which utilizes PCA and VARIMAX, was used to investigate the validity of the variables, group measurement items into latent factors, and calculate factor loadings. To examine the suitability of the data for factor analysis, various measures were applied. Specifically, Bartlett's test of sphericity (Chi-square = 3079.784, $p < 0.001$) verified that the correlation matrices had significant correlations among the variables. The Kaiser-Meyer-Olkin (KMO) measure was 0.883, and the measurement of sampling adequacy (MSA) ranged from 0.574 to 0.952, indicating that both values were acceptable. These MSA values were all higher than 0.50 (Hair et al., 2014). Finally, to examine the reliability, convergent, and discriminant validity, Cronbach's alpha test, Composite Reliability (CR), and average variance extracted (AVE) values were utilized. Factor loadings ranged from 0.540 to 0.911 (Table 59.4) and were high in all cases (>0.4), Cronbach's alpha values surpassed the threshold of 0.7 (Bentler, 1990), ranging from 0.821 to 0.847 (Table 59.4), whereas Composite Reliability (CR) also surpassed 0.6 (Bagozzi & Yi, 1998), ranging from 0.828 to 0.851 (Table 59.4), and Average Variance Extracted (AVE) surpassed 0.5, ranging from 0.532 to 0.708 (Table 59.4).

Structural Model

The analysis of the structural model (as depicted in Fig. 59.1) aimed to provide an empirical evaluation of the hypothesized relationships among the research variables and constructs. The standardized parameters were utilized to quantify the strength of these relationships, with solid lines representing the major pathways. Furthermore, the examination of goodness-of-fit measures indicated a favorable fit for the model, suggesting that it adequately represents the data. Specifically, the model's overall goodness of fit was assessed using a combination of measures. As suggested by these measures, the data fit the model well; the recommended values are presented in Table 59.3. Thus, the chi-square/df ratio should be lower than 5 (Bentler, 1990); the goodness-of-fit index (GFI), the comparative fit index (CFI), the incremental ft. index (IFI), and the Tucker-Lewis index (TLI) values should exceed 0.90 (Hu & Bentler, 1999); and the root mean square error of approximation (RMSEA) should be lower than 0.08 (Muthén & Muthén, 2015). Therefore, the structural model illustrated in Fig. 59.2 was satisfactory (see Table 59.3) because the model indicators were satisfactory according to the values recommended in the literature.

Table 59.4 Standardized factor loadings and individual item reliability

Construct	Item	Loading	Mean statistic	Std. deviation	CR	AVE	Cronbach's Alpha
Characteristics (CHA)	1	0.635	2.74	1.086	0.849	0.532	0.827
	2	0.811	2.30	1.146			
	3	0.771	2.24	1.068			
	4	0.775	2.03	1.025			
	5	0.639	1.59	0.828			
Incentive (INC)	1	0.642	2.20	1.139	0.849	0.590	0.847
	2	0.830	3.10	1.232			
	3	0.654	2.20	1.165			
	4	0.911	2.86	1.241			
Frequency (FRE)	1	0.900	2.89	1.288	0.828	0.708	0.827
	2	0.778	2.75	1.291			
Type of email (TYP)	1	0.540	2.10	0.947	0.840	0.574	0.821
	2	0.814	2.32	1.169			
	3	0.842	2.00	1.042			
	4	0.796	1.98	1.011			
Effectiveness of email marketing (EFE)	1	0.795	1.85	0.809	0.851	0.589	0.847
	2	0.794	1.96	0.897			
	3	0.743	1.54	0.713			
	4	0.736	1.70	0.726			

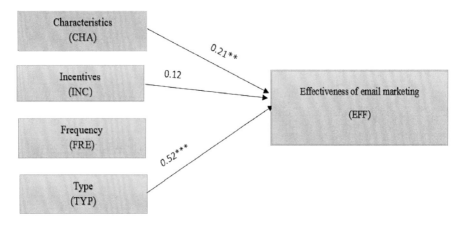

Fig. 59.2 Results of the structural equation modelling

Table 59.5 Path coefficients (standardized regression coefficients)

Hypothesis	Path	Coefficient
H1	CHA → EFF	0.21**
H2	INC → EFF	0.12
H3	FRE → EFF	Nonsignificant
H4	TYP → EFF	0.52***

Note: $p < 0.1$, * $p < 0.05$; ** $p < 0.01$; *** $p < 0.001$

The path diagram with the resulting standardized regression coefficients indicating the direction and magnitude of relationships among variables is demonstrated in Fig. 59.2. The structural model revealed that one (H3) of the four hypotheses is rejected (Table 59.5). The results support the hypothesis that email characteristics (CHA) have a significant positive effect on the effectiveness of email marketing (EFF) (H1: $b = 0.21$, $p = 0 < 0.01$), and email incentives have a positive effect on effectiveness (H2: $b = 0.12$, $p < 0.1$). Finally, the type of email used was found to significantly affect effectiveness (H4: $b = 0.52$, $p < 0.001$), suggesting that different types of email have varying levels of impact on achieving marketing objectives. Therefore, these findings suggest that the characteristics of email marketing, incentives, and type of email marketing are determining factors in terms of the effectiveness of email marketing.

59.5 Conclusions

The reach and potential of email marketing should not be overlooked by businesses. Email marketing is an effective means for customer outreach, communication, content promotion, building brand awareness, and gaining a competitive advantage.

After the literature review, a conceptual framework was created according to which the measurement model and the structural model followed, specifically the assessment of the structural model. The findings from this assessment of the structural model are that the characteristics of email marketing, which include subject line, length of email, images, number of links, and emoji, significantly influence the effectiveness of email marketing (hypothesis H1). These findings are consistent with previous research that highlights the importance of creating attention-grabbing subject lines, visually appealing content, and maintaining the appropriate length for emails (Rettie & Chittenden, 2003a, b). Indeed, incentives that are usually economic and include subscription to a newsletter (which usually offers a discount), discount coupons, offers, and customized emails, offered in the promotional activities of the sellers, significantly influence consumers (hypothesis H2). By offering attractive incentives, businesses can increase the effectiveness of their email campaigns and achieve better results (Gamage, 2021). Furthermore, the type of emails (hypothesis H4) that include newsletters, personalization, welcome emails, and reengagement emails significantly influence consumers. These findings align with prior researches that underscore the increased effectiveness of email marketing when there is a focus on empowering consumers. This can be achieved by sending them relevant emails with their consent and actively encouraging their participation in the communication process (Hartemo, 2016). The literature review has shown that the sources of the factors that affect the effectiveness of email marketing are incomplete; therefore, this area needs further investigation and study. After conducting the research, according to the literature, further research on the effectiveness of personalized and segmented email campaigns on customer engagement and conversion rates is suggested. In addition, mobile devices are increasingly preferred regarding the means used to connect to the Internet. For this reason, further research is proposed, which will focus on the optimization of email campaigns for the specific users. Finally, considering all the above, we concluded that email marketing has many indications of an efficient digital tool for promoting products at low cost, as long as there is a proper strategy, planning, and implementation.

References

Ansari, A., & Mela, K. F. (2003). Customization. *Journal of Marketing Research, 40*, 138.

Antoniadis, I., Assimakopoulos, C., & Koukoulis, I. (2019a). Attitudes of college students towards online advertisement in social networking sites: A structural equation modelling approach. *International Journal of Internet Marketing and Advertising, 13*(2), 137–154.

Antoniadis, I., Kontsas, S., & Spinthiropoulos, K. (2019b). Blockchain and brand loyalty programs: A short review of applications and challenges. *International Conference on Economic Sciences and Business Administration, 5*(1), 8–16.

Antoniadis, I. I., Saprikis, V. S., & Karteraki, E. E. (2019c). Consumers' attitudes towards advertisement in YouTube. *Strategic Innovative Marketing and Tourism*, 253–261.

Antoniadis, I., Paltsoglou, S., Vasios, G., & Kyratsis, P. (2020). Online engagement factors on posts in food Facebook brand pages in Greece. In E. K. A. Kavoura (Ed.), *Strategic innovative marketing and tourism* (pp. 365–373). Springer Proceedings in Business and Economics.

Baggott, C. (2007). *Email marketing by numbers*. Wiley.
Baggott, C. (2011). *Email marketing by the numbers: How to use the world's greatest marketing tool to take any organization to the next level*. Wiley.
Bagozzi, P., & Yi, Y. (1998). On the evaluation of structural equation models. *Journal of Academic Marketing Science*, 74–94.
Balakrishnan, R., & Parekh, R. (2014). Learning to predict subject-line opens for large-scale email marketing. *IEEE International Conference on Big Data*, 579–584.
Bawm, Z. L., & Nath, R. P. D. (2015). *A conceptual model for effective email marketing* (pp. 250–256). 17th International Conference on Computer and Information Technology (ICCIT).
Bentler, M. (1990). Comparative ft indexes in structural models. *Psychological Bulletin, 107*, 238–246.
Biloša, A., Turkaljb, D., & Kelićc, I. (2016). *Open-Rate Controlled Experiment in E-Mail Marketing Campaigns*. Trziste.
Chaffey, D. (2003). *Total E-mail marketing*. Marketing Insights Ltd.
Chang, H. H., Rizal, H., & Amin, H. (2013). *The determinants of consumer behavior towards email advertisement*. Internet Research.
Julián Chaparro-Peláez, Ángel Hernández-García, Ángel-José Lorente-Páramo. (2022, April). May I have your attention, please? An investigation on opening effectiveness in e-mail marketing. Review of Managerial Science, pp. 1–24.
Chittenden, L., & Rettie, R. (2003). Evaluation of e-mail marketing and factors affecting response. *Journal of Targeting, Measurement and Analysis for Marketing, 3*, 208.
Ellis-Chadwik, F., & Doherty, N. (2012). Web advertising: The role of email marketing. *Journal of Business Research, 65*, 843–848.
Fariborzi, E., & Zahedifard, M. (2012). E-mail marketing: Advantages, disadvantages and improving techniques. *International Journal of e-Education, e-Business, e-Management and e-Learning, 2*(3), 234–236.
Feld, S., Frenzen, H., & Krafft, M. (2012). The effects of mailing design characteristics on direct mail campaign performance. *International Journal of Research in Marketing*, 1–17.
Feld, S., Frenzen, H., Krafft, M., Peters, K., & Verhoef, P. C. (2013). The effects of mailing design characteristics on direct mail campaign performance. *International Journal of Research in Marketing, 30*, 143–159.
Gamage, T. C. (2021). Boost your email marketing campaign! Emojis as visual stimuli to influence customer engagement. *Management Digest*, 26–31.
Goic, M., & Rojas, A. (2021). The effectiveness of triggered email Marketing in Addressing. *Journal of Interactive Marketing, 55*, 121.
Hair, J., Black, W., Babin, B., & Anderson, R. (2014). *Multivariate data analysis*. 3rd Pearson/Prentice Hall.
Hartemo, M. (2016). Email marketing in the era of the empowered consumer. *Journal of Research in Interactive, 10*, 212–230.
Hu, L. T., & Bentler, P. M. (1999). Cutof criteria for ft indexes in covariance structure analysis: Conventional criteria versus new alternatives. *Structural Equation Modeling: A, 6*, 1–55.
Hudak, M., Kianičková, E., & Madleňák, R. (2017). The importance of e-mail marketing in e-commerce. *International Scientific Conference on Sustainable, Modern and Safe Transport*, 342–347.
Iliopoulou, E., & Vlachvei, A. (2022). Clustering the social media users based on users' motivations and social media content. In *Advances in quantitative economic research* (pp. 553–568). International Conference on Applied Economics (ICOAE).
Jenkins, S. (2009). *The truth about email marketing*. FT Press.
Kanich, C., Kreibich, C., & Levchenko, K. (2008). Spamalytics: An empirical analysis of spam marketing conversion. *International Computer Science Institute*, 27–31.
Khedkar, C. E., & Khedkar, A. E. (2021). Email MArketing: A cost-effective marketing method. *Vidyabharati International Interdisciplinary Research Journal*, 207–210.

Kline, R. B. (2016). *Principles and practice of structural equation modeling*. 2nd The Guilford Press.

Koronaki, E., Vlachvei, A., & Panopoulos, A. (2023). Managing the online customer experience and subsequent consumer responses across the customer journey: A review and future research agenda. Electronic commerce research and applications. *Electronic Commerce Research and Applications, 58*(C), 1–36.

Kotler, P., & Armstrong, G. (2009). *Principles of marketing*. Learned Nshrasly.

Kumar, A. (2021). An empirical examination of the effects of design elements of email newsletters on consumers' email responses and their purchase. *Journal of Retailing and Consumer Services, 58*, 1–13.

Lewis, H. G. (2002). *Effective e-mail marketing: The complete guide to creating successful campaigns*. American Management Association.

Lorente-Páramoa, Á.-J., Hernández-García, Á., & Chaparro-Peláezb, J. (2020). Modelling e-mail marketing effectiveness—An approach based on the theory. *Management Letters / Cuadernos de Gestión*, 19–27.

Mahmoud, A. B., Grigoriou, N., Fuxman, L., Mahmoud, F. B., Yafi, E., & Tehseen, S. (2019). Email is evil!Behavioural responses towardspermission-based direct emailmarketing and gender differences. *Journal of Research in Interactive Marketing, 13*(2), 227–248.

McKinsey & Company by Aufreiter, N., Boudet, J., & Weng, V. (2014, January 1). Why marketers should keep sending you e-mails. *Growth, Marketing & Sales* (p. 3). Retrieved from https://www.mckinsey.com/capabilities/growth-marketing-and-sales/our-insights/why-marketers-should-keep-sending-you-emails

Merisavo, M., & Raulas, M. (2004). The impact of e-mail marketing on brand loyalty. *Journal of Product & Brand Management, 13*(7), 498–505.

Micheaux, A. L. (2011). Managing e-mail advertising frequency from the consumer perspective. *Journal of Advertising, 40*, 47.

Miranda, M. F., & d'Angelo, M. J. (2019). Limitations of the use of E-mail as communication strategy in downstream social Marketing for the People from Espirito Santo – Brazil. *Brazilian Journal of Marketing*, 119–223.

Muthén, L. K., & Muthén, B. O. (2015). *Mplus for windows 731*. Muthén & Muthén.

Namira, S. R., & Wandebori, H. (2016). Measuring the effectiveness of email marketing toward the consumer decision journey. *Journal of Business and Management, 5*(6), 727–738.

National Statistical Service of Greece (NSSG). (2022). *National Statistical Service of Greece (NSSG)*. Retrieved from https://www.statistics.gr/

Nussey, B. (2009). *The quiet revolution in email marketing*. NE: iUniverse.

Paulo, M., Miguéis, V. L., & Pereira, I. (2022). Leveraging email marketing: Using the subject line to anticipate the open rate. *Expert Systems With Applications., 207*, 117974.

Reimers, V., Chao, C.-W., & Gorman, S. (2016). Permission email marketing and its influence on online shopping. *Asia Pacific Journal of Marketing, 28*(2), 308–321.

Rettie, R., & Chittenden, L. (2003a). Email marketing: Success factors. *Kingston University, Occasional Paper Series No, 50*, 1–15.

Rettie, R., & Chittenden, L. (2003b). An evaluation of e-mail marketing and factors affecting response. *Journal of Targeting, Measurement and Analysis for Marketing, Henry Stewart Publications 1479-1862, 7*, 203–217.

Saprikis, V. (2013). Consumers' perceptions towards E-shopping advertisements and promotional actions in social networking sites. *International Journal of E-Adoption, 5*, 12.

Saprikis, V., Avlogiaris, G., & Katarachia, A. (2021). Determinants of the intention to adopt Mobile augmented reality apps in shopping malls among university students. *Journal of Theoretical and Applied Electronic Commerce Research*, 491.

The Radicati Group, Inc. (2018, March). *Email statistics report, 2018–2022*. Retrieved from A Technology Market Research Firm: https://www.radicati.com

Thomas, J. S., Chaoqun, C., & Iacobucci, D. (2022). Email marketing as a tool for strategic persuasion. *Journal of Interactive Marketing, 57*(3), 377–392.

Tiwari, A., Ansari, M. A., & Dubey, R. (2018). An effective email marketing using optimized email cleaning process. *International Journal of Computer Sciences and Engineering, 6*, 277–285.

Verma, S., Sharma, R., Deb, S., & Maitra, D. (2021). Artificial intelligence in marketing: Systematic review and future research direction. *International Journal of Information Management Data Insights, 1*, 2–8.

Chapter 60
E-commerce to Increase Sales in a Peruvian Importer of Hardware Items

Guillermo S. Miñan Olivos, María Y. Del Busto Valdez, Johan H. Espinoza Tumpay, Williams E. Castillo Martínez, and Jairo Jaime Turriate Chávez

Abstract The present chapter sought to demonstrate how e-commerce could increase sales in a Peruvian company importing hardware items. The chapter had a quantitative approach, a nonexperimental cross-sectional design, and a descriptive level. The study population was represented by all company sales and historical sales from 2020 to 2021 were sampled, as well as a sales projection for 2022; therefore, a non-probability sampling was used for convenience. The quantitative evaluation of sales was able to demonstrate that e-commerce managed to increase sales, even predicting a pessimistic behavior in the volume of these through the digital channel of Mercado Libre. Therefore, the study was able to conclude that e-commerce would increase sales in a Peruvian importer of hardware items, so it should proceed with the administrative and operational design so that sales begin their operation in the recommended Marketplace.

Keywords E-commerce · Sales · Marketplace · Regression

60.1 Introduction

Nowadays, e-commerce is at its peak and growing sustainably, both in number of users and in marketing channels and technological progress has contributed to a fast

---

G. S. Miñan Olivos (✉) · J. J. T. Chávez
Universidad Tecnológica del Perú, Chimbote, Peru
e-mail: c20342@utp.edu.pe; e20207@utp.edu.pe

M. Y. Del Busto Valdez · J. H. Espinoza Tumpay
Universidad Cesar Vallejo, Lima, Peru
e-mail: mdelbustov@ucvvirtual.edu.pe; espinozat@ucvvirtual.edu.pe

W. E. Castillo Martínez
Universidad Cesar Vallejo, Chimbote, Peru
e-mail: wcastillom@ucv.edu.pe

© The Author(s), under exclusive license to Springer Nature Switzerland AG 2024
N. Tsounis, A. Vlachvei (eds.), *Applied Economic Research and Trends*, Springer Proceedings in Business and Economics,
https://doi.org/10.1007/978-3-031-49105-4_60

expansion nationally and internationally. It increased by 22.9% in 2018 with sales of $ 2928 billion and it is estimated that, by the end of 2019, e-commerce will grow by 20.7% with sales around $ 3535 billion. China leads the e-commerce market in the world, with an annual turnover of $ 636,087 billion (Cordero Linzán, 2019). On the other hand, the gross domestic product of Latin America and the Caribbean increased by 1.5% in the second quarter of 2018.

This factor gradually decreased compared to the 1.9% growth registered by the sector in the first quarter of 2018. However, the advance of economic activity in these quarters has been very different between countries, because while in economies such as Mexico, Chile, Colombia, and Peru the increase has recovered, in Argentina, Brazil, and Venezuela, it has decreased (Economic Commission for Latin America and the Caribbean, 2018). Likewise, Colombia and Mexico are Latin American countries that have managed to get many benefits through e-commerce, taking into consideration that more than 3% of the GDP of these countries are received from e-commerce sales, establishing an economic growth that has allowed entrepreneurs to implement business models based on these platforms, due to the little capital that is needed and the great social coverage that can arrive (Medina Cadena, 2018).

According to the Daily El Peruano (2020), before the mandatory immobilization order due to the advance of COVID-19, most commercial premises had to deepen the implementation of a digital sales resource, taking into consideration that it was already being applied in much of the world; at the local level in Peru, its implementation was not yet clear in this situation. Thus, e-commerce began to take center stage in the national economy.

Mucha Paitan (2019) indicates that at the national level, it is evident that some companies still do not use e-commerce; like the SME producers of footwear in the city of Trujillo, who are not trained in this kind of trade, reaching a low level of knowledge by 85%. Because of this, they do not know how to use this tool to increase their sales, causing problems such as low income and absorption by the competition. On the other hand, the Peruvian Chamber of Electronic Commerce (2021) pointed out that the MYPES are very sensitive to the commissions charged by the various platforms, and we noticed in the offline market they charge 5% for the use of the POS, and to avoid this expense, it is transferred to the end user, distorting the shopping experience and its outcome. In this case, the use of digital wallets such as Yape has had a relevant role and their opening with Yape Companies and its 400,000 registered companies, orienting themselves about the great advantages of digitizing money, not only for their own security but also to validate that the money they do not have physically; it is the money which is not spent and can be saved.

The Daily Gestión (2019) commented that e-commerce in Peru has produced 5.75% in favor of the national GDP in 2018; all this expresses a sales volume of S /11,500 expressed in millions, taking as a reference that the gross domestic product increased to S /200,000 expressed in millions, mentioned Helmut Cáceda, Founding CEO of the Peruvian Chamber of Electronic Commerce (Capece). From another perspective, the Central Reserve Bank of Peru applied an innovative and objective system of allocation of liquidity and contribution to the credit of the production sector, with a guarantee of state reserves that has achieved the stability of several companies and has avoided the fall of the payment chain, with the economic program Reactiva Peru. This economic program, which consists of S/60,000 expressed in millions of soles, has covered more than 480,000 organizations, 98% is made up of Small and Medium size Enterprises (SMEs), and has managed to reduce active interest rates for a diverse number of sectors and sizes of companies. In this way, interest rates are activated for large, medium, small, and micro-organizations; today they are equivalent, respectively, to 71%, 42%, 27%, and 24% of those that are executed at the beginning of this year (Vega Castro, 2020).

On the other hand, with reference to the company's problems, the company in the hardware wholesale sector for 2 years has been decreasing in its traditional sales channel, and what continues to affect are the continuous cases of COVID-19 infections; consequently, the client portfolio was reduced due to death in some cases and, in others, the change of commercial line or the bankruptcy of the business. However, since March 16, 2020, when the total quarantine began, sales began to gradually reduce due to social immobilization and the restriction of national trade. The continuous infections of COVID-19 caused the lifting of the quarantine to be postponed on many occasions; customers in Lima and the Province refused to make payments prior to the attention of their products for convenience issues since the cash on delivery service was deleted, which generated the loss of customers due to the breakdown of their businesses and the increase in their level of indebtedness; Faced with this situation, the company had to reduce the salary of all staff and restructure the profile of some employees to meet the new market needs.

Given the problematic reality exposed, the following research problem has been formulated: How would e-commerce increase sales in a Peruvian importer of hardware items?

Therefore, this research is justified from the practical point of view since it will focus on the digital transformation of the company and will allow it to control the flow of information from an initial point to an endpoint. That is why the e-commerce proposal will serve to increase sales, which in turn will help the rapid rotation of stored products and reduce the risk of expiration of some additive products. Likewise, the current situation of the company is that it only has a sales channel that is the traditional one, which due to the current situation is losing market coverage due to its null digital presence, which will allow the entry of other competitors that market the same products in different brands of the portfolio. On the other hand, an e-commerce proposal will generate a positive impact on other aspects, such as: visibility of the product portfolio, a new revenue channel, and a new customer portfolio; being of great relevance for end users because the purchase and sale of goods and services is not relevant to be done physically, originating new forms of payment, such as credit cards and debit cards (Meléndrez, 2018).

From a social perspective, the study is relevant because it will provide greater capacity to the company to show its product portfolio and to benefit final consumers by getting imported products at a fair price. In this sense, the diagnosis of the research will allow to identify if the e-commerce proposal is suitable for the development of commercial and logistics tasks; if the product portfolio is digitized, access to the online marketing channel will be allowed. According to Rubio Tauma (2018), e-commerce seen from an online store will allow the exposure of products in all time ranges, allowing the end user to visualize the virtual store from any electronic device connected to Internet, having a didactic purchase from the place where he is.

60.2 Materials and Methods

The National Council of Science, Technology and Technological Innovation of Peru (2018) indicates that applied research allows to conclude, through the scientific method, the methodical process, the records, or the means through which a coverage of multiple observed needs can be given or certain problems solved. Likewise, the research design was descriptive. Guevara Alban et al. (2020) mentioned that the descriptive study aims to analyze various specific characteristics of sets of the same category, using various systematic management indicators that manage to standardize the processes in the scheme or behavior of the variables to be investigated, providing comparable management data from the other sources of information. On the other hand, the research was nonexperimental, since according to Hernández and Mendoza (2018), the nonexperimental research study is one that is executed without constantly changing the variables; this is how the research was carried out without any modification and only the possible impact of e-commerce on the company's sales was described.

In the same way, the population of the study was represented by all the sales of the company and the historical sales from 2020 to 2021 were taken as a sample as well as a projection of sales for 2022; therefore, a non-probability sampling was used for convenience.

60.3 Results and Discussion

Nowadays, the importer of hardware does not have a digital presence; consequently, many of its potential customers do not manage to have easy communication with the organization, which causes these potential customers to disclose unfavorable comments causing the loss of business opportunities. In that sense, the research sought to propose a way to achieve an increase in sales using digital media in order to adequately expose the image of the company and its product portfolio. To achieve this measure, it was decided to evaluate the possibility of starting online sales operations through a Marketplace and to be able to distribute resources efficiently for the attention of this new commercial channel (Fig. 60.1).

Subsequently, the alternatives to carry out the implementation of e-commerce in the company were evaluated. Therefore, the web tool SimilarWeb in its Pro version was used to visualize the current panorama of the Marketplace at the national level

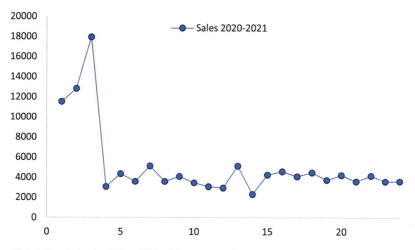

Fig. 60.1 Historical sales 2020–2021 of the company importing hardware articles

Fig. 60.2 Conversion rate in sales by type of Marketplace based on visits received per page

Marketplace	Pages / Visit
mercadolibre.com.pe	6.944%
promart.pe	4.366%
plazavea.com.pe	4.168%
linio.com	1.711%
falabella.com.pe	1.620%

taking into consideration the information of the first quarter of the current year. Figure 60.2 shows that Mercado Libre has the highest sales conversion indicator (6.944%).

In the same way, three indicators were used through a Marketplace comparison matrix. For this, the three most important aspects in the management of a Marketplace were considered, which are: commercial-economic, business, and technical. The technical aspects valued the following criteria: quality of service, veracity of information, support to the provider, dispute policy, and policy of use and treatment of data. The commercial and economic aspects valued the following criteria: commissions, forms, and deadlines for withdrawing money, logistics, and guarantees. The business aspects valued the following criteria: stability, advice to the supplier, ease of understanding, recognition/experience, and training to the supplier.

The comparison matrix used scores from 1 to 5 for each aspect, in which 1 is a low rating of appearance and 5 is the highest rating of appearance. The commercial-economic aspect had a weight of 52%, the business aspect 22%, and the technical aspect 26%.

Table 60.1 Evaluation of alternatives for the implementation of e-commerce in the importing company of hardware items

E-commerce	Technical appearance	Commercial and economic aspects	Business appearance	Total score
Mercado Libre	1.16	2.60	1.00	4.76
Plaza Vea	0.75	1.88	0.85	3.48
Promart	0.49	1.84	0.75	3.08
Linio	0.68	1.28	0.90	2.86

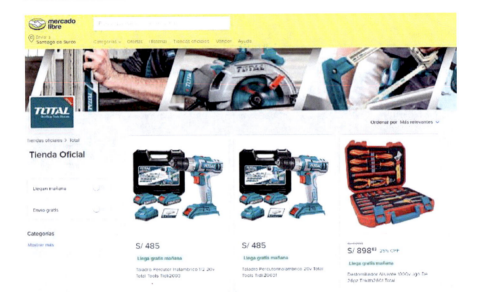

Fig. 60.3 Design of the e-commerce channel for the importer of hardware items

The tool used allowed to have a broader vision of the current panorama of the available Marketplaces. As a final result, the Mercado Libre Marketplace got 4.76 points, which is why it was the most recommended online sales platform for the e-commerce proposal (Table 60.1).

After having analyzed the different alternatives of Marketplace and opting for Mercado Libre, we proceeded to design the platform and show the way through which you could see the products and buy them online. Figure 60.3 shows the proposed final version.

Another important point was the perception of customers regarding e-commerce. Therefore, a questionnaire was applied to recurring users of the company. Figure 60.4 shows that customers got an acceptable perception regarding e-commerce since the data showed a tendency to the average value (asymmetry $= 0.07$). The questionnaire quantified the perception of customers getting a minimum value of 42 (highly negative perception) and a maximum of 80 (highly positive perception). About 50% of the achieved data was between 42 and 59, while the rest fluctuated

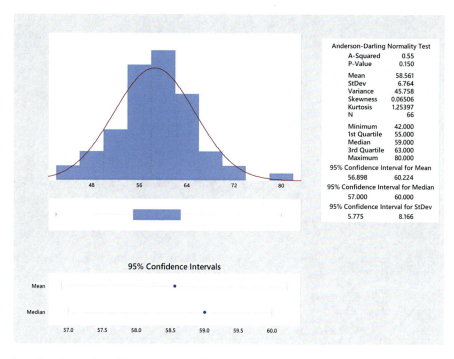

Fig. 60.4 Perception of the customers of the company importing hardware articles regarding e-commerce

between 60 and 80. Likewise, a 95% confidence interval was established for the mean, fluctuating between 57 and 60.

As a complementary part of the research, an analysis was carried out on the possible impact on sales from the proposal designed for e-commerce of the company importing hardware items. As a first point, the behavior of sales was estimated if the company kept traditional sales without using e-commerce. To this end, a regression analysis was carried out for the historical behavior of sales. In Fig. 60.5, sales had a better fit to a potential behavior ($R^2 = 0.509$) compared to other regression models (exponential $R^2 = 0.3295$, linear $R^2 = 0.2752$, logarithmic $R^2 = 0.4717$). From the selected model, sales without e-commerce could be projected.

On the other hand, to estimate the impact of e-commerce on the company importing hardware items, the products with the highest inventory turnover were selected and, in parallel, the number of visits to the Marketplace was estimated. In Table 60.2, there were three scenarios: one optimistic, one probable, and one pessimistic; In this way, it was possible to reduce uncertainty in decision-making. Likewise, it was taken into consideration that according to Fig. 60.2, the indicator of conversion into sales of Mercado Libre was 6.944%, so the calculations were made with an average of 3.9%.

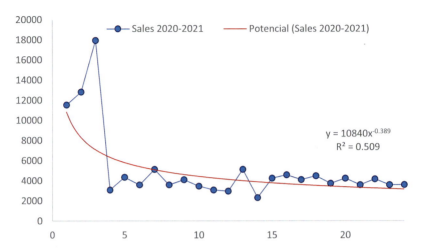

Fig. 60.5 Potential regression for the historical sales 2020–2021 of the company importing hardware articles

Table 60.2 Estimation of possible scenarios in the implementation of e-commerce of the company importing hardware items

2022	Visitas (Optimista)	Visitas (Probable)	Visitas (Pesimista)
Enero	2015	1008	403
Febrero	3015	1508	603
Marzo	1000	500	200
Abril	2015	1008	403
Mayo	1500	750	300
Junio	2000	1000	400
Julio	1600	800	320
Agosto	550	275	110
Setiembre	1000	500	200
Octubre	3000	1500	600
Noviembre	3000	1500	600
Diciembre	6000	3000	1200

After that, sales revenue was calculated for each of the scenarios and added to the initial projection to evaluate whether a statistically significant increase was achieved.

According to Fig. 60.6, e-commerce increases sales in an optimistic scenario, that is, with a high level of visits and a conversion indicator greater than 4%. The sales of the year 2022 without e-commerce were estimated at $ 34,527 and adding the sales by e-commerce (optimistic scenario) would reach $ 55,003 having a positive percentage variation of 59%.

According to Fig. 60.7, e-commerce increases sales in a probable scenario, that is, with an average level of visits and a higher conversion indicator around 4%. The sales of the year 2022 without e-commerce were estimated at $ 34,527 and adding

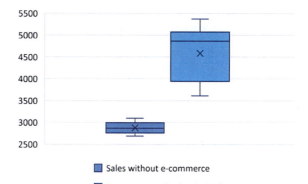

Fig. 60.6 Sales with projection to 2022 estimating the impact of e-commerce in an optimistic scenario

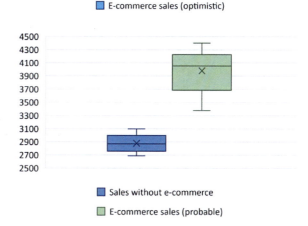

Fig. 60.7 Sales with projection to 2022 estimating the impact of e-commerce in a probable scenario

the sales by e-commerce (probable scenario) would reach $ 47,772 having a positive percentage variation of 38%.

According to Fig. 60.8, e-commerce increases sales in a pessimistic scenario, that is, with a low level of visits and a conversion indicator higher than 4%. The sales of the year 2022 without e-commerce were estimated at $ 34,527 and adding the sales by e-commerce (pessimistic scenario) would reach $ 40,637 having a positive percentage variation of 18%.

Table 60.3 shows that e-commerce would achieve a significant increase ($p < 0.05$) in sales, including a pessimistic scenario.

60.4 Conclusions

The study was able to determine that the Peruvian importer of hardware articles showed a negative trend in the behavior of its sales. Therefore, it was necessary to implement strategies aimed at increasing the volume of sales. So, e-commerce was a

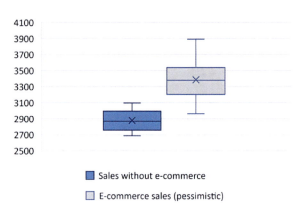

Fig. 60.8 Sales with projection to 2022 estimating the impact of e-commerce in a pessimistic scenario

Table 60.3 Comparison of scenarios for sales

Scenarios for e-commerce sales	Differences with respect to selling without e-commerce	Significance
Optimistic scenario	1706 ± 688	$p < 0.05$
Probable scenario	603 ± 540	$p < 0.05$
Pessimistic scenario	595 ± 278	$p < 0.05$

cutting-edge alternative to explore new mechanisms that manage to reach potential users or strengthen business relationships with current customers.

There are several technological alternatives to implement e-commerce according to the needs and characteristics of each company. In this study, the first option was a Marketplace with a large number of visits received per page and with a high level of conversion in sales. That is why Mercado Libre was chosen, which had a sales conversion indicator of almost 7% and was superior to other options regarding commercial-economic, business, and technical criteria.

Another point that could be concluded is that Peruvian buyers do not have a negative perception regarding online purchases. This perception has improved as a result of the events associated with the COVID-19 pandemic where e-commerce has boomed due to limitations in free transit. Although the results do not show a very high value in terms of the preference for digital sales channels, it has been possible to identify a regular level that would promote sales with a tendency to continue growing in the medium term.

The quantitative evaluation of sales was able to demonstrate that e-commerce managed to increase sales, even predicting a pessimistic behavior in the volume of these, through the digital channel of Mercado Libre. There, the study was able to conclude that e-commerce would increase sales in the Peruvian importer of hardware items, so it should proceed with the administrative and operational design so that sales begin their operation in the recommended Marketplace.

References

Cordero Linzán, M. (2019). *E-commerce e-commerce, current analysis from the perspective of the consumer in the city of Guayaquil, province of Guayas and effective strategies for its development.* http://repositorio.ucsg.edu.ec/handle/3317/14064

Daily El Peruano. (2020). *E-commerce grew 400% during the quarantine.* https://elperuano.pe/noticia/99199-comercio-electronico-crecio-400-durante-cuarentena

Daily Gestión. (2019). *E-commerce contributes 5.75% to the national GDP.* https://gestion.pe/tecnologia/comercio-electronico-aporta-5-75-pbi-nacional-capece-263849-noticia/?ref=ges

Economic Commission for Latin America and the Caribbean. (2018). *Economic Survey of Latin America and the Caribbean. Evolution of investment in Latin America and the Caribbean: Stylized facts, determinants and policy challenges.* (146), 1–248. https://www.cepal.org/es/publicaciones/43964-estudio-economico-america-latina-caribe-2018-evolucion-la-inversion-america

Guevara Alban, G., Verdesoto Arguello, A., & Castro Molina, N. (2020). Educational research methodologies (descriptive, experimental, participatory, and action research). *Editorial Saberes del Conocimiento – Article RECIMUNDO, 4*, 163–173. https://recimundo.com/index.php/es/article/view/860/1363

Hernández, R., & Mendoza, C. (2018). *Research methodology: The quantitative, qualitative and mixed routes* (1st ed., pp. 1–714). McGraw-Hill/Interamericana Editores, S.A. https://virtual.cuautitlan.unam.mx/rudics/?p=2612

Medina Cadena, S. (2018). *The influence of e-commerce on the dynamization of international business between 2008 and 2018: A comparative analysis between Colombia and Mexico.* https://hdl.handle.net/20.500.11839/6936

Meléndrez, V. (2018). E-commerce logistic: Cross docking, merge in transit, drop shipping y ick and collect. *Científica, 22*(2), 105–112. Obtained from https://www.redalyc.org/jatsRepo/614/61458109003/61458109003.pdf

Mucha Paitan, M. E. (2019). *Electronic commerce and its relationship with the level of sales of SMEs, footwear producers – Province of Trujillo.* National University of Trujillo. https://doi.org/10.17268/sciendo.2018.023

National Council of Science, Technology and Technological Innovation of Peru. (2018). *Presidential Resolution N 216. Technical guidelines for the execution of science, technology and technological innovation projects financed with public resources from the canyon in public universities*, 1–10. http://resoluciones.concytec.gob.pe/subidos/sintesis/RP-214-2018-CONCYTEC-P.pdf

Peruvian Chamber of Electronic Commerce. (2021). *Official report of the E-commerce industry in Peru.* https://www.capece.org.pe/wp-content/uploads/2021/07/0-Observatorio-Ecommerce-Peru-2020-2021-V.2.pdf

Rubio Tauma, J. A. (2018). *Business plan for the implementation of an online store of electronic products in the city of Chachapoyas 2016* (Bachelor's thesis). Cesar Vallejo University. Repository of Cesar Vallejo University. https://hdl.handle.net/20.500.12692/44544

Vega Castro, J. (2020). *Chronicle of the Peruvian economy in times of pandemic.* Department of Economics-Pontificia Universidad Católica del Perú. (No. 2020-495). https://doi.org/10.18800/2079-8474.0495

Chapter 61
Big Data in Economics Research

Aristidis Bitzenis and Nikos Koutsoupias

Abstract The relationship between Big Data Technologies (BDs) and Economics Research has experienced significant growth, offering possibilities for systematic and bibliometric evaluations. Surprisingly, no bibliometric study has yet been conducted on the association between Big Data Technologies and Economics Research (BDER). To bridge this gap, our research utilizes a bibliometric analysis to conduct a statistical evaluation of published studies and assess the impact of these publications within the scientific community. We performed an extensive bibliometric analysis, both qualitative and quantitative, utilizing Scopus indexed articles from Economics fields spanning for the last decade, along with the R-language data analysis package, bibliometrix. Our analysis yielded various findings, including insights on the most influential authors, journals. We also explored the theoretical foundations, themes, and current research trends within the field of BDs and its impact on economic issues. Additionally, we investigated the evolution of research streams and trends in BDER areas and highlighted several potential avenues for future research.

Keywords Big Data · Economics research · Bibliometric data analysis · Applied research · Research Analytics

61.1 Introduction

The concept of "Big Data" (BD) has gained popularity recently in both academic and nonacademic media. The idea has really taken off, especially online and on social media. When this paper was being written (in March 2023), a Google Scholar search using the term "Big Data" turned up about two million results. BD refers to the massive amount of data, both structured and unstructured, that have been

---

A. Bitzenis (✉) · N. Koutsoupias
University of Macedonia, Thessaloniki, Greece
e-mail: bitzenis@uom.edu.gr

© The Author(s), under exclusive license to Springer Nature Switzerland AG 2024
N. Tsounis, A. Vlachvei (eds.), *Applied Economic Research and Trends*, Springer Proceedings in Business and Economics,
https://doi.org/10.1007/978-3-031-49105-4_61

produced by modern advancements and the rapidly rising use of devices that can be automated and connected to the internet. Data have exploded due to the use of networked devices like tablets and smartphones (Kibria et al., 2018), a great deal of the time with relation to user-generated content originating from online social networks (Leung et al., 2013; Ghani et al., 2019). Due to their volume and features, BD is challenging to handle using conventional statistical techniques and tools (Chen et al., 2014; Wang et al., 2016a). Yet, BD is quickly gaining popularity as an innovative new topic of study in the social sciences, where it has been recognized as an indispensable component to promote prosperity and economic development and address societal issues (Mayer-Schonberger & Cukier, 2013) in addition to being a significant force behind the development of value for companies and consumers (Wang et al., 2016b).

In terms of methodology, BD-based techniques help researchers get beyond the challenges of using representative samples because BD essentially enables dealing with the complete population under study (Fan et al., 2015). It is claimed to be able to address any inquiry on people's beliefs, attitudes, ideas, and behaviors. In addition, it appears to be an effective instrument for addressing unique research issues, creating creative research designs beneficial to the scientific advancement, and eventually producing both management and policy decision support (George et al., 2016).

Several contexts have investigated economics-related uses of BD technologies with general reviews (Sangwan et al., 2019; Court, 2015; Yang et al., 2018) or with focus on agricultural economics (Lusk, 2017), auditing (Appelbaum et al., 2017), capital markets (Bukovina, 2016), forecasting (Bok et al., 2018; Elliott & Timmermann, 2016), risk analysis (Kou et al., 2019), supply chain (Wang et al., 2016a, b; Kamble et al., 2020), sustainability (Jin et al., 2019; Hua et al., 2021), management (Finger et al., 2019), and marketing (Balducci & Marinova, 2018), among others.

To the best of our knowledge, the field of BD and associated technologies' literature reviews on Economics subjects using state-of-the-art scientometric tools is limited (Ahmed et al., 2022) or it is concentrated in specialized areas such as production economics (Kaffash et al., 2021), marketing (Ghorbani et al., 2022), and supply chain research (Argumedo-García et al., 2021).

Unlike previous review studies, the literature search process in the present study focuses on top Scopus-indexed economics-related academic journals. In establishing the conceptual framework of the subject and pinpointing potential directions for further investigation, we analyze published papers that address BDER. As a result, we address four research goals. The first step is to establish whether BDER is a separate research field. The second is to identify the important journals and authors within this study topic. The third step entails locating frequent words and trendy terms as well as examining underlying research clusters to map the conceptual structure of BDER. The goal is to identify and offer potential directions for further investigation.

The results of this study have several ramifications for academia and business. It offers a systematic introduction of the study subject and introduces readers to the most important papers, authors, journals, concepts, and methodologies for academics and industry professionals interested in BDER. The principles and techniques mentioned can help economics organizations and regulatory bodies improve resource use, coordination between key stakeholders, environmental performance, and navigational safety.

The following is the organization of the remaining sections of this study. In Part II, a method description is provided. Section 61.3 contains the presentation of the main bibliometric analysis and results. Term frequencies, trend topics, and a thematic BDER map can be found in Sect. 61.4. Section 61.5 concludes the study with future research suggestions.

61.2 Research Methodology

The BD economics related published research was selected utilizing Scopus' online search service, querying the term "Big Data" excluding 2023 and 2024 papers. The initial query returned more than 4,000 records. To concentrate further to economics-oriented research, the results were filtered using the corresponding "Subject area" option, producing 1449 Scopus-indexed economics-related journal articles. The full dataset analyzed resides in a scientific data repository (Koutsoupias, 2024). After the dataset was compiled, it was fed into bibliometrix, an R language package that specializes in scientometrics (Aria & Cuccurullo, 2017).

Table 61.1 displays the primary findings of the analyzed publications, providing essential information about the dataset.

Specifically, Table 61.1 presents several noteworthy details, including the significant annual growth rate of publications which is close to 35%, the impressive count of authors and co-authors totaling approximately 3500, and the average number of co-authors per document (2.81).

Table 61.1 Dataset description

Description	Results
Timespan	2013:2022
Sources (Journals, Books, etc.)	491
Documents	1449
Annual growth rate %	35.63
Document average age	3.49
Average citations per doc	19.9
Author's keywords (DE)	4196
Authors	3509
Authors of single-authored docs	287
Single-authored docs	310
Co-authors per doc	2.81
International co-authorships %	25.12

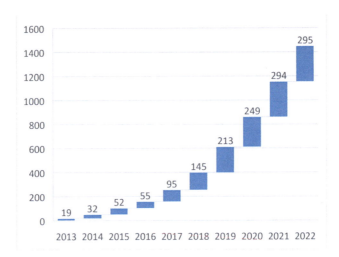

Fig. 61.1 Annual scientific production

Figure 61.1 illustrates a noticeable surge in the yearly interest in BDER. It is particularly noteworthy that almost two-thirds of the articles were published between 2019 and 2022, highlighting the significant increase in research output during that period.

61.3 Main Findings

Nearly 180 of the analyzed documents are contributed by the top five journals, namely *Journal of Financial Data Science*, the *International Journal of Production Economics*, the *Statistical Journal of the IAOS*, the *Journal of Advanced Transportation*, and the *Journal of Self-Governance and Management Economics* which have the highest number of BDER papers (Table 61.2). The most impactful journal is the *International Journal of Production Economics* with a TotalCitations (TotCit)/Articles ratio of 183.45 with two of its most popular BDER articles obtaining more than 1000 references each (Frank et al., 2019; Fosso Wamba et al., 2015).

Table 61.3 lists the BDER authors who have been the most prolific, indicating both their total number of citations (TotCit) and the year in which they published their first article (PY_start).

Zhang has been identified as the author who has published the highest number of articles, with one of his most cited works having received 36 references (Shen et al., 2017). On the other hand, Akter is the most frequently referenced co/author in the BDER field, and his most well-received article has been cited 1021 times (Fosso Wamba et al., 2015).

Table 61.2 Journals by published BDER papers

Source	Articles	TotCit
Journal of Financial Data Science	45	243
International Journal of Production Economics	37	6788
Statistical Journal of the IAOS	36	84
Journal of Advanced Transportation	31	174
Journal of Self-Governance and Management Economics	27	540
Economics, Management, and Financial Markets	25	432
Journal of Open Innovation: Technology, Market, and Complexity	20	376
Frontiers in Energy Research	19	28
Electronic Markets	14	1672
Electronic Commerce Research	14	160
Humanities and Social Sciences Communications	14	171

Table 61.3 Most active authors

Author	TC	Articles	PY_start
Zhang Y	101	13	2017
Wang Y	178	11	2018
Liu Y	42	10	2018
Li Y	348	9	2017
Wang X	188	9	2017
Li H	37	8	2018
Lu W	289	7	2015
Li S	65	7	2018
Wang Z	28	7	2020
Kim J	7	7	2018

Table 61.4 presents the most frequently cited papers in BDER, including their total number of citations and the ratio of citations per year. *International Journal of Production Economics* contributed seven titles in the list, mainly in relation to economics applications of big data methods and techniques. Also, *Electronic Markets* with two articles related to tourism and e-commerce. Additionally, *Intelligent Systems in Accounting Finance and Management*, the *Journal of Economic Perspectives,* and the *Journal of Marketing Research* show one article each in the top article list, investigating correspondingly, issues related to supply chain, econometrics, and brand analysis.

61.4 Frequent Words, Trend Topics, and Thematic Map

Table 61.5 displays the author keywords that were used most frequently across the analyzed papers. These popular keywords, each occurring 25 times or more, apart from "big data," include "machine learning," "big data analytics," "artificial

Table 61.4 Most cited papers

Paper	TC	TC/year
Frank AG, 2019, Int J Prod Econ	1110	222.00
Fosso Wamba S, 2015, Int J Prod Econ	1021	113.44
Gretzel U, 2015, Electron Mark	875	97.22
Akter S, 2016, Int J Prod Econ	663	82.88
Varian HR, 2014, J Econ Perspect	642	64.20
Hazen BT, 2014, Int J Prod Econ	553	55.30
Tirunillai S, 2014, J Mark Res	431	43.10
Kim HM, 2018, Intell Syst Account Finance Manag	394	65.67
Akter S, 2016, Electron Mark	379	47.38
Opresnik D, 2015, Int J Prod Econ	350	38.89
Zhong RY, 2015, Int J Prod Econ	345	38.33
Chae B, 2015, Int J Prod Econ	335	37.22

Table 61.5 Most frequent keywords

Words	Occurrences
Big data	623
Machine learning	80
Big data analytics	75
Artificial intelligence	73
Big data/machine learning	38
Internet of things	36
Social media	36
Covid-19	32
Industry 4.0	31
Data analytics	27
Privacy	26
Sustainability	25

intelligence," "big data/machine learning," "internet of things," "social media," "covid-19," " industry 4.0," "data analytics," "privacy," and "sustainability."

Figure 61.2 illustrates the shift in focus of author keywords from the initial emphasis on "business analytics" and "business intelligence" in BDER to the current emphasis on "auditing" and "digital platforms."

Furthermore, the analysis reveals that "machine learning" and "big data analytics" have become increasingly important in recent years. This shift in emphasis is evident from the longitudinal examination of author keywords in the set of articles examined.

To classify BDER themes we utilized co-word analysis techniques (Callon, et al., 1991; Donthu, et al., 2021). When mapping science using co-word analysis, themes are identified by analyzing clusters of keywords and their interconnections. Each research theme is characterized by two parameters, namely "density" and "centrality." These parameters can be used to classify themes into four groups using the median and mean values for both density and centrality. A "thematic

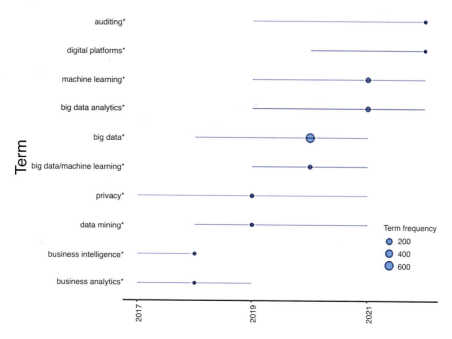

Fig. 61.2 BDER trend topics

network" is created in a theme through the interconnections between keywords, forming a network graph with "centrality" as the horizontal axis and "density" as the vertical axis. Nodes with many relations with others have higher centrality and are in essential positions in the network. Centrality is used to measure the degree of connection between different topics. Similarly, higher density indicates higher cohesiveness and the internal correlation between nodes. The density of a research field reflects its ability to maintain and develop itself. The thematic map provides an intuitive plot where themes can be analyzed based on the quadrant, they are located in Fig. 61.3.

The upper-right quadrant pertains to motor themes, while the lower-right quadrant pertains to basic themes. The lower-left quadrant involves emerging or disappearing themes, and the upper-left quadrant deals with specialized or niche themes. Themes situated in the upper-right quadrant are crucial to the organization of the BDER field, such as "privacy" and "digitization" and "digital economy" are both well-established and significant. Conversely, themes located in the upper-left quadrant possess well-developed internal connections but have unimportant external connections, making them only marginally relevant to the field, such as "big data/machine learning," "performance measurement," and "portfolio construction." Themes in the lower-left quadrant are weakly established and marginal, often repre-

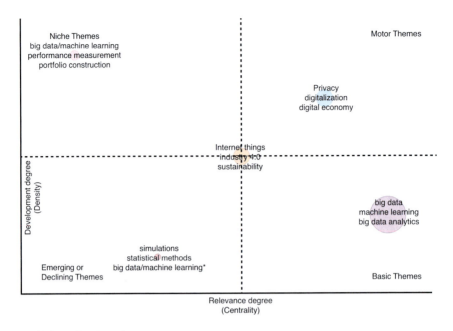

Fig. 61.3 BDER thematic map

senting emerging or vanishing topics, such as "simulations," "statistical methods," and "big data/machine learning." Lastly, the lower-right quadrant groups essential, crosscutting, and general themes, such as "big data," "machine learning," and "big data analytics," which are important to a research field but not yet fully developed.

61.5 Concluding Remarks and Future Work

The present study endeavors to offer a comprehensive review of the literature on big data and Economics Research. By utilizing descriptive and network bibliometric analysis techniques, this paper makes three contributions to the current literature on Big Data and Economics Research (BDER). The first contribution entails exploring the most distinguished and influential authors, publications, and journals in this field. The second contribution involves identifying the most used author keywords and BDER themes. Lastly, the third contribution focuses on identifying current research trends and gaps to be addressed in future research studies.

In our future work, we aim to identify significant institutions and countries associated with BD economics-related research, examine author collaboration and co-word networks, and analyze research collaboration among different countries.

Acknowledgment This research was funded by the Greek Ministry of Education and Religious Affairs for the project "Enhancing Research and optimizing UOM's administrative operation."

References

Ahmed, S., Alshater, M. M., Ammari, A. E., & Hammami, H. (2022). Artificial intelligence and machine learning in finance: A bibliometric review. *Research in International Business and Finance, 61*, 101646. https://doi.org/10.1016/j.ribaf.2022.101646

Appelbaum, D., Kogan, A., & Vasarhelyi, M. A. (2017). Big data and analytics in the modern audit engagement: Research needs. *Auditing: A Journal of Practice & Theory, 36*(4), 1–27. https://doi.org/10.2308/ajpt-51684

Argumedo-García, M., Salas-Navarro, K., Acevedo-Chedid, J., & Ospina-Mateus, H. (2021). Bibliometric analysis of the potential of technologies in the humanitarian supply chain. *Journal of Open Innovation: Technology, Market, and Complexity, 7*(4), 232. https://doi.org/10.3390/joitmc7040232

Aria, M., & Cuccurullo, C. (2017). bibliometrix: An R-tool for comprehensive science mapping analysis. *Journal of Informetrics, 11*(4), 959–975. https://doi.org/10.1016/j.joi.2017.08.007

Balducci, B., & Marinova, D. (2018). Unstructured data in marketing. *Journal of the Academy of Marketing Science, 46*(4), 557–590. https://doi.org/10.1007/s11747-018-0581-x

Bok, B., Caratelli, D., Giannone, D., Sbordone, A. M., & Tambalotti, A. (2018). Macroeconomic nowcasting and forecasting with big data. *Annual Review of Economics, 10*(1), 615–643. https://doi.org/10.1146/annurev-economics-080217-053214

Bukovina, J. (2016). Social media big data and capital markets—An overview. *Journal of Behavioral and Experimental Finance, 11*, 18–26. https://doi.org/10.1016/j.jbef.2016.06.002

Callon, M., Courtial, J. P., & Laville, F. (1991). Co-word analysis as a tool for describing the network of interactions between basic and technological research: The case of polymer chemistry. *Scientometrics, 22*(1), 155–205. https://doi.org/10.1007/BF02019280

Chen, M., Mao, S., & Liu, Y. (2014). Big data: A survey. *Mobile Networks and Applications, 19*(2), 171–209. https://doi.org/10.1007/s11036-013-0489-0

Court, D. (2015). Getting big impact from big data. *McKinsey Quarterly*, (Issue 1) McKinsey and Co. Inc. https://www.scopus.com/inward/record.uri?eid=2-s2.0-84946165107&partnerID=40&md5=a88b7e93c940f09baba2935c0baa130b

Donthu, N., Kumar, S., Mukherjee, D., Pandey, N., & Lim, W. M. (2021). How to conduct a bibliometric analysis: An overview and guidelines. *Journal of Business Research, 133*, 285–296. https://doi.org/10.1016/j.jbusres.2021.04.070

Elliott, G., & Timmermann, A. (2016). Forecasting in economics and finance. *Annual Review of Economics, 8*(1), 81–110. https://doi.org/10.1146/annurev-economics-080315-015346

Fan, S., Lau, R. Y. K., & Zhao, J. L. (2015). Demystifying big data analytics for business intelligence through the lens of marketing mix. *Big Data Research, 2*(1), 28–32. https://doi.org/10.1016/j.bdr.2015.02.006

Finger, R., Swinton, S. M., El Benni, N., & Walter, A. (2019). Precision farming at the nexus of agricultural production and the environment. *Annual Review of Resource Economics, 11*(1), 313–335. https://doi.org/10.1146/annurev-resource-100518-093929

Fosso Wamba, S., Akter, S., Edwards, A., Chopin, G., & Gnanzou, D. (2015). How "big data" can make big impact: Findings from a systematic review and a longitudinal case study. *International Journal of Production Economics, 165*, 234–246. https://doi.org/10.1016/j.ijpe.2014.12.031

Frank, A. G., Dalenogare, L. S., & Ayala, N. F. (2019). Industry 4.0 technologies: Implementation patterns in manufacturing companies. *International Journal of Production Economics, 210*, 15–26. https://doi.org/10.1016/j.ijpe.2019.01.004

George, G., Osinga, E. C., Lavie, D., & Scott, B. A. (2016). Big data and data science methods for management research. *Academy of Management Journal, 59*(5), 1493–1507. https://doi.org/10.5465/amj.2016.4005

Ghani, N. A., Hamid, S., Targio Hashem, I. A., & Ahmed, E. (2019). Social media big data analytics: A survey. *Computers in Human Behavior, 101*, 417–428. https://doi.org/10.1016/j.chb.2018.08.039

Ghorbani, Z., Kargaran, S., Saberi, A., Haghighinasab, M., Jamali, S. M., & Ale Ebrahim, N. (2022). Trends and patterns in digital marketing research: Bibliometric analysis. *Journal of Marketing Analytics, 10*(2), 158–172. https://doi.org/10.1057/s41270-021-00116-9

Hua, Y., Liu, X., Zhou, S., Huang, Y., Ling, H., & Yang, S. (2021). Toward sustainable reuse of retired lithium-ion batteries from electric vehicles. *Resources, Conservation and Recycling, 168*, 105249. https://doi.org/10.1016/j.resconrec.2020.105249

Jin, R., Yuan, H., & Chen, Q. (2019). Science mapping approach to assisting the review of construction and demolition waste management research published between 2009 and 2018. *Resources, Conservation and Recycling, 140*, 175–188. https://doi.org/10.1016/j.resconrec.2018.09.029

Kaffash, S., Nguyen, A. T., & Zhu, J. (2021). Big data algorithms and applications in intelligent transportation system: A review and bibliometric analysis. *International Journal of Production Economics, 231*, 107868. https://doi.org/10.1016/j.ijpe.2020.107868

Kamble, S. S., Gunasekaran, A., & Gawankar, S. A. (2020). Achieving sustainable performance in a data-driven agriculture supply chain: A review for research and applications. *International Journal of Production Economics, 219*, 179–194. https://doi.org/10.1016/j.ijpe.2019.05.022

Kibria, M. G., Nguyen, K., Villardi, G. P., Zhao, O., Ishizu, K., & Kojima, F. (2018). Big data analytics, machine learning, and artificial intelligence in next-generation wireless networks. *IEEE Access, 6*, 32328–32338. https://doi.org/10.1109/ACCESS.2018.2837692

Kou, G., Chao, X., Peng, Y., Alsaadi, F. E., & Herrera-Viedma, E. (2019). Machine learning methods for systemic risk analysis in financial sectors. *Technological and Economic Development of Economy, 25*(5), 716–742. https://doi.org/10.3846/tede.2019.8740

Koutsoupias, N. (2024). Big Data in Economics Research Dataset. https://doi:10.17605/OSF.IO/AZ58D

Leung, R., Rong, J., Li, G., & Law, R. (2013). Personality differences and hotel web design study using targeted positive and negative association rule mining. *Journal of Hospitality Marketing & Management, 22*(7), 701–727. https://doi.org/10.1080/19368623.2013.723995

Lusk, J. L. (2017). Consumer research with big data: Applications from the food demand survey (FooDS). *American Journal of Agricultural Economics, 99*(2), 303–320. https://doi.org/10.1093/ajae/aaw110

Mayer-Schonberger, V., & Cukier, K. (2013). *Big data: The essential guide to work, life and learning in the age of insight*. Hachette UK.

Sangwan, V., Harshita, H., Prakash, P., & Singh, S. (2019). Financial technology: A review of extant literature. *Studies in Economics and Finance, 37*(1), 71–88. https://doi.org/10.1108/SEF-07-2019-0270

Shen, D., Zhang, Y., Xiong, X., & Zhang, W. (2017). Baidu index and predictability of Chinese stock returns. *Financial Innovation, 3*(1), 4. https://doi.org/10.1186/s40854-017-0053-1

Wang, C., Chen, M.-H., Schifano, E., Wu, J., & Yan, J. (2016a). Statistical methods and computing for big data. *Statistics and Its Interface, 9*(4), 399–414. https://doi.org/10.4310/SII.2016.v9.n4.a1

Wang, G., Gunasekaran, A., Ngai, E. W. T., & Papadopoulos, T. (2016b). Big data analytics in logistics and supply chain management: Certain investigations for research and applications. *International Journal of Production Economics, 176*, 98–110. https://doi.org/10.1016/j.ijpe.2016.03.014

Yang, D., Chen, P., Shi, F., & Wen, C. (2018). Internet finance: Its uncertain legal foundations and the role of big data in its development. *Emerging Markets Finance and Trade, 54*(4), 721–732. https://doi.org/10.1080/1540496X.2016.1278528

Chapter 62
Testing Horizontal Support and Resistance Zones on Cryptocurrencies

Prodromos Tsinaslanidis

Abstract We examine the price behavior of three cryptocurrencies around algorithmically derived horizontal support and resistance zones. The dataset considered in this study is composed of daily prices of Bitcoin, Ethereum, and BNB for a period spanning from 2018 to 2022. We find in our sample that prices are more likely to bounce on support than on resistance zones. Three dynamic trading strategies based on price bounces are also proposed, tested, and compared with a buy-and-hold benchmark. Results are mixed with two out of the three proposed strategies performing better (in terms of risk-adjusted returns) than the benchmark, in only one of the three examined series.

Keywords Technical Analysis · Support and Resistance · Cryptocurrencies · Bitcoin · Trading

62.1 Introduction

Technical analysis (TA) is a method used in finance, to analyze primarily graphically the history of financial assets' price series such as stocks, currencies, commodities, and indices to make predictions of future price movements. Proponents of technical analysis argue that history tends to be repeated forming patterns that can be used to exploit profits. The efficacy of TA has been a controversial topic with mixed results provided by the bibliography, and although many academics regard TA with great skepticism, a significant proportion of practitioners include TA's recommendations within their trading activities (Tsinaslanidis & Zapranis, 2016).

Technicians use various tools and techniques to interpret market data and make trading decisions. Among them, some commonly used tools include (a) technical indicators such as moving averages, relative strength index, and Moving Average

---

P. Tsinaslanidis (✉)
Department of Economics, University of Western Macedonia, Kastoria, Greece
e-mail: ptsinaslanidis@uowm.gr

© The Author(s), under exclusive license to Springer Nature Switzerland AG 2024
N. Tsounis, A. Vlachvei (eds.), *Applied Economic Research and Trends*, Springer Proceedings in Business and Economics,
https://doi.org/10.1007/978-3-031-49105-4_62

Convergence Divergence, (b) chart patterns such as "head and shoulders," "double tops/bottoms," "triangles," and "flags," and (c) support and resistance levels. Regarding the latter tool, support levels are price levels where buying pressure is expected to outweigh selling pressure, leading to a potential price increase. On the other hand, resistance levels are price levels where selling pressure is expected to exceed buying pressure, potentially causing a price decline. These levels are determined based on previous price movements and act as reference points for traders.

Consequently, TA contradicts implications derived from the weak form of the efficient market hypothesis (Fama, 1970). In other words, in an efficient market it is not possible to systematically achieve abnormal returns by using information embedded in historical prices and the use of TA should be preferred in markets that are not efficient. Furthermore, Tsinaslanidis and Zapranis (2016) demonstrated through a simulation experiment that the volatility rate of the series is positively related to the number of regional locals (minima and maxima), and thus, technical patterns and other technical tools that depend on regional locals are more likely to appear on volatile series. This paper assesses the price behavior of three cryptocurrencies on horizontal support and resistance levels derived by historical regional locals. The choice of cryptocurrency series is justified due to their high unconditional volatility (Chaim & Laurini, 2018) and the significant bulk of existing academic work that provides evidence in favor of market inefficiency (Kyriazis, 2019).

The rest of this chapter is organized as follows. Section 62.2 presents the relevant literature review. Section 62.3 presents the methodology and the data used in the empirical analysis. Section 62.4 presents the empirical results and Sect. 62.5 conclusion.

62.2 Related Literature

Support and resistance levels can be identified with various methods, and according to Tsinaslanidis and Zapranis (2016), in most studies, they are identified by historical regional locals, i.e., minima or maxima (Kavajecz & Odders-White, 2004).

Another way to define SAR levels is by using, as Osler (2000) states, simple numerical rules. A simple example of this case is the 50% rule where prices halt, i.e., find support around 50% of a major market correction. A similar approach is to define support and resistance levels on specific percentages such as 61.80%, 38.20%, and 23.61% deriving from $\lim_{n\to\infty} \frac{F_n}{F_{n+k}}$, for $k = 1, 2, 3, \ldots$, where F_n is a Fibonacci sequence where each number results by the sum of the previous two numbers (Banik et al., 2022; Gurrib et al., 2022; Tsinaslanidis et al., 2022).

Market psychology is another way by which these SAR levels can be derived. For example, according to the round number syndrome (Osler, 2002, 2003), prices seem to cluster near round numbers. Chen (2018) considered a large sample of 2629 stocks from 41 countries and demonstrated that returns are shown to be the highest at prices ending in 9 and lowest at prices ending in 1, while Chen (2021) explored the presence of round number bias in trading time. Regarding cryptocurrency markets, the clustering of Bitcoin prices on round numbers is demonstrated by Baig et al. (2019) and Urquhart (2017).

Osler (2000) used published SAR levels provided by six firms, for three currency pairs. However, the firms did not specify how these SAR levels had been derived. The profitability of those levels was examined using a bootstrapped technique. Among her main results, she mentioned that published levels performed better than those produced artificially, a finding in favor of the efficacy of TA.

62.3 Data and Methodology

62.3.1 Data

This study considers the daily prices of three cryptocurrencies with great market capitalization. More precisely, for the period spanning from 1-Jan-2018 until 31-Dec-2022, 1826 daily prices of BTC-USD, ETH-USD, and BNB-USD were downloaded from coinmarketcap.com. Our choice of these crypto series can be justified due to the increased scrutiny of their characteristics from academia and practitioners. Furthermore, for the evaluation of the performance of the examined trading algorithm, the risk-free rate from French (2023) is being used.

Table 62.1 presents the descriptive statistics of the arithmetic returns of the examined series. Daily returns are highly volatile and not normally distributed as indicated by the Kolmogorov Smirnov (KS)-statistics and the corresponding *p*-values. For the period examined, the mean return of BNB is positive and statistically significant and different than zero for a 5% significance level, while the mean returns of the other two cryptos are not significant. The risk inherited by those investing is significant as indicated by the extreme values of the range, standard deviation, and other risk measures reported later in Sect. 62.4.

62.3.2 Methodology

62.3.2.1 Identification of HSAR Zones

In this paper, we test the price behavior of these series on horizontal support and resistance (HSAR) zones derived by adopting the methodology proposed in Zapranis and Tsinaslanidis (2012). The algorithm identifies on a daily and rolling basis horizontal support and resistance levels by grouping historical locals (minima

Table 62.1 Descriptive statistics

	BTCUSD	ETHUSD	BNBUSD
Mean	0.0009	0.0015	0.0035
Standard error	0.0009	0.0012	0.0014
Median	0.0010	0.0008	0.0007
Standard deviation	0.0385	0.0500	0.0586
Sample variance	0.0015	0.0025	0.0034
Excess kurtosis	7.2811	5.2533	24.9533
Skewness	−0.3909	−0.3075	1.9326
Range	0.5592	0.6829	1.1167
Minimum	−0.3717	−0.4235	−0.4190
Maximum	0.1875	0.2595	0.6976
Count	1825	1825	1825
Confidence bound (95.0%)	−0.0009	−0.0008	0.0008
Confidence bound (95.0%)	0.0026	0.0038	0.0062
KS-statistic	0.088	0.075	0.104
KS p-value	0.000	0.000	0.000

and maxima) in price bins of equal percentage width. Subsequently, bins with frequencies greater than 2 signify a support and resistance zone.

A preliminary process is required for the identification of HSAR levels, and for this reason, the first 250 days of our dataset are being used to identify the first (if any) HSAR zones. Figure 62.1 presents the daily identification of HSAR levels (black horizontal dotted lines) on the BTCUSD series. The algorithm starts to identify the first HSAR levels after the first 250 days and generates the corresponding trading signals (discussed later in Sect. 62.3.2.3) after bounces on the HSAR levels. It is also worth noting that during the period Dec 2020 and July 2021, no HSAR levels have been identified because the price series entered this price level for the first time and therefore there was no precedent for the algorithm to be trained and identify SAR levels. However, during the period succeeding July 2021, the algorithm starts to identify HSAR levels again and generate signals. In this example, a drawback of the algorithm is illustrated. When prices move for the first time to new price levels at which the crypto has not been traded in the past, the algorithm is unable to identify HSAR levels. Of course, this is aligned with a fundamental convention of TA where the price tends to behave repetitively, and thus to use TA for trading purposes, a similar price history is required. Of course, this does not apply to all technical tools. For example, using "moving average crossovers" should be able to generate trading signals on a series that fluctuates on new price levels because in this case, a technician would use the historical crossovers of moving averages instead of historical price levels. Figure 62.2 presents a zoom perspective of Fig. 62.1 during the period July 2021 until May 2022.

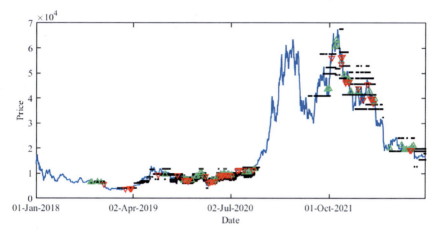

Fig. 62.1 BTCUSD price series with horizontal SAR levels identified with their corresponding bounce signals

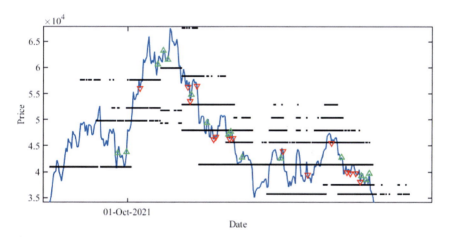

Fig. 62.2 Zoom perspective of Fig. 62.1. Green upward triangles indicate bounces on support zones, while red downward signals indicate bounces on resistance zones

62.3.2.2 Bounces and Failures

Figure 62.3 depicts a theoretical example of the definition of bounces and failures with respect to a support situation. We keep the same terminology as that of Zapranis and Tsinaslanidis (2012), and a support hit is defined when the price enters from above an HSAR zone for the first time. Afterward, on the first day when the

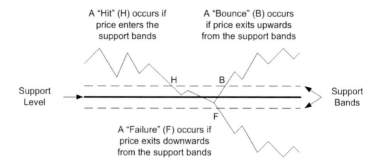

Fig. 62.3 A theoretical example of bounces and failures on a horizontal support level. Support Bands define the support zone around the support level

price exits the zone either upwards or downwards, a bounce or a failure occurs, respectively. The description of a resistance level is analogous. A resistance hit is defined when the price enters from below an HSAR zone for the first time and a bounce (failure) occurs the first day the price exits the zone downwards (upwards). A bounce frequency is defined as the number of bounces over the number of hits. For the construction of zones, a desired distance of 5% has been used (Zapranis & Tsinaslanidis, 2012).

62.3.2.3 Trading Rules

Although in Zapranis and Tsinaslanidis (2012) a holding period is used after each signal, in this chapter a more dynamic approach is being used and three different trading strategies are employed. More precisely, the algorithm generates signals $s_t = \{0, 1, -1\}$ based on bounces.

$$s_t = \begin{cases} 1, \text{ if price bounces on a support level at time } t \\ -1, \text{ if price bounces on a resistance level at time } t \\ 0, \text{ otherwise.} \end{cases}$$

Then we test three different trading strategies based on the generated signals. According to the first trading strategy, dubbed (LN: Long or Neutral), long positions are taken after price bounces on a support level (support-bounces) and these positions are closed after resistance-bounces. Let $p_t = \{0, 1\}$ be a variable describing the position taken in the previous day, i.e., $p_t = 1$ when a long position is taken and $p_t = 0$ when a neutral position is taken. If the price bounces on a support zone on day $t - 1$, then a long position is taken and the algorithm benefits from the arithmetic return of day t, $r_t \frac{P_t}{P_{t-1}} - 1$, where P_t is the daily price of the cryptocurrency considered. Table 62.2 describes the manner variable p_t takes values based on p_{t-1} and s_t.

Table 62.2 First Trading strategy. Value of p_t based on p_{t-1} and s_t

	$s_t = -1$	$s_t = 0$	$s_t = 1$
$p_{t-1} = 0$	0	0	1
$p_{t-1} = 1$	0	1	1

Table 62.3 Second Trading strategy. Value of p_t based on p_{t-1} and s_t

	$s_t = -1$	$s_t = 0$	$s_t = 1$
$p_{t-1} = -1$	−1	−1	1
$p_{t-1} = 0$	−1	0	1
$p_{t-1} = 1$	−1	1	1

Table 62.4 third Trading strategy. Value of p_t based on p_{t-1} and s_t

	$s_t = -1$	$s_t = 0$	$s_t = 1$
$p_{t-1} = -1$	−1	−1	0
$p_{t-1} = 0$	−1	0	1
$p_{t-1} = 1$	0	1	1

The second trading strategy (LS: Long or Short, rarely Neutral) is designed according to Table 62.3 and allows for short positions after short signals. Within this framework $p_t = \{-1, 0, 1\}$, and once a position is opened, it will be either long or short. In the third trading strategy though, dubbed (LSN: Long, Short, Neutral) positions are closed whenever an opposite signal is generated (Table 62.4). This implies that to move from a long position to a short position, two short signals are required; one to close the initial long position and a second one to open the short position.

62.4 Empirical Results

Table 62.5 presents the first results of our analysis regarding the breakdown of bounce frequencies. As implied by the bounce frequencies (BF) which are greater than 50% across all three examined series, bounces are more often than failures. Examining further the tabulated bounce frequencies, our results corroborate the findings in Zapranis and Tsinaslanidis (2012), highlighting the superiority of support levels compared to resistance levels.

The accumulated return in all for all trading strategies has been derived from the following equation assuming an initial value of 100€.

$$V_t = V_{t-1}\left(1 + p_t r_t + ||p_t| - 1| r_f\right),$$

where $V_0 = 100€$ and r_f is the risk-free rate. From the above expression, it is obvious that the risk-free rate is gained whenever neutral positions are considered. The accumulated returns from all trading strategies are then compared with a "buy and hold" (BH) benchmark for all three cryptocurrencies and results are presented in Figs. 62.4, 62.5, and 62.6. Several performance measures are also estimated for comparison reasons and presented in Table 62.6.

Table 62.5 Results for Bounce frequencies (BF) across the examined dataset

	ALL HSARS			Supports			Resistances		
Locals	Hits	Bounces	BF (%)	Hits	Bounces	BF (%)	Hits	Bounces	BF (%)
Panel A: BTCUSD									
2	92	51	55%	48	28	58%	44	23	52%
3	52	31	60%	27	18	67%	25	13	52%
4	36	24	67%	18	12	67%	18	12	67%
5	5	3	60%	2	2	100%	3	1	33%
Total	**185**	**109**	**59%**	**95**	**60**	**63%**	**90**	**49**	**54%**
Panel B: ETHUSD									
2	107	65	61%	55	39	71%	52	26	50%
3	45	24	53%	22	14	64%	23	10	43%
4	2	0	0%	1	0	0%	1	0	0%
Total	**154**	**89**	**58%**	**78**	**53**	**68%**	**76**	**36**	**47%**
Panel C: BNBUSD									
2	84	52	62%	39	28	72%	45	24	53%
3	57	41	72%	27	20	74%	30	21	70%
4	17	11	65%	10	7	70%	7	4	57%
5	14	7	50%	7	4	57%	7	3	43%
6	7	5	71%	5	4	80%	2	1	50%
7	2	0	0%	1	0	0%	1	0	0%
Total	**181**	**116**	**64%**	**89**	**63**	**71%**	**92**	**53**	**58%**

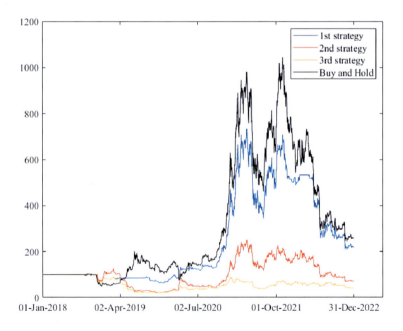

Fig. 62.4 Accumulated returns for the "Buy and Hold" and the three trading strategies for the BTCUSD series

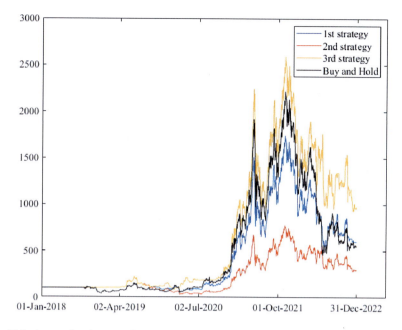

Fig. 62.5 Accumulated returns for the "Buy and Hold" and the three trading strategies for the ETHUSD series

Regarding BTCUSD, the use of HSAR levels did not produce higher returns than the BH strategy. In fact, of the three trading strategies examined, only the first one performed positively, providing positive mean and accumulated returns and better risk measures. However, when considering excess returns per unit of risk, the BH case was the best as illustrated by the highest Sharpe ratio. Similar was the performance of the algorithm on the BNBUSD series, with improved risk measures but with deteriorated returns.

On the other hand, two of the three trading strategies beat the BH benchmark in the ETHUSD series. More precisely, the LSN produced a cumulative return of 857%, which is roughly twice as the BH method, with reduced risk. However, even these "reduced" levels of risk are undoubtedly high compared to those obtained from investments in mainstream financial assets such as stocks. Indicatively, the VaR of 6.1% implies that using the third strategy, someone would have realized a daily loss greater than 6.1% every 20 days, with an expected value of 9.7% for these extreme losses.

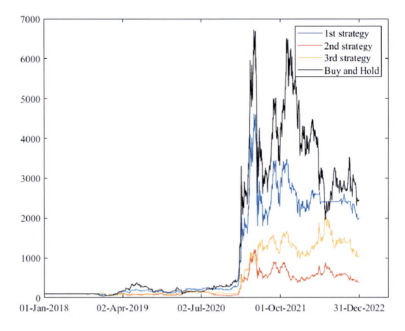

Fig. 62.6 Accumulated returns for the "Buy and Hold" and the three trading strategies for the BNBUSD series

62.5 Conclusions

In this article, three algorithmic trading strategies have been devised and tested on three Bitcoin, Ethereum, and BNB cryptocurrencies. The trading rules are based on horizontal support and resistance zones that were identified automatically by employing the methodology proposed in Zapranis and Tsinaslanidis (2012).

Among our main findings, we observed that prices are more likely to bounce on identified support than on resistance zones. This is aligned with results obtained from the stock price series reported in the existing bibliography. In terms of profitability, three different trading strategies were designed, and their performance has been compared to a buy-and-hold benchmark. Results were mixed since we did not discover any consistent superior performance of a strategy. They were, however, promising since enhanced performance has been reported in some cases in terms of risk-adjusted returns.

We believe that future studies on the evaluation of trade signals produced by integrating HSAR levels with other technical tools, "stop-loss" or "take-profit" orders, would be an intriguing area to pursue.

Table 62.6 Performance measures for the BH and the three trading strategies

Panel A: BTCUSD	LN	LS	LSN	BH
Mean	0.1%	0.0%	0.0%	0.1%
Standard deviation	**2.9%**	3.7%	**3.0%**	3.7%
Sharpe	3.0%	1.2%	−0.5%	3.4%
Value-at-risk (95%)	**0.042**	0.056	**0.046**	0.057
Expected shortfall	**7.1%**	8.8%	**7.7%**	8.6%
Cumulative return	115.8%	−29.0%	−59.1%	155.9%
Maximum drawdown	**71.7%**	83.2%	80.8%	76.6%
Panel B: ETHUSD				
Mean	0.2%	0.2%	0.2%	0.2%
Standard deviation	**4.2%**	**4.5%**	**4.1%**	4.9%
Sharpe	**0.048**	0.038	**0.055**	0.046
Value-at-risk (95%)	**6.4%**	**6.7%**	**6.1%**	7.3%
Expected shortfall	**10.2%**	**10.7%**	**9.7%**	11.3%
Cumulative return	**495.7%**	195.8%	**857.8%**	451.0%
Maximum drawdown	**77.0%**	86.3%	**65.4%**	79.4%
Panel C: BNBUSD				
Mean	0.3%	0.2%	0.2%	0.3%
Standard deviation	**4.5%**	**5.3%**	**4.3%**	5.4%
Sharpe	0.063	0.041	0.054	0.064
Value-at-risk (95%)	**5.7%**	7.2%	**5.2%**	7.2%
Expected shortfall	**9.1%**	**10.4%**	**8.3%**	11.1%
Cumulative return	1889.8%	298.9%	947.1%	2354.3%
Maximum drawdown	**61.3%**	**74.4%**	**54.2%**	75.8%

Notes: Bold values indicate better performance of a strategy compared to the BH benchmark

References

Baig, A., Blau, B. M., & Sabah, N. (2019). Price clustering and sentiment in bitcoin. *Finance Research Letters, 29*, 111–116.

Banik, S., Sharma, N., Mangla, M., Mohanty, S. N., & Shitharth, S. (2022). LSTM based decision support system for swing trading in stock market. *Knowledge-Based Systems, 239*, 107994.

Chaim, P., & Laurini, M. P. (2018). Volatility and return jumps in bitcoin. *Economics Letters, 173*, 158–163.

Chen, T. (2018). Round-number biases and informed trading in global markets. *Journal of Business Research, 92*, 105–117.

Chen, T. (2021). Round-number biases on trading time: Evidence from international markets. *Journal of Financial Research, 44*(3), 469–495.

Fama, E. (1970). Efficient capital markets: A review of theory and empirical work. *Journal of Finance, 25*(2), 383–417.

French, K. R. (2023). *Kenneth R. French - data library*. Retrieved 10 January 2023 from https://mba.tuck.dartmouth.edu/pages/faculty/ken.french/data_library.html

Gurrib, I., Nourani, M., & Bhaskaran, R. K. (2022). Energy crypto currencies and leading US energy stock prices: Are Fibonacci retracements profitable? *Financial Innovation, 8*, 1–27.

Kavajecz, K. A., & Odders-White, E. R. (2004). Technical analysis and liquidity provision. *Review of Financial Studies, 17*(4), 1043–1071. http://rfs.oxfordjournals.org/content/17/4/1043.abstract

Kyriazis, N. A. (2019). A survey on efficiency and profitable trading opportunities in cryptocurrency markets. *Journal of Risk and Financial Management, 12*(2), 67.

Osler, C. L. (2000). Support for resistance: Technical analysis and intraday exchange rates. *FRBNY Economic Policy Review, 6*(2), 53–68.

Osler, C. L. (2002). *Stop-loss orders and price cascades in currency markets.* Mimeo.

Osler, C. L. (2003). Currency orders and exchange rate dynamics: An explanation for the predictive success of technical analysis. *The Journal of Finance, 58*(5), 1791–1819. https://doi.org/10.1111/1540-6261.00588

Tsinaslanidis, P. E., & Zapranis, A. D. (2016). *Technical analysis for algorithmic pattern recognition.* Springer.

Tsinaslanidis, P., Guijarro, F., & Voukelatos, N. (2022). Automatic identification and evaluation of Fibonacci retracements: Empirical evidence from three equity markets. *Expert Systems with Applications, 187*, 115893.

Urquhart, A. (2017). Price clustering in bitcoin. *Economics Letters, 159*, 145–148.

Zapranis, A., & Tsinaslanidis, P. E. (2012). Identifying and evaluating horizontal support and resistance levels: An empirical study on US stock markets. *Applied Financial Economics, 22*(19), 1571–1585. https://doi.org/10.1080/09603107.2012.663469

Chapter 63
Pre-bankruptcy Consolidation Process and Business Reorganization: A Case Study

Araviadi Ioanna and Katarachia Androniki

Abstract This chapter concerns the consolidation process after the amendments to Law 4738/2020. Specifically, the new consolidation process is presented, aiming at rescuing companies in economic crisis. In times of severe economic crisis, as many businesses are overwhelmed by enormous financial difficulties, it is necessary to change and modernize the legislative framework that has been made to facilitate the rescue of viable businesses.

An attempt is made by the legislator to restore the debtor to the market and its business. The consolidation process could succeed with a collective and honest effort by all parties involved. With these modifications, an attempt is made to address the disadvantages of the process, and in general, to strengthen the consolidation and prevention of operational bankruptcy, so that it becomes a modern and effective tool for dealing with commercial insolvency for sustainable businesses.

In the same direction and after studying and analyzing the case of the consolidation and rescue of Boutaris Company, some proposals are made for the existing legislative framework. Our main goal should be to attract investments so that investors and investment funds could give the opportunity to acquire an existing business that needs liquidity. The interests and claims of the creditors are better secured since as a rule the creditors will be satisfied more by a functioning company than they would be by the forced sale of its assets. Creating an effective bankruptcy system that will faction as a tool for business recovery would open up a new market.

Keywords Reorganization · Consolidation · Bankruptcy · Economic dimensions

A. Ioanna (✉) · K. Androniki
Department of Accounting & Finance, School of Economics, University of Western Macedonia, Kozani, Greece
e-mail: akatarachia@uowm.gr

© The Author(s), under exclusive license to Springer Nature Switzerland AG 2024
N. Tsounis, A. Vlachvei (eds.), *Applied Economic Research and Trends*, Springer Proceedings in Business and Economics,
https://doi.org/10.1007/978-3-031-49105-4_63

63.1 Introduction

Business bankruptcy is an important issue and at the same time a pervasive problem in modern society. Over the past twenty years, the dramatic socioeconomic effects of liquidation have become clear in several cases of companies that bankrupted. (General Motors, Toys 'R' Us, Schlecker). Therefore, research on bankruptcy and company survival is essential, and for this reason, recovery strategies are gaining significant interest in failed companies and the economy, in general. From the recent literature review, it is obvious that the resolution of "troubled" companies, which are either on the verge of bankruptcy or already in bankruptcy, is now of great importance, not only in terms of satisfying the creditors of the debtor companies but, mainly, in terms of their ability to reorganize and possibly be able to reactivate/recover the whole business (Broude, 2005). Due to the importance of the issue, reorganization law (Müller, 2002) as a set of legal rules is gaining more and more importance nowadays (Baird, 2010).

In 2019, an EU directive (directive 2019/1023/20-07-2019 and amending directive 2017/1132) invited all member states to introduce a court-supervised preventive procedure for businesses into their trade laws. The rationale for a proactive process is that the earlier the difficulties are addressed, the better its chances of survival.

In Greece, due to the crises that have intervened, it is an interesting challenge to study and research from an economic-social point of view the possibilities offered today by the legislative/institutional framework for the consolidation of troubled companies, as well as the proposal of possible future modifications, in the direction of restructuring these businesses instead of bankruptcy while simultaneously safeguarding all parties (Rokas, 2014).

The new Law 4738/2020 introduces a reformed framework for dealing with insolvency for the collective satisfaction of creditors. It also offers arrangements regarding the relief from debt of any person, natural or legal. Its aim is to ensure sustainable businesses and entrepreneurs facing financial difficulties and to enable them to continue their normal operation. The provisions for the pre-bankruptcy reorganization procedure are found now in Chapter B and in particular in articles 31 to 64 of Law 4738/2020.

With this law, an attempt is made to remedy the disadvantages of the older procedures and, in general, to strengthen the sanitizing and preventive operation of bankruptcy, so that it becomes a modern and effective tool for dealing with commercial insolvency for viable businesses. A business that does not go bankrupt may become more attractive and attract new investments, since the investor will prefer to start his investment from an existing business that needs liquidity to save and grow than to start again from scratch (Angelakis, 2010).

An interesting case study, which implemented the procedures of this law, is the consolidation of the "Boutaris" company, a company with many years of history and tradition in winemaking and one of the most powerful companies in Greece.

63.2 The Institution of Pre-bankruptcy Consolidation Process in Foreign Countries

The legal and institutional framework of business restructuring presents different characteristics in each country, but the general trend that prevails has as its ultimate goal the acceleration of the business restructuring process and its greater efficiency.

In France, there are two different procedures for a company seeking debt restructuring under judicial supervision: Sauvegarde and RJ. The main difference between the two is the extent of the financial difficulties faced by the business. An insolvent company has access to RJ, while the business that is not (yet) insolvent, but can demonstrate that it is in serious financial trouble, has access to Sauvegarde (Epaularda & Zapha, 2022).

In Italian law, there are several pre-bankruptcy procedures. Businesses with serious financial problems, as well as those in default of payments, can join. A court order is issued, and with that, starts the process and at the same time defines the protection of the debtor from individual prosecutions of creditors in order to facilitate negotiations. The compromise is reached by a simple majority of the creditors and is binding for all the creditors (Rokas, 2014). Due to the commitment of all creditors to the compromise, it is required to be ratified by a court decision. In contrast, restructuring agreements require a majority of 60% of creditors. Finally, a special procedure is foreseen for large companies employing more than 200 employees, which have the prospect for consolidation.

In English law, in 1870, Schemes of Arrangements had been introduced as an insolvency procedure, while in 1986, with the new Insolvency Law, Company Voluntary Arrangements (CVAs) and Administration were introduced (Rokas, 2011). The Act was intended to modernize insolvency law and was later amended in 2002 with the Enterprise Act (Perakis, 2017). Company Voluntary Arrangements (CVAs) are agreements between the company and its creditors through which the possibility of consolidation is achieved.

In the United States of America, the basic orientation of American law, from the nineteenth century, when they faced the threatened bankruptcy of the railway companies, is the reorganization of companies with financial difficulties and not their liquidation. Its contribution to global bankruptcy law is significant, mainly with the reorganization methodology and also with the rapid settlement of procedures. The most important chapters of the American bankruptcy code (Bankruptcy Code of 1978) are Chap. 7 and the famous Chap. 11 (Chap. 11), which concern the reorganization of natural or legal persons, but also Chap. 13, which concerns the bankruptcy of natural persons (consumers). The process is not considered pre-bankruptcy but a form of bankruptcy, with the main difference being that it is not aimed at liquidation but at rescuing the business.

63.3 Pre-bankruptcy Consolidation Procedure in Greece

The new business recovery framework aims to support the national economy and its function within the market. As long as the acceleration of prevention and restructuring processes is achieved and productive means are returned to productive uses as soon as possible, the country will immediately become more attractive for investments, while at the same time, sustainable businesses will have been preserved. In addition, by providing the possibility of consolidation, potentially viable businesses will not be led to liquidation—divestment and the loss of jobs will be avoided (Avgitidis, 2017).

In general, any person or company, who carries out a business activity and has the center of its main interests in Greece, can be the subject to the consolidation process. The exceptions are credit institutions and insurance companies. More specifically, if a company is in a present or threatened inability to fulfill its overdue financial obligations, in a general way, or simply if there is a possibility of insolvency, it has the possibility by law to draw up an agreement with the majority of its creditors, and if it is ratified by the court, it avoids the bankruptcy (Psychomanis, 2021). In addition, the same possibility is provided to the debtor's creditors, who can request their debtor to be included in the consolidation, without the debtor himself participating, as long as certain conditions are met.

The stages of the consolidation process, according to the recent law, briefly are the following:

a. Initiate informal negotiations with creditors on the basis of a business plan.
b. Applying for precautionary measures to facilitate negotiations.
c. Conclusion of agreement with only their signature or approval by electronic voting.
d. Submit a request for validation of the agreement.
e. New application for preventive measures or extension of the granted ones.
f. Issuance of a decision on validation or non-validation.

The content of a resolution agreement may include, for example:

- Any adjustment of assets and liabilities (adjustment/deletion/change of repayment terms).
- Disposal of assets.
- Renting a business.
- Suspension of individual prosecutions of non-contracting parties for 3 months.
- Selling the business.
- Hiring a person who will oversee the implementation of the agreement.
- Obtaining interim or new financing, in case of business transfer → super-privilege.

63.4 The "Boutaris" Winery

Starting in 1879 and with five generations of uninterrupted family identity—the Boutaris family—the Boutaris Company belongs to the limited and elite circle of the powerful historical European family winemaking.

Since its establishment in 1879 in Naoussa, the Boutaris winery has had an upward trajectory, and since 1930, it has implemented internationalization strategies towards large foreign markets. Giannis and Konstantinos Boutaris, who took over the leadership of the company in 1968, implemented vertical integration strategies and the company also turned to viticulture. In 1978, a new state-of-the-art winery was inaugurated in Stenimahos, Naoussa. From 1980 to 2015, the winemaking activity expanded to the most important wine-producing regions in Greece, but also outside Greece, and more specifically in the South of France where the company acquired a winery, Domaine de Mayrac, surrounded by a vineyard of 700 hectares of organic cultivation.

The company developed rapidly and in 1987 was listed on the Athens Stock Market and the Boutaris Group (I. Boutaris & Sons Holding A.E.) was founded, which took first place in the bottled wine market. In 1989, the Boutaris group acquired the exclusive representation and marketing of the alcoholic beverages of the multinational United Distillers Plc. (now Diageo).

In the early 1990s, Boutari's journey was marked by the acquisition of Kamba SA, the oldest wine and beverage industry in Attica, which since the early 1930s had passed (due to pledges) to the National Bank. At the beginning of the 90 s, the Boutaris winery innovated by opening the doors of its wineries to the public, and now every Boutaris winery actively participates in the viticultural, cultural, and socioeconomic development of its region.

In 1992, the Boutaris group expanded into the brewing market. A few years later, in 1996, the two brother-partners, Konstantinos and Yiannis Boutaris, separated their business activities and Konstantinos Boutaris took over the leadership of the group. In 2006, the management of the group decided to focus on the core business, wine, and sold the company's entire participation to "Mythos Brewery S.A." and at the same time regained overall control of "Boutaris Winery S.A." by buying the entire stake held by Global Finance on behalf of its strategic investors.

63.5 Financial Impasse and Consolidation Attempts

The financial difficulties for the company, which erupted from time to time, not only could not be managed but became more and more every year. In 2016, the company had begun efforts to restructure its debt obligations, through agreements that had been signed with the four systemic banks; however, the road to consolidation proved to be difficult along the way. Among the moves that the Boutaris winery had to proceed with, as foreseen in the business plan, was the sale of the subsidiary company Millesime S.A. in France with a binding price of two million euros, as well as a property in Hydra owned by the main shareholder of the company Mr. K. Boutaris as a guarantor for an amount of 1.3 million euros. The above sales were not possible due to the negative economic circumstances that prevailed in 2017 and 2018 and the suffocating time margin given to the management of the company to look for buyers.

Boutaris Winery, which belonged to the Boutaris Holdings group, had in the past received the approval of the creditor banks, Eurobank, Alpha Bank, National Bank, and Piraeus for the consolidation of its debt. The agreement, which was also judicially approved by the Court of First Instance of Imathia, defined, among other things, the regulation of bank lending over a period of 15 years and the financing of the company's short-term obligations with a simultaneous grace period of one year with the obligation to pay only the interest.

However, the non-fulfillment of specific terms of the reorganization agreement, among which was the sale of the subsidiary company and the winery maintained by the Boutaris group in the South of France, brought specific delays and the failure of the original agreement. It is noted that the total borrowing in the year of the first consolidation agreement exceeded 25 million euros.

Two years later, the banks rejected the offer made by the NPL management company, Pillarstone, in collaboration with the European Investment Bank, to buy Boutaris. The effort to find a solution this time with a proposal from a domestic investor was also fruitless.

In 2019, the adventure of auctions had begun for the famous company, which saw the postings for the sale of its properties in Thiva, Naoussa, Nemea, Crete, Paros, Paiana, and Pikermi. However, in the majority, the electronic hammer did not strike as there were moves that prevented the auctions.

Given the inability to repay the subsidiary Company's loan obligations, the continuation of its activity and, by extension, the group's, was put at risk. Given the circumstances, as mentioned above, the options for the continuation of the Company that remained were either the forcible liquidation of the Company's current assets or the implementation of a viable resolution plan.

Taking into account the aforementioned and in view of the amendments brought about by Law 4738/2020, the Company and the subsidiary company decided to follow the reorganization plan by starting new negotiations with the aim of the uninterrupted continuity of its operation and the maintenance of jobs.

63.6 The Consolidation of "Boutaris"

Premia Properties, with the main shareholder Sterner Stenhus Greece, with basic stakeholder the Greek-Swedish businessman Mr. Ilias Georgiadis, came to put an end to the slippery course of the company. The two sides began negotiations in the summer of 2021 in order to find a common ground to save the historic wine company.

According to the reorganization agreement, the following day would find the Boutaris winery with the sector related to its purely winemaking and commercial activity separated, which passed to a new entity, SSG Hellenic Wineries S.A., and its estate division, which was transferred to Premia's portfolio.

After lengthy negotiations, Premia Properties announced that the discussions with the Boutaris company and its creditors have been completed, thus opening the way for the consolidation of the companies "I.BOUTARIS & SON SA" & "I.BOUTARIS & SON HOLDINGS COMPANY & INVESTMENT SA". A few months later, it was officially announced that the discussions had a positive outcome, while in August 2022 the reorganization agreement between Premia and Boutari's creditors was ratified by the Court of First Instance of Veria.

The structure of the deal included the separation of the properties from the winemaking/commercial activity, creating greater value for all investors. Premia participates as an investor for the real estate, while the company "SSG Hellenic Wineries SA" (a subsidiary of STERNER STENHUS GREECE AB which is the largest shareholder of Premia) participates as an investor and would take over the wine production and commercial activity through the transfer of the trademarks, production machinery, stocks, and reformed claims and liabilities. SSG Hellenic Wineries after the validation of the consolidation would start with zero bank borrowings and would have no overdue debts to the Greek State or insurance funds.

More specifically, the Consolidation Agreement of the Parent and Subsidiary Company predicted:

- All the real estate of the Parent and Subsidiary Company (plots and buildings), except for the historical winery of the Subsidiary Company in Naoussa, to be transferred to the Investor or a Company of his interests.
- All other assets of the Parent and Subsidiary Company, including the Company's historical winery in Naoussa, to be transferred to the New Company (with the exception of assets of zero value).
- Part of the Company's liabilities (€3.6 million for the subsidiary and 0.1 million for the Parent Company) to be transferred to the New Company.

The Exchange-Price for the transfer of the assets of the Companies consisted of:

- The value of the transferred liabilities to the New Company, amounting to €3.6 million for the subsidiary and 0.1 million for the Parent Company.
- The payment of €2.3 million for the subsidiary and €0.9 million for the Parent by the New Company for the repayment of liabilities remaining in the Companies.
- The payment of an amount of €10.4 million for the subsidiary and €1.9 million for the Parent by the Investor or by a Company of his interests for the repayment of obligations remaining in the Companies.
- In the context of facilitating the parent and subsidiary companies and since cash crunch was observed, the New Company would finance the possible cash needs of the subsidiary and the Parent company in the interim period up to the amount of €1.0 million. This financing would only be given if needed and in order to

ensure the continuation of the activity, to cover urgent needs of the subsidiary and the parent company, including the supply of raw materials, to cover the current payroll, and to maintain the prospect of its resolution through the Agreement.
- Employees to be transferred to the New Company, so that they do not lose their jobs and their rights.

The properties acquired by Premia Properties would include buildings with a total area of 28,000 square meters (5 wineries, an office building in Pikermi Attica as well as other buildings) and 5 vineyards of an area of 600 acres, which are located in the best wine-producing locations of the country (Naoussa, Goumenissa, Mantineia, Nemea, Santorini, Crete). Some of the properties (such as those in Santorini and Knossos) are properties with particular potential for tourism development in the wine tourism industry.

On the other hand, the new company, Sterner Stenhus Greece, the domestic arm of the group of brothers Ilias and Thomas Georgiadis from Sweden, operates Boutaris Winery since November 2022, aiming to keep it at the top by maintaining the brands and machinery of the former winery, while all the employees were transferred to it. The winemaker-entrepreneur Konstantinos Boutaris now has the honorary position of consultant in the new company.

Also, the sale of the four houses of Mr. K. Boutaris—in Hydra, Kefalari of Kifissia, Thessaloniki, and Amyntaio of Florina—and subsequently their purchase by Sterner Stenhus Greece companies at prices higher than the prices at which they would be auctioned was the last act of Boutari's entry into the new era. The utilization of these properties by Sterner Stenhus is being considered, while their resale is not excluded. The total price for their acquisition amounted to 4.885 million euros.

The business plan for the next 5 years includes significant investments in the Boutaris brand, trademarks, production facilities, modernization of systems, and organizational structures, as well as environmental upgrades and real estate utilization. Now, in addition to the basic activity of winemaking, the goal is the parallel development of the tourism industry that will also include the operation of boutique hotels in some of the wineries of Boutaris, such as in Santorini and Crete.

63.7 Summary: Conclusions and Proposals for Future Improvements of the Law

After the bibliographic review and the analysis and study of the "Boutaris" case, the following are concluded:

Consolidation preserves the value of the business as a "going concern", i.e., as an economic unit that continues its operation, in contrast to the (destructive) scenario of liquidation of the individual assets of the business that leads to liquidation; in addition to the procedural and organizational aspects of the reform of Law 4738/2020, which aims at a more effective consolidation process, the change of direction of bankruptcy law, from the interests of creditors, to the emergence as its fundamental objective, of providing a second opportunity, in the company that bankrupted or is at risk of going bankrupt (Avgitidis, 2017; Kavadella, 2018).

The institution of the consolidation of companies that are in a state of imminent bankruptcy offers a socially important second chance to save jobs, both in the company itself and in other cooperating companies that do business with it. A successful business rescue helps attract investments since it gives investors and investment funds the opportunity to acquire an already existing business that needs liquidity, but does not lose its intangible value and does not interrupt its productive activity. Creditors' interests and claims are better secured, since as a rule creditors will be more satisfied with a functioning business than they would be satisfied with a forced sale—divestment of its assets.

The progressive implementation of the institution of business consolidation will gradually change the perception of business failure in Greece, where the bankruptcy and liquidation of a business is a heavy stigma and will cultivate a culture of rescue, with an emphasis on reorganization. It is necessary to "cultivate" a culture of consultation of all parties involved and to adopt a more sympathetic attitude towards the debtor and his business in order to put the agreements in a different context. It is important to have a forecast so that the entrepreneur is not damaged at all levels; to preserve his name and not to be put in social, economic, and moral exclusion because of his debts.

Also, there is a need for a legislative calm in the immediate future, which will allow familiarization with the new provisions. The institution of business consolidation, as regulated by the new law 4738/2020, will take time and smooth operating conditions for the national economy and market to be assessed and valued in terms of its efficiency and effectiveness.

There is room for improvement/reform of the reorganization law, despite its modernization, which briefly concerns its flexibility and attractiveness for all parties involved, in order to further improve the process, and also to safeguard the interests of all parties (creditors, debtors, judicial authorities, etc.). The process must be adapted to the current socioeconomic reality, international trends, and judicial practice so that the second chance will return dynamically to the area of bankruptcy law and to everyone's satisfaction.

It is very important that the companies, which have the possibility to reorganize, present a realizable plan for their reorganization, with the effort of all the parties involved and with legislative support. The continuance of the business ensures that there will be no financial loss. Finally, in time, collective effort and flexibility will be needed from all those involved in the process of restructuring a business in order to keep the business "alive," with the ultimate goal of satisfying everyone who depends on the viability of the business.

The points that need to be addressed in the future and improved in the next improvement/change of the relevant article of the bankruptcy law are:

A. The utilization of real estate with preservation of their objective value: the proposal here is related to the utilization of the debtor's property in the best possible way so that it is not liquidated in a hurry, so that the creditors are immediately satisfied by zeroing the debtor morally, psychologically, financially, and ethically. The assets of companies and individuals must be better utilized at a fair price both in the context of consolidation and liquidation. Perhaps the value of the debtor's real estate should be preserved at the level of their fair value, in order to avoid their violent and hasty liquidation, leaving the companies helpless and without any protection under the pressure of the creditors.

B. The training of the involved parties. It is proposed to create an environment that will guarantee and enhance the education and training of the involved parties. Bankruptcy and liquidation law judges should be continuously trained, to have the appropriate knowledge and qualifications, as well as research activity on these subjects. An important component for the development of "rescue culture" is the training of all parties involved (business managers, lawyers, judges) for the operation and unlimited possibilities of the institution of consolidation.

C. Establish rules of supervision in professional organizations that will help their members dealing with bankruptcy, in order to ensure high standards of adequacy and integrity.

D. The handling of the consolidation procedures should be done by special Courts and these cases to be undertaken by judges, with experience and combined knowledge in tax, accounting, and labor law.

References

Angelakis, M. (2010). The *changes that occurred in the Bankruptcy Code with law 3588/2007* (p. 856).

Avgitidis, D. (2017). *Business fertilization through bankruptcy agreements* (1st ed.). Sakkoulas Publications.

Baird, D. G. (2010). *The elements of bankruptcy* (p. 256).

Broude, R. F. (2005). *Reorganizations under chapter 11 of the bankruptcy code (Bankruptcy Series, Lslf Edition).*

Epaularda, A., & Zapha, Ch. (2022). *Bankruptcy costs and the design of preventive restructuring procedures.*

Kavadella, E. (2018). Forms, conditions and procedure of article 99 et seq. Of the Bankruptcy Code after law 4446/2016—Pre-bankruptcy process of business consolidation as well as proposals de lege ferenda. Diploma Thesis, University of Piraeus.

Müller, H.-F. (2002). *Der Verband in der Insolvenz* (p. 261).

Perakis, E. (2017). *Bankruptcy Law* (3rd ed., p. 38). Law Library.

Psychomanis, S. (2021). *Bankruptcy law (based on law 4738/2020)* (9th ed., p. 104). Sakkoulas Publications.

Rokas, A. (2011). *Pre-bankruptcy process of restructuring companies* (pp. 25–41). Sakkoulas Publications.

Rokas, A. (2014). *Bankruptcy process of business consolidation* (p. 281). Sakkoulas Publications.

Chapter 64
Tourist Clusters and the Tourist Experience as a Tool for Smart, Sustainable, and Integrated Development of Rural Areas: The Case of Troodos in Cyprus

Electra Pitoska and Panayiotis Papadopoullos

Abstract Cluster theory has been developed for two decades. Initially, it was a tool for better describing the economic activity of companies that were geographically concentrated and based on knowledge. In practice, the cluster model helps to understand how the companies that make it up are connected, how they are interdependent, and also how they will become more competitive, appreciating how important each of them is.

The aim is to clearly define the concept of a cluster today, as well as the reasons that make its creation beneficial for all the companies that make it up without being competitive and since the companies themselves create an added value.

Choosing the correct research methodology can determine the success and overall quality of the report as well as the impact of the project. Choosing Qualitative research method to collect the data for this report, achieved by interviewing key persons of the Troodos Region, from different sectors of the daily life, i.e., tourism industry, local authorities, Troodos organizations using a semi-structured questionnaire giving them the opportunity to express their thoughts and feelings regarding the creation of a new cluster in the local tourism industry and facing their worries and potential risks. From the other side, focus groups in each subregion of Troodos offer the chance of inviting a limited number of individuals in common physical environment to discuss in an organized way with the help of one or more mediators about clustering in Troodos region and a series of interrelated issues.

Through this study answer the question: How the tourism clusters in Troodos and a pilot project began from Platres, will provide platforms of local economic development, growth and innovation of new and existing enterprises in the tourism industry, through trusted cooperation and creative complementarity, especially in a

E. Pitoska (✉) · P. Papadopoullos
Department of Accounting & Finance, University of Western Macedonia, Kozani, Greece
e-mail: ipitoska@uowm.gr

small economy like Platres, whereas as the economists state "Small is beautiful", in the sense that tourism clusters in Platres, can be easily managed with a great impact and results.

From what has been said above, there is no doubt that a number of actions should be taken with the ultimate goal of strengthening clusters in the tourism, in order to stimulate and develop innovation, but also competitiveness between companies of all sectors of the wider economy and especially the tourism sector. In fact, by strengthening the clusters, it is possible to promote competitiveness, as well as encouraging businesses to be productive, as well as developing entrepreneurship. Finally, it is important to emphasize the need to strengthen the clusters, as well; through them, it is possible to encourage the local economic development and the growth of new enterprises in the market.

Keywords Tourism experience · Tourism clusters · Smart · Sustainable · Inclusive growth · Rural areas

64.1 Introduction

Human needs are unlimited and the means to satisfy them are limited. Tourism is a temporary movement of people from one place to another with a design to meet tourism needs and is a phenomenon that can observed from many angles. Tourism products in relation to other products are characterized by high heterogeneity, seasonality, and geographical concentration. The objectives of tourism policy cannot be achieved if they are not supported by the wishes and needs of tourists, which should be reflected in one qualitative and flexible tourism product.

Business clusters, according to scientific definitions, are the set of businesses operating in a specific area of society and aim to develop the economy. The tourism cluster consists of any cluster of companies with different elements and activities but always with a common goal of increasing and optimizing tourism in the geographical area where the cluster operates. This cluster may include services tourism businesses, such as accommodation, travel agencies, aquariums, theme parks, public transport, etc. Also, the infrastructure and superstructures of the area are optimized and also support services.

It is a fact that the presence of clusters can affect the overall economic performance of a region and consequently a country. First of all, we cannot fail to mention at this point that the share of employment of an area in cluster categories is statistically significantly correlated and positively with a higher average salary (Ketels, 2003). In addition, it has been concluded through relevant studies that the larger the share of employment in large clusters, and also the larger the number of areas that direct and eventually concentrate their employment on business clusters, the higher the wage growth expected (Ketels, 2003). Also, one of the main characteristics of a cluster is innovation, or more precisely, the production and marketing of a good with different characteristics compared to the goods of the competition. It is a fact that clusters play a major role in endurance to innovate in the sector in which the latter operates, as there is no doubt that clusters have the opportunity to benefit from a more direct access to market, compared to isolated companies (Galindo et al., 2009).

Beni (2003, p. 74) then focused his study on coherence and cooperation which govern the activity of the participants in the tourism cluster, conceptually defining the latter as a set consisting of turn of important tourist destinations, but which are located within a limited geographical context, while in these destinations guests are offered services which are of high quality (da Cunha & da Cunha, 2005). But the main feature of tourist clusters, according to Beni (2003), concerns the fact that these clusters of companies are distinguished from their cohesion, both socially and politically, as well as their connection with the productive process and culture is obvious, and have excellent management, which in turn leads to achieving competitive advantages for the companies participating in the tourism cluster (Beni, 2003, p. 74, in da Cunha & da Cunha, 2005).

In order for such a cluster of businesses to grow, it must innovate, improve its productivity, and also access human resources, suppliers, technology, and information resources; also take advantage of complementarity to create new businesses and participate locally, improving competitiveness. The cluster should reach a level where businesses respond to each other collectively and new conditions are created for public-private partnerships. The achievement of a cluster is that the number of all the companies that set up the cluster should exceed the sum of those that operated individually. The phenomenon of synergy, which arises from the establishment and efficient operation of a cluster of companies, the world market through real examples, from the whole world around, proves the success of the clusters.

This report covers the theoretical background referring to tourism and its main elements, in theory of clusters and how these clusters can affect a city and a society in general. The purpose of this work is the development of clusters and how their creation positively or negatively affects a society, especially in the tourism industry. Over the years, countries are looking for ways in which they will manage to stimulate local economies, which in turn will help the national economy. Tourism is a key pillar and an important economic factor for Cyprus and the whole world market and, for this reason, has been researched in recent years' various methods for its development. The leading role in these researches is played by business clusters and more specifically business clusters for the common purpose of tourism. We should explore the major issue of creation of local clusters in the field of tourism, and also their function and importance as an effective tool for strengthening the local economy and sustainable development.

Finally, after the finish of the research will be able to have the results about the questions:

1. If and how much is their knowledge about clusters in order to guide us to farther steps that we have to follow to reach our goals.
2. If they had any experience of clustering, participating in a cluster, or even cooperating with other companies at least in the philosophy of clustering.

3. And finally, what will be the benefits of adapting to this model of working and whether they believe this model will help their companies to develop.

64.2 The Background

The issue of business networking and business clusters was highlighted academically in the early 1990s by Michael Porter. Porter (1998) provided a definition for business networking, which to this day is the most common and commonly accepted definition of business networking among members of the scientific community. In particular, Porter pointed out that networks are a set consisting of many companies, which are interconnected geographically, but also by cooperating institutions, in a clearly defined field of business activity (Porter, 1998). The main characteristic of these businesses and institutions is that they are governed by common interests, common pursuits and goals, and in the majority of cases, they complement each other (Porter, 1998). Enright and Flowcs-Williams (2001) defined business clusters as "geographic concentrations of interconnected and interconnected firms that produce and sell a range of related or complementary products". The definition of Enright and Flowcs-Williams (2001) had much in common with the one originally introduced by Porter in 1998.

Despite the strong mobility of the component parts of a cluster, a cluster obeys a clearly defined outline, which consists of parameters, which according to Andersson et al. (2004), can be summarized in the following seven components: the geographical concentration, distinct economic specialization, or sectoral specialization, the large number and range of participants, longevity, critical mass, competition and close cooperation between participating firms, and innovation.

With regard to the stages of creation of business clusters, although the starting point of business clusters differs from case to case, as it is influenced and partly determined by the circumstances at hand, but also the factors that motivate their creation, the four main stages of creation of a cluster are as follows:

1. The development of social capital and the establishment of a mutual relationship.
2. trust,
3. The development of strategic cooperations.
4. The creation of a common vision and mission.
5. Taking action and implementing the common strategy.

As regard the distinction of business clusters in individual categories, it is important that the criterion on the basis of which this distinction will be made plays a major role. Business clusters differ in a wide range of dimensions, the most important of which are follows:

- The type and diversification of products and services they provide.
- The dynamics of the geographical location in which they are established.
- The stage of their development, and.
- The business environment that surrounds them (Ketels, 2003, p. 4).

One of the strategies applied is the concentration of businesses in a geographical area and the development of cooperation links between them, since it is now commonly accepted among the members of the scientific community that the formation of business clusters can promote the level of competitiveness between cluster member firms (Feurer & Chaharbaghi, 1994). Business clusters affect competition in various ways, and more specifically, they positively affect the businesses participating in each cluster.

In general, experts have concluded in the context of their research that the way in which business clusters ultimately increase the competitiveness of their member companies is based on their main characteristics, the most important of which is the cooperation of its members' cluster (Feurer & Chaharbaghi, 1994).

The presence of clusters can affect the general economic performance of a region, and by extension, a country. Besides, the employment share of an area in cluster categories is statistically significantly and positively correlated with a higher average salary (Ketels, 2003). Also, clusters play a major role in the continuous ability of a firm to innovate in the field in which it operates, as firms that are members of a cluster have the ability to benefit from a more direct access to the market, compared to isolated firms (Galindo et al., 2009).

Innovative activities, which are created within a cluster, enable the cluster itself to compete successfully against its dispersed competitors. However, innovative performance and incentives to innovate are influenced and partly determined by the nature of competition, and also by the structure of the market, in which the cluster is located and operates (Piperopoulos, 2007, p. 201). In addition, Tracey and Clark point out, in the context of their scientific research, how important the geographical proximity of businesses is, as it is, according to them, a factor that encourages and also maintains over time all the types of relationships deemed necessary for the development of innovation.

Several studies have been conducted regarding the effect of business clusters on sustainable or otherwise green development, one of which is those of Triga et al. (2011, p. 1). The scientists investigated this major issue and managed to draw important conclusions, so that it is possible to identify the degree of importance of the individual factors, which are related to the operation of a sustainable building cluster, and also the way in which this will contribute to the green economy. As Hoppwood et al. typically state, "actions to deal with climate change must include a change in the existing development model, in the direction of a sustainable, green economy with low or even zero carbon emissions with the use of modern technology".

A business cluster in the tourism sector refers to a particularly complex group, which consists of a multitude of different elements and includes tourism business services, such as:

- The accommodations, hotels, and Agro tourism establishments,
- Travel agencies,
- Thematic and theme parks such as aquariums, Rope parks, etc.

It also includes a wide range of heterogeneous companies and industries, including even communication and transport infrastructure, complementary activities, and support services, as well as the natural resources of the region and the policies adopted, according to the policy of the area. All of the above constitute the tourism business cluster, which provides interested consumers with a multitude of tourism experiences, due to the varied characteristics and individual elements that make it up (Montfort & Masure, 2000, p. 46, in da Cunha & da Cunha, 2005).

Beni (2003, p. 74) focused his study on the cohesion and cooperation that governs the activity of the participants in the tourism cluster, conceptually defining the latter as a set which in turn consists of important tourist destinations, which however, they are located within a limited geographical framework, while in these destinations visitors are offered services that are of high quality (da Cunha & da Cunha, 2005). However, the main characteristic of tourism clusters, according to Beni (2003), concerns the fact that these clusters of businesses are distinguished by their cohesion, both at a social and political level, while their connection with the productive process and culture and have excellent management, which in turn leads to the achievement of competitive advantages for participating firms in the tourism cluster (Beni, 2003, p. 74, in da Cunha & da Cunha, 2005).

The development of clusters in the tourism sector can be a new perspective, but also a direction towards the development of the specific sector of the economy; however, innovation in this sector is quite incomplete. More specifically, the main reasons for non-diffusion of innovation and incomplete application of clusters in the tourism sector are mainly the particularities and characteristics that distinguish the tourism market.

All of the above have been the subject of careful research, but also of intense reflection, with experts holding discussions regarding the various issues and problems that emerge, as well as the obstacles that arise during the efforts to implement business clusters in practice and the diffusion of innovation in tourism (Jackson & Murphy, 2002).

64.3 The Empirical Research

64.3.1 The Methodology

Choosing the correct research methodology can determine the success and overall quality of the report as well as the impact of the project. Research methods are divided into qualitative and quantitative. The quantitative methods analyze the amount of occurrence of the phenomenon under consideration and qualitative ones refer to the species, to the specific character of the phenomenon (Kvale, 1996: 67). Both methods enable the researcher to approach a research field and focus on it. Important elements that characterize the quality methods have a normal flow, and to a large extent, are not directed by the researcher. Lincoln and Guba, moreover, wrote in 1985 that quality methods are natural (Lincoln & Guba, 1985). The researcher thus can penetrate the personality of the subjects and understand the social ones' influences that the subjects have accepted.

Within this research, we need to take into consideration and understand the thoughts and individual's perspectives of specific tourism experts and the stakeholders in order to meet the study's aim and find out: If and how the tourism clusters can be the right tool for sustainable development? For Platres Resort as a pilot project for the Troodos Region. This aim determined the study's research design.

The qualitative methodology was considered the more appropriate for this research, in terms of gathering information and data from the stakeholders, the representatives of the three Troodos Companies, Troodos Regional Tourism Board, the Troodos Development Board, and the Troodos Network of the thematic centers, the representatives of the local authorities and of the five subregions of Troodos, the representatives of the hoteliers, restaurants, and cafes owners, the traditional products workshops, and the youth centers. In research where the main goal of the researcher is the in-depth understanding of, qualitative research, is the most appropriate method to achieve this goal. The researcher making a qualitative study immerses himself in the social space he studies and tries to see things from the point of view of the investigated (Kyriazi, 1999).

A qualitative research is chosen because of the flexibility it offers during its conduct, as well as because of the immediacy and familiarity that the interviewee feels. It enables the researcher to obtain a more direct and clearer picture of the positions and views of the informants. Many researchers (e.g., Kvale, 1996) emphasize the value of interviews because in-depth information can be gathered by achieving direct interaction between the researcher and the informant. It is a very demanding process for its design and time consuming to carry out, as the selection and formulation of questions play an important role in the processing, analysis, and utilization of results (Cohen et al., 2000).

64.3.2 Method of Data Collection

The method of data collection has been determined by the study's aim and research questions and linked to theoretical framework of the research. For this research, two types of collecting data were used, namely, semi-structured interviews and focus groups.

The semi-structure type gave the opportunity to hear ideas and discover difficulties and find solutions for topics you never thought about. Semi-structured interviews can be used in explanatory studies, i.e., those that we seek to understand relationships between variables. In the personal interview, an important stage is the selection and training of interviewers. The target group of the interviews covers the whole society of the local communities in Troodos region by interviewing key persons of local authorities, local entrepreneurs, youngsters who decided to invest in families' business and stay in the region, but also persons from the tourist industry of the Troodos region, hoteliers, agro tourism establishments owners, café owners, and craftsmen.

The interview is one of the most well-known methods of collecting material, where the researcher submits to the respondent a series of questions to be answered (Tsiolis, 2014). The interview is one of the main tools of the quality method. It is about the interaction, the communication between persons, that guided the researcher or questioner with the aim of extracting information related to the object of research. In other words, it is the method which has as its object to form one "Mental content" (Mialaret, 1997: 148) to reveal aspects of personality and recognize behaviors. Its main tool is a conversation that takes place between two or more persons. Tuckman defined interviews as an opportunity to "enter" into what takes place in the subject's mind (Tuckman, 1972). The interviews show the knowledge that the subject possesses (information and knowledge), his likes and dislikes (values and preferences), and especially what he thinks (opinions and perceptions).

Within the context of this study, the interviewer asked questions, such as "If and what they know about cluster" in order to understand how familiar participants are with the concept and help me at the focus group discussion. The other question asked was "If they had any cooperation in the concept of a cluster" in order to understand about their experience of the concept which will be useful for the procedure, either avoid any problems of bad experiences, or encourage them of good experiences. The most important question was "Their feelings about clustering and if they were ready to try this concept" which was a nodal point of the future of the research.

Apart from the interviews in this research, the focus groups were used, which were the think tank consisting of the representatives of all parts of the community and the economic factors as well as members of the public entities that are directly involved with Troodos, as the ultimate aim of the whole research was based on the idea of clusters as being a tool of sustainable development in Troodos and in Platres Resort, especially. The aim of this is to gather important opinions by having the focus group discuss the topic and offer solutions where needed, on one hand, whereas offering a ground for the creation and development of the clusters.

The methodological approach of the focus groups consists of an organized collective interview and interaction of a number of participants for one focused topic or for a series of interrelated phenomena and processes. Focus group is a title given to a specific type of group interview which is structured in order to gather detailed knowledge about one specific issue by selected participants. The essential purpose of the focus groups is to explore a range of perceptions and views on a research object and the acquisition of understanding of the subjects under investigation through the point of view of the participants themselves (selected participants). A concentration of a limited number of individuals in common physical (or virtual) environment to discuss in an organized way with the help of one or more mediators a specific issue or a series of interrelated issues. Participants are substantially related, but are usually from different positions with different perspectives on the subject under the investigation process.

64.3.3 Sampling

Through this research interviewing key persons from local authorities and young entrepreneur's, which decided to invest in families' business and stay in the region but also persons from the tourist industry of the Troodos region, hoteliers, agro tourism establishments owners, café owners and craftsmen's, 30 interviews in total with questions asked in person, so that a full explanation given to the stakeholders and together with their answers having the chance to open their heart and express their feelings, thoughts, aspirations and objectives. The conversations were semi-structured, giving the opportunity to express their thoughts and feelings regarding the creation of a new cluster in the local tourism industry and facing their worries and potential risks. The questionnaires were semi-structured, giving the opportunity to express their thoughts and feelings regarding the creation of a new cluster in the local tourism industry and their worries and potential risks. At the same time, they enabled us to find out how much they knew about the clusters and if they believe that they are beneficial for their village.

Through the research also 5 focus groups organized, cover the 5 sub areas of the Troodos region as Solea Valley, Marathasa Valley, Wine villages, Pitsilia Villages and Mountain Resorts region which located in the center and it's the region where Platres Resort is located. Each focus group was consisting of 5 local persons in each sub area as follows: The representative of the local authorities, of the hotelier's, of the youth, of the restaurant and cafes owners and of the traditional products producers. Also was very important having with us representatives of the 3 Troodos Region companies as follows: The Troodos Regional Tourism Company, The Troodos Development company, and The Troodos Network of Thematic Centers.

Some of the stakeholders involved were very positive and they could see their profit in this joining of forces; from the other side, were few stakeholders skeptical because of the bad experiences they had in the past through some cooperation they had; also were few stakeholders who were looking to find out more information, feel more secured, and then to decide. Very positive was the involving of the 3 Troodos companies into the procedure as was familiar with the concept of the clusters, and their support for the pilot application of the concept in Platres Resort in order to give the opportunity to the other villages to realize the profit of the cooperation and join forces together, was also very important of the support at the implementation of the results of the study.

64.3.4 Method of Data Analysis

In the diverse field of qualitative research, there are many different approaches and analyses of research material. Some ways are more general and others more specific depending on the research material available to the researcher and based on the research planning that has been followed to conduct the research. Qualitative research usually produces a large volume of material, which can be particularly rich, "dense", complex, or even chaotic due to the nonstandard in advance which is mainly due to semi-structured methods. The "Theoretical freedom" or "flexibility" was the main reason for using the thematic analysis of data in this research; also, thematic analysis is an easy-to-use method that is widely used in qualitative research. It is considered especially important for new researcher, as it provides basic skills that are useful for conducting more specialized qualitative analysis approaches. In particular, it is a method of identifying, describing, reporting, and "thematizing" repetitive semantic patterns, i.e., "themes" arising from research data, and is a key tool for all researchers involved in qualitative research (Braun & Clarke, 2006). One of the advantages of this analysis is that it is characterized by "theoretical freedom" or "flexibility", as its choice as a method of analysis does not require, alone, the commitment of researchers to specific ontological or epistemological positions, as with other qualitative analyses (e.g., interpretive phenomenological analysis is bound to a phenomenological orientation) (Braun & Clarke, 2006).

64.4 The Research Findings

64.4.1 Interviews' Results

Through the interviews, focus group, and general discussion about tourism and clustering in tourism, the stakeholders mention that tourism is a complex, unbounded phenomenon that, according to international organizations, includes: Economic activities, such as accommodation services of various types, catering services with food and beverages, private accommodation, information services, transportation services, and also rental of cars and motorcycles, Cultural services (cultural production, museums, archeological and historical sites and individual monuments, botanical and natural areas), and Sports services and leisure (sports facilities, theme parks and leisure parks, hiking trials, biking trails), without this list being closed. At the same time, the tourist uses local, shared natural and cultural resources, without a direct financial transaction.

First, through the 30 interviews, it was found that the main difficulties in order for the Troodos region to become an attractive destination and reach at least 5% of the incoming tourism flows are as follows: The Product fragmentation, the lack of funds, the branding of the Troodos products, the establishment of a Tourism and Hospitality School, the creation of the Tourism Experience, the lack of cooperation, the Sustainable Development of the Troodos region, and the poor Public Transport.

After the records of the views and discussion with the stakeholders of the Tourism industry and Local authorities of the Troodos region, we have a common finding that tourism is the main sector or the "locomotive" of the Troodos economy. Despite this fact—and especially in the last decade—everyone (experts, businessmen, politicians) also agrees that the tourism product is degrading and not competitive. The basic conditions for a sustainable tourism development and for a better future are discussed in the following:

1. *The differentiation of the development model* chosen in the first decades of the establishment of the Republic of Cyprus period and which is exclusively related to organized mass holiday tourism is a first precondition. This pattern is identified with the short tourist season and its consequent problems, the unambiguous and often dependent connection with specific European markets, and the "monoculture" of tourism to the detriment of other sectors of the local economy. The massive demand for the services and infrastructure of this model gradually led to the degradation of the competitiveness of the Troodos tourist product, which now need the help of all stakeholders in order to establish a new model of development with many benefits. Indeed, both the region in which the cluster is developing and the local community benefit to an extremely high degree from the cluster business activity, with the main benefits, always at the level of local communities, being: The development of the local economy, the promoting collective learning and innovation, and the reduction of unemployment (Piperopoulos, 2007).

2. *The enrichment of the Troodos tourism product* with infrastructures, products, and services of the Special and Alternative Forms, which are based on the experience, forming an important and quality market, is a second prerequisite. Efforts in this direction have been made in the last 10 years with the establishment of the Troodos Regional Tourism Board and the Troodos Development Board and recently the establishment of the Troodos Geopark, but are characterized by lack of coordination and insufficient marketing. At the same time, most of our competitors have similar products since the first postwar decades, which allowed them both the qualitative differentiation of their product and the extension of the tourist season.

    The underlying advantage of Troodos is that it is a virgin area, completely unexploited from human interventions; therefore, Troodos offers something authentic to tourists, either this is a traditional village and scrolling into the narrow paths discovering legends and traditions, discovering nature with a bike or a walk to the forest or by the river, or by visiting a winery or a small workshop taste the tradition and learn the stories behind them, and visiting a chapel of thirteenth century with unique frescos or a medieval bridge, listed of the World protected Heritage of UNESCO.

    "This illustrates the potential of the Troodos area to become an authentic tourism destination. Seeking authenticity is an important attribute for contemporary tourists, which can provide unique experiences".

    "Within the context of Cyprus and predominance of a mass tourism model, the Troodos region represents a setting where authentic experiences cab be build, contributing to the enrichment of the tourism product and repositioning the island as a unique destination" (Katherine Desper, Rural Tourism: An international Perspective, p. 398).

3. *The geographical dispersion of the tourism offers*, in order to reverse the current negative phenomenon of spatial overconcentration in a relatively small number of traditional Troodos resorts (like Platres, Omodos, Pedhoulas, Kakopetria, and Agros), is the third condition. In these areas, environmental problems, high infrastructure costs, local product degradation, over-professionalism, and consequent low incomes are some of the main effects of this situation. In addition, many other areas of the region with rich tourist resources have been deprived due to this overconcentration of the benefits of decades of tourism development. Tourism destinations are commonly planned and managed following the administrative boundaries of the corresponding territorial administration without considering how tourists geographically consume destinations. This means that a destination may not be adapted to consumers' needs. The destination may thus be missing out on the opportunity to improve planning and management to the detriment of sustainability and business-favorable circumstances. Furthermore, tourism mobility patterns have become more massive and complex, providing more evidence that the destination model based on administrative boundaries is severely outdated. There is thus a need to bring back previously unsolved debates on destination planning models and the definition of tourism destination boundaries.

4. *The lack of consistency and continuity in the institutional framework of strategic planning* and tourism representatives. The oxymoron is that while everyone involved in politics emphasizes the economic and developmental importance of tourism, it has been deprived of its specific field of reference in politics, legislation, and development. Even the few attempts that were undoubtedly made were fragmentary and short-lived, with contradictory results. At the same time, other sectors such as industry, agriculture, and shipping with less contribution to income, GDP, or employment and especially less competitive products have their own body (ministry) and institutional framework that tourism for decades—for micro-political reasons—does not have. The recent establishment of the Deputy Ministry of Tourism is clearly a positive development, but in relation to most of our competitors in the international arena, it is too late and its importance remains to be seen in practice. From the other side, the fragmentation of Troodos into two districts and 100 villages with their own President and budget doesn't help the strategic planning of the region with a common vision and mission.

    In the last two decades, the globalization process made the business environment highly turbulent and the concern of 'change' has received immense interest both by strategic thinkers and practitioners. Many new theories, such as crafting strategy, strategic flexibility, complexity and chaos, and strategic change and transformation, have taken the center stage.

5. *Upgrading and diversifying the offer* (infrastructure, services, activities, human resources) of Troodos tourism is also urgently needed if we do not want to lose in the game of international competition, which is constantly growing with new countries, new destinations, new products, lower prices, but limited development prospects of tourist-sending countries. In this gloomy reality, courageous

decisions are needed (incentives and institutional framework) with the aim of improving the quality, on the one hand, and the gradual "exit" (through change of use or permanent closure) of many companies, mainly accommodation, from the market, on the other. These measures are necessary not only to improve the image of the Troodos tourism product, but also to control over-professionalism, part of which is related to poor quality or illegal business activities. The application of the Strategy of the European Union for 2020 for Smart Specialization is the tool of the upgrading and diversifying the product of Troodos region.

"The National Strategy for Research and Innovation for Smart Specialization 2014–2020" seeks the efficient, effective and collaborative use of the (limited) resources available in direction of enhancing innovation, upgrading human resources as well as strengthening or creating competitive advantages in sectors of the economy that meet the relevant conditions. In addition to its horizontal components (development of innovative products and services, creating research and innovation infrastructures, taking advantage of the opportunities they offer emerging technological fields, excellence in research, development of human research potential, interconnection of science with society, production of new knowledge, international cooperation), the National RTD Strategy has a specific sectoral dimension, which emerged through the application of the business discovery process "The Goals of Smart Specialization", S3 policy brief series, No1/2013, Dominique Foray and Xabier Goenaga, European Commission Joint Research Centre, Institute for Prospective Technological Studies.

6. *The repositioning of the priorities of the demand and specialization of the tourism marketing,* in order to upgrade and dynamically promote the "image" of the region. The era of a few stable markets and one tourist product has now given way to the many unstable markets, the new and varied consumer incentives, and the many specialized tourism products. In this context, Troodos must now look for new markets or new target groups in the existing ones, constantly seeking to increase and improve the quality of tourists. Two important examples are the decades-long underestimation of the importance of domestic tourism and the lag in the development of a marketing plan for Special and Alternative Tourism.

   What Is Repositioning? Repositioning refers to the process of altering the existing space a brand occupies in the brains of the customers. In simple terms, it is a process of changing how the target market perceives the brand or its offering with respect to its—Features, and Competitors. With repositioning, the business tries to change the way the customer views the brand without always altering the bond between the customer and the business. It involves changing the brand's promise and personality with an updated or refreshed—Marketing mix, Brand identity, Target customer, and Brand essence. (Aashish Pahwa, Marketing Essentials, 2020).

7. *Planning of sustainable development,* which requires participatory processes and upgrading of the role of the "partners" who are professionally involved in it, plan it, or manage it. The international experience in developed—and not only—countries is that these partners are usually four: The Regional Tourism Board, the Regional Development Board, local authorities and specialists (scientists or

tourism experts), and in some cases, citizen representatives are added (consumer or travel tourism organizations, environmental associations) directly related to tourism and development. In Troodos, almost throughout the establishment of the Republic of Cyprus period, planning remained a matter for the central government and less for local authorities, and in terms of tourism policymakers, it was almost exclusively the state and the private sector with the least contribution from local authorities, while the other two partners have little or no participation. "Locality", as a key dimension of the development of sustainable tourism, but also the transition from empirical to scientific planning of sustainable tourism, requires substantial changes in this issue as well. In general, rural tourism development often fails due to the lack of strategic and participatory planning capable of bringing together all the community stakeholders group. The root cause of this failure primarily lies in the clash between planner's worldviews and those of residents (Chalip & Costa, 2012). Chalip and Costas' (2012:25) ethnographic study of a Portuguese rural community illustrated this clash of worldviews; this clash in the worldviews of planners and locals seems to also exist in y = the case of Troodos creating a number of problems which constrain the mutual understanding, empathic communication, and efficient collaboration. The convergence of different worldviews is a social-cultural process that inevitably takes a lot of time to be completed. However, community negotiation and adoption of a common vision for a rural area could facilitate this process and put in place the operational mechanisms needed for sustainable development.

64.5 Conclusions

One of the main conclusions drawn from our work concerns with the fact that we found that clusters are growing, which as time goes by and, without a doubt, is dynamic and timeless phenomenon, which supports the local productive and socioeconomic structure. The concept of clusters has not been fully clarified among members of the scientific community, but instead continues to arouse their scientific interest, mainly due to their multidimensional nature and breadth; concepts that clusters can cover. It is important to mention that there are specific factors as well specific stages of the development of a cluster. The main goals of the clusters are to achieve the increase of the competitive advantage of the participating companies and to face the growing demands of the current economic "globalized" reality, with the specific objectives of promoting competitiveness and innovation, encouraging entrepreneurship, his motivation entrepreneurship, economic growth, as well as the creation of new businesses and the increase in the number of existing ones. Clusters are especially important for small- and medium-sized enterprises, due to some particular difficulties and problems that the latter are called upon to overcome. In particular, due to the lack of business and scientific knowledge and skills on the part of their owners-managers, and also due to the lack of large production capacities, capital, and homogenized standards, collectively, do not allow these companies to take advantage of market opportunities.

The advantages of clusters are derived from geographical concentration, and also from the existence of relations of cooperation and simultaneous competition between the member companies of each cluster, which are also the pillars of innovation, which is more directly accessible among members of the cluster. Unlike individual companies, those participating in a cluster are encouraged to increase, increasingly, their business activity, while they often created economies of scale, as there will always be substantial cooperation between cluster members. Indeed, this structure affects competition in a variety of ways, and more specifically, it positively affects the companies participating in each case cluster, through the increase of the produced innovation, the increase of their general productivity, and also through the promotion of the establishment of new enterprises that in turn support, further, the innovation and the cluster extension.

In addition to the benefits that cluster companies can reap, the existence of the latter in one area can lead to multiple benefits for the region itself, the local economy, and for the inhabitants themselves, since collective learning and innovation are promoted, while at the same time unemployment is reduced in the specific area where the cluster exists and operates, aiming at the same time, especially on us, in sustainability and sustainability. As far as the tourism cluster is concerned, this refers to one particularly complex group, or more precisely, a wide range of heterogeneous companies and industries, e.g., tourism business services, communications and transport infrastructure, complementary activities and support services, as well as natural resources of the area but also policies adopted, according to the institutions. The most important factors in creating a cluster in tourism are the nature of the tourism product, the hotel services, the access to specialized guides—entrepreneurs, the collection and circulation of ideas and knowledge, the exchange of experiences, and technological development and innovations. It is a fact that nowadays the importance is recognized more and more in the creation of tourist clusters, since especially in the tourism sector, it is a new perspective, but also at the same time a new direction towards the development sector of the economy, but nevertheless there is insufficient growth of clusters and non-diffusion of innovation in the tourism sector, something which has occupied experts for a long time.

In order for a cluster to prove successful, they must be met at the same time with many factors, the most important of which is willingness of member companies for cooperation, mutual assistance, and complementarity in business level, mutual trust, the development of a collaborative culture, as well as the flexibility to adapt companies to modern competitive requirements with the adoption of modern technologies and innovations. It is a fact that our country does not have organized business clusters; however, an informal interface as well as a limited number of conventional business clusters can be perceived, while in the tourism sector, it is estimated by experts that business clusters should be created at two different levels, but aimed at different goals and, more specifically, to act at both national and local or regional level.

From what has been said above, there is no doubt that a number of actions should be taken with the ultimate goal of strengthening clusters in the tourism, in order to stimulate and develop innovation, and also competitiveness between companies of all sectors of the wider economy and especially the tourism sector. In fact, by strengthening the clusters, it is possible to promote its competitiveness, as well as encouraging businesses to be productive, as well as developing entrepreneurship. Finally, it is important to emphasize the need to strengthen the clusters as through them the local economic development and the growth of new enterprises in the market are possible.

Following the procedure and analyses of the results of the research, it's proved that the geographical proximity of interconnected hotels, restaurants, thematic tourism centers, wineries, museums, etc. helps the cluster to develop more easily; the equal participation in the cluster as a separate entity and the independence of the participants in the cluster make them all feel acting in a partnership with commonly accepted terms and objective; common goals aimed at the mutual benefit of the participants.

Cluster in Cyprus is a new concept, and for that, there is not enough academic bibliography, it's a promising concept with many benefits found out through this report and through the international experience research through this project. The research covers a part of this concept, but needs to expand and go deeper in order to help the local society. The research flows through the pandemia with lockdowns, openings, and new lockdowns again, which was a difficult situation for researchers.

Platres can be a pilot project, which will provide platforms for local economic development, growth, and innovation in the tourism industry, through trusted cooperation and creative complementarity, especially in a small economy. "Small is beautiful", in the sense that tourism clusters in Platres can be easily managed with a great impact and results. Finally, even the research flows through the pandemia with the lockdowns, which was a difficult situation for researchers, the results are here and a small project can start and become a part of the future research in the field.

References

Andersson, T., Schwaag-Serger, S., Sorvik, J., & Hansson, E. W. (2004). *The cluster policies Whitebook. IKED*. Holmbergs. 266 p.
Beni, M. C. (2003). *Globalização do turismo: megatendências do setor e a realidade brasileira*. Aleph.
Braun, V., & Clarke, V. (2006). Using thematic analysis in psychology. *Qualitative Research in Psychology, 3*(2), 77–101. ISSN 1478-0887 Available from: http://eprints.uwe.ac.uk/11735
Chalip, L., & Costa, C. A. (2012). Clashing worldviews: Sources of disappointment in rural hospitality and tourism development. *Hospitality & Society, 2*, 25.
Cohen, L., Manion, L., & Morrison, K. (2010). The basis of distinction between qualitative and quantitative research in social science: Reflection on ontological, epistemological and methodological perspectives. *Ethiopian Journal of Education and Sciences*.
da Cunha, S. K. & da Cunha, J. C. (2005, July/December). Tourism cluster competitiveness and sustainability: Proposal for a systemic model to measure the impact of tourism on local development. *BAR*, D. 2, n. 2, art 4, 47–62.

Enright, M., & Flowcs-Williams, I. (2001). *Local partnership, clusters and SME globalization.* Organization for Economic Co-operation and Development.

Feurer, R., & Chaharbaghi, K. (1994). Defining competitiveness: A holistic approach. *Management Decision, 32,* 49–58.

Galindo, et al. (2009). *Entrepreneurship and business: A regional perspective.* Publisher by Springer.

Jackson, J., & Murphy, P. (2002). Tourism destinations as clusters: Analytical experiences from the New World. *Tourism and Hospitality Research, 4,* 36.

Ketels, C. M. (2003). *The Development of the cluster concept–Present experiences and further developments.*

Kvale, S. (1996). *"The 1,000-Page Question" (First Published September 1, 1996, Research Article).*

Kyriazi, N. (1999). *Sociological research: Critical review of methods and techniques.* Ellinika Grammata.

Lincoln, Y. S., & Guba, E. G. (1985). *Naturalistic inquiry* (Vol. 9, 1st ed., p. 438). Sage publications.

Mialaret, G. (1997). *Le funzioni educative dello sport.*

Montfort, K. V., & Masure, E. (2000, July 1). *Business economics the service industries.*

Piperopoulos, P. (2007). Barriers to innovation for SMEs: Empirical evidence from Greece. *International Journal of Business Innovation and Research, 1*(4), 365–386.

Porter, E. M. (1998). *Clusters and the new economics of competition.* Harvard.

Tsiolis, G. (2014). *Methods and techniques of data analysis for social qualitative research.*

Tuckman, B. W. (1972) *Conducting educational research* (402 + xiii pp). New York: Harcourt Brace Jovanovich.

Electronic Resources: Websites

Commissioner of Mountainous Areas - Presidency of the Republic of Cyprus. https://www.presidency.gov.cy › cypresidency.nsf › all.

National Strategy for the Development of Troodos Mountain Communities. https://www.pio.gov.cy › newsroom › 2022/03 PDF.

Regional Tourism Strategy and Action Plans for the Mountain Resorts of Cyprus. (2007). Cyprus Tourism Organisation. http://media.visitcyprus.com (Oreina Theretra (SPEED Development consultant).

The National Strategy for the development of the Troodos Mountain communities. (2020). https://medmountains.com (Thessaly University).

Troodos Development Company (**ANET**). http://www.troodos-geo.org

Troodos Network. http://lovetroodos.com

Troodos Regional Tourism Board. https://mytroodos.com

Chapter 65
Entrepreneurship of Winemaking Enterprises in Mountain Less-Favored Areas: An Empirical Study

Electra Pitoska, Evagelia Theodorli, and Agapi Altini

Abstract Entrepreneurship, a highly intriguing and fairly new scientific and scholarly field, has generated outstanding global research for the last three decades. The present research investigates entrepreneurship in mountain less-favored areas, a poorly researched topic, by mainly focusing on the winemaking industry.

The research, exploring the conclusive conditions and opportunities for the rapidly growing wine sector in mountain less-favoured areas, which is a critical sector for the local communities and economy, was carried out in a less-favoured area, Amynteo, Florina, located away from major hubs for economic activity, displaying low prosperity indicators, and suffering the consequences of dwindling population in the context of the prolonged financial crisis.

Data collection relied both on a semi-structured interview and a questionnaire answered by 9 (out of 15) local winemaking enterprises. The research findings demonstrate that entrepreneurship in a mountain less-favored area can exploit potential disadvantages, such as isolation and adverse climate, and turn them into significant growth advantages for local entrepreneurship, and more specifically, for the local winemaking and wine tourism enterprises. The findings also highlight the critical role of development programs during the transition to the post-lignite era and the significance of state support actions aimed at increasing the competitive advantage of such areas by engaging stakeholders in promoting local state-of-the-art PDO products and the special regional features and potential.

Keywords Mountain less-favored areas · Winemaking enterprises · Amynteo

E. Pitoska (✉) · E. Theodorli
School of Economic Sciences, University of Western Macedonia, Kozani, Greece
e-mail: ipitoska@uowm.gr

A. Altini
School of Engineering, University of Western Macedonia, Kozani, Greece

65.1 Entrepreneurship in Mountain Less-Favoured Areas

Entrepreneurship is defined as a field that aims to understand how opportunities are discovered, created, and pursued, by whom, and with what consequences (Neck et al., 2020). Entrepreneurship, a multifaceted and complex process affected by various different factors both at the start and during a business lifetime, has been widely researched. According to Gaddam (2007), the six major determinants of successful business activities involve economic, psychological, social, environmental, demographic, and cultural considerations.

Describing an area as mountainous might appear simple; however, establishing official definitions is a complex process. In Greece, the definition of mountainous areas is determined by legislative criteria related to altitude and slope of land. According to the initiative opinion CES 461/88, published in the official journal of the European Union, a mountain area is defined as "a physical, environmental, socio-economic and cultural region in which the disadvantages deriving from altitude and other natural factors must be considered in conjunction with socio-economic constraints, spatial imbalance and environmental decay," also characterized by "a considerable limitation of the possibilities for using the land and an appreciable increase in the cost of working it" (Regulation (EC) 1257/1999). Overall, the Council Directives 75/268 and 81/645 define mountain areas in terms of geomorphological, socio-economic, and demographic criteria.

In addition, the term "less favored" implies farming areas scoring lower in competitiveness indices, either due to adverse climate conditions or low productivity as a result of poor infrastructure (Paschalidou, 2010). According to NORDREGIO (2004), mountain areas in Greece account for 77.9% of the total country area, thus, classifying Greece as a predominantly mountainous country.

Mountain areas, despite being generally perceived as "problematic" and less favored, can, under certain circumstances, turn their own disadvantages into advantages and compete with other more favored areas. Table 65.1 includes a summary of the advantages and disadvantages of such areas.

Social and economic marginalization of rural and, primarily, mountain areas, has caused the emergence of special local economies for these regions, based exclusively on the local comparative advantage they possess.

Enterprises operating in mountain areas, typically family-owned home-making businesses, are encountered with various restraints and problems with engaging in innovative activities. Their location away from urban centers and markets has significantly increased production and distribution costs and reduced alternative policy-focused processes. The relationship of distance-proximity to large urban centers affects access to capital and information sources, skilled labor force, consulting services, and specialized business institution services, and places further constraints on business creation and growth.

Entrepreneurship in mountain areas is determined by entrepreneurial attempts to turn disadvantages into advantages and discover new business opportunities. Despite

Table 65.1 Advantages and disadvantages of mountain areas

Disadvantages	Advantages
Isolation, poor road networks, and access	Rich cultural heritage, heritage protection, and promotion
Poor infrastructure	Protection, promotion, and preservation of the natural environment
Inadequate organisation of economic activities	Production of state-of-the-art PDO products
Ageing population	Alternative forms of tourism
Low employment rates, increased unemployment	Leverage of national and EU funds via entrepreneurship development programs
Inability to adopt, use, and diffuse new technologies	Promotion of renewable energy sources
Long distance from central administration services	Low impact of business activities on the natural environment

the fact that the natural environment of mountain areas tends to deter business growth, it offers business development prospects, which cannot be promoted in urban areas.

A major constraint to entrepreneurship in mountain areas involves the reduced number of human resources, as labor migration has substantially aggravated the availability of workforce in the specific areas.

65.2 The Vine Growing and Wine Tourism Industry in Amynteo

The Region of Florina, a purely mountain and less-favoured area, is one of the "energy" counties in Greece. Amynteo, with its famous wineries, is a leading Greek vine growing zone, declared a PDO (Protected Designation of Origin) region for its Xinomavro wine variety. In the current post-lignite era, agriculture, livestock farming, and, to a greater extent, tourism will take a dominant role in entrepreneurship growth.

Local vineyards in Amynteo, the largest vineyards in Northern Greece, are among the largest ones in Southern Europe, and, remarkably, the largest vineyards of the Xinomavro grape variety worldwide. Vine growing in the wider region of Amynteo, dating back to ancient times, and high-quality wine products have been an integral part of the long-established tradition of the area, contributing to the local economy over time. Nowadays, the vine growing zone of Amynteo includes state-of-the-art wineries producing various high-quality wines, thus offering significant benefits to the wider area. Local wineries are active winemaking enterprises bottling and labeling wines produced from local and other Greek or international varieties with the geographical indication "Amynteo" (visitAmynteo.com).

Remarkably, Amynteo is classified among the few AOQS (Designation of Origin of Superior Quality) winemaking regions, in accordance with article 40 of the regulation (EC) no. 607/2009, as amended and in force by regulation (EC) 670/2011 of the Commission, as defined and registered in the "E-Bacchous" database (minagric.gr).

Present and future vine growing prospects appear to be very positive, due to efforts made by local stakeholders, who have contributed to building and improving relevant production facilities and infrastructures. The winemaking industry has been a major asset for the region, as it enables the production of "branded" products of premium quality, well known for their high export rates. This is also endorsed evidence in international contexts (trade, consumption), where the consumption of quality wine products has been constantly increasing (lifeamybear.eu).

In 2020, according to data from the General Directorate of Regional Agricultural Economy and Veterinary Medicine, vine growing areas accounted for 10,970.30 acres, which implies an increase of approximately 1%.

With regard to the wine tourism industry, the specific area is a member of the wine tourism network of the "Wine Roads of Northern Greece" under the name "Wine Route of the Lakes." The network was awarded the honorary distinction of the "Top Practices of Greek Tourism" organized by the Tourism Awards 2014 for its contribution to the development and promotion of wine tourism in Greece (visitAmynteo.com). Membership in wine route networks contributes to improving winery corporate image, increasing wine reputation, and promoting tourism growth. Several local wineries are members of the "Winemakers of North Greece" (WNG), a union that contributes to promoting and strengthening wine tourism and membership revenues, by organizing various events, such as Open Doors, World Wine Tourism Day, World Xinomavro Day, etc., aimed at increasing the number of visits to wineries.

Despite the health crisis measures in 2020, the number of visits to wineries in Amynteo was fairly high, given that the regional health level was excellent compared to other areas in Northern Greece, thus making the specific area a leading destination at that time.

Figure 65.1 shows the number of visits to WNG member wineries in Amynteo, compared with the total number of visits to other member wineries (30 members), which illustrates that in 2020, wine tourism in the specific region was superior.

Notably, the best wineries to visit in the area have been awarded the Winery to Visit Label by the Ministry of Tourism, certifying that they meet all required conditions to be classified as wineries to visit. In this context, they offer reception services, guided tours, and hospitality and catering services in functionally integrated winemaking or wine-producing (vineyard) facilities, in addition to vine growing and winemaking activities, during which visitors have the opportunity to learn about wines and wineries.

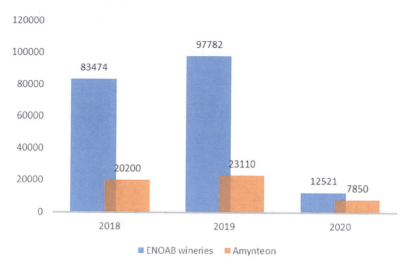

Fig. 65.1 Comparison of number of visits to wineries. (Source: Winemakers of North Greece (WNG))

65.3 The Vine Growing and Wine Tourism Industry: A Driver for Regional Growth

The role of the wine industry is substantial for regional economic growth. In Amynteo, local wineries have highlighted the exceptional quality of their premium branded wine products. The growth of the local vine growing and wine tourism industry has offered a number of benefits, both to wineries and locally-owned enterprises, which employ a large number of permanent and seasonal workers, thus, improving the local economy and promoting hospitality and catering enterprises, which also contribute to increasing visits to wineries.

Wine reputation and delivery of quality services have created trust relationships with visitors generating increased direct sales and word-of-mouth reputation, thus, increasing corporate profits and enhancing the economic, social, and cultural value of the specific region. Investments in wine tourism facilities and infrastructure funded by relevant actions and programs have offered a competitive strong advantage, which is critical to promoting local image and reputation and rank the area among the best wine tourism destinations.

In addition, the local vine growing and wine tourism industry contribute to sustainable rural development, by creating new jobs and partnership relations with other local businesses.

To conclude, the contribution of the vine growing and wine tourism industry involves the following:

- Enhancing economic growth and creating new jobs.
- Promoting the image and reputation of the area as a tourist destination.
- Improving local wine reputation.
- Promoting the regional gastronomy, environmental, and cultural features.
- Creating added value by exploiting the unique natural environment and local gastronomy.

65.4 Empirical Study

65.4.1 Research Methodology

To investigate entrepreneurship in mountain less-favored areas, the present research carried out a series of surveys focusing on the winemaking – wine tourism industry in the mountain less-favored area of Amynteo, called the "Wine Route of the Lakes," member of the wine tourism network "Wine Roads of Northern Greece." The specific area belongs to the region of Western Macedonia and is typical of a mountain less-favored winemaking and wine tourism area suffering all economic and social consequences of the transition towards the post-lignite era.

To ensure research reliability, a combination of two methods was applied. First, a semi-structured interview with Mr. Panagiotis Dimopoulos, an expert local businessman, knowledgeable of "business development" of the surveyed mountain less-favored area, and owner of the Dimopoulos Wine Estate, a fairly new and thriving local winemaking and wine tourism enterprise. The interview included 10 five-item questions about local entrepreneurship, local winemaking and wine tourism industry growth, modern winery facilities, and support programs. In addition, it explored the effect of local disadvantages and advantages on the winemaking and wine tourism industry and, thus, on local growth.

Second, the research employed a structured questionnaire, which was sent to a sample of 15 winemaking enterprises in Amynteo, followed by personal meetings with nine (out of 15) local winery owners. The research was carried out from October to December 2022.

The questionnaire includes 13 questions and is structured in three sections. The first section is focused on the factors perceived as comparative advantages and disadvantages for the area, whereas the second section includes the subjects' views on the strengths and weaknesses of the surveyed mountain less-favored area, the potential opportunities and threats, as well as the subjects' comments and suggestions about entrepreneurship. Finally, the third section involves information about the participating enterprises, such as year of establishment, legal status, and number of employees.

65.4.2 Research Findings

65.4.2.1 Interview

Data analysis demonstrated that the surveyed region has had a long and unbroken tradition in vine growing and winemaking activities (since the Turkish occupation period). Vineyard revival in the wider area of Amynteo took place after the establishment of the Union of Agricultural Cooperatives of Amynteo in 1945 and the Union winery in 1959. In 1972, the wine-growing zone of PDO "Amynteo" branded wines was established.

With regard to the relevant comparative advantages, the interview demonstrated that the natural disadvantages of the region, such as altitude and slopes of land as well as climate, have been practically turned into advantages and created particularly favorable conditions for local vine growing and winemaking, thus, contributing to a wider economic development. It was also stated that according to the ministerial decision no. 866/86629/18-3-2020 of the Ministry of Rural Development and Food on the "Establishment of the necessary additional measures for the implementation of Regulations (EC) no. 1308/2013, (EU) no. 2018/273 and (EU) no. 2018/274, for the management of the scheme of authorizations for vine plantings", altitude was included among eligibility criteria, thus, giving an additional competitive advantage to the areas above 500 m.

In addition, continental climate with relatively low average temperatures, despite being generally considered a disadvantage, is significantly conducive to the growth of the winemaking industry in the specific region. Remarkably, in 2021, despite the prolonged heat wave, vineyards in the wider area of Amynteo were completely unaffected, in contrast to other vineyards in the rest of the country, most of which had suffered significant damage, which implied low production levels. In mountain areas, such as Amynteo, despite any extreme weather conditions during summer days, temperatures drop in the evening and, thus, allow vines to "rest."

It was also emphasized that land slopes contribute to vine growing, as good soil drainage has a favourable impact on the health and quality of grapes and, therefore, enhances winemaking competitiveness.

As regards the contribution of the vine growing and wine tourism industry to the local economy, it was demonstrated that in the post-lignite era, it will become very significant. Accordingly, state development support programs, such as the Just Development Transition Plan, are essential to winemaking enterprises, despite the fact that strict eligibility criteria have frequently excluded small-sized businesses from relevant programs and favored large-sized ones.

Great emphasis was also placed on the need to modernize winery facilities and adjust winemaking institutional frameworks, as most winemaking enterprises do not use modern facilities and advanced production equipment.

In addition, it was demonstrated that in the wine tourism industry, fundamental improvements are required, mainly to sales and promotion processes as well as the use of new equipment and quality service delivery, which most local wine tourism enterprises cannot make. Remarkably, only three wineries in Amynteo have been awarded the Winery to Visit Label by the Ministry of Tourism, which is virtually a certificate of quality winery service and strong branding.

With regard to investment attraction policies in the winemaking and wine tourism industry, due consideration should be currently given not only by local entrepreneurs but also by other stakeholders in the rest part of the country, who have been either already engaged in the relevant business industry or wish to diversify business. Remarkably, a significant investment asset of the researched area is an increase in investment funding from 40% before the post-lignite period to 65% or 70% in the framework of the Just Development Transition Plan. Prospective investments will enhance the local economy and will contribute to reducing high unemployment rates caused by the shutdown of the coal-fired power plants, in which a large part of the local population had been employed. An innovative action can also be the possibility to organise bicycle wine tours, or weekly dinners, in collaboration with Nomade et Sauvage.

To conclude, the interview demonstrated that a potential threat, which has already caused problems to the local tourism industry and is likely to undermine regional growth, is the possibility of uncontrolled installation of wind turbines, which may cause regional decline. In addition, a significant threat is the rapid energy price increase and, overall, increased inflation and interest rates, as well as problems in the supply chain as a consequence of the Covid-19 pandemic combined with economic instability and uncertainty. However, great emphasis was placed on the regional growth potential in winemaking and wine tourism activities and their contribution to the overall economic growth, which, under current circumstances, is most indisputable.

65.4.2.2 Questionnaire

Data analysis, based on descriptive statistics, demonstrated that the vast majority of the research sample (77%) consider that the greatest advantage of the specific mountain less-favored area for the winemaking and wine tourism industry is the natural environment, followed by local climate conditions and the long tradition of winemaking (67%) as well as the high quality of grapes and wine products (55%). As regards altitude, the subjects' views are similar ("moderately significant" or "very significant") accounting for 33.3%. It is also worth noting that a smaller number of subjects (11.5%) do not feel that promoting the local natural environment and the local cultural identity is an advantage. Table 65.2 shows relevant information about the significance of the comparative advantages of the researched mountain less-favored area.

Remarkably, high energy costs and low rates of skilled staff are considered major disadvantages (88% and 77%, respectively), similar to high transportation costs, due to the long distance from major urban centers and markets. Adverse weather conditions during winter as well as mountain road networks are highlighted among the comparative disadvantages by 55% of the subjects, whereas demographics and

Table 65.2 Significance of comparative advantages

	Not significant	Slightly significant	Moderately significant	Significant	Very significant
Climate	0%	0%	0%	33%	67%
Altitude			33.3%	33.3%	33.3%
Natural environment	0%	0%	0%	77%	23%
Grapes and wine product quality	0%	0%	12%	55%	33%
Long tradition in winemaking	0%	0%	22%	67%	11%
Cultural legacy	11.25%	11.25%	55%	11.25%	11.25%
Special incentives	0%	11.35%	33.3%	44%	11.35%
Protection and promotion of the natural environment	11.5%	0%	22%	55%	11.5%

unpredictable weather disasters are perceived moderately significant. In addition, four out of the nine surveyed enterprises feel that increased unemployment rates are a major disadvantage.

Among the main strengths of the researched area is the natural environment with its exceptional ecosystem as well as climate and altitude. Similarly, the subjects highlighted the significance of local PDO products, gastronomy, and the variety of alternative tourism activities and placed great emphasis on the long tradition of winemaking enterprises.

On the other hand, the respondents demonstrated that poor infrastructure and mountain road networks, as well as transportation problems and long distance from urban centers, are among the most common weaknesses (44%). In addition, the subjects highlighted the significance of the demographic problem (67%), aggravated by the rapid population decline due to labor migration, the small number of skilled employees, and the current high energy costs.

As regards opportunities, the majority of the research participants consider that promoting the natural environment, the positive outlook of the tourism industry, and particularly alternative forms, such as wine, mountain, and culinary tourism are major opportunities. In addition, they emphasize opportunities for partnerships with tourist enterprises.

Potential threats mainly involve the demographic problem, which is essential to maintaining and enhancing prosperity, the high unemployment rates (55%), and low yields and income. Similarly, the participating companies place special emphasis on the uncontrolled installation of wind and photovoltaic farms in the specific area, as they perceive that they undermine business activities, do not create jobs, and contribute to regional tourism decline.

It is also worth noting that the subjects believe that tax incentives (88%) and recruitment of qualified staff can contribute to the growth of the local businesses industry. With regard to cooperation between local wineries, there are various and divergent views covering all five items; however, 55% of the respondents place special emphasis on cooperation initiatives with wineries in other regions. The contribution of wine tourism is also considered critical by 77% of the subjects, and seven out of the nine surveyed enterprises emphasise promoting alternative tourism. Significantly, 88% of the sample agree that cooperation with tourism businesses contributes to regional growth. Additional support actions, such as promotion of the specific area, farmers' training and education, admission to relevant national and EU programmes, and employee specialized training, are considered essential by most participating enterprises.

However, 67% of the surveyed enterprises highlighted the absence of external investment funds, and 55% stated that bank lending is limited, whereas 67% maintained that admission to various development programs is fairly difficult. In addition, the majority of respondents answered that the number of national development and funding programs is not satisfactory, and collaboration with specialized research centres is rather poor. However, 55% of the participants also placed special emphasis on the absence of professional bodies and employment counseling centers. Remarkably, three out of nine of the surveyed enterprises answered that the number of available professional bodies and employment counseling centers is "very small" whereas two answered "fairly small." Access to business information is considered "moderately significant" (44%), similar to collaboration opportunities with research bodies. In addition, with regard to collaboration with local wine-making enterprises, there are divergent views equally encompassing all items, whereas collaboration with tourism enterprises is "moderately significant" (55%). Finally, a large number of subjects (67%) highlighted that bureaucracy growth and understaffing of state services is "moderately significant" or "very significant."

Data analysis also demonstrated that 33.3% of the surveyed enterprises are sole proprietorships and the rest are various other legal entities. In addition, most enterprises (67%) were established in the last 20 years, two were established in 1997, and one in 1959 as a Legal Entity under Private Law. However, it is worth noting that in the last 5 years, no winemaking enterprises were established in the surveyed area. Most enterprises employ six to 10 people and only two employ more than 15 people.

Remarkably, all participating wineries, except for only one, are wineries to visit, and six have been awarded a Winery to Visit Label by the Ministry of Tourism. As regards the degree of satisfaction with the number of visits, 67% of the subjects are not satisfied, and 1/3 of the enterprises also highlighted that they do not follow food and wine social media. In addition, 55% offer modern visitor reception facilities, whereas 33% are going to invest in facility renovation works. It is also worth noting that eight out of nine enterprises offer modern facilities and equipment and apply advanced technology methods. Remarkably, the majority have already engaged in investments, which are still in progress.

Data analysis also demonstrated that six out of nine enterprises had engaged in development programmes in the past and only three out of nine have successfully applied in the current period. With regard to collaboration with research centers

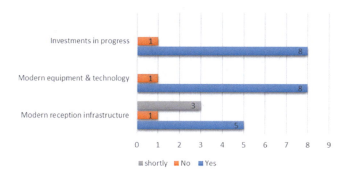

Fig. 65.2 Infrastructure and investment

and universities, 67% gave a positive answer and highlighted they are partners in clusters. Finally, the vast majority of wine enterprises (88%) have won wine awards and competitions in Greece and other countries and have engaged in export business.

Figure 65.2 provides summarised information on infrastructure and investments in the wine tourism industry.

In addition, the majority of winemaking enterprises (77%) consider that the impact of the transition to the post-lignite era on new business activities will be significant. However, 44% of the participants highlight the significance of the natural environment, whereas 33% maintain it is very significant. As regards the impact of the transition on the number of visitors – tourists and the prospects of wine tourism, only 1/3 of the enterprises answered they are significant.

In contrast, an increase in unemployment rates appears to be "significant" or "very significant" for 88% of the participants. Reduced yields and income are "significant" or "very significant," and 44% of the subjects believe that the creation of new diversified jobs will be "not significant." In addition, five out of nine enterprises state that the impact on land use, the microclimate, and soil and water resources is "significant" or "very significant." Remarkably, 77% of the surveyed enterprises advocate that the local economy will suffer the serious consequences of the transition to the post-lignite era.

As regards the participants' suggestions and comments, the majority emphasized the need for strategic planning aimed at regional growth, by adopting realistic and needs-related plans, in compliance with the current transition to the post-lignite era. To enhance entrepreneurship, the subjects made suggestions about tax relief measures and reduced energy and transport costs as well as increased development funding and more favorable eligibility criteria to facilitate successful application to development programs. The subjects demand state efforts against economic and social decline and suggest easy access to financial tools and promotion actions to enhance local tourism growth organized by competent public tourism bodies and agencies.

Given the strong regional demographic problem, it is essential that employment be maintained, and new jobs be created to enable economic prosperity and deter depopulation.

In addition, enhancing collaboration between enterprises or public stakeholders, and continuous education and training of entrepreneurs and employees will increase the competitive advantage of enterprises and will facilitate digital transformation.

Placing special emphasis on the significance of the natural environment, especially during the transition period, can contribute to the growth of alternative forms of tourism. This requires improvements of infrastructure, such as modern road networks and connection to major roadways, and implies that state funding is critical. Finally, advertising and promotion of local products are imperative.

65.5 Conclusions

In international literature, mountain less-favored areas are mainly described as areas with permanent natural disadvantages. Isolation, long distance from large cities and trade zones, and dwindling population caused by labor migration imply reduced human resources. In addition, poor infrastructure and understaffing or centralized administrative services, as well as inadequate mountain road networks and ageing population, further enhance the potential disadvantages of the specific areas. Notably, however, perceived disadvantages, such as isolation, have a positive impact on the preservation of the natural environment, thus offering the specific areas a significant comparative advantage.

Mountain less-favored areas are also described as PDO-producing areas, which also encourage promotion of alternative forms of tourism as well as leverage of national and EU funding via special development programs aimed at encouraging entrepreneurship. Entrepreneurship in such areas mainly relies on agriculture, livestock farming, and alternative forms of tourism, and is focused on turning disadvantages into advantages.

Remarkably, the findings of the present empirical investigation, compliant with relevant findings in the extant literature, demonstrate a number of constraints and obstacles to promoting entrepreneurship in mountain less-favored areas. More specifically, perceived drawbacks, such as isolation, inadequate road networks, and distance from major cities and markets, significantly increase business operating costs, which, in addition to increased energy costs during winter, have a negative impact on the local economy and, thus, render local enterprises less competitive. The dwindling population is also a critical factor resulting in low rates of skilled staff and local economic growth, with a substantial impact on unemployment rates and, thus, depopulation. In addition, poor available infrastructure tends to restrain business functions and renders the specific area less attractive for investment initiatives.

On the other hand, the result findings demonstrate that the rich natural environment and special ecosystem with Natura protected areas, the climate, local premium quality products, and the long tradition in vine growing and winemaking are unique comparative advantages contributing to regional promotion and growth. The findings also demonstrate the great development potential of the winemaking and wine tourism industry in the surveyed area, despite the rather poor state promotional support practices and policies.

Low investment capital and the small number of development programs aimed at local economy support during transition to the post-lignite era were emphasized as major threats. In contrast, actions towards reducing energy costs, tax relief, increased funding, and improved eligibility and access to development programs are critical to enhancing the local economy.

However, economic instability caused by the financial and health crisis in Greece is perceived as a major threat by the enterprises, which also have a negative attitude towards photovoltaic and wind farms, likely to undermine regional tourism growth. In contrast, the great regional development potential of the winemaking and wine tourism industry, combined with the rich natural environment, local gastronomy, and alternative tourist activities integrated in the winemaking and vine growing industry, can become pillars of regional growth in the post-lignite era, and contribute to reducing the underlying impacts (i.e., high unemployment rates). Thus, a state-based realistic approach aimed at engaging local stakeholders in actions focused on the special regional features and potential, and promoting partnerships and collaboration between stakeholders is critical.

In conclusion, entrepreneurship in mountain less-favored areas will be encouraged by offering equal opportunities to those of the most favored and privileged areas, and by deploying regional development prospects, with a view to enhancing the economic, social, cultural, and environmental role of such regions.

Bibliography

CES 461/88, *Official Journal of the European Union*. Available at: https://eur-lex.europa.eu/LexUriServ/ LexUriServ.do?uri=OJ:C:2003:128:0025:0040:EL:PDF, [Accessed 20/05/2023].

Community Directives 75/268 and 81/645. Available at https://eur-lex.europa.eu/legal-content/EN/TXT/?uri=CELEX%3A31981L0645 [Accessed 20/05/2023].

Gaddam, S. (2007). A conceptual analysis of factors influencing entrepreneurship behavior and actions. *ICFAI Journal of Management Research, 6*(11), 46–63.

Neck, H., Neck, C., & Murray, E. (2020). *Επιχειρηματικότητα, Νοοτροπία και Πρακτική, Κριτική, Αθήνα*.

NORDREGIO. (2004). *Mountain areas in Europe: Analysis of mountain areas in EU member states, acceding and other European countries*, European Commission contract No 2002, CE.16.0.AT.136, Final report.

Paschalidou, A. (2010). Desertification as a factor of degradation of the natural environment and creation of less-favoured areas. In G. Arabatzis (Ed.), *Development of mountains and less-favoured areas* (Forestry and environmental and natural resource management issues) (Vol. 2). Democritus University of Thrace.

Regulation (EC) 1257/1999. Available at https://eur-lex.europa.eu/LexUriServ/ LexUriServ.do?uri=OJ:L:1999:160:0080:0102:EN:PDF [Accessed 17/05/2023].

Online Sources

European Commission website/E-BACCHUS wine database. http://www.gaiapedia.gr/gaiapedia/index.php/%CE%99%CF%83%CF%84%CE%BF%CF%83%CE%B5%CE%BB%CE%AF%CE%B4%CE%B1_%CE%95%CF%85%CF%81%CF%89%CF%80%CE%B1%CF%8A%CE%BA%CE%AE_%CE%95%CF%80%CE%B9%CF%84%CF%81%CE%BF%CF%80%CE%AE/%CE%92%CE%AC%CF%83%CE%B7_%CE%B4%CE%B5%CE%B4%CE%BF%CE%BC%CE%AD%CE%BD%CF%89%CE%BD_%CF%84%CE%BF%CF%85_%CE%BF%CE%AF%CE%BD%CE%BF%CF%85_E-BACCHUS

Executive Regulation (EU) No. 670/2011 of the Commission, of July 12, 2011. https://eur-lex.europa.eu/legal-content/EL/TXT/?uri=CELEX%3A32011R0670

LIFE AMYBEAR. https://lifeamybear.eu/, http://lifeamybear.eu/sites/default/files/a5.1.pdf

REGULATION (EC) no. 607/2009 OF THE COMMISSION of July 14, 2009. https://eur-lex.europa.eu/legal-content/EL/TXT/PDF/?uri=CELEX:32009R0607

VISIT AMYNTEO. https://www.visitAmynteo.com/wine.html

Wine Producers Association of The Northern Greece. https://winemakersofnorthgreece.gr/en/

Chapter 66
Consumer Attitudes Toward Artificial Intelligence in Fashion

Katerina Vatantzi, Aspasia Vlachvei, and Ioannis Antoniadis

Abstract Given the growing interest in converging fashion with digital technologies, it becomes important for fashion researchers and businesses to research and understand new technologies and artificial intelligence. This work examines whether the adaptation of Technology Acceptance Model (TAM) by incorporating some additional factors (attitude toward AI, degree of engagement with fashion) can predict consumers' fashion behavior (purchase intention). For this purpose, a conceptual model related to consumer attitude and purchase intention toward an AI product was constructed and tested. Results confirmed the findings of studies reporting that perceived usefulness and perceived ease of use were significant in predicting consumers' attitudes toward AI as well as their purchase intention. Also, consumers' attitudes toward technology positively influence purchase intention and also attitudes toward AI, while fashion involvement does not affect the effect of attitude toward technology on purchase intention and the effect of attitude toward AI on purchase intention.

Keywords Artificial intelligence · Consumer attitudes · Fashion

66.1 Introduction

Technological progress has brought about dramatic changes in consumer behavior. Consumers' self-awareness and fashion sense are being transformed by technology. As combinations of fashion and digital innovations emerge, it is important for researchers, as well as fashion businesses, to understand consumer reactions to new technologies (Bues et al., 2017; Kim et al., 2017). As artificial intelligence (AI) has emerged as an important field of technological innovation (Vlačić et al., 2021), it has also begun to be used as a new application in the fashion industry

---

K. Vatantzi · A. Vlachvei (✉) · I. Antoniadis
University of Western Macedonia, Kozani, Greece
e-mail: avlahvei@uowm.gr

© The Author(s), under exclusive license to Springer Nature Switzerland AG 2024
N. Tsounis, A. Vlachvei (eds.), *Applied Economic Research and Trends*, Springer Proceedings in Business and Economics,
https://doi.org/10.1007/978-3-031-49105-4_66

(Luce, 2018). Because AI can deliver significant improvements in speed, cost, and flexibility throughout the fashion supply chain, it is important to use AI to redefine design, merchandising, and marketing (Mohiuddin Babu et al., 2022). By analyzing and storing information from thousands of images and videos using data from the internet, AI can help designers incorporate trendy colors, key patterns, and styles, which can reduce overall lead times and expand designers' creative discovery (Liang et al., 2019). AI is also used to help fashion businesses recommend items based on each customer's preferences for price, size, general style, order history, and social media activity, such as fashion photos that have been saved to Pinterest (Giri et al., 2019). Additionally, AI has been used by fashion retailers (such as Nordstrom, Nike, Macy's, Farfetch) in chatbots, virtual assistants, and product navigators to improve and integrate online and offline consumer experiences (Gu et al., 2020).

According to a recent report by McKinsey & Company (2018), fashion companies expect to deploy artificial intelligence to redefine customer interactions and engagement in the near future. As retailers study consumer buying behavior and drive the future of on-demand manufacturing, a better understanding of consumer acceptance of AI in fashion is needed. However, because the development and application of fashion AI is in its early stages, the research is still in its infancy. Relatedly, few researchers have examined and developed studies on consumer acceptance of fashion AI.

With the current study, we aim to develop and empirically test the technology acceptance model (TAM) in the context of AI acceptance in fashion, incorporating perceived usefulness, perceived ease of use, and perceived risk. Therefore, the purpose of the study is to examine the effects of perceived usefulness, perceived ease of use, perceived risk, and attitude toward technology on consumer attitude and intention to purchase a fashion product and to test the influence of the degree of consumer involvement in fashion on attitudes toward technology and intention to purchase a product. The research findings will be beneficial for industry professionals to better understand consumer preferences and acceptance in relation to the application of artificial intelligence in the fashion industry.

66.2 Literature Review and Hypotheses

More than creating new technology, it is important to ensure that people will accept and use it. Otherwise, the technologies will never become an innovation and will not be useful. In order for technology to be useful and useful, it is important to understand how it can be introduced into the daily routine, convincing people that it will improve their quality of life or their daily routine (Marangunić & Granić, 2014). It is important to understand how people, individually, accept new technologies and also how companies can exploit and use them, as marketing tools or as tools to improve their overall customer experience. Furthermore, it is interesting to understand how receptive people are to new technologies and what can be done to ensure a smoother transition (Momani & Jamous, 2017).

Researchers have studied the impact of users' internal beliefs and attitudes on their usage behavior (Davis, 1989). Researchers in the field of adoption of new systems and technologies have proposed intention models from a social psychology perspective as a possible theoretical basis for research on the determinants of user behavior (Marangunić & Granić, 2014). Among the many theories used by researchers, Fishbein and Ajzen's (1975) theory of reasoned action (TRA) is considered a researched model of intention assessment that has proven successful in predicting and explaining behavioral intention in a wide range of domains (Montaño & Kasprzyk, 2008). Davis (1986) finally developed TAM by adapting TRA to the field of information systems and new technologies.

The TRA model is a social psychology model used to study determinants of consciously intended behaviors (Fishbein & Ajzen, 1975). The TRA model as defined by Fishbein and Ajzen (1975) and adopted by Davis (1986) is thought to offer a useful conceptual starting point for a range of factors that can enable researchers to explore the extent to which individuals engage in specific procedures or actions. The TRA model consists of three dimensions: behavioral intention, subjective norm, and attitude. For example, behavioral intention (BI) is defined as a measure of the strength of one's intention to perform a specific behavior (Jen et al., 2009). Attitude refers to a person's positive or negative feeling (evaluative affect) about performing a behavior (Fishbein & Ajzen, 1975). Subjective norm refers to the individual's perception that others important to him/her believe they should or should not adopt the behavior in question (Davis, 1986). According to TRA, a person's intention to perform a particular behavior is a causal determinant of the actual occurrence of that behavior, and the intention is determined by his attitude toward performing the behavior, as well as the perceived social influence of important people for them (Fishbein & Ajzen, 2015). Davis (1986) conducted a literature review of a number of technology adoption studies to determine the structure of factors that determine an individual's beliefs and attitudes toward technology use.

Davis (1986) adopted TRA as the theoretical base model for TAM. A key purpose of TAM is to provide a basis for identifying the influence of external factors on internal beliefs, attitudes, and intentions (Taherdoost, 2018), perceived usefulness and perceived ease of use. Perceived usefulness is defined as the degree to which a person believes that using a certain system will help him in his daily life or in a certain area of interest (Marangunić & Granić, 2014). Individuals view a system positively (attitude) if they believe it improves a particular area of interest (where they perceive its usefulness). They develop a positive attitude and increase their readiness to engage (behavioral intention) in using the system. On the other hand, perceived ease of use is defined as the degree to which a person believes that the use of a particular system could be achieved without much effort (Davis, 1989). Attitude refers to the degree of evaluative feeling (Fishbein & Ajzen, 1975) with which a person associates using the target system (Davis, 1986). An easy-to-use system will have a positive impact on people's feelings toward it. According to Davis (1989), perceived usefulness and perceived ease of use are statistically distinct dimensions (Koronaki et al., 2023a, b).

Perceived usefulness is the degree to which a person believes that using a particular system would enhance their work performance or improve some aspect of their daily life (Davis, 1989). Perceived usefulness in the TAM model has been found to have a significant impact on attitudes toward the use of technology as well as the use of artificial intelligence (Belanche et al., 2019; Notta et al., 2022). AI in fashion can enhance perceived usefulness as consumers can get help choosing clothing and footwear faster, get help choosing more fashionable clothing and increase their efficiency in choosing a more fashionable outfit (Liang et al., 2019). With these AI functions and interactions, the efficiency of consumers in choosing the most fashionable clothing will be improved, and these functions can make it easier for consumers to choose what to wear. Therefore, consumers will likely have a positive attitude toward AI and are expected to have an increased intention to purchase a product (Silva & Bonetti, 2021; Sohn & Kwon, 2020). Therefore, we propose the hypotheses:

Hypothesis 1: Perceived usefulness will positively influence consumer attitudes toward artificial intelligence.

Hypothesis 2: Perceived usefulness will positively influence consumers' intention to purchase a product from a business that uses AI applications.

Perceived ease of use is an important determinant of the use of a new technology or system (Davis, 1989; Tao & Xu, 2020). The importance of perceived ease of use has been emphasized in the TAM model because of the impact of the potential difficulty the user may have in rejecting the technology (Mohr & Kühl, 2021). Perceived ease of use in the TAM model is the extent to which a person believes that using a particular system will greatly facilitate what they wish to do or obtain (Venkatesh, 2000). Previous researchers have validated a positive relationship between perceived ease of use and consumer attitudes toward new technologies (Vlachvei et al., 2022). For example, Kim et al. (2017) found that perceived ease of use is an important factor in determining the adoption of smart retail technologies, and Lunney et al. (2016) showed that perceived ease of use positively influenced the attitude of consumers toward a new technology in the field of retail trade. The ease of use of an AI system is primarily about how easy it is for someone to use and interact with the AI application (Sadriwala & Sadriwala, 2022). To have the desired level of convenience, an AI application in fashion must be easy to use, clear, and understandable; make it more flexible to interact with fashion companies; and be able to offer more options (Liang et al., 2019). These could contribute to consumers having a more positive attitude toward AI and an increased intention to purchase a product. Therefore, we propose the hypotheses:

Hypothesis 3: Perceived ease of use will positively influence consumer attitudes toward artificial intelligence.

Hypothesis 4: Perceived ease of use will positively influence consumers' intention to purchase a product from a business that makes use of AI applications.

Perceived risk refers to an individual's subjective assessment of the unexpected performance of a product's attributes or outcomes (Hasan et al., 2021). It has been defined as the probability that a system or new technology will not work as expected and/or not provide the desired benefits (Al-Gasawneh et al., 2022). Previous researchers found that perceived risk negatively affected attitude (Chang, 2005; Hwang et al., 2016; Lăzăroiu et al., 2020; Liang et al., 2019) and purchase intention (Choon Ling et al., 2011; Kamalul Ariffin et al., 2018; Liang et al., 2019) using a new technology.

Key consumer concerns about AI applications are that a product advertised through AI systems is different from the real product or will not have the quality they expect (Al-Gasawneh et al., 2022). Thus, if consumers are concerned that AI will not perform as expected their expectations will not be met and a negative attitude will likely result (Liang et al., 2019). Therefore, we propose the hypotheses:

Hypothesis 5: Perceived risk of use will negatively influence consumers' attitudes toward AI.

Hypothesis 6: Perceived risk of use will negatively influence consumers' intention to purchase a product from a firm that uses AI applications.

Several researchers have reported that the technology tends to evoke both positive and negative emotions, which result in positive or respectively negative effects (Taherdoost, 2018). Previous researchers have reported that positive attitudes toward technology are generally positively associated with favorable attitudes or willingness to adopt a new technological product or application (Belanche et al., 2019). Lin and Hsieh (2006) also showed that the more favorable an individual feels about technology in general, the more likely they are to have favorable attitudes or greater willingness to purchase new technology products. Thus, more positive attitudes toward technology in general may lead to more favorable attitudes toward a new technological product and subsequently to greater purchase intention (Chang & Jai, 2015; Masukujjaman et al., 2021). Consumers tend to have more positive attitudes toward technology when the use of technology has more benefits compared to disadvantages and when the use of technology has improved many aspects of everyday life and has provided solutions to many problems in everyday life (Sánchez & Hueros, 2010). Therefore, we propose the hypotheses:

Hypothesis 7: Consumers' positive attitudes toward technology will positively influence their attitudes toward AI.

Hypothesis 8: Consumers' positive attitude toward technology will positively influence their intention to buy a product from a firm that makes use of AI applications.

Hypothesis 9: Consumers' positive attitude toward AI will positively influence their intention to buy a product from a company using AI applications.

Engagement is a measure that can be used to examine consumer behavior and provide useful information on consumer purchases (Darley et al., 2010). Engagement defines one's tendency to pay close attention to products or to actively participate in specific product acquisition activities (Parment, 2013). Fashion engagement is defined as the extent to which consumers see fashion-related activities as a central part of their lives, care about their outfits, and want to keep up to date with fashion trends (Liapati et al., 2015). Fashion engagement has been used primarily to predict behavioral variables related to apparel and footwear products (Bhaduri & Stanforth, 2017). Previous researchers have found that consumers with higher levels of fashion engagement value fashion more, care less about cost, and engage more in fashion-related activities such as searching for new news and trying new fashion-related technologies (Kautish et al., 2020; Sun & Guo, 2017). Celik and Kocaman (2017) concluded that fashion engagement has significant and direct influences on consumers' attitudes toward the application of new technologies in fashion. In this thesis, we hypothesize that consumers with higher fashion engagement will be more likely to be more positive about interacting with an AI application. Therefore, we propose the hypothesis:

Hypothesis 10: The effects of (a) attitudes toward technology and (b) attitudes toward AI on purchase intention are stronger for consumers with higher (vs. lower) levels of fashion engagement.

66.3 Research Methodology

For this research, a quantitative research based on the principles of positivism was conducted. According to this theory, observation and reason are the best means of understanding human behavior. True knowledge is based on sensory experience and can be assessed by conducting a social survey (Saunders et al., 2009). At the ontological level, positivists assume that reality is objective and measurable using properties that are independent of the researcher. In other words, knowledge is objective and quantifiable. In addition, in quantitative research, the researcher adopts scientific methods and through them, the researcher can highlight correlations between different concepts such as people's perceptions of AI and technology with their intention to buy a product through an AI application (Bryman & Bell, 2011). The quantitative method is chosen due to its objectivity and the attempt to highlight general trends of individuals. Also, this method is suitable for investigating the explanation and correlation between variables. In addition, the quantitative method is considered more appropriate as data can be collected quickly with the possibility of studying the sample in a short period of time. Based on the above, quantitative research based on the principles of positivism was considered the most appropriate for this thesis.

66.3.1 Sampling

The population of this study was chosen to be Greek citizens/consumers aged 18 years and above. The convenience sampling technique was used to select the sample. Sampling is a technique of selecting a subset of individuals from the entire population in order to participate in a study. Sampling is an important step because it is included in almost all surveys as it is not practical to study all individuals in the entire population. In sampling, the selection method is based on two ways: probability sampling and non-probability sampling. Non-probability sampling is appropriate for this study because the research questions describe something about a distinct phenomenon (the selection of participants in this research is Greek citizens/consumers), their willingness to participate, to answer questions such as "why," "what," and "how." In non-probability sampling, participants are selected on the basis of their ability or availability to participate. The sample was approached by sending the online questionnaire to social media platforms and forums as well as to the researcher's acquaintances. A total of 221 consumers/citizens participated in the survey who agreed to participate voluntarily and anonymously in the survey.

66.3.2 Data Collection Instrument

The collection of primary data for this study was based on the use of a self-report questionnaire. The questionnaire was divided into five parts. The first part of the questionnaire consisted of a total of six questions regarding the demographic information of the participants such as gender, age group, marital status, occupational status, educational level, and annual family income. The second part of the questionnaire consisted of 15 questions formulated on a Likert scale between 1 = Strongly Agree and 5 = Strongly Agree. Questions 1–4 related to the dimension "Perceived Usefulness," questions 5–9 related to the dimension "Perceived Ease of Use," questions 10–12 related to the dimension "Perceived Risk," and questions 13–15 related to the dimension "Attitude toward technology." The questions were drawn from Liang et al. (2019). The third part of the questionnaire consisted of seven questions formulated on a Likert scale between 1 = Strongly Disagree and 5 = Strongly Agree. The questions were intended to explore the participants' level of engagement with fashion. The questions were drawn from O'Cass' (2004) research. The fourth part of the questionnaire consisted of 10 questions formulated on a Likert scale between 1 = Disagree Strongly and 5 = Agree Strongly. The questions were intended to explore the participants' attitudes toward AI. The questions were drawn from the research by Liang et al. (2019) and Schepman and Rodway (2020). The fifth part of the questionnaire consisted of 5 questions formulated on a Likert scale between 1 = Strongly Disagree and 5 = Strongly Agree. The questions were intended to explore the participants' intention to purchase products/services from companies in the fashion industry that make use of AI applications.

Statistical analysis of the primary data collected through the survey questionnaire was conducted using the data processing and analysis software, SPSS version 26. The analysis of the primary data was done through the calculation of descriptive statistics and criteria and methodology indicators and inferential statistics. The investigation of consumer/citizen perception regarding the use of AI in fashion was done through the calculation of descriptive statistics measures such as Mean (denoted by MT) and Standard Deviation (denoted by TA) as all questions were Likert type. A higher mean value in a question indicates that consumers agree to a greater extent with the respective proposal.

66.4 Results

Aggregated results for the demographic characteristics of the 221 participants are given in Table 66.1.

Table 66.2 shows the results of the exploratory factor analysis for the questions assessing the dimensions of the Technology Acceptance model. The exploratory factor analysis confirmed that the 15 questions generate four factors (CMO = 0.903, Bartlett's test $p = 0.000$). The four factors explained 71.8% of the variability in the data. The results show that questions 1–4 indeed assess perceived usefulness (first

Table 66.1 Demographic characteristics of the 221 consumers surveyed

		N	%
Sex	Male	42	19.0%
	Female	179	81.0%
Age	Up to 25 years old	25	11.3%
	26–35 years old	61	27.6%
	36–45 years old	69	31.2%
	46–55 years old	55	24.9%
	56 years old and above	11	5.0%
Educational level	Secondary school graduate	97	43.9%
	Graduate of a university/technical school	94	42.5%
	Master's degree	27	12.2%
	Doctoral degree	3	1.4%
Marital status	Unmarried	60	27.1%
	Married	140	63.3%
	Divorced	18	8.1%
	Widowed	3	1.4%
Occupation	Student	19	8.6%
	Freelancer	34	15.4%
	Private employee	79	35.7%
	Civil servant	41	18.6%
	Pensioner	7	3.2%
	Unemployed	41	18.6%
Annual family income	Up to 5000	36	16.3%
	5001–10,000	67	30.3%
	10,001–20,000	77	34.8%
	20,001–30,000	28	12.7%
	30,001 and up	13	5.9%

66 Consumer Attitudes Toward Artificial Intelligence in Fashion

Table 66.2 Results of exploratory factor analysis for the questions assessing the dimensions of the Technology Acceptance Mode

	Factors			
	1	2	3	4
The use of artificial intelligence can help me choose clothing and footwear items more quickly	0.753			
The use of AI can help me choose more fashionable clothing the use of AI can increase my efficiency in choosing more fashionable clothing	0.862			
The use of AI can increase my efficiency in choosing more fashionable clothing	0.864			
Using AI can make it easier for me to choose what to wear	0.765			
It would be easy to use AI applications to help me choose clothing and footwear		0.632		
My interaction with AI applications is clear and understandable		0.786		
AI apps make it more flexible to interact with companies in the fashion industry		0.706		
It would be easy for me to make use of AI applications for selecting clothing and footwear		0.776		
AI marketing technology can offer me more choices		0.581		
I am worried that a product advertised through AI systems is different from the real product				0.917
I am afraid that the product advertised through AI systems will not have the quality I expect				0.914
When I shop online, AI marketing technology may prevent me from accurately retrieving goods				0.792
Technology can provide solutions to many everyday problems			0.875	
The use of technology has improved many aspects of everyday life			0.862	
The use of technology has more benefits than disadvantages			0.746	

factor), questions 5–9 indeed assess perceived ease (second factor), questions 10–12 indeed assess perceived risk (fourth factor), and questions 13–15 indeed assess attitude toward technology (third factor). The Cronbach's α reliability coefficient showed that the dimension "Perceived usefulness" shows a reliability of $\alpha = 0.911$ (very high), the dimension "Perceived ease" shows a reliability of $\alpha = 0.902$ (very high), the dimension "Perceived risk" shows a reliability of $\alpha = 0.885$ (very high), and the dimension "Attitude towards technology" shows a reliability of $\alpha = 0.906$ (very high).

Table 66.3 shows the results of the exploratory factor analysis for the questions assessing the degree of involvement in fashion. The exploratory factor analysis confirmed that the six questions create one factor (CMO = 0.894, Bartlett's test $p = 0.000$). The factor generated explained 69.4% of the variability in the data. The results show that the questions do assess the degree of individuals' involvement

Table 66.3 Results of exploratory factor analysis for questions assessing the degree of involvement in fashion

	Factor 1
Fashion means a lot to me	0.898
Fashion is an important part of my life	0.884
I think a lot about fashion	0.888
I want to be informed about fashion matters	0.864
I know a lot about fashion	0.824
I would describe myself as an expert in fashion matters	0.745

Table 66.4 Results of exploratory factor analysis for questions assessing attitudes toward AI

	Factor 1
I am confident in my ability to make the best choice in my outfit	0.699
AI can provide solutions to many everyday problems	0.783
I am interested in using AI applications in my daily life	0.848
People like me will suffer if AI is used more and more	−0.718
AI systems can perform better than humans	0.552
I have discomfort when I think about future uses of artificial intelligence	−0.781
Much of society will benefit from the use of AI.	0.779
Artificial intelligence is used to record people's habits	−0.556
I think artificial intelligence systems make a lot of mistakes	−0.689
I would visit a website that has AI applications	0.799
I like applications that make use of artificial intelligence	0.812

in fashion. The Cronbach's α reliability coefficient showed that the dimension "Fashion involvement" shows a reliability of $\alpha = 0.922$ (very high).

Table 66.4 shows the results of the exploratory factor analysis for the questions assessing attitudes toward AI. The exploratory factor analysis confirmed that the 11 questions create one factor (CMO = 0.923, Bartlett's test $p = 0.000$). The factor generated explained 68.8% of the variability in the data. The results show that the 11 questions do assess attitudes toward AI. The Cronbach's reliability coefficient α showed that the dimension "Attitude toward AI" shows a reliability of $\alpha = 0.918$ (very high).

Table 66.5 shows the results of the exploratory factor analysis for the questions assessing purchase intention. The exploratory factor analysis confirmed that the five questions create one factor (CMO = 0.883, Bartlett's test $p = 0.000$). The factor generated explained 67.2% of the variability in the data. The results show that the five questions do assess the intention of consumers/citizens to buy fashion products from companies/companies that make use of AI applications. The Cronbach's reliability coefficient α showed that the dimension "Purchase intention" shows a reliability of $\alpha = 0.906$ (very high).

Table 66.5 Results of exploratory factor analysis for questions assessing purchase intention

	Factor 1
The use of AI applications by companies in the fashion industry increases the likelihood of buying a product	0.792
I would choose to buy a fashion product from a company that uses AI applications on its website	0.848
AI applications on a website that markets fashion products would prevent me from buying a fashion product	−0.701
I am willing to browse products or services on a web platform supported by AI technology and applications	0.749
I am likely to buy unplanned fashion products when I shop on an online platform supported by AI marketing technology and applications	0.748

66.5 Conclusions

This work examines whether the adaptation of Davis' (1989) Technology Acceptance Model (TAM) by incorporating some additional factors (attitude toward AI, degree of engagement with fashion) can predict consumers' fashion behavior (purchase intention). For this purpose, a conceptual model related to consumer attitude and purchase intention toward an AI product was constructed and tested.

Initially, the first four research hypotheses (perceived usefulness and perceived ease of use positively influence consumers' attitudes toward AI and their intention to purchase a product from a company that makes use of AI applications) were confirmed. These results confirmed the findings of studies reporting that perceived usefulness and perceived ease of use were significant in predicting consumers' attitudes toward AI as well as their purchase intention (Belanche et al., 2019; Liang et al., 2019; Lunney et al., 2016; Sadriwala & Sadriwala, 2022; Silva & Bonetti, 2021; Sohn & Kwon, 2020). A logical explanation is that consumers appreciate the functions of AI and recognize the significant benefits and conveniences it provides. With these features and the user-friendly system, consumers' efficiency in selecting fashion products is highly enhanced, which leads to a more positive attitude toward AI and ultimately to an increased intention to purchase a product from a company that makes use of AI applications (Mohr & Kühl, 2021).

Furthermore, based on the results of the model, it was found that perceptions do not negatively affect consumers' attitudes toward AI and their intention to purchase a product from a firm that makes use of AI applications (Hypotheses 5 and 6). This contradicts with findings in the literature that argue that perceived risk negatively affects consumer behavior (Chang, 2005; Hwang et al., 2016; Ling et al., 2011; Kamalul Ariffin et al., 2018; Liang et al., 2019).

In addition, research confirmed that consumers' attitudes toward technology positively influence purchase intention and also attitudes toward AI (Hypotheses 7, 8, and 9). A logical extension of this idea is that consumers who are more positive about technology will be more likely to try new technologies such as AI (Chang & Jai, 2015; Masukujjaman et al., 2021).

Finally, from the results, it was shown that fashion involvement does not affect the effect of attitude toward technology on purchase intention and the effect of attitude toward AI on purchase intention (Hypotheses 10 and 11). These results are not in agreement or with previous studies reporting that consumers with higher fashion engagement are more likely to be ready to use a new technology such as AI (Kautish, Khare, & Sharma, 2020; Sun & Guo, 2017).

66.5.1 Research Limitations

The research conducted has a number of limitations that need to be addressed in order to make recommendations for future research in an attempt to draw safer and more reliable conclusions. The first limitation to be mentioned is that the sample of the survey consisted of 221 Greek citizens/consumers. This indicates that the survey sample is small in relation to the size of the population; therefore, there are limitations in terms of the generalisability of the results and the representativeness of the sample. Similarly, an important limitation is the use of convenience sampling. A key limitation of this type of sampling is that the findings may not be generalizable to the entire population, but are an indication that can be used in future larger-scale surveys (Saunders et al., 2009). Given these two limitations, further empirical data are needed to test whether a larger and more reliable sample could lead to stronger results or different conclusions.

In addition, a major limitation of the study was that citizens/consumers' attitudes and intentions toward AI were assessed with a self-report tool (questionnaire) that captures their opinions but not their actual behavior. Research based on self-report tools has the risk of bias in the results (underestimation or overestimation of a situation). Therefore, future studies should try to collect more objective data, perhaps using experimental or semi-experimental research.

66.5.2 Theoretical and Practical Implications of Research

The results of the study have theoretical and practical implications and implications. The study contributed theoretically to the Technology Acceptance Model (TAM) by extending the model to consumer evaluation of a new technology in the fashion industry, artificial intelligence applications. In addition, technological behaviors were incorporated into the TAM framework and the results of the analyses, and a positive effect on purchase intention was demonstrated. The addition of these variables provided insights for future research on the application of AI in the fashion industry. From a practical perspective, the structure and results of this study provided evidence for a systematic strategic plan to improve AI applications in the fashion industry. First, we showed that consumers' evaluation of perceived usefulness and perceived ease of use significantly influenced their attitudes toward

AI, which confirmed findings from previous researchers that the functions and interactions with the technology enhanced consumers' expectations and satisfaction as well as their attitudes toward the use of these technologies. Entrepreneurs in the fashion industry could continuously upgrade their platforms with AI applications with an emphasis on utility and convenience to keep them at a user-friendly interface level, improve consumer attitudes toward AI applications and ultimately increase the likelihood of purchasing one of their products.

References

Al-Gasawneh, J. A., Alfityani, A., Al-Okdeh, S., Almasri, B., Mansur, H., Nusairat, N. M., & Siam, Y. A. (2022). Avoiding uncertainty by measuring the impact of perceived risk on the intention to use financial artificial intelligence services. *Uncertain Supply Chain Management, 10*(4), 1427–1436. https://doi.org/10.5267/j.uscm.2022.6.013

Bhaduri, G., & Stanforth, N. (2017). To (or not to) label products as artisanal: Effect of fashion involvement on customer perceived value. *Journal of Product & Brand Management, 26*(2), 177–189. https://doi.org/10.1108/jpbm-04-2016-1153

Belanche, D., Casaló, L. V., & Flavián, C. (2019). Artificial intelligence in FinTech: Understanding robo-advisors adoption among customers. *Industrial Management & Data Systems, 119*(7), 1411–1430. https://doi.org/10.1108/imds-08-2018-0368

Bues, M., Steiner, M., Stafflage, M., & Krafft, M. (2017). How Mobile in-store advertising influences purchase intention: Value drivers and mediating effects from a consumer perspective. *Psychology & Marketing, 34*(2), 157–174. https://doi.org/10.1002/mar.20981

Bryman, A., & Bell, E. (2011). *Business research methods* (3rd ed.). Oxford University Press.

Celik, H., & Kocaman, R. (2017). Roles of self-monitoring, fashion involvement and technology readiness in an individual's propensity to use mobile shopping. *Journal of Systems and Information Technology, 19*(3/4), 166–182. https://doi.org/10.1108/jsit-01-2017-0008

Chang, H. J. J., & Jai, T. M. C. (2015). Is fast fashion sustainable? The effect of positioning strategies on consumers' attitudes and purchase intentions. *Social Responsibility Journal, 11*(4), 853–867. https://doi.org/10.1108/srj-07-2014-0095

Chang, M. (2005). The effects of trust and perceived risk on attitude and purchase intension in internet shopping malls. *Journal of Information Systems, 14*(1), 227–249. http://www.koreascience.or.kr/article/ArticleFullRecord.jsp?cn=JBSTB0_2005_v14n1_227

Choon Ling, K., Bin Daud, D., Hoi Piew, T., Keoy, K. H., & Hassan, P. (2011). Perceived risk, perceived technology, online trust for the online purchase intention in Malaysia. *International Journal of Business and Management, 6*(6), 167. https://doi.org/10.5539/ijbm.v6n6p167

Darley, W. K., Blankson, C., & Luethge, D. J. (2010). Toward an integrated framework for online consumer behavior and decision making process: A review. *Psychology & Marketing, 27*(2), 94–116. https://doi.org/10.1002/mar.20322

Davis, F. D. (1986). *A technology acceptance model for empirically testing new end-user information systems: Theory and results*. Massachusetts Institute of Technology.

Davis, F. D. (1989). Perceived usefulness, perceived ease of use, and user acceptance of information technology. MIS Quar.

Fishbein, M., & Ajzen, I. (1975). *Belief, attitude, intention, and behavior: An introduction to theory and research*. Addison-Wesley.

Fishbein, M., & Ajzen, I. (2015). *Predicting and changing behavior: The reasoned action approach* (1st ed.). Psychology Press.

Giri, C., Jain, S., Zeng, X., & Bruniaux, P. (2019). A detailed review of artificial intelligence applied in the fashion and apparel industry. *IEEE Access, 7*, 95376–95396. https://doi.org/10.1109/access.2019.2928979

Gu, X., Gao, F., Tan, M., & Peng, P. (2020). Fashion analysis and understanding with artificial intelligence. *Information Processing & Management, 57*(5), 102276. https://doi.org/10.1016/j.ipm.2020.10227

Hasan, R., Shams, R., & Rahman, M. (2021). Consumer trust and perceived risk for voice-controlled artificial intelligence: The case of Siri. *Journal of Business Research, 131*, 591–597. https://doi.org/10.1016/j.jbusres.2020.12.012

Hwang, C., Chung, T. L., & Sanders, E. A. (2016). Attitudes and purchase intentions for smart clothing: Examining US consumers' functional, expressive, and aesthetic needs for solar-powered clothing. *Clothing and Textiles Research Journal, 34*(3), 207–222.

Jen, W., Lu, T., & Liu, P. (2009). An integrated analysis of technology acceptance behaviour models: Comparison of three major models. *MIS REVIEW: An International Journal, 15*(1), 89–121. https://doi.org/10.6131/misr.200909_15(1).0004

Kamalul Ariffin, S., Mohan, T., & Goh, Y. N. (2018). Influence of consumers' perceived risk on consumers' online purchase intention. *Journal of Research in Interactive Marketing, 12*(3), 309–327. https://doi.org/10.1108/jrim-11-2017-0100

Kautish, P., Khare, A., & Sharma, R. (2020). Influence of values, brand consciousness and behavioral intentions in predicting luxury fashion consumption. *Journal of Product & Brand Management, 30*(4), 513–531. https://doi.org/10.1108/jpbm-08-2019-2535

Kim, H. Y., Lee, J. Y., Mun, J. M., & Johnson, K. K. P. (2017). Consumer adoption of smart in-store technology: Assessing the predictive value of attitude versus beliefs in the technology acceptance model. *International Journal of Fashion Design, Technology and Education, 10*(1), 26–36. https://doi.org/10.1080/17543266.2016.1177737

Koronaki, E., Vlachvei, A., & Panopoulos, A. (2023a). Managing the online customer experience and subsequent consumer responses across the customer journey: A review and future research agenda. *Electronic Commerce Research and Applications, 58*, 101242.

Koronaki, E., Vlachvei, A., & Panopoulos, A. (2023b). Shaping the online customer experience through website elements: An integrated framework. In N. Tsounis & A. Vlachvei (Eds.), *Advances in empirical economic research. ICOAE 2022. Springer proceedings in business and economics*. Springer. https://doi.org/10.1007/978-3-031-22749-3_60

Lăzăroiu, G., Neguriță, O., Grecu, I., Grecu, G., & Mitran, P. C. (2020). Consumers' decision-making process on social commerce platforms: Online trust, perceived risk, and purchase intentions. *Frontiers in Psychology, 11*, 890.

Liapati, G., Assiouras, I., & Decaudin, J. M. (2015). The role of fashion involvement, brand love and hedonic consumption tendency in fashion impulse purchasing. *Journal of Global Fashion Marketing, 6*(4), 251–264. https://doi.org/10.1080/20932685.2015.1070679

Liang, Y., Lee, S. H., & Workman, J. E. (2019). Implementation of artificial intelligence in fashion: Are consumers ready? *Clothing and Textiles Research Journal, 38*(1), 3–18. https://doi.org/10.1177/0887302x19873437

Lin, J. S. C., & Hsieh, P. L. (2006). The role of technology readiness in customers' perception and adoption of self-service technologies. *International Journal of Service Industry Management, 17*(5), 497–517.

Ling, K. C., Daud, D. B., Piew, T. H., Keoy, K. H., & Hassan, P. (2011). Perceived risk, perceived technology, online trust for the online purchase intention in Malaysia. *International journal of Business and Management, 6*(6), 167.

Luce, L. (2018). *Artificial intelligence for fashion: How AI is revolutionizing the fashion industry* (1st ed.). Apress.

Lunney, A., Cunningham, N. R., & Eastin, M. S. (2016). Wearable fitness technology: A structural investigation into acceptance and perceived fitness outcomes. *Computers in Human Behavior, 65*, 114–120. https://doi.org/10.1016/j.chb.2016.08.007

Marangunić, N., & Granić, A. (2014). Technology acceptance model: A literature review from 1986 to 2013. *Universal Access in the Information Society, 14*(1), 81–95. https://doi.org/10.1007/s10209-014-0348-1

Masukujjaman, M., Alam, S. S., Siwar, C., & Halim, S. A. (2021). Purchase intention of renewable energy technology in rural areas in Bangladesh: Empirical evidence. *Renewable Energy, 170*, 639–651. https://doi.org/10.1016/j.renene.2021.01.125

McKinsey & Company. (2018). *The state of fashion 2018.* Ανακτήθηκε από: https://cdn.businessoffashion.com/reports/The_State_of_Fashion_2018_v2.pdf

Mohiuddin Babu, M., Akter, S., Rahman, M., Billah, M. M., & Hack-Polay, D. (2022). The role of artificial intelligence in shaping the future of agile fashion industry. *Production Planning & Control*, 1–15. https://doi.org/10.1080/09537287.2022.2060858

Mohr, S., & Kühl, R. (2021). Acceptance of artificial intelligence in German agriculture: An application of the technology acceptance model and the theory of planned behavior. *Precision Agriculture, 22*(6), 1816–1844. https://doi.org/10.1007/s11119-021-09814-x

Momani, A. M., & Jamous, M. (2017). The evolution of technology acceptance theories. *Social Science Research Network.* https://papers.ssrn.com/sol3/Delivery.cfm/SSRN_ID2971454_code1450767.pdf?abstractid=2971454&mirid=1

Montaño, D. E., & Kasprzyk, D. (2008). Theory of reasoned action, theory of planned behavior, and the integrated behavioral model. *Health Behavior and Health.*

Notta, O., Raikou, V., & Vlachvei, A. (2022). Social media usage and business competitiveness in Agri-food SMEs. In N. Tsounis & A. Vlachvei (Eds.), *Advances in Quantitative Economic Research*, Springer Proceedings in Business and Economics, Springer International Publishing AG 2022, pp. 531–538.

O'cass, A. (2004). Fashion clothing consumption: antecedents and consequences of fashion clothing involvement. *European Journal of Marketing, 38*(7), 869–882.

Parment, A. (2013). Generation Y vs. Baby Boomers: Shopping behavior, buyer involvement and implications for retailing. *Journal of Retailing and Consumer Services, 20*(2), 189–199.

Sadriwala, M. F., & Sadriwala, K. F. (2022). Perceived usefulness and ease of use of artificial intelligence on marketing innovation. *International Journal of Innovation in the Digital Economy, 13*(1), 1–10. https://doi.org/10.4018/ijide.292010

Saunders, M., Lewis, P., & Thornhill, A. (2009). Research methods for business students. Pearson education.

Sánchez, R. A., & Hueros, A. D. (2010). Motivational factors that influence the acceptance of Moodle using TAM. *Computers in Human Behavior, 26*(6), 1632–1640. https://doi.org/10.1016/j.chb.2010.06.011

Schepman, A., & Rodway, P. (2020). Initial validation of the general attitudes towards Artificial Intelligence Scale. *Computers in Human Behavior Reports, 1*, 100014.

Silva, E. S., & Bonetti, F. (2021). Digital humans in fashion: Will consumers interact? *Journal of Retailing and Consumer Services, 60*, 102430. https://doi.org/10.1016/j.jretconser.2020.102430

Sohn, K., & Kwon, O. (2020). Technology acceptance theories and factors influencing artificial Intelligence-based intelligent products. *Telematics and Informatics, 47*, 101324.

Sun, Y., & Guo, S. (2017). Predicting fashion involvement by media use, social comparison, and lifestyle: An interaction model. *International Journal of Communication, 11*, 24.

Taherdoost, H. (2018). A review of technology acceptance and adoption models and theories. *Procedia Manufacturing, 22*, 960–967. https://doi.org/10.1016/j.promfg.2018.03.137

Tao, Q., & Xu, Y. (2020). Consumer adoption of fashion subscription retailing: antecedents and moderating factors. *International Journal of Fashion Design, Technology and Education, 13*(1), 78–88.

Venkatesh, V. (2000). Determinants of perceived ease of use: Integrating control, intrinsic motivation, and emotion into the technology acceptance model. *Information Systems Research, 11*(4), 342–365. https://doi.org/10.1287/isre.11.4.342.11872

Vlachvei, A., Notta, O., & Koronaki, E. (2022). Effects of content characteristics on stages of customer engagement in social media: Investigating European wine brands. *Journal of Research in Interactive Marketing, 16*(4), 615–632.

Vlačić, B., Corbo, L., Costa e Silva, S., & Dabić, M. (2021). The evolving role of artificial intelligence in marketing: A review and research agenda. *Journal of Business Research, 128*, 187–203. https://doi.org/10.1016/j.jbusres.2021.01.055

Chapter 67
What Determines Supply and Demand for Occupational Pension Provision in Germany? Results of a Current Expert Surveys

Robert Piotr Dombek

Abstract Retirement at 70, old-age poverty, the importance of private and occupational pension schemes are all topics that have been discussed in German politics for years. Experts agree that the statutory pension insurance of the Federal Republic of Germany, which is financed on a pay-as-you-go basis, is facing a massive problem due to demographic developments. Therefore, effective and sustainable solutions are needed. The idea of pension provision must be strengthened again among citizens in order to create incentives for their own provision in old age. With the introduction of the Act to Strengthen Occupational Pensions on 1 January 2018, the legislator pursued the goal of promoting occupational pension provision in Germany, making it more interesting and thus achieving an increase in demand. Unlike private pension provision, where the customer decides whether or not to take out a contract, in occupational pension provision, the employer plays a decisive role in addition to the employee. Based on this insight, expert interviews were conducted with a mix of small, medium, and large companies in Germany in 2023. This chapter presents the results of the qualitatively analyzed interviews. In the first step, the currently available literature is analyzed and evaluated. In the further course, the results of the conducted expert interviews are presented and evaluated, before further approaches for increasing the demand for occupational pension provision are identified and summarised on the basis of the information gained in order to provide an outlook for further research.

Keywords Demand for Occupational pension provision · Occupational Strengthening Pensions Act · Pensions maps · Spread of occupational pension provision

JEL Classification C12, C24, G22, J53, K00

R. P. Dombek (✉)
Economics and Management, Mendel University Brno, Brno, South Moravia, Tschechien, Czech Republic

© The Author(s), under exclusive license to Springer Nature Switzerland AG 2024
N. Tsounis, A. Vlachvei (eds.), *Applied Economic Research and Trends*, Springer Proceedings in Business and Economics,
https://doi.org/10.1007/978-3-031-49105-4_67

67.1 Introduction

The current scientific literature is strongly concerned with old-age poverty and the reforms of the German old-age security system. For example, there are numerous scientific publications on old-age poverty (Bäcker, 2008), (Bäcker & Schmitz, 2013), (Goebel & Grabka, 2011) and also (Seils, 2020) and the pension reforms (Bonin, 2001), (Börsch-Supan & Wilke, 2004) and also (Tiefensee, 2020). When dividing occupational pension provision into old world (contracts before 01.01.2018) and new world (contracts after 01.01.2018), one finds a great deal of the scientific literature that deals exclusively with the old world of occupational pension provision. The possible causes for the low level of Ruprecht deals with the penetration rate of occupational pension provision and the option of automatic occupational pension provision for employees in his article (Ruprecht, 2004). In her article, Leiber takes stock of the forms and spread of occupational pension provision 4 years after the 2001 Retirement Assets Act came into force. The results of this article were based on a survey of works and staff councils in the private sector and staff councils in the public sector conducted in 2004/05 (Leiber, 2005). The Federal Ministry of Labour and Social Affairs provides a good overview of the spread of occupational pension provision in the period 2001–2015 in its 2016 Old-age Security Report (Bundesministerium für Arbeit und Soziales, 2016). In their report on funding opportunities for occupational pension provision, Kiesewetter et al. deal with the decline in occupational pension provision in recent years and at the same time, point out that the aspects for the decline in occupational pension provision have not yet been sufficiently researched. As a possible solution to the decline in occupational pension provision, they examine the option of a new regulation under tax and social security law for the promotion of occupational pension provision (Kiesewetter et al., 2016). Due to the concern of a low diffusion rate of occupational pension provision, the focus of the microdata analysis conducted by Beznoska & Pimpertz is on the diffusion of occupational pension provision in German households. The aim of this microdata analysis is to better classify the subsidy options for occupational pension provision in particular (Beznoska & Pimpertz, 2016).

There is also some scientific literature on the new world of occupational pension provision. Schwark, for example, devotes his report to the Occupational Strengthening Pensions Act (OSPA). In his report, however, Schwark quickly comes to the conclusion that it is too early for a significant interim result after only one year since the Occupational Strengthening Pensions Act came into force (Schwark, 2019). The author Augustin provides a brief overview of possible motives for a low penetration rate of occupational pension provision in their position paper. The authors identify the dependence on employers and collective bargaining parties as possible reasons for the decline in occupational pension provision (Augustin, 2019). Menzel clearly presents the new world of occupational pension provision in his work. In his work, the author provides a good overview of the model-theoretical consideration of occupational pension provision from the perspective of employees and employers and almost summarises the results in the context of an advantage analysis (Menzel, 2019). In cooperation with the F.A.Z. Institute, Generali Germany AG conducted a study in 2019 that looked specifically at the spread of occupational pension provision among small- and medium-sized companies in Germany. Companies with 50–100 employees were defined as smaller, 100–250 employees as medium-sized, and 250–500 employees as larger companies. According to the initial results of this study, no positive spread of occupational pension provision has been seen since the introduction of the Occupational Strengthening Pensions Act on 1 January 2018, but rather the opposite, with a slight stagnation (F.A.Z. – Institut & Generali Deutschland AG, 2019). This study showed that the market penetration of occupational pension provision has stagnated among middle and top management employees and that there has been only a minimal increase among the remaining employees. As for the old world of occupational pension provision, the Federal Ministry of Labour and Social Affairs provides a good overview of the spread of occupational pension provision in the period from 2001 to 2019 in its Old Age Security Report 2020 (Bundesministerium für Arbeit und Soziales, 2020a).

The recording of the benefits and the spread of occupational pension provision in Germany is carried out on the basis of the already mentioned and other significant existing data sets, which are mentioned in the next chapter. In particular, the limitations and associated gaps of these analysis methods will be highlighted. Decisive for the further course of this chapter are the databases with the character of the recorded variables and the respective advantages and disadvantages. First, the previous larger and/or repeated surveys at the individual, household, and company level are presented, followed by the smaller surveys of insurers or associations.

67.2 Literature Review and Current State of Research

67.2.1 *Employer and Agency Survey (EaS)*

As mentioned earlier in this research chapter, the Federal Government's Old Age Security Report provides good information on the general spread of occupational pension provision. This report is published once per legislative period, in addition to the pension insurance report, and provides information on the income situation of older persons and on current pension benefits. The Federal Ministry of Labour and Social Affairs' own survey of providers provides the data basis for this. Since 2001, companies and providers of occupational pension provision have been surveyed six times on existing entitlements to occupational pension provision. The most recent survey dates from 2019. The data is completed with information from the Federal Financial Supervisory Authority (BaFin), the German Insurance Association (GDV), and the Pension Assurance Association (PSV). In the survey of companies and providers of occupational pension schemes, the measures of existing entitlements and contribution amounts are evaluated in particular. The evaluation is carried out according to gender and the type of implementation method of occupational pension provision (Bundesministerium für Arbeit und Soziales, 2020b, c).

Since this survey covers the male and female members of an institution, there may be double entries among the institutions, which makes it difficult to answer the question of how many people have at least one occupational pension contract. Therefore, the average number of contracts per capita is determined and the amount of pension entitlements adjusted by this factor. Using this data, a time series can be formed which can provide further information on various developments in occupational pension provision. Changes in the demand for occupational pension provision in the various implementation channels can be well documented and are thus important for an initial investigation of the effects of the Occupational Pensions Strengthening Act (Bundesministerium für Arbeit und Soziales, 2020b, c).

However, this survey comes up against the following characteristic limits of the insured persons:

- From the concentrated data of the carrier survey, it is not possible to determine the prevalence of occupational pension provision of different possible underserved groups of people.
- A closer look at the asset and income situation is excluded.
- The ratio of the savings contribution of occupational pension provision to other savings contributions of the old-age provision portfolios of individuals or households cannot be determined.
- It is also not possible to say whether the pension entitlements in retirement must be sufficient for one person or for several.
- No consideration at the level of individual households.
- No information on the cost composition of existing contracts (Bundesministerium für Arbeit und Soziales, 2020b, c).

In summary, it can be said that, from a macroeconomic perspective, the survey of providers offers a good data basis for obtaining an overall view of the development and spread of occupational pension provision. However, it has its limits for analyses from a microeconometric perspective. Likewise, the data are insufficient for recording insufficiently provided groups of people or for future pension reforms. Due to the problems mentioned above, the remainder of this section presents survey data that identifies further variables in the context of occupational pension provision, such as household and person level.

67.2.2 Dissemination of Old-Age Provision (DP)

On behalf of the Federal Ministry of Labour and Social Affairs (BMAS), three studies have already been carried out since 2011 with the study "Dissemination of old-age provision" (DP), which aimed at the written survey of employees subject to social security contributions between the ages of 25 and 65. With the current study from 2019 alone, 11,906 people were surveyed. The focus of these surveys is information on occupational pension provision. The studies record, among other things, contracts that are currently being saved for and also the amount of one's own savings rate. A special feature of this study is that it is noted whether an information provision letter is available. If such an information provision letter is available, the respondents are asked to indicate the total savings contributions. Thus, in addition to personal contributions, the contributions made by employers are also recorded and respondents are asked about pension entitlements and the actual capital stock (Social Affairs, 2020) and (Bundesministerium für Arbeit und Soziales, 2020c).

In summary, it can be said that certain trends can be derived from the data sets obtained from these surveys in order to gain initial insights into the role of occupational pension provision in the respondents' pension portfolios. Although many assets are not recorded in detail, at least an initial picture can be gained of how occupational pension provision is used. Another important feature of these surveys is the clear differentiation between occupational pension provision for employees in the private sector and those in the public sector.

However, this survey also reaches its limits and, in addition to the advantages already mentioned, also offers some disadvantages such as:

- The results are only available in aggregated form within the studies and not also in the form of a data set.
- Due to the unavailability of the data set, microeconometric analyses, such as multivariate analysis, are not possible.
- Underserved groups of people can only be recorded on the basis of the combinations of characteristics presented in the studies.
- Each survey in these studies is always an independent sample and therefore not a panel study.
- The savings behavior over the life cycle can therefore not be answered in concrete terms because the savings behavior of the individual is not observed at specific points in time.
- Exclusion of analyses of effects on certain legal or personal changes.

67.2.3 Old Age Security in Germany (OASG)

On behalf of the Federal Ministry of Labour and Social Affairs, a study was conducted for the first time in 1986 and since 1995 every 4 years. This study also involves repeated surveys of independent samples. Within the framework of this study, persons between 55 and 80 years of age were asked about their income situation in old age at the beginning and, since 2019, for the first time between 60 and 85 years of age (Bundesministerium für Arbeit und Soziales, 2021). In contrast to the studies described so far, the conclusions of the studies of old-age provision in Germany do not provide any new insights into future gaps in provision, but rather more about the current level of provision of the persons surveyed in the age cohorts 55–80 and 60–85 (Beznoska & Pimpertz, 2016).

In the case of occupational pension provision, the survey refers in particular to the pensions received by pensioners. For the respondents still in employment, on the other hand, it refers to whether they receive benefits from occupational pension schemes when they retire. Furthermore, in this survey, the variables are recorded separately for married couples. A special feature of this study is that the results become more conditional over time, since, for example, 55-year-olds surveyed in 2011 were already 60-years-old in 2015 and were also recorded in the survey round. The study thus captures the changing concentrated patterns of provision over time. (Bundesministerium für Arbeit und Soziales, 2021). The next survey on old-age security in Germany will take place in 2023 and will include approximately 16,000 people (Institut für angewandte Sozialwissenschaft, 2023).

In addition to the aforementioned advantages of this study, the study of old-age provision in Germany also has its weaknesses such as:

- The study is not a panel survey, which is why dynamic processes, such as dissaving processes, cannot be recorded.
- This study is not suitable for savings and dissaving processes.

67.2.4 Life Courses and Retirement Provision (LCRP)

On behalf of the German Pension Insurance and the Federal Ministry of Labour and Social Affairs, the survey "Life Courses and Retirement Provision" (LCRP) was conducted in 2016. In this study, persons aged between 40 and 60 born between 1957 and 1976 were questioned in detail about their personal employment biographies in addition to their pension situation in old age. Respondents from the new German federal states and with a migration background were given special consideration. The fact that persons with a migration background were given special consideration is due to the fact that the concept of migration experience used in the study for life courses and old age was applied to the individual mobility of immigration or mobile employment biographies across transnational borders. In this context, people who were born abroad and moved to Germany were also interviewed. By taking these two characteristics into account, it was possible for the first time to document foreign employment and entitlements and to assess them in relation to possible influencing factors and outcomes of migration (Heien & Krämer, 2018).

The special feature of this study was that the survey data of this study were linked via the national insurance number with existing data from the statutory pension insurance. This had the advantage that employment biographies could be traced precisely, which made it possible to draw cohort comparisons (Heien & Krämer, 2018).

The disadvantages of this survey are briefly presented:

- Survey has only been conducted once before.
- Total population not covered.
- Occupational pension provision cannot be researched without a panel structure over the life cycle.
- There is no data access for scientific use.

67.2.5 Survey of Health Ageing and Retirement in Europe (SHARE)

The panel study "Survey of Health Ageing and Retirement in Europe" (SHARE), which is managed by the Munich Center for the Economics of Ageing (MEA), refers to a population of people aged at least 50. The study now surveys people from 26 European countries in Switzerland and Israel on retirement planning topics. Data from England and Ireland are collected in the harmonised studies English Longitudinal Study of Ageing (ELSA) and the Irish Longitudinal Study on Ageing (TILDA). A special feature of this study is that it documents the payout phases of occupational pension provision and any occupational pension. Similarly, this study is able to capture dynamics, the types of payouts, and the year of first pension withdrawal. In addition, the study also asks people who are not currently drawing a pension about any future occupational pension entitlement, the duration of savings, the average savings contribution and the possible future occupational pension amount. In the surveys, this study does not differentiate between occupational pension provision in the private sector and the public sector, but it is possible to draw conclusions about past employment in various stages of life as to whether the respondent has worked in the private sector or the public sector (Börsch-Supan et al., 2013, 2020, 2022).

This study has the following disadvantages:

- Detailed statements about current savings processes are not possible.
- Statements on current savings and pension levels of younger generations can only be observed to a limited extent, as these are not recorded.

67.2.6 Savings and Old-Age Provision in Germany (SOG)

The study "Savings and Retirement Provision in Germany" (SOG), also conducted by the MEA, surveys a broader section of the population. The first time this study was conducted was in 2001 as part of a preliminary survey, and subsequently in 2003/04, from 2005 to 2011 annually and the last time in 2013. The aim of this panel study was to document dynamic changes in savings behavior over time. With the financial coefficients, variables on occupational pension provision were also surveyed. The explicit questionnaire differed slightly from survey to survey. In almost every survey, the number of contracts, the monthly savings contributions, and the current credit balance were asked. In the case of spouses, it was not possible to distinguish the person making the contributions. In the 2007 survey, it was also asked whether the answers were taken from current documents or whether they were only estimates. In addition, it was theoretically possible to make statements about the composition of savings contributions for occupational pension provision through these studies. That is, what proportion of the total contribution was made by the employee and what proportion by the employer (Coppola & Lamla, 2013).

The study recorded variables of occupational pension provision, private pension provision, and other assets, which made it possible to present the savers' portfolios more transparently. A special feature of this study is the recording of sociological and behavioral psychological character traits, which in turn enables the analysis from a behavioral economics perspective. In principle, the study can provide information on which group of people make provisions for occupational pensions (Beznoska & Pimpertz, 2016; Coppola & Lamla, 2013). The advantage of this panel structure is that it offers insights into possible savings and their changes over time, but the sample size is often not particularly large when analyzing certain individuals, with the result that it is difficult to make statements about certain groups (Kröger et al., 2011).

The main disadvantages of this study are as follows:

- The data was collected only up to the year 2013.
- The effects on demand behavior due to the introduction of the Betreiebsrentenstärkungsgesetz in 2018 have therefore not been researched.
- Details on existing occupational pension contracts are not covered by this study.

67.2.7 Socio-Economic Panel (SOEP)

The survey within the framework of the "Socio-Economic Panel" (SOEP) is a panel household survey conducted by the German Institute for Economic Research (DIW). This survey was conducted for the first time in 1984 (Schupp, 2009). The Socio-Economic Panel currently surveys about 30,000 people from about 15,000 households every year. To date, about 15,000 households have been surveyed regarding their savings behavior for occupational pension provision. Special surveys on occupational pension provision were conducted in the 2013 and 2018 surveys. The surveys of the 2 years focused in particular on the acquired occupational pension entitlements and the type of financing (Deutsches Institut für Wirtschaftsforschung, 2013). Due to the data basis, the Socio-Economic Panel offers a further data basis, which can be useful for further research on the spread of occupational pension provision. A survey at periodic intervals of the status of occupational pension provision can also increase the learning curve and lead to more detailed information from the respondents.

However, this survey also comes up against certain limits such as:

- Limited data potential due to the larger time frame of the survey.
- The described learning effects are not to be expected on the occasion of the temporary survey on the prevalence of occupational pension provision.

67.2.8 *Private Households and Their Finances (PHF)*

The representative panel study "Private Households and their Finances," which has been conducted regularly by the Deutsche Bundesbank since 2010, provides a further database for the financial structure of private households with at least one adult household member over the age of 18. The second and third surveys took place in 2014 and 2017. The data collected includes household asset balances and other variables, as well as the number of occupational pension contracts and other information on contributions and expected pensions or one-off capital payments. Furthermore, respondents are asked about the replacement ratio of old-age pensions in relation to their net income (Deutsche Bundesbank, 2017). However, this study has one disadvantage:

- This study does not allow for a differentiation of savings contributions according to employer and employee share.

The various data sets described at the household and person level are summarised in Table 67.1 according to the survey years, the client, the structure, and sample size.

Some of the studies presented differ greatly in the variables they contain for occupational pension provision. Therefore, Table 67.2 summarises the variables.

Data sets from surveys at the company level are available from the Federal Statistical Office from the years 2008 and 2012. With the survey "Earnings and labour costs – Expenses and entitlements of occupational pension schemes" (Elc), the payments of employers and pension entitlements were differentiated according to the industry, the size of the company, and the type of implementation method (Federal Statistical Office, 2012; Wallau et al., 2014). As only companies with more than 10 employees were surveyed in this study, the results are not representative of all companies in Germany. Furthermore, the data is only available in concentrated form (Beznoska & Pimpertz, 2016).

The survey "Verdienststrukturerhebung" (VSE) is also the responsibility of the Federal Statistical Office. It was first conducted in 1951 and has been conducted at regular four-year intervals since 2006. In 2010 and 2014, this survey was the first to register data on the prevalence of occupational pension provision in the context of deferred compensation of employees (Geyer & Himmelreicher, 2021; Statistisches Bundesamt, 2016). The first survey in 2010 took into account companies with more than 10 employees, while the second in 2014 also included companies with fewer than 10 employees, which is why the VSE from 2014 is significant. The special feature of this survey is its accuracy due to the availability of information on occupational pension schemes from the pay slips of the respondents. Even though only deferred compensation is analyzed here, this survey is extensive with a

Table 67.1 Data sets on occupational pension provision at the individual and household level in Germany (own representation)

Data set	Years of survey	Client	Structure	Sample size and sample characteristics
DP	2011, 2015, 2019	BMAS	Cross section	N (2019): Approx. 11.906 employees subject to social insurance contributions aged 25–65 years
OASG	1986, 1992 and from 1995 all 4 years	BMAS	Cross section	N (2019): Approx. 30.431 persons age: 60–85
LCRP	2016	DRV & BMAS	One-off survey	N: Approx. 10.000 persons
				40–60 year-olds (birth cohorts 1957–1976)
				Disproportionate consideration: Persons from East Germany and with migration experience
SHARE (SHARE-RV)	From 2004 all 2 years	MEA	Panel	N for Germany: Approx. 2.700 persons for wave 8, age: 50+
SOG	2001–2013	MEA	Panel	N (2013): 1.430 households
				Documents dynamic changes in savings behavior over time
SOEP (SOEP-RV)	2013, 2018	DIW	Panel	N (2018): Approx. 15.000 households & approx 30.000 people special surveys on occupational pension provision were conducted in the 2013 and 2018 surveys
PHF	2010/11, 2014, 2017	Deutsche Bundesbank	Panel	N (2017): Approx. 4.942 households
				Households are randomly selected age of respondents 18+

Table 67.2 Contents of the data sets on occupational pension provision at the individual and household level in Germany (own representation)

Question		DP	OASG	LCRP	SHARE	SOG	SOEP	PHF
Number of occupational pension contracts		Is a contract currently being used for savings	Existence can result from services received/expected can be concluded	Existence is requested	Was paid in or not; on public service can possibly be concluded via SHARELIFE can be closed	Asked for last year [all years except 2011] 2011: Do you or your partner (separately for both of you) acquire both	[2013]: Only the existence of occupational rights to occupational pensions is queried [2018]: Additionally: How many occupational pension contracts from different employers	Is queried
		Number of current entitlements		Amount of entitlements in year 2016				
Contributions paid in the last year		Employee contribution for all	×	×	×	Will be asked (but for "you or your partner") for the last year (monthly contributions) [all years except 2011].	×	Is queried
		Employer contribution if information letter						
Credit		If information letter is available	×	×	×	Will be asked (but for "you or your partner") [all years except 2011]	Is queried ("entitlements acquired so far") (2013, 2018)	×

(continued)

Table 67.2 (continued)

Question	DP	OASG	LCRP	SHARE	SOG	SOEP	PHF
Financing type	Is recorded	×	×	×	Identifiable (AN/AG contributions asked separately) [all years except 2011]	To be queried [2013, 2018]	×
Share of employee and employer contributions	If information letter is available	×	×	×	Calculable (employer and employee contributions requested separately) [all years except 2011]	×	×
Implementation channel	Seems present, but little broken down	×	×	×	Distinction between indirect vs. direct implementation possible [2013, 2010, 2009, 2008, 2007]	×	Company pension scheme, direct insurance, contract taken out yourself?
Commitment type	×	×	×	×	×	×	×
Expected benefits	If information letter is available	If not retired: Expected future benefits	×	Is queried	Which benefits do you expect to receive [all years except 2011]	×	Expected monthly amount of the retirement income, expected amount one-off payment

		Recorded separately for women and men	Is queried	Is queried	Will be queried [all years except 2011]	Queried regularly	Can be tapped
Drawings from occupational pension schemes	×						
Characteristics of the people	New/old federal states; age groups; occupational education; number of children under 18; level of employment; gross wage; nationality (German/non-German); since when employed by employer	Questions about the living and living situation (household members, income, age, …), education and employment status, housing costs, sources of income	Age; gender; origin/migration; education; income; employment history	Age, gender, income, household structure and information about partner:In, employment history, education, financial planning, also health variables	Many characteristics including, socio-demographic characteristics, satisfaction, health, savings behavior, financial knowledge, forms of income, expectations, and self-assessment	Age, gender, etc., income, household structure, etc.	Age, gender, etc., income, household structure, financial education, financial planning, expectations, etc.
Characteristics of the companies	Sector; company size (number of employees)	Company of the last activity	×	Industries of current job	Information on IAB link in the ninth survey	Branch of the company	×
		Size of enterprise, (number of employees)		Industries of previous jobs			
Contract details	×	×	×	×	×	×	×
Other savings/portfolios	Detailed information on Riester contracts	Income from other other forms of pension provision	Vested rights from all three pillars of the AV	Further AV savings benefits are queried	Forms of wealth and private pension provision	Is partially recorded	Is queried

(continued)

Table 67.2 (continued)

Question	DP	OASG	LCRP	SHARE	SOG	SOEP	PHF
	Detailed information on GRV existence of additional forms of provision and type of provision form is recorded	Expected future benefits from other AV		Assets module ("assets") available, imputations so far until wave 7, from 2022 also for wave 8			
Other	Reasons against additional pension provision	Payment of the occupational pension as a one-off lump sum is recognized	Survey data are linked with DRV process data	Supplementary or lump-sum payments from company pension and its amount	Does the company offer a pension scheme [2013, 2011]?	"make use of the deferred compensation"	Percentage GRV/civil servant pension and bAV/pAV measured against final net salary
	Ever received an information letter?		Receipt since when	Information on occupational pensions when joining the company? [2013]			

Did you receive an information letter?				In which jobs were contributions were paid	Would you like to acquire rights to a pension? [2013]	Are the details of the already acquired entitlements accurate or approximate?
Evaluation of the information letters					Source (information letter/self-disclosure) when contributions to occupational pensions is specified [2013, 2010, 2009, 2008, 2007]	
					Attitude "occupational pension provision is safe" [2013]	
					Since when do you acquire rights to occupational pension/public service [2011]	

sample of about 60,000 companies and about one million documented employment relationships (Statistisches Bundesamt, 2016).

Another survey was conducted by the Economic and Social Research Institute (ESRI) in 2010 and 2015. In this survey, approximately 2000 works councils of companies with more than 20 employees were interviewed. These surveys provided information on the implementation methods of occupational pension schemes offered in different sectors and of different sizes. Furthermore, far-reaching information was obtained on the composition of the type of financing. That is, whether the employee, the employer, or even both participate in the savings contributions in the form of mixed financing. However, in the case of mixed financing, it is unfortunately not possible to draw any conclusions about the proportionality of the employee and employer contributions. However, in order to estimate the proportionality, the works council's obstruction is used. However, this survey makes it difficult to determine the prevalence of occupational pension provision, as it is not asked about on a continual basis. No survey has yet been carried out following the introduction of the Company Pension Reinforcement Act (BRSG) (Baumann & Blank, 2016).

The survey of the Institute of the German Economy (IGE) also deals with questions on occupational pension provision. Within the framework of this survey, persons with personnel responsibility in 1000–1500 companies have been interviewed up to three times a year since 2010 within the "IW-Personalpanel" on topics of the labor market and personnel policy. The survey refers to companies with at least five employees, which means that no statements can be made about the overall economic situation. In the 2013 and 2017 waves of data collection, information on occupational pension provision was provided on the basis of five questions. These questions were aimed in particular at the implementation methods and the contribution financing of the employers. In the 2017 survey wave, employers were asked about their knowledge of the German Occupational Pensions Strengthening Act (Betriebsrentenstärkungsgesetz—BRSG) and their expectations regarding the possible effects (Pimpertz & Stettes, 2018).

For a better understanding of the declared surveys at the company level, Table 67.3 serves as an illustration.

As part of the literature research, a further 14 studies by insurers and associations were identified that deal specifically with the spread of occupational pension provision in companies of different sizes and corresponding industries. In these studies, employers were mainly asked about the offer of occupational pension provision in the company. These studies are summarised in Table 67.4 according to the survey characteristics, such as target group, number of respondents, and deviation characteristics of the respective study by company size.

67.3 Results of the Available Data Sets

In summary, the data situation on occupational pension provision in Germany is as follows. Of the data sets presented at the individual and household level, the employer and sponsor survey on the distribution of occupational pensions by the

67 What Determines Supply and Demand for Occupational Pension Provision... 1159

Table 67.3 Data sets on occupational pension provision at company level in Germany (own representation)

Date set	Year of survey/rhythm	Client	Sample size and sample
Elc	2008, 2012	Federal Statistical Office	Only companies with 10 or more employees and female employees
VSE	2010, 2014	Federal Statistical Office	2010: Only companies with 10 or more employees
			2014: All establishments
ESRI	2010, 2015	ESRI	2000 works council members; only companies with more than 20 employees and a works council
IGE	Since 2010, up to three times a year	IGE	HR managers in 1000–1500 companies; companies with 5 employees or more

Federal Ministry of Labour and Social Affairs from 2019 is the most up-to-date. However, due to the introduction of the Act to Strengthen Occupational Pensions on 1 January 2018, it is not yet possible to derive any meaningful results from this survey that speak for the spread of occupational pension provision due to the Act to Strengthen Occupational Pensions. In 2023, there will be another employer and sponsor survey on the spread of occupational pension provision. However, no statement can be made about the results at the present time. The OASG study, which will also be conducted in 2019 and again in 2023, does not currently provide any relevant results, as is the case with the employer and sponsor survey. In the case of the other studies mentioned in Table 67.1, it is also not possible to draw any conclusions about the spread of occupational pension provision, as these studies were all carried out before 2018 and thus before the introduction of the Act to Strengthen Occupational Pensions. With the exception of the SOEP study conducted in 2018. However, this study does not provide an answer either, as the period under consideration was too short.

The data sets at the company level, which are summarised in Table 67.3, also do not provide any results on the spread of occupational pensions, as these were also collected before the introduction of the Act to Strengthen Occupational Pensions.

The surveys of insurers and associations shown in Table 67.4 also do not provide any clear results on the spread of occupational pension provision due to the introduction of the Occupational Pensions Strengthening Act, as these were also all conducted before the introduction of the Occupational Pensions Strengthening Act, with the exception of the Gothaer SME study from 2022.

67.4 Methodology

Expert interviews can be used as a method most frequently employed in qualitative empirical research. Expert interviews are used in particular to provide the researcher with an initial overview of the research topic or to further develop scientific problem

Table 67.4 Target groups of the analyzed studies, sorted by ascending years in descending order (own representation based on Wallau et al., 2014. Modified)

Data set	Year of survey	Survey of employer
Gothaer Allgemeine Versicherung AG: Gothaer KMU-Studie 2022 Versicherungen	2022	$N = 1.000$
Zurich Group Germany 2012: Occupational pension schemes—what moves employers	2015	N: 600 BAV managers, 550 of whom were in companies with up to 500 employees. In companies with up to 500 employees; differentiated evaluations according to six employee size categories (1–10, 11–20, 21–50, 51–100, 101–500, 1.000, and more employees)
Generali insurances: Occupational pension schemes in small and medium-sized enterprises 2013	2013	N: 100 HR managers in German medium-sized enterprises with 50 to 500 employees; differentiated. Evaluations according to three employee size classes (50–99, 100–249, and 250–500 employees)
Gothaer Allgemeine Versicherung AG: Gothaer KMU-Studie 2013 Versicherungen	2013	N: 1016 persons responsible in SMEs with up to 500 employees, differentiated evaluations according to four employee size classes (less than 10, 10–19, 20–199, 200–500 employees)
Longial: 14th Handelsblatt Annual Conference – Company Pension Schemes 2013	2013	N: 300 employers and providers of occupational pension schemes
Federal Ministry of Labour and Social Affairs: Situation and development of occupational pension provision in the private and public sectors (BAV 2011) (FB 429)	2012a	N: 3590 employers in the private sector, differentiated evaluations by nine employee size classes (1–4, 5–9, 10–19, 20–49, 50–99, 100–199, 200–499, 500–999, 1.000, and more employees)
Federal Statistical Office: Low Wage and Employment 2010	2012	N: 32,000 companies; differentiated evaluations according to five employee size classes (10–49, 50–249, 250–499, 500–999, 1.000, and more employees)
Federal Statistical Office (2012): Earnings and labour costs 2008	2012	N: 32,000 companies with more than ten employees; differentiated evaluations according to five employee size classes (10–49, 50–249, 250–499, 500–999, and 1.000 employees)
Standard Life Insurance/Personnel Magazine (2011): The company pension scheme in the	2011	N: 251 occupational pension managers, 199 of them with occupational pension offer in their company (9–500 employees), no further differentiation according to company size

(continued)

Table 67.4 (continued)

Data set	Year of survey	Survey of employer
YouGov/Psychonomics: BAVReport 2011, Occupational pension provision from the perspective of employees, entrepreneurs, and brokers	2011	N: 500 SMEs, differentiated evaluations according to five employee size classes (1–10, 11–20, 21–50, 51–100, and 101–500 employees)
Allianz Global Investors: Study on company pension schemes for SMEs – financing pension obligations as a challenge for the future	2010	N: 89 SMEs; no disclosure of the SME definition and no differentiation according to company size classes possible
ERGO Insurance Group: The occupational pension is massively underestimated	2010	N: Approx. 3500 employers with 2 to 499 employees
		Employees, differentiated evaluations according to five employee size classes (2–4, 5–9, 10–19, 20–99, and 100–499 employees)
Rathje: The company pension scheme in SMEs according to the Retirement Assets Act and retirement income	2007	N: 15 companies with 10 to 200 employees
Paffenholz et al.: Occupational pension schemes in the medium	2005	N: 500 companies; differentiated
		Evaluations according to four employee size classes (less than 10, 10–1 9, 20–49, 50, and more employees)

awareness for the matter under investigation. On the basis of the insights gained, they make it possible to formulate hypotheses in relation to the main research object, which can then be empirically tested using quantitative research methods (Bogner et al., 2014). Actors who have special knowledge regarding the field of investigation required by the researcher are called experts. The expert himself does not necessarily represent the research object, but can also function as a kind of medium through which the researcher obtains information about the research object (Gläser & Laudel, 2010). Since the experts have a special knowledge based on experience, which stands for the number of actors in the target group, they can also be seen as a kind of multiplier. In this way, the researcher gains a data basis with regard to a defined target group already in the exploration phase of the study, which in turn enables a clear entry into the field of study (Bogner et al., 2002). The expert interviews were conducted by the author using an interview guide with open questions. The questions were very detailed from the beginning. The concrete questions, including any further questions, were included. The questionnaire was designed in such a way that the interviews could be completed within 30 minutes. The experts were contacted partly in person, via telephone calls, and a cover letter sent by e-mail. In this letter, the explicit object of research and the objective of the

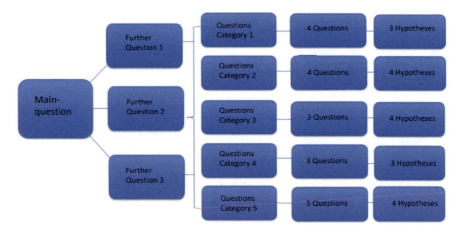

Fig. 67.1 Overview of the derivation of the questions and hypotheses (own representation)

work were explained. After positive feedback, face-to-face as well as telephone and video appointments were arranged by Microsoft teams.

In the context of preparing the interview guide and the main introductory question:

"What determines supply and demand in occupational pension provision in Germany"?

Three further questions were initially derived, which in turn formed the five following question categories with their own questions.

- Category 1 = General level of knowledge.
- Category 2 = Interest in occupational pension provision.
- Category 3 = Motives for and against an occupational pension scheme.
- Category 4 = Communication.
- Category 5 = Effectiveness and suggestions for improvement.

An overview of the derivation of the questions and hypotheses is provided by Fig. 67.1.

A total of 18 hypotheses were formed from the questions in the question categories. Table 67.5 gives an overview of the derivation of the questions and hypotheses.

67.5 Data

With the current status of this chapter as of June 2023, expert interviews were conducted. The interviews lasted for an average of 20 min and were conducted in German. Women accounted for 14.29% of the interviewees and men for 85.71%. The interviewees were between 22 and 63 years old and all were employed. Of

Table 67.5 Hypotheses of the categories (own representation)

Category	Hypotheses
1. General level of knowledge	*H1*: Parts of the persons examined have a moderate basic knowledge of occupational pension provision
	H2: People with moderate basic knowledge view occupational pension provision as skeptical
	H3: People with a certain basic knowledge see occupational pension schemes as a good instrument to provide for old age
2. Interest in occupational pension provision	*H4*: Being male increases the likelihood of taking out an occupational pension plan
	H5: Employers are often not approached by their employees about occupational pension schemes
	H6: Interest in occupational pension provision is low if it is not actively offered by the employer
	H7: The rate of employees with a company pension scheme did not increase after the introduction of the OSPA
3. Motives for and against an occupational pension scheme	*H8*: Employers see it as their duty to offer their employees a company pension scheme
	H9: Most employers fear a pension problem in old age
	H10: Employers with little knowledge of occupational pension schemes, are not convinced by it
	H11: There is a fundamental distrust of occupational pension schemes
4. Communication	*H12*: Employers do not inform sufficiently about the possibilities of a company pension scheme
	H13: In most cases, the information is only provided after the employee has asked for it
	H14: Information on occupational pension schemes is provided by third parties and not directly by the employer
5. Effectiveness and suggestions for improvement	*H15*: The mandatory employer subsidy does not trigger an increase in demand for occupational pensions
	H16: Occupational pension provision is perceived as too complex
	H17: One does not want to acquire a certain basic knowledge due to its complexity
	H18: Mandatory occupational pension provision is seen as critical

these, 71.45% were employed and 28.58% were self-employed. Experts from the insurance, fitness, high-tech, opticians & acoustics, and consumer goods sectors were interviewed, as well as from management consultancy. The selection of experts was not limited to small, medium-sized, or larger companies, but experts from companies employing between 10 and 16,000 workers in Germany were interviewed. However, 28.58% of the interviews were conducted in person and 71.42% via Microsoft Teams with camera.

Table 67.6 Hypothesis testing to explain general knowledge of occupational pensions (own representation)

Research question	Hypothesis	Result
Do persons with management responsibility and senior executives have a certain basic knowledge of occupational pension provision and are therefore convinced of it?	*H1*: Parts of the persons examined have a moderate basic knowledge of occupational pension provision	N
	H2: People with moderate basic knowledge view occupational pension provision as skeptical	Y
	H3: People with a certain basic knowledge see occupational pension schemes as a good instrument to provide for old age	Y

Y = The hypothesis was confirmed
N = No, the hypothesis was not confirmed

67.6 Evaluation and Results

To answer the research question already mentioned, the expert interviews were analyzed qualitatively. The evaluation took place on the basis of the five previously defined categories, which allowed the derived hypotheses to be confirmed or rejected. In addition, the interviews were evaluated by regression analyses.

67.6.1 Factor Influencing Supply and Demand in Occupational Pension Provision in Germany: General Level of Knowledge

The fact that HR managers and other executives have a certain general knowledge about occupational pension schemes and are therefore convinced of them was partly confirmed by the expert interviews conducted. The results of the hypothesis testing to explain general knowledge of occupational pension provision are shown in Table 67.6.

The survey revealed that managers from smaller companies in particular have little basic knowledge about occupational pension schemes. But even a manager from a global corporation had only a very marginal knowledge.

67.6.2 Factor Influencing Supply and Demand in Occupational Pension Provision in Germany: Interest in Occupational Pension Provision

Interest in occupational pension schemes must be aroused by employers. Many employees do not approach their employer on their own initiative and ask about

Table 67.7 Hypothesis testing to explain the interest in occupational pension provision (own representation)

Research question	Hypothesis	Result
How has interest in occupational pension provision changed since the introduction of the Occupational Pensions Strengthening Act?	H4: Being male increases the likelihood of taking out an occupational pension plan	Y
	H5: Employers are often not approached by their employees about occupational pension schemes	Y
	H6: Interest in occupational pension provision is low if it is not actively offered by the employer	N
	H7: The rate of employees with a company pension scheme did not increase after the introduction of OSPA	Y

Y = Yes, the hypothesis was confirmed
N = No, the hypothesis was not confirmed

the possibility of occupational pension provision. The results of the hypothesis tests to explain interest in occupational pension provision are shown in Table 67.7.

Of the experts surveyed, 85.72% were male, all of whom had an occupational pension contract. The female expert herself did not have an occupational pension contract. The experts also stated that they were not often approached by employees about the possibilities of occupational pension provision. The fact that interest in occupational pension provision is low if it is not offered by the employer could be refuted, as the experts interviewed here stated that in principle between less than 20% and 95% of employees were interested in occupational pension provision.

To the question: What percentage of your employees do you think are generally interested in taking out a company pension scheme?

The experts gave the following answers:

> Well, I can only answer that from a distance, because I don't have any direct employees, but I assume that there is an interest of at least 60% to 70% of the employees, even if it is not actually implemented that way. (Expert 1, 2023)

> I would even put it at 95%. (Expert 2, 2023)

> I assume between 30 and 35%, I could imagine in any case. But I also think that many people don't even know that it works like that and that the path exists at all. (Expert 3, 2023)

> I would have to guess. So less than 20%, but not interested in the sense that they don't want to secure tax advantages or anything, but that the inhibition threshold to deal with it is too high. Yes, it's too complicated and they don't give you enough guidance. (Expert 4, 2023)

> I can say pretty accurately. After all workers have been interviewed. It is 30–40%. (Expert 5, 2023)

> Interested? 50%. (Expert 6, 2023)

As things stand, I would say a maximum of 50%. (Expert 7, 2023)

To the question: Do you think that the demand for occupational pension provision in your company has rather increased decreased or remained the same since the introduction of the Company Pension Strengthening Act?

The experts gave the following answers:

In my opinion, some factors have led to an increase in interest. For example, through the increased funding amounts. Unfortunately, however, there has not been much of a surge in demand. (Expert 1, 2023)

It has definitely increased. (Expert 2, 2023)

So, I guess I would imagine it's stayed the same because I joined the company in 2017 and now I've been running the studio since 2021 in that case and since then as I said I haven't heard of it, no one has ever asked about it and before that I wouldn't have heard of anyone being interested in it or anything like that. (Expert 3, 2023)

Remained the same! No one, no one has perceived in any way, in my opinion, that anything has changed. (Expert 4, 2023)

Remains the same. (Expert 5, 2023)
   Remains the same. (Expert 6, 2023)

I think it has remained the same, because I don't think the broad mass of people who work are necessarily familiar with it. (Expert 7, 2023)

The following regression analysis in Fig. 67.2 shows the results of the evaluated expert interviews on the basic interest of employees in occupational pension provision and the percentage of employees who already had occupational pension provision before the introduction of the Act to Strengthen Occupational Pensions.

The regression analysis clearly shows that although according to the experts' statements the interest in taking out an occupational pension is between 20 and 95%, according to the experts' own statements the demand has remained the same in 71.42% of the cases. Two experts stated that the interest in occupational pension provision is higher than people actually own one. Especially, the statement of expert 2 was very interesting. He stated that probably 95% of his employees were interested in a company pension scheme, but only 50% had one.

When asked if the experts could roughly estimate what percentage of their workforce in the company had a company pension scheme after the introduction of the Company Pension Strengthening Act, 71.42% of the experts stated that there had been an increase in the number of employees with a company pension scheme. However, 14.28% of the experts felt that it was not possible to give any information on this and the remaining 14.28% saw no change. The regression analysis in Fig. 67.3 shows the increasing interest in occupational pension provision after the introduction of the Act to Strengthen Occupational Pensions compared to before the introduction of the Act to Strengthen Occupational Pensions.

It can be clearly seen that interest and the associated demand for occupational pension provision has increased between 5% and 40% due to the Company Pension Strengthening Act, according to the experts' statements. Since some experts only

67 What Determines Supply and Demand for Occupational Pension Provision...

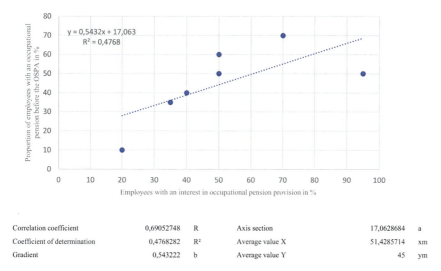

Correlation coefficient	0,69052748	R	Axis section	17,0628684	a
Coefficient of determination	0,4768282	R²	Average value X	51,4285714	xm
Gradient	0,543222	b	Average value Y	45	ym

Fig. 67.2 Results of the basic interest of employees in occupational pension provision and the development of demand before the introduction of the OSPA (own calculations and representation)

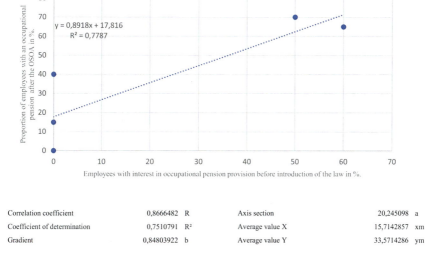

Correlation coefficient	0,8666482	R	Axis section	20,245098	a
Coefficient of determination	0,7510791	R²	Average value X	15,7142857	xm
Gradient	0,84803922	b	Average value Y	33,5714286	ym

Fig. 67.3 Interest in occupational pension provision after the introduction of the Act to Strengthen Occupational Pensions compared to before (own calculations and representation)

gave percentages in response to the question, which refer to after the introduction of the law, and others answered that after the introduction of the law, there was an increase of, e.g., 5%, the value 0 was assumed in this regression in the cases of these answers from before the introduction of the law. The expert who could not give an answer to this question could not be taken into account in the regression analysis.

Table 67.8 Hypothesis testing to explain the motives for and against an occupational pension scheme (own representation)

Research question	Hypothesis	Result
What are the reasons for and against occupational pension provision?	*H8*: Employers see it as their duty to offer their employees a company pension scheme	Y
	H9: Most employers fear a pension problem in old age	N
	H10: Employers with little knowledge of occupational pension schemes, are not convinced by it	Y
	H11: There is a fundamental distrust of occupational pension schemes	N

Y = Yes, the hypothesis was confirmed
N = No, the hypothesis was not confirmed

67.6.3 Factor Influencing Supply and Demand in Occupational Pension Provision in Germany: Motives for and Against an Occupational Pension Scheme

There are reasons for and against a company pension scheme. The results of the hypothesis tests to explain the motives for and against an occupational pension scheme are shown in Table 67.8.

The experts mentioned numerous reasons for and against occupational pension schemes. However, the hypothesis could be confirmed that employers consider it their duty to at least offer pension provision to their employees, even though they are not necessarily concerned about a pension problem in old age. The interviews also revealed that ignorance does not lead to conviction, but neither does it lead to mistrust of occupational pension schemes.

67.6.4 Factor Influencing Supply and Demand in Occupational Pension Provision in Germany: Communication

The company pension scheme is communicated differently in the companies. It does not matter whether the company is small, medium-sized, or even large. The results of the hypothesis tests to explain the to show the channels of communication are shown in Table 67.9.

According to the experts, employers do provide sufficient information about the possibilities of occupational pension schemes, but in most cases only when asked by the employee.

Table 67.9 Hypothesis testing to explain the communication (own representation)

Research question	Hypothesis	Result
How are employees informed about the possibilities of occupational pension provision?	*H12*: Employers do not inform sufficiently about the possibilities of a company pension scheme	N
	H13: In most cases, the information is only provided after the employee has asked for it	Y
	H14: Information on occupational pension schemes is provided by third parties and not directly by the employer	N

Y = Yes, the hypothesis was confirmed
N = No, the hypothesis was not confirmed

Table 67.10 Hypothesis testing to explain the effectiveness and suggestions for improvement (own representation)

Research question	Hypothesis	Result
Occupational pension provision is generally considered to be good, but there is some need for optimization	*H15*: The mandatory employer subsidy does not trigger an increase in demand for occupational pensions	N
	H16: Occupational pension provision is perceived as too complex	N
	H17: One does not want to acquire a certain basic knowledge due to its complexity	N
	H18: Mandatory occupational pension provision is seen as critical	N

Y = Yes, the hypothesis was confirmed
N = No, the hypothesis was not confirmed

67.6.5 Factor Influencing Supply and Demand in Occupational Pension Provision in Germany: Effectiveness and Suggestions for Improvement

Even if the occupational pension scheme is considered good by most experts, the experts still see a certain need for optimization in the design of the occupational pension scheme. The results of the hypothesis tests to explain the effectiveness and suggestions for improvement are shown in Table 67.10.

The experts do not see the mandatory 15% employer contribution as a demand turbo for occupational pension provision. The experts also do not consider the current occupational pension scheme to be too complicated, which is why they would also be willing to acquire a certain basic knowledge. Although it could not be confirmed that occupational pension provision is seen as too complex, there are suggestions for improvement.

67.7 Discussion

In summary, it can be stated that from the current expert survey from 2023 on the question "What determines supply and demand in occupational pension provision in Germany"? of the 18 hypotheses, 10 hypotheses were rejected and 8 hypotheses were confirmed.

When looking at the individual categories asked, it became clear that in the first category "General level of knowledge," not every expert who has a management function or personnel responsibility among the respondents is really familiar with the topic of occupational pensions. In the second category "Interest in occupational pensions," it was found that more male than female experts have a basic interest in occupational pensions. It was also found that employers are mostly not approached by employees about occupational pensions. Despite the fact that employers are not actively approached, the hypothesis that interest in occupational pensions is low if they are not actively offered by the employer could not be confirmed. The regression analysis in Fig. 67.2 showed that interest in occupational pension provision on the part of employees was already present before the introduction of the Occupational Pensions Act. As a result, the experts assume that the share of employees with occupational pension provision has increased since the introduction of the Occupational Pensions Strengthening Act. This assumption was supported by the regression analysis in Fig. 67.3. In the evaluation of the third category "Motives for and against occupational pension provision," it became clear that employers take it for granted to offer their employees an occupational pension provision, although most employers do not assume that their employees will have a pension problem in old age. It also became clear that a lack of knowledge leads to a lack of conviction of employers in favor of occupational pensions, but not to a distrust of occupational pensions. The "communication" about occupational pensions is mostly done by the employers themselves. However, the detailed information is usually only given upon request by the employees. The information is usually given by the employers themselves without using external consultants. This was the result of the assessments of the fourth category. The fifth category, which focused on "effectiveness and suggestions for improvement," produced the following results. It could not be confirmed that the mandatory employer subsidy has not led to an increase in demand for occupational pension provision. Nor is occupational pension provision seen as too complicated, which is why people would be willing to acquire some basic knowledge. The experts would also not necessarily reject mandatory occupational pension provision.

67.8 Conclusion

In summary, the following findings were obtained in the context of this chapter with regard to the in-depth question in the expert interviews conducted in 2023. Not every person responsible for human resources or with managerial responsibility in small, medium, to large corporations is familiar with the topic of occupational pension provision. Despite the lack of knowledge, employers feel responsible for their employees and see it as their duty to offer their employees a company pension. Employers must communicate the issue of occupational pensions more because the interest on the part of the employees is basically given and they must not wait for the demand of the employees. In order to investigate the effect of the Act to Strengthen Occupational Pensions on the dissemination of occupational pensions, I see the following data needs: On the one hand, further expert surveys should be conducted in order to obtain more information on the supply of and demand for occupational pensions in Germany. Secondly, in order to be able to concretely assess the determinants of supply and demand for occupational pension provision in the overall context, further analyses should be conducted on individuals or households. Survey data sets at the individual or household level contain important information on socio-demographic characteristics to estimate the distribution of occupational pension provision in different groups. Thirdly, it is essential to link administrative data and survey data for the evaluation of short- and medium-term effects of the Act to Strengthen Occupational Pensions. These data should at least include: (i) the existence of an occupational pension scheme, (ii) the year of the conclusion of the occupational pension scheme, and (iii) the type of implementation mode. An annual data frequency would be appropriate to identify effects over longer time horizons. Here one could build on the experience of the linked data sets mentioned in Table 67.2. In addition, heterogeneity can be traced by socio-demographic characteristics. From the employers' point of view, a better understanding of the decision-making situation would also be important. For example, the exact study of the implementation of collective agreements would be interesting. An examination of the number and type of contracts offered by employers to their employees would be significant in order to obtain information on how decision-making behavior is influenced. This could be done, for example, in cooperation with a company. In summary, it can be said that the picture of the data situation on occupational pension provision in Germany is very heterogeneous overall. In further reforms of occupational pension provision in Germany, existing data gaps should therefore firstly be closed by recording further variables in existing data sets. In addition, the data situation should be improved by providing administrative data from employers and institutions and linking it to survey data. Finally, researchers should have easier access to existing data sources. Thus, the determinants of supply and demand in occupational pension provision can be estimated and possible socio-political action can be identified in time.

References

Augustin, F. (2019). *Positionspapier zur Reform der staatlich geförderten Altersvorsorge in Deutschland*. CFA Society Germany e.V. Available via DIALOG. https://www.cfa-germany.de/media/03/3d/3a/1669891313/CFASocietyGermany_Positionspapier_Altersvorsorge_2019.pdf. Accessed 30 Mar 2023.

Bäcker, G. (2008). Altersarmut als soziales Problem der Zukunft? In *Deutsche Rentenversicherung*. Available via DIALOG. http://www.sozialpolitik-aktuell.de/files/sozialpolitik-aktuell/_Politikfelder/Alter-Rente/Dokumente/AltersarmutDRV.pdf. Accessed 29 Mar 2023.

Bäcker, G., & Schmitz, J. (2013). Altersarmut und Rentenversicherung: Diagnosen, Trends, Reformoptionen und Wirkungen. In C. Vogel & A. Motel-Klingebiel (Eds.), *Altern im sozialen Wandel: Die Rückkehr der Altersarmut?* (Vol. 23, pp. 24–53). Springer.

Beznoska, M., & Pimpertz, J. (2016). Neue Empirie zur betrieblichen Altersvorsorge Verbreitung besser als ihr Ruf. In *Vierteljahresschrift zur empirischen Wirtschaftsforschung*. Institut der deutschen Wirtschaft Köln. Available via DIALOG. https://www.iwkoeln.de/fileadmin/publikationen/2016/277844/IW-Trends_2016-02-01_Beznoska-Pimpertz.pdf. Accessed 7 Feb 2023.

Bogner, A., Littig, B., & Menz, W. (Eds.). (2002). *Das Experteninterview*. Springer.

Bogner, A., Littig, B., & Menz, W. (Eds.). (2014). *Interviews mit Experten*. Springer.

Bonin, H. (2001). *Will it last? An assessment of the 2001 German pension reform*. IZA – Institute of Labor Economics. Available via DIALOG. https://www.econstor.eu/bitstream/10419/21201/1/dp343.pdf. Accessed 7 Mar 2023.

Börsch-Supan, A. (2022). *SHARE Survey of Health, Ageing and Retirement in Europe*. Mannheim Research Institute for the Economics of Aging. https://doi.org/10.6103/SHARE.w8.800

Börsch-Supan, A., & Wilke, C. B. (2004). *Reforming the German Public Pension System*. Mannheim Research Institute for the Economics of Aging, National Bureau of Economic Research. Available via DIALOG. Microsoft Word – Tokyo-GermanPensionReform-30Aug04.doc (hit-u.ac.jp). Accessed 9 Mar 2023.

Börsch-Supan, A., Brandt, M., Hunkler, C., et al. (2013). Data resource profile: The Survey of Health, Ageing and Retirement in Europe (SHARE). *International Journal of Epidemiology, 42*, 992–1001. https://doi.org/10.1093/ije/dyt088

Börsch-Supan, A., Czaplicki, C., Friedel, S., et al. (2020). SHARE-RV: Linked data to study aging in Germany. *Journal of Economics and Statistics, 240*, 121–132. https://doi.org/10.1515/jbnst-2018-0034

Baumann, H., & Blank, F. (2016). *Die Betriebliche Altersversorgung: Verbreitung und Finanzierung-Ergebnisse der WSI-Betriebsrätebefragung 2015* (No. 30). WSI Report.

Bundesministerium für Arbeit und Soziales. (2016). Ergänzender Bericht der Bundesregierung zum Rentenversicherungsbericht 2016 gemäß § 154 Abs. 2 SGB VI. In: Alterssicherungsbericht 2016. Available via DIALOG. https://www.bmas.de/DE/Service/Presse/Pressemitteilungen/2016/rentenversicherungsbericht-2016.html. Accessed 1 Oct 2022.

Bundesministerium für Arbeit und Soziales. (2020a). Ergänzender Bericht der Bundesregierung zum Rentenversicherungsbericht 2020 gemäß § 154 Abs. 2 SGB VI. In: Alterssicherungsbericht 2020. Available via DIALOG. http://www.sozialpolitik-aktuell.de/files/sozialpolitik-aktuell/_Politikfelder/AlterRente/Dokumente/2020_11_BuReg_Alterssicherungsbericht%202020.pdf. Accessed 5 Oct 2022.

Bundesministerium für Arbeit und Soziales. (2020b). Forschungsbericht 565, Verbreitung der Altersvorsorge 2019 (AV 2019)—Abschlussbericht. Available via DIALOG. https://www.bmas.de/SharedDocs/Downloads/DE/Publikationen/Forschungsberichte/fb-565.pdf?__blob=publicationFile&v=1. Accessed 10 Oct 2022.

Bundesministerium für Arbeit und Soziales. (2020c). Forschungsbericht 565, Verbreitung der Altersvorsorge 2019 (AV 2019)—Methodenbericht. Available via DIALOG. https://www.bmas.de/SharedDocs/Downloads/DE/Publikationen/Forschungsberichte/fb-565-methodenbericht.pdf?__blob=publicationFile&v=3. Accessed 15 Oct 2022.

Bundesministerium für Arbeit und Soziales. (2021). Forschungsbericht 572/Z, Alterssicherung in Deutschland 2019 (ASID 2019)—Zusammenfassender Bericht. Available via DIALOG. https://www.bmas.de/SharedDocs/Downloads/DE/Publikationen/Forschungsberichte/fb-572-alterssicherung-in-deutschland-2019.pdf?__blob=publicationFile&v=2. Accessed 21 Oct 2022.

Coppola, M., & Lamla, B. (2013). Saving and old age provision in germany (save): Design and enhancements. *Journal of Contextual Economics–Schmollers Jahrbuch, 1*, 109–116.

Expert 1. (2023). Transcript interview. The effects on demand behaviour for occupational pensions through the Occupational Strengthening Pensions Act (OSPA). Available via: On request from the author.
Expert 2. (2023). Transcript interview. The effects on demand behaviour for occupational pensions through the Occupational Strengthening Pensions Act (OSPA). Available via: On request from the author.
Expert 3. (2023). Transcript interview. The effects on demand behaviour for occupational pensions through the Occupational Strengthening Pensions Act (OSPA). Available via: On request from the author.
Expert 4. (2023). Transcript interview. The effects on demand behaviour for occupational pensions through the Occupational Strengthening Pensions Act (OSPA). Available via: On request from the author.
Expert 5. (2023). Transcript interview. The effects on demand behaviour for occupational pensions through the Occupational Strengthening Pensions Act (OSPA). Available via: On request from the author.
Expert 6. (2023). Transcript interview. The effects on demand behaviour for occupational pensions through the Occupational Strengthening Pensions Act (OSPA). Available via: On request from the author.
Expert 7. (2023). Transcript interview. The effects on demand behaviour for occupational pensions through the Occupational Strengthening Pensions Act (OSPA). Available via: On request from the author.
F.A.Z.-Institut. (2019). Betriebliche Altersversorgung im Mittelstand 2019. In *Vorsorge und Personalplanung aus der Sicht von bAV-Verantwortlichen*. Generali Deutschland AG. Available via DIALOG. https://umdenken.diebayerische.de/wp-content/uploads/2019/05/Generali_bAV-Studie-2019.pdf. Accessed 28 Jan 2023.
Geyer, J., & Himmelreicher, R. K. (2021). *Charakteristika der Entgeltumwandlung: Wer sorgt in welchem Umfang für das Alter vor?* (No. 1929). DIW Discussion Papers.
Gläser, L., & Laudel, G. (2010). *Experteninterviews und qualitative Inhaltsanalyse als Instrumente rekonstruierender Untersuchungen*. VS Verlag für Sozialwissenschaften.
Goebel, J., & Grabka, M. M. (2011). *Entwicklung der Altersarmut in Deutschland*. Deutsches Institut für Wirtschaftsforschung. Available via DIALOG. https://elibrary.duncker-humblot.com/zeitschriften/id/25/vol/80/iss/1455/art/5508/. Accessed 12 Nov 2022.
Heien, T., & Krämer, M. (2018). Lebensverläufe und Altersvorsorge der Personen der Geburtsjahrgänge 1957 bis 1976 und ihrer Partner. *Forschungsprojekt im Auftrag der Deutschen Rentenversicherung Bund und des Bundesministeriums für Arbeit und Soziales. DRV Schriften, 115*. Available via DIALOG. https://www.researchgate.net/publication/339800433_Lebensverlaufe_und_Altersvorsorge_der_Personen_der_Geburtsjahrgange_1957_bis_1976_und_ihrer_Partner?enrichId=rgreq-32a1566d5cc40e566079f130b5fd7913-XXX&enrichSource=Y292ZXJQYWdlOzMzOTgwMDQzMztBUzo4NjgwMDc1MDUwNTE2ND1AMTU4Mzk2MDUyNDU5Nw%3D%3D&el=1_x_2&_esc=publicationCoverPdf Accessed 08. Oct 2021.
Kiesewetter, D., Grom, M., Menzel, M., et al. (2016). *Optimierungsmöglichkeiten bei den bestehenden steuer- und sozialversicherungsrechtlichen Förderregelungen der betrieblichen Altersversorgung*. Würzburg University Press. Available via DIALOG. https://nbn-resolving.org/urn:nbn:de:bvb:20-opus-128597. Accessed 8 Dec 2022.
Kröger, K., Fachinger, U., & Himmelreicher, R. K. (2011). Empirische Forschungsvorhaben zur Alterssicherung. *Einige kritische Anmerkungen zur aktuellen Datenlage*.
Leiber, S. (2005). *Formen und Verbreitung der betrieblichen Altersvorsorge—Eine Zwischenbilanz*. Wirtschafts- und Sozialwissenschaftliches Institut. Available via DIALOG. https://www.boeckler.de/data/wsimit_2005_06_leiber.pdf. Accessed 12 Dec 2022.
Menzel, M. (2019). *Das Betriebsrentenstärkungsgesetz und seine Auswirkungen auf Geringverdiener: Eine modelltheoretische Analyse*. https://doi.org/10.25972/WUP-978-3-95826-127-3

Pimpertz, J., & Stettes, O. (2018). Neue Impulse für die betriebliche Altersvorsorge? Status-quo-Messung zur Einführung des Betriebsrentenstärkungsgesetzes. *IW-Trends-Vierteljahresschrift zur empirischen Wirtschaftsforschung, 45*(3), 3–19.

Ruprecht, W. (2004). Automatische Entgeltumwandlung in der betrieblichen Altersversorgung: Eine Replik. *Leibniz Information Centre for Economics, 84*(10), 651–656.

Schupp, J. (2009). Twenty-five years of the German Socio-Economic Panel-An infrastructure project for empirical social and economic research in Germany. *Zeitschrift fur Soziologie, 38*(5), 350–357.

Schwark, P. (2019). *Betriebsrenten: Reformen wirken lassen, Nachbesserungen angehen.* Gesamtverband der Deutschen Versicherungswirtschaft e. V. Available via DIALOG. https://www.gdv.de/resource/blob/48272/2348d198658ed3ed8a19c317a04b62e4/altersvororge-kompakt%2D%2D-betriebsrenten%2D%2D-download-data.pdf. Accessed 17 Dec 2022.

Seils, E. (2020). Wiederanstieg der Altersarmut: Eine Kurzauswertung aktueller Daten für 2019 auf Basis des Mikrozensus. *The Institute of Economic and Social Research (WSI), Hans Böckler Foundation, 45*, 2–8.

Statistisches Bundesamt. (2016). *Verdienststrukturerhebung. Erhebung der Struktur der Arbeitsverdienste nach § 4 Verdienststatistikgesetz. VSE 2014 Qualitätsbericht.* Available via DIALOG. https://www.destatis.de/DE/Methoden/Qualitaet/Qualitaetsberichte/Verdienste/verdienststrukturerhebung-2014.pdf?__blob=publicationFile&v=3. Accessed 27 Nov 2021.

Tiefensee, A. (2020). Altersarmut—(k)ein Problem? Aktuelle und zukünftige Entwicklungen in Deutschland. In F. Blank, M. Hofmann, & A. Buntenbach (Eds.), *Neustart in der Rentenpolitik. Analysen und Perspektiven* (1st ed., pp. 157–170). Nomos.

Wallau, F., Gädckens, C., Werner, J., et al. (2014). Machbarkeitsstudie für eine empirische Analyse von Hemmnissen für die Verbreitung der betrieblichen Altersversorgung in kleinen und mittleren Unternehmen (Machbarkeitsstudie BAV in KMU)—Endbericht-. Bundesministerium für Arbeit und Soziales. Available via DIALOG. Machbarkeitsstudie für eine empirische Analyse von Hemmnissen für die Verbreitung der betrieblichen Altersversorgung in kleinen und mittleren Unternehmen (Machbarkeitsstudie BAV in KMU): Endbericht (ssoar.info). Accessed 19 Jan 2023.

Chapter 68
Population Aging: How Much Time Do We Still Have?

Jure Miljevič and Cveto Gregorc

Abstract Most of the developed world today is facing an aging population, and Slovenia is no exception. Moreover, Slovenia is a country with one of the highest average ages of the population in Europe. According to the EUROSTAT forecasts from 2015, the number of inhabitants in Slovenia is projected to decrease absolutely over the next 50 years. This entails altering the relationships that today's population perceives as more or less acceptable socio-economic circumstances in which they fulfill their living and their life needs and aspirations. The cause of these changes—decreasing population growth—occurred many years ago and gradually, which resulted in it not being adequately perceived by society and addressed in a timely manner. The consequences, particularly the structural imbalances in the functioning of society, are challenging to eliminate within a short period of time. Taking a long-term perspective on the demographic transition and its resulting consequences for the structure and functioning of society is crucial. As a result, it becomes necessary to describe social interdependencies in a tangible and quantitative manner, considering the long-term perspective.

Keywords Demographic transition · Population ageing · Age group relationships · Multi-relational platform · GDP · Services for people · Social needs · Employment · Productivity · Long-term debt · Retirement age

68.1 Introduction

Humanity is experiencing constant growth, becoming bigger and younger with each passing moment, although this trend does not apply universally to every continent. This situation differs for the European Union, which has been undergoing an aging process for some time, as well as for Slovenia. In this paper, we summarize the

---

J. Miljevič (✉) · C. Gregorc (✉)
Eintegra MG, Ltd., Ljubljana, Slovenia
e-mail: jure.miljevic@eintegra-mg.si; cveto.gregorc@eintegra-mg.si

© The Author(s), under exclusive license to Springer Nature Switzerland AG 2024
N. Tsounis, A. Vlachvei (eds.), *Applied Economic Research and Trends*, Springer Proceedings in Business and Economics,
https://doi.org/10.1007/978-3-031-49105-4_68

results of a broader survey on the demographic development in Slovenia since 1982 and its long-term trajectory. Alongside examining dynamic year-to-year changes, we also explore shifts in population structure and size, considering factors such as sex and age within each year. The dynamics of changes are mainly conditioned by the number of newborns each year and, to a much lesser extent, by migration from and to the surrounding regions.

Different demographic transitions condition different circumstances for the GDP generation. Assuming the same level of GDP in various potential demographic transitions throughout the projected population forecast in a quantitative model enables the assessment of changing structural conditions concerning GDP generation based on these transitions. With a more detailed breakdown of GDP into stakeholder models, it is possible to observe these aggregate indicators of change in more detail, thereby enhancing the analytical capacity to measure the long-term impacts of potential demographic changes.

The main driver of this change is the vitality of the population across all age groups. The model encompasses three default groups: from birth to entering the labor market at the age of 20, dependents; between 20 and 65 years of age, active population, and after 65 years old, retired population group. Each of these groups plays a distinct role depending on socio-economic characteristics, which directly affects the overall functioning of the entire society. These specificities and the overall performance of society are covered in socio-economic sub-models, which are mutually conditioned but not necessarily balanced. These sub-models differ across each version of demographic development.

The research examines two distinct scenarios of the demographic transition, both quantified by assuming identical socio-economic conditions as those achieved in 2019. To estimate the changed socio-economic efficiency—GDP for a particular year—we used the socio-economic organization and efficiency parameters of the neighboring Republic of Austria instead of the Slovenian parameters used in the demographic transition versions.

The entire model is evaluated on a multi-relational platform,[1] incorporating parameters of population morbidity by age and sex sourced from the state of Florida, as the structure in both states is entirely based on the international classification of diseases.

68.2 Model of Population Aging in Slovenia Until the Year 2078

The aging of the population is defined through a present demographic pyramid. Slovenia's demographic development in the past was characterized by a "baby boom" in the 1960s and 1970s. However, in the 1980s and 1990s, there was a

---

[1] Eintegra_MG® platform.

significant decline in the birth rate. As a result, there is a relatively higher number of residents in the age group between 20 and 65 years, who will gradually transition into the elderly population (over 65 years) in the coming years. Due to the significant decrease in the birth rate, making accurate predictions about the demographic transition becomes risky. The challenges of a shrinking active population and an increase in the elderly population are expected to worsen in the near future.

The motive behind defining the demographic transition as an independent endogenous variable stems from the uncertainty associated with forecasting other interdependent variables of socio-economic development. By selecting the demographic transition as an independent variable, we gain the advantage of observing the effects of individual or group measures on both the demographic scenarios themselves, or on all other interdependent relationships, on the socio-economic relations subordinated to this variable.

68.2.1 Formalization of the Demographic Model

The demographic pyramid undergoes changes over time. The change in the demographic pyramid at time t_i is a function of the demographic pyramid at the previous time t_{i-1}, incorporating the number of newborns at time t_i, subtracted by the number of deaths at time t_i, and further adjusted by the balance of migration during the same period.

$$P(t_i) = \sum_{a=0}^{100} N_F(a, t_i) + \sum_{a=0}^{100} N_M(a, t_i) \tag{68.1}$$

$$P(t_i) = P(t_{i-1}) + B(t_i) - D(t_i) + M(t_i) \tag{68.2}$$

t_i ... current year.
$P(t_i)$ ... population size in year t_i.
$N_F(a, t_i)$ ... size of female population in year t_i who are of age a
$N_M(a, t_i)$ ... size of male population in year t_i who are of age a
$B(t_i)$ ... number of births in year t_i
$D(t_i)$ ... number of deaths in year t_i
$M(t_i)$ ... number of migrations in year t_i

The number of children born in the selected time interval is a function of all potential mothers – women in the childbearing period. The potential birth interval is considered to be the age of girls from 15 years to the biological wall of women at 45 years, and this range remains constant throughout the analyzed period. However, the actual distribution within this interval changes over time due to prevailing societal values or conditions. We assume that societal measures can impact the population's attitudes towards motherhood, resulting in earlier childbirth and an increase in the number of newborns. Nevertheless, these measures themselves are not the focus of this research.

$$B(t_i) = \sum_{a=15}^{45} N_F(a, t_i) \times \overline{b}(a, t_i) \qquad (68.3)$$

$\overline{b}(a, t_i)$ ... probability of birth in year t_i for a woman of age a

The variable of demographic development can be defined using any other forecast that possesses a similarly described structure of the independent variable. This flexibility allows us to apply it in other scenarios of demographic development:

$$P(t_i) = P(t_{i-1}) + \sum_{a=15}^{45} N_F(a, t_i) \times \overline{b}(a, t_i) - D(t_i) + M(t_i) \qquad (68.4)$$

68.3 Demographic Development of Slovenia After 1982

The demographic transition is mainly determined by two natural processes:

- The birth process.
- The process of aging and dying.

Migrations also contribute to the transition, but their contribution is not typical. Migrations are both internal (between regions or municipalities) and external (between countries) and are always included in the models.

68.3.1 Births

In Slovenia, the birth process has changed considerably[2] between 1982 and 2019, both in terms of the number of newborns and its structure. Advances in medicine have expanded the possibilities for a larger proportion of women to become mothers. However, an increasing trend has emerged where women are opting to have only one child. This shift can be attributed to the growth of the standard and the construction of the position of women in society, which pushed the age of mothers at the birth of their first child towards the physiological limit, where the ability to conceive falls sharply. Thus, the peak age of mothers moved from the age of 21 in 1982 to 29 in

---

[2] Teja Drofelnik, Phd, Jure Miljevič, MSc, Cveto Gregorc, MSc, A dynamic forecast of changes in the population according to births and deaths, OMEGAconsult, Ltd., Dec 2020.

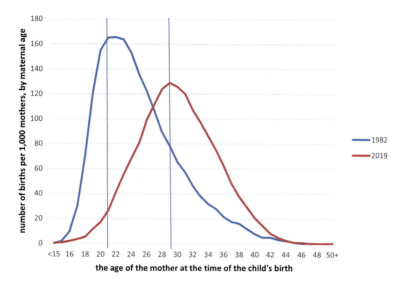

Source: SORS (Statistical Office of the Republic of Slovenia), 2023; own calculation.

Picture 68.1 Number of children born per 1000 mothers by maternal age for the years 1982 and 2019. (Source: SORS (Statistical Office of the Republic of Slovenia), 2023; own calculation)

2019, i.e., by 8 years in just under 40 years. In the last 10 years, the birth rate in Slovenia has stabilized. Therefore, in the base model of changes in the demographic pyramid, we assumed the same change in the endogenous variable throughout the observed period (Picture 68.1).

Based on the statistical results, two demographic scenarios are created, which will be further examined in terms of their societal consequences. The first – basic demographic scenario is characterized by the same – current constant probability distribution of births throughout the observed period. For this probability distribution, the statistics show that it has not changed significantly in the last period. In the second scenario, which aims to maintain the current population number until 2078 (conservation scenario), a measure is assumed to be implemented. This measure is expected to lead to a gradual increase in the number of births, from 19,238 to 20,600, over the observed period.

The results of the two scenarios differ in the number of newborns. In the first scenario, despite the constant probability distribution of births, the general trend of decreasing newborns continues and falls below 17,000 per year at the end of the observed period. In the second scenario, however, the trend reverses and starts to rise above 20,000 per year (Picture 68.2).

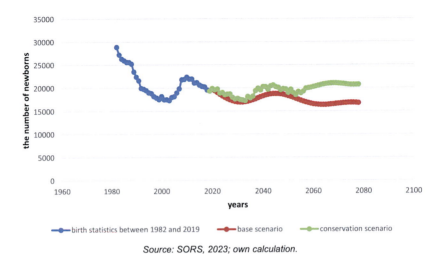

Picture 68.2 Number of newborns according to the first and second scenarios by year. (Source: SORS, 2023; own calculation)

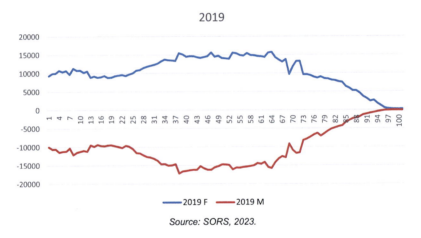

Picture 68.3 Demographic pyramid of Slovenia for 2019. (Source: SORS, 2023)

68.3.2 The Demographic Pyramid

Both scenarios share the same probability distribution of mortality by age and gender, as well as the same migration dynamics, which, as previously mentioned, have a limited impact on the overall outcome. The ultimate result is the formation of an age pyramid representing the country's population (Picture 68.3).

The blue curve represents the female population, while the red the male population. Both curves exhibit a higher number of inhabitants (around 15,000 people per year) between the ages of 40 and 65. These individuals were born between

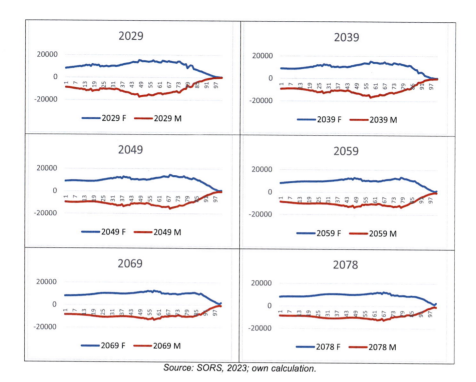

Picture 68.4 The course of the demographic transition in 10-year intervals, base scenario. (Source: SORS, 2023; own calculation)

1955 and 1980. For the population under 40 s, a gradual decline in births can be observed, with the number of people decreasing in each successive generation, with the total number settling at 20,000 people per generation. In the case of the elderly population, the longer life expectancy of women is evident, as the male curve approaches zero at an earlier age.

In the upcoming 25 years, the demographic pyramid in Slovenia will flatten out. The population group aged between 40 and 65 will gradually transition into the elderly population over 65 during this period. Advances in medicine and a generally higher standard will allow these people to live longer compared to previous generations. Stagnation of births at approximately 20,000 newborns per year will lead to an unfavorable change in the relationship between social needs and available resources in the future (Picture 68.4).

In the initial year of 2019, Slovenia had a population of 2,071,804 inhabitants. However, according to the base scenario, by the target year of 2078, this number is projected to decrease to 1,840,672 individuals due to the stagnation of births. In the conservation scenario, which assumes an increase in the number of births, the population is estimated to reach 1,969,875 by the same target year (Pictures 68.5, 68.6 and 68.7 and Table 68.1).

Picture 68.5 Age structure change by years—base scenario. (Source: SORS, 2023; own calculation)

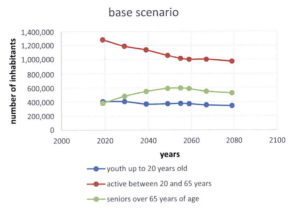

Source: SORS, 2023; own calculation.

Picture 68.6 Age structure change by years—conservation scenario. (Source: SORS, 2023; own calculation)

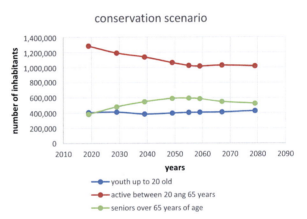

Source: SORS, 2023; own calculation.

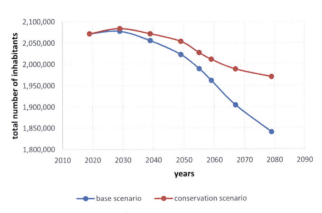

Source: SORS, 2023; own calculation.

Picture 68.7 Change in total population by year—both demographic scenarios. (Source: SORS, 2023; own calculation)

Table 68.1 The course of the demographic transition in time intervals

	Base scenario				Conservation scenario			
	Youth up to 20 years old	Active between 20 and 65 years	Seniors over 65 years of age	Total	Youth up to 20 years old	Active between 20 and 65 years	Seniors over 65 years of age	Total
2019	405,759	1,283,055	382,989	2,071,804	405,759	1,283,055	382,989	2,071,804
2029	405,723	1,191,332	480,402	2,077,458	411,996	1,191,332	480,402	2,083,730
2039	369,579	1,138,174	547,756	2,055,509	385,514	1,138,174	547,756	2,071,444
2049	373,673	1,057,636	591,429	2,022,738	398,091	1,063,892	591,429	2,053,411
2055	377,674	1,015,732	595,636	1,989,042	405,884	1,025,589	595,636	2,027,109
2059	373,453	1,001,056	586,910	1,961,419	407,485	1,016,940	586,910	2,011,335
2067	354,781	1,000,618	548,655	1,904,054	410,773	1,028,659	548,655	1,988,087
2079	343,817	972,798	524,057	1,840,672	426,827	1,018,991	524,057	1,969,875

Source: SORS, 2023; own calculation

68.3.3 3D Display of Demographic Model Result (Pictures 68.8, 68.9, 68.10 and 68.11)

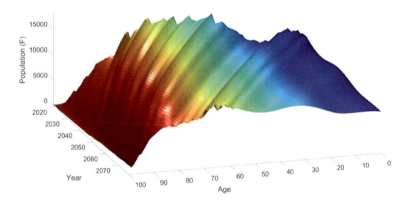

Picture 68.8 3D model of demographic transition, base scenario, women. (Source: SORS, 2023; own calculation)

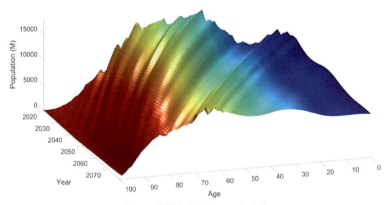

Picture 68.9 3D model of demographic transition, base scenario, men. (Source: SORS, 2023; own calculation)

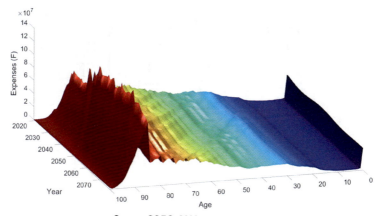

Picture 68.10 3D model of healthcare costs, base scenario, women. (Source: SORS, 2023; own calculation)

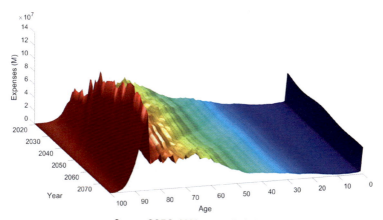

Picture 68.11 3D model of healthcare costs, base scenario, men. (Source: SORS, 2023; own calculation)

68.3.4 Influence of the Demographic Transition on the Spatial Distribution of the Population

The total population under the base scenario shows a significant difference at the aggregate level compared to the conservation scenario. An even bigger difference emerges when we look at the distribution of the population across geographical

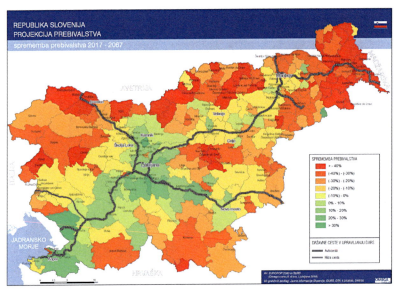

Source: EUROSTAT 2021, SORS, 2021; own calculation.

Picture 68.12 Change in the spatial distribution of the population by municipalities from 2017 to 2067. (Source: EUROSTAT 2021, SORS, 2021; own calculation)

areas. In the paper,[3] the impact of demographic changes was shown in the areas—by statistical regions and municipalities, where the problem of structural disparities is getting worse. In the paper, this dimension is shown for the overall population and the age group of individuals aged 65 years and above. The analysis is based on the population trends forecast for Slovenia according to EUROSTAT 2015.

A closer examination of the spatial distribution reveals a trend of population preservation or even growth in areas surrounding highway intersections, accompanied by an aging population. On the other hand, other regions are experiencing both population aging and a decline in population size. Notably, the number of elderly residents aged 65 and above is also on the rise along the motorway corridors (Pictures 68.12 and 68.13).

The social sectors of healthcare, elderly care, and the increase in the mass for pensions are directly a function of the characteristics of the population in the demographic transition. They exhibit the same temporal characteristics—dynamics as the demographic transition. However, these characteristics reflect differently across various age groups within the population, leading to dynamic changes in the relationships between different age groups over time.

---

[3] A different view of regional development on the example of the demand for medical care specialties in the light of demographic changes; J.Miljevič et al.; Regional development yesterday, today tomorrow; Založba ZRCM Ljubljana 2021.

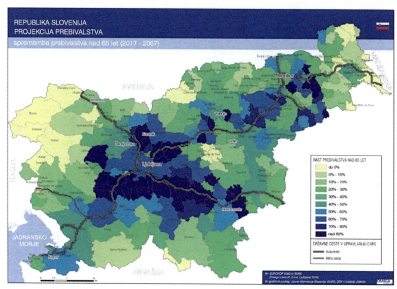

Source: EUROSTAT 2021, SORS, 2021; own calculation.

Picture 68.13 Changes in the spatial distribution of the elderly by the municipality from 2017 to 2067. (Source: EUROSTAT 2021, SORS, 2021; own calculation)

68.4 Employment

Population employment in the model is defined as the second age group, comprising individuals between the ages of 20 and 65. The first and third groups consist of Slovenia's population before entering the labor market (up to the age of 20) and those over the age of 65. The second group, known as the active residents, comprises individuals qualified to provide services—services for people (quaternary) and engage in business activities in society (primary, secondary, and tertiary). The combined number of employees from both groups corresponds to the total active population and is influenced by the scope and dynamics of the overall demographic transition. In the base year of 2019, there were 901,537 employees in Slovenia.

$$E(t_i) = \sum_{EA} E(t_i, EA) + E_H(t_i) + E_{ss}(t_i) + E_E(t_i) = \sum_{a=20}^{65} (N_F(a, t_i) + N_M(a, t_i)) \tag{68.5}$$

$$E(t_i, EA) = E(t_0, EA) \times \frac{(E(t_i) - E_H(t_i) - E_{ss}(t_i) - E_E(t_i))}{(E(t_0) - E_H(t_0) - E_{ss}(t_0) - E_E(t_0))} \tag{68.6}$$

EA ... economic activities except healthcare, social services and education

Table 68.2 Number of employees according to both demographic scenarios by year

	Base scenario			Conservation scenario		
	Employed	Business	Services for people	Employed	Business	Services for people
2019	901.537	678.732	222.805	901.537	678.732	222.805
2029	837.088	612.909	224.178	837.088	612.184	224.904
2039	799.736	581.754	217.983	799.736	579.257	220.479
2049	743.146	530.066	213.080	747.542	529.864	217.678
2055	713.703	502.904	210.799	720.628	503.632	216.997
2059	703.391	494.183	209.207	714.551	498.025	216.526
2067	703.083	498.313	204.770	722.786	506.850	215.936
2078	683.535	487.475	196.060	715.993	500.684	215.309

Source: SORS, 2023; own calculation

$E(t_i)$ ... employed population in year t_i as a function of independent variable (population in demographic transition)

$E(t_i, EA)$ ... number of employees in EA in year t_i

The structure of the second age group of the population is conditioned by the size and dynamics of the other two groups. In the field of healthcare, which impacts the overall vitality of the entire population, for example, employees in this sector cater to the entire population. In the case of education, which plays a crucial role in the development of society, their activities encompass pre-school education, primary, secondary, and higher education, adult education, and research. In short, the education sector plays a critical role in equipping the population with the necessary skills and knowledge for their active age, addressing the challenges posed by demographic development for society as a whole.

Based on these starting points, an employment model was created for the observed period between 2019 and 2078. The model assumes that the employment structure by activity remains constant, with only the number of employed individuals changes based on a function of the available number of the active population. However, there are a few exceptions to this assumption:

- Healthcare sector: The number of employees follows the expected incidence of disease as a function of population aging.
- Social sector: The number of employees follows the number of elderly residents aged 65 and above.
- Education sector: The number of employees is associated with the dynamics of the youth population under 20 years of age (Table 68.2).

The demographic transition, or the changing dynamics of transition, directly influences the shifting needs of the population, which is reflected in the ratio between employees in service-related sectors and employees in the business sector. This impact can be observed both in terms of the overall volume and the structural composition of employees in the business sector.

A health sub-model was developed to manage the aforementioned consequences of the demographic transition. In addition, the social needs perspective was also presented.

68.4.1 The Healthcare Sub-model

The basis for the health sub-model is the database of recorded health episodes in the US state of Florida[4] in 2020. This state has approximately 10 times the population of Slovenia. Episodes are classified by patient age, gender, and diagnosis using the International Classification of Diseases (ICD-10). The data includes information on the duration of treatment (from admission to discharge) and the value of measures/interventions during the course of treatment for each patient.

The model describes the societal activity dedicated to ensuring the well-being and vitality of the entire population. It is part of the services for people,[5] specifically focused on managing the population's health through the healthcare system, including healthcare facilities and personnel. Through various forms of health insurance, resources are provided to cover the operation of this activity, and in this respect, it is also a part of the generated GDP. Demand is defined by the following:

- The age and gender structure of the population.
- Incidence of a disease classified by ICD-10 according to the WHO, which represents the probability that an individual of a certain age and gender will suffer from this specific disease or what is the proportion of individual groups of the population as an element of the population structure of the entire population at a given moment in the same age group susceptible to a certain disease according to the share of this disease in relation to all other diseases for this population element. Such is the probability that a representative of a certain population element will fall ill with this disease in a specific population.

$$\overline{noe}_F(a, \text{ICD}) = \frac{noe_F^{Fl}(a, \text{ICD})}{N_F^{Fl}(a)}; \quad \overline{noe}_M(a, \text{ICD}) = \frac{noe_M^{Fl}(a, \text{ICD})}{N_M^{Fl}(a)} \quad (68.7)$$

$$NoE(t_i) = \sum_{a=0}^{100} \sum_{\text{ICD}} N_F(a, t_i) \times \overline{noe}_F(a, \text{ICD}) + \sum_{a=0}^{100} \sum_{\text{ICD}} N_M(a, t_i) \times \overline{noe}_M(a, \text{ICD})$$

$$(68.8)$$

---

[4] Florida, State Inpatient Database (SID), State Ambulatory Surgery and Services Database (SASD), State Emergency Department Database (SEDD), Healthcare Cost and Utilization Project (HUCP), Agency for Healthcare Research and Quality, 2020.

[5] Alan J. Horowitz, "Lowry-Type Land Use Models", Handbooks in Transportation Planning, No 5, Transport Geography and Spatial Systems, 2004, pp. 167–182.

ICD ... International classification of a disease
$\overline{noe}_F(a, \text{ICD})$ ... probability of a disease ICD-10 for age a, women
$\overline{noe}_M(a, \text{ICD})$ ... probability of a disease ICD-10 for age a, men
$noe_F^{Fl}(a, \text{ICD})$ ... number of episodes by ICD-10 for age a, women in Florida
$N_F^{Fl}(a)$ ... size of female population of age a in Florida
$NoE(t_i)$ ... number of episodes in year t_i
$N_F(a, t_i)$ ... size of female population in year t_i who are of age a
$N_M(a, t_i)$ ... size of male population in year t_i who are of age a

On the side of health service providers, the database also contains information on the time spent by staff and the costs of utilizing various medical devices, infrastructure, and medications that were used to perform a treatment measure—an episode—from the beginning to the end of the treatment of a specific disease.

$$\overline{th}_F(a, \text{ICD}) = \frac{th_F^{Fl}(a, \text{ICD})}{N_F^{Fl}(a)}; \quad \overline{th}_M(a, \text{ICD}) = \frac{th_M^{Fl}(a, \text{ICD})}{N_M^{Fl}(a)} \quad (68.9)$$

$$\overline{ch}_F(a, \text{ICD}) = \frac{ch_F^{Fl}(a, \text{ICD})}{N_F^{Fl}(a)}; \quad \overline{ch}_M(a, \text{ICD}) = \frac{ch_M^{Fl}(a, \text{ICD})}{N_M^{Fl}(a)} \quad (68.10)$$

$$TH(t_i) = \sum_{a=0}^{100}\sum_{\text{ICD}} N_F(a, t_i) \times \overline{th}_F(a, \text{ICD}) + \sum_{a=0}^{100}\sum_{\text{ICD}} N_M(a, t_i) \times \overline{th}_M(a, \text{ICD})$$
$$(68.11)$$

$$CH(t_i) = \sum_{a=0}^{100}\sum_{\text{ICD}} N_F(a, t_i) \times \overline{ch}_F(a, \text{ICD}) + \sum_{a=0}^{100}\sum_{\text{ICD}} N_M(a, t_i) \times \overline{ch}_M(a, \text{ICD})$$
$$(68.12)$$

$TH(t_i)$ ... accumulated durations of episodes in year t_i
$CH(t_i)$ ... accumulated costs of episodes in year t_i
$N_F(a, t_i)$ ... size of female population in year t_i who are of age a
$N_M(a, t_i)$ ... size of male population in year t_i who are of age a

The results of the sub-model are used to estimate the following:

- The required number of healthcare employees based on the total treatment time of all patients.
- The necessary amount of resources in healthcare based on the total value of the measures/interventions.

As an example of the impact of demographic transition on both age and spatial structure, we present the morbidity for the Neoplasm diagnosis group in the Ljubljana urban region. Due to demographic changes, an increase in the number

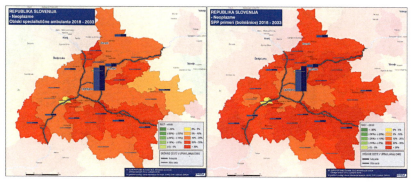

Source: NIPH (The National Institute of Public Health) 2021, SORS, 2021; own calculation.

Picture 68.14 Change in needs at the specialist (left) and hospital level (right) for the Neoplasm diagnosis group in the Ljubljana urban region. (Source: NIPH (The National Institute of Public Health) 2021, SORS, 2021; own calculation)

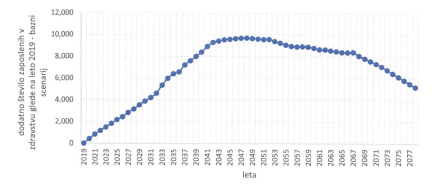

Source: SORS, 2023; own calculation.

Picture 68.15 Additional required employees in healthcare based on the base year 2019. (Source: SORS, 2023; own calculation)

of cases for both specialist examinations and hospitalizations is anticipated in the next 15 years (Picture 68.14).

The organization of primary healthcare, particularly through health centers, was established based on the present needs of the population, which is also reflected in the employees and their qualifications.

The changing conditions in the demographic transition will have an impact on both the quantity and specialization of healthcare sector employees in the future, as a result of changes in the local demand for health services. The number of healthcare employees is considered at the national level in Slovenia, and the spatial organization or changes in the number of employees due to aging and concurrent spatial shifts in demand are not covered (Picture 68.15 and Table 68.3).

Table 68.3 Required number of employees in healthcare

	Base scenario	Conservation scenario
2019	45.468	45.468
2029	49.005	49.085
2039	53.472	53.698
2049	55.126	55.419
2055	54.541	54.958
2059	54.350	55.068
2067	53.863	54.895
2078	50.646	52.036

Source: HCUP 2020, SORS, 2023; own calculation

$$E_H(t_i) = E_H(t_0) \times \frac{TH(t_i)}{TH(t_0)} \quad (68.13)$$

$E_H(t_i)$ ... number of healthcare employees in year t_i
$TH(t_i)$ ... accumulated durations of episodes in year t_i

The curve of additional needs for employees in healthcare reaches its peak in 2048, when 9700 additional employees will be needed compared to the base year of 2019.

68.4.2 Social Aspect

In the base year of 2019, employees in social activities accounted for 2.2% of all employees in Slovenia, totaling 20,106 individuals. The majority of these employees were working in daycare centers and centers for social work, while a smaller portion was engaged in the field of long-term care for elderly residents.

The demand for employees in long-term care is increasing with the increasing population of elderly residents in Slovenia aged 65 and above. Consequently, the need for these employees is on the rise, with the peak demand projected to occur in 2053, when almost 4300 employees are additionally needed (Table 68.4).

$$E_{SS}(t_i) = E_{SS}(t_0) \times \frac{\sum_{a=66}^{100}(N_F(a,t_i) + N_M(a,t_i))}{\sum_{a=66}^{100}(N_F(a,t_0) + N_M(a,t_0))} \quad (68.14)$$

$E_{ss}(t_i)$ ... number of social services workers in year t_i
$N_F(a,t_i)$ ... size of female population in year t_i who are of age a
$N_M(a,t_i)$ ... size of male population in year t_i who are of age a

The same applies to employees in education (Picture 68.16).

Table 68.4 Employees in homes for the elderly and labor protection centers and centers for social work, by years

	Base scenario			Conservation scenario		
	DSO[a]	DVC in CSD[b]	Total	DSO	DVC in CSD	Total
2019	7.625	12.481	20.106	7.625	12.481	20.106
2029	9.549	12.476	22.025	9.565	12.553	22.117
2039	10.859	12.472	23.332	10.906	12.479	23.384
2049	11.790	12.463	24.252	11.775	12.370	24.145
2055	11.896	12.453	24.349	11.859	12.211	24.071
2059	11.676	12.450	24.125	11.685	12.116	23.802
2067	10.945	12.454	23.399	10.924	11.976	22.900
2078	10.466	12.474	22.940	10.434	11.867	22.301

Source: SORS, 2023; own calculation
[a]DSO—retirement home
[b]DVC in CSD—day care center and social work center

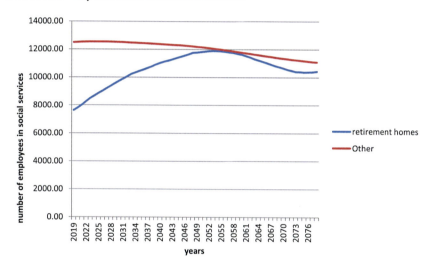

Source: SORS, 2023; own calculation.

Picture 68.16 Additional necessary employees in social security based on the starting year 2019. (Source: SORS, 2023; own calculation)

$$E_E(t_i) = E_E(t_0) \times \frac{\sum_{a=0}^{19}(N_F(a, t_i) + N_M(a, t_i))}{\sum_{a=0}^{19}(N_F(a, t_0) + N_M(a, t_0))} \qquad (68.15)$$

$E_E(t_i)$ ... number of employees in education in year t_i
$N_F(a, t_i)$ ... size of female population in year t_i who are of age a
$N_M(a, t_i)$ ... size of male population in year t_i who are of age a

68.5 Domestic Product

68.5.1 Formalization of the Model

According to the EUROSTAT forecasts from 2015, the number of inhabitants in Slovenia is projected to decrease absolutely over the next 50 years.

In the fourth chapter, the required number of employees in the health, social care, and education sectors was defined. It was assumed that, from the available quota of the active population, the necessary employees in the listed sectors will first be added, and the rest of the available employees will be distributed proportionally according to the ratios in the starting year. By accounting for the changing needs in healthcare, social care, and education through the number of employees in these sectors, and assuming a constant density of GDP per employee applies, the change in productivity in these industries remains the same as the productivity in the base year.

$$\text{prod}_{sfp}(t_i) = 1 \qquad (68.16)$$

The independent variable is therefore the dynamics of the demographic transition and the extent of the social product to ensure the already achieved standard expressed by the GDP.

The basic assumption for the calculation of GDP in year t_i is the equality of socio-economic conditions and efficiency for any category of economic activity as it was achieved in the base year 2019—the same value of produced GDP per employee in a certain industry. The same applies when considering GDP in terms of expenditure – the same specific consumption per capita for each category of expenditure per unit of population as was achieved in the base year 2019. The same applies to all taxes and duties which are intended for public consumption (costs of the healthcare system, pensions, state investments, etc.). In this macro-model, we assume the balance of foreign trade, which means that the impact of imports and exports is considered neutral.

The aggregate GDP defines the amount of products necessary to sustain the current socio-economic conditions. However, the demographic transition and the resulting aging of society will lead to changes in the composition of social groups, including young people (up to 19 years old), the active population (20 to 65 years old), and seniors (over 65 years old). These demographic changes have specific impacts on various sectors, such as healthcare and social care, which are expressed in specific sub-models described in previous chapters. In the following, the effects under the models are monetized in the form of GDP.

We have divided the GDP into GDP generated by services for people (quaternary) and GDP generated by economic activities for the economy (primary, secondary, and tertiary).

$$\text{GDP}(t_i) = \text{GDP}_{sfp}(t_i) + \text{GDP}_{sfb}(t_i) \tag{68.17}$$

$\text{GDP}_{sfp}(t_i)$ ... GDP generated by services for people in year t_i
$\text{GDP}_{sfb}(t_i)$ ... GDP generated by services for business in year t_i

$$\text{GDP}_{sfp}(t_i) = \text{GDP}_H(t_i) + \text{GDP}_E(t_i) + \text{GDP}_{SS}(t_i) + \text{GDP}_{OTH}(t_i) \tag{68.18}$$

$\text{GDP}_H(t_i)$ ... GDP generated by healthcare in year t_i
$\text{GDP}_E(t_i)$ ... GDP generated by education in year t_i
$\text{GDP}_{SS}(t_i)$ ... GDP generated by social services in year t_i
$\text{GDP}_{OTH}(t_i)$ ... GDP generated by culture, defense, security, public services, and others in year t_i

$$\text{GDP}_H(t_i) = CH(t_i) + E_H(t_i) \frac{\text{GDP}_H^W(t_0)}{E_H(t_0)} \tag{68.19}$$

$CH(t_i)$ ... accumulated costs of episodes in year t_i
$E_H(t_i)$ ... number of healthcare employees in year t_i
$\text{GDP}_H^W(t_0)$ ... GDP generated by healthcare employees in year t_i

$$\text{GDP}_E(t_i) = E_E(t_i) \frac{\text{GDP}_E(t_0)}{E_E(t_0)} \tag{68.20}$$

$E_E(t_i)$ ... number of employees in education in year t_i

$$\text{GDP}_{SS}(t_i) = E_{SS}(t_i) \frac{\text{GDP}_{SS}(t_0)}{E_S(t_0)} \tag{68.21}$$

$E_{ss}(t_i)$ ... number of social services workers in year t_i

$$\text{GDP}_{OTH}(t_i) = \sum_A E_A(t_i) \frac{\text{GDP}_A(t_0)}{E_A(t_0)} \tag{68.22}$$

A ... activities of culture, defense, security, public services, and others
$E_A(t_i)$ ... number of employees in activity A in year t_i

In Eq. (68.17), GDP_{sfb} is expressed as follows:

$$\text{GDP}_{sfb}(t_i) = \text{GDP}(t_i) - \text{GDP}_{sfp}(t_i) \tag{68.23}$$

The general expression in Eq. (68.23) can be written in a way that expresses the condition of maintaining the specific GDP per employee in an individual economic activity, namely[6]:

$$\text{GDP}_{sfb}(t_i) = \sum_{EA_{sfb}} E_{EA_{sfb}}(t_i) \frac{\text{GDP}_{EA_{sfb}}(t_0)}{E_{EA_{sfb}}(t_0)} = \text{gdp}_{sfb}(t_0) \quad (68.24)$$

$$\times \left(E_{sfb}^{AV}(t_i) + E_{sfb}^{R}(t_i) \right)$$

$$\text{gdp}_{sfb}(t_0) = \frac{\text{GDP}_{sfb}(t_0)}{E_{sfb}(t_0)} \quad (68.25)$$

$\text{GDP}_{sfb}(t_i)$ ... GDP of services for business in year t_i
$E_{sfb}(t_i)$ ... employees in services for business in year t_i
$E_{sfb}^{AV}(t_i)$ ... available employees in services for business in year t_i
$E_{sfb}^{R}(t_i)$ ... required employees in services for business in year t_i

$$\text{gdp}_{sfP}(t_0) = \frac{\text{GDP}_H(t_0) + \text{GDP}_E(t_0) + \text{GDP}_{SS}(t_0) + \text{GDP}_{OTH}(t_0)}{E_{sfP}(t_0)}$$
$$(68.26)$$

$$E_{sfp}(t_0) = \sum_{OTH} E_{OTH}(t_0) + E_H(t_0) + E_{ss}(t_0) + E_E(t_0) \quad (68.27)$$

$$E_{sfb}^{AV}(t_i) + E_{sfb}^{R}(t_i) = E(t_i) - E_{sfp}(t_i) \quad (68.28)$$

$$E_{sfp}(t_i) = E_{sfp}(t_0) \times \frac{\text{GDP}_{sfp}(t_i)}{\text{GDP}_{sfp}(t_0)} \quad (68.29)$$

$$E_{sfb}(t_i) = E_{sfb}^{AV}(t_i) + E_{sfb}^{R}(t_i) \quad (68.30)$$

Equation (68.30) in the model ensures the balance between the needs of the population and the social product, when changing the independent variable—the structure and size of the population in accordance with the expected demographic transition (necessary condition—responsiveness to demography) and subject to the ceteris paribus limitation of all subordinate variables, which today's population perceives as more or less acceptable socio-economic circumstances in which they fulfill their life needs and aspirations.

---

[6] $E_{sfb}^{R}(t_i) <> 0$; in amount of exogenous workers if available.

68.5.2 Quantification of Demographic Scenarios

The interdependence of GDP and the demographic transition is indirect. It is connected through an active population that generates GDP. Interdependence is reflected in the ratio between the number of employees in services for people and those working in the business activities.

Each of the two groups (services for people and business) has its own function in socioeconomic reproduction and each of them has specific limitations. If the first group is characterized by the ability to ensure the greatest possible vitality and performance of the population as a whole, the second group is the one that ensures the material side of this society, i.e., the GDP from which all the needs of society are met, including the repayment of the state's overdue debts. The aging population is already changing the numerical ratios between the first and the second group and those over 65, whose needs increase more intensively with aging.

We calculated the long-term changes in GDP for two versions of the demographic transition: the base scenario and the conservation scenario. In the conservation scenario, we further analyzed an additional assumption regarding performance, specifically considering the performance level currently observed in neighboring Austria, while keeping all other socio-economic conditions unchanged.

In addition to value-added, social revenue also includes taxes on the turnover of goods and services, excise duties, and other taxes on production, while subsidies to the economy are subtracted. The densities of individual categories in relation to the achieved added value and the volumes of the relevant age demographic groups were used below to estimate the tax component of GDP (Table 68.5).

Social consumption consists of the state budget and the pension and health fund. In addition to employees and economic entities, the state also contributes partially to both funds from the annual budget. To avoid potential double counting of expenses, the budget was reduced for these components.

Table 68.5 GDP and available resources for social services, by years (in millions of EUR)

	Base scenario		Conservation scenario		Organization and performance of the Republic of Austria	
	GDP	Resources for services for people	GDP	Resources for services for people	GDP	Resources for services for people
2019	48.499,8	19.136,0	48.499,8	19.136,0	96.281,7	39.177,8
2029	43.828,3	16.733,3	44.540,1	17.028,2	88.417,9	34.915,4
2039	41.537,4	15.478,3	42.455,0	15.872,9	84.278,9	32.584,5
2049	39.174,2	14.059,0	39.417,8	14.269,5	78.250,0	29.344,0
2055	38.144,6	13.370,1	37.788,2	13.401,0	75.016,6	27.590,7
2059	37.753,9	13.077,9	37.412,3	13.178,4	74.271,6	27.143,7
2067	37.286,3	12.753,4	37.868,7	13.337,6	75.179,8	27.474,0
2078	35.849,3	11.948,2	37.423,8	13.079,0	74.298,0	26.954,4

Source: SORS, 2023; own calculation

The same applies to the education and sports segment. This is fully covered by the state budget, so this cost component was subsequently excluded from the budget (Table 68.6).

Consumption consists of:

- Health fund.
- Pension fund.
- Costs of education and sports.
- National budget with the above components excluded.

The basic assumption in the model of the demographic transition or the aging of the population assumed that:

> all relationships are maintained, which today the population perceives as more or less acceptable socio-economic circumstances in which they realize their living and their life needs and aspirations.

Compared to the base year, in both demographic scenarios, the resources created to cover the obligations arising from the increased needs of the demographic transition are insufficient.

In other words, it is not possible to meet the growing needs associated with population aging using the current level of efficiency and the efforts of the active population to generate GDP, especially considering the declining number of employees in the economy. Achieving a balance between needs and capabilities requires an increase in productivity.

68.6 Scenario Evaluation

In the formalization of the model, we expressed the fundamental interdependence of the target condition of maintaining the standard in socio-economic relations as achieved in the base year and the endogenously derived independent variables in relation to the demographic pyramid encountered.[7]

$$E_{sfb}(t_i) = E_{sfb}^{AV}(t_i) + E_{sfb}^{R}(t_i) \qquad (68.31)$$

$E_{sfb}^{AV}(t_i)$ ... available employees in services for business in year t_i
$E_{sfb}^{R}(t_i)$ ... required employees in services for business in year t_i
$E_{sfb}(t_i)$ ... employees in services for business in year t_i

Equation (68.31) represents the requirements for employees in economic activities to achieve the current level of productivity. However, the demographic transition

---

[7] No exogenous workers are assumed; $E_{sfb}^{R}(t_i) = 0$.

Table 68.6 Resources, social needs, and surplus/deficit, by year (in million EUR)

	Base scenario			Conservation scenario			Organization and performance of the Republic of Austria		
	Resources	Needs	Surplus/deficit	Resources	Needs	Surplus/deficit	Resources	Needs	Surplus/deficit
2019	19.136,0	18.734,4	401,6	19.136,0	18.734,4	401,6	39.177,8	18.734,4	20.443,4
2029	16.733,3	20.554,2	−3.820,9	17.028,2	20.579,3	−3.551,1	34.915,4	20.579,3	14.336,0
2039	15.478,3	21.531,9	−6.053,6	15.872,9	21.596,8	−5.723,9	32.584,5	21.596,8	10.987,7
2049	14.059,0	22.057,8	−7.998,8	14.269,5	22.179,9	−7.910,4	29.344,0	22.179,9	7.164,0
2055	13.370,1	21.976,6	−8.606,5	13.401,0	22.132,6	−8.731,6	27.590,7	22.132,6	5.458,0
2059	13.077,9	21.733,6	−8.655,7	13.178,4	21.946,6	−8.768,2	27.143,7	21.946,6	5.197,1
2067	12.753,4	20.840,3	−8.086,8	13.337,6	21.192,5	−7.854,9	27.474,0	21.192,5	6.281,5
2078	11.948,2	19.899,8	−7.951,6	13.079,0	20.442,6	−7.363,6	26.954,4	20.442,6	6.511,8

Source: SORS, 2023; own calculation

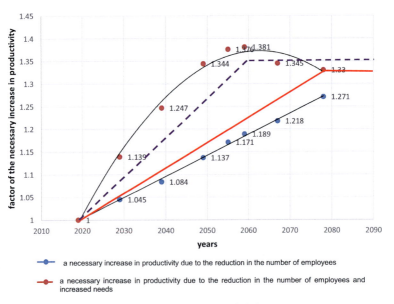

Picture 68.17 The necessary increase in productivity to ensure the balance of resources and needs, base scenario. (Source: SORS, 2023; own calculation)

defines the current state of needs. In the diagram (Picture 68.17), this is shown as the need for a gradual increase in the productivity of economic sectors, indicating that by 2060, productivity should rise to factor 1.381 of the present. If productivity were perfectly elastic, the federal equilibrium would be ensured with such productivity as indicated by the red points. For each point, the equation would apply (Picture 68.17):

$$E_{sfb}(t_i) = \left(E_{sfb}^{AV}(t_i) + E_{sfb}^{R}(t_i)\right) \times f_{\text{prod}}(t_i) \tag{68.32}$$

$$\text{GDP}_{sfb}(t_i) = \text{gdp}_{sfb}(t_0) \times \left(E_{sfb}^{AV}(t_i) + E_{sfb}^{R}(t_i)\right) \times f_{\text{prod}}(t_i) \tag{68.33}$$

$\text{GDP}_{sfb}(t_i)$ ... GDP of services for business in year t_i
$f_{\text{prod}}(t_i)$ ... productivity factor in year t_i relative to 2019

Three scenarios were evaluated, representing the initial boundary conditions for defining fundamental measures or restrictions in the demographic transition, given the current state of the demographic pyramid. Baseline measures are shown for each scenario as time-varying curves as a function of the measure under the influence of the scenario-specific demographic development and the associated GDP over time. It is assumed, however, that if a balance of resources and needs is to be achieved under such a scenario, the efficiency that ensures this is required—the volume of

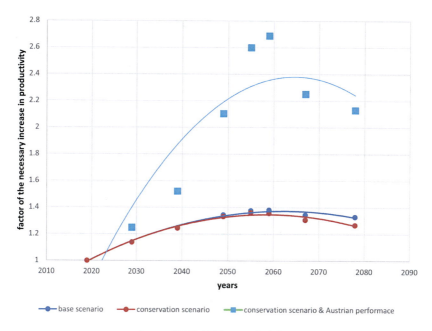

Picture 68.18 Comparison of scenarios. (Source: SORS, 2023; own calculation)

the corresponding GDP by years to ensure socio-economic conditions as they were in the base year (Picture 68.18).

According to the available forecasts on the demographic transition, none of them indicate that Slovenia will reach its current population level by the year 2078. This applies to the base scenarios (1,840,672 inhabitants in 2078 with a peak of 2,080,808 in 2025), the conservation scenario (final 1,969,875 with a peak of 2,084,730 in 2029), as well as the EUROSTAT 2015 demographic forecast (final 1,939,768 with a peak of 2,083,271 in 2025) and EUROSTAT 2019 forecast (final 1,908,156, with a peak of 2,115,598 in 2024).

Simultaneously, in the base scenario, the number of residents over 65 years of age is projected to increase continuously from 382,989 in 2019 to 524,057 in 2078. On the other hand, the number of active individuals is expected to decrease from 1,283,055 to 972,798 during the same period. This shows that achieving a sustainable balance between needs and available resources in the long term will be challenging without implementing additional measures.

The third scenario considers a demographic transition based on the conservation scenario, but with the assumption of specific production density per employee in each economic activity, similar to what is currently achieved in neighboring Austria.

With the social efficiency and productivity achieved today by neighboring Austria and with a demographic transition by conservation scenario, Slovenia could successfully manage the transition of the baby boom generation from the 1960s and 1970s to the population group over 65 years of age. However, it should still provide sufficient numbers of medical staff and staff to provide permanent care for the elderly due to the increase in the needs of the over-65 group. It will have to appropriately strengthen sectors that ensure higher performance of the active population, e.g., upbringing and education.

Slovenia has the possibility of taking simultaneous action in several ways. For example, increasing productivity with simultaneous robotization, which would help offset the decline in the number of employees in the economy. Measures to increase performance in the social sector naturally remain, as does state borrowing.

But the question arises as to what is the most effective measure and its extreme limit that can be reached. If the lower point on the graph represents a demographic pyramid in the starting year and the second point represents the demographic pyramid in the year 2078, their combination represents the change in productivity that society at that time should achieve, taking into account the demographic structure at that time, in order to maintain the current socio-economic conditions derived in the model.

The straight red line in Picture 68.17 delimits the graph with the minimum necessary productivity growth that the society at that time must achieve in order to maintain the current living conditions experienced in the starting year. If this border line could not be reached, it would be necessary to reduce consumption.[8] Productivities marked on the line below the marginal productivity require an urgent reduction in aggregate consumption by the population.

The demographic transition of the baby boom generation to the age group over 65 leads to an increase in needs, as represented by the square curve above. Assuming that the red dividing line represents maximum efficiency in the long run, this burden can be bridged with external resources and subject to external conditions.

In the event that higher productivity can be achieved, as indicated by the dashed line, we can determine the most efficient ratio based on the maximum point of consumption and borrowing conditions.

However, if the Slovenian economy was flexible enough to achieve productivity levels that meet the federal demand, the same assumptions would apply as we have shown with suitably reduced productivity, as achieved by neighboring Austria.

In this model, we assume that the generational transition until the year 2078 is not burdened by previously accepted obligations. The obligation, which we considered as optimizing the transition of the baby boom generation shown in graph 6.1, indicates the possibility of easing the pressure on the future generation through acceptable borrowing.

---

[8] Easterlin noted that the numerically small generations born during the Great Depression of the 1930s in the United States experienced high wages and easy entry into the labor market during their active years. That is why they married early and had a high birth rate in the 1950s and 1960s. A small generation of parents produced a large generation of children, resulting in the Baby Boom. Easterlin predicted that the aging of this great generation would usher in a period of relatively lower wages, slower advancement, later marriage, and lower birth rates—all of which occurred in the Baby Bust of the 1970s.

68 Population Aging: How Much Time Do We Still Have?

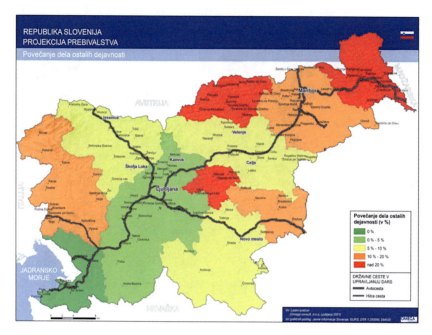

Source: EUROSTAT 2021, SORS, 2021; own calculation.

Picture 68.19 A regional view of needed increased productivity by statistical region. (Source: EUROSTAT 2021, SORS, 2021; own calculation)

To present a regional perspective on the required changes in GDP, we display the gap in the social product in 2067, which would have been produced based on the demographic transition according to the EUROPOP forecast from 2015 (Picture 68.19).

68.7 Sensitivity Analysis

In addition to assessing the demographic scenarios, sensitivity analysis was conducted by incorporating modifications into the healthcare model. This included reducing healthcare costs, extending the retirement age to 67 years, and exploring a combination of both measures.

In all cases, the necessary increase in productivity was estimated to balance the projected needs for social services for the demographic scenario of conservation (Picture 68.21).

In order to reduce costs in healthcare, the assumption was made that until 2030, costs increase in line with projected needs. After this year, however, they increase linearly to the value of healthcare needs, as reached in the target year 2078.

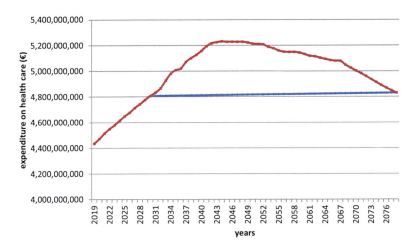

Source: SORS, 2023; own calculation.

Picture 68.20 Assumed cost reduction in healthcare, conservation scenario. (Source: SORS, 2023; own calculation)

The resulting difference between needs and assumed costs can be compensated by increased productivity in healthcare, improved organization and rationalization, and automation of processes (Picture 68.20).

By implementing cost reduction measures in healthcare, the demand for additional employees in the healthcare sector decreases. This allows more individuals to be available for employment in other sectors of the economy, thereby potentially boosting GDP.

The assumed extension of the retirement age to 67 years in the following scenarios also leads to an additional increase in GDP.

For the model, we made the assumption that productivity would increase linearly until the year 2049, (midpoint of the observed period). In that year, it is assumed that the resources for services for people would reach the required value for the target year 2078 in order to achieve a balance between resources and needs. This value would then remain constant until the end of the period. The shortfall between actual social needs and bridging the demographic transition would be covered through long-term borrowing (Picture 68.21).

The assumed measures reduce the necessary burden on employees in the economy by reducing the target productivity growth in the period between 2019 and 2049. By decreasing the estimated amount of debt necessary to bridge the demographic transition, the future generations of employees after 2078 will be relieved of a significant burden.

In the case of a pure conservation scenario, in order to meet the same level of needs as in the target year 2078, the productivity in 2049 would need to be 1.21 times higher than in the baseline year 2019. Additionally, to bridge the demographic transition in the entire observed period up to 2078 and at the assumed discount

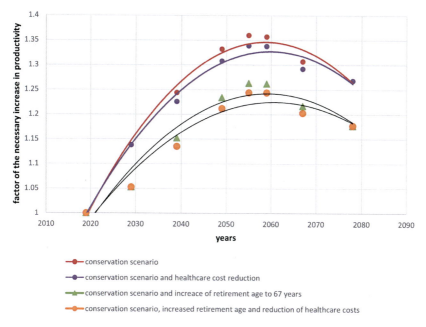

Picture 68.21 Productivity increase needed to ensure balance of resources and variant needs, conservation scenario. (Source: SORS, 2023; own calculation)

rate of 3%, long-term debt in the net present value of almost EUR 27.8 billion is required. If, alongside the conservation scenario, healthcare costs are reduced according to the described model, the necessary productivity in 2049 would be 1.205 times higher than in the starting year 2019. To bridge the demographic transition until 2078 in this case, a long-term debt of around EUR 23 billion, in net present value terms, would be required. In the case of the conservation scenario combined with the extension of the retirement age to 67 years, the required productivity increase would be 1.12 times higher than in 2019, and the current value of debt would amount to almost EUR 13.5 billion. However, if we also include the reduction of healthcare costs alongside the extension of the retirement age, the productivity increase factor would decrease to 1.116, and the required current value of debt would be just over EUR 8.5 billion.

68.8 Summary

The main problem at this moment of the demographic transition is the decline in births that we have witnessed since 1982. An even bigger problem is the stagnation of the number of births due to the ever-later average year of the first birth. Slovenian society was not aware of the drop in population in the demographic pyramid in time and is now faced with the retirement of the baby boom generation. The next generation is numerically smaller by a third, and due to the period between 1990 and 2005, when the birth rate was the lowest, this is also reflected in the lower number of women who are entering childbearing age at this time. Demographic policy, which would accelerate the number of births, seen from this moment, will achieve its first effects only at the end of the sixties of this century, when the reduction of a large number of elderly residents already begins.

However, in none of the forecasts, the total number of inhabitants in 2078 exceeds 1,970,000, as projected by the conservation demographic scenario. This indicates an unfavorable population distribution across the age groups of 0–20 years, 20–65 years, and over 65 years. Consequently, there is increased pressure on employees, both those who are supposed to provide for people's needs, as well as those in the economy. The pressure is also reflected in ensuring a sufficient number and qualifications of both those employed in the provision of social services and those in the economy, which also requires appropriate organization and implementation of the schooling and education sector. The healthcare system, in particular, is highly sensitive, as it will require nearly 25% more medical personnel during the peak demand for health services. All of the above aggravates the problem of the availability of personnel in the economy, which will be forced to provide resources to cover all these needs with increased productivity.

The growing problem of the gap between the needs of an aging population and the limited number of employees can be managed by increasing productivity. This requires the entire society to be oriented towards this goal. In one of the scenarios, we showed that the otherwise challenging demographic transition in Slovenia would not exist if our current level of development and efficiency matched that of the Republic of Austria.

While most predictive models take into account changes in socio-economic variables in the long term, the specificity of the presented model is a starting assumption about the perception of socio-economic events in the base year. The fundamental reason for this specificity is the very motive behind the need for long-term research into a possible future that is largely unknown to us. This awareness is the main lever in the perception of limitations, which are inevitable on the way to the future. Limitations and imbalances can only be overcome if the society as a whole takes necessary measures in time to maintain or increase the standard as achieved in the base year.

The research used methods and tools that enable multi-relational and systematic analysis of interdependent processes. Although it is a macro-model, it has also proven to be a suitable tool for observing and analyzing the effects of specific parameters at a more detailed level, while at the same time, the responsiveness of the related interactions of the model to changes in these parameters is shown. This property is essential in assessing the possible contributions of various solutions or independent scenarios to the development of coordinated strategies.

The EintegraMG platform is based on standards and databases that are collected and edited by EUROSTAT for each EU member state. In this regard, the results are comparable to one another, but it is important to note that their interpretation is subjective and left to the discretion of each individual analyst.

References

Easterlin, R. A. (1968). *Population, labor force, and long swings in economic growth: The American experience.* Columbia University Press.

Eurostat: Population projections – Population (Demography, Migration and Projections). Medmrežje: https://ec.europa.eu/eurostat/web/population-demography-migration-projections/population-projections-data (17. 2. 2021).

Florida, State Inpatient Database (SID), State Ambulatory Surgery and Services Database (SASD), State Emergency Department Database (SEDD), Healthcare Cost and Utilization Project (HUCP), Agency for Healthcare Research and Quality. (2020).

Ministry of Health: Public Health Service Network. Internet: https://www.gov.si/teme/mreza-javne-zdravstvene-sluzbe/ (March 1, 2021).

National Institute of Public Health (NIJZ): Data portal. Internet: https://podatki.nijz.si/pxweb/sl/NIJZ%20podatkovni%20portal?px_language=sl&px_db=NIJZ%20podatkovni%20portal&rxid=3fffd693-9111-41fc-856d-2f5522f81e9d (2018).

SURS: Statistical Office of the Republic of Slovenia. Internet: https://pxweb.stat.si/SiStat/si (March, April, May 2023).

Chapter 69
The Impact of Capital Adequacy on Banking Risk-Evidence from Emerging Market

Osama Samih Shaban

Abstract This study aimed to examine the impact of capital adequacy on banking risks in Jordanian commercial banks. In order to achieve the objectives of the study, the quantitative approach was adopted in this study, which focuses on describing the study sample and its variables, and then testing the hypotheses. The study population included all the Jordanian commercial banks in the Amman Stock Exchange (ASE). After verifying the published financial reports, all 13 commercial banks were accredited during the time period (2016–2021). The results of the study concluded that capital adequacy has a statistically significant effect in reducing risks in Jordanian commercial banks. The main recommendation encourages banks to focus on maintaining high levels of capital adequacy in order to reduce both credit risk and liquidity risk.

Keywords Capital adequacy · Banking risks · Liquidity risk · Quantitative approach

69.1 Introduction

Banks play an important role in the national economy as one of the economic growth levers, as evidenced by a number of characteristics related to the size of their operations and their role in distributing wealth to members of society, as well as being a pillar of the financial market. These banks also differ from other businesses in terms of ownership structure and capital adequacy.

Whereas the concept of capital adequacy has gained prominence in accounting literature, particularly in recent years, due to its impact on the behavior of corporate management when developing policies and making future decisions, as capital

---

O. S. Shaban (✉)
Department of Accounting, Faculty of Business, Al-Zaytoonah University of Jordan, Amman, Jordan
e-mail: drosama@zuj.edu.jo

© The Author(s), under exclusive license to Springer Nature Switzerland AG 2024
N. Tsounis, A. Vlachvei (eds.), *Applied Economic Research and Trends*, Springer Proceedings in Business and Economics,
https://doi.org/10.1007/978-3-031-49105-4_69

adequacy is regarded as one of the most important mechanisms contributing to the effective implementation of corporate governance, this prompted the majority of capital market authorities to request that all companies registered with them disclose their capital adequacy in order to improve stock market transparency and disclosure (Ismail et al., 2020; Feng et al., 2020).

The adequate amount of capital (shareholder money) that a bank must hold as a percentage of its risk-weighted assets is referred to as capital adequacy. Bank capital adequacy is strictly regulated around the world to improve the financial system and global economy stability and to provide additional protection for depositors (Chowdhury & Zaman, 2018; Chun & Lee, 2017).

The research problem is reflected by the risk associated with capital adequacy. Banking risks are regarded as one of the most serious issues confronting banks and their exposure to economic crises, so it is critical to prevent the occurrence of this type of risk and manage it if it does occur. In general, businesses, particularly banks, measure and analyze potential risks in a systematic manner in order to avoid exposure to them or mitigate their effects if they occur (Alzoubi, 2017).

Many studies have discussed the impact of capital adequacy on banking risks, as having an efficient capital adequacy that balances its financial system, and leads to better identification of banking risks, and thus reduces or eliminates them (Chun & Lee, 2017; Blanch, 2010).

The current research seeks to investigate the impact of capital adequacy on banking risks in Jordanian commercial banks. To achieve the objectives of the study, the published financial reports of all 13 commercial banks will be investigated during the time period (2016–2021).

69.2 Literature Review

Bank capital adequacy is a crucial element in maintaining the stability of financial systems and protecting depositors. Regulated globally, it ensures that banks have sufficient capital to withstand potential losses and prevent insolvency. Various methods are employed to assess capital adequacy, including the capital adequacy ratio, tier 1 leverage ratio, economic capital measure, and liquidity ratios (Hakimi & Zaghdoudi, 2017a, b).

The capital adequacy ratio measures a bank's available capital as a percentage of its risk-weighted credit exposures. It aims to ensure that banks possess enough capital to absorb losses before reaching insolvency (Gallati, 2022; Saleh & Abu Afifa, 2020a, b, c). Risk-weighted assets, such as loans and other assets, are weighted based on their risk of loss to the bank. The resulting capital adequacy ratio, also known as the capital-to-risk-weighted assets ratio (CAR), reflects the financial health of a bank and contributes to the dependability and effectiveness of the global financial system (Hassan et al., 2019a, b).

The capital adequacy ratio consists of two tiers of capital. Tier 1 capital, also referred to as core capital, includes equity capital, ordinary share capital, intangible assets, and audited revenue reserves. This capital is available to absorb losses and supports banks during risky transactions such as trading, investing, and lending (Gallati, 2022; Hassan et al., 2019a, b).

Tier 2 capital, on the other hand, comprises unaudited retained earnings, reserves, and general loss reserves. It acts as a buffer against losses in the case of a bank's winding-up or liquidation. While tier 2 capital provides additional protection, it is considered less secure compared to tier 1 capital. The capital adequacy ratio is calculated by combining both tiers of capital and dividing them by risk-weighted assets, which are determined by assessing the risk associated with a bank's loans and assigning appropriate weights (Gallati, 2022).

Relevant literature discussed many theories and concepts related to capital adequacy and banking risk in emerging markets include (Basel III, 2011; Borio & Drehmann, 2009; Demirgüç-Kunt & Detragiache, 1998; Nier & Baumann, 2006; Saleh & Abu Afifa, 2020a, b, c).

1. Basel Accords: The Basel Accords, particularly Basel III, provide a regulatory framework for capital adequacy and risk management in banking. These accords set out guidelines for calculating capital requirements based on the risk profile of banks' assets and activities. They aim to ensure that banks maintain sufficient capital buffers to absorb losses and enhance the stability of the financial system.
2. Capital Adequacy Ratio (CAR): The Capital Adequacy Ratio is a key measure used to assess a bank's capital adequacy. It represents the ratio of a bank's capital to its risk-weighted assets. A higher CAR indicates a stronger capital position and implies a lower probability of insolvency. Regulators set minimum CAR requirements to safeguard depositors and promote financial stability.
3. Systemic Risk: Systemic risk refers to the risk of disruption to the entire financial system due to the failure of one or more banks or other financial institutions. In emerging markets, where financial systems may be more vulnerable and interconnected, systemic risk can pose significant challenges. Capital adequacy regulations aim to mitigate systemic risk by ensuring that banks have sufficient capital to absorb losses and maintain their stability.
4. Moral Hazard: Moral hazard arises when banks take excessive risks because they expect to be bailed out by the government or central bank in case of financial distress. In the context of capital adequacy, imposing higher capital requirements can mitigate moral hazard by reducing the likelihood of bank failures and the need for taxpayer-funded bailouts.
5. Procyclicality: Procyclicality refers to the tendency of the financial system to amplify economic cycles. In periods of economic expansion, banks may have higher capital levels and take on more risk, potentially exacerbating the boom-bust cycle. Conversely, during downturns, banks may face capital constraints and reduce lending, amplifying the economic downturn. Addressing procyclicality is an important consideration in designing capital adequacy frameworks to promote financial stability.
6. Liquidity Risk: Liquidity risk refers to the risk of a bank's inability to meet its obligations when they come due. In emerging markets, where liquidity

conditions can be less stable, ensuring sufficient liquidity buffers becomes crucial. Capital adequacy regulations often incorporate liquidity requirements to mitigate liquidity risk, ensuring that banks can withstand liquidity pressures and continue to fulfill their obligations.
7. Stress Testing: Stress testing is a tool used to assess a bank's resilience to adverse scenarios and potential shocks. It involves subjecting banks' balance sheets and capital positions to severe but plausible stress scenarios. Stress testing helps identify vulnerabilities, evaluate the adequacy of capital, and assess the impact of adverse events on a bank's risk profile. It is an important component of risk management and capital adequacy assessment in emerging markets.

These theories and concepts can provide valuable insights into the relationship between capital adequacy and banking risk in emerging markets. They guide the development of effective regulatory frameworks, risk management practices, and supervisory approaches to enhance the stability and resilience of banking systems. By considering these aspects, this research examines the relationship between capital adequacy and banking risk in emerging markets. It seeks to contribute to the understanding of how capital adequacy measures impact the stability and risk levels of banks in these markets.

Bank financial condition monitoring is also important because banks must deal with a liquidity mismatch between their assets and liabilities. Very liquid accounts, such as demand deposits, appear on the liabilities side of a bank's balance sheet. However, the majority of a bank's assets are rather illiquid loans. While banks can (and frequently do) sell loans, they can only be quickly converted to cash by selling them at a significant discount (Karamoy & Tulung, 2020; Hakimi & Zaghdoudi, 2017a, b).

Banks in Jordan are regulated under the Central Bank of Jordan (CBJ), while banks are regulated at the federal level in the United States by the Federal Deposit Insurance Corporation (FDIC), the Federal Reserve Board, and the Office of the Comptroller of the Currency (OCC). Banks in the United States are required to maintain a minimum capital adequacy ratio. The capital adequacy ratio represents a bank's risk-weighted credit exposure (Gallati, 2022).

The importance of minimum capital adequacy ratios in preventing banks from going bankrupt and losing depositor money is underscored by their ability to withstand a tolerable level of losses. Currently, Basel II and Basel III stipulate minimum capital-to-risk-weighted assets ratios of 8% and 10.5%, respectively. High capital adequacy ratios exceed Basel II and Basel III's basic standards (Adequacy, 2019).

The study of risks is crucial in the business sector since, according to its financial definition, risk is an anticipated direct harm to an economic company's operation. Economic, human, political, and natural disasters may result in a variety of losses for the firm as a whole, which has a detrimental effect on the likelihood that the company will continue to engage in its economic activity (Alqirem et al., 2020; Shingjergji & Hyseni, 2015).

The banking industry experienced an accelerated series of technological and financial developments that made its operations more complex and diversified. This led to a significant increase in risks relating to borrowers' ability to pay their debts or the bank's ability to meet its obligations on time, which made it necessary to concentrate on risk management. Banks must develop thorough procedures with adequate senior management oversight to identify risks and their sources, measure them, and monitor them in order to deal with and manage these risks (Milojevi & Redzepagic, 2021).

The term risk derives from the Latin term Riscass or Risque, which means the occurrence of a change in comparison to what was expected or a deviation from what was expected. A deviation from the desired objectives, risk can also express uncertainty about the occurrence of a specific loss or the expected material loss as a result of the occurrence of a specific accident (Chakroun & Abid, 2016; Gallati, 2022).

Legally, risk is described as a contractual occurrence that causes a string of losses in financial institutions and markets. This occurrence frequently originates from one party's breach of contract, which causes a string of losses owed to the other party (Gallati, 2022; Zhongming et al., 2019).

In the United States of America, the Bank Assurance and Risk Management Committee defines banking risk as: the possibility of loss, either directly through losses in business results or in capital, or indirectly through the presence of restrictions that limit the ability of the bank to continue to provide and practice its activities on the one hand, and limiting its ability to invest in the opportunities available in the banking environment on the other hand (Van Greuning & Bratanovic, 2020; Sadgrove, 2016).

Risks in the banking environment can be classified into the following categories: (Daly et al., 2019; Chakroun & Abid, 2016; Gallati, 2022; Saleh & Abu Afifa, 2020a, b, c).

- Financial risks: These risks are associated with financial institutions, which face unique risks as a result of the nature of their business, which is represented by providing financial services to customers, such as market risks, interest rate risks, credit risks, currency risks, and liquidity risks.
- Operational risks: It is defined as the risks posed by insufficient internal processes, systems, and individuals. It also refers to the risks posed by insufficient internal activities and operations in the bank as a result of human errors, design flaws, and natural disasters.
- Electronic risks: It includes fraudulent operations, the disclosure of customer secrets, and other risks associated with the increased use of software and computers.
- Non-financial risks: These are the risks that banks face in their daily operations, and they include reputational risks which arise from general negative customer opinions, which result in large losses for banks and are caused by negative rumors or mismanagement of bank ownership. Non-financial risk also includes legal risks, and this risk is caused by inadequacies or scarcity of bank operations docu-

ments, which renders them legally unacceptable. These risks are unintentionally introduced when clients provide guarantees that later prove to be unacceptable in court. These risks are also related to the lack of clarity of financial contracts in terms of implementation, as they are linked to legislation, the main system, and regulatory orders governing compliance with deals and contracts.

Banking risk management is regarded as one of the most important topics that concern bankers and attract their attention, particularly in recent years, when many internal and external factors, such as external factors related to the global or national economy, or internal factors such as weak internal and external control and mismanagement, have contributed to the occurrence of banking crises (Leo et al., 2019). General risk management policies are not founded on broad and comprehensive regulatory frameworks. This means that identifying, managing, and evaluating risks is one of the most important factors influencing banks' success and growth, as well as their ability to meet their objectives (Milojević & Redzepagic, 2021; Van & Bratanovic, 2020).

Banking risk management is defined as the process of detecting, tracking, and monitoring risks in order to report, control, and mitigate their negative consequences. This process aims to identify and evaluate potential risks' expected losses, study alternatives, and select the best method for dealing with them. Banking risks can be managed by following a series of actions: (Daly et al., 2019; Van & Bratanovic, 2020).

- The first stage in risk management is to determine the anticipated hazards and the likelihood that they will materialize. There are several hazards associated with every good or service the bank offers. It is important to remember that the process of risk identification must be ongoing and that these risks must be understood at the level of both individual business and the bank as a whole.
- Risk measurement: Following the process of identifying banking risks, it is required to ascertain and quantify the scope, persistence, and likelihood of these risks.
- Risk control: There are three main methods for controlling banking risks. The first is to set limits for the bank's activities, then analyze the risks, and finally eliminate the impact of these risks. It is worth noting that management must balance the return on risks with the expenses incurred to control these risks, implying that banks must set risk limits through standards, policies, and procedures that demonstrate accountability.

Banking risk dimensions can be classified as follows:

Credit risk: When granting credit to borrowers, it is critical to consider their credit capacity, as this ability is likely to deteriorate over time, resulting in an inability to repay. Where credit risk or customer failure to meet its obligations is regarded as one of the most significant risks confronting banks, in addition to the risk of credit concentration resulting from the bank's dealings with one or a group of customers or a lack of diversification of activities (Zamore et al., 2018).

Liquidity risk: This risk refers to the ability of a bank to convert assets into cash as quickly as possible without incurring losses in cases of sudden demand or current dues, such as facing demand or sudden withdrawals in the event of a crisis. As a result, we discover that banks keep specific percentages of deposits in the form of cash assets that are determined by prior legislation and laws. While banking liquidity is defined as: the bank's ability to fulfill all of its commercial obligations and respond to credit requests, which requires the presence of liquid cash with banks or obtaining it through facilitating some of its assets in an easy and fast way, the concept of bank liquidity may refer to the availability of assets that convert into cash quickly and without any loss in value in order to meet the due debts on time and without any delay (Alzoubi, 2017; Chowdhury & Zaman, 2018).

Bank growth (ROA): The amount that the bank invests its assets in making a profit is tracked by one of the operational performance indicators called return on assets (ROA), which is largely dependent on the size of the assets used in production and the type of industry. In order to gauge the size of emerging profits, it is also used to compare businesses in the same industry. Since the company's assets are made up of capital and total liabilities and these funds are used to finance its operations, the rate of return on assets (ROA) measures the company's capacity to invest its assets by demonstrating the effectiveness of utilizing the invested assets to generate the desired profits (Langfield & Pagano, 2016).

Bank size: The size of the bank is regarded as one of the most significant factors affecting the financial structure because numerous studies have shown that it has an effect on borrowing within the financial structure due to the lower likelihood of bankruptcy in large banks because they are more likely to turn to borrowing on favorable terms. Additionally, large banks' operations are distinguished by a high degree of diversification, which reduces their risk exposure and provides an incentive for them to increase borrowed funds. Due to its simplicity and clarity, the logarithm of total assets can be used to determine the size of the bank (Hasan et al., 2020; Sensoy, 2017).

69.3 Methodology

In this study, the quantitative approach was used, which focuses on describing the study sample and its variables before testing the hypotheses (Wilson, 2014). Because the study data included several cross-sections with time series, it is referred to as mixed data or panel data. According to (Greene, 2012), this data is the most common and used in economic, accounting, and financial studies for a number of Jordanian commercial banks during the period (2016–2022). Secondary sources were used entirely in the data collection process in this study, as scientific papers, books, and academic periodicals were used as secondary sources to construct the study methodology, variables, and theoretical and conceptual framework, while secondary sources such as data and financial reports published for service companies listed on the Amman Stock Exchange were used for the study's test variables.

69.3.1 Study Population

All (13) Jordanian commercial banks were included in the study population. The researcher presented the data of these banks from annual reports published in the Amman Stock Exchange. During the time period, (13) commercial banks were approved after verifying the published reports.

69.3.2 Study Design

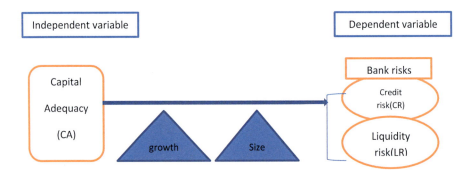

69.3.3 Descriptive Statistics Results

Extraction of descriptive statistics' results, which aims to interpret various scientific phenomena, is one of the fundamental methodological steps that must be followed in any scientific study (Sekaran & Bougie, 2016). Descriptive statistics allows for a simpler understanding of scientific phenomena through the use of numbers and calculations to understand the study data in a way that is understandable to other researchers.

In this section, the variables from the independent, dependent, and control studies' descriptive statistics (arithmetic means, standard deviations, median, largest value, and least value) were calculated and extracted (2016–2022). The outcomes of these values are shown in Table 69.1.

The results of the descriptive statistics of the study variables are shown in Table 69.1, and it is evident that the results of the descriptive statistics are as follows:

Capital adequacy: The capital adequacy variable's arithmetic mean was (0.451) and its standard deviation was (0.270). This value demonstrates the importance of capital adequacy in Jordanian commercial banks. This demonstrates the effec-

Table 69.1 Descriptive statistics outcomes

Variable	Arithmetic mean	Standard deviation	Greatest value	Lowest value
Capital adequacy (CA)	0.451	0.270	0.883	0.015
Credit risk (CR)	0.067	0.023	0.118	0.016
Liquidity risk (LR)	0.702	0.112	0.997	0.474
Bank growth	0.083	0.143	0.860	0.243-
Bank size	9.41	0.371	10.42	8.90

tiveness of the management at Jordanian commercial banks and the effectiveness of the capital policies adopted by the institutions, which promote investment in Jordanian commercial banks. The data's largest value was (0.883), while its smallest value was (0.015).

Credit risk (CR): The credit risk variable's arithmetic mean was (0.067) and its standard deviation was (0.023). The study's data had the highest value (0.118) and the lowest value (0.118), (0.016).

Liquidity risk (LR): The liquidity risk variable's arithmetic mean was (0.702), and its standard deviation was (0.112). As more loans are granted by Jordanian commercial banks than there are deposits held by banks, this value denotes a high percentage of liquidity risk in those institutions, and liquidity therefore carries significant risks. The highest value found in the study data for the period (2016–2022) was (0.997), and the lowest value found in the study data for the same period was (0.474).

Bank growth: The bank growth variable's arithmetic mean was (0.083) and its standard deviation was (0.143). This figure shows that the growth of loans from Jordanian commercial banks during the research period was modest, at 8.3%. There may be political and economic unrest at the time of this outcome. Environmental factors in Jordan, such as the Syrian crisis and subsequent economic crises, have made it difficult for people and businesses to get loans and investments over the past six years. According to the study's data, the highest growth value was (0.860), while the slowest growth rate was (−0.243).

Bank size: The bank size variable's arithmetic mean was (9.41) and its standard deviation was (0.371). When converting the logarithmic number into a real unit, this value (10.42) is the highest in the data and shows that the total assets of Jordanian commercial banks are substantial. In the study's data, (8.90) had the smallest value.

69.3.4 Hypothesis Testing and Results

The researcher used the linear model to estimate the regression equation for the purpose of hypothesis testing, as the regression equations are as follows:

Table 69.2 Regression analysis outcomes (H01, H01:1, H01:2)

Variable	Regression coefficient, beta	Standard error	t-test	P-Value
Capital adequacy (CA)	0.024-	0.009	2.46-	0.016
Bank growth	0.048-	0.012	3.78-	0.000
Bank size	0.004-	0.002	1.57-	0.120
R^2	0.468			
The value of the modified coefficient of determination	0.423			

$$CR = \beta_0 + \beta_1 CA i.t + \beta_2 GROWTH i.t + \beta_3 SIZE i.t + \varepsilon i.t$$

$$LR = \beta_0 + \beta_1 CA i.t + \beta_2 GROWTH i.t + \beta_3 SIZE i.t + \varepsilon i.t$$

H01: There is no statistically significant effect of capital adequacy on credit risk in Jordanian commercial banks.

H01:1: There is no statistically significant effect of Bank Growth on credit risk in Jordanian commercial banks.

H01:2: There is no statistically significant effect of Bank Size on credit risk in Jordanian commercial banks.

Table 69.2 illustrates the outcomes of the regression analysis of the first hypotheses and its sub-hypotheses. It appears that the capital adequacy factor has a statistically significant effect on credit risk in Jordanian commercial banks, as indicated by the "regression coefficient" value of 0.024 and the "t-test" and "P-Value" values of 2.46 and 0.016, respectively. This means that the first hypothesis (H01) is rejected and that capital adequacy does indeed have an impact on credit risk.

The bank growth factor also appears to have a significant effect on credit risk in Jordanian commercial banks, with a "regression coefficient" of 0.048 and "t-test" and "P-Value" values of 3.78 and 0.000, respectively. This means that the second hypothesis (H01:1) is also rejected and that bank growth does have an impact on credit risk.

However, the bank size factor does not seem to have a statistically significant effect on credit risk, as indicated by the "regression coefficient" of 0.004 and the "t-test" and "P-Value" values of 1.57 and 0.120, respectively. This means that the third hypothesis (H01:2) is accepted and that bank size does not have a significant impact on credit risk.

Overall, the analysis shows that both capital adequacy and bank growth have a significant impact on credit risk in Jordanian commercial banks, while bank size does not seem to have a significant effect.

Table 69.3 Regression analysis outcomes (H02, H02:1, H02:2)

Variable	Regression coefficient, beta	Standard error	t-test	P-Value
Capital adequacy (CA)	0.124	0.053	2.33	0.022
Bank growth	−0.169	0.079	−2.11	0.037
Bank size	−0.082	0.022	−6.91	0.000
R^2	0.260			
The value of the modified coefficient of determination	0.198			

H02: There is no statistically significant effect of capital adequacy on liquidity risk in Jordanian commercial banks.

H02:1: There is no statistically significant effect of Bank Growth on liquidity risk in Jordanian commercial banks.

H02:2: There is no statistically significant effect of Bank Size on liquidity risk in Jordanian commercial banks.

Table 69.3 illustrates the outcomes of the regression analysis of the second hypotheses and its sub-hypotheses. The capital adequacy factor appears to have a statistically significant effect on liquidity risk in Jordanian commercial banks, as indicated by the "regression coefficient" of 0.124, the "t-test" value of 2.33, and the "P-Value" of 0.022. This means that the first hypothesis (H02) is rejected and that capital adequacy does indeed have an impact on liquidity risk.

The bank growth factor also appears to have a statistically significant effect on liquidity risk, but in the opposite direction of what was hypothesized. The "regression coefficient" of −0.169, "t-test" value of −2.11, and "P-Value" of 0.037 all suggest that higher bank growth is associated with lower liquidity risk. This means that the second hypothesis (H02:1) is also rejected and that bank growth does indeed have an impact on liquidity risk.

The bank size factor appears to have a strong and statistically significant effect on liquidity risk, as indicated by the "regression coefficient" of −0.082, the "t-test" value of −6.91, and the "P-Value" of 0.000. This means that the third hypothesis (H02:2) is rejected and that bank size does indeed have an impact on liquidity risk, with larger banks generally having lower liquidity risk.

Overall, the analysis suggests that both capital adequacy and bank size have significant effects on liquidity risk in Jordanian commercial banks, with higher capital adequacy and larger size being associated with lower risk. Bank growth also has an effect, but in the opposite direction of what was hypothesized.

69.4 Conclusions and Recommendations

- Capital adequacy has a statistically significant effect on both credit risk and liquidity risk in Jordanian commercial banks, with higher capital adequacy being associated with lower risk in both cases.
- Bank growth has a statistically significant effect on credit risk, but in the opposite direction of what was hypothesized, with higher growth being associated with lower credit risk. Bank growth also has a statistically significant effect on liquidity risk, but again in the opposite direction of what was hypothesized, with higher growth being associated with lower liquidity risk.
- Bank size has a statistically significant effect on liquidity risk, with larger banks generally having lower liquidity risk. However, bank size does not appear to have a statistically significant effect on credit risk.
- Overall, these results suggest that capital adequacy and bank size are important factors to consider when assessing the risk profile of Jordanian commercial banks, while the effect of bank growth is more complex and may vary depending on the type of risk being considered.

According to the result obtained, the study recommends the following:

- Jordanian commercial banks should focus on maintaining high levels of capital adequacy in order to reduce both credit risk and liquidity risk.
- Banks should carefully consider the potential impacts of growth on both credit risk and liquidity risk and ensure that their risk management strategies are able to effectively address any potential negative effects.
- Larger banks may have an advantage in terms of liquidity risk, but they should still be mindful of this risk and have appropriate strategies in place to manage it.
- Further research could be conducted to more fully understand the relationship between bank growth and risk, and to identify any potential mitigating factors or strategies that could be employed to address any negative effects.

Based on the research study, the following potential limitations can be stated:

- The study is based on a relatively small sample of Jordanian commercial banks, which may not be representative of the entire population of banks in the country. This could limit the generalizability of the findings.
- The study relies on a single snapshot of data, which means that it may not capture changes in risk over time or the full range of risk experienced by the banks in the sample.
- The study only considers a few potential factors that may affect risk, and there may be other important variables that are not being taken into account.
- The statistical analysis used in the study may not fully capture the complexity of the relationships between the various factors being considered and risk.
- The study does not consider the potential impact of external factors, such as macroeconomic conditions or regulatory changes, on risk.

- Overall, these limitations may affect the accuracy and completeness of the findings, and further research would be needed to more fully understand the relationships between the various factors being considered and risk in Jordanian commercial banks.

References

Adequacy, C. (2019). Capital adequacy, cost income ratio and performance of banks in Ghana. *International Journal of Academic Research in Business and Social Sciences, 9*(10), 168–184.

Alqirem, R., Afifa, M. A., Saleh, I., & Haniah, F. (2020). Ownership structure, earnings manipulation, and organizational performance: The case of Jordanian insurance organizations. *The Journal of Asian Finance, Economics and Business (JAFEB), 7*(12), 293–308.

Alzoubi, T. (2017). Determinants of liquidity risk in Islamic banks. *Banks & bank systems, 12*(3), 142–148.

Basel Committee on Banking Supervision. (2011). *Basel III: A global regulatory framework for more resilient banks and banking systems.* Bank for International Settlements.

Blanch, J. (2010). Financial risk identification based on the balance sheet information. *Managing and Modelling of Financial Risks*, 10–19.

Borio, C., & Drehmann, M. (2009). *Assessing the risk of banking crises—Revisited* (pp. 29–46). BIS Quarterly Review.

Chakroun, F., & Abid, F. (2016). Capital adequacy and risk management in banking industry. *Applied Stochastic Models in Business and Industry, 32*(1), 113–132.

Chowdhury, M., & Zaman, S. (2018). Effect of liquidity risk on performance of Islamic banks in Bangladesh. *IOSR Journal of Economics and Finance, 9*(4), 1–09.

Chun, S., & Lee, M. (2017). Corporate ownership structure and risk-taking: Evidence from Japan. Journal of Governance and Regulation. Volume 6 Issue 4, 39, 52.

Daly, K., Batten, J. A., Mishra, A. V., & Choudhury, T. (2019). Contagion risk in global banking sector. *Journal of International Financial Markets, Institutions and Money, 63*, 101136.

Demirgüç-Kunt, A., & Detragiache, E. (1998). The determinants of banking crises in developing and developed countries. *IMF Staff Papers, 45*(1), 81–109.

Feng, Y., Hassan, A., & Elamer, A. A. (2020). Corporate governance, ownership structure and capital structure: Evidence from Chinese real estate listed companies. *International Journal of Accounting & Information Management.*

Gallati, R. (2022). Risk management and capital Adequacy. In *Risk management and capital adequacy* (2nd ed., pp. 11–35). Wiley.

Greene, W. (2012). *Econometric analysis* (7th ed.). Prentice Hall.

Hakimi, A., & Zaghdoudi, K. (2017a). Liquidity risk and bank performance: An empirical test for Tunisian banks. *Business and Economic Research, 7*(1), 46–57.

Hakimi, A., & Zaghdoudi, K. (2017b). The determinants of bank capital adequacy in developing countries: Evidence from MENA region. *Journal of Emerging Market Finance, 16*(3), 303–329.

Hasan, M. S. A., Manurung, A. H., & Usman, B. (2020). Determinants of bank profitability with size as moderating variable. *Journal of Applied Finance and Banking, 10*(3), 153–166.

Hassan, M. K., Khan, A., & Paltrinieri, A. (2019a). Liquidity risk, credit risk and stability in Islamic and conventional banks. *Research in International Business and Finance, 48*, 17–31.

Hassan, M. K., Monir, T., & Rashid, A. (2019b). Capital adequacy and bank risk in South Asia. *Review of Economics and Finance, 18*(3), 111–134.

Ismail, S. M., Aris, N. M., Mohamed, A. S., Yusof, S. M., & Zaidi, N. S. (2020). Ownership structure and firms' performance: evidence from finance sector in Malaysia. *International Journal of Academic Research in Business and Social Sciences., 10*(7), 319–329.

Karamoy, H., & Tulung, J. E. (2020). The impact of banking risk on regional development banks in Indonesia. *Banks and Bank Systems, 15*(2), 130–137.

Langfield, S., & Pagano, M. (2016). Bank bias in Europe: Effects on systemic risk and growth. *Economic Policy, 31*(85), 51–106.

Leo, M., Sharma, S., & Maddulety, K. (2019). Machine learning in banking risk management: A literature review. *Risks, 7*(1), 29.

Milojević, N., & Redzepagic, S. (2021). Prospects of artificial intelligence and machine learning application in banking risk management. *Journal of Central Banking Theory and Practice, 10*(3), 41–57.

Nier, E., & Baumann, U. (2006). Market discipline, disclosure and moral hazard in banking. *International Journal of Central Banking, 2*(2), 129–160.

Pearson Education Limited Sekaran, U., & Bougie, R. (2016). *Research methods for business: A skill building approach*. John Wiley & Sons.

Sadgrove, K. (2016). *The complete guide to business risk management*. Routledge.

Saleh, A., & Abu Afifa, H. (2020a). Determinants of banks' capital adequacy: Empirical evidence from Jordan. *Journal of Risk and Financial Management, 13*(5), 86.

Saleh, I., & Abu Afifa, M. (2020b). The effect of credit risk, liquidity risk and bank capital on bank profitability: Evidence from an emerging market. *Cogent Economics & Finance, 8*(1), 1814509.

Saleh, N. S., & Abu Afifa, R. M. (2020c). The effect of capital adequacy ratio on the risk of Jordanian commercial banks. *Journal of Economic Sciences, 4*(3), 8–22.

Sensoy, A. (2017). Firm size, ownership structure, and systematic liquidity risk: The case of an emerging market. *Journal of Financial Stability, 31*, 62–80.

Shingjergji, A., & Hyseni, M. (2015). The determinants of the capital adequacy ratio in the Albanian banking system during 2007–2014. *International Journal of Economics, Commerce and Management, 3*(1), 1–10.

Van Greuning, H., & Bratanovic, S. B. (2020). Analyzing banking risk: A framework for assessing corporate governance and risk management. *World Bank*. Publications.

Wilson, J. (2014). *Essentials of business research: A guide to doing your research project*. Sage.

Zamore, S., Ohene Djan, K., Alon, I., & Hobdari, B. (2018). Credit risk research: Review and agenda. *Emerging Markets Finance and Trade, 54*(4), 811–835.

Zhongming, T., Frimpong, S., & Guoping, D. (2019). Impact of financial risk indicators on Bank's financial performance in Ghana. *Business and Economic Research, 9*(4), 23–52.

Chapter 70
Digital Entrepreneurship Activities Among Gender Groups in Greek Agrifood Firms

Afroditi Kitta, Ourania Notta, and Aspasia Vlachvei

Abstract The purpose of this chapter is to provide insight into digital entrepreneurship through the gender lens in Greek agrifood firms. Especially, the study brings to light cultural factors, digital behaviour, marketing activities, and communication media towards e-marketing through gender differences. To achieve this aim, a survey of 91 participants (65 men and 26 women entrepreneurs) was conducted and the data were analyzed using the Principal Component Analysis.

Keywords Digital entrepreneurship · Gender differences · Cultural factors · Digital behaviour · Marketing activities · Communication media · Greek agrifood firms

70.1 Introduction

Entrepreneurship is very important for female empowerment, highlighting gender equality and human progress. Entrepreneurial activities have consequences for the economy and society. Thompson (2009) defines entrepreneurial intention as "a person's self-admitted conviction that they intend to establish a new business venture and consciously plan to do so at some point in the future." Given that digital entrepreneurship is a subset of traditional entrepreneurship, digital entrepreneurial intention can be defined as an individual's proclivity to start a new technology-based business (Chang et al., 2020; Huang et al., 2022; Wang et al., 2016). Digital entrepreneurial intention demonstrates a person's mental state and behavioral attributes. The person shows eagerness and decisiveness to use digital technologies for his/her digital business. Therefore, digital entrepreneurship

---

A. Kitta · O. Notta (✉)
Department of Agriculture, International Hellenic University, Thessaloniki, Greece
e-mail: ournotta@ihu.gr

A. Vlachvei
Department of Economics, University of Western Macedonia, Kastoria, Greece

is added to traditional entrepreneurship as activities and digital technologies lead to change in the business model and new opportunities.

In recent years, digital entrepreneurship has been a developing field of research for many academics, professionals, and policymakers (Kitta et al. 2023; Notta et al., 2022; Vlachvei et al., 2022; Notta & Kitta, 2021; Beliaeva et al., 2019; Kraus et al., 2019). Nonetheless, the concept is in its infancy in entrepreneurship research, and little is known about its determinant factors (Darmanto et al., 2022; Mir et al., 2022; Nambisan, 2017). Furthermore, the factors that drive people to become digital entrepreneurs and influence their goals and desires for a successful digital entrepreneur are not fully understood.

According to Anderson et al. (2014), innovation is defined as a new and improved way of doing things, something original and valuable. The knowledge of women entrepreneurship is a valid topic for research because gender is relevant to the performance and women entrepreneurship for economic growth. Particularly, there is a lack of knowledge in developing countries about this topic, so the study attempts to describe the case of a developing country, namely, Greece. Scholars are increasingly interested in the relationship between gender and innovation. Furthermore, digital technology has made female-led entrepreneurship possible. As a result, a growing corpus of scholars has begun to focus on female entrepreneurs and gender inequities in digital environments.

Consequently, the study provides a review of gender digital entrepreneurship's previous studies by analysing and identifying the differences between male and female entrepreneurs in Greek agri-food firms. To achieve the aim of the study, this chapter is structured as follows. In Sect. 70.2, previous studies related to (a) cultural factors towards e-marketing activities, (b) entrepreneurial digital behaviour, and (c) marketing activities and communication media are presented below. In Sects. 70.3 and 70.4, research methodology and data analysis are demonstrated, respectively. Then, a discussion of the research findings is presented in Sect. 70.5. Finally, conclusions are highlighted in Sect. 70.6.

70.2 Theoretical Background and Hypothesis Development

70.2.1 Cultural Factors Toward Electronic Marketing Activities

Researchers accumulate their search for cultural factors towards gender role expectations and identities, societal cultural dimensions, and entrepreneurial environment. Low female entrepreneurial activity is associated with structural and cultural obstacles in societies with fatherly authority. Female entrepreneurs face gender biases, so culture encompasses beliefs, norms, and expectations in a community.

Funding plays a pivotal role in innovation (Bates et al., 2007). When economic opportunity is high for women, companies grasp the chance to "gender-balanced ownership structure and workforce" to bring about innovation. New entrepreneurs face difficulties in financing start-up costs, but they may be able to use their social networks. Mekonnen and Cestino (2017) advocate for the relevance of social networks in knowledge transfer and innovation adaption.

Motherhood plays a significant role in women's life. It is an essential micro-level component that has an impact on innovators' success. They may abandon their inventive endeavors in favor of family. However, there are more favorable perspectives on culture and women's entrepreneurship, since women have discovered ways to balance their personal and professional life.

Feminine skills have been developed from household responsibilities, such as multitasking, interpersonal skills, and emotional empathy (Ruderman et al. 2002). Women as leaders in a business limits barriers and this notion gains admittance towards cultural and economic context. Leadership characteristics that demonstrate women's skills are being nurturing, collaborative, cooperative, affectionate, and concerned for others in the community (Yoder 2001). Researchers have claimed that women outperform men in empathy, emotion judging, friendship, community building, and sensitive relationship management. Passion for variety, intercultural empathy, and diplomacy are included among their global leadership abilities. Also, they highlighted that women are influenced by their close relationships. Women can connect to, be inspired, and imitate peers formulating role models (Markussen & Røed, 2017). Thus, we propose the following hypothesis:

H1 Are there differences in cultural factors that support e-marketing activities between gender groups?

70.2.2 Digital Behavior Toward E-Marketing Adoption

Opportunities are not limited to a select few but rather are available to anyone who has the vision to see them. There are three complementary but mutually exclusive constructs: "scanning and searching for information," "connecting previously disparate information," and "making evaluations on the existence of profitable business opportunities." As a result, those who are aware of entrepreneurial opportunities are more inclined to pursue them. Additionally, "innovativeness is more likely to occur when individuals are passionate about the task at hand." Furthermore, when there is a strong desire to create, creativity and overall innovativeness are enhanced.

According to *Robert* Adams (2008, p. 16), empowerment is "the ability of individuals, groups/communities to take control of their positions, exert power, and achieve their own goals." They can improve the quality of their life both individually and collectively. In method and practice, the concept of empowerment remains multidimensional (Pekonen et al., 2020). Empowerment is a commonly used idea that can be implemented at the individual, community, or organizational levels. Individuals can obtain psychological empowerment when they are given opportunities to direct their life on intrapersonal, interpersonal, and behavioral levels (Zimmerman, 1995).

Psychological empowerment consists of four cognitions: meaning, competence, self-determination, and impact. The guiding dimensions for psychological empowerment are goal internationalization, perceived control, and perceived competence. Other researchers consider psychological empowerment traits such as meaning, impact, self-determination, and self-esteem. Also, scholars looked into four different female psychological empowerment cognitions: internationalization, perceived control, perceived competence, and effect. "Meaning" is defined as "a fit between the requirements of a job and a person's beliefs, values, and behaviors," which is the same as goal internalization.

Goal internalization is defined as female entrepreneurs' beliefs and values in becoming digital entrepreneurs (Crittenden et al., 2019). Female entrepreneurs' participation in social media supports and strengthens their intention to become digital entrepreneurs. Furthermore, it encourages female entrepreneurs to consider the internet presence of their businesses as one of their goals.

Entrepreneurs should learn how to leverage current technologies to transform their company model, do things differently, produce new products and services, and engage with their customers in novel ways. In the realm of technology, digital competence is related to ICT self-efficacy, computer self-efficacy, and digital technology self-efficacy. Previous studies asserted that successful entrepreneurs must have faith in their abilities in order to recognize untapped business opportunities.

Perceived control can be defined as the level of authority and independence gained by female entrepreneurs through social media participation, which determines their intention to engage in digital entrepreneurship. One of the psychological states of female empowerment that women encounter when conducting business on digital platforms such as social media is perceived control.

70.2.2.1 Empowerment and Women Entrepreneurship

Scholars are increasingly emphasizing a larger understanding of the function of entrepreneurship, one that incorporates individual and group emancipatory elements (Gaddefors & Anderson, 2017). Entrepreneurial efforts frequently involve breaking away from the authority and dominance of others in order to achieve individual and collective progress. Thus, starting a business allows people to connect with the resources and social networks needed to complete entrepreneurship projects that involve social transformation and freedom from dominant power structures (Alkhaled & Berglund, 2018). Different entrepreneurial practices and outcomes reaching personal and communal freedom and autonomy from unequal social systems and authority structures are vital. Furthermore, entrepreneurship encourages a "social turn," resulting in more egalitarian and inclusive communities and is a significant driver of poverty reduction and human evolution.

Entrepreneurship has an inherent empowering component related to the improvement of human happiness through the development of capacities that people may use to practically fulfill their goals. Empowerment seeks to alter power dynamics and shift power inequalities in favor of persons who previously had little control over their life.

Control over resources (physical, financial, human, etc.) and control over ideology (beliefs, values, and attitudes) are important strategies of attaining agency and power. As a result, empowerment methods should aim to increase women's self-esteem and assertiveness, or consciousness. Consciousness is also a social change in which women are able to express opinions or ideas that differ from dominant mainstream attitudes, become role models in communities and society, and mobilize and organize individually and collectively. Thus, we propose the following hypothesis:

H2 Are there differences in digital behavior towards E-Marketing adoption between gender groups?

70.2.3 Marketing Activities and Communication Media

New digital technologies have opened new avenues for organizations, allowing them to interact with customers through online channels including websites, social networks, and mobile apps, in addition to traditional offline channels. In an omnichannel trip, consumers can browse product information and read online reviews before making a purchase in a store, or they can experience offline after-sales and delivery services after purchasing a product online.

Female entrepreneurs have been observed to be actively engaged in terms of reading numerous messages, posting various comments, and sharing knowledge. Previous research has identified three categories of engagement in social media communities: informative, actionable, and attitudinal. Female entrepreneurs are being mobilized through social media for informational, actionable, and attitudinal participation.

Such sorts of engagement also build the attitude and spirit of female entrepreneurs reading many messages, posting a variety of comments, and exchanging knowledge. If the opinion is favorable, it increases the members' loyalty to the products or services, and vice versa. Furthermore, brand, as a cognitive and emotional medium, plays an important role in the transition from encounters to co-creation. Cross-channel consistency (CCC) is an important consideration in the omnichannel context. Firms are actively investing in expanding the channels via which they may engage with their clients, who move freely across channels and want a seamless purchasing experience.

In omnichannel engagements, customers use many online and offline channels to gather information, communicate, and complete transactions for a single purchase. Channel interactivity refers to the level of contact initiated by enterprises from the consumer's perspective. Interactions with both information technologies and humans are referred to as interactivity. Interactivity can thus be described as the degree to which one or more individuals respond to specific resources, such as

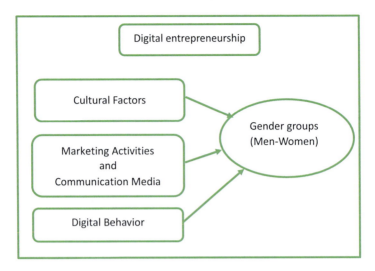

Fig. 70.1 Theoretical framework

objects and content. Coproduction and value-in-use are two prevalent variables in value co-creation.

In addition, the researchers measured customer value co-creation (VCB) behavior on two aspects: (i) customer engagement behavior (in a role), divided into information seeking, sharing, responsibility, and personal interaction behavior, and (ii) customer citizenship behavior (outside of roles), divided into feedback, advocacy, mutual help, and tolerance. Cognitive activities, cooperation, information seeking and gathering, complementary activities, habit modification, co-production, joint learning, and association are all examples of VCB. Figure 70.1 depicts our conceptual model. Thus, we propose the following hypothesis:

H3 Are there differences in marketing activities and communication media between gender groups?

70.3 Methods

Structured interviews (questionnaires) were performed with entrepreneurs from agri-food enterprises to obtain primary data. IBM SPSS Statistics 29.0 software was used for statistical analysis. The sample was chosen at random, and businesses were looked up using online business directories (www.xo.gr and www.vrisko.gr) and exhibitor information leaflets at food and beverage exhibits (Detrop, Expotrof, and Food Expo).

However, 200 surveys were sent, of which 91 were completed and returned. This means that the sample response rate is 45.5%. Our survey participants were 65 male entrepreneurs and 26 female entrepreneurs.

70.4 Analysis and Results

To develop our measures for this construct, we relied on *Chakraborty U., & Biswal S. K. (2023)*. Managers were asked to express their opinion about the cultural factors and digital behavior that support e-marketing activities, as well as the exploitation of Marketing activities and communication media. The final measure included: regarding the cultural factors 11 items for men and 8 items for women. About digital behaviour 16 items for men and 13 items for women were included. Taking into consideration Marketing activities and communication media, 8 items for men and 6 items for women, all were assessed on a five-point Likert scale with the anchors 1: very much disagree, 5: very much agree.

First, data were analyzed using principal component factor analysis. To extract some specific elements, research was based on Guttman-Kaiser Criterion. Therefore, elements with Eigenvalues greater than 1 are eligible. Through the analysis of the principal component method, three factors have been identified explaining together 74.1% for men and 78.2% for women of the variance in the items concerning the cultural factors that support E-Marketing activities. Refer Tables 70.1 and 70.2 for the exact item clarifications and factor analysis results.

The first factor, named as *"Entrepreneurial Opportunity,"* accounts for 32.43% for men and 40.5% for women of Total Variance Explained. This factor is characterized by significant correlation for the two gender groups in parameters concerning the competitors' pressure and avoidance of losing market share. The second factor (explains 21.46% for men and 23.17% for women of Total Variance Explained) is assigned the characterization *"Government support"* as there is a high correlation between the parameters that refer to the adoption of e-marketing because of the: (a) incentives, (b) protection provided by the government, and (c) government influences, for both men and women. The third factor named as *"Perceived interactivity"* explains 20.21% for men and 14.61% for women of Total Variance Explained. In this category, men respondents assert that: (a) Customers prefer to pay in cash instead of electronic payment methods, (b) there is lack of trust between enterprises conducting E-Marketing activities, (c) customers do not trust E-Marketing due to security issues, (d) customers do not trust E-Marketing due to issues of privacy about personal data, and (e) customers distrust firms that provide products using E-Marketing tools. On the contrary, women respondents argued that: (a) there are enough legal acts to provide a supportive business environment for E-Marketing, and (b) majority of customers are able to utilize technology.

Tables 70.3 and 70.4 present the results from the creation of three components that have been identified corresponding to 69.87% of Total Variance Explained for men and 81.58% for women. Findings are about the digital behavior towards e-

Table 70.1 Cultural factors that support e-marketing activities

Rotated component matrix[a, b]

	Component		
	Entrepreneurial opportunity	Government support	Perceived interactivity
Competitors pressure is one reason for e-marketing adoption	**0.645**[c]	−0.032	−0.014
Competitors pressure is the main reason for e-marketing adoption	**0.881**	0.035	0.135
Adopted e-marketing to avoid losing market share from competitors	**0.905**	0.045	−0.005
Adopted e-marketing because of the incentives provided by the government	−0.026	**0.942**	0.166
Adopted e-marketing because of the protection provided by the government	−0.053	**0.969**	0.119
Adopted e-marketing because of government influences	0.089	**0.962**	0.035
Customers prefer to pay in cash instead of electronic payment methods	0.096	0.124	**0.744**
There is lack of trust between enterprises conducting e-marketing activities	0.031	0.107	**0.685**
Customers do not trust e-marketing due to security issues	0.061	0.082	**0.923**
Customers do not trust e-marketing due to issues of privacy about personal data	−0.013	−0.002	**0.883**
Customers distrust firms that provide products using e-marketing tools	−0.480	0.093	**0.609**

Extraction Method: Principal Component Analysis
Rotation Method: Varimax with Kaiser Normalization
[a]Rotation converged in 4 iterations
[b]Only cases for which GENDER = MAN are used in the analysis phase
[c]Kaiser-Meyer-Olkin (KMO) Measure of Sampling Adequacy: 0,70 Sig. level for the Bartlett's test : 0,000

marketing adoption. To extract a specific number of factors, the research was based on the Guttman-Kaiser Criterion. Therefore, factors with Eigenvalue greater than 1 are eligible. The factor *"Digital Entrepreneur Intention"* (explains 42.51% for men and 60.6% for women of Total Variance Explained) reveals that there is significant correlation in the following parameters: for men entrepreneurs, it is essential to adopt e-marketing because its usage: (a) helps when firm size increases, (b) enables to accomplish tasks more quickly, (c) improves job quality, (d) makes it easier to do their job, (e) increases productivity, (f) gives greater control over their job, and (g) enhances effectiveness on their job. Women entrepreneurs claimed that e-marketing usage: (a) improves their job quality, (b) makes it easier to do their job, and c) improves job performance. The second factor, *"Digital presence goals achievement"* (explains 19.1% for men and 12.29% for women of Total Variance Explained), demonstrates that there is significant correlation between the two gender

Table 70.2 Cultural factors that support e-marketing activities

Rotated component matrix[a, b]	Component		
	Entrepreneurial opportunity	Government support	Perceived interactivity
Competitors pressure is one reason for e-marketing adoption	**0.682**[c]	−0.091	−0.366
There are enough legal acts to provide a supportive business environment for e-marketing	0.187	0.137	**0.791**
Competitors pressure is the main reason for e-marketing adoption	**0.891**	0.191	0.059
Adopted e-marketing to avoid losing market share from competitors	**0.877**	0.138	0.126
Adopted e-marketing because of the incentives provided by the government	0.084	**0.976**	−0.058
Adopted e-marketing because of the protection provided by the government	0.141	**0.942**	0.078
Adopted e-marketing because of government influences	0.057	**0.938**	−0.046
Majority of customers are able to utilize technology	−0.321	−0.274	**0.632**

Extraction Method: Principal Component Analysis
Rotation Method: Varimax with Kaiser Normalization
[a]Rotation converged in 4 iterations
[b]Only cases for which GENDER = WOMAN are used in the analysis phase
[c]KMO Measure of Sampling Adequacy: 0,67 Sig. level for the Bartlett's test : 0,000

groups in parameters regarding the following: (a) the important role to conduct business activities through e-marketing tools, (b) there is enough support from the management towards e-marketing tools, (c) personnel attitude and behavior goes in line with e-marketing adoption, (d) marketing team use e-marketing tools with a beneficial manner, (e) e-marketing tools correspond with enterprise beliefs and values, and (f) entrepreneurs believe that e-marketing is easy to use. The last factor for the digital behavior towards e-marketing adoption is *"Perceived control"* (refers to 8.2% for men and 8.6% for women of Total Variance Explained). Men expressed that e-marketing: (a) fits absolutely with their job, (b) Interaction with e-marketing is clear and understandable, and (c) it is easy to do what they want with e-marketing. Women argued that (a) they adopted e-marketing due to the existence of sufficient financial resources and (b) e-marketing usage fits absolutely with their job and is compatible with their work style.

Tables 70.5 and 70.6 present the research results on the Marketing activities and communication media. Variables were classified into two categories according to the Guttman-Kaiser Criterion describing 59% for men and 69.37% for women of the Total Variance. Elements with Eigenvalues greater than 1 are eligible. The first factor is defined as *"One-way communication"* (refers to 38.84% for men

Table 70.3 Digital behavior towards e-marketing adoption

Rotated component matrix[a, b]

	Component		
	Digital entrepreneur intention	Digital presence goals achievement	Perceived control
e-marketing tools are very important to conduct business activities	0.350	**0.641**[c]	−0.124
Enough support from the management	0.228	**0.841**	0.009
Personnel attitude goes in line with e-marketing adoption	−0.090	**0.777**	0.413
e-marketing tools go in line with enterprise beliefs	0.097	**0.886**	0.108
Personnel behavior goes in line with e-marketing adoption	0.095	**0.811**	0.325
Marketing team use e-marketing tools with a beneficial manner	0.074	**0.656**	0.145
You will adopt e-marketing when you will increase firm size	**0.482**	−0.288	0.272
e-marketing usage enables to accomplish tasks more quickly	**0.732**	0.307	0.300
e-marketing usage improves job quality	**0.850**	0.312	0.100
e-marketing usage makes it easier to do your job	**0.827**	0.120	0.285
e-marketing usage increases productivity	**0.914**	0.098	0.132
e-marketing usage gives greater control over your job	**0.876**	0.039	0.029
e-marketing usage enhances effectiveness on your job	**0.891**	0.196	−0.007
e-marketing usage fits absolutely with your job	0.400	0.462	**0.499**
Interaction with e-marketing is clear and understandable	0.216	0.092	**0.625**
It is easy to do what you want with e-marketing	0.090	0.228	**0.862**

Extraction Method: Principal Component Analysis
Rotation Method: Varimax with Kaiser Normalization
[a]Rotation converged in 5 iterations
[b]Only cases for which GENDER = MAN are used in the analysis phase
[c]KMO Measure of Sampling Adequacy: 0,78 Sig. level for the Bartlett's test : 0,000

and 52.58% for women of Total Variance Explained). In this category, for men participants, there is significant correlation in parameters concerning the usage of E-Marketing resources (website, e-mail) to communicate with customers, to support firm traditional commercial activities. Also, they use the Internet to access other companies' websites. Women participants support that: they use e-marketing resources (website, e-mail) to communicate with customers, to advertise products,

Table 70.4 Digital behaviour towards e-marketing adoption

Rotated component matrix[a, b]

	Component		
	Digital entrepreneur intention	Digital presence goals achievement	Perceived control
Enough support from the management	0.186	**0.798**[c]	0.342
e-marketing tools go in line with enterprise values	0.231	**0.886**	0.272
Personnel attitude go in line with e-marketing adoption	0.359	**0.870**	−0.033
e-marketing tools go in line with enterprise beliefs	0.295	**0.882**	0.252
Personnel behavior goes in line with e-marketing adoption	0.316	**0.838**	0.276
Marketing team use e-marketing tools with a beneficial manner	0.386	**0.685**	0.188
e-marketing adoption due to the existence of sufficient financial resources	−0.071	0.091	**0.889**
e-marketing usage improves job quality	**0.892**	0.310	0.210
e-marketing usage makes it easier to do your job	**0.919**	0.236	0.099
e-marketing usage improves job performance	**0.782**	0.390	−0.030
e-marketing usage fits absolutely with your job	0.454	0.481	**0.594**
e-marketing usage fits into work style	0.232	0.344	**0.844**
Believe that e-marketing is easy to use	0.380	**0.447**	0.351

Extraction Method: Principal Component Analysis
Rotation Method: Varimax with Kaiser Normalization
[a]Rotation converged in 5 iterations
[b]Only cases for which GENDER = WOMAN are used in the analysis phase
[c]KMO Measure of Sampling Adequacy: 0,77 Sig. level for the Bartlett's test : 0,000

and to support the firm's traditional commercial activities. The second component is called *"Interactive communication"* (refers to 20.24% for men and 16.78% for women of Total Variance Explained). Significant correlations revealed for men in parameters concerning: (a) systematic or regular updates to their firm website, (b) their enterprise interacts with its customers through registration forms, newsletters, and e-mail accounts, and (c) they have a customer database that they use to perform marketing activities. About women high correlations presented in parameters that are associated with: (a) their firm website is connected to a customer database, (b) they have a customer database that they use to perform marketing activities, and (c) they conduct B2B marketing activities.

Table 70.5 Marketing activities and communication media

Rotated component matrix[a, b]	Component	
	One-way communication	Interactive communication
Conduct marketing activities according to traditional marketing	**−0.688**[c]	−0.117
Do not have any access to the internet or any Electronic Marketing means	**−0.663**	0.246
Use e-marketing resources (website, e-mail) to communicate with customers	**0.689**	0.136
Use Internet in accessing other companies' websites	**0.771**	0.121
Use e-marketing resources to support firm traditional commercial activities	**0.704**	0.343
Carry out systematic or regular updates to website	0.433	**0.608**
Enterprise interacts with its customers through registration forms, newsletters, and e-mail accounts	0.162	**0.868**
Have a customer database that use to perform marketing activities	−0.105	**0.824**

Extraction Method: Principal Component Analysis
Rotation Method: Varimax with Kaiser Normalization
[a]Rotation converged in 3 iterations
[b]Only cases for which GENDER = MAN are used in the analysis phase
[c]KMO Measure of Sampling Adequacy: 0,73 Sig. level for the Bartlett's test : 0,000

Table 70.6 Marketing activities and communication media

Rotated component matrix[a, b]	Component	
	One-way communication	Interactive communication
Use e-marketing resources (website, e-mail) to communicate with customers	**0.935**[c]	0.018
Use e-marketing resources (website, e-mail) to advertise products	**0.853**	0.275
Use e-marketing resources to support firm traditional commercial activities	**0.613**	0.607
Website is connected to a customer database	0.111	**0.599**
Have a customer database that use to perform marketing activities	0.489	**0.710**
Conduct B2B marketing activities	0.035	**0.791**

Extraction Method: Principal Component Analysis
Rotation Method: Varimax with Kaiser Normalization
[a]Rotation converged in 3 iterations
[b]Only cases for which GENDER = WOMAN are used in the analysis phase
[c]KMO Measure of Sampling Adequacy: 0,58 Sig. level for the Bartlett's test : 0,000

70.5 Discussion

This chapter explores how cultural factors, digital behavior, marketing activities, and communication media towards e-marketing stimulate differences in gender groups. To start with, three factors were formed according to cultural factors that support e-marketing activities. Results about the first factor *"Entrepreneurial Opportunity"* revealed that both men and women entrepreneurs will be motivated to venture into digital marketing because of the competitors' pressure and avoidance of losing market. Competitive pressure can be influenced by factors such as rapid dissemination of innovation, globalization, and technical improvement. It has been stated that the bigger the number of rivals in an industry, the greater the adoption of new technology among SMEs. Since digital innovation is defined as the unique application of digital technology in a business context to the introduction of new products, services, processes or business models as a means or end, it is important to note that technology-related skills and abilities are required to get the most out of digital technologies; otherwise, innovation will remain an abstract notion that cannot be realized.

Furthermore, results for the second factor "Government *support"* revealed that entrepreneurs consider government incentives/protection and influences very important to expand their digital business. A productive and helpful entrepreneurial ecosystem for women entrepreneurs is comprised of unbiased legal and commercial frameworks that secure equitable access to financial resources and increase cultural expectations and practices that promote women's companies. Policies that encourage financial institutions to advertise investment funds and lending products directly to women, as well as produce specific financial products for women entrepreneurs, are examples of a helpful entrepreneurial climate.

Moreover, results for the factor *"Perceived interactivity"* revealed differences in gender groups. Specifically, men conveyed that there is a distrust towards digital technologies from their customers conducting online payments, share content related to marketing activities. This content reinforces their concerns for its credibility about security and personal data. On the other hand, women asserted that customers can utilize technology and their environment support e-marketing without gender discriminations by the state. These results can be explained from different aspects. Researchers believe that a range of presenting formats allows customers to exchange information or ideas, which promotes value co-creation behavior. Customized information can help clients understand the supplier and eliminate transactional uncertainty. Effective channel interactivity in the digital context suggests that the provider can deliver tailored material and diversify its message presentation. If a company responds quickly to a customer's question, the good interaction experience increases the customer's perceived value of the company and its products. Digital entrepreneurs can achieve a better work-life balance by having greater adaptability and freedom in terms of work time and location. Researchers examined the relationship between social media and female entrepreneurs and discovered that there are low investment and operating costs in a social media start-up venture, which incentivizes female entrepreneurs.

Furthermore, three factors were created regarding digital behavior toward e-marketing adoption. Findings concerning the first factor *"Digital Entrepreneur Intention,"* men described that they will adopt e-marketing when they will increase firm size. Also, e-marketing usage enables to accomplish tasks more quickly, makes it easier to do their job, gives greater control over their job, and enhances effectiveness on their job. It seems that e-marketing adoption depends on their firm financial resources and towards this sense of purpose, they plan how to achieve marketing performance. On the part of women, it seems that to use e-marketing tools is independent of financial support in case they want to expand their digital business and accomplish their purposes expressing persistence. So, they can increase firm performance through paid content to different digital channels. Many women run their enterprises from home, where they can efficiently manage both their professional and personal life.

Additionally, results for the second factor *"Digital presence goals achievement"* revealed that both men and women declared that there is enough support from the management towards e-marketing adoption. Also, digital tools go in line with enterprise values, personnel behavior goes in line with their adoption, and the marketing team uses digital platforms in a beneficial manner. Managerial support is critical in creating a welcoming climate and allocating the necessary resources for innovation adoption. Furthermore, by incorporating social media activities into business operations in a way that is consistent with the firm's aims, principles, and values, companies will be able to effectively reach their target audiences by instantaneously disseminating information about the firm's services.

According to the last factor, *"Perceived control"* for agri-food entrepreneurs revealed the following: Men expressed that perceived control is associated towards interaction with e-marketing that is clear and understandable. Also, it depends on the degree of convenience to do what they want using e-marketing tool. Male participants associate e-marketing tools with personality traits to exploit entrepreneurial opportunities across time. About women participants, they pointed out that perceived control encompasses sufficient financial resources and compliance with work style. This means that integrating applications into their sites will increase interactive communication between the company and consumers. As a result, superior firm performance is relevant to financial sources.

In the end, two factors were created concerning Marketing activities and communication media. Findings about the first factor *"One-way communication,"* men claimed that they communicate with customers using website or email and they have access to other firms' websites. This is encouraged by employing low-cost and easily accessible channels such as online videos, tweets, Facebook pages, and email campaigns. Women asserted that they use e-marketing tools to communicate with customers and advertise their products. Female entrepreneurs are active in marketing their business activities on social media through information involvement. Female entrepreneurs' social media participation boosts their client engagement. The higher the level of interaction, the higher the level of digital platform business activity. Increased social media contact with clients boosts customer motivation. In addition, Chakraborty and Biswal (2023) discovered through data analysis that female entrepreneurs are found as opinion leaders in social media groups to supply new information on products or services. Their actions, such as liking, sharing, and commenting on various messages, satisfy opinion-seekers on social media networks.

Moreover, the last factor *"Interactive communication"* demonstrated the following results: men expressed that they carry out regular updates to website and interact with customers through registration forms, newsletters, and e-mail accounts. Also, they have a customer database that is used to perform marketing activities. About women respondents, they clarified that their website is connected to a customer database and they conduct B2B marketing activities. Taking into consideration these results and comparing gender groups, women coordinate their marketing activities through online and offline contexts to increase a firm's appeal and achieve value co-creation behaviors. The halo effect is caused by a highly integrated cross-channel arrangement, which mutually enhances the positive perception of the interaction for distinct channels.

70.6 Conclusion

In conclusion, this study aims to explore digital entrepreneurship revealing differences between gender groups. To achieve this aim, this chapter gathered the recent literature and synthesized the proposed model, which was tested with Principal Component Analysis. This model is divided into (a) cultural factors towards e-marketing activities: entrepreneurial opportunity, government support, perceived interactivity, (b) digital behaviour towards e-marketing adoption: digital entrepreneur intention, digital presence goals achievement, perceived control, and (c) marketing activities and communication media: one-way communication, interactive communication. Based on data collected online from 91 agrifood firms in Greece, male participants 65 and female 26, the results provide useful insights for both managers and policymakers for developing digital marketing strategies related to gender differences.

References

Adams, R. (2008). *Empowerment, participation and social work*. Macmillan International Higher Education.

Alkhaled, S., & Berglund, K. (2018). 'And now I'm free': Women's empowerment and emancipation through entrepreneurship in Saudi Arabia and Sweden. *Entrepreneurship & Regional Development, 30*(7–8), 877–900.

Anderson, N., Potočnik, K., & Zhou, J. (2014). Innovation and creativity in organizations: A state-of-the-science review, prospective commentary, and guiding framework. *Journal of Management, 40*(5), 1297–1333.

Bates, M., Manuel, S., & Oppenheim, C. (2007). *Models of early adoption of ICT innovations in higher education.*

Beliaeva, T., Ferasso, M., Kraus, S., & Damke, E. J. (2019). Dynamics of digital entrepreneurship and the innovation ecosystem: A multilevel perspective. *International Journal of Entrepreneurial Behavior & Research, 26*(2), 266–284.

Birkner, S., Ettl, K., Welter, F., & Ebbers, I. (2018). Women's entrepreneurship in Europe: Research facets and educational Foci. *Women's Entrepreneurship in Europe: Multidimensional Research and Case Study Insights*, 3–13.

Bullough, A., Guelich, U., Manolova, T. S., & Schjoedt, L. (2022). Women's entrepreneurship and culture: Gender role expectations and identities, societal culture, and the entrepreneurial environment. *Small Business Economics, 58*(2), 985–996.

Chakraborty, U., & Biswal, S. K. (2023). Impact of social media participation on female entrepreneurs towards their digital entrepreneurship intention and psychological empowerment. *Journal of Research in Marketing and Entrepreneurship*. (ahead-of-print).

Chang, S. H., Shu, Y., Wang, C. L., Chen, M. Y., & Ho, W. S. (2020). Cyber-entrepreneurship as an innovative orientation: Does positive thinking moderate the relationship between cyber-entrepreneurial self-efficacy and cyber-entrepreneurial intentions in non-IT students? *Computers in Human Behavior, 107*, 105975.

Chatterjee, S., Chaudhuri, R., Mikalef, P., & Sarpong, D. (2023). Coopetition in the platform economy from ethical and firm performance perspectives. *Journal of Business Research, 157*, 113576.

Crittenden, V. L., Crittenden, W. F., & Ajjan, H. (2019). Empowering women micro-entrepreneurs in emerging economies: The role of information communications technology. *Journal of Business Research, 98*, 191–203.

Cui, X., Xie, Q., Zhu, J., Shareef, M. A., Goraya, M. A. S., & Akram, M. S. (2022). Understanding the omnichannel customer journey: The effect of online and offline channel interactivity on consumer value co-creation behavior. *Journal of Retailing and Consumer Services, 65*, 102869.

Darmanto, S., Darmawan, D., Ekopriyono, A., & Dhani, A. (2022). Development of digital entrepreneurial intention model in Uncertain Era. *Uncertain Supply Chain Management, 10*(3), 1091–1102.

Elnadi, M., & Gheith, M. H. (2023). The role of individual characteristics in shaping digital entrepreneurial intention among university students: Evidence from Saudi Arabia. *Thinking Skills and Creativity, 101236.*

Feng, C. X., & Wang, X. F. (2003). Surface roughness predictive modeling: Neural networks versus regression. *IIE Transactions, 35*(1), 11–27.

Gaddefors, J., & Anderson, A. R. (2017). Entrepreneurship and context: When entrepreneurship is greater than entrepreneurs. *International Journal of Entrepreneurial Behavior & Research.*

Huang, T. C., Wang, Y. J., & Lai, H. M. (2022). What drives internet entrepreneurial intention to use technology products? An investigation of technology product imagination disposition, social support, and motivation. *Frontiers in Psychology, 13*, 829256.

Jia, S., Tseng, H. T., Shanmugam, M., Rees, D. J., Thomas, R., & Hajli, N. (2022). Using new forms of information and communication technologies to empower SMEs. *British Food Journal.*

Kitta, A., Notta, O., & Vlachvei, A. (2023). Social media engagement: What matters? An empirical study on Greek agri-food firms. In N. Tsounis & A. Vlachvei (Eds.), *Advances in empirical economic research. ICOAE 2022. Springer proceedings in business and economics*. Springer. https://doi.org/10.1007/978-3-031-22749-3_61

Kraus, S., Palmer, C., Kailer, N., Kallinger, F. L., & Spitzer, J. (2019). Digital entrepreneurship: A research agenda on new business models for the twenty-first century. *International Journal of Entrepreneurial Behavior & Research, 25*(2), 353–375.

Markussen, S., & Røed, K. (2017). The gender gap in entrepreneurship – The role of peer effects. *Journal of Economic Behavior & Organization, 134*, 356–373.

Mekonnen, H. D., & Cestino, J. (2017). The impact of the institutional context on women's entrepreneurship in Ethiopia: Breaking the cycle of poverty? In *Contextualizing entrepreneurship in emerging economies and developing countries* (pp. 65–79). Edward Elgar Publishing.

Mir, A. A., Hassan, S., & Khan, S. J. (2022). Understanding digital entrepreneurial intentions: A capital theory perspective. *International Journal of Emerging Markets*. (ahead-of-print).

Mohammed, S. A. S. A., Bamahros, H. M. A., Grada, M. S., & Alaswadi, W. (2023). EC-education, gender disparity, and digital entrepreneurship intention: The moderating role of attitude components; a competitive advantage of the Ha'il region. *International Journal of Information Management Data Insights, 3*(2), 100179.

Nambisan, S. (2017). Digital entrepreneurship: Toward a digital technology perspective of entrepreneurship. *Entrepreneurship Theory and Practice, 41*(6), 1029–1055.

Notta, O., & Kitta, A. (2021). Factors affecting e-marketing adoption and implementation in food firms: An empirical investigation of Greek food and beverage firms. In *Advances in longitudinal data methods in applied economic research: 2020 international conference on applied economics (ICOAE)* (pp. 509–526). Springer.

Notta, O., Raikou, V., & Vlachvei, A. (2022). Social media usage and business competitiveness in agri-food SMEs. In *International conference on applied economics* (pp. 531–538). Springer.

Nwokah, N. G., & Irimagha, B. B. (2017). E-marketing orientation and social media implementation in the banking industry in Nigeria. *iBusiness, 9*(4), 111–133.

Pekonen, A., Eloranta, S., Stolt, M., Virolainen, P., & Leino-Kilpi, H. (2020). Measuring patient empowerment – A systematic review. *Patient Education and Counseling, 103*(4), 777–787.

Qalati, S. A., Ostic, D., Sulaiman, M. A. B. A., Gopang, A. A., & Khan, A. (2022). Social media and SMEs' performance in developing countries: Effects of technological-organizational-environmental factors on the adoption of social media. *SAGE Open, 12*(2), 21582440221094594.

Ruderman, M. N., Ohlott, P. J., Panzer, K., & King, S. N. (2002). Benefits of multiple roles for managerial women. *Academy of Management Journal, 45*(2), 369–386.

Sultan, S., & Sultan, W. I. (2020). Women MSMEs in times of crisis: Challenges and opportunities. *Journal of Small Business and Enterprise Development, 27*(7), 1069–1083.

Thompson, E. R. (2009). Individual entrepreneurial intent: Construct clarification and development of an internationally reliable metric. *Entrepreneurship Theory and Practice, 33*(3), 669–694.

Vlachvei, A., Notta, O., & Koronaki, I. (2022). How do post characteristics affect the stages of customer engagement in social media? An investigation of European wine brands. *Journal of Research in Interactive Marketing, 16*(4), 615–632. https://doi.org/10.1108/JRIM-12-2020-0275

Wang, Y. S., Lin, S. J., Yeh, C. H., Li, C. R., & Li, H. T. (2016). What drives students' cyber entrepreneurial intention: The moderating role of disciplinary difference. *Thinking Skills and Creativity, 22*, 22–35.

Yoder, J. D. (2001). Making leadership work more effectively for women. *Journal of Social Issues, 57*(4), 815–828.

Zerwas, C. S., & Zerwas, C. S. (2019). Expert study: Factors influencing women entrepreneurs' work-life balance. *Work-Life Balance and Women's Entrepreneurship: An Exploration of Influencing Factors*, 101–194.

Zhang, R. R., Abd Rahman, A., Aziz, Y. A., & Sidek, S. (2023). Unpacking technological and interpersonal interaction on value co-creation and outcomes in trade show: A dyadic examining view. *Journal of Hospitality and Tourism Management, 55*, 334–343.

Zimmerman, M. A. (1995). Psychological empowerment: Issues and illustrations. *American Journal of Community Psychology, 23*, 581–599.

Chapter 71
The Dynamics of Tourist Flows in Greece

G. Bertsatos, Z. Kalogiratou, Th. Monovasilis, and N. Tsounis

Abstract In this chapter the destination life cycle and product life cycle frameworks are used to develop an overall mathematical model to determine the different stages of the tourist product offered by Greece through time. An Ordinary Differential Equation (ODE) will be used, and its solution will be fitted to a long time series data (1955–2019) from tourist arrivals in Greece. Then using simple calculus, the five different periods of the Greek tourist product, i.e., exploration, involvement, development, consolidation, and stagnation, have been identified.

Keywords Digital entrepreneurship · Gender differences · Cultural factors · Digital behavior · Marketing activities · Communication media · Greek agrifood firms

71.1 Introduction

As a service sector, tourism has grown greatly through time and is crucial to the growth of many nations. As a result, in many nations, including Greece, which is the topic of this chapter, tourism today contributes significantly to the Gross Domestic Product (GDP) and employment. For the Greek economy, it is one of the most important sectors. In 2019 over 30 million tourists from over 40 countries visited Greece contributing 27% of the GDP and over 30% of the total employment. Since the 1960s and 1970s, Greece's tourism industry has grown significantly from a promising luxury good to a significant industry. The tourist industry proved to be both the key engine of the Greek economy's post-crisis recovery and the main

---

G. Bertsatos · T. Monovasilis · N. Tsounis
Department of Economics, University of Western Macedonia, Kastoria, Greece
e-mail: decon00001@uowm.gr; tmonovasilis@uowm.gr; ntsounis@uowm.gr

Z. Kalogiratou (✉)
Department of Informatics, University of Western Macedonia, Kastoria, Greece
e-mail: zkalogiratou@uowm.gr

embankment in the recession during the financial crises of 2007 and 2008. Before the pandemic period, between 2005 and 2019, the number of inbound tourists climbed by 136.34% (from 14.4 to 34 million), and their receipts were anticipated to have increased by 69.4% (from 10.7 to 18.2 billion euros), respectively. The percentage of workers in the tourism industry relative to all employment has climbed from 17.7% in 2009 to 25.9% in 2018 (INSETE 2019), continuing the increasing trend. With sales of 17.7 billion euros and 31.3 million visitors, the tourism sector contributes to the Greek economy by 20.8% of GDP in 2019 and by 21.7% of all jobs, according to SETE statistics (INSETE 2021). According to the Greek Statistic Office's estimate, the impact of one euro spent in the tourism industry on the Greek economy is between 2.2 and 2.65 times greater (ibid.). The significance of the tourism industry for Greece, a small open economy with a trade to GDP ratio of nearly 90% (World Bank 2023), is made clear by this straightforward list of data. It has significant macroeconomic effects in that it has an impact on the growth, income, employment, revenue, and balance of payments. Tourism has also significant microeconomic effects since it has an impact on a variety of industries, including transportation, lodging and food, rental and leasing, travel agencies, tour operators and reservation services, entertainment and cultural services, sports, amusement, and recreation services.

In this chapter we will use the product life cycle analysis to identify the stages of the tourist product of Greece through its life span. Usually, the model can be used to assess an individual firm's products, a type of product, or an industry. Different variations of the model can show between four and six stages which are development, introduction, growth, maturity, saturation, and decline. Specifically for the tourist product offered by a country (or a destination), Butler (1980) identified tourist product evolution in five stages:

- Exploration
- Involvement
- Development
- Consolidation
- Stagnation

We will use this approach to study the conceptual life cycle of Greek tourist product.

The chapter proceeds as follows: in Sect. 71.2 the data used are described, Sect. 71.3 presents a mathematical model developed to identify the different stages of the Greek tourist product, and Sect. 71.4 presents the results from the data fitting and finally concludes.

71.2 Data Description

Data of arrivals in Greece of non-Greek citizens are reported since 1955 by the Hellenic Statistical Authority (2023) (see Fig. 71.1). In 1955 there have been 208 thousand arrivals, and by 1965 the number of arrivals climbed to almost one million.

Fig. 71.1 Tourist arrivals in Greece 1955–2019

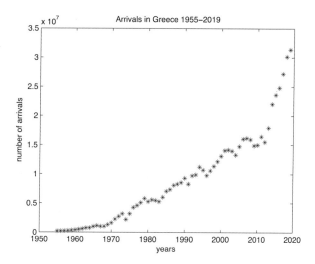

The rate of change was positive apart from the years 1966–1967 where from 1.132 million arrivals in 1966 the next year the number reduced to 996 thousands. The next negative sign in the rate of change appears in 1974 with a reduction of 31% from 1973; arrivals dropped from 3.178 to 2.188 million, to overcome in 1975 with 3.172. In years 1967 and 1974 the country experienced political instability that seems to have affected the incoming tourism.

The rapid increase continued until 1979 when the arrivals reached 5.798 million. In the following years the rate of change is positive apart from 1979–1980 with a reduction of 9% and 1990–1991 with a reduction of 11% which balanced with an increase of 18% in 1991–1992.

From 2006 to 2012 arrivals vary in the interval between 15 and 16.5 million; these may be considered as the last two stages of the product life. Year 2012 seems to be a critical year since from this year on the tourist arrivals increase rapidly to reach 31 million in 2019. We observe that a full product cycle has been completed in 2012 and a new cycle has started with a rejuvenation stage from 2012 onward where a sharp increase in tourist arrivals is observed.

71.3 Mathematical Modelling

Let $x(t)$ denote the tourist number at time t. The simplest model is

$$x'(t) = mx(t), \qquad (71.1)$$

and the solution is

$$x(t) = x_0 e^{mt_0}.$$

For $m > 0$, the number of tourists will increase, and this can explain the first three stages of Butler's theory. The number of facilities at a destination increases upon increase in the tourist demand, and this in turn reciprocally influences the demand over time.

According to Butler (1980) the tourist number approaches a maximum that accounts for a flattening in numbers over time reaching the so-called stagnation period. Over time a destination may not be as desired as earlier commonly due to social, economic, or environmental issues. This will imply a decline that will balance with the increase to a peak of tourist number called the *capacity of growth*.

Following the approach of Shobeiri Nejad and Tularam (2010), let X be the maximum tourist number, and then growth is assumed proportional to $(X - x(t))/X$.

The differential equation that describes this situation is

$$x'(t) = mx(t)\left(\frac{X - x(t)}{X}\right) \tag{71.2}$$

or

$$x'(t) = mx(t) - m\frac{x^2(t)}{X}.$$

The analytical solution is

$$x(t) = \frac{X}{1 + e^{-m(t-a)}},$$

where a is a constant that depends on the initial condition.

Define

$$\beta(t) = \frac{1}{1 + e^{-m(t-a)}};$$

then

$$\beta(t) = \frac{x(t)}{X},$$

the proportion of tourists at time t to the capacity X.

The function $x(t)$ will be fitted to real data to determine the values of the parameters m and a.

Following the approach of Shobeiri Nejad and Tularam (2010), the stage of the tourism product (exploration, involvement, development, consolidation, and stagnation) will be determined using the derivatives of $\beta(t)$ (see Fig. 71.2).

$$\beta'(t) = m(-\beta^2 + \beta)$$
$$\beta''(t) = m^2\beta(2\beta^2 - 3\beta + 1)$$

71 The Dynamics of Tourist Flows in Greece

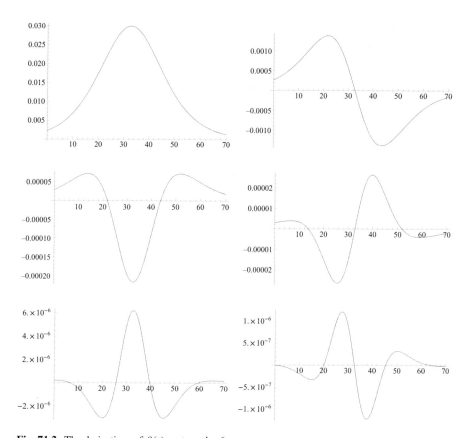

Fig. 71.2 The derivatives of $\beta(t)$ up to order 6

$$\beta^{(3)}(t) = m^3\beta(-6\beta^3 + 12\beta^2 - 7\beta + 1)$$
$$\beta^{(4)}(t) = m^4\beta(24\beta^4 - 60\beta^3 + 50\beta^2 - 15\beta + 1)$$
$$\beta^{(5)}(t) = m^5\beta(-120\beta^5 + 360\beta^4 - 390\beta^3 + 180\beta^2 - 31\beta + 1).$$

The critical points of the first derivative are 0 and 1 and of the second derivative are 0, 0.5, and 1. For higher order derivatives the critical points are given in the next table.

Derivative	Critical values
3	0, 0.2113, 0.7887, 1
4	0, 0.0917, 0.5, 0.9082, 1
5	0, 0.0413, 0.3010, 0.6990, 0.9587, 1
6	0, 0.0192, 0.1804, 0.5, 0.8196, 0.9809, 1

71.4 Data Fitting and Conclusions

From the form of the data we notice the five stages of the tourist product up to 2012. From 2012 we observe rejuvenation; $x(t)$ increases up to 2019 when it reaches a maximum over that 31 million arrivals. For this reason we choose to fit the data with model (71.2) (see Fig. 71.3) up to 2012 and with model (71.1) for the period 2012–2019 (see Fig. 71.4).

For the period up to 2012, we obtain $m = 0.12$ and $a = 32.8$ the function $x(t)$ is

$$x(t) = \frac{X}{1 + e^{-0.12(t-32.8)}}$$

and make the following comments:

- Over the whole period examined, the first derivative is positive indicating a continuous increase of $x(t)$.
- The maximum growth rate is observed for the year 1988.
- The first derivative has the form of normal distribution with mean 1988. In the bibliography, the product cycle has been studied by normal distribution, and the following three stages are identified: introduction, growth, and maturity.
- From the second derivative we find the maximum and the minimum acceleration of tourist arrivals (the maximum or minimum rate of change).
- The zeroing of the third derivative corresponds to the years 1974 and 2003.
- From the sign of the fourth derivative, we find that the maximum of acceleration is in 1974 and the minimum is in 2003.

According to Butler (1980) the exploration and involvement stages are located within the introduction stage of the life cycle. On the same pace, the consolidation

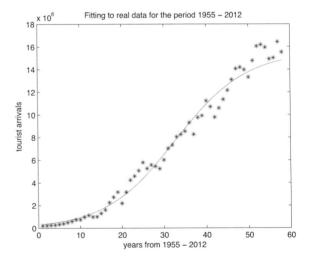

Fig. 71.3 Fitting data 1955–2012

Fig. 71.4 Fitting data 1955–2019

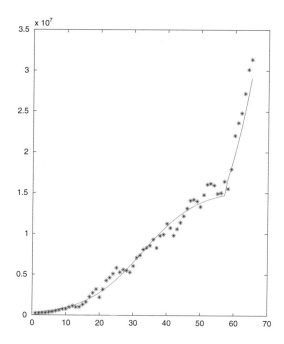

and stagnation stages are located within the maturity stage. Therefore, the stages of the Greek tourist product have been identified to be the following:

- Exploration stage 1965–1966
- Involvement stage 1967–1973
- Development stage 1974–2004
- Consolidation stage 2005–2010
- Stagnation stage 2011–2012

For the years 2012–2019 a significant increase in the number of tourist arrivals is observed. We have chosen to fit the data with model (71.1) and find $m = 0.09$.

References

Butler, R. W. (1980). The concept of a tourist area cycle of evolution: Implications for management of recourse. *Canadian Geographer, 24*, 5–12.

Hellenic Statistical Authority (ELSTAT) (2023) *Annual Tourist Arrivals, Athens*.

Shobeiri Nejad, S.A.H., & Tularam, G. A. (2010). Modeling tourist arrivals in destination countries: An application to Australian tourism. *Journal of Mathematics and Statistics, 6*(4), 431–441.

Index

A
Altini, A., 1113–1125
Androniki, K., 1085–1094
Antoniadis, I., 487–495, 987–1006, 1127–1139
Antoniadis, I. Dr., 1035–1047
Avlogiaris, G., 487–495
Avlogiaris, G. Dr., 1035–1047

B
Bagnasco, A.M., 867–885
Baranowska-Prokop, E., 235–241
Bartošová, S., 701–725
Bertsatos, G., 187–204, 1241–1247
Besana, A., 393–408, 445–461
Bitzenis, A., 1063–1070
Bohdalova, M., 939–954
Bohušová, H., 321–332
Botha, I., 37–47
Bouloumpasi, E., 839–848
Broni, G., 427–443

C
Caballero, L.A.V., 521–528
Castillo Martínez, W.E., 1051–1060
Chaiboonsri, C., 63–75
Chatzitheodoridis, F., 641–662
Chávez, J.J.T., 521–528, 1051–1060
Chinoracky, R., 337–347
Clavenna, V., 867–885
Collazos Alarcón, M.A., 521–528

Corejová, T., 337–347
Crisafulli, E.G.D., 393–408

D
Dang, T.D., 413–423
Dash, A., 283–295, 741–755
Del busto Valdez, M.Y., 1051–1060
del Pilar Pintado Damián, M., 521–528
de Wet, M.C., 1–14
Dimitrios, D., 487–496
Dombek, R.P., 1143–1171
Dritsaki, C., 159–183
Dritsaki, M., 159–183
Duda, Jirí, 205–215
Ďurian, J., 815–829
Duru, E., 113–140

E
Ebomuche, N.C., 113–140
Efthalitsidou, K., 91–109
Elexa, L., 593–608
Espinoza Tumpay, J.H., 1051–1060
Esposito, A., 445–461
Evangelou, P., 427–443

F
Ferro-Gonzales, P., 969–984
Fisichella, C., 445–461
Forshaw, R., 667–699

Fortunato, F., 867–885
Friel, M.M., 393–408
Fulajtarova, Z., 701–725

G
Giantsis, I.A., 853–864
Gregorc, C., 1175–1027
Grofčíková, J., 351–365, 499–517
Gupta, A.K., 283–295, 741–755

H
Haberer, N., 939–954
Haller, R.K., 245–260
Hosseinmardi, H. Ph.D., 17–35

I
Ihugba, O.A., 113–140
Ikášová, T., 1021–1032
Izáková, K., 351–365

K
Kalfas, D., 583–864
Kalogiannidis, S., 367–388, 641–662
Kalogiratou, Z., 1241–1247
Kamenidou, I. (Eirini), 839–848
Kano, M.I., 465–484
Karampatea, A., 839–848
Karamperidis, S., 531–536
Karantonis, Z., 367–388
Karnachoritis, D., 889–903
Kiki, M., 427–443
Kitta, A., 1223–1237
Klacsanova, K., 939–954
Klement, L., 907–920
Klementová, V., 907–920
Koutouzidou, G., 583–864
Koutsoupias, N., 1063–1070
Kremeier, P., 613–623
Kropf, S.L., 537–553

L
Lee, W., 219–232
Liu, M., 757–789, 793–812
Loudovaris, S., 583–864
Lourdes, V.T.S., 521–528

M
Mamalis, S., 839–848
Ma, Q.-P., 757–789, 793–812

Melas, K., 531–536
Melfou, K., 583–864
Metsios, I., 987–1006
Metsiou, A., 427–443
Miñan Olivos, G.S.M., 521–528, 1051–1060
Michail, N.A., 531–536
Miljevic, J., 1175–1027
Monovasilis, T., 1241–1247
Muradoglu, G., 465–484
Musa, H., 575–589
Musova, Z., 575–589, 701–713

N
Nguyen, M.T., 413–423
Notta, O., 1223–1237

O
Olbrys, J., 77–87
Olukuru, J., 465–484
Orji, A.A., 113–140

P
Papachristou, E., 427–443
Papadopoullos, P., 1095–1110
Papaevangelou, O., 367–388
Papapanagos, H., 299–318
Papathanasopoulos, A., 923–935
Papík, M., 729–738
Papíková, L., 729–738
Patitsa, C., 641–662
Petrakos, G., 143–156
Pintér, L., 575–589
Pitoska, E., 1095–1110, 1113–1125
Pražák, T., 1009–1018
Prokop, J., 235–241

R
Rech, F., 575–589
Rontos, K., 143–156
Rossi, C., 393–408
Ruf, T., 559–572

S
Samanta, I., 889–903
Saprikis, V., 487–496, 987–1006
Sariannidis, N., 91–109
Savvidou, D., 367–388
Ščerba, K., 831–849
Sedliačik, I., 831–837

Sempelidou, L.M., 1035–1047
Shaban, O.S., 1209–1221
Shah, A., 17–35
Shah, K., 17–35
Shaikh, I., 283–295, 741–755
Simockova, I., 815–829
Singvejsakul, J., 63–75
Skendi, A., 839–848
Skupieňová, M., 955–968
Smerek, L., 815–829
Spinthiropoulos, K., 91–109
Srivastava, M.K., 283–295, 741–755
Stalmasekova, N., 337–347
Sucaticona-Aguilar, V., 969–984
Svoboda, P., 321–332
Syndoukas, D., 367–388, 641–662

T
Tam, V.N.N., 265–281
Thanh, C.T., 265–281
Theodorli, E., 1113–1125
Thompson, C., 37–47

Touitou, M., 51–61
Tsinaslanidis, P., 1073–1083
Tsitouras, A., 299–318
Tsounis, N., 187–204, 299–318, 1241–1247

V
Vannini, M.C., 445–461
Vatantzi, K., 1127–1139
Vavoura, C., 143–156
Vavouras, I., 143–156
Vezou, M., 91–109
Vinczeová, M., 907–920
Vlachvei, A., 1127–1139, 1223–1237

W
Wieke, S., 625–638

Y
Yan, C., 575–589